AIR International — VOLUME TEN

ILLUSTRATIONS

Photographs — half-tone and (c) colour

Line illustrations and cut-away (c/a) drawings

Tone illustrations and colour (c) drawings

AIR International

Volume 10   Number 1   January 1976

Managing Editor   William Green
Editor   Gordon Swanborough
Modelling Editor   Fred J Henderson
Contributing Artists   Dennis Punnett
                        John Weal
Cover Art   W R Hardy
Contributing Photographer
                        Stephen Peltz
Editorial Representative, Washington
                        Norman Polmar
Publisher   Donald Hannah
Circulation Director   Donald Syner
Subscription Manager   Claire Sillette
Advertising/Public Relations
                        Elizabeth Baker
Advertising Manager   Jim Boyd

Editorial Offices:
The AIR INTERNATIONAL, PO Box 16, Bromley, BR2 7RB Kent.

Subscription, Advertising and Circulation Offices:
The AIR INTERNATIONAL, De Worde House, 283 Lonsdale Road, London SW13 9QW. Telephone 01-878 2454. US and Canadian readers may address subscriptions and general enquiries to AIR INTERNATIONAL PO Box 353, Whitestone, NY 11357 for onward transmission to the UK, from where all correspondence is answered and orders despatched.

MEMBER OF THE AUDIT BUREA OF CIRCULATIONS   ABC

Subscription rates, inclusive of postage, direct from the publishers, per year:
United Kingdom   £5·50
USA $17·50
Canada $17·50

Rates for other countries and for air mail subscriptions available on request from the Subscription Department at the above address.

The AIR INTERNATIONAL is published monthly by Fine Scroll Limited, distributed by Ducimus Books Ltd and printed by Jayprint Holdings Ltd, Pinfold Road, Thurmaston, Leicester, England. Editorial contents © 1976 by Pilot Press Limited. The views expressed by named contributors and correspondents are their own and do not necessarily reflect the views of the editors. Neither the editors nor the publishers accept responsibility for any loss or damage, however caused, to manuscripts or illustrations submitted to the AIR INTERNATIONAL.

Second Class postage approved at Long Island City, NY 11101. USA Mailing Agents: Air-Sea Freight Inc, PO Box 1305, Long Island City, NY 11101.

CONTENTS

**WRENDEZVOUS
WITH WREN**

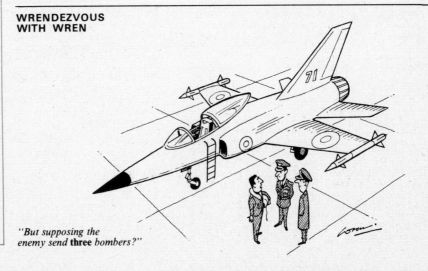

"But supposing the enemy send **three** *bombers?"*

AIRSCENE

MILITARY AFFAIRS

AUSTRALIA

The **first** RAAF pilot **training course on** the NZAI CT-4 **Airtrainer** was scheduled to commence on 28 November at No 1 Flying Training School at Point Cook, near Melbourne, instructor conversion having begun on 1 September at the Central Flying School, East Sale, Victoria. No 1 FTS anticipates having received its full complement of Airtrainers by March, almost a year behind the original schedule which called for the initiation of training courses on the Airtrainer at Point Cook in January 1975. Although the Winjeel has now been phased out of the initial training rôle, four are being retained by the Forward Air Control Flight at Williamtown and a few remain in the communications rôle.

The **Wessex** AS Mk 31s now being replaced in the ASW rôle by Sea King Mk 50s are being **transferred** from the Royal Australian Navy's No 817 Squadron to No 723 Squadron with which they are **to** serve in the **utility rôle** alongside the unit's UH-1D Iroquois and Bell 206B JetRanger II helicopters.

Although the RAAF originally hoped to replace the C-130A Hercules of No 36 Squadron with new C-130Hs on a one-for-one basis, it now seems likely that the **procurement of only eight** new **Hercules** will be possible. The aged C-130As may be passed on to third-world countries through Australian aid programmes after arrival of the C-130Hs.

BELGIUM

The elements of the *Ecole de Pilotage Avancé* and the *Entrainement de Pilotage de Transition* at Brustem have **recently** been **assigned squadron numbers.** The Magister-equipped basic training component has now been divided into the 7ème and 9ème escadrilles, while advanced and refresher training on T-33As is now the responsibility of the 11ème Escadrille. The last-mentioned unit is scheduled to commence conversion to the Alpha Jet from late 1978, and the basic training squadrons will convert from mid 1979 to mid 1980.

The *Aviation Légère de la Force Terrestre* (ALFT), the Belgian **Army's aviation** component, is **to receive** 12 Britten-Norman **Islanders** to replace its Dornier Do 27Bs. This primarily helicopter-equipped force is now seeking a successor for the Alouette II and Alouette-Astazou LOH helicopters operated by the 16ème, 17ème and 18ème Escadrilles d'Observation Légère. It is anticipated that some 80 helicopters will be acquired in two batches, the initial batch filling the LOH and anti-armour rôles with the second batch being intended for the assault task. The Islanders will be operated by the 15ème Escadrille at Brasschaat, near Antwerp.

BRAZIL

While the *Fôrça Aérea Brasileira* has stated its anxiety that the production line of the Neiva T-25 **Universal** basic trainer be kept open, **negotiations** with the Air Ministry **for a follow-on contract** have now been **continuing** for a year without agreement being reached. The principle problem involves the French ERAN-manufactured undercarriage which costs almost $20,000 (£9,900), the total unit cost of a fully-equipped Universal being $70,000 (£34,500). Neiva is anxious that any follow-on contract covers the production of at least two aircraft per month, but until the undercarriage cost problem is resolved, the Air Ministry is unlikely to finalize a contract and at least one export order (see news item under Chile) is apparently awaiting a Brazilian ministerial decision concerning a follow-on order for the FAB. It will be recalled that Neiva manufactured 132 Universals and a prototype Universal II.

In early November, the Air Ministry completed **negotiations** with EMBRAER **for** the **follow-on batch of** EMB 326GC **Xavante** trainer and light strike aircraft for the FAB and it is hoped that this order will carry EMBRAER until production can commence of the planned AX light attack aircraft now deferred until the 1977-78 period. Xavante production is currently running at two per month and number 105 is expected to be completed this month (January), leaving only seven of the initial contract for 112 Xavantes to be completed. Production tempo is likely to fall to 1·5 aircraft per month towards the end of this year. The follow-on contract will enable the FAB to carry through its full Xavante re-equipment programme.

CANADA

The Defence Ministry is considering **proposals to transfer** the Canadair-built **CF-5A** tactical **fighters** of the Canadian Armed Forces' Air Command **to Europe** for the ground support rôle, according to Defence Minister James Richardson, thus increasing the Canadian NATO contingent. The Air Command possesses two CF-5A squadrons — No 433 and No 434 at Bagotville and Cold Lake respectively, the latter having a dual operational/ training rôle — and these are currently committed to NATO's ACE Mobile Force (Denmark-Norway) on an emergency fly-over basis. These proposals have been interpreted in some quarters as a means of displaying Canada's good intentions towards NATO and Europe while delaying a decision concerning a replacement for Air Command's CF-101 Voodoos and CF-104 Starfighters.

CHILE

It is reported that the Chilean and Brazilian governments are currently **negotiating** a **follow-on contract for** a further eight Neiva **Universal** trainers for the *Fuerza Aérea de Chile*, the contract depending on acceptable financing arrangements. The FAC has already received 10 Universals (delivered May-June) and the Aerotec company has now received a contract from the Chilean government for the manufacture of underwing gun pods for these aircraft to suit them for the dual armament training/counter-insurgency task.

EGYPT

In recent months, the **range of equipment** studied by the Egyptian Air Force has been **extended** to include Italian aircraft. Aeritalia recently demonstrated the G.91T to the Egyptian Air Force and is making a strong bid to sell the G.222 transport in which the EAF has evinced some interest. However, Italian sources report that any Egyptian purchase contract for the G.222 — 10-12 aircraft having been mentioned — is contingent on Italy's ability to supply the EAF quickly with some 30 G.91Y tactical fighters. While Aeritalia's G.91Y assembly line is still open, budgetary considerations having dictated the stretching of the delivery tempo to the *Aeronautica Militare* (AMI) of the final batch of 10 aircraft, only the last three or four aircraft on the line could be delivered within the Egyptian time scale, assuming that the AMI is willing to relinquish them, and no substantial quantity of G.91Ys could be delivered by Aeritalia much before mid-1977. The Egyptian condition can thus be met only by dint of withdrawing aircraft from the AMI inventory, a proposal that the service is most unwilling to entertain. Aermacchi has recently demonstrated the single-seat MB 326K and two-seat MB 326L to the EAF at Almaza Airport, Cairo, and has apparently tendered proposals to the Egyptian government concerning licence production of the MB 326L or more advanced MB 339 by the domestic arms complex when it is finally set up, these proposals reportedly embracing the Agusta A 109C Hirundo. Apart from the Italian company's wide experience and good track record in licensing its aircraft for manufacture in other countries, the Aermacchi aircraft also offers significant financial advantages.

During his October-November visit to the USA, President Anwar el-Sadat discussed his military equipment interests with President Ford and Secretary-of-State Henry Kissinger, and among longer-term requirements allegedly expressed **interest in** the General Dynamics **F-16A** as a potential successor to the MiG-21 in the air superiority rôle from the beginning of the next decade. A US spokesman subsequently commented that the US government is not ready at the moment to make any specific commitments, but it would seem improbable that Congressional approval would be granted the supply of this warplane to Egypt.

It has been unofficially reported that an Egyptian Air Force **delegation** recently **evaluated** the McDonnell Douglas F-4E **Phantom** in Iran.

While visiting the UK in November, President **Sadat** is understood to have **renewed** his **request for** the supply to the EAF of the SEPECAT **Jaguar International** and, in something of a *volte face*, the French government is apparently now encouraging Egyptian acquisition of the Anglo-French strike fighter rather than the Mirage F1 — 22 examples of which were "ordered" by Egypt early last year but for which a contract has still to be signed at the time of closing for press! Any Egyptian Jaguar contract will, of course, depend on bilateral talks with France on production sharing, but despite press reports that the British government is now unlikely to object, sale of the Jaguar to the EAF is by no means certain as the supply of this warplane to Egypt is particularly sensitive owing to Israeli concern over new weaponry being delivered to the Middle East that could affect the balance of power, and the British Foreign Office has apparently received strong representations from both the Israeli and US governments to embargo any Jaguar sale to Egypt. The EAF reportedly has a requirement for up to 200 Jaguar International strike fighters, but any contract is likely to call for an initial batch of 50-60 aircraft to be delivered 1977-78, with follow-up batches into the 'eighties, perhaps eventually involving some assembly work in Egypt.

FEDERAL GERMANY

The **Army** air component, the *Heeresflieger*, was expected to select a missile-armed **anti-armour helicopter** shortly after this column closed for press. The *Heeresflieger* apparently preferred the MBB BO 115 which it believed would offer superior agility to competitive helicopters owing to its rigid rotor system, but there was doubt that the BO 115 with a capable anti-armour missile and associated visionics could achieve production status earlier than 1980, by which time the *Heeresflieger* plans to have a proportion of its projected anti-armour helicopter force in service owing to the tempo at which the Warsaw Pact countries are introducing improved tanks, which, it is anticipated, will endow them with a qualitative superiority by 1980 to add to their existing quantitative edge.

GREECE
The Hellenic **Air Force,** currently awaiting delivery of the first of its 40 Rockwell T-2E Buckeye trainer and light attack aircraft, is now **working up** its first LTV Aerospace A-7H **Corsair and** Dassault-Breguet **Mirage** F1CG **squadrons.** Deliveries of these aircraft to Greece commenced in June and August respectively, 60 of the former and 40 of the latter being on order. Apart from the A-7H Corsairs and Mirage F1CGs, recent deliveries to the HAF have included 33 Lockheed T-33As transferred from the *Luftwaffe,* while the Army air component has received 10 Bell UH-1D Iroquois from the USA and 40 Agusta Bell AB 204Bs and AB 205s from Italy. The Army has a requirement for about a dozen armed helicopters and the Navy is seeking a half-dozen or so ASW helicopters. Greece is now spending approximately 25 per cent of her national budget on defence and arms purchases are expected to average some £167m annually for the next five years.

INDIA
Consideration is being given by the Indian Navy to **possible procurement of** a small number of Kamov **Ka-26** ASW helicopters for operation from the new series of *Leander* class Seacat-equipped frigates currently being built by the Mazagan Dockyard, Bombay. The Ka-26s, if acquired, will serve as interim equipment pending availability of the navalized ASW version of HAL's ALH (Armed Light Helicopter) which is under development. These helicopters will presumably be operated by INAS 331 which was formed in May 1972 with an establishment of eight torpedo-carrying Alouette IIIs.

Although the Indian **Navy** is **still** actively **promoting** the **Maritime Harrier** for use from INS *Vikrant,* the service is now virtually resigned to the fact that no funding can be found for such a purchase owing to the higher priorities assigned to the acquisition of maritime patrol aircraft, submarines and missile boats.

IRAN
The Iranian Imperial **Air Force** is currently **negotiating** with Lockheed **for two specially-configured P-3 Orions** for use in connection with the so-called Ibex airborne and ground-based communications and radar monitoring system which it is planned to establish in Iran and for which the Autonetics group of Rockwell International is acting as programme adviser to the Iranian government. The Orions (which are in addition to the six P-3F models already delivered to the IIAF for long-range maritime patrol tasks) will be fitted with receiving antennæ and will be modified to accommodate racks of electronic and communications intelligence equipment, plus wideband tape recorders. Current planning also calls for the similar modification of two of the 13 Boeing 707-3J9C refuelling boom-equipped tanker-transports currently on order for the IIAF (six of which have been delivered).

Delivery of the **first** Grumman F-14 **Tomcats** to Iran will be made late **this month** (January) when either one or two of the fighters will be ferried to the Isfahan air base, south of Teheran. Further aircraft are expected to be delivered at a rate of three-four per month through late 1977.

KOREA (NORTH)
Gen Binyamin Peled, C-in-C of the Israeli air arm, recently revealed that, on 25 October 1973, during the Middle East conflict, Israeli aircraft shot down two **MiG-21s flown by North Korean pilots** seconded to the Egyptian Air Force. Gen Peled commented that the North Koreans had generally endeavoured to avoid combat with the Israelis but did engage on this one occasion. He added that the Israelis bombed an Egyptian airfield from which the North Korean pilots were flying.

KOREA (SOUTH)
It was announced on 21 October that the US government is to sell South Korea a further 18 F-4E Phantom fighters at a cost of $177·9m (£88·5m) which, together with the 18 additional F-4D Phantoms that it was announced in the previous month were to be supplied to **South Korea,** effectively **double the Phantom-equipped component** of the Republic of Korea Air Force (ROKAF), this having previously comprised one (18-aircraft) squadron each of the F-4D and F-4E versions of the Phantom. On 10 October, the appropriate Congressional Committee had been informed of proposals to furnish the ROKAF with 60 additional Northrop F-5Es and F-5Fs (see *Airscene*/December) valued at approximately $205m (£102m).

NORWAY
A White Paper to be published shortly by the Norwegian Government is expected to include the main recommendations of a Ministry of Defence special committee which has investigated future requirements **for the surveillance of Norwegian** fishing and oil **interests in the North Sea.** The recommendations include the acquisition of at least six new helicopters and three more fixed-wing maritime patrol aircraft. The helicopters, which the committee considers should be somewhat smaller than the RNoAF's Sea Kings, should be organized as a separate squadron, estimated expenditure being NKr99m (£8·6m) with an annual operating cost of the order of NKr13m (£1·15m). On grounds of standardization, the committee recommended that the fixed-wing maritime patrol aircraft be Lockheed Orions — of which five currently serve with the RNoAF — and that these be integrated into the Orion-equipped SKv 333, the estimated investment being NKr120m (£10·5m) with annual operating expenditure being approximately NKr19m (£1·65m). Delivery of the aircraft is recommended as quickly as possible (ie, at a rate commensurate with trained personnel availability).

OMAN
The third **BAC One-Eleven 475** for the Sultan of Oman's Air Force and the first to incorporate BAC's newly-developed upward-opening freight door in the port side of the forward fuselage and a removable freight handling system was **delivered** from Hurn **to Muscat** in November. The first two SOAF One-Eleven 475s, which have been serving with No 4 squadron, are now to be returned to Hurn to be similarly converted.

SAUDI ARABIA
A Syrian military spokesman in Damascus confirmed, in November, that **elements of the** Royal Saudi Air Force are **now based in Syria** for the support of Saudi ground forces deployed on the Golan Heights. The spokesman commented on the participation of the RSAF aircraft — Northrop F-5E Tiger IIs — in manœuvres held recently in the vicinity of the Heights. Also during November, Jordanian Television showed King Hussein of Jordan greeting RSAF pilots who had arrived at Mafraq (King Hussein Air Base) with their F-5E Tiger IIs on detachment. It was not revealed if the Saudi squadron was in Jordan

to participate in joint exercises with the RJAF or is to be permanently based at Mafraq.

SOVIET UNION
According to US Defense Department analysts, construction of a **third aircraft carrier** of the *Kiev* class has begun in a Leningrad shipyard (presumably the Zhdanov or the Baltic) whereas the first of the class, the *Kiev* now working up, was built in the Nikolayev Nosenko yard where the second carrier, the *Minsk,* is currently under construction. The third carrier, which, like its predecessors, is expected to displace 45,000 tons, is unlikely to join the Soviet Navy before 1979-80.

US Defense Department now contends that the *Backfire-B* variable-geometry supersonic **bomber can strike** major portions of the **USA without** any requirement for **aerial refuelling.** The 285,000-lb (129 280-kg) *Backfire,* which is approximately four-fifths of the size of the Rockwell International B-1, is now being configured for electronic countermeasures and reconnaissance missions, and is the primary reason for the recent impasse in the SALT negotiations, deadlock arising when the Soviet government rejected US proposals to impose minimal restraints on the deployment of *Backfire,* indicating that no restraints on the deployment of this warplane would be acceptable.

Pentagon officials are evincing increasing **concern at** the pace at which the Soviet Union is outstripping the USA in the **introduction of new warplanes** into its operational inventory as well as in research and development. One official recently commented that the US is "busy talking about the F-15 and F-16 which are not going to be meaningful operationally until 1980 at least", adding that the MiG-23 is "vastly superior" to the F-4 Phantom in the air combat rôle, with greater range, speed and mobility, and almost 1,000 MiG-23s have already been produced! The MiG-23S interceptor and air superiority fighter is now referred to as the *Flogger-B* by NATO whereas the fighter-bomber MiG-23B is now the *Flogger-D,* the tandem two-seat MiG-23U being the *Flogger-C.*

SPAIN
The *Ejército del Aire* is to receive this month (January) the **first** of three KC-130H **Hercules tanker-transports** ordered early in 1975. The KC-130Hs (designated TK 10 by the EdA) are to be operated by *Escuadrón núm* 301, the second and third aircraft being scheduled for delivery in February and March respectively. In addition to the KC-130Hs the EdA anticipates receiving a further five C-130Hs (four having been taken into the inventory during 1974). With the arrival of these aircraft, *Escuadrón núm* 301 will be split into two six-aircraft squadrons forming *Ala núm* 31.

The two surviving examples of the three Aérospatiale **SA 330 Puma** helicopters delivered to the EdA have now been included in the inventory of the recently-created *Unidad Especial de Helicopteros* and a **replacement** Puma for the one that crashed early in 1975 has been ordered.

SYRIA
According to well-informed sources in Damascus, **France** is **to supply** the Syrian Arab Air Force (SAAF) with between 15 and 40 Aérospatiale SA 321 **Super Frelon** heavy-duty helicopters in the first major military hardware procurement deal concluded by the Syrian government outside the Soviet bloc in many years. However, the deal does not signify any change in the Syrian attitude towards the Soviet Union as the country's primary source of military equipment, the procurement of French helicopters

having been dictated by Saudi Arabia which is funding the purchase and has a long record of seeking to persuade the so-called Arab confrontation states bordering Israel to buy western weapons.

Some concern has been expressed in Washington over the recent **deployment of** a **V-VS unit** of MiG-25R *Foxbat-B* reconnaissance aircraft **to** a **Syrian base.** It will be recalled that a detachment of V-VS MiG-25Rs was withdrawn from Cairo West airfield in September as a result of strained relations between Egypt and the Soviet Union (see *Airscene*/December).

According to a New York Times report, **deliveries of Soviet weapons** to the Syrian armed forces have **accelerated** since the visit of Syrian President Hafez al-Assad to Moscow in October, and the first-line combat strength of the Syrian Arab Air Force now exceeds 300 aircraft, including 45 MiG-23s. The number of Soviet technical advisers in Syria now totals some 3,500.

THAILAND
The **first** batch **of** an **additional** 20 Fairchild **AU-23A Peacemaker "minigunship" aircraft** ordered for the Royal Thai Air Force in 1974 will arrive shortly in Bangkok for assembly by RTAF personnel. The first of the new AU-23As, which differ from those already serving with the RTAF (the survivors of the 15 involved in the USAF "Credible Chase" evaluation) in being fitted with armour to protect crew, oil cooler and fuel system from small arms fire, was accepted at Hagerstown, Maryland, on 21 October by Air Marshal Leelasiri Kamron, CO of the RTAF Tactical Air Command, and production of the AU-23A was increased from one to three a month in December, with the last of the 20 aircraft for the RTAF being scheduled for May delivery. The Thai AU-23As are armed with a side-firing General Electric XM-197 20-mm cannon and can carry up to 1,400 lb (635 kg) of ordnance on four underwing stores stations.

TURKEY
The Soviet Union has finally overcome Turkey's long-standing anti-Soviet policy in weapon procurement with the sale of a substantial number of helicopters to the Ankara government. The **Soviet Union** is to **supply** Turkey with 60 **helicopters** of unspecified type but believed to be Mil Mi-8s. Other Turkish helicopter procurement includes an order on behalf of the naval air component for Agusta Bell AB 212ASWs.

Turkish and Federal German officials have

Artist's impressions of (above) the EMBRAER EMB-121 Xingu and (below) the EMB-123 Tapajos, respectively short and long-fuselage versions of the pressurized Bandeirante.

been discussing the **possible procurement** by the Turkish Air Force of 50-plus Dassault-Breguet/Dornier **Alpha Jets** to replace both its T-33As and T-37Bs. If a contract is signed, final assembly of a proportion of the Alpha Jets will be undertaken in Turkey with, possibly, progressive licence manufacture to follow. However, it seems unlikely that the Turkish Air Force could begin to take the Alpha Jet into its inventory before 1980–81 at the earliest. Discussions concerning possible Alpha Jet procurement have been held with Federal German rather than French officials owing to the fact that Federal Germany is one of Turkey's traditional defence suppliers.

UNITED KINGDOM
The RAF's **No 23** (Red Eagle) **Sqdn disbanded** as a Lightning unit at RAF Leuchars on 31 October **and reformed** at RAF Coningsby on 17 November with Phantom FGR Mk 2s. No 23's place at Leuchars has been taken by the Phantom FGR Mk 2-equipped No 111 Sqdn, formerly based at Coningsby.

USA
The **last** Fairchild C-119L **"Flying Boxcars"** of the Air National Guard were **retired** in October when the remaining five transports of this type belonging to the 130th Special Operations Group left Kanawha County Airport, Charleston, West Virginia, four being flown to the Military Aircraft Storage and Disposition Center at Davis-Monthan AFB, Arizona, and the fifth being flown to Little Rock AFB, Arkansas, where it has been placed on permanent static display.

AIRCRAFT AND INDUSTRY

BRAZIL
EMBRAER has concluded an agreement with **Piper** providing for the latter **to market** about 24 **pressurized Bandeirantes** each year from 1977, leaving about eight a year to be sold by EMBRAER in Brazil. First flight of the prototype EMB-121 (*Airscene*/November 1975) is expected by the end of January, with an eight-month flight test programme to be undertaken and a static test specimen to be completed by July.

EMRAER's **production of Piper models** is gathering momentum and by 30 September the company had completed 16 EMB-810 (Seneca II), 12 EMB-720 Minuano (Cherokee Six), 29 EMB-710 Carioca (Pathfinder) and 17 EMB-711 Corisco (Arrow II). The first EMB-820 (Navajo) flew at the end of October. Basic production of the three single-engined models is handled by Neiva at its Botucatu City plant under sub-contract to EMBRAER at a rate of three a week, together with fuselages for the Ipanema ag-plane and parts of the EMB-810 and EMB-820. EMBRAER is expected to obtain 25 per cent of Neiva stock in a re-arrangement of the latter company which will leave the present owners in control but with some stock being available for public purchase. The two companies are working together on improvements for the T-25 Universal, these including an indigenous undercarriage to replace the French gear, the imported price of which now amounts to just over 25 per cent of the total cost of the Universal.

FEDERAL GERMANY
MBB's Hamburg Division has proposed the development of suitable equipment to adapt **Transall C 160s** in service with the *Luftwaffe* for use **as water bombers.** The proposal comes in the wake of the disastrous forest fires suffered in Lower Saxony last August, in which French Canadair CL-215s were called upon to help German fire fighting services. The Transall scheme involves the installation of a

3,300-Imp gal (15 000-l) water tank on a pallet in the fuselage, with a high-speed discharge nozzle through the lowered rear ramp, permitting the whole water load to be dumped in about 3·5 secs. Using high pressure pumps available to airfield fire brigades, the tank could be refilled in 6 minutes but the aircraft would lack the ability to refill its tanks without landing. To permit operations from very small or rough fields, MBB also suggests the development of a built-in air cushion landing system for the Transall.

FRANCE
During a recent press conference in Paris, M Marcel Dassault confirmed that the prototype **Super Mirage** currently under construction would make its first **flight at** the **end of 1976,** and commented that the French government should waste no time in reaching a decision on the future of the aircraft which, he said, would have a unit cost of Fr75m (£8·06m) on the basis of a French order for 100 aircraft and would carry an export price of Fr60m (£6·45m). Indeed, he said, the export fly-away price *could* be as low as Fr55m (£5·91m) — he discounted allegations that the unit cost would be as high as Fr100m (£10·73m), pointing out that such would include amortisation of prototypes, flight and ground testing, production tooling, provision of technical publications, etc. He stressed that removal of these fixed costs from the Super Mirage resulted in the previously-mentioned Fr75m unit price which included 20 per cent tax.

Although Aérospatiale has a major stake in the Airbus programme, there is a degree of overlap between projected future versions of the A300 and a series of **projects** studied by **Aérospatiale** under the designation **AS-200.** The latter are Aérospatiale's contribution to the studies being made by the group of six European manufacturers in an attempt to meet the future aircraft requirements of Air France, British Airways and Lufthansa. Two, three-and four-engined versions of the AS-200 have been studied, using underwing pods and, for the tri-jet, a single rear fuselage engine installation, with the CFM-56 or JT10D as the favoured power plant. A supercritical wing aerofoil is projected, for a low-mounted wing with modest sweepback, and the possible application of CCV (control-configured vehicle) principles has been studied, together with the use of new materials and advanced avionics. Capacities range from 120-170 for the twin to 180-220 for the largest four-engined variant, and a wide spectrum of payload/range variations has been embraced by the studies.

Dassault-Breguet Aviation has confirmed that preliminary discussions have been held with McDonnell Douglas and Lockheed with a view to establishing co-operative **development of the Mercure 200** with one or other of these companies. The Mercure 200 is a slightly-stretched version of the Mercure 100 now used by Air Inter, with GE/SNECMA CFM-56 turbofans replacing the JT8Ds. The French government has informed Dassault-Breguet that Aérospatiale would be nominated as the French partner in any such Franco-US deal, although Dassault would form the final assembly line for the aircraft at Istres.

Dassault-Breguet has **plans to introduce** a new version of the Mystère 20/Falcon as **the Falcon G,** with 5,000-lb (2 270-kg) thrust class Rolls-Royce RB.401 or Garrett AiResearch ATF3-6 turbofans in place of the General Electric CF700s of the Falcon F. Improvements are expected to include a 10 per cent reduction in field lengths, better rate of climb, reduced noise levels and 20 per cent range increase for the same speed. To be available in 1980, the Falcon G will also provide the basis for further development of the airframe, including eventually increased fuel and a stretched fuselage.

The first two Dassault-Breguet **Mercures** in service with Air Inter have been **fitted with DARD** (Dispositif Anti-Rafale Dassault) anti-gust devices. Other aircraft in the fleet will be progressively equipped. DARD is a gust alleviator linked to the aircraft's yaw damper, to reduce the Mercure's sensitivity to lateral gusts when flying at high speed at low altitude.

INTERNATIONAL
Agreement in principle has been reached between **Rolls-Royce and United Technologies** for **collaboration** by the British company in development and production of the Pratt & Whitney JT10D "ten-tonne" commercial turbofan. Details of the agreement, which is subject to British Government approval and other formalities, may be announced by the time this issue appears, and are expected to provide Rolls-Royce with a 34 per cent share, including responsibility for the fan, combustor and diffuser. MTU in Germany and Fiat in Italy already have agreements with Pratt & Whitney to participate in the JT10D programme and are expected to have shares of 10 per cent and 2 per cent respectively, leaving the parent company with 54 per cent, including the core compressor and turbine. Collaboration by Pratt & Whitney in the Rolls-Royce RB.401 development programme for a 5,000 lb st (2 270 kgp) turbofan, in place of the Canadian company's projected JT25D, may be part of the deal.

Dornier, the Federal German partner in the Franco-German **Alpha Jet** programme, has initiated **studies for a single-seat version** of the aircraft, which, the company believes, will be more in keeping with the requirements of the *Luftwaffe* for a daylight/VFR (visual flight rules) close air support aircraft. The *Luftwaffe*, which has requested the studies, originally accepted the proposition that the trainer with strengthened wing for external stores would be suitable for the close air support mission in two-seat configuration, cost of developing a single-seat variant being considered too high to be justified. The *Luftwaffe* now believes, however, that the additional range and payload possible if the rear cockpit is eliminated may make the single-seat Alpha Jet economically feasible.

JAPAN
The definitive **configuration of** the National Aerospace Laboratory's **VTOL research aircraft** was finally **agreed** early in October and the Laboratory now anticipates that construction will commence early in 1977. The experimental aircraft is to be powered by four 3,196 lb (1 450 kg) NAL JR-100V lift engines and a 3,086 lb (1 400 kg) General Electric CJ-610-9 propulsion engine, and take-off gross weight will be 9,920 lb (4 500 kg). Performance is expected to include a max speed of 260 mph (418 km/h) and a range of 190 miles (306 km), and the aircraft will be able to hover for a maximum of seven minutes at low altitude. Overall dimensions will include a span of 30 ft 6 in (9.30 m), a length of 37 ft 8½ in (11.50 m) and a height of 14 ft 1¼ in (4.30 m). During Fiscal 1976, NAL effort will centre on the development of new control and instrumentation systems for the vehicle, and will conduct a basic study of the upper-surface blowing concept utilising a large fanjet, this being directly applicable to a projected four-engined experimental STOL aircraft for which wind tunnel tests will commence during the course of 1976, and on which it is hoped that prototype construction may begin before the end of the present decade.

(Above) The first of six prototypes of the pressurized, 6-9 seat Rockwell Commander 700/Fuji FA-300 that made its initial flight at Utsunomiya on 13 November. Powered by 340 hp Lycoming TIO-540-R2AD engines, the FA-300 is subject of collaborative design and development by the two companies, and the third and fourth airframes are now in the USA for assembly and flight tests by Rockwell International's General Aviation Division. (Below) Beech is continuing to flight test this Super King Air with JT15D turbofans replacing the PT6A turboprops; known as the Fan Jet 400, it may provide the basis for Beech to enter the biz-jet market in due course.

NETHERLANDS
The Fokker **F28 Mk 6000** Fellowship has received its Dutch **certificate of airworthiness** on 5 November, after a 350-hr test programme involving the prototype and first production aircraft. The Mk 6000 has the same long fuselage as the Mk 2000, but with increased wing span, leading edge slats and power plant improvements.

Possible power plants for the Fokker-VFW F28-2 — **a planned Fellowship derivative** for production in the 'eighties (*Airscene*/December 1975) are the 14,000 lb st (6 356 kgp) Rolls-Royce RB.183-72 (a refanned, high BPR version of the Spey 555 used in the present Fellowship) or uprated variants of the Rolls-Royce/SNECMA M45H or General Electric TF34. The F28-2 proposal as at present under study has a 9 ft 10 in (3.01-m) fuselage stretch in two plugs, to increase seating to 110 in a high-density layout, and a 96-ft 6 in (29.4-m) span wing with a supercritical section with six flight spoilers for direct lift control and six lift dumpers, plus leading edge high-lift devices and double-slotted Fowler flaps. A three-engined F28 derivative with M45H engines has also been studied.

SOVIET UNION
The Soviet Union has recently submitted to the FAI for homologation four **speed records for helicopters** set in August by a woman pilot, Galina Rastorgueva flying a Mil A-10 helicopter powered by two 1,500 shp Izotov TV-2-117A turboshafts. The records are as follows: 205.67 mph (331 km/h) over a 310.69-mile (500-km) closed circuit; 206.59 mph (332.65 km/h) over a 621.37-mile (1 000-km) closed circuit; 212.09 mph (341.32 km/h) over a 9.3-15.53 mile (15-25 km) distance, and 207.82 mph (334.46 km/h) over a 62.1-mile (100-km) closed circuit. The A-10 is presumably a special version of the Mi-24 (Hind) military helicopter.

It was anticipated at the time of closing for press that Rolls-Royce would initiate negotiations with the Soviet government during December for the supply of **RB.211-524**

engines for a **new** airbus being developed by the Antonov design bureau. The new **Antonov transport** is reportedly based on the 300-seat fuselage of the Ilyushin Il-86, will be powered by four RB.211-534s and will have a range of 6,910 mls (11 120 km).

USA
Two short-fuselage versions of the L-1011 TriStar are currently being studied by Lockheed, one for short ranges and one for long ranges. The latter variant, designated L-1011-500, is thought to be of more immediate interest to potential customers — including British Airways — as a replacement for early-model jet transports on "long lean" routes on which larger capacity aircraft are not justified. This model would make use of 50,000 lb st (22 700 kgp) RB.211-524B engines and would have a gross weight of 490,000 lb (222 460 kg) — 60,000 lb (27 240 kg) more than the current L-1011-1. Combined with a reduction in fuselage length of 20 ft 2 in (6.15 m), this extra weight would allow the L-1011-500 to carry 212,000 lb (96 248 kg) of fuel, providing a range of 6,200 mls (9 970 km). The L-1011-500 would have redesigned shorter wing root fairings, developed for the TriStar as a fuel economy measure, and might also benefit from various other modifications currently being studied, including 3-ft (0.92-m) wing tip extensions that were recently tested in flight. The short-fuselage TriStar, which Lockheed indicates would not be available until 1979/80, would have the same fuselage length as the L-1011-500, providing up to 231 seats, but would have de-rated RB.211-36 engines of about 36,000 lb st (16 344 kgp) thrust, and the longer-span, high aspect ratio wings. Both these new TriStar variants would probably have improved engine nacelle afterbodies to reduce fuel consumption; the first improvement has been introduced with effect from the 97th production TriStar, comprising the so-called 11-deg afterbody which eliminates the hot core spoiler and reverses only the by-pass fan flow. A 15-deg afterbody, giving a further 1.5-2 per cent improvement in fuel efficiency, is expected to become available later this year.

McDonnell Douglas has proposed a **new version of the DC-10** to British Airways as a prospective replacement for the Boeing 707 and Super VC10. Designated DC-10-30R, it would have Rolls-Royce RB.211-542B engines rated at 50,000 lb st (22 700 kgp) and other items to bring the total British content to about 30 per cent. With a new high gross weight of 572,000 lb (259 690 kg), the -30R would have a range of over 5,750 mls (9 260 km). In an unrelated programme that might eventually produce refinements applicable to the -30R, McDonnell Douglas has flown a DC-10 with modifications to the wing roots and tail fairings to investigate means of reduce drag and, therefore, fuel consumption.

The **first** of the 52 **production** Fairchild **A-10** close-support aircraft so far funded was **flown** at Farmingdale on 21 October, and delivery of the first four production aircraft to Edwards AFB began mid-November. The first A-10 squadron is scheduled to be formed next month (February) at the Davis-Monthan AFB. Considerable effort is currently being expended to ascertain the reasons for a preformance decrease in the pre-production A-10, which, it was anticipated, would display a 10 per cent improvement over the performance attainable by the prototypes. Instead, the performance of the pre-production aircraft has been rated 20-30 per cent *lower*. The pre-production and production A-10s are not as clean aerodynamically as the prototypes and possible aerodynamic drag problems are being investigated, and the installed thrust of the General Electric TF34 turbofan has been found to be 1,000 lb (453 kg) lower than the static thrust rating of the engine, a contributory factor possibly being gun gas residue. Furthermore, as a result of a fatigue test failure (at 81·5 per cent of the load that the A-10 is expected to encounter during an operational lifetime), the fuselage attachment fittings have to be redesigned and strengthened at the point where they meet the forward edge of the wing. The R & D aircraft and the first 18 production A-10s will have to be retrospectively modified.

On 6 November, the US Senate Appropriations Committee approved $132·7m (£66m) **funding for** the McDonnell Douglas/Northrop **F-18 shipboard fighter,** enabling full development to proceed. The first flight of the development F-18 is now scheduled for July 1978, with initial sea trials commencing in August 1979 and a full production go-ahead in March 1980. Initial operational capability is to be achieved in 1981, and of the 800 aircraft planned, approximately 500 will be configured as fighters and the remainder as attack aircraft. The latest complete programme cost to be quoted is $10,487m (£5,243m).

Flight development of the production-configured **Boeing E-3A** AWACS aircraft entered a new phase with the **first flight** of the second Test System (T/S) aircraft at Seattle on 31 October, to be followed by the third and final T/S E-3A early this year. The first Test System E-3A flew last February, actually being one of the original EC-137D prototypes updated (see *AWACS — A Better Balloon/* Vol 8 January 1975); the second and third are new airframes, to be followed by the first of six production E-3As by the end of 1976. The contract for a second batch of six, which the USAF requested in the FY76 Budget, is still the subject of Congressional consideration. The designation of the engines for the production E-3As is now TF33-PW-100/100A, these being derivations of the commercial JT3D with the thrust rating increased to 21,000 lb (9 535 kg).

Boeing is maintaining a small design effort

on an advanced version of the 707, known provisionally as the **Boeing 707-500,** powered by GE/SNECMA CFM-56 or Pratt & Whitney JT10D "ten-tonne" engines. With a fuselage stretch of 23 ft 3 in (7,10 m), the 707-500 would accommodate 60 more passengers than present high-density versions, and would have a gross weight of 354,000 lb (160 700 kg). A one-year flight-test programme is projected, providing certification of the 707-500 by the end of 1979, some eight months after the CFM-56 is planned to be approved for commercial service. A military tanker variant is also proposed, with dual underwing refuelling pods in addition to a centre-line boom; operating at a ramp weight of 378,000 lb (171 600 kg), this could transfer up to 185,000 lb (83 990 kg) of fuel at a distance of 1,380 mls (2 220 km) from base.

Boeing has confirmed that General Electric **CF6-50E engines** are to be available, as a customer option, **on the 747SP** as alternatives to the JT9Ds. The CF6-50E is rated at 52,500 lb st (23 835 kgp) compared with 46,950-50,000 lb (21 315-22 700 kgp) for the JT9D, according to model.

Grumman American has adopted the **name Cheetah for the AA-5A** in its 1976 range of single-engined lightplanes, which also embraces the AA-5B Tiger, TR2 and Trainer. The Cheetah has similar characteristics to the AA-5, which was itself a four-seat derivative of the original AA-1.

Rockwell International's Sabreliner Division is completing design definition of two alternative **developments of the Sabre,** aimed at providing about 25 per cent more range, and better field performance especially at hot and high airfields. An extensive survey of the military and civil market for such an aircraft is to be made later this year to permit selection of the preferred configuration. Basis of the proposals is to use the Sabre 40 or Sabre 60 airframe, with either two 3,960 lb st (1 800 kgp) Garrett AiResearch TFE731-4 engines or three 2,310 lb st (1 048 kgp) Pratt & Whitney JT15D-4s. The twin-engined variant would use the enlarged tailplane of the Sabre 75 and extended wing tips, and could be available in 1978, offering a range of 1,530 mls (2 460 km) cruising at Mach = 0·75, with a gross weight of 21,000 lb (9 534 kg). The three-engined version, which could be available in 1980, would also have the Sabre 75 tailplane, with a new rear fuselage increasing overall length by 8 in (20 cm). Cruising at Mach = 0·75, this variant would have a range of 2,185 mls (3 513 km), the take-off weight being 21,500 lb (9 761 kg).

Rockwell's General Aviation Division has expanded its **range of single-engined aircraft** to three models for 1976. The Model 112A, previously available, has several minor improvements for 1976 and is termed the "value leader" of the Rockwell range, being powered by a 200 hp Lycoming IO-360-C1D6 and having a basic price of $35,900 (£17,690). It is now joined by a turbocharged variant, the Model 112TC and a more powerful version, the Model 114. With a 210 hp Lycoming engine, the 112TC has an increased wing span of 35 ft 7½ in (10,86 m), 2 ft 10½ in (0,88 m) greater than the basic model, and a basic price of $42,900 (£21,130). The Model 114 is powered by a 260 hp Lycoming IO-540-T4A5D engine, has the same wing as the Model 112A, and is priced at $46,900 (£23,100). All three models are certificated to FAR 23·7, the highest standards currently applicable to aircraft of this class. Full data for the new models will appear in the *Air Data File* section of a subsequent issue.

Following Rockwell's interest in the 600 hp

LIT-3S engine as a prospective power plant for future models of its Thrush Commander agplane (*AirScene*/August 1975), Grumman American is investigating the use of this engine **in the AgCat** biplane. The engine, also now referred to as the PZL-3S, is a Polish-built variant of the Ivchenko AI-26W, originally developed in the Soviet Union as a helicopter power plant. A Thrush Commander with the Polish engine is undergoing flight testing in Poland, with a four-blade Polish propeller and a three-blade Dowty Rotol unit being evaluated as alternatives. Grumman American has set aside three AgCats to test the LiT-3S installation and the first of these is now flying at Elmira, where the ag-plane is built under Grumman licence by Schweizer Aircraft Corp. If the new installation is successful, AgCats with Polish engines will be available commercially in 1977.

Piper's tapered wing design, introduced two years ago on the Cherokee Warrior, has been made a feature of the **1976 Archer II,** the four-seat business variant of the Cherokee, with fixed undercarriage. The new wing increases the span by 3 ft (0,92 m) without changing the area, and gives a 3 mph (4,8 km/h) improvement in cruising speed and 100-lb (45-kg) increase in useful load. With a 180 hp Lycoming O-360 engine, the Archer II cruises at 144 mph (232 km/h) and has improved control responses. All seven variants of the Cherokee in the 1976 range, including the Archer II and the new Lance (*AirScene*/December 1975) incorporates a newly engineered door design that "virtually eliminates air and moisture leakage and makes for a much quieter cabin", Piper claims.

Optional internal wing-tip tanks with a capacity of 20 US gal (75,7 l) each are one of the **new features of the Aztec F** and Turbo Aztec F, offered by Piper in this 1976 range. They offer a 300-ml (482-km) increase in range, to 1,500 mls (2 412 km) for the normally-aspirated Aztec and 1,310 mls (2 106 km) for the turbocharged model. Other new features are a flap-to-stabilator twin interconnect, which automatically retrims to neutralize pitch control pressures when flaps are actuated, and a new brake assembly. The TBO of the engines has been increased.

Longest flight to date **by the Rockwell B-1** was made on 24 October, this being the 19th flight, with a duration of 7 hr 52 min. Two aerial refuellings were made, and two supersonic flutter tests were completed — at Mach 1·3 at 25,000 ft (7 625 m) and Mach 1·4 at 27,500 ft (8 388 m). The structural mode-control system was also investigated. On the 18th flight, on 9 October, the intermediate weapons bay, containing a rotary launcher loaded with eight dummy SRAM missiles, was opened in flight. On the 20th flight, low-level penetration was investigated, Mach 0·85 being maintained at altitudes down to 1,000 ft (305 m).

The US Army will begin the **Government Competitive Tests (GCT) on the** two **UTTAS helicopter** designs on 1 February. Both Sikorsky and Boeing Vertol were scheduled to hand over three prototypes of their respective designs — the YUH-60A and YUH-61A — in late January. One instrumented prototype of each design was to be sent to Edwards AFB to undergo testing by the US Army Aviation Engineering Flight Activity and the other four prototypes should be tested in an operational configuration under tactical conditions at Fort Rucker, Alabama, and Fort Campbell, Kentucky. Prior to the hand-over, the Army conducted a Preliminary Evaluation (APE) on each type; that on the YUH-60A was completed on 6 November 1975, five days ahead

continued on page 50

THE ALL-WEATHER TACTICIANS

Attack and electronic countermeasures aircraft are an indispensable team in the US Navy, the ECM aircraft making it possible for the strike aeroplanes to survive in a hostile missile and intercept-radar environment during an attack mission. David W H Godfrey, C Eng, P Eng, MRAeS, AFAIAA, here describes the development and operational use of such a team, represented by the latest versions of the Grumman Intruder and Prowler, the A-6E and EA-6B.

THREE significant factors govern the nature of naval aircraft — the operational requirement, the technology available, and the options developed by planning and weapon system analysis. To these must be added overall aircraft carrier suitability or, in the vernacular of the 'seventies, "platform compatibility". These aspects apply to the three distinct areas of US naval aviation as it is structured in the present decade — attack carrier wings (CVW), each of which is a composite element of fighter, attack, surveillance, reconnaissance and support aircraft, with the main mission of projecting air power ashore primarily in support of amphibious operations: sea-based anti-submarine warfare (ASW) groups (CVSG), comprising fixed and rotary-wing aircraft specializing in providing concentrated ASW protection to localized forces such as those in the objective area of an amphibious operation, and shore-based patrol squadrons consisting of long-range aircraft for open-ocean ASW.

With the elimination of the USN's dedicated ASW carriers (CVSs), ASW squadrons are being integrated with attack carrier air wings (CVAs) and the latter are being redesignated simply as aircraft carriers (CVs). The carrier establishes the first and primary operational requirement for naval aircraft, but the two other basic naval aviation systems that have a far-ranging influence on future aircraft procurement are shore-based ASW patrol aeroplanes and non-carrier ship-based aircraft (eg, the LAMPS light airborne multi-purpose system, selection of which was recently delayed by the US Department of Defense to provide a more stable production pattern for military helicopters).

The workhorse tactical aircraft of the US Navy are the attack aeroplanes for close air support and interdiction missions — the contemporary equivalent of the old dive-bombers and torpedo-droppers. After World War II, the Grumman TBM Avenger torpedo-bomber and Curtiss SB2C

Helldiver dive-bomber were phased out and replaced by the Douglas AD Skyraider and the larger North American AJ Savage three-engined* attack aircraft. After the Korean War, all-jet equipment gradually took over and was universal by 1966, with classifications of light, medium and heavy attack aeroplanes typified by the Douglas A-4 Skyhawk, Grumman A-6 Intruder, and Douglas A-3 Skywarrior. Apart from size and weight classification, the A-4 was intended as a small, tactical, nuclear daylight-only bomber (used also for close air support by the Marine Corps); the A-6 was a general-purpose all-weather interdiction aircraft, and the A-3 was deployed primarily for delivery of nuclear weapons.

All-weather capability appeared first as a radar bomb sight in the AJ Savage. The A-4's only all-weather or night capability was for dropping on-signal, either while flying in formation with a radar-equipped A-3 or by using flares and bombing visually. The A-3 replaced the AJ (by this time redesignated A-2) and had night/all-weather capability, but was primarily a nuclear bomber. The A-6 was the first true all-weather tactical attack aircraft and replaced the AD (later redesignated A-1), the A-4 being replaced by the LTV A-7 Corsair II. (At first, the A-7 was restricted to the day or clear-air mass delivery rôle, but a systems update gave it some all-weather weapon-delivery capability. However, this remained limited since a two-man crew is a requirement in other than a very benign environment.

Having run the gamut of various electronic and photographic systems for gathering information, Navy reconnaissance aircraft have included photo versions of the Grumman Hellcat

---

* The original AJ-1 and AJ-2 had a tail-mounted Allison J33 turbojet in addition to two wing-mounted Pratt & Whitney R-2800 piston engines; they were later converted to become tankers with the jet removed to provide room for the hose and reel unit.

and Panther, and McDonnell Banshee (F6F-4P; F9F-5P; -6P and -9P and F2H-2P), and the shore-based Lockheed RC-121 Constellation with electronic equipment. The RA-3 version of the Skywarrior was the first carrier-based aeroplane to have both photographic and electronic reconnaissance capabilities, and the only shipboard aircraft to have reconnaissance as its sole mission was the Rockwell RA-5C Vigilante. However, the original procurement plan for the RA-5C was cut back as an economy measure and those that remain have only a few years of service life left (see *Eyes of the Fleet* November 1975). Continued financial stringencies have resulted in a move to develop reconnaissance camera pods that may be attached to the Grumman F-14A Tomcat fighter and to the A-7E, plus the probable use of remotely piloted vehicles (RPVs) and satellites for reconnaissance.

Thus, with reconnaissance limited to photography, other intelligence must be acquired either (strategic) from satellites or (tactical) from aircraft flying with the strike force to neutralize hostile electronic systems — an electronic counter-measures (ECM) aeroplane that can survive defensive radar detection and surface-to-air missile (SAM) launches by jamming radar and sending decoy signals to missiles. The Grumman EA-6B (which replaces the EKA-3B, the final ECM/tanker variant of the Skywarrior) is the current ECM

aircraft of the US Navy and will also be supplied to the US Marine Corps which has been the only user of the earlier and less capable EA-6A in support of Navy operations.

Intruder development

Initial version of the Intruder was the A2F-1, which first flew from Calverton, Long Island, NY on 19 April 1960, piloted by Bob Smyth (now Flight Acceptance Director at Grumman). The A2F (redesignated A-6A in 1962 — the later designation is used throughout this account for simplicity) began with a 1956 operational requirement followed by a request for proposals in May 1957 to design the first US Navy aeroplane to feature an integrated weapon system including a digital computer, radar, inertial navigation platform and displays to assist the two-man crew in navigation, attack bombing and terrain-avoidance. The aircraft was to be capable of detecting, identifying and destroying radar-significant tactical and stra-tegic targets under conditions of zero visibility.

Eleven designs were submitted by eight aircraft companies (in addition to Grumman, responses to the RFP came from Bell, Boeing, Douglas, Lockheed, Martin, North American, and Vought), and on the last day of 1957 Grumman's single entrant, Design 128, was announced to be the winner. A development contract was signed in May 1958, and a \$101m cost-plus-incentive-fee production contract was awarded in April 1959. Another important new naval tactical aeroplane was on the way from Grumman's renowned "Ironworks" at Bethpage, Long Island, a term that reflects the traditional strength of the company's airframes under the most adverse conditions.

A fully equipped A-6A flew in November 1960, and the first Navy Preliminary Evaluation (NPE1) was made in September 1961. The airframe Board of Inspection and Survey (BIS) trials started at Naval Air Test Center, Patuxent River, Maryland in November 1962, and the next month NPE2 was made. On 1 February 1963 formal delivery of two A-6As was taken by Vice Admiral Frank O'Breirne, Commander of US Forces Atlantic, and these aircraft were issued to Attack Squadron Forty-Two (VA-42 *Green Pawns*) at Naval Air Station Oceana.

The Intruder was designed as a carrier-borne low-level attack aircraft for delivery of nuclear or "iron" bombs in all weathers and with targets obscured by cloud or darkness. A basic part of its concept was the digital integrated attack navigation equipment (DIANE) system* based on 'fifties state-of-the-art first-generation electronics. This system included high-resolution radars, a digital ballistics computer, an inertial navigation platform and cockpit displays integrated with each other as well as with standard aircraft instruments.

For all-weather attack, radar is used continuously from take-off to landing for navigation to, in, and from the target area; for pin-pointing the target relative to the aircraft in range, bearing and elevation, and for low-level escape. In the target area, the radar must provide ground mapping, terrain avoidance and three-dimensional target tracking. Since these functions must be provided simultaneously, the high resolution needed results in a large dish-type antenna. For visual attack, radar is used as required for ground mapping and terrain-avoidance during navigation to and from the target area, and for target-range measurement during the attack.

Other than a larger core memory for special all-weather modes such as nuclear weapon delivery, the computer needs for all-weather and for visual attack are the same. Inertial

Comparative side views below show (1), the A2F-1 development aircraft with hinged jet tailpipes, narrow rudder, test nose probe and hinge fairings on upper tailplane surface; (2) early production A-6A with fixed jetpipes, perforated air brakes, broad rudder, in-flight re-fuelling probe, and aft-positioned tailplane; (3), A-6B with Standard ARM missiles; (4), A-6C with FLIR and LLLTV in ventral fairing; (5), KA-6D tanker; (6), new-production A-6E, without fuselage air brakes and with TRAM sensors under nose; (7), EA-6A and (8), EA-6B Prowler.

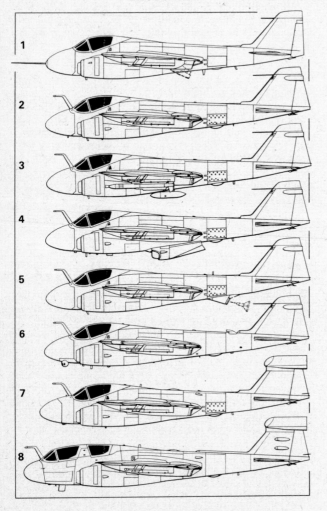

* DIANE included the AN/APQ-92 search radar; AN/APQ-112 track radar; AN/ASQ-61 ballistics computer; AN/ASN-31 inertial navigation system; AN/ASW-16 automatic flight control system; CP-729A (or CP-863A or CP-864A) air data computer; AN/AVA-1 vertical display; AN/APN-141 radar altimeter; AN/APN-153 Doppler navigation; AN/ASQ-57 integrated electronic control and AN/AIC-14 intercom system with IFF, TACAN, and ADF.

The first ECM version of the Grumman Intruder was the EA-6A (above), produced between 1965 and 1969 and now operated by the US Marine Corps' VMAQ-2 squadron at Cherry Point. The EA-6B Prowler (below) is a more extensively equipped ECM variant with four-man crew, still in production for the US Navy. The example illustrated is carrying four sensor pods and one fuel tank.

requirements for both navigation and wind-velocity correction during attack are identical for both types of mission. Both attack capabilities require a vertical display indicator for the attack/navigation situation, and a radar display of horizontal flight-path/mapping information. For all-weather capability, a larger indicator of the radar display is presented to the bombardier/navigator, the pilot's horizontal situation display being presented as a radar monitor. The major difference between the visual and the all-weather capabilities is the radar performance and aperture needed to achieve the higher

resolution required and the two-man workload resulting from the continuous use of radar in the all-weather case. A basic effect of this on the A-6 configuration was to produce relatively large frontal area for a small aircraft, so advantage was taken of this to seat the two crew members side-by-side.

Since the A-6A was to have high subsonic speed, a moderate wing sweepback angle of 25 deg at the quarter-chord line was chosen, with root leading edges swept more sharply and fitted with stall-warning strips to cause a flow burble at high angles of attack. Leading-edge slats were combined with very

wide-span slotted area-increasing trailing-edge flaps. No ailerons were used, lateral control being provided by upper-surface spoilers operating selectively; lift-dumping was achieved by operating the spoilers together when the aircraft had alighted ashore with weight on the main wheels and the engine throttles closed. The tail surfaces comprised a horizontal "flying stabilizer" with 30-deg quarter-chord sweepback and a conventional fin/rudder vertical stabilizer with 28-deg quarter-chord sweepback. (The flying stabilizer had been proved earlier on the Grumman F11F Tiger, in addition to the mechanical artificial feel systems because of its good stick-force-per-*g* feel characteristics; the slat/flap/spoiler combination had likewise been used with great success on the Tiger). Fuselage-side air brakes were located aft of the wings.

Air intakes of the "cheek" type were located well forward of the wings, on the lower sides of the fuselage. Power was provided by a pair of Pratt & Whitney J52-P-6 turbojets each of 8,500 lb st (3 855 kgp). To reduce stalling speed, for

launching and alighting, the A-6A prototype had jet pipes that could be tilted down hydraulically 23 deg from the horizontal, but this feature was found to be unnecessary and was deleted. However, to avoid redesigning to keep exhaust away from the rear fuselage and tail, production aircraft had their tailpipes fixed at a downward angle of 7 deg. Another change for the production Intruder was the addition of a fixed flight-refuelling probe directly in front of the windshield. In all, 488 A-6As were built between 1959 and December 1970 when the last was delivered. The 26th and subsequent aircraft used wingtip air brakes; these opened above and below the wings to an included angle of 120 deg and were located at the trailing edge outboard of the flaps. Subsequently, the original fuselage-side air brakes were deactivated on all aircraft prior to the 310th, and were deleted on subsequent aeroplanes because it was found that they blanked off the engine exhaust and reduced thrust. (Since all EA-6As were modified early A-6As, built before the wingtip brakes were introduced, they had fuselage

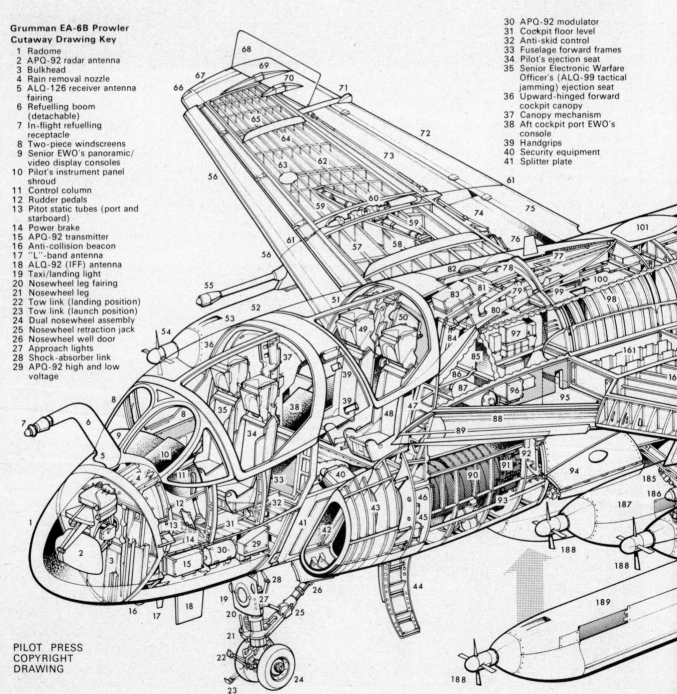

Grumman EA-6B Prowler
Cutaway Drawing Key

1 Radome
2 APQ-92 radar antenna
3 Bulkhead
4 Rain removal nozzle
5 ALQ-126 receiver antenna fairing
6 Refuelling boom (detachable)
7 In-flight refuelling receptacle
8 Two-piece windscreens
9 Senior EWO's panoramic/video display consoles
10 Pilot's instrument panel shroud
11 Control column
12 Rudder pedals
13 Pitot static tubes (port and starboard)
14 Power brake
15 APQ-92 transmitter
16 Anti-collision beacon
17 "L"-band antenna
18 ALQ-92 (IFF) antenna
19 Taxi/landing light
20 Nosewheel leg fairing
21 Nosewheel leg
22 Tow link (landing position)
23 Tow link (launch position)
24 Dual nosewheel assembly
25 Nosewheel retraction jack
26 Nosewheel well door
27 Approach lights
28 Shock-absorber link
29 APQ-92 high and low voltage

30 APQ-92 modulator
31 Cockpit floor level
32 Anti-skid control
33 Fuselage forward frames
34 Pilot's ejection seat
35 Senior Electronic Warfare Officer's (ALQ-99 tactical jamming) ejection seat
36 Upward-hinged forward cockpit canopy
37 Canopy mechanism
38 Aft cockpit port EWO's console
39 Handgrips
40 Security equipment
41 Splitter plate

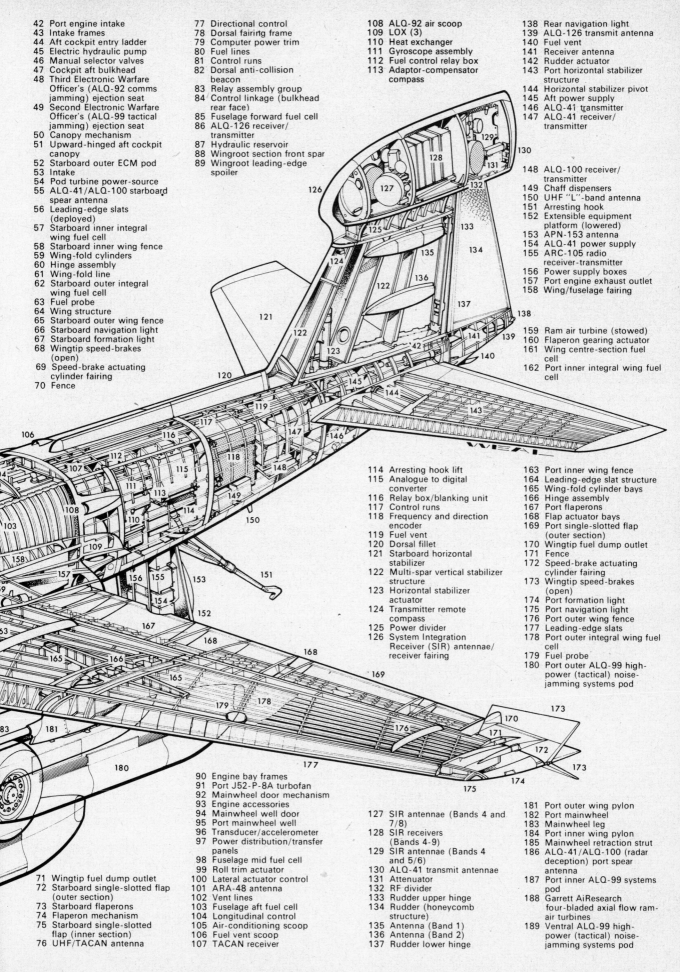

42 Port engine intake
43 Intake frames
44 Aft cockpit entry ladder
45 Electric hydraulic pump
46 Manual selector valves
47 Cockpit aft bulkhead
48 Third Electronic Warfare Officer's (ALQ-92 comms jamming) ejection seat
49 Second Electronic Warfare Officer's (ALQ-99 tactical jamming) ejection seat
50 Canopy mechanism
51 Upward-hinged aft cockpit canopy
52 Starboard outer ECM pod
53 Intake
54 Pod turbine power-source
55 ALQ-41/ALQ-100 starboard spear antenna
56 Leading-edge slats (deployed)
57 Starboard inner integral wing fuel cell
58 Starboard inner wing fence
59 Wing-fold cylinders
60 Hinge assembly
61 Wing-fold line
62 Starboard outer integral wing fuel cell
63 Fuel probe
64 Wing structure
65 Starboard outer wing fence
66 Starboard navigation light
67 Starboard formation light
68 Wingtip speed-brakes (open)
69 Speed-brake actuating cylinder fairing
70 Fence

71 Wingtip fuel dump outlet
72 Starboard single-slotted flap (outer section)
73 Starboard flaperons
74 Flaperon mechanism
75 Starboard single-slotted flap (inner section)
76 UHF/TACAN antenna

77 Directional control
78 Dorsal fairing frame
79 Computer power trim
80 Fuel lines
81 Control runs
82 Dorsal anti-collision beacon
83 Relay assembly group
84 Control linkage (bulkhead rear face)
85 Fuselage forward fuel cell
86 ALQ-126 receiver/ transmitter
87 Hydraulic reservoir
88 Wingroot section front spar
89 Wingroot leading-edge spoiler

90 Engine bay frames
91 Port J52-P-8A turbofan
92 Mainwheel door mechanism
93 Engine accessories
94 Mainwheel well door
95 Port mainwheel well
96 Transducer/accelerometer
97 Power distribution/transfer panels
98 Fuselage mid fuel cell
99 Roll trim actuator
100 Lateral actuator control
101 ARA-48 antenna
102 Vent lines
103 Fuselage aft fuel cell
104 Longitudinal control
105 Air-conditioning scoop
106 Fuel vent scoop
107 TACAN receiver

108 ALQ-92 air scoop
109 LOX (3)
110 Heat exchanger
111 Gyroscope assembly
112 Fuel control relay box
113 Adaptor-compensator compass

114 Arresting hook lift
115 Analogue to digital converter
116 Relay box/blanking unit
117 Control runs
118 Frequency and direction encoder
119 Fuel vent
120 Dorsal fillet
121 Starboard horizontal stabilizer
122 Multi-spar vertical stabilizer structure
123 Horizontal stabilizer actuator
124 Transmitter remote compass
125 Power divider
126 System Integration Receiver (SIR) antennae/ receiver fairing

127 SIR antennae (Bands 4 and 7/8)
128 SIR receivers (Bands 4-9)
129 SIR antennae (Bands 4 and 5/6)
130 ALQ-41 transmit antennae
131 Attenuator
132 RF divider
133 Rudder upper hinge
134 Rudder (honeycomb structure)
135 Antenna (Band 1)
136 Antenna (Band 2)
137 Rudder lower hinge

138 Rear navigation light
139 ALQ-126 transmit antenna
140 Fuel vent
141 Receiver antenna
142 Rudder actuator
143 Port horizontal stabilizer structure
144 Horizontal stabilizer pivot
145 Aft power supply
146 ALQ-41 transmitter
147 ALQ-41 receiver/ transmitter

148 ALQ-100 receiver/ transmitter
149 Chaff dispensers
150 UHF "L"-band antenna
151 Arresting hook
152 Extensible equipment platform (lowered)
153 APN-153 antenna
154 ALQ-41 power supply
155 ARC-105 radio receiver-transmitter
156 Power supply boxes
157 Port engine exhaust outlet
158 Wing/fuselage fairing

159 Ram air turbine (stowed)
160 Flaperon gearing actuator
161 Wing centre-section fuel cell
162 Port inner integral wing fuel cell

163 Port inner wing fence
164 Leading-edge slat structure
165 Wing-fold cylinder bays
166 Hinge assembly
167 Port flaperons
168 Flap actuator bays
169 Port single-slotted flap (outer section)
170 Wingtip fuel dump outlet
171 Fence
172 Speed-brake actuating cylinder fairing
173 Wingtip speed-brakes (open)
174 Port formation light
175 Port navigation light
176 Port outer wing fence
177 Leading-edge slats
178 Port outer integral wing fuel cell
179 Fuel probe
180 Port outer ALQ-99 high-power (tactical) noise-jamming systems pod

181 Port outer wing pylon
182 Port mainwheel
183 Mainwheel leg
184 Port inner wing pylon
185 Mainwheel retraction strut
186 ALQ-41/ALQ-100 (radar deception) port spear antenna
187 Port inner ALQ-99 systems pod
188 Garrett AiResearch four-bladed axial flow ram-air turbines
189 Ventral ALQ-99 high-power (tactical) noise-jamming systems pod

Four colourfully-marked A-6As of the US Marine Corps squadron VMA-324, one of five Marine units currently flying the Intruder (now re-equipped with A-6Es).

brakes only). The A-6A was capable of 6·5g manœuvres and carried 18,000 lb (8 165 kg) of stores on four underwing hardpoints and a fuselage-centreline station.

Early variants

The A-6B was an A-6A modified in 1968 to carry the General Dynamics AGM-78 Standard anti-radiation missile (ARM) designed to home onto radiation emissions from ground radars such as those used to direct surface-to-air (SAM) weapons or for ground-controlled intercept (GCI) of defending fighters. The first 10 A-6Bs were stripped A-6As with navigation equipment only and no attack capability. These were known as partial-systems aircraft. The next three A-6Bs were taken from the A-6A production line in 1969 and modified into passive-angle-tracking anti-radiation-missile (PAT/ARM) configuration. The last A-6Bs were selected from fleet aircraft in 1970 and modified into the target identification acquisition system (TIAS) configuration. Thus, there were three basic configurations of A-6B, all capable of firing the AGM-78 missile.

The A-6C trails, roads interdiction multisensor (TRIM) aircraft was an adaptation of a fully-equipped A-6A to incorporate electro-optical sensors for use against targets that could be neither seen visually nor detected by radar. For this version of the Intruder, 12 A-6As were taken from the production line and modified to carry forward-looking infra-red (FLIR) and low light-level television (LLLTV) mounted on a limited-coverage, gimballed platform all located in a cupola faired under the fuselage. The A-6C TRIM entered fleet service in 1970 and has been used in the western Pacific and Mediterranean. It is no longer operational, but there are contingency plans to reactivate a minimum number if required.

The KA-6D tanker version of the Intruder is the replacement for the Douglas KA-3B. Basically an A-6A with DIANE computer and search and track radars removed, a demonstrator tanker flew on 23 May 1966, but the first production standard KA-6D did not fly until 16 April 1970. In this tanker version, the vertical display indicator is retained and other equipment including Doppler navigation and antenna relocated to accommodate the flight-refuelling hose and reel installation. Candidate A-6A airframes for conversion to the KA-6D standard were selected from the fleet, based on high wing-fatigue life since the tanker is limited to 4g loads. In addition to the hose and reel, the KA-6D has four 300-US gal (1 136 l) external fuel tanks under the wings and a fifth tank or a "buddy" store back-up refuelling system under the fuselage. Total fuel carried is 3,844 US gal (14 547 l) of which 3,000 US gal (11 365 l) is transferrable to another aircraft at a rate of 350 US gal (1 323 l) a minute. The first four tankers were modified at Calverton by engineering changes and the first of these flew on 16 April 1970. Fifty more were modified by Grumman at Stuart, Florida, between 1970 and 1972. The US Navy later modified three KA-6Ds in 1973 and five in 1974; eight more were under conversion in 1975. In addition, Grumman modified three of the original development-batch A-6As to serve as tankers for the F-14A during the latter's early flight trials; these modified aircraft were designated NA-6As.

The Intruder improved

Successor to the A-6A for production is the A-6E, which is an electronic "resuiting" of the Intruder to take advantage of 'seventies technology to replace the "bit and piece" improvements made to the original DIANE installation. Thus, the A-6E is a second-generation aeroplane with a new general-purpose digital computer, multimode radar and a new weapons-release system. The basic A-6A airframe/power plant/flight-instrumentation combination is retained, the engines initially being J52-P-8A/B turbojets of 9,300-lb (4 218-kgp) thrust.

The A-6E story began in July 1967, when Grumman made the Design 128S proposal to update the Intruder, subsequently gaining USN support. The prototype A-6E first flew on 27 February 1970 and was used to evaluate the IBM AN/ASQ-133 solid-state digital computer which had already been used in the EA-6B Prowler (as described later in this article), LTV A-7 Corsair II and General Dynamics F-111. Flight testing of the solid-state weapons-release system began in

(Above) A Grumman A-6A engaged in weapons trials, carrying a Rockwell AGM-53A Condor air-to-surface missile on the port wing pylon. The Condor is in process of being added to the inventory of weapons carried by the Intruder. (Below) An A-6A and EA-6B on board the USS Independence. The EA-6Bs carry a cross marking on the nose to distinguish them from A-6Es on the final approach to deck.

August that year, and by November the Norden AN/APQ-148 multimode (instead of separate track and search) radar was flying. This modern avionics equipment significantly improved reliability (more than 90 per cent probability of trouble-free operation of the attack/navigation system during a typical two-hour mission) and maintainability of the weapon system, and added such new features as built-in test equipment (BITE), dynamic calibration and fault isolation to significantly reduce the direct maintenance manhours per flight hour (28·9 DMMH/FH and 2·3 hours mean flight time between maintenance actions), and the shop overhaul space required aboard the carrier (decreased to 234 sq ft/21,7 m² from 516 sq ft/47,9 m²). The BITE has simplified ground support by eliminating all line-test equipment for the attack/navigation system. The number of onboard equipment boxes is reduced to 14 from 26 and 20 fewer technicians are needed.

There are several new systems scheduled for progressive incorporation in the A-6E to enhance its all-weather attack capability. The first of these adds the Rockwell AGM-53A Condor air-to-surface missile to the Intruder's inventory of weapons, giving it a stand-off delivery capability of up to 70 miles (111 km). Condor is guided to the target by the bombardier/navigator (B/N) who monitors the display transmitted from the missile's television sensor. Once the Condor has been launched, the Intruder can break off the attacking run and escape while the missile navigates its way to the target area, at which time the B/N takes over control for terminal guidance to impact.

Two other forthcoming refinements are the installation of the automatic carrier landing system (ACLS) for one-way data-link control of the aircraft in various operational situations, and of a communication/navigation/identification (CNI) package with dual UHF transceivers and AN/ARN-84 TACAN for greater reliability and less maintenance. The fourth new system is the target recognition attack multisensor (TRAM) which presents real-time television-type imagery of non-visual and/or non-radar significant targets; permits delivery of autonomous laser-guided weapons ("smart" bombs) and enables more precise target discrimination during the final phase of an attack. First flight of an A-6E with the TRAM turret installed was made on 22 March 1974, but the FLIR equipment was not available until October, the first flight being made in the TRAM prototype on 29 October.

The TRAM system integrates forward-looking infra-red (FLIR) and laser sensors provided by Hughes Aircraft with the multimode radar target identification tracking and ranging, under any combination of lighting and weather conditions, with higher accuracy than before. TRAM makes it possible to view terrain features such as road patterns, cultivated areas, ploughed fields and wooded regions as well as traditional radar targets. It provides inflight video-recording replay for target classification and damage assessment as well as post-flight debriefing for operations, intelligence and maintenance requirements. These new capabilities match such weapons as the television-guided Condor and Walleye, the enemy-radar-homing Standard ARM and laser-guided bombs; they also allow implementation of 24-hour broad-ocean search and ship identification for the US Navy rôles of sea control and projection of power ashore.

The fifth new feature for the A-6E, development of which is concurrent with the TRAM programme, is the adoption of the carrier airborne inertial navigation system (CAINS) for reduced maintenance, shorter alignment time for the inertial system and increased accuracy of navigation. For CAINS, the AN/ASN-31 inertial navigation system of the A-6E is replaced by the Litton AN/ASN-92 system used also in the Grumman F-14A Tomcat, E-2C Hawkeye and Lockheed S-3A Viking. CAINS comprises an inertial measuring unit, power supply, control panel and data link. It is compatible with the versatile avionic shop test (VAST) system used both on board carriers and ashore to provide a unified method of testing for the latest US Navy aircraft. Also, extensive built-in test equipment is used for on-board checkout in preflight, flight, post-flight and ground tests. Primary inertial system alignment is by using the ship inertial navigation system (SINS) by cable or radio-frequency link.

As of September 1975, 66 new A-6Es had been built and

continued on page 29

The tone drawing below depicts an A-6E of Navy Squadron VA-65, carrying five drop tanks.

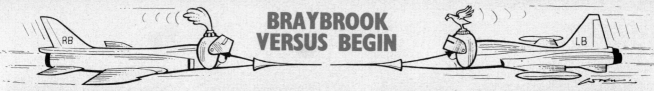

FIGHTER DESIGN PHILOSOPHY

Firstly, let me give you some background. There are certain ideas on fighter design that Lee Begin and I *have* in common; on other points it is a case of total war. Both of us are project engineers by training and each has had the priceless benefit of working under the guidance of an elder statesman of the fighter business. We both accept the fact that preliminary design is a highly specialized field and are, of course, obsessed with getting the early decisions right.

However, Begin has a penchant for a straight-wing and twin engines, whereas I was weaned on the single-motor and moderate sweep concept. All my best leading edges were drawn with a 45 deg setsquare; it's easier, too! He is a transonic air combat expert, whereas (apart from an early stint on an interceptor) I have been mainly concerned with subsonic attack aircraft. If you want to be analytical, forthright and toothless, you might add that Begin has been more successful. Or *just* successful! I would prefer to say that somebody in the US made some sensible decisions, while one halfwit in the UK threw away a 20-year leap in V/STOL technology and some Whitehall genius later turned down the best thing I ever originated and elected to go for a twin-engined advanced trainer that turned out to be too expensive for advanced training!

On occasion, talking to Begin is like trying to converse with someone freshly disembarked from a spaceship. For example, consider engine change technique. Now you may feel that rotating machinery is the ultimate dregs; the very antithesis of the pure, graceful shapes that Begin and I knock out. But this sordid side of the business cannot be ignored. When we discuss changing an engine, he is talking of large stressed access panels made of composite material, with strength and stiffness orientated to suit requirements, a piano hinge along one edge and quick-release latches on the others. On my side of the Atlantic, there is no law to stop me using that approach, but there is an army of characters with perfectly good reasons why it can't be done! Not only have I never seen such a panel (whatever the material) on a European fighter; I have never even seen a machine that would drill out a long piano hinge!

Despite the mind-boggling technology at his disposal, in one respect Begin still has, in my view, to be coaxed reluctantly into the Twentieth Century. He has never accepted the need for thrust reversal, believing that adequate landing performance can be achieved via a low wing loading (and Northrop has quite a nifty single-slotted flap on its later series aircraft), plus an optional drag chute. He also feels that all the deceleration needed in combat can be had via speed brakes and by cranking on some attitude (and high angle operation is certainly an area in which Northrop excels).

In so far as this particular argument goes, I have seen more studies on thrust vectoring in combat than has Lee. I would never try to sell him on full thrust vectoring, because it puts constraints on engine configuration and aircraft layout that he would (perhaps rightly) find unacceptable, and because the fantastic attitude tolerance of his aircraft makes it possible to vector thrust in flight over large angles while keeping the powerplant fixed. However, as a last-ditch effort, the computers say that there is a tremendous advantage in being able to force the character on your tail to overshoot. If you try to slow down by

Lee Begin is one of the principal members of the distinguished Northrop design team. The T-38 Talon and the F-5 "Freedom Fighter" saw their birth on his drawing board; he later became Cobra programme manager and is now concerned with advanced developments of the Cobra family. Roy Braybrook, who retired from the drawing board a few years ago, exchanging his drawing instruments for a typewriter to become — in his view — a grossly underpaid aviation writer, has for long held some diametrically opposed views on fighter design to those promoted by Lee Begin and the editors suggested — with tongue in cheek — that a verbal punch-up between the two could well prove instructive, at least, to our readers!

pulling incidence, Red Baron will see it all happening, go up in a high-speed yo-yo and zap you on the way down. On the other hand, if you can simply go into reverser, he has no visual warning. All he knows is that suddenly you've disappeared from his windscreen and his aluminium is getting the Henry Moore treatment!

North Cape caper

Another advantage that this writer possesses is that of having spent more time talking to pilots of the four Scandinavian air forces and more time above the Arctic Circle. Consider a possible scenario. You're leading a section trying to land at Banak,

The Northrop YF-17 — unsuccessful candidate for the USAF lightweight fighter selection but progenitor of the US Navy's F-18 — is the ultimate expression of Lee Begin's design art, as discussed in this article.

The Northrop F-17 in flight. Two prototypes were built for the fly-off with the General Dynamics F-16 prototypes and completed about 350 hrs in 288 flights for the USAF's accelerated flight test programme. High angle of attack manœuvrability was demonstrated, with no departure tendencies or loss of pilot control at angles of attack up to 63 deg at 20 knots (37 km/h) and sideslip angles of 36 deg at 40 deg angle of attack. 6g and 7g turns were made without buffet at transonic and supersonic speeds and more than 9g was reached in one part of the flight envelope.

which used to be a *Luftwaffe* base for plastering the Murmansk convoys and is now a forward fighter strip with all of 8,500 ft (2 600 m) of runway. In summer, the mosquitoes are so big they need intake guards to keep the F-5s out (that's an old RNoAF joke). Now it's winter and the night lasts all day, it's minus 40 deg and the runway is all ice. For this scenario the balloon has gone up; Ivan has just planted a Mk 84 roughly half-way down the runway, although no one knows exactly where. The clouds are full of rocks and the 40 kt (74 km/h) crosswind (which is full of sleet showers and seagulls) has just produced a snow drift across the arrester. If you divert to nearby Alta, Ivan will wipe you out on the ground, because there is nowhere to disperse and no flak. If you go all the way back to Bodø or Bardufoss, you might as well throw away Finnmark and the North Cape. Your wingman says that if you don't come up with a decision soon, his engine will be sucking on fumes. *Now* do you want a thrust reverser?

Before some gullible reader asks whether it is purely a question of finance that Northrop doesn't fire Begin and hire Braybrook, let me give you just one example where he walked all over me. We argued once (once was enough!) about engine changing. Being brought up on aircraft of F-86 generation, in which you jack the thing up on trestles, remove the rear fuselage at the transport joint and slide the engine away horizontally, I take a dim view of this modern technique of slashing enormous holes in the primary structure to drop the engine out. This saves trestling the aircraft and you can nail the gearbox directly on the engine, but what a terrible thing to do to the airframe!

In line with my "horizontal extrusion" philosophy, the ultimate is the Mirage F1 engine change, in which the engine and afterburner appear simply to slide out through the hole left by the final nozzle. I assume that the engine trolley is adjusted in height, rather than trestling the fuselage. In the early days Northrop used much the same process, although it involved removing the tail cone aft of the tailplane hinge. They abandoned horizontal engine removal for the Cobra series in favour of dropping the engines out. The access panels that make this possible are (of necessity) fully stressed primary structure, since the central fuselage keel disappeared along with the centre-line fin. The residual strength of the rear fuselage with both sets of panels open must be ziltch, but presumably you have armed guards to see nobody leans on the tailplane and accidentally tears the aircraft in two!

Begin's first argument against a horizontal engine change via the nozzle aperture was that the power plant design then dictates the fuselage boat-tail shape, which is highly sensitive drag-wise. I didn't completely buy this, especially in the case of designing a new airframe with a new engine, although it certainly means close collaboration between the two design teams. However, he then pointed out that changing an engine my way couldn't be done inside a NATO aircraft shelter and that the entire Gray Funnel Line would have died laughing if anyone had suggested pulling an engine longitudinally out of the F-18 in a carrier hangar. I don't think there can really be an answer to that!

One all
There is a part of fighter design philosophy that might be described as avoiding superimposing problems. For example, it is Northrop philosophy to have no structure aft of the jet-pipe nozzles. I approve of this: it means in practice that the tailplane cross section has tapered off before the steep part of the boat-tail and there are no possible acoustic fatigue problems. The back end of the Cobra series is very neat, with mechanically-variable, convergent-divergent nozzles mounted on the airframe and no surrounding gap. Northrop philosophy is that the engine nozzles should be as close together as possible, thus avoiding the enormous wetted areas of the F-14 and F-15.

The opposite approach to nozzle location (which you see in the F-4 and F-15) is to cut the afterburner short and pick up

some supersonic post-exit thrust as the jets expand against the afterbody. Short jetpipes also reduce wetted area and give the option of building in some thrust inclination to improve take-off performance. Northrop's main objection is that there is inevitably a base drag penalty when such nozzles are closed down for cruise.

In the Cobra series this matter of separating out problem areas is carried further in that the "vertical" tails have been brought well ahead of the tailplane (I suppose Begin would call it the stabilator). This spreads out the cross section areas and also results in fin effectiveness being maintained up to incredible angles. Northrop philosophy is that the pilot should be able to operate the aircraft with complete confidence over the entire performance spectrum and the YF-17 certainly lived up to this goal.

While admiring the handling characteristics that result, I am inclined to part company with Begin on fin design, in the belief that he has accepted too much wetted area and weight penalty in keeping all the fin above the fuselage. My inclination would be to rely to some extent on ventral fins which provide a long tail arm and operate in really clean air, even if this approach means a fin fold with the undercarriage down (*à la* MiG-23). Begin rejects ventrals as cluttering up engine access and removal.

Deriving from F-5 experience, all the Cobra series have the gun in the upper front fuselage, with blast deflectors to throw the gases even further from the underwing intakes. My only reaction is that it would be interesting to talk to the pilot who carried out the night firings on the YF-17 — the character with the white stick! However, Begin says, "Braybrook, try closing one eye, like your mother taught you before turning on the bathroom light in the dead of night and you might have a neat solution to the problem, as most F-5 pilots know!" I say, "Bring on the photochromic goggles!"

If you define the objective in choosing a gun location as to avoid (a) pitching and yawing disturbances, (b) blinding the pilot, (c) surging the engines and (d) disintegrating the avionics, then there is probably no entirely satisfactory solution. I once praised a design for having the maximum possible vertical separation between intake and gun, only to learn that the first airborne trials had broken up the compressor!

Northrop story
Such matters as gun location and fin configuration, though illustrating quite important aspects of design philosophy, are still far from the core of Begin's thinking. To discuss how the Northrop family of supersonic fighters and trainers developed, we must refer back to 1952, when the N-102 Fang project was offered to the USAF. This aircraft was an 18-20,000 lb (8 165-9 070 kg) fighter powered by a single J79. It had a low tailplane, chin inlet, single fin and two ventrals. In the USAF competition it lost out to the similarly-powered Lockheed F-104, and Northrop then dropped the N-102 as too "pointed" (specialized?) to justify development for the overseas market.

Because he could "make quick drawings", Lee Begin was then taken into the preliminary design section where he came under the guidance of Jack Northrop, "a designer's designer". Later in the Fang period, he was influenced by another great designer, Ed Schmued of P-51 fame, who migrated to Northrop in the early '50s. Begin was instructed to "use technology to simplify and miniaturize" in designing the follow-on to the N-102 project, which was seen in the very early days as a potential naval fighter. At that stage the US Navy had a lot of small carriers, which they could either scrap or fit out with lightweight fighters — the former won out.

In essence, Begin achieved his design aim by combining the bare minimum of armament (ie, two lightweight Sidewinder missiles) with the new aerodynamics of Mach One Area Rule and a power plant of exceptional thrust/weight ratio. Northrop's choice of engine fell on the General Electric J85, which

(Above) An illustration showing that the YF-17's tailplanes need no support when the engines are removed. Notice also that the engine bays are completely plumbed to receive the engine and are remarkably clean (by design) to facilitate quick engine changes and to reduce the probability of plumbing damage, etc. (Below) The integrated nozzle afterbody: an example of remarkable aerodynamic cleanliness.

was then used only in the McDonnell Green Quail missile. It had a 25-hour life and no reheat, and its accessories were on top rather than being configured for ventral access in a fighter. The one possible alternative was the Fairchild J83, but this was judged less suitable.

The aircraft depicted in the first three-view arrangement drawing had a 27-ft (8,23-m) span including the tip-mounted missiles. It had a T-tail and a wing planform almost identical with that of the subsequent F-5A. Begin's philosophy is that flying qualities start with the wing-body combination. "Leading-edge sweep of more than 30 or 35 deg causes more problems than it's worth", he believes, "since the swept wing stalls at the tips and you lose the ailerons". Northrop investigated the effects of varying b/t (ie, span/thickness, a parameter of which I had never heard) while holding sweep angle constant. In the end, a 4·8 per cent section was chosen, although this was as much to suit main gear retraction as for any other reason.

The striking thing about the preliminary design was North-

rop's obsession with weight saving to achieve the maximum possible performance from two minimal engines. For example, the project adopted mid-span ailerons (sacrificing flap effectiveness) and used the Sidewinder launchers as anti-flutter weights (just as Soviet designers put lead in the leading edge) to minimize the need for wing torsional stiffness.

Begin emphasizes the value of low speed wind tunnels in developing an aircraft's handling characteristics, an area in which the straight wing excels. He feels that this planform also has an advantage in producing less drag due to lift, giving an exceptional transonic manœuvrability, although he admits that it penalizes transonic acceleration.

The first N-156F flew on 30 July 1959. During its development a contract had been issued for a two-seat derivative to meet USAF advanced training needs, resulting in the first flight of the YT-38 on 30 April, just ahead of the privately-funded single-seater. The two-seat Talon became operational with USAF Air Training Command in 1961, but it was only in 1964 that MAP deliveries of the F-5A began.

In assessing this first generation, of which well over 2,500 have been produced, I would say that the T-38 was one of the great classics of high performance design. Perhaps it was the only aircraft in history to have been too good for its own good, since its ease of piloting throughout the speed range appears to have killed off most future plans for supersonic flying training! USAF Air Training Command's major accident rate on the T-38 is almost precisely 2/100,000 hours, the lowest for any supersonic machine in the world. The single-seat F-5 is one of the most controversial aircraft of our time, although there can be no doubt of its importance, in giving the less wealthy air forces of the Free World a start in the supersonic combat aircraft business. One interesting aspect of the series is that they pioneered the concept of spin resistance, partly by retaining aileron control beyond the stall and partly through the flat elliptic sections of the front fuselage. The T-38 has never been spun in over five million flying hours and the F-5 can only be made to spin with extreme difficulty.

Laurels and brickbats

Having said all that, however, I would add that, in my opinion, Northrop was absolutely wrong to use a straight wing in designing a supersonic fighter around that level of power plant technology. Things are different now, but in those days a straight wing meant either a moderate wing loading and very little supersonic performance, or a high loading, good supersonics and a dangerously high landing speed. A moderately swept wing would have given a better speed range (through reduced transonic drag and greater wing thickness, making possible more effective flaps) plus simpler construction. This is a question of design priorities: you have to get the speed range before you start looking for better handling, turning performance and load-carrying capability.

As Begin says, the aerodynamic drawback of the swept wing is that its lifting performance is restricted by the spanwise drift of boundary layer, making it prone to tip-stall. This can be alleviated by an array of vortex generators, leading edge extensions, notches, or fences, but there is no cure for its limitation in regard to stores carriage. Outboard loads are invariably aft of the CG (and hence pitch the aircraft nose down on release) and the tip is aerodynamically limited as a mounting point. My opinion doesn't stop the Mirage F1 carrying Magic missiles on the wingtips, but not even Dassault-Breguet would put fuel tanks out there! If any reader should wonder how the Corvette can do it, I can only suggest that this executive jet doesn't operate to the lift coefficients that fighters use. In addition, the wing sweep is relatively small.

As a platform for external loads, the straight wing is unequalled and the Swiss were quite right to choose it for their FFA P.16 subsonic attack aircraft, the same basic wing being used (without Krueger flaps) for the Learjet. But for a supersonic fighter the straight wing was, in my view, definitely wrong prior to the recent advent of US advanced technology engines. By increasing engine thrust/weight ratio from 5:1 to 8:1, they have made it possible to design a high performance fighter that can live with a comparatively low wing loading and in so doing they have made the straight wing a viable supersonic choice for the first time. .

Should the reader be puzzled as to why Begin and I have such contrasting views, I would explain that each designer has a set of graphs for estimating weight and drag, based on his own analysis of past aircraft. There are no internationally accepted standards (otherwise all projects intended to do the same task would look alike) and Begin has naturally had access to different information from my own.

What was of historical significance in the first supersonic Northrop series was not the straight wing itself, but the way in which it was developed to improve the aircraft's cross section area distribution. Figuratively speaking, our paths crossed at that point, since we were both designing from the basis of the T-38. Begin adopted an approach that I considered unattractive, but which turned out (to his surprise perhaps as much as mine) to provide the key to the new wave of aerodynamics, which has now been developed and refined for the Cobra series.

For my part, I was trying to design an advanced trainer, with a good secondary ground attack capability (effectively a scaled-down F-100), for the export market. It was to have employed a single turbofan (the Adour being a "rubber" engine in those days), and improve on the T-38 wave drag by using swept surfaces and by carving off the basic fuselage shape below the front cockpit floor line. The control runs went back in an external tunnel that would have been wiped off each time the thing landed with gear up.

From an area distribution viewpoint, the main problem was to fair the cross section of the front fuselage into the sudden increase provided by the wing. I proposed to do this by two "bullet" fairings of semi-circular section, extending forward from the wing roots and conceivably providing some sort of gun location. As I recall, this type of fairing was first used on the Breguet Taon. The idea of using a swept-forward wing root to achieve the desired smoothing of cross section did not appeal

to me: you didn't need a crystal ball to see short-span vortices and more induced drag.

Fortunately oblivious to such misguided thoughts, when Northrop came to optimize the area distribution of the F-5A, they merely increased the sweep of the inboard leading edge to give extra cross section between the canopy and the basic wing. The result was not only reduced wave drag, but a 10 per cent increase in usable lift coefficient (based on the original wing area). My interpretation of Begin's account is that, although aspect ratio had decreased, lift curve slope had effectively increased and (while optimum lift/drag ratio was little different) turning performance was markedly improved.

Lucky is best

In later (post-Cobra) development, the F-5E intake was moved forward and a much larger root extension fitted. As before, and completely at variance with my predictions, turning performance was improved throughout the speed range.

For the Cobra, preliminary work on which began in 1966, the LEX (leading edge extension) concept was taken much further, since virtually any wetted area penalty could be absorbed. Begin admits that in level flight the hybrid wing gives a slight degradation, but the LEX adds up to 50 per cent to the trimmed lift of the basic wing in turning flight and also maintains aileron. effectiveness to 10-15 deg higher incidence, much as a fence on a swept wing.

In the case of what might now be termed the Cobra I, area ruling was computed for minimum drag in a turn at Mach 1·2. The aircraft was designed with sufficient thrust to maintain maximum g up to 20,000 ft (6 100 m) and with sufficiently low wing loading to reach the same g (unsustained) at twice that height. Stall speed was to have been less than 100 kt (185 km/h).

During wind tunnel development, the shape of the Cobra's "hood" was considerably refined. It was designed so that the LEX span placed the vortices over the optimum part of the basic wing (about 30 per cent span outboard of the wing root), and the LEX area, planform and cross section were adjusted to give the necessary vortex strength. The principle is that the vortices create suctions, giving extra lift on the main wing, and simultaneously these vortices clean up the boundary layer to delay the stall and maintain aileron effectiveness. The fact that

The Northrop family of supersonic twins on display at the company's California plant on the occasion of the roll-out of the YF-17 (extreme right). In the background above, a T-38A Talon trainer is flanked by an F-5B (left) and F-5A (right), respectively two-seat and single-seat versions of the Northrop Freedom Fighter. In the foreground above is the F-5E Tiger II, derivative of the earlier fighter variants.

A head-on view of the Northrop YF-17, showing its unique leading edge extensions (LEX) — the so-called Cobra hood — with long slots at their roots to prevent build up of boundary-layer air ahead of the air intake.

the LEX works primarily by creating extra lift on the main wing explains why the aerodynamic centre of the wing-body combination does not move forward with angle of attack, which is the destabilizing effect that might be anticipated if the forward surface were operating alone.

One further advantage of the Cobra's "hood" is that it exerts significant control over the direction of the flow approaching the underwing intakes, which consequently only experience half the aircraft's incidence changes. This intake location suits a short duct, which is quite feasible for a twin-engined aircraft, provided that there are no sudden changes in duct cross section. One of Begin's constant themes is that the intake duct is one of the most expensive parts of the structure, hence the shorter the better.

Long slots were cut in the LEX root to prevent the build-up of fuselage boundary layer air ahead of the intake, especially at high incidence. These slots make little difference to lift, as might be expected by analogy with a wind tunnel model that almost spans the working section. Small strakes were fitted to the Cobra's extreme nose to improve directional stability at high attitudes by controlling the vortices flowing from the front fuselage — in effect simulating the elliptical nose shape of the F-5 series.

Northrop thus introduced a completely new approach to fighter aerodynamics. The SST people may describe such vortex lift as a straightforward extension of their work, but this would be to understate a brilliant piece of original development. Historically, it *may* be seen as the next important step beyond the canard layout of the Viggen, in which — to judge from the NATO assessment leaked to the US press — the favourable interference between foreplane and mainplane is reduced significantly in turning flight. Perhaps the real advance of the Northrop layout is that, by connecting the foreplane directly to the wing, the trailing vortex is held close to the main lifting surface over a wide range of incidences. In addition, the conventional tailplane is retained to provide longitudinal control inputs with a large effective tail arm.

In giving credit for this tremendous advance in fighter design, two names that might be singled out for attention are Walt Fellers and John Patierno. Fellers joined Northrop in 1954, having worked on the P-51, FJ-1, F-86 and F-100 for North American Aviation. He is now Chief Designer of Northrop Corporation's Aircraft Division and recently received the AIAA's 1975 Aircraft Design Award. Patierno is a pure-bred

Northrop aerodynamicist with an MIT background.

My main regret about the Northrop configuration is that it rules out the use of a low wing, which is certainly preferable for a simple, wide-track undercarriage and for directional stability in flight at high angles of attack. The Viggen layout has no such restriction and it would be interesting to see how much it could be improved by a LEX. I also have a feeling that the canard may be more amenable to in-flight thrust reversal than a tail-aft layout, so all is not lost at Linköping!

Twins and singles

Readers may have gathered that Begin is something special in the fighter world. In one respect he is not only special but quite unique: he is the only designer I have ever met who claims that a twin-engined fighter can be built *lighter* than the equivalent single-engined one! The basis for his belief is that by halving the thrust of an engine, you achieve a better thrust/weight (T/W) ratio through disproportionate savings on both the casing and rotating parts. Any theoretician will bear this out, from simple hoop stress and centrifugal load considerations.

This really is the crunch point for the reader, who now has to decide whether to accept the word of this Lee Begin person, backed by every theoretician this side of the Mexican border, or the opinion of your's truly. To me the idea of a lighter twin is so ridiculous that if anyone but Begin had said it I would have keeled over laughing. In the circumstances, I telephoned the only rotating machinery merchant that I trust (as a taxpayer I own the company — why shouldn't I ask him?) and put the point to him. He failed to produce the anticipated expressions of scorn. On the contrary, he said that halving the thrust would certainly improve T/W, provided this wasn't carried so far that engine details reached minimum gauge sizes. Making a note to have him certified, I asked him to find out what would be the T/W degradation from a 4-tonne to an 8-tonne dry engine and in due course back came the computer's reply: *all of 2 per cent*!

Well, in my opinion, a 2 per cent saving in dry weight is easily offset by the better fuel consumption of the larger engine. Add to this the effects of the much wider fuselage required for the twin and of its more complex installations, and you are back with the old rule-of-thumb that a twin-engined fighter is roughly 10 per cent heavier than a single of the same performance and that the cost differential is even higher. Begin's computer is obviously throwing him different data!

Having said all that, I am still not opposed to the use of twin engines in combat aircraft. It is up to the operator to decide whether a cost increment in the region of 10 per cent is justified by the improvement in aircraft attrition, which logically may be anything from zero to 30 per cent. For a service that operates over water or that intends to go to war, this may well be the more important consideration.

In addition, there are some practical design problems that favour the twin. Begin points out that one big advantage is the reduced length of the power plant, resulting in increased fuel space ahead of the compressor. The twin also facilitates a wide track undercarriage. Aside from having a sneaking regard for a good, solid keel member, I like the twin as a means of straightening out the intake ducts. Straight ducts mean shorter, lighter ducts, less flow distortion at the compressor face and fewer problems with the boundary layer ramps. The other attraction of the twin is that it gets away from the messy fuel tankage almost invariably caused by the V-planform intake ducts of the single engine. General Dynamics avoided this problem with the single ventral intake of the F-16, but I might just wait for the FOD statistics before copying that idea!

Consolations for the loser

Returning to the Northrop story, in 1972 the USAF ordered two prototypes of the Cobra-derived YF-17 under the LWF low-cost technology demonstration programme, for testing alongside two YF-16s from General Dynamics. Intent on providing the maximum flying time within the funding available, Northrop went to bat with a minimum-cost aeroplane, using an off-the-shelf undercarriage and two engines which could have benefitted from a lot more development. Suddenly, in April 1974, the USAF switched the trials objective from technology demonstration to ACF selection, and there was *no way* that the YF-17 could have won. The subsequent choice of the YF-16 for production was the zero-shock decision of a decade.

The first YF-17 began flight trials on 9 June 1974 and the second aircraft on 21 August of the same year. Technologically, the most interesting part of the programme was the fantastic range of flying attitudes explored by the YF-17, confirming Northrop's ideas on planforms and handling qualities, and proving that the LEX was straightening the airflow into the intakes, there being no stall-induced flame-outs. Although designed to retain stability and control to 45 deg AOA (angle of attack), which is about 50 per cent more than normal, the YF-17 in flight showed no departure tendencies even at 63 deg! It also reached a sideslip angle of 36 deg at 40 deg AOA. For comparison, published AIAA data indicate that the YF-16 reached a peak of only 28 deg AOA.

Whatever the success in technology demonstration, the USAF production contract had been lost and Northrop joined with the McDonnell Douglas Corporation to develop from the YF-17 a carrier-suitable ACF project to offer to the US Navy, with MDC assuming the prime contractor rôle in view of its naval aviation experience. The resulting F-18 was selected by the US Navy to be its new lightweight fighter to replace the F-4J and ultimately the A-7D; in effect completing the cycle that Begin had started 20 years earlier. Compared with the YF-17, it has a larger nose, extra graphite composites, more powerful controls, a wet wing with outboard fold and further aerodynamic refinements to the LEX. The General Electric F404 engines will give 8 per cent better cruise fuel consumption and 25 per cent more transonic thrust. The F-18 weighs 8,142 lb (3 693 kg) more than the YF-17, giving a normal gross of 33,642 lb (15 267 kg), but 3,000 lb (1 360 kg) of this increase is fuel, resulting in a total internal capacity of 10,000 lb (4 535 kg).

The Cobra series does not stop with the F-18. By de-navalizing it, Northrop will benefit (relative to the YF-17) from the much more advanced 16,000 lb (7 256 kg) thrust F404

engines, the greater fuel volume provided by more efficient packaging of the F-18, and the 28-in (71-cm) radar dish and all-weather, all-aspect missiles. The resulting Cobra II will have a substantially better radius-SEP combination than the F-16 and the option of a vastly improved weapons system, including better air-surface delivery accuracies than the A-7D!

To get the fighter business in perspective, I have written in the past about the analogy to the 1930s, with many fighter manufacturers still turning out low-performance "biplanes" which were clearly obsolete before they ever flew. Today, the analogy continues, but with American manufacturers at last producing the modern equivalents of the '40s' outstanding monoplanes. Thus, to my mind the F-14 and F-15 are up-dated P-38s, providing long-endurance combat air patrols and air superiority at long radius, but also representing enormous targets. The F-16 may similarly be the modern equivalent of the Zero; a remarkably manœuvrable aircraft with surprisingly long range for its small size. By the same token, the F-18 and Cobra II should prove analogous to the F6F and P-51; medium-size fighters with a war-winning combination of performance and equipment.

If Begin really has initiated the '80s' equivalent of the P-51, then is it sackcloth-and-ashes for Braybrook? Not entirely and for two good reasons. Firstly, in the mid-'50s I drew a fighter around a single afterburning Spey (half the power plant of the British F-4). It had a low wing of moderate sweep, half-scale F-4 intakes and it would have been a reasonably useful aircraft at that time. However, I then tore it up and threw it away, not just because the RAF had lost interest in fighters, but because it was obvious to anyone with a sense of perspective that the design was too easy; that it would inevitably be wiped out conceptually before it amounted to anything. If I don't feel too bad today, it is firstly because 10 years ago I knew something about the business that one European so-called fighter manufacturer is still trying to come to terms with!

Secondly, I take consolation from the fact that fighter contests are like horse races: there is always another one tomorrow and the prizes are getting bigger every time. All it takes to compete is a certain talent, a wealthy sponsor and the belief that today's winner was a little bit lucky. If you scratch around right now, you can find some splendid fellows who are anxious to convert their incredible wealth into certain forms of technological leadership. I think I might bone up on my Arabic, get my drawing board out of hock and just beat old Lee Begin into the dirt. The P-51 was the greatest in its day, but it didn't last for ever! □

THE HIGH WIND FROM OTA

THE PACIFIC WAR had barely entered its third year when Allied Intelligence became aware that Japan's Imperial Army Air Force was phasing into service what was reported to be an appreciably more potent air superiority fighter than the widely-used Nakajima Hayabusa, the measure of which had only relatively recently been taken. Nothing was known of the physical appearance of the new warplane. Indeed information was restricted to the fact that it was again a creation of the Nakajima organization; that it was powered by the 18-cylinder Homare engine and that its *Kitai* (experimental airframe) designation was Ki.84. It was accordingly assigned the reporting name *Frank* under the ATIU-SWP (Air Technical Intelligence Unit — South-West Pacific) system and reports of its combat début were keenly awaited.

Some seven months passed and suddenly, early in August 1944, the sorely beleaguered US 14th Air Force in China, with almost half its combat force committed to the Burma campaign, critically low on fuel reserves and short on supplies, and struggling to provide air cover for the Chinese and US forces endeavouring to stem the Japanese advance towards the Yangtze, found itself confronted by yet another problem in the shape of a new and formidable Japanese fighter. A truly redoubtable opponent possessing a performance far in excess of anything previously fielded by the Imperial Army Air Force and coupling this with very respectable firepower, outstanding manœuvrability and the ability to withstand battle damage to an extent hitherto unknown in Japanese fighters, signifying the use of a markedly sturdier structure than customary and the provision of protection for both pilot and fuel tankage. This could only be *Frank*!

In the few weeks that followed before this newcomer disappeared from Chinese skies as suddenly as it had appeared, the new fighter had a dramatic effect on the balance of airpower in the area and an equally dramatic effect on the morale of the 14th AF fighter element, which had vacated its vital base at Hengyang on 8 August, saw other of its forward bases seriously threatened and now found itself opposed by a warplane that outclassed its own equipment. It seemed to the hard-pressed USAAF pilots that *Frank* enjoyed all the virtues displayed by earlier Japanese fighters yet suffered none of their shortcomings.

The début of this new combat aircraft had indeed been auspicious and the interest with which a crashed specimen found on Hsian airfield in September was examined by a TAIC (Technical Air Intelligence Command) field team can well be imagined. Its findings did little to alleviate the concern that had followed the new fighter's appearance in battle; it had no readily apparent Achilles Heel such as had been found in its predecessors. If conventional enough by western standards, it was *radically* different from what had come to be expected of Japanese fighters. Whereas such types as the Hayabusa had featured well-designed but relatively lightly constructed airframes mated to low-powered engines, rudimentary if any pilot and fuel tank protection and firepower in keeping with this lightweight concept, *Frank* was a bird of very different feather. Characterized by an extremely sturdy structure, it had all the advantages of a really powerful engine utilizing water-methanol injection, self-sealing fuel tanks, pilot armour and bullet-proof windscreen, and highly destructive armament. From every aspect this was a formidable warplane indeed, and 14th AF pilots had had good reason to view it with something akin to awe.

From bird of prey to wind of change

When Major Iwashi first led his newly-mounted 22nd *Sentai* into its temporary base on the outskirts of Hankow in August 1944, he and his pilots fully anticipated the impact that their appearance would have. The 14th AF had succeeded in establishing a meagre edge in the northern Chinese skies, but logistical problems compounded by escalating combat losses as the Japanese offensive gained momentum had imposed serious strain on the relatively limited USAAF resources and the 22nd *Sentai* was enabled to blood its new fighter in combat under just the conditions for which it had been designed; conditions that it was destined rarely to enjoy throughout the remainder of its combat life which was to be spent primarily in a defensive rôle with all its attendant disadvantages.

Established at Fussa, Yokota, on 5 March 1944, the 22nd *Sentai* had been the first recipient of the Army Type 4 Fighter Model 1-ko Hayate (Gale), or Ki.84-I-ko, its pilot cadre having been drawn from the Hayate service trials *Chutai* which had conducted intensive operational evaluation of the new warplane in Japan from October 1943. This evaluation, like the service trials at the Tachikawa Army Air Arsenal that had preceded it, had proceeded remarkably smoothly with few of the teething troubles usually associated with such initiation. Such minor problems as were encountered (eg, occasional and inexplicable drops in fuel and hydraulic pressures) were considered to be of relatively minor nature and as such would be eliminated in the normal course of service development. It was thus that only 16 months elapsed between the commencement of prototype flight testing at Ojima in April 1943 and the operational début of the fighter over China at the hands of the 22nd *Sentai*.

Work on the Ki.84 had been initiated early in 1942 by Yasumi Koyama to meet a requirement for a successor to the Ki.43 Hayabusa (Peregrine Falcon), which, just committed to combat, was already establishing an impressive ascendancy over the semi-obsolescent Allied fighters by which it was being opposed. The Army Air Headquarters, the *Koku Hombu*, was sufficiently realistic to appreciate the fact that the maintenance of air superiority could not be assured by the Hayabusa for very long, despite the success that had attended its operational committal — success that was undoubtedly due in some part to the mystique with which, in so far as the Allies were concerned, this Japanese fighter was enveloped. The appearance of higher calibre Allied fighters was only a matter of time, the Nakajima Shoki (Devil-Queller) interceptor was too specialized in application to succeed the Hayabusa, and thus the development of a new all-purpose, long-range fighter with characteristics superior to those of the best western fighter known to be under development at that time was adjudged a matter of high priority.

The *Koku Hombu* therefore prepared a specification for a new fighter which was issued to Nakajima within a few weeks of the Pearl Habour attack. Assigned the *Kitai* designation

Ki.84, the new fighter had, in essence, to combine the manoeuvrability of the Hayabusa with the speed and climb of the Shoki, relatively heavy firepower, armour protection and self-sealing fuel tanks being mandatory. A maximum speed of 400-420 mph (640-680 km/h) was called for, together with the ability to operate 250 miles (400 km) from base at combat rating for one-and-a-half hours. Wing loading was not to exceed 34·8 lb/sq ft (170 kg/m²), the specified power plant was an Army version of the Navy's NK9A Homare 18-cylinder two-row radial and armament had to comprise a pair of 20-mm Ho-5 cannon and two 12,7-mm Ho-103 machine guns.

Nakajima's study to meet this requirement was approved by the *Koku Hombu* on 27 May 1942, and Koyama and his team immediately initiated detail design. Such was the effort placed behind the project at Nakajima's Ota plant that the first prototype of the new fighter was rolled out of the experimental hangar almost exactly 11 months later, during the last week of March 1943, flying for the first time the following month in strict secrecy at the Ojima airfield.

(Above) The first prototype of the Ki.84 Hayate. Note collected exhaust stubs and prominent gun ports. (Immediately below) One of the pre-production Ki.84 Hayates at Tachikawa.

(Head of opposite page) A Ki.84-I-ko Hayate of the 104th Sentai at Ota airfield. This Sentai was originally formed on Hayates at Heizan, Manchuria. (Below) Hayates of the 101st Sentai during the Okinawa invasion. The 101st was formed specifically for Okinawa defence.

Nakajima (Ki.84-I-ko) Army Type 4 Fighter Model 1-ko Hayate specification

Power Plant: One Nakajima (Ha-45-21) Army Type 4 Model 21 18-cylinder radial air-cooled engine rated at 2,000 hp at 3,000 rpm for take-off, 1,860 hp at 3,000 rpm at 5,905 ft (1 800 m) and 1,620 hp at 3,000 rpm at 20,995 ft (6 400 m), driving four-bladed constant-speed electrically-operated Pe-32 propeller of 10 ft 2 in (3,10 m) diam. Total internal fuel capacity of 153 Imp gal (697 l) distributed between one 47·7 Imp gal (217 l) fuselage tank, two 40 Imp gal (173 l) wing centre section tanks and two 14·7 Imp gal (67 l) outboard wing leading-edge tanks.

Performance: (At 7,965 lb/3 613 kg with 124 Imp gal/563 l fuel) Max speed, 325 mph (523 km/h) at sea level, 362 mph (582 km/h) at 9,840 ft (3 000 m), 388 mph (624 km/h) at 21,325 ft (6 500 m), 374 mph (602 km/h) at 29,530 ft (9 000 m), 340 mph (547 km/h) at 34,450 ft (10 500 m); normal cruise, 236 mph (380 km/h) at 19,685 ft (6 000 m); initial climb rate, 3,790 ft/min (19,25 m/sec); time to 16,405 ft (5 000 m), 6·42 min, to 26,245 ft (8 000 m), 11·66 min; service ceiling, 36,090 ft (11 000 m); range (full internal fuel) at 1 640 ft (500 m), 1,025 mls (1 650 km) at 178 mph (286 km/h), 780 mls (1 255 km) at 254 mph (408 km/h), with two 44 Imp gal (200 l) drop tanks, 1,815 mls (2 920 km) at 173 mph (278 km/h), 1,410 mls (2 270 km) at 241 mph (388 km/h); stalling speed (flaps down), 86 mph (138 km/h).

Weights: Empty equipped, 5,864 lb (2 660 kg); normal loaded (full internal fuel), 8,192 lb (3 716 kg); max overload, 9,195 lb (4 171 kg).

Dimensions: Span, 36 ft 2 in (11,24 m); length, 32 ft 6½ in (9,92 m); height, 11 ft 1 in (3,38 m); wing area, 226·04 sq ft (21,0 m²).

Armament: Two fuselage-mounted 13-mm Ho-103 machine guns with 350 rpg and two wing-mounted 20-mm Ho-5 cannon with 150 rpg. Provision for two 66-lb (30-kg), 220-lb (100-kg) or two 551-lb (250-kg) bombs on underwing racks.

A conventional low-wing cantilever monoplane, the Ki.84 had a flush-riveted semi-monocoque light alloy fuselage structure of oval section and a single-spar wing with light alloy stressed skinning. The structural design followed the common Japanese practice of building the wing integral with the centre fuselage in order to save the weight of heavy attachment points, but the Ki.84 was very much sturdier than any of its predecessors. Of particular interest was the heavy mainspar built up of half-inch extruded A1 angles into an I-beam design. The wing carried metal-framed fabric-covered ailerons and hydraulically-operated Fowler-type flaps with a maximum deflection of 35 deg. The fuselage centre section embodied two firewalls between which was mounted a 35 Imp gal (160 l) water-methanol tank, and 162 Imp gal (737 l) of fuel was distributed between the main tank aft of the cockpit, a pair of wing tanks inboard of the main undercarriage members and two outboard wing leading edge tanks. The windscreen incorporated 65-mm armourglass, the pilot was provided with 13-mm head and back armour, and the paired synchronized Ho-103 machine guns in the forward fuselage had 350 rpg while the two wing-mounted Ho-5 cannon each had 150 rounds. From the outset provision was made for underwing racks capable of lifting two bombs of up to 551 lb (250 kg) weight or 44 Imp gal (200 l) drop tanks. The initial Army version of the Homare installed in the prototypes, the Ha-45-11, offered a take-off rating of 1,800 hp

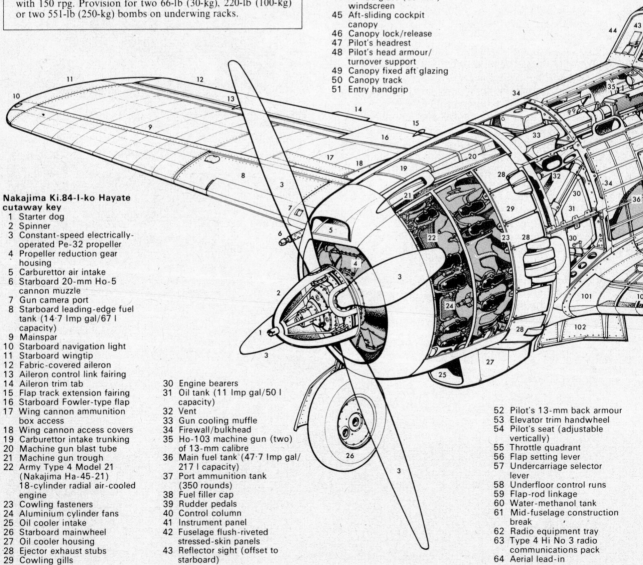

44 Armourglass (65-mm) windscreen
45 Aft-sliding cockpit canopy
46 Canopy lock/release
47 Pilot's headrest
48 Pilot's head armour/turnover support
49 Canopy fixed aft glazing
50 Canopy track
51 Entry handgrip

Nakajima Ki.84-I-ko Hayate cutaway key
1 Starter dog
2 Spinner
3 Constant-speed electrically-operated Pe-32 propeller
4 Propeller reduction gear housing
5 Carburettor air intake
6 Starboard 20-mm Ho-5 cannon muzzle
7 Gun camera port
8 Starboard leading-edge fuel tank (14·7 Imp gal/67 l capacity)
9 Mainspar
10 Starboard navigation light
11 Starboard wingtip
12 Fabric-covered aileron
13 Aileron control link fairing
14 Aileron trim tab
15 Flap track extension fairing
16 Starboard Fowler-type flap
17 Wing cannon ammunition box access
18 Wing cannon access covers
19 Carburettor intake trunking
20 Machine gun blast tube
21 Machine gun trough
22 Army Type 4 Model 21 (Nakajima Ha-45-21) 18-cylinder radial air-cooled engine
23 Cowling fasteners
24 Aluminium cylinder fans
25 Oil cooler intake
26 Starboard mainwheel
27 Oil cooler housing
28 Ejector exhaust stubs
29 Cowling gills
30 Engine bearers
31 Oil tank (11 Imp gal/50 l capacity)
32 Vent
33 Gun cooling muffle
34 Firewall/bulkhead
35 Ho-103 machine gun (two) of 13-mm calibre
36 Main fuel tank (47·7 Imp gal/217 l capacity)
37 Port ammunition tank (350 rounds)
38 Fuel filler cap
39 Rudder pedals
40 Control column
41 Instrument panel
42 Fuselage flush-riveted stressed-skin panels
43 Reflector sight (offset to starboard)
52 Pilot's 13-mm back armour
53 Elevator trim handwheel
54 Pilot's seat (adjustable vertically)
55 Throttle quadrant
56 Flap setting lever
57 Undercarriage selector lever
58 Underfloor control runs
59 Flap-rod linkage
60 Water-methanol tank
61 Mid-fuselage construction break
62 Radio equipment tray
63 Type 4 Hi No 3 radio communications pack
64 Aerial lead-in

at sea level and drove an electrically-operated four-blade constant-speed Pe-32 propeller.

A batch of no fewer than 83 service trials aircraft was initiated in the early summer of 1943, immediately upon confirmation by Army test pilots at the Tachikawa Air Arsenal of the Nakajima test pilot's enthusiastic report on the capabilities of the Ki.84, the first of these pre-production fighters following closely on the heels of the second Ki.84 prototype from the Ota plant in August 1943. Although in some respects performance fell short of that requested by the specification, the capabilities of Nakajima's new warplane were undoubtedly impressive, and one of the Army test pilots at Tachikawa, Lt

Funabashi, attained a maximum level speed of 394 mph (634 km/h) at 21,800 ft (6 645 m) in the second pre-production example which embodied the various minor modifications resulting from the prototype test programme. During diving trials, the aircraft attained a speed of 496 mph (798 km/h), at which point the test pilot experienced difficulty with his oxygen supply, necessitating termination of the test.

The pre-production aircraft were largely hand-built, despite the quantity involved, and differed one from another in minor details, these including various detail changes to the vertical tail surfaces, the application of different types of ejector exhausts and the provision of a centreline rack for a drop tank. Individual aircraft were tested with longer-span wings and at least two of the pre-production examples were evaluated with retractable skis in Hokkaido during the winter of 1943-44. A total of 24 pre-production fighters had left the Ota line by the end of 1943, a service trials *Chutai* being formed with a number of these in October of that year, but the primary factor governing deliveries was, at this time, availability of Ha-45 engine.

The pre-production engines had revealed a number of design deficiencies that were not proving easily rectified and although

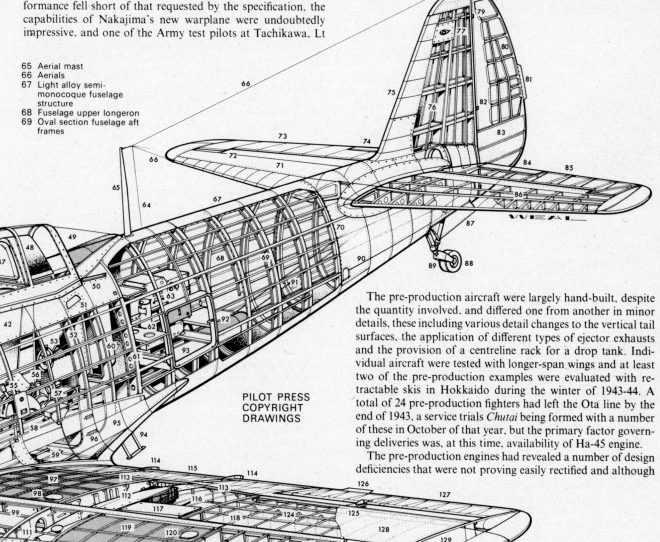

PILOT PRESS
COPYRIGHT
DRAWINGS

65 Aerial mast
66 Aerials
67 Light alloy semi-monocoque fuselage structure
68 Fuselage upper longeron
69 Oval section fuselage aft frames
70 Aft fuselage construction break
71 Starboard tailplane
72 Elevator balance
73 Starboard elevator (fabric covered)
74 Elevator trim tab
75 Tailfin leading edge
76 Tailfin structure
77 Rear navigation/formation light
78 Aerial stub attachment
79 Rudder upper hinge
80 Rudder frame (fabric covered)
81 Rudder trim tab
82 Rudder centre hinge
83 Rudder lower section
84 Elevator trim tab
85 Elevator frame (fabric covered)
86 Tailplane structure
87 Tailwheel doors
88 Solid rubber tyre
89 Aft-retracting tailwheel
90 Fuselage lower longeron
91 Tail surface control cables
92 Oxygen cylinders
93 Radio access
94 Retractable entry step
95 Wing root fairing
96 Fairing former
97 Port main wing tank (40 Imp gal/173 l capacity)
98 Fuel filler cap
99 Wing spar
100 Undercarriage leg cut-outs
101 Mainwheel wells
102 Mainwheel doors
103 Port 20-mm Ho-5 cannon muzzle
104 Wheel brake hydraulic lines
105 Shock-absorber links
106 Port mainwheel
107 Axle
108 Mainwheel leg fairing
109 Underwing auxiliary fuel tank (44 Imp gal/200 l capacity)
110 Landing light
111 Cannon blast tube
113 Flap tracks
114 Flap track extension fairings
115 Fowler-type flap structure
116 Rear auxiliary spar
117 Cannon ammunition tank (150 rounds)
118 Spar join
119 Port auxiliary leading-edge tank (14·7 Imp gal/67 l capacity)
120 Fuel filler cap
121 Pitot tube
123 Main spar outer section
124 Wing ribs
125 Aileron control rod link fairing
126 Aileron trim tab
127 Aileron frame (fabric covered)
128 Wing skinning
129 Port wingtip
130 Port Navigation light

(Above) A Hayate of the 52nd Sentai taking-off with a drop tank beneath the port wing and a 551-lb (250-kg) bomb beneath the starboard wing. (Below) A Hayate captured by the Nationalist Chinese forces and believed to have belonged to the 25th Sentai.

development personnel at Nakajima's No 11 plant at Musashi — where preparations for the large-scale production of this power plant were being made — evinced confidence that all teething troubles would be overcome without delaying the achievement of full production status, engine maintenance problems seriously inhibited the test programme. Sudden and inexplicable drops in fuel pressure and power losses were reported by test pilots, leading to some redesign of the fuel system without tangible results.

Engine apart, the only major teething trouble encountered with the Ki.84 throughout its test programme stemmed from the hydraulic system which was found to be insufficiently powerful and to lack reliability. The consensus of opinion was that both power plant and hydraulics difficulties were not sufficiently serious to warrant delaying full-scale production as the fighter fully met the Army Air Force's requirements in every other respect and its service introduction was becoming vitally urgent.

Nakajima's Ota factory had meanwhile completed tooling and was to deliver its first production Ki.84 as the Army Type 4 Fighter Model 1-ko Hayate in April 1944, and the Utsunomiya plant had also attained an advanced stage in tooling, the two factories being the recipients of orders calling for the delivery of 2,565 Hayates by the end of the year. From the outset, the structure of the Hayate had been designed with a view to facilitating production, calling for 44 per cent less tooling than the Hayabusa and 42 per cent less than the Shoki, and production tempo built up extremely rapidly. At the same time as the first production Hayates began to leave the Ota assembly line, a further pre-production batch of 42 fighters was laid down; these, to be produced in parallel with the initial production fighters, were intended primarily to evaluate improvements and changes suggested by initial service experience and modifications proposed by the design team to increase performance.

In the meantime, output of Ha-45 engines at Musashi had suffered a number of setbacks, these largely stemming from inadequate preparations which were resulting in serious shortages of jigs, tools and skilled personnel. Indeed, only 66 engines had been completed by the end of 1943, and it was to be April 1944 before a production tempo in excess of 100 engines per month could be attained. Another inhibiting factor was the failure of sub-contractors to attain planned component output,

and although the Ota and Utsunomiya assembly lines were never to be stalled for lack of component parts, neither were they ever to achieve capacity output.

Rapid regimental status

Despite shortfalls in engine and component deliveries, Hayate output climbed rapidly during the summer months of 1944, the new fighter achieved widespread regimental status extremely quickly, several *Sentais* having converted from the Hayabusa to the Hayate before the autumn and others being formed directly on the Hayate. While the ground handling characteristics left much to be desired and were to be largely responsible for a fairly high rate of training attrition, the flying characteristics were generally conceded to be first class. The Hayate was simple to fly and relatively inexperienced pilots could convert to the new fighter after only a brief training period on the Hayabusa. By comparison with the very much lighter Hayabusa, the Hayate displayed several poor control characteristics — the elevators heavied up at high speeds and the rudder was somewhat mushy at low speeds — but such shortcomings were considered a small price to pay for the dramatic improvements in other respects offered by the new fighter.

The first *Sentai* to convert, the 22nd which was to blood the Hayate in action over China, was formed with highly experienced pilots and, pending availability of the new fighter in quantity, flew it in concert with the Ki.44 Shoki. The China deployment of this *Sentai* was to last no more than five weeks, the unit being reassigned to Leyte in the Philippines immediately Japanese Intelligence became aware that this would be the next primary objective in General MacArthur's strategy following the fateful Battle of the Philippine Sea and as a prelude to Allied seizure of the Philippines. The 51st *Sentai* had been formed with the Hayate at Ozuki on 28 April 1944, specifically for Philippines defence, the 52nd *Sentai* being formed simultaneously at Bofu for the same purpose, both converting to the Hayate after preliminary working up on the Hayabusa. On 30 June, the 71st, 72nd and 73rd *Sentais* were formed and subsequently assigned to the Philippines with Hayates, these new regiments being joined by the 1st and 11th *Sentais* which converted from the Hayabusa to the Hayate during the autumn.

While the Philippines had priority in Hayate assignments, the 103rd *Sentai* was formed on 25 August with Hayates for home defence, and in the remaining months of 1944, the Shoki-equipped 29th *Sentai* added Hayates to its inventory in the Philippines; the 50th *Sentai* converted from the Hayabusa to the Hayate for Philippines defence, together with the newly-established 200th *Sentai*; the 101st and 102nd *Sentais* were formed on the Hayate for Okinawa defence; the 85th *Sentai* had begun to operate the Hayate in concert with the Shoki in China, and the 104th *Sentai* had formed with Hayates at Heizan, Manchuria. Thus, within nine months of the first production Hayate leaving Ota, some 16 *Sentais* were, for the most part, exclusively equipped with the new fighter, a total of 1,670 pre-production and production Hayates having been delivered into the Imperial Army Air Force's inventory by the end of the year, 373 being delivered during the course of December alone — the highest monthly production rate attained by any Army aircraft.

The Hayate was much vaunted by service pilots — it was alleged that the Nakajima fighter translated a tyro into a competent combat pilot and a run-of-the-mill pilot into an ace — and there could be no doubt that it was a formidable warplane, capable of out-climbing and out-manœuvring all opponents. Like most thoroughbreds, it was amenable to adaptation. It fulfilled the high-, medium- and low-altitude interception rôles, and was utilised for close support and dive bombing, although it was really in its element when performing the air superiority task for which it was conceived. For the

MRCA on target

Flight testing of the avionics system in the fourth prototype is well advanced

The rate of progress on the tri-national MRCA programme – particularly on flight development – has sharply accelerated. But the brake has been successfully kept on cost escalation.

" ... clearly the most successful international collaborative project ever, in which the real escalation of costs has been minimal and has been carefully controlled ..."

Mr Brynmor John, Under-Secretary of State for RAF.

By mid-November 1975, five **MRCA** prototypes had joined the flight development programme – two in Britain, two in Germany, one in Italy – and the flying rate had risen sharply. The emphasis has shifted from proving the basic handling and performance of the aircraft to proving its systems. Flight clearance of the integrated avionics system is well advanced, and clearance of the flight

Government test pilots have flown the first prototype

cond prototype (above and below) flew with external stores in October and has proved the flight refuelling system

The first trainer prototype made 11 flights in four days

envelope with external stores has begun. The flight re-fuelling system was cleared in an unprecedentedly short time – substantially in one flight – and has since been used to extend the duration of some test flights. The first two-seat trainer prototype has also begun flight development.

MRCA will equip the German air force and navy, the Royal Air Force, and the Italian air force. With a total production requirement for over 800 aircraft already stated by the Governments of the three participating nations, **MRCA** is ensured of low unit costs which cannot be rivalled in the world by any other aircraft of comparable performance and versatility.

"... The Bundeswehr needs a good aircraft and the Bundeswehr will get a good aircraft ... There is no alternative to the MRCA at a comparable cost ..." Herr Leber, German Minister of Defence.

The fifth prototype is extending the external stores flight test programme

"... The system has confirmed its full validity ... the programme is of prime importance to the Italian air force and Italian industry ..."
General Ciarlo, Italian Chief of Air Staff.

MRCA – the largest and most exacting military equipment programme Europe has ever seen – is backed by the resources of three of Europe's most powerful aerospace industries, who have at their command massive research, design, development and production strength. The air-craft meets the operational needs of three of the world's most experienced air forces and the German Navy. The programme mobilises the skills and experience of thousands of workers in Britain, Germany and Italy. It has established in Europe a military aviation capability second to none in the world. Authorisation of full production will ensure the continuing employment of a still larger workforce in all three countries for years to come.

PANAVIA MRCA

Panavia Aircraft GmbH, München, Arabellastrasse 16, Germany
AERITALIA
BRITISH AIRCRAFT CORPORATION
MESSERSCHMITT-BÖLKOW-BLOHM

PRODUCT OF EUROPE

dive bombing mission, the Hayate normally carried either 66-lb (30-kg) or 110-lb (45-kg) bombs on its wing racks, the dive normally being commenced at 4,920 ft (1 500 m) at a 55 deg angle with wing flaps depressed five degrees. The bombs were normally released at about 1,970 ft (600 m) and at an airspeed of 342 mph (550 km/h), the pull-out being commenced immediately and about 985 ft (300 m) being required for recovery.

In so far as the Allies were concerned, the Hayate established an awesome reputation in the skies above the Philippines, but it fought at constant disadvantage. It suffered numerical inferiority which dictated consistent use in the defensive rôle, and the extreme pressure under which it had been manufactured and the inevitable lowering of production standards in consequence produced serious maintenance problems. The Ha-45 was an excellent power plant but the fuel pressure problem that had plagued its early development had proved more difficult of solution than had been anticipated.

The Ha-45 Model 11 largely gave place to the Model 12 with a marginal increase in take-off rating from 1,800 to 1,825 hp, and this was to give place, in turn, to the Ha-45 Model 21 affording 1,970 hp for take-off, a low-pressure fuel-injection version of the last-mentioned engine, the Model 23, being introduced late in the production life of the fighter, this finally eliminating the problem of fluctuating fuel pressure. The hydraulic system, too, presented continuous maintenance problems in the field; the brakes were untrustworthy and the use of metal of insufficient tensile strength for the mainwheel legs resulted in the loss of many Hayate fighters owing to undercarriage failure on landing. These problems placed an impossible burden on ground personnel, a high proportion of fighters being written off without suffering serious combat damage, and most Hayate-equipped *Sentais* participating in the Philippines campaign were decimated.

Progressive development

The initial production Ki.84-I-ko was followed by the Ki.84-I-otsu which differed in having the synchronized fuselage-mounted machine guns supplanted by a second pair of 20-mm Ho-5 cannon, and a relatively small number were completed as specialized bomber destroyers as the Ki.84-I-hei, these having the 20-mm wing cannon replaced by 30-mm Ho-105 weapons. A more radically modified version of Hayate resulted from the increasingly critical light alloy supply situation as the war progressed. Late in 1943, Nakajima had been asked to investigate ways of conserving aluminium and had begun to consider the possibility of introducing wooden components into the Hayate airframe. A wooden rear fuselage was designed and, together with wooden wingtips, was produced by the Tanuma shadow factory, these components being delivered to the Ota plant for application to otherwise standard airframes which were referred to under the designation Ki.84-II Hayate-Kai. A small series of aircraft of this version was delivered during the late spring and early summer of 1945, but a more thoroughgoing redesign of the airframe to conserve strategic materials had by this time attained an advanced stage in development under the designation Ki.106.

The Ki.106 stemmed from an instruction issued on 8 September 1943 for the redesign of the entire Hayate airframe for wooden construction, utilizing a high proportion of semi-

The Ki-84-I-ko Hayate illustrated by the general arrangement drawing below was flown by Corporal Noboru Naito of the 520th Provisional Intercept Sentai operating from Nakatsu airfield between December 1944 and March 1945. The upper surfaces of this aircraft were finished in a two-tone green dapple (with substantial areas of flaked paint showing natural metal) and the undersides were pale blue. Standard yellow identification striping appeared on the inboard wing leading edges, the spinner and upper section of the wheel cover were painted in the Chutai colour (ie, red) and the tail stripe was red outlined with white. The three "kill" markings on the engine cowling comprised white star with blue disc and red tail.

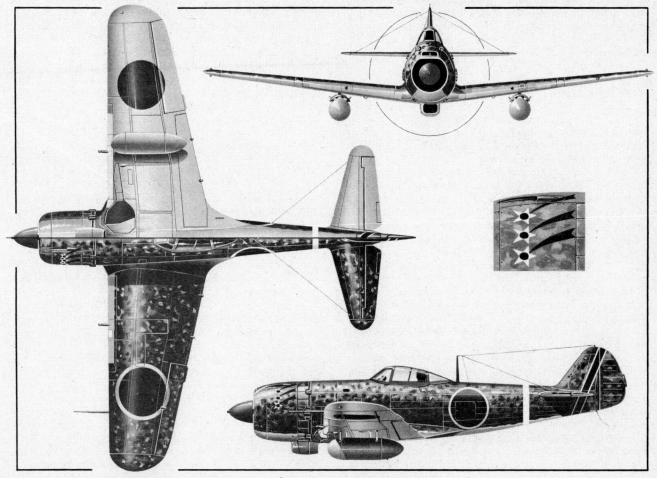

One of the three examples of the Ki.106, a wooden derivative of the Ki.84 Hayate. Prototype construction was sub-contracted to Ohjo Koku and the example illustrated is seen at Tachikawa Airfield prior to shipment to the USA for examination.

skilled and unskilled labour. It was proposed that the wooden Hayate's components would be produced by small woodworking shops grouped around designated assembly points, and Tachikawa Hikoki was assigned the task of structural redesign in collaboration with the Army Aerotechnical Research Institute at Tachikawa. The actual work was supervised by 1st Army Air Arsenal engineer Shinagawa and Tachikawa designer Moriyuki Nakegawa, prototype construction being sub-contracted to Ohjo Koku (Prince Aircraft) KK at Ebetsu, Ishikari, where manufacture of three examples of the Ki.106 finally began in the autumn of 1944.

Owing to a variety of factors, the first of these prototypes was not to be completed and flown until July 1945, by which time the capabilities of the Ki.106 were to be of little more than academic interest. The external characteristics of the standard Hayate were retained, apart from some minor revision of the vertical tail surface contours, and an outstanding external finish was achieved by applying a thick coat of polish to the plywood skin.

Flown by a prominent Army pilot, Major Yasuhiko Kuroe, the first prototype Ki.106 carried an armament of four 20-mm Ho-5 cannon and was powered by the standard Ha-45 Model 21. At 6,900 lb (3 130 kg), the Ki.106 was 952 lb (432 kg) heavier than the standard Ki.84-I-ko in empty equipped condition, the loaded wight at 9,259 lb (4 200 kg) being 683 lb (310 kg) heavier. The higher weights had an adverse effect on climb rate and manœvrability, 7·85 minutes being required to attain 16,405 ft (5 000 m), but maximum level speed was virtually unchanged at 385 mph (620 km/h) at 21,325 ft (6 500 ft). During initial trials, the plywood wing skinning failed on the upper surface of the port wing, but Maj Kuroe succeeded in landing the aircraft safely and after modifications no further problems of this nature were experienced. The armament of the second and third Ki.106s was reduced to a pair of 20-mm cannon as a weight-saving measure, the former commencing its flight test programme during the last week of the war.

Yet another attempt to economize on the use of light alloys was represented by the Ki.113 which was an experimental Hayate utilizing carbon steel for the main and auxiliary spars, main longitudinal members, ribs, ailerons, flaps and elevators, and steel sheet for the engine cowling and fuel tanks, the rear fuselage and tailplane being of wooden construction. Design work on the Ki.113 was begun by Nakajima in September 1944, planning calling for three prototypes and 30 pre-production aircraft. It was calculated that empty and normal loaded weights would be barely higher than those of the standard Hayate at 6,349 lb (2 880 kg) and 8,708 lb (3 950 kg) respectively, and anticipated performance included a maximum speed of 385 mph (620 km/h) at 21,325 ft (6 500 m) and climbing

times of 6·9 min to 16,405 ft (5 000 m) and 13·3 min to 26,245 ft (8 000 m), service ceiling being 33,790 ft (10 300 m). The three prototypes were powered by the Ha-45 Model 21 and standard Ki.84-I-ko armament was proposed, but in July 1945, with the first prototype within three weeks of commencing its flight test programme, force of circumstances necessitated the abandoning of the Ki.113 programme.

Numerous other variants of Hayate were to be proposed before Japan's final defeat, but only one of these was destined to be tested. This, the Ki.116, resulted indirectly from the successful adaptation of the Kawasaki Ki.61-II-KAI Hien (see August 1975 issue) to take the Mitsubishi Ha-112-II 14-cylinder air-cooled radial rated at 1,500 hp for take-off. Nakajima's aero engine plant at Musashi had been attacked by B-29 Superfortresses of the US 20th Air Force based in the Marianas for the first time on 24 November 1944, and again on 3 December — Musashi was, in fact, to become the most frequently bombed factory in the Japanese aircraft industry. Neither of the first two attacks did a great deal of damage, but the possibility of the sole source of the Hayate's engine being knocked out resulted in urgent consideration being given to the Ha-112-II as an alternative to the Ha-45.

Mansyu Hikoki Seizo at Harbin, Manchuria, which was in process of tooling for Hayate production, was instructed to engineer the conversion of the Nakajima fighter to take the Mitsubishi engine and, in the event, adapted the fourth Mansyu-built airframe to serve as a prototype, utilising a three-blade propeller from a Mitsubishi Ki.46-III. The Ha-112-II was substantially lighter than the Ha-45 that it replaced, necessitating the lengthening of the engine mounts to maintain the CG position and some enlarging of the vertical tail surfaces to compensate for this additional length forward. The prototype Ki.116, which commenced its flight test programme in July 1945, was found to possess an empty equipped weight of only 4,980 lb (2 259 kg), or some 900 lb (410 kg) less than that of the standard Hayate, normal loaded weight being commensurately lower. The reduced loadings resulted in truly spectacular manœuvrability, but before the full capabilities of the Ki.116 could be explored, hostilities had ceased and with them further work on this Hayate derivative.

Although the writing had for long been on the wall in so far as Japan was concerned, as late as 4 June 1945, a conference was held by the *Koku Hombu* to determine the most suitable means of adapting the basic Hayate as a specialized high-altitude interceptor, and three projected derivatives of the Hayate were tendered by the Nakajima design office, these being assigned the provisional designations Ki.84R, Ki.84N and Ki.84P. The Ki.84R was the least ambitious of

continued on page 43

104 more modified from A-6A standard to this latest configuration. The modification programme is planned to extend through 1979, by which time 228 earlier Intruders (including B and C models, as well as all available A-6As) will have been converted to the A-6E TRAM standard. Production of the A-6E is at present expected to be concluded when 94 new-build aircraft have been delivered, the last 12 of these being finished in February 1976. The Navy currently has 15 squadrons of A-6s in service and the Marine Corps has five squadrons; Navy plans include maintaining 12 squadrons of A-6Es and four squadrons of KA-6Ds into the 'eighties, although there are some doubts that the extent of A-6E procurement will be sufficient to maintain the force at this level, with 12 aircraft per squadron and allowing for the five Marine A-6E units.

Prowler Genesis

Derived from the A-6A airframe/engine combination, the EA-6A version of the Intruder is a tactical electronic countermeasures (ECM) aircraft whose primary rôle is support of strike aircraft and ground forces. It detects, locates, classifies, records and jams radiation; suppresses enemy electronic activity and obtains tactical electronic intelligence within the combat area. The EA-6A differs from the A-6A in having a faired radome atop the fin and pods containing ECM equipment on the underwing stores hardpoints. In addition to its new electronics equipment, the EA-6A retains partial strike capability.

A contract was placed for the EA-6A (initially as the A2F-1H) by the US Marine Corps in March 1962, to provide a replacement for the Douglas EF-108 (F3D) Skyknight, and the first aircraft flew on 26 April 1963. The first six aircraft were modified A-6As and a second batch of six was manufactured on the A-6A production line, but to EA-6A configuration. These aircraft were delivered between August 1965 and January 1967. A further 15 aircraft were built on an EA-6A production line and were delivered between December 1968 and November 1969.

Experience gained with this modified ECM version of the A-6 airframe* led to a new model, the EA-6B Prowler, with more major modifications. A 40-in (103-cm) extension of the forward fuselage made room for two more crew members and additional avionics. The airframe was strengthened to increase fatigue life at high weights and was stressed for 5·5g manœuvres. The partial strike capability was deleted, as were the fuselage air brakes. Avionics equipment carried was increased to a total of 8,000 lb (3 629 kg) internally and up to 950 lb (431 kg) on each of the five external stores positions. Maximum take-off weight was 51,000 lb (23 133 kg) including five pods; overload weight was 65,000 lb (29 484 kg), and maximum landing weight was 45,500 lb (20 639 kg).

The first EA-6B (one of three A-6A conversions) made its initial flight on 25 May 1968, powered by J52-P-8A engines of 9,300 lb st (4 218 kgp) and 22 aircraft were built to the initial basic standard. A switch was then made to 11,200 lb st (5 080 kgp) J52-P-408 engines and the capability of the jamming pods was extended to cover eight frequency bands compared with the original four. These later production aircraft are known as EXCAP (expanded capability). After completion of BIS and carrier-suitability trials in 1970 with the development aircraft aboard the USS *Midway*, production deliveries began in January 1971. After a lengthy working up period, operational deployment of the first two Navy squadrons of EA-6Bs began in mid-1972, and these two squadrons engaged in a total of 720 combat sorties in support and strike operations over North Vietnam, including support of the final B-52 attacks in Operation Linebasher at the end of 1972.

The EXCAP version of the EA-6B was first deployed to the Mediterranean in January 1974 and is now also serving in the Pacific. A further improved version of the Prowler, known as ICAP (improved capability), made its first flight in July 1975 and deliveries are to begin in February, the modifications including the use of digitally tuned receivers, human engineering

---

* *The EA-6A never had a name. The appellation "Prowler" belongs exclusively to the EA-6B.*

Grumman A-6E Intruder Specification

Power Plant: Two Pratt & Whitney J52-P-8A/B turbojets each rated at 9,300 lb st (4 218 kgp) for take-off and military power at 12,060 rpm and 0·86 sfc; and at 8,200 lb st (3 720 kgp) at 11,660 rpm and 0·81 for normal power. Internal fuel (JP5), 1,326 US gal (1,104 Imp gal/5 019 l) in three fuselage tanks and 1,018 US gal (848 Imp gal/3 855 l) in five wing tanks. External fuel, 1,477 US gal (1 230 Imp gal/5 592 l) total in five drop tanks. Equipped for in-flight refuelling.
Performance (cose support rôle, with 28 Mk 81 Snakeye 1 bombs, take-off weight of 52,749 lb/23 927 kg, full internal fuel): take-off run, nil wind, 3,590 ft (1 095 m); distance to 50 ft (15,2 m), 4,380 ft (1 336 m); max speed, 557 mph (896 km/h) at 5,000 ft (1 525 m); initial rate of climb, 4,570 ft/min (23,2 m/sec); time to 20,000 ft (6 100 m), 6·1 min; time to 30,000 ft (9 150 m), 13·4 min; service ceiling, 34,300 ft (10 460 m); combat range, 1,127 mls (1 813 km) at 458 mph (737 km/h) average at 30,800-42,700 ft (9 395-13 023 m); combat radius, 370 mls (595 km) at 464 mph (747 km/h) average.
Performance (as above, at combat weight of 46,373 lb/21 053 kg, at military thrust rating with 1,400 US gal/1 166 Imp gal/5 300 l fuel remaining): max speed, 564 mph (907 km/h) at 15,000 ft (4 575 m); rate of climb, 4,800 ft/min (24,4 m/sec) at 5,000 ft (1 525 m); combat ceiling, 35,000 ft (10 675 m); landing distance from 50 ft (15,2 m) 2,205 ft (672 m), ground roll, 1,590 ft (485 m); stalling speed, 104 mph (167 km/h) power on, 97 mph (156 km/h) at approach power at landing weight of 30,457 lb (13 827 kg).
Performance (clean, HI-HI-HI mission, full internal fuel, take-off weight 42,866 lb/19 460 kg): max speed, 654 mph (1 052 km/h) at sea level; initial rate of climb, 8,600 ft/min (43,7 m/sec); time to 20,000 ft (6 100 m), 2·7 min; time to 30,000 ft (9 150 m), 4·6 min; service ceiling, 44,600 ft (13 600 m); combat range, 2,320 mls (3 733 km) at 482 mph (776 km/h) average speed at 37,700-44,600 ft (11 500-13 600 m).
Weights: Empty, 25,980 lb (11 795 kg); basic, HI-LO-HI, 27,519 lb (12 494 kg); design, 36,526 lb (16 583 kg); combat,

HI-LO-LO-HI, 45,543 lb (20 677 kg); max take-off (field), 60,400 lb (27 420 kg); max take-off (catapult), 58,600 lb (26 605 kg); max landing (field), 33,637 lb (15 271 kg); max landing (arrested), 36,000 lb (16 344 kg).

Dimensions: Span, 53 ft 0 in (16,15 m); folded span, 25 ft 4 in (7,72 m); wing aspect ratio, 5·31 :1; quarter-chord wing sweepback angle, 25 deg; wing area, 528·9 sq ft (49,14 m²); overall length, 54 ft 9 in (16,69 m); height to fin top, 16 ft 2 in (4,93 m); wing-folding max height, 21 ft 11 in (6,68 m); wing-folded height, 16 ft 3 in (4,95 m); horizontal tail area, 117 sq ft (10,87 m²); tailplane quarter-chord sweepback angle, 30 deg; vertical tail area, 79·25 sq ft (7,36 m²); quarter-chord fin-and-rudder sweepback angle, 28 deg; undercarriage track, 10 ft 10½ in (3,33 m).

Armament/Stores (All external on one fuselage and four underwing pylons, 3,600 lb/1 635 kg capacity each): 28 Mk 82 bombs, or eight Mk 83 bombs and one 300-US gal (250-Imp gal/1 136-l) drop tank, or 12 Mk 20 Rockeye II and three tanks, or five Mk 84 bombs, or four Mk 84 bombs and one tank, or three Mk 84 bombs and two tanks, or six Mk 83 bombs and three tanks, or 18 Mk 82 bombs and two tanks, or 28 Mk 36 Snakeye I. A wide variety of stores may be carried including normal or retarded-fall "iron" bombs of 250- to 2,000-lb (113- to 907-kg) weight; cluster bombs (Mk 20 Rockeye II; CBU-1A/A and -9A/A, CBU-24, -29 and -49); incendiary bombs (Mk 77 Mod 1); missiles (Sidewinder 1A and 1C; AGM-45A Shrike; Aero 7D, LAU 3A/A; Aero 6A, LAU-32 A/A; LAU-10/A, -61A and -69A); drop tanks; mines (Mk 25, 36, 50 and 52; Mk 53, 55 and 56); practice bombs (Mk 76, Mk 106); pyrotechnics (Mk 24, 45 and 58); and launching racks (A/A 37B-3 PMBR, A/A 37B-5 TER, A/A 37B-6 MER, ADU-315 dual adaptor, and Aero 5A-1 launcher). The centre-line station is never used for mounting either missiles or rockets. Nuclear weapons (Mk 28/Mk 104, Mk 43, Mk 57/BDU-11E) are carried only on the centreline station and the two inboard wing pylons.

(Above) The first A2F-1 development aircraft, showing the jet tailpipes fully deflected and (below) the fourth development aircraft, showing the perforated fuselage air brakes.

An early production A-6A, with the definitive tail unit, including a small radome above the rudder, and a slab tailplane in place of elevators.

changes to provide a more equal distribution of the in-flight work load and improvements in the mission response time and effectiveness. The basic EA-6Bs are to be modified to ICAP standard and the EXCAP aircraft will be updated in due course to a similar or even more advanced configuration. Maximum level speed of the EA-6B is 574 kts (1 064 km/h); cruising speed is 415 kts (769 km/h) and combat radius with four jamming pods and one external fuel tank is 710 naut mls (1 316 km).

The EA-6B has the first fully integrated airborne tactical jamming system, the AN/ALQ-99 (a modified form of which is to be used in the EF-111 being developed by Grumman for the US Air Force), which is carried in pods under the wings and fuselage. This system generates high-power noise or jamming signals, power being provided in each pod by its own windmill-driven electrical alternator. A radar-deception transmitter and a communications jamming system are also carried by the Prowler. The aircrew comprises a pilot and three electronic countermeasures officers (ECMOs). The senior ECMO sits beside the pilot and operates half of the frequency coverage of the jamming system; the second ECMO deals with the other half of the jamming system; and the third ECMO operates the communications jamming equipment. The Prowler is equipped for stand-off jamming, ECM escort and penetration-protection of strike aircraft.

All 27 EA-6A aircraft built went to the US Marine Corps and are now in service with VMAQ-2 at Cherry Point. The EA-6B Prowler for the US Navy and, in due course, the Marine Corps remains in production, present plans covering a total of 77 aircraft up to 1978. The Navy will dispose its Prowlers in 12 squadrons of four aircraft each, one to serve aboard each carrier; eight squadrons are currently in commission. By the end of 1975, nearly 200,000 deck landings will have been made by Intruders and Prowlers which have flown more than one million hours. The carrier safety record of these aircraft is the best of all US types by a large factor.

Intruders and Prowlers in action

With justification, Grumman terms the A-6E TRAM "the world's most advanced electro-optical attack aircraft". In a typical attack mission the bombardier/navigator (B/N) uses simultaneous search radar at relatively long range for initial target detection and identification. The circular radar display in the centre of his instrument panel allows him to track the radar-derived target until it becomes clearly visible on the rectangular infra-red display above the radar 'scope. From that point on, the FLIR display is used for the terminal phases of identification and attack.

The FLIR installation consists of detecting/ranging set (DRS) sensors mounted on a turret-stabilized platform (TSP) in a cupola under the fuselage just aft of the nose radome. The TSP can be slewed through a full circle for complete lower-hemisphere coverage, and is gimballed for target tracking during all normal aircraft manœuvres. The DRS includes the FLIR display and controls; the TSP-mounted sensors consisting of the FLIR receiver, laser ranger/designator (LRD) transceiver; the forward air controller (FAC) receiver and related avionics.

The FLIR receiver provides extended day or night vision capability, featuring continuous optical zoom with 13-power magnification. Zooming permits the B/N to "frame" the target while maintaining resolution without losing target orientation. All FLIR and laser alignments are maintained mechanically, the centre of the laser beam being aligned to keep it directly under the reticle of the FLIR display. The reticle is placed on the target, the laser is turned on, and the weapon release computed, small corrections being made to the FLIR reticle until weapon impact. Meanwhile, the pilot is free to leave the target area and perform relatively unrestricted manœuvres for survival.

When there is a forward air controller (FAC) on the ground to direct the attack with a laser beacon, the FAC receiver provides a wide-angle laser spot-seeker that permits acquisition and attack of beacon-designated targets. Using the FAC receiver to locate the remotely designated target, the B/N in the A-6E TRAM aircraft has the option of attacking the FAC's target or using the onboard LRD narrow-beam transceiver to designate the attack. Concurrent operation of both FAC receiver and LRD transceiver does not compromise the performance of either and this, with the radar beacon capability of the TRAM system, provides an outstandingly effective close air support weapon for the US Marine Corps. As an example,* suppose that a Marine FAC calls for a strike against an enemy tank. He specifies targeting geometry and weapon conditions, and activates his portable radar beacon transponder, signalling his identity and position to the Intruder. The B/N enters aimpoint with range and bearing to the target in the aircraft's computer, selects navigation, attack and sensor modes and sits back as the aircraft flies to the target area. After the B/N acquires the beacon on the radar display, he tracks it with the radar range and azimuth cursors. Since the TRAM sensors are slaved to the radar, plus aimpoint range and bearing to target, the FLIR cupola points to the general target area defined by the radar cursors and aimpoint-offset data.

On radio command from the aircraft, or as otherwise pre-arranged, the FAC "lasers" the target. The airborne laser receiver detects the illuminated target anywhere within a rather broad field of view and many miles off, angle and distance depending on weather, target reflectance and laser power. A square symbol appearing on the FLIR display shows that the laser receiver has acquired the target and is giving its location relative to the TRAM cupola line-of-sight axis. The B/N selects

---

* *Condensed from "Grumman Horizons".*

A-6E Avionics Equipment	
Attack navigation instruments	
Compass system	MA-1
Air data computer	CP 1005/A
Computer set, ballistics	AN/ASQ-133
Search radar	AN/APQ-148
Track radar	AN/APQ-112
Doppler radar	AN/APN-153
Inertial platform	AN/ASN-31
Radar altimeter	AN/APN-141(V)
Integrated display system	AN/AVA-1
AFCS	AN/ASW-16
Video recorder	AN/USH-17(V)
Communications	
CNI Package (AN/ASQ-57)	
UHF receiver/transmitter	RT542A/ASQ-57
UHF auxiliary receiver	AM2310/ASQ-57
UHF/ADF antenna	AS-909/ARA-48
IFF	KY-533A/ASQ-57
TACAN	
Receiver/transmitter	RT-541/ASQ-57
Pulse decoder	KY-309/ASQ-57
ICS	AN/AIC-14
Ground control bombing	AN/ARW-67
Countermeasures	
Repeater jammer	AN/ALQ-41
Repeater jammer	AN/ALQ-100
Chaff dispenser	AN/ALE-29
Warning receiver	AN/APR-25
Warning receiver	AN/APR-27

With wing slats extended and air brakes open, an A-6E Intruder from VA-34 comes aboard the USS John F Kennedy. *The large nose radome covers a Norden AN/APQ-48 all-weather radar system which simultaneously provides a mapping display for detection, identification and acquisition of the target; terrain-avoidance information and aircraft-to-target position for precision bombing.*

the TRAM track mode and positions the line-of-sight cross-hairs over the square FAC symbol by rotating the cupola. Estimated errors in aimpoint-offset data are eliminated by then directly tracking the target with the aircraft's FLIR and its own laser system. Radar cursors are slaved onto the cupola line-of-sight plus offset distance to the radar aimpoint. The B/N can complete the run by tracking either the laser receiver symbol or the FLIR image of the target if it can be seen on the display.

Unguided ordnance ("iron" or "dumb" bombs, or missiles) is released at the tracked target position in the same manner as with radar tracking. For laser-guided weapons ("smart" bombs or missiles), the choice of aircraft or FAC designation of the target is usually prearranged, depending on whether the target is considered FLIR-significant or susceptible to FLIR imagery. This is the first time that infra-red imaging, currently immune to ECM jamming, has been coupled with laser designation in one fully integrated system in an all-weather attack aeroplane. The cupola has proved its ability to keep the laser (active) and infra-red (passive) sensors stably trained on targets throughout high-*g* attack manœuvres.

Electronic warfare has developed rapidly in the past few years and an ECM aircraft that is to protect a strike force adequately must have the ability to intercept, sort and identify each of the dozens of radars "painting" the attack force. The

ECM crew has to decide quickly when to jam signals and in what direction — to use barrage noise jamming might disrupt several radar 'scopes, but it lacks precision and finesse since the transmitters could be wasting power on frequencies where no threat exists, while the power is desperately needed to jam threats of higher priority. Also, this brute-force method might jam friendly radar.

Since the current hostile environment has reduced drastically the time available for manually selected ECM operation, computer-control is essential. This has led to development of the tactical jamming system (TJS) used in the EA-6B Prowler. Each of the five pods carried by this aircraft contains two jammers; there is also an integrated all-weather navigation

One of the 12 A-6Cs, modified A-6As carrying TRIM (trails, roads interdiction multi-sensor) equipment for use against targets that could not be seen visually nor detected by radar. One US Navy squadron used the A-6Cs for several years but they are now in storage.

This illustration of an EA-6A undergoing deck-handling trials prior to delivery to the Marine Corps shows the ECM radomes on each wing and the top of the fin; note also the special equipment pods inboard, the wing fold and the retractable access steps to the cockpit.

system for support of single or multiple strike groups, warning receivers and deceptive jammers for self-protection.

In a typical penetration mission* the Prowler's objective might be to jam enemy radar at five known sites, allowing accompanying A-6E Intruders to bomb an inland target with minimum risk. Before launching from the carrier, the Prowler crew assign frequency bands and radar threat types among the ECMOs; insert in the AN/ALQ-99 TJS computer such information as electronic order of battle data known beforehand about the five sites and their radars (position, pulse-repetition interval, frequencies, associated weapons) and adjust detection capability to cover the threat sectors of interest.

As the Prowler climbs through 34,000 ft (9 144 m), the TJS receivers are scanning in an acquisition mode, looking for possible threat-frequency activity. The ECMOs are monitoring their displays and listening for the characteristic sounds of the various types of radar making emissions. Eventually, an ECMO observes activity in several frequency bands and each ECMO reviews his threat assignments. About 250 miles (408 km) from the target and nearing the detection range of each site, the senior ECMO pushes the "master radiate" control to start jamming.

The operators monitor their displays for jammer and emitter

* *Condensed from "Grumman Horizons".*

frequency and for direction coincidence to ensure that good jamming is maintained while the surveillance receivers continue to scan their bands, intercepting and processing signals of interest. At one point in the flight, Site 3 becomes unmasked when the Prowler flies past the hill concealing its radar signals. Such new emitters are processed automatically with either the ECMOs or the computer assigning jammers, depending on system mode, threat and priority. The operators observe the detected signals and monitor the jamming/emitter coverage on their displays. Two signals from Site 3 appear in one band and are jammed. At another point, four additional emitters from Site 4 are detected. Site 1 masks itself and its emitters disappear. But an unanticipated surface-to-air (SAM) missile site is detected in a second band from an unknown location. Its characteristics were stored in the TJS central computer before the mission began. Now, the TJS automatically processes the new SAM emitters with those from Site 4 and the computer re-optimizes the distribution of jammers to include them.

One ECMO reviews the jamming of Site 1 and confirms the computer's redistribution of transmitters. Another ECMO studies data from the new SAM site and tries to locate it more exactly, while the computer maintains the jamming. A little later, a new signal is acquired in a third band and the Prowler's jammers engage it. With all threats countered by jamming, the EA-6B now climbs to loiter altitude of 34,000 ft (10 363 m) while the strike aircraft attack the target. Because of its high-powered jammers, the Prowler can remain outside the lethal range of SAM threats while providing protection for the strike force. After the attack, it maintains an ECM screen during the bombers' escape and/or rendezvous with them *en route* for the carrier.

Throughout the years, the A-6/EA-6 series has changed hardly at all externally, the only noticeable variation being the longer fuselage of the EA-6B (the prototype A2F-1 had slightly smaller horizontal and vertical tail surfaces). Higher-powered engines and updated avionics have served not only to keep the stubby, purposeful Grumman aeroplane in the front rank of military aircraft, but also to confirm the basic soundness of the design during a period of rapid technological change. No better tribute is needed to the engineers of the Bethpage "Ironworks". □

An EA-6B Prowler of Navy Squadron VAQ-129, without the sensor pods usually carried beneath wing and fuselage — a fuel tank is visible on the outer wing pylon. The long dorsal spline is a feature of later production EA-6Bs.

FIGHTER A TO Z

(Above) The S-3 (described last month) photographed on 8 August 1917 in its ultimate form with raised centre wing, the ducted spinner having been removed.

(Above) The S-4 during initial trials with wheel undercarriage and (below) the S-6 with Lewis guns mounted between fuselage and upper wing.

CURTISS S-4 AND S-5   USA

During the course of 1917, the Curtiss Aeroplane Company evolved two float seaplane variants of the S-3 "Triplane Speed Scout" which retained the 100 hp OXX-3 engine and fuselage of the landplane but featured an additional wing bay on each side with an increase in span and gross area. The S-4 featured a twin-float arrangement while the S-5 had a single central float with small outrigger stabilizing floats. Both S-4 and S-5 performed their initial trials with a standard S-3 type wheel undercarriage before being fitted with float undercarriages for water trials. No records would seem to have survived concerning the results of these trials but it may be assumed that they were insufficiently successful to warrant further development of either type.

CURTISS S-6   USA

A refined version of the S-3 with revised strutting carrying the centre section of the upper wing and the root attachments of the centre wing, a modified undercarriage and other changes, the S-6 triplane of 1917 was the first US "scout" to be fitted with twin forward-firing machine guns, these being gas-operated Lewis guns which were mounted side-by-side on inverted and inclined "V" struts immediately beneath the centre section of the upper wing and firing outside the propeller disc. Only a single example of the S-6 was built and tested. Max speed, 110 mph (117 km/h). Loaded weight, 1,377 lb (625 kg). Span, 25 ft 0 in (7,62 m). Length, 19 ft 6 in (5,94 m). Height, 8 ft 7 in (2,62 m). Wing area, 142·6 sq ft (13,25 m²).

CURTISS GS   USA

During 1917, the US Navy issued the Curtiss company with a contract for five single-seat fighting scout float seaplanes powered by a US-built version of the 100 hp Gnome nine-cylinder rotary, the GS designation indicating "Gnome Scout". These were completed under the designation GS-2 when a supplementary contract was issued for a sixth aeroplane which was assigned the designation GS-1. The GS-1 was a single-seat triplane with a single central float and outrigger stabilizing floats which drew heavily on Curtiss S-3 experience, and an unusual feature was the introduction of shock absorbers in the struts between the fuselage and the central float. These resulted in the float angle being subject to change at high speed on the water and producing an undesirable porpoising. Delivered to the US Navy early in 1918, the GS-1 was flown several times by US Navy acceptance pilots but was eventually damaged beyond repair as a result of a heavy landing. The five similarly-powered GS-2s differed from the GS-1 primarily in being of biplane configuration, but little is recorded of these aircraft apart from the fact that they suffered from tail heaviness. No data are available for either GS-1 or GS-2.

CURTISS CB   USA

The CB (Curtiss Battleplane), unofficially known as the "Liberty Battler", was an experimental two-seat fighter developed and flown early in 1918 as a result of difficulties being experienced with the Liberty-engined version of the Bristol F2B. Powered by a 425 hp 12-cylinder Liberty 12 water-cooled engine, the CB two-bay biplane was an early example of "Curtiss ply" construction — two layers of 2-in (5,08-cm) wide wood veneer being cross-laminated over a form to build up a monocoque fuselage shell — and in an effort to maintain fuselage streamlining, the radiators were slung under the upper wing centre section where they were found to have a seriously detrimental effect on the airflow. The fairing of the upper wing into the top fuselage contour resulted in a very narrow wing gap with aerodynamic penalties and while it provided the rear gunner with an excellent field of fire, it impaired the forward and downward view of the pilot, necessitating the provision of

The GS-1 (Gnome Scout) fighting scout floatplane which drew heavily on experience gained by Curtiss with the S-3.

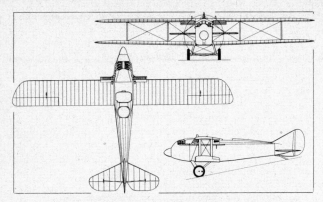

(Above and below) The CB, unofficially known as the "Liberty Battler" two-seat fighter. The heads of the pilot and gunner may just be seen projecting above the top wing in the photograph below.

small windows in the fuselage sides. Flown early in 1918, the sole prototype CB proved to have extremely poor handling characteristics and crashed early in its test programme. No data for the CB are available.

CURTISS HA   USA

Designed by Capt B L Smith of the US Marine Corps as a two-seat patrol fighter floatplane for use in the Dunkirk-Calais area, the HA — known unofficially as the "Dunkirk Fighter" — was intended to combat the Brandenburg float fighters and was built at the experimental plant of the Curtiss Engineering Corporation. Of conventional wooden construction with fabric skinning, the HA was powered by a 425 hp Liberty 12 engine and featured an unusually rotund fuselage. Proposed armament comprised two synchronized 0·3-in (7,62-mm) Marlin machine guns and two Lewis guns of similar calibre on a scarf mounting in the rear cockpit. The HA was flown for the first time on 21 March 1918 but was found to be unstable longitudinally and seriously tail heavy, and the initial test terminated in a crash. Curtiss was then awarded a contract for two further prototypes, the first of which, the HA-1, utilized salvaged components from the original HA and featured revised vertical tail surfaces, an annular-type radiator and relocated wings. The HA-1 demonstrated appreciably improved handling qualities but was written off after a fire in the air. The third HA prototype, the HA-2 (which see) differed appreciably from the HA-1. In 1919, a single-seat landplane version of the HA-1 was developed for use as a mailplane by the US Post Office Department, initially being flown as a single-bay biplane of reduced span. Similar two-bay wings to those of the HA-1 floatplane prototype were fitted after initial trials and two examples of the aircraft in this form were subsequently used on mail services. The following data apply to the HA-1 float fighter. Max speed, 126 mph (203 km/h). Time to 9,000 ft (2 743 m), 10 min. Empty weight, 2,449 lb (1 111 kg). Loaded weight, 3,602 lb (1 634 kg). Span, 36 ft 0 in (10,97 m). Length, 30 ft 9 in (9,37 m). Height, 10 ft 7 in (3,23 m). Wing area, 387 sq ft (35,95 m²).

CURTISS HA-2   USA

The third HA float fighter prototype embodied considerable redesign as the HA-2. Powered by a similar 12-cylinder Liberty 12 water-cooled engine to that of the preceding

prototypes, the HA-2 had longer-span wings of marginally increased chord and gap, the upper wing being raised clear of the fuselage, the decking of which was lowered. The radiator was redesigned but cooling problems were encountered and although the HA-2 proved more docile than the lighter HA-1, it possessed insufficient promise to warrant further development. Max speed, 118 mph (190 km/h). Time to 7,900 ft (2 408 m), 10 min. Empty weight, 2,946 lb (1 336 kg). Loaded weight, 3,907 lb (1 772 kg). Span, 42 ft 0 in (12,80 m). Length, 30 ft 9 in (9,37 m). Height, 11 ft 5 in (3,48 m). Wing area, 490 sq ft (45,52 m²).

(Above and below) The HA "Dunkirk Fighter" in HA-1 form, this embodying components of the first HA prototype which crashed during trials.

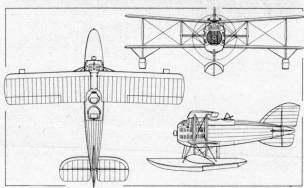

(Below) The HA-2 differed appreciably from the HA-1, having longer-span wings, lowered fuselage decking and a redesigned frontal radiator.

The genesis of the kit

WHEN APPRAISING the boxed contents of a newly-issued kit, how many of us spare a thought for — or, for that matter, are aware of — the fact that many months and perhaps even a year or more have gone into its preparation; that the kit making its début on your stockist's shelves in January of 1976 was possibly conceived as long ago as mid-1974. That there is quite a long leadtime between a new kit translating from a gleam in the eye of a project manager or designer to the collection of polystyrene components that finds its way to our modelling bench and that a very substantial organisation indeed is necessary to create and market the modern mass-produced plastic kit are facts that were brought home to us somewhat forcibly when we recently had the opportunity to visit Lesney's large new factory on the outskirts of Peterborough; a factory devoted entirely to the production and distribution of the already extensive and ever-growing "Matchbox" kit range.

The true genesis of a kit is usually as an idea of the chief designer, almost invariably a dedicated individual with a keen appreciation of modelling, both as a pastime and as a business; he must tread a wary line between subjects that would be considered esoteric by other than the more ardent modeller and therefore a sales gamble, and the more mundane which, if following a well-trodden path, is nevertheless assured of reasonable commercial success. He must always keep in mind the fact that a kit must sell in hundreds of thousands if it is to be commercially viable and lacking a crystal ball he must perforce ignore accusations of timidity in choice of subject matter levelled by the self-styled *aficionados*, or else his employers will be advertising his position in the "situations vacant" column.

Assuming that his proposal for a new kit is accepted by his directors, who, with little or no practical modelling interest, have examined it in a hard commercial light, the process of gathering suitable reference and examining and measuring up, if available, a full-scale example of the selected subject commences. The designer that knows his job must be highly discriminating in his choice of reference sources — how many aircraft model kits have their commercial potential marred at this stage — and once these have been finalised, the task of breaking down the projected model into practical components for manufacturing is initiated. These separate components are created as individual hand carvings from blocks of an easily-worked resinous material but to a much larger scale than that of the eventual model — Lesney, for example, employ 1/24th scale at this stage for a future 1/72nd scale "Matchbox" kit. As yet, no external detail is applied, and the steel moulds, which will eventually be utilised in the production of the kit parts, are made from the large-scale hand-carved patterns, the

reduction to 1/72nd scale being effected by a pantograph arrangement. Once the basic die has been obtained in this fashion, the surface details have to be added, together with the channels through which the heated plastic will flow and which must be carefully calculated in varying sizes to ensure that the plastic finds its way into every crevice and corner.

Next comes the most tedious and time-consuming process of all. This is the hand-polishing of the surfaces of the moulds to a mirror-like finish without scratch or blemish, no plating being used. When trial runs have been made and test shots have passed the close scrutiny of the inspectors, the kit finally goes into production. The set of moulds is inserted into the injection moulding machine, measured quantities of plastic granules are fed from a hopper, heated and forced into the moulds, and a frame of plastic parts is ejected roughly every 17 seconds — with more than 60 of these injection moulding machines at Lesney's Peterborough factory, the output of kits in an eight-hour working day can well exceed 100,000! Incidentally, transparencies — being in smaller frames — are moulded in groups and separated manually before mating with their respective kits.

Simultaneous with the creation of the moulds has been the researching of colour schemes and markings, and the printing of decals, instruction sheets and boxes by specialist firms. Lesney's policy of moulding its individual kits in two or three different colours of plastic — each colour of course being moulded separately — means that the individual frames of parts are quite compact. These are brought together in the packing department to be manually inserted into the boxes, together with the transparencies, stand, decals and instruction sheet. Each kit box is sealed with transparent tape and then packed into a carton for dispatch.

The production tempo is remarkable and a tour of Lesney's new factory impresses one with the fact that, today, the manufacture of plastic model kits is a colossal business and it is big export business, too, for more than 50 per cent of the output of this one factory goes to overseas customers.

A lead Lightning

Revell has made it a practice to issue most of its 1/32nd scale kits in more than one version and the latest to receive the "treatment" is the Lockheed P-38J Lightning. First issued in standard fighter form, this kit now reappears in revised form to represent the so-called "droop-snoot" variant evolved as a lead aircraft for formations of bomb-carrying Lightnings, a transparent nose and a station for a bombardier, complete with Norden sight, being provided and gun armament being sacrificed. The "droop-snoot" modification changed the appearance of the Lightning quite radically and Revell has made a neat job of

adapting the existing kit to represent this variant, giving added interest to a basically accurate and well-detailed product.

The 103 component parts of the kit are moulded in olive drab plastic, apart from the very clear transparencies. Cockpit detail is very complete, as is also that in the wheel wells, and a feature of the kit is the very detailed port engine with removable cowling. The hatch in the top of the pilot's canopy is hinged and the undercarriage is particularly neatly and accurately moulded, with very realistic wheels. The turbo-superchargers in the tops of the booms are separate mouldings and two bombs are included for good measure. We can see no possible way in which sufficient weight can be incorporated to balance the tail, so recourse must be made to the support provided with the kit and which, fitting under the tailplane, is reasonably unobtrusive. The decal sheet provides markings for an aircraft of the 77th Fighter Sqdn, 20th Fighter Group, 8th AF, and includes many small stencil markings. We do not have a retail price for this kit at the time of closing for press but it should be generally available from stockists in the UK.

This month's colour subject

It would be idle to claim that float seaplane addicts among the modelling fraternity have been well catered for by the kit manufacturers, but at least the most important among Allied floatplanes of WW II, the Vought OS2U Kingfisher, has fared rather well and three kits depicting this type have so far appeared. The Kingfisher was a noteworthy aircraft from both the manufacturing and operational viewpoints: it was the first aircraft to utilise spot welding in its primary structure and to employ a non-buckling fuselage structure, and it was to undertake a wide variety of tasks not envisaged by its designers nor the specification to which it was created, even performing dive-bombing missions on occasions. The Kingfisher was, of course, used primarily by the US Navy, most of the 100 transferred to the Royal Navy serving in the training rôle in the West Indies. It also found its way into the inventories of Chile, Argentina, Uruguay, Cuba, Dominica and Mexico, but perhaps the least known were those assigned to the Netherlands East Indies of which 18 found their way into service with the Royal Australian Air Force.

Among several consignments of aircraft on their way to the Netherlands East Indies when this territory was finally overrun by the Japanese was a quantity of OS2U-3 Kingfishers destined for use with the *Marine Luchtvaartdienst*. Three vessels carrying a total of 24 of the floatplanes, in Dutch markings, were re-routed to Australian ports where the Kingfishers were off-loaded. Carrying the MLD identification numbers V-1 to V-24 inclusive, 18 of the Kingfishers were promptly assigned to the RAAF as A48-1 to -18, eventually serving (with the exception of A48-8 lost at sea while with No 3 Operational Training Unit) with No 107 Squadron on convoy duties and anti-submarine patrols. For the modeller with a penchant for the more esoteric in markings, we are devoting our colour page this month to the handful of Kingfishers which, ordered for the Netherlands East Indies, saw service with the RAAF.

Of the three Kingfisher kits that have been issued, that from Monogram to 1/48th scale is undoubtedly the best, being both accurate and well detailed, with good cockpit interior and alternative parts enabling either float- or wheel-equipped version to be built. A beaching trolley is provided for the floatplane. The cockpit canopy is in five sections and may be assembled with one or both sliding sections open. Surface detailing is of a very high order, with finely raised panel lines and some rivets, all discretely proportioned. Assembly is quite simple, the centre float being moulded in halves with the fuselage, the lower wing section being manufactured in one piece and fitting through a shaped slot in the fuselage to fix the dihedral angle. The decal sheet provides markings for both a US Navy OS2U-3 and a Royal Navy Kingfisher I.

Airfix's 1/72nd scale kit follows generally similar lines, again being essentially accurate, well detailed and offering alternative parts for float or wheel versions. The decals in this case cover both pre-WW II and wartime US Navy machines, the former being quite colourful. This kit is included in Series 2. Both the Monogram and Airfix kits should be readily obtainable, while the third Kingfisher kit, a Lindberg product to 1/72nd scale, may well present problems, at least, in so far as UK modellers are concerned. In any case, we do not have an example of this last-mentioned kit for comparison purposes. However, both Monogram and Airfix kits are to be recommended.

What . . . another stuka?

At first sight, yet *another* kit of Junkers' notorious Ju 87 is needed by the modelling fraternity like a slipped disc, but another look reveals the fact that Revell's new 1/72nd scale "stuka" is something more than another example of unnecessary duplication. There has been no shortage of attempts to produce kits of the Ju 87 to this scale, with varying degrees of success but without complete satisfaction. Happily, the Revell product comes close to being definitive, being, in our opinion, the most accurate yet offered in 1/72nd by quite a margin.

This kit may be assembled either as the extended-wing Ju 87D-5 or its anti-armour derivative, the Ju 87G-1, and with alternative component parts for the two variants, there is a total of 59 in this kit, moulded in a medium green plastic and with neat surface detailing of the fine raised-line variety. The cockpit interior is quite well furnished and an unusual feature at this scale is the detailed engine with removable top cowling. A 551-lb (250-kg) bomb is provided for the swing-link crutch under the fuselage of the Ju 87D-5, plus two 110-lb (50-kg) bombs for each of the underwing racks, while the Ju 87G-1 is provided with the two underwing 37-mm BK 3,7 cannon. The propeller is arranged so that it does not have to be fitted until all assembly and painting is completed, a useful feature. The decal sheet is very good indeed, including the instrument panel and many small markings. The units to which belonged the aircraft for which markings are provided are not specified, although the Ju 87D-5 (T6+BK) belonged to 2.*Staffel* of *Stukageschwader 2* "*Immelmann*". In the case of the Ju 87G-1,

the coding DJ+FT is offered and we would assume this to have been *Werk-Nr* 1097 of the *Versuchsverband für Panzerbekampfung*, the experimental tank-fighting unit that appeared on the Eastern Front early in 1943, this particular aircraft, which retained the factory call sign letters, having been shot down near Lepeschino. The accompanying instruction sheet is most lucid and includes adequate painting information.

A Gamma from Williams Brothers

The US company of Williams Brothers is a relative newcomer to the plastic model aircraft kit business, having previously issued only two kits — both excellent — representing the Boeing 247D and the Martin B-10, and both to 1/72nd scale. We have now received an example of this company's third offering, which, to the same scale and from the same period of aviation history, represents the pace-setting Northrop Gamma; an aerodynamically clean monoplane that was to be the progenitor of the line of aircraft culminating in the Douglas Dauntless. The quality of this kit is fully up to the standard established by its predecessors and the choice of subject matter and the treatment of this kit indicate a real understanding of the connoisseur among modellers. This kit is quite obviously the end product of extensive research and fully justifies the effort that must have gone into its creation.

The Gamma was not a mass-produced aircraft, each example being hand-built to the individual customer's requirements. So, if it is to be authentic, a model of the Gamma must represent a specific example and Williams Brothers have elected to offer the necessary parts and instructions enabling the kit to be completed as either Frank Hawks' single-seat *Texaco Sky Chief* with a 14-cylinder radial and three-bladed propeller, or Dr Lincoln Ellsworth's two-seat *Polar Star* with a nine-cylinder radial and two-bladed propeller. All necessary alternative parts are provided for the two machines, while different modifications carried out subsequent to the actual construction of the aircraft are fully detailed by the instruction sheet.

There are 52 component parts in all, these being moulded in light grey plastic with very little flash, and the fit of the parts is precise, no filling being needed, although to achieve some variations the cutting and fitting of certain parts is necessary — all clearly explained. Interior details are engraved on the sides of the cockpits, which have floors, seat(s), instrument panel (with decal) and controls. This is all that is needed as the canopy windows are small and strictly limit what may be seen of the internals.

Both engines are very good and each has its individual cowling, and the "trousered" undercarriage gives the model a really offbeat appearance which is increased by the "parkbench" type ailerons utilised by the *Texaco Sky Chief* and the *Polar Star* in its original form — the latter was eventually modified with conventional inset ailerons. Surface detailing consists primarily of beautifully fine raised lines and is as neat as one could desire. Indeed, so fine is this detailing that the painting process must be carried out with extreme care if the raised lines are not to be obscured. The decal sheet, by Micro Scale, fully maintains the standard set by the remainder of the kit. The US price of the kit is $2.95

(plus postage) from Williams Brothers of 181 B Street, San Marcos, California 92069, but Gamma will be available from specialist dealers in the USA and UK in due course.

A vac-form pick-a-back

Flying boats have become something of a speciality with Contrail which has produced no fewer than six as vacuum-formed kits and to these is now added the company's most ambitious project to-date, the Short-Mayo Composite comprising the S.20 *Maia* and the S.21 *Mercury* which effected their first combined flight on 20 January 1938. The kits for *Maia* and *Mercury* are packaged individually and may be purchased separately, but as these two aircraft are as inseparable as bacon and eggs, we cannot envisage anyone wanting the one without the other!

These are *not* kits for the beginner for they require more than a little know-how in their assembly; all of the major component parts are provided but the modeller has to use his initiative in many areas and a great deal of filling and fairing is called for, and particularly so in respect of *Mercury,* an outstandingly clean design in which any disruption of the smoothly flowing lines would stand out like pimples on ducks' . . . . ! The mouldings are clean and sturdy, and internal reinforcements are provided. Windows are marked but have to be cut out and glazed with clear plastic sheet, and there is not much surface detailing; what there is is rather coarse. The struts for the *Mercury* floats have to be cut from plastic sheet and need careful measuring from the 1/72nd scale drawings provided by Contrail with the kits — their assembly is a rather tricky operation. The propellers utilized by *Mercury* were of carved wood and are best represented on the model in the same way, for those that accompany the kit are really quite useless. The H-type Napier-Halford Rapier engines had air intakes above and below the thrust line, and these must be cut out after the engine halves are assembled.

The *Maia* was a large aircraft generally similar to the S.23 C-Class Empire boat, but there were *many* differences, such as the proportionately wider hull planing bottom, larger chord wings, etc, of *Maia*, all features included in the Contrail kit, together with the rather complex cradle which was mounted above the hull to support *Mercury*. The drawings give full details of the cradle and include a perspective sketch, but we would recommend that the struts provided be retained only as a guide to length, those to be utilised by the model being cut from plastic sheet.

Cowlings are included but no engines or propellers, and we suggest that, despite the expense, these be obtained from one of the existing injection-moulded kits including Pegasus engines (or Hercules which are externally similar in this scale, although, to be correct, push rods should be added). The Airfix kit of the Sunderland will provide engines, cowlings and propellers, but nothing else is useable.

These are a fascinating pair of kits, priced in the UK at £2·42 for *Maia* and £2·20 for *Mercury*, the apparently disproportionate price of the latter being due to the fact that it is imported from Canada. Postage is additional to these prices and the kits may be obtained from Sutcliffe Productions of Westcombe, Shepton Mallet, Somerset. □

F J HENDERSON

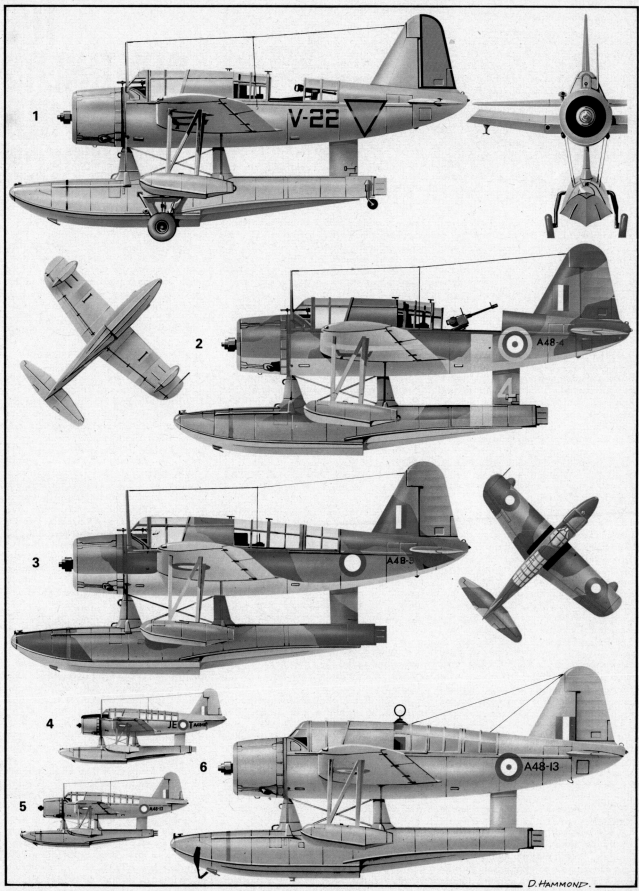

Depicted at No 1 above is the *Vought-Sikorsky OS2U-3 as delivered for service with the Marine Luchtvaartdienst; of 24 such aircraft that arrived in Australia in March 1942, 18 entered service with the RAAF. The plan and side views at No 2 show Kingfisher I A48-4 in RAAF service as a trainer at Rathmines in late 1942, and the two views at No 3 show A48-9 in the markings of No 107 Squadron. No 4 shows A48-18, also with No 107 Squadron, in bare metal finish. Kingfisher A48-13 is shown at No 5 as prepared for the RAAF Antarctic Flight in 1947 and at 6 in its ultimate finish in 1948.*

D. HAMMOND.

THE OLD-TIMERS OF OLD RHINEBECK

BY DENNIS O NORMAN

THE DRIVE to Old Rhinebeck from my home takes about six hours, and that is time enough to savour the pleasant memories of previous visits to the airfield and museum owned and operated by Cole Palen just a few miles north of the historic and peaceful Hudson River community of Rhinebeck, New York.

Palen, at 50, is a small, wiry, dynamo of a man with an explosive laugh and a ready sense of both history and humour. He is constantly on the move. When I last saw him, he was standing in the front cockpit of a 1930 two-seat Aeromarine Klemm lightplane which was being hoisted for suspended display from the ceiling of Palen's latest museum building. An hour before, he had been both host and guest of honour at a picnic held by a women's flying club at the recreation area near the several hangars where his substantial collection of antique and replica aircraft sit awaiting the next call to thrill and entertain the crowds that come each weekend from mid-May throughout October.

The Old Rhinebeck Aerodrome is open to visitors daily from 10.00 am to 5.00 pm. Visitors are encouraged to photograph the aircraft, engines and other aeronautic memorabilia found in the hangars and in the museum complex. Flying demonstrations, however, are confined to the weekends. From mid-May until early July the flying shows are on Sundays only and feature World War I aircraft. Beginning in July there is also a Saturday show, at which aircraft of the "pioneer" and "Lindbergh" eras are flown. Each of these shows lasts 1½ hrs, starting at 2.30 p.m. There is a small admission charge.

The Aerodrome's flying area is entered by crossing a quaint wooden bridge over a peaceful stream flowing from a large pond upon which ducks and geese frolic in noisy disregard of camera-laden visitors who often pause to record the charm of the spot. The last portion of the bridge is covered and its walls are decorated with handsome colour photographs of the people and machines that recapture the thrill and excitement of flying in the pre-jet age.

Palen's flying shows customarily begin with a venerable type such as a Thomas Morse Scout or a Curtiss JN-4H Jenny lumbering overhead in a steady circular crawl to an altitude of 1,000 ft (305 m). As that "work" goes on, the crowd of spectators on the west side of the field stands to attention for the playing of the National Anthem. This is followed by an enthusiastic greeting from an announcer dressed in a World War I officer's uniform atop the Aerodrome's 1918 control tower (a wooden platform about 20 ft (6 m) high) which is festively decked in red, white and blue bunting. The announcer explains that the crowd is about to witness a flying demonstration of one of the largest private collections of flying antique aircraft in the world.

By this time, the lumbering veteran is directly overhead and the crowd's attention is directed to it. The announcer explains that the show will begin with a "ribbon-cutting ceremony" in which the pilot will attempt to sever a long tissue paper "ribbon" as many times as possible before it reaches the ground. Suddenly a hundred feet of white streamer plummets from the cockpit. The aircraft now twists and turns slicing the ribbon as it falls toward the air strip. One, two, three, four times! The last "snip" is at tree top level directly before the cheering crowd.

In the typical Saturday show, the next flying activity is that of the pre-World War I types. Each of these, whether it be the Bleriot XI, Short S.29 pusher biplane, 1913 Derperdussin, Curtiss Model D pusher, or some other type, begins its performance on a hill at one end of the airstrip. The engine starting procedure is usually laborious and requires the co-ordinated efforts of the pilot and a husky lad at the propeller while several other sturdy fellows firmly grasp the airframe. Ignition is followed by a loud roar and billowing blue-grey smoke which clears to reveal the pilot, in vintage attire including leather helmet and flying goggles, beaming in triumph. At his signal, the "ground crew" releases the machine and it lurches forth with all the power that its antique engine can muster.

As early types were notoriously underpowered, no attempt is made to circle the Aerodrome. The "flight" consists of taking the aircraft aloft for a distance of 100 ft (30 m) or less, covered a few feet above the ground. It then touches down and is greeted by the firm but loving hands of the more youthful and robust members of the ground crew who have raced along to be ready to grab struts to slow and steady the veteran's return to Mother Earth.

When the pre-World War I types have completed their presentations, the display of the "Lindberg-era" types begins. These aircraft, from the 1920's and 1930's, are, of course, considerably more sophisticated and flying demonstrations with them involve not only circling the field, but also performing aerobatics. To meet the need to entertain the crowd which always includes wives and children who would soon tire of watching a succession of aircraft flying overhead, Palen arranges such antics as the "Pants Race," an event featuring three lightplanes in which the pilots line up and, at the sound of a starting gun, remove their trousers, race to their aircraft, take off, circle the field once, land and scramble back into the limits of propriety. It is, of course, hilarious and well spiced with "dirty tricks" played by loyal ground crews who are given to turning trousers inside out, tying knots in the legs, etc. While the merriment progresses, there are dozens of opportunities to photograph or film the aircraft both on the ground and in the air.

The Sunday shows are given over entirely to the flight of World War I types. Again to meet the need to entertain potentially restless spectators, Palen arranges the demonstration in the context of an appropriately uproarious melodrama centering around the antics of such characters as "Sir Percy Goodfellow," ostensibly of the Royal Flying Corps, the allegedly notorious "Black Baron" (portrayed by Palen himself, dressed in a black uniform with outsized riding breeches, swagger stick and a face covered with grease-painted scars). Our principal characters vie for the attention of none other than "Miss Trudy Truelove" (a shapely blonde who, although flirting with the Black Baron, is in truth an Allied spy). These characters are backed by a dozen or so non-flying personnel operating such lumbering earth-bound antiques as the Morgan Space 3 Wheeler, an early English sports car, and a genuine 1917 Renault tank. These vehicles, surrounded by people in authentic period costumes, serve to distract the crowd and add a touch of continuity while the aircraft take off and are flown into position. Further excitement is added through the use of smoke bombs, tossed as the planes swoop by at, or below, tree top level.

Typically, in the course of the Sunday afternoon show, the crowd is treated to flights by such types as an Avro 504K, FE-8, Sopwith Pup, Camel and Snipe. The opposing forces are represented by such types as an Albatros D Va, Fokker Dr I triplane and D VII and/or a Siemens Schuckert D III. From the French, we may see the Nieuport 28 or a Spad XIII, and even the fledgeling United States Army Air Service is represented by a Thomas-Morse S-4B and Curtiss JN-4H Jenny. All of these types twist and turn at low altitude permitting the audience to relive the sights and smells of aviation's childhood. Even the most amateur photographer is assured of beautiful footage of these vintage types as they swoop through the melodrama.

The set-piece itself ends, appropriately enough, with the Black Baron's death. Palen acts out the death scene with great flourish. No detail is overlooked — not even the "rigor mortis" which leaves the villain's torso and legs at a near perfect right angle with each other. In what must surely be a demonstration of Palen's physical fitness, the Black Baron remains at right angles with himself while "medics" appear with a stretcher, to remove the "corpse" in an original World War I ambulance.

Until its purchase by Palen in November 1958, the Aerodrome was a modest 100-acre Hudson Valley farm. There were no flying facilities and the only aircraft seen were those flown by local crop dusters; the farm itself had been abandoned and was badly overgrown. The first order of business was the clearing of the 1,000-ft (305-m) strip of the land for a runway. As the majority of the aircraft that would use the facility lacked brakes, the grass landing strip was carefully contoured several feet below the edges of the field so as to minimize problems with ground looping aircraft. The Aerodrome is privately owned, but open for public use and sport flyers are welcome at their own risk to visit, refuel and enjoy a cold soft drink.

Palen grew up next to the Red Oaks Mills Airport at Poughkeepsie, New York, and like so many who were children in the 1920's and 1930's, he obtained his first flight experience at the age of ten as a passenger in a barnstorming White Standard. After wartime service in the infantry, Palen's interest in aviation continued to grow and blossomed fully in 1947 when he purchased, for $250.00, a 1929 Viele Monocoupe. A visit to Roosevelt Field that year further stimulated his interest when he discovered a considerable number of old aircraft sitting in storage. Palen "barnstormed" in the late 'forties and by 1951 was able to begin his collection of antique types by purchasing most of the collection surviving at Roosevelt Field.

Although continuing to occasionally "barnstorm" until as late as 1968, Palen's activity centred more and more on the Aerodrome after its purchase in 1958. The long flights and rigorous schedules of "barnstorming" at state fairs, airshows, etc, resulted in much wear and tear on the aircraft and, with makeshift facilities, performances given could be neither as entertaining nor as profitable as those possible in a fixed locale. Since 1968 Palen has been busy each flying season and has done, and intends to do, no barnstorming whatsoever.

Until 1966, the Aerodrome activity was centred on developing the flying field and the hangars and workshop facilities needed to store the collection. Occasionally aircraft used in the flying shows would be severely damaged or fatigued to the point where they could not be safely flown. Palen was also accumulating a substantial collection of engines and other aircraft memorabilia which could not be adequately presented in the existing facilities. Thus it was that Old Rhinebeck Aerodrome Museum began.

The museum presently consists of two large corrugated hangars and a small workshop and

(Above) The Nieuport 28C-1 at Rhinebeck, in the markings of the famous "Hat in Ring" squadron of the AEF (the 94th Aero Squadron), is a comparatively recent addition, having taken the place of a restored Nieuport 24 bis in the markings of Charles Nungesser.

(Above The Sopwith Pup at Rhinebeck was built some years ago by Dick King, one of two aero-modelling brothers who are among Palen's regular helpers. (Below) The Fokker Dr I triplane used by Palen when he flies as the "Black Baron" is also a replica.

VETERAN & VINTAGE

fices, but they are large, well lit, and open to all visitors — including a sparrow last seen nesting in the empennage of the 1908 Voisin Flyer!

Although scarce, original engines are still available. Airframes, however, of the period have nearly ceased to exist outside of museums. Considering the well known ravages of time on wood, it is understandable that original airframes existing today are seldom put to the stress of flight. Palen has solved this problem by carefully rebuilding the airframes he acquires. Where an original is unavailable, as with the Albatros D V currently entering Palen's Flying Show, Palen journeys hundreds or even thousands of miles to carefully photograph and measure original examples residing in the protective custody of the world's leading aviation museums. With the photographs, drawings and notes made from personal inspection, Palen returns to Rhinebeck with the ingredients needed to reproduce the original airframe as faithfully as possible.

Since the flying season is very hectic and busy, Palen saves his construction work for the winter months in Florida. Among his most recent achievements has been the construction of a replica 1913 French Deperdussin which, because of the unavailability of the original power plant, is powered by a 160 hp Gnome engine. The Deperdussin struggles its way aloft on the Saturday shows and, as mentioned, is frequently preceded or followed by replicas of a 1909 Curtiss Pusher Model D (powered by a 50 hp engine and copied from the famous "Rheims machine" in which Glenn Curtiss won the first speed event in history, the Gordon Bennett Trophy, at the astonishing speed of 46 mph (74 km/h), a 1909 Bleriot XI and a 1910 Short S.29.

As indicated by the list accompanying this article, Palen's aircraft collection is sizable and filled with an enviable number of famous types. When asked which aircraft in the collection is his favourite, Palen readily answers that he has no favourite — his collection is his "harem" and each aircraft

is located on a hill to the west of the flying strip. Although the aircraft housed in the museum are occasionally returned to flying status, the static display consists of approximately two dozen aircraft, including such pioneer types as a 1909 Demoiselle, a 1910 Bleriot and the 1912 Passett Ornithopter replica featured in the Twentieth Century Fox film "Those Magnificent Men in Their Flying Machines." Also housed in the museum are such World War I types as the Spad XIII, Sopwith Snipe, and the very rare (and unsuccessful) Pigeon Fraser Pursuit which was powered by a 100 hp Gnome engine and featured an "all moving" rear fuselage elevator control. The Golden Age of flying is also well represented by such types as the previously-mentioned Klemm, a 1931 Bird Model CK, a 1932 de Havill and Puss Moth, and a 1937 Fairchild 24R

whose checkered career began with its purchase new in 1937 for $10,000 by a prominent New York stockbroker as a gift to his wife with the stipulation that she always be accompanied by a fully certificated pilot on all flights and that the aircraft not be flown after dark or in inclement weather. Years later, the story goes, the aircraft was purchased (for an undisclosed sum) by Palen as a gift, with "stipulations," to his wife, Rita, for St Swithin's Day (better known as "Groundhog Day" in the United States).

The museum buildings also contain a substantial number of vintage aircraft engines and instruments. These and the aircraft displayed are clearly identified and are frequently accompanied by signs which explain their history both as to Palen's involvement and as to their place in aviation history. The museum buildings are not sleek air-conditioned edi-

The Fokker D VII used in the Sunday displays at Rhinebeck was originally flown commercially, as a two-seater, by Bert Acosta. It has been restored to fighting configuration and is still powered by its original Mercedes engine.

has its own personality and must be loved for what it is. Not all of them are easy to maintain or fly, but, even if eccentric, he loves them for their eccentricities.

Although a member of the Experimental Aircraft Association and Antique Airplane Association, Palen is not affiliated with any other museum. He also, occasionally, will trade or sell rare aircraft parts or instruments, but requires substantial proof that they will be used in completing an existing restoration or replica construction project. Old Rhinebeck Aerodrome is self-supporting, but occasionally receives cash gifts and testimentary donations from admiring patrons. The Aerodrome's staff consists of 25 to 30 non-flying personnel and a half-dozen or so

pilots for the weekend shows.

Virtually all of the aircraft in Palen's collection have been flown. A few, such as the Passett Ornithopter, were really never capable of flying even when new. Others, such as the experimental Pigeon Fraser Pursuit, were highly erratic and dangerous in flight and are kept only for static display. The principal attraction of Old Rhinebeck is in the flying of antique types and it is important that the aircraft in the Aerodrome be able to "pay their own way." The collection is expanded by two or three aircraft annually. As favourites, such as Palen's replica Fokker D VII, reach the limits of their operational lives, they are retired to the museum for eventual overhaul and reconstruction, but are replaced

by the newer additions. The collection at present consists of only single-engine types, but Palen has been considering the construction of a replica of a twin-engine French Caudron bomber from World War I. He already has the engines, instruments, wheels, etc, and the airframe dimensions have been taken from an original Caudron at the Smithsonian Institution. The project will be monumental and no starting date has been set.

Palen is occasionally criticized for making compromises in airframe construction and engine type. He candidly admits that deviations result both from the pressures of time in constructing the airframes and from the limits of his technical abilities. Metal work, in

Palen's Spad XIII is a 1918 original and is no longer airworthy, although it was flown for a time after Palen acquired it from the Roosevelt Field Museum. It is painted to represent the aircraft used in 1918 by Capt Eddie Rickenbacker.

THE AIRCRAFT OF OLD RHINEBECK (AS AT MID-1975)

Aircraft	Marking (c/n)	Notes
Aeromarine 39B	347N (55923)	1918 biplane under restoration. 90 hp Hall Scott engine
Aeromarine-Klemm	N320N (2-59)	Static display. US licence-built Klemm, 1930. 70 hp Le Blond
Aeronca C-3	N17447 (A-754)	Airworthy. 36 hp Aeronca engine
Albatros D Va	N12156	Static display. Palen replica 1972. 120 hp Mercedes
Albree Pigeon Frazer	—	1917 rebuild on static display. 100 hp Gnôme
Avro 504K	N4929	Airworthy replica (UK-built). 110 hp Le Rhône
Bird CK	N850W (4012)	1931 airworthy biplane. 125 hp Kinner
Bleriot XI	N60059 (56)	1909 monoplane in static display. 35 hp Anzani engine
Bleriot XI	N60094 (153)	1910 monoplane airworthy. 35 hp Anzani engine
Breguet	—	1911 biplane in storage
Curtiss D pusher	N4124A	Replica of 1910 biplane, under restoration. Rausenberger engine
Curtiss JN-4H Jenny	N3918 (38262)	Airworthy 1918 example. 180 hp Hispano engine
Curtiss-Wright Junior	N605EB	1931 monoplane, airworthy. 45 hp Szekely engine
De Havilland Puss Moth	N770N	1930 monoplane in static display. 135 hp Gipsy
Deperdussin	N8448	Replica of 1913 monoplane. Static display. 160 hp Guerne engine
Dickson glider	N5666	Replica of 1930 primary glider
Fairchild 24-C8F	N19129 (3224)	1937 monoplane in static display. 150 hp Ranger
Fleet Finch 16B	N666J	1942 biplane, airworthy. 125 hp Kinner engine
F.E.8	N17501	Airworthy 1970 replica from original drawings. 80 hp Le Rhône
Fokker D VII	N10408 (286/18)	Airworthy 1918 original, was used by Bert Acosta. 180 hp Mercedes
Fokker Dr I	N3221	1965 airworthy replica. 100 hp Gnôme
Funk Model B-85C	N24115	1939 biplane, airworthy. 85 hp Continental
Gazelle	N6551	Airworthy. 65 hp Continental
Great Lakes	N304Y	1930 biplane under restoration. 125 hp Menasco
Hanriot	N8449	Flying replica of 1910 biplane. 50 hp Franklin engine
Monocoupe 113	(332)	1929 monoplane in static display. 65 hp Velie engine
Nieuport 28C-1	N4123A (10)	1917 original in static display. 160 hp Gnôme
Passett Ornithopter	—	Replica of 1910 machine for "Those Magnificent Men" film. Static
Piper J-2 Cub	N17834	1936 monoplane, airworthy. 40 hp Continental
Raab Katzenstein	—	1921 primary glider, stored incomplete
Santos Dumont Demoiselle	—	Airworthy 1969 replica, under restoration. 65 hp Continental
Short S.29	N4275 (7")	Airworthy, replica built by Palen. 60 hp ENV
Siemens–Schuckert D III	N1918G	1969 replica of 1917 biplane, in static display. 160 hp Gnôme
Sopwith Pup	N5139 ("4")	1965 flying replica (owner Dick King). 80 hp Le Rhône
Sopwith Snipe 7F1	N8737R (9262/E8100)	1918 original in static display. 230 hp Bentley BR2
SPAD XIII	N2030A (16541)	1918 original in static display. 180 hp Hispano
Spartan C-3	NC285M	1929 biplane, airworthy. 165 hp Wright J6-5
Standard J-1	—	1918 biplane stored incomplete
Taylorcraft BC-65	N27558	1939 monoplane (owner G Bainbridge). 65 hp Continental
Thomas Morse S-4B	N74W	Airworthy 1917 biplane. 80 hp Le Rhône
Thomas Pusher	—	1911 original, stored incomplete
Thomas Pusher	N4720G	1912 original in static display. 90 hp Curtiss OX-5
Voisin	N38933	1908 original built for Norvin Rinek, in static display. 50 hp Rinek
Waco 9	N2574	Airworthy 1926 biplane (owner Martin Horan). 90 hp Curtiss OX-5
Waco 10	N9401	Airworthy 1928 biplane. 90 hp Curtiss OX-5

The FE 8 at Rhinebeck is an airworthy replica, added only recently to the Palen collection. The Flying Circus is constantly adding new aircraft to its collection as others are retired, sold or "swapped".

making cowlings for instance, is a difficult area for Palen. His skills are improving and are being augmented by those of others working with him; working not only in metal, but also in modern synthetics which permit the accurate reproduction of cowlings and other difficult-to-reproduce shapes originally fashioned from metal. As noted, the emphasis is on performing aircraft and, perhaps because of this, no special attempts are made to preserve old airframes or engines in their original state. As parts weaken or wear out, they are unceremoniously replaced although all original rejected parts are saved. The Aerodrome's non-flying staff constantly goes over both airframes and engines to be sure that they are in the best possible operating condition.

Cole Palen is obviously a man happy with his work. His immediate plans are to continue collecting, building, and demonstrating antique types. For 1976, the United States' Bi-Centennial Year, he hopes to add a flying replica of a 1911 Wright Flyer used in the famous "Vin-Finn" promotional tour across the USA.

The "Rhinebeck Experience" is one suited to and recommended for the entire family. Were it not for Palen's efforts, the visiting children and probably many of the parents would never have the opportunity to witness the sights, smells and sounds of aviation's youth. For the historian or collector, there is the opportunity to closely examine numerous original engines, instruments and airframes. For others there is the colour and good natured humour of Palen's entertaining shows. In any case, a visit to the Old Rhinebeck Aerodrome is a thoroughly pleasurable and wholly worthwhile experience. □

the proposals, calling simply for the Ha-45/44 engine with a mechanically-driven two-stage three-speed supercharger to be married to a standard Ki.84-I airframe, and installation design was to be 80 per cent complete by the time the war terminated. The Ki.84N and Ki.84P were both based on the use of the new 2,500 hp Ha-44-13 engine and differed only in the extent to which wing area was increased, that of the Ki.84N being increased by 16·15 sq ft (1,50 m²) and that of the Ki.84P being increased by 37·68 sq ft (3,50 m²). While neither project was to progress further than preliminary design, plans were already being formulated for the production of the Ki.84N as the Ki.117 when hostilities ended.

The wind begins to drop

By the beginning of 1945, the Hayate was by far the most numerous of the Imperial Army's fighters but the bulk of those assigned to the Philippines had been largely dissipated. Although the Hayates had given an extremely good account of themselves, being employed for every conceivable type of mission, ranging from long-range penetration, fighter sweeps and interception to dive bombing and ground strafing, attrition had been inordinately heavy and the bulk of the output of the Ota and Utsunomiya factories had been absorbed in enabling the Hayate-equipped *Senais* to maintain some semblance of operational strength. Relatively few Hayates were available for assignment to other theatres of operations and the early months of 1945 saw the re-equipment of only three more *Sentais* from the Hayabusa, these being the 20th on Formosa and the 13th in Indo-China in February, and the 25th in China during the course of March. As the remnants of those units that had fought in the Philippines straggled back to the home islands during the early months of 1945, they were hastily re-equipped and reassigned to home defence.

Meanwhile, the Okinawa campaign had begun, Hayate regiments deployed in defence of the island comprising the 47th, 52nd, 101st and 102nd *Sentais*. Although their bases suffered heavily as a result of the Allied air operations that preceded the invasion of Okinawa, the Hayate units were extremely active and achieved particularly good results in day and night sweeps over airfields established by the US forces in northern Okinawa. In one sortie conducted by 11 Hayates of the 101st *Sentai* on 15 April, the installations at two airfields were heavily damaged, one airfield being put temporarily out of action, and a considerable number of aircraft were either destroyed or damaged on the ground, but eight of the Hayates were brought down by the airfield defences and another was damaged, making a forced landing on an islet.

While production of the Hayate had peaked at 373 in December 1944, such a production rate could not be maintained in the face of growing shortages of components and power plants compounded by a steadily escalating USAAF bombing offensive against the airframe and engine factories. The Musashi engine plant was to be the recipient of no fewer than

12 bombing attacks between 24 November 1944 and 8 August 1945, although some production of the Ha-45 was maintained at Musashi until 20 April when the factory was finally brought to a standstill. Earlier, in January, production of the Ha-45 had been launched at Nakajima's Hamamatsu works, and assembly of the engine was transferred from Musashi to an underground plant at Asakawa where production continued until the end of the war to bring total Ha-45 output to 4,066 units. The first direct attack on the Hayate assembly plant at Ota came on 10 February 1945, a total of 84 Superfortresses inflicting heavy damage and 74 Hayates being seriously damaged or destroyed on the assembly lines. The Ota plant was also damaged as a result of attacks by US carrier aircraft, necessitating acceleration of the plant dispersal programme and a serious drop in output in consequence.

Production standards had begun to slip badly by early 1945, and inevitably serviceability in the Hayate-equipped units suffered. The performances of individual aircraft varied greatly as a result of the general lowering of manufacturing standards and this became increasingly noticeable as the plant dispersal programme accelerated. New pilots converted to the Hayate with barely more than 200 flying hours and operational training had to be conducted *on operations*! Virtually all Hayates were used to make up attrition in existing units as they came off the assembly lines and few were available for the conversion of more units still mounted on the obsolete Hayabusa, although the 246th *Sentai* supplemented its Shokis with the Hayate, the 111th *Sentai* was formed on 10 July 1945 with a mix of Hayates and Ki.100s, the 112th *Sentai* being formed on the same day as a Hayate-equipped unit, and the 64th *Sentai* was to be in process of converting from the Hayabusa to the Hayate in Manchuria as the war ended.

Mansyu Hikoki Seizo at Harbin contributed 94 Hayates during the closing months of the war, but output fell far short of target, the Utsunomiya facility, for example, delivering only 727 Hayates by July 1945 as compared with 1,606 scheduled. Thus, apart from two prototypes and 125 pre-production examples, the total number of Hayates delivered was 3,382, Army acceptances of pre-production and production Hayates totalling 3,470 aircraft.

The Hayate fought to the end in the skies above the home islands under increasingly chaotic conditions, its bases under frequent attack and servicing and maintenance rendered a nightmare by the disruption of supplies of spares. Supplies of aviation fuel became increasingly critical, seriously curtailing operations, and some of the Hayate-equipped units had to be held in reserve for the anticipated assault on Japan. In the final weeks of the war, a substantial proportion of the Hayates remaining in the inventory of the Imperial Army Air Force were grounded through lack of spares, and thus the gale (Hayate) that had begun to manifest itself with such force a year earlier died to a feeble breeze.

The Hayate had been, during the final phases of the Pacific War, numerically the most important Army fighter and during

The Ki.84-I-ko Hayate of the 2nd Chutai, 11th Sentai, which was destined to survive to the present day. This aircraft, seen below as originally captured at Clark Field, Manila, was utilised at Wright Field in 1946 for the flight evaluation appearing on pages 44-46.

The much-travelled Ki.84-I-ko Hayate C/N 1446, originally used for the flight evaluation which commences below, is seen here landing at Iruma after its return to Japan.

its operational life it had never been outclassed by its opponents. Typifying the changing fighter requirements of the Imperial Army Air Force during the conflict, the Hayate was a brilliant design; its misfortune was that it could so rarely be employed in the offensive rôle for which it had been primarily intended. □

Viewed from the cockpit

The following account of the characteristics of the Hayate was prepared by one of the USAAF test pilots responsible for evaluating a Ki.84-I-ko which had been recovered at Clark Field, Luzon, and transported to Wright Field, Dayton, Ohio, after preliminary testing by a Technical Air Intelligence Unit pilot in situ whose task was to ready the fighter for the subsequent tactical trials in the USA. The evaluation at Wright Field comprised a total of 11½ flying hours but the test programme was frequently interrupted by failure of exhaust stacks as a result of the poor materials used in their manufacture coupled with inefficient welding. Problems were also experienced with the hydraulics.

THE COCKPIT of the Hayate was entered from the port wing root walkway and was facilitated by a retractable step and a push-in type handhold at the wing trailing edge, and a second retractable step just below the cockpit sill, these being extremely well located and making for easier access than offered by contemporary AAF fighters. The stamped metal pilot's seat could

be adjusted vertically by means of a handle on the left side, but the locking pin in this particular aircraft did not always engage, with the result that the seat had an annoying tendency to shift under g force changes. The AAF shoulder harness that had been fitted for the test programme was anything but satisfactory, affording no protection for the pilot whatsoever in the event of a crash landing as no stress member had been installed over which the straps could be passed and in the event of an accident involving longitudinal deceleration, the sheet metal seat back would undoubtedly have failed and the pilot would have struck his head on gunsight or instrument panel.

The layout of the cockpit itself was, in general, satisfactory, with the flight and engine instruments logically grouped, the former being arranged on the upper centre portion of the panel with the latter below. The flap and undercarriage controls were situated on the lefthand side of the floor, with the elevator trim wheel and engine control quadrant against the lefthand sidewall. No flight-adjustable aileron or rudder trim tabs were provided, preventing the aircraft being trimmed for hands-off flight. The auxiliary electrical panel and ignition boost control containing circuit breakers were below the instrument panel on the right; the internal and external fuel selector valves and fuel cooler and primer controls were on the righthand side of the floor, and the cowling and oil cooler flap controls were on the upper right cockpit side, together with the radio equipment. The auxiliary hydraulic pump was further aft on the righthand side and the mechanical up-lock release was on the left side of the cockpit floor.

The wobble pump, primer and starter button, all being on the right, kept one hand rather busy in starting, and it soon became obvious that the Hayate handled rather poorly in taxying owing to inadequate braking action, a condition aggravated by the inefficient design of the rudder bar and toe brake assembly. Use of the brakes was mandatory for "S"-ing in order to obtain a measure of forward vision. At the same time, braking had to be strictly limited in order to prevent overheating and locking as a consequence. It proved difficult to get the tailwheel to castor and vision for taxying was certainly not improved by the narrow cockpit and rearward position of the seat, but the actual take-off characteristics were good, with negligible torque effect if rated power was applied gradually. On the other hand, if power was piled on, full right rudder and some braking were necessary to counter the strong pull to port. Three-point take-offs could be safely executed at 95 mph (153 km/h) IAS with normal rated power or above, initial acceleration being normal with either 15 deg flap or no flap at all. At 150 mph (241 km/h) IAS only some four seconds were required for undercarriage retraction, this process producing no loss in altitude or sinking feeling and negligible trim change,

The surviving Hayate is superbly if not entirely accurately finished as may be seen from this photograph which makes interesting comparison with that at the foot of page 43 which illustrates the same aircraft as captured by US forces at Clark Field, Manila (Photograph courtesy of Koku Fan).

and it was immediately obvious that initial climb rate was extremely good, although no performance climbs could be attempted owing to flying time restrictions.

Excellent handling and control

Once the canopy was shut it became apparent that the cockpit left something to be desired from the viewpoint of comfort for a normal-sized pilot owing to the severely restricted head-room, and the design of the seat coupled with lack of provision for rudder pedal adjustment would obviously have resulted in some discomfort during extended operations. However, body room was ample and heat level and ventilation volume were found to be good for warm weather operation at low and medium altitudes — cold weather operation would have been another story owing to lack of cockpit heat. Despite a some-what narrow canopy, combat vision was excellent in climbing flight when gentle "S"-turns were necessary. The cockpit noise level proved to be fairly normal for a radial-engined fighter without an exhaust collector ring, and the vibration level was definitely lower than that of the A6M5 Zero-Sen, especially at high speed, and comparing fairly closely with that of most contemporary US fighters.

It was quickly ascertained that, in general, the handling and control characteristics of the Hayate were superior to those of comparable US fighters and particularly in the low speed regime. The roll rate and turning radius were found to be slightly inferior to those of the A6M5, but control feel was very good; rudder and aileron forces were light, well correlated and produced quick, positive changes of attitude. Elevator forces, although heavier than those of the rudder and ailerons, were not objectionable and progressed with g forces with no apparent lightening. No flat spots or control reversal tendencies were encountered over an IAS range of 74 to 350 mph (119 to 563 km/h). There were little changes in directional trim be-tween 150 and 350 mph (241 and 563 km/h), but the rudder control became extremely sensitive at 300 mph (483 km/h) IAS, sensitivity reducing somewhat at higher speeds.

As previously mentioned, flight adjustable trim was provided for the elevators only and the trim control worked easily, but excessive play at the cockpit end of the device resulted in some difficulties in the initial pre-setting of the tab, although very little trim change was necessary throughout the level flight speed of the aircraft. Only slight longitudinal trim changes occurred with operation of the undercarriage and flaps. The lack of in-flight trimming for the ailerons or rudder did not seem serious, although a rudder trimmer would undoubtedly have improved the Hayate's capabilities as a gun platform. As flown, the Hayate had been rigged with too much right rudder trim and the attendant starboard wing heaviness proved something of a handicap in evaluating stall and handling characteristics accu-rately. However, the stability of the aircraft appeared to be very satisfactory. Yaw tests indicated some lateral oscillation, although not of a serious nature.

The stalling characteristics of the Hayate proved to be quite normal and stall warning occurred early enough to prevent a stall developing if recovery procedure was initiated promptly. In clean condition with power off at 8,000 ft (2 440 m) the stall warning consisted of shudder and elevator buffet at 108 mph (174 km/h) IAS. The actual stall, which came at 102 mph (164 km/h), proved clean and the Hayate was stable with little tendency to drop off on a wing, and the ailerons and rudder remaining effective well below stalling speed. With the wheels and flaps down and the oil cooler shutters open, but the cowl flaps and canopy closed, the stall warning — occasionally accompanied by severe canopy buffet — came at 92 mph (148 km/h) IAS and the actual stall occurred at 90 mph (145 km/h) with the nose dropping straight through. Again, there was no indication of instability.

With power on, undercarriage down and full flap, the Hayate did not stall. The rudder became inadequate below 81 mph

(Above) Hayate No 1446 seen above during preliminary flight trials as S17 with Technical Air Intelligence Unit in the Philippines and (immediately below) as tested at Wright Field in 1946 as "302".

(Immediately below) Hayate No 1446 as N3385G with Col Walker "Bud" Mahurin at the controls during the run up for the first flight after complete restoration of the fighter by Air Research Manufacturing.

(130 km/h) IAS and at this speed heading could be maintained by use of full right rudder and right aileron. The ailerons be-came inadequate for maintaining altitude below 74 mph (119 km/h), the Hayate yawing left at this speed and then rolling with any further decrease in speed, but control was readily recovered by an increase in airspeed and a slight de-crease in power.

Manœuvrability was good; rolls, loops, Immelmanns and turns being executed with ease at normal speed, although well co-ordinated manœuvres proved somewhat difficult owing to the lack of in-flight aileron and rudder trimming. Handling on the approach and during landing was very good, with no undesirable characteristics or ground looping tendencies mani-festing themselves, and vision, too, was good during the ap-proach, although less than adequate after the flare was made. After extension of the undercarriage below 160 mph (257 km/h) and the application of full flap at 130 mph (209 km/h), a three-point landing could be satisfactorily executed (with elevator trim set for zero stick force) using speeds of 120 mph (193 km/h) over the fence and 110 mph (177 km/h) just off the runway, the actual touch-down being made at 92 mph (148 km/h). The Hayate landed easily, with all oleos soft, and was stable during the landing run which was pleasantly short. Crosswind landings could be made comfortably, but the brakes were relatively poor, although rather better than those encountered on the Ki.43-II Hayabusa.

General functioning

The Japanese instruments functioned well and appeared re-liable with one or two noteworthy exceptions. The gyro turn indicator appeared to be binding inasmuch as only one-third needle width right or left was the maximum indication obtainable under any attitude or rate of turn; the caging knob was missing (or had been omitted) from the artificial horizon, making it impossible to cage the instrument for aerobatics or to erect the gyro after it had been upset — no gyro erection tendency was apparent in five minutes of level flight after upsetting, and the left fuel gauge consistently read lower than the righthand gauge although the fuel tanks theoretically fed evenly. Control friction was nominal on the ground, with no binding or roughness present, but interference between the auto mixture control and the stick became evident when an attempt was made to apply full left aileron when the mixture control was set normal.

The operation of the Nakajima Ha-45 18-cylinder radial was generally satisfactory throughout the series of flight tests, but while easy to start cold proved somewhat difficult when hot, the externally energized starter apparently having an insufficient torque rating. The engine ran somewhat roughly between 1,400 and 1,600 rpm and between 1,900 and 2,100 rpm, but the engine controls were smooth in operation with positive response. The engine control quadrant friction locks were unreliable, however, and rarely held the controls in fixed position, the auto mixture and supercharger controls creeping and the propeller control tending to vibrate at low rpm positions. Operation of the four-bladed electrically-controlled constant-speed Pe-32 propeller was good, although it displayed a tendency to overspeed excessively unless extreme care was taken when power was being applied after a prolonged dive.

The hydraulic system usually worked smoothly but some difficulty was experienced with the hydraulically-operated undercarriage. On one flight, the mainwheels retracted only partway and on another retraction was completed but the up-locks would not engage. On both occasions repeating the cycle of operations appeared to clear the trouble. Prior to the delivery of this particular Hayate to Wright Field, the hydraulic pump had failed completely on one flight with the result that the wheels crept down. The auxiliary hand pump, which was connected to the reserve portion of the main hydraulic tank, worked well and its capacity was such that approximately 100 strokes were required to retract or extend the flaps, but its efficacy in so far as the undercarriage was concerned was not checked. In the event of a complete hydraulic fluid failure, the undercarriage could be unlocked manually and allowed to fall into place, the process being aided by yawing the aircraft until the indicator lights showed that the down-locks had engaged. One poor feature of the hydraulic system was the need to open and shut the by-pass. This had to be opened below 1,200 rpm to prevent the pump from overheating. The electrical system functioned well, with the exception of one instance of generator failure prior to take-off, but the location of the generator switch in the baggage compartment (which could not be reached by the pilot) was poor.

It was concluded from the test programme carried out at Wright Field that Hayate was essentially a *good* fighter which compared favourably with the P-51H Mustang and the P-47N Thunderbolt. It could out-climb and out-manœuvre both USAAF fighters, turning inside them with ease, but both P-51H and P-47N enjoyed higher diving speeds and marginally higher top speeds. The light power loading and control forces of the Japanese fighter were to be admired, but it was not so well constructed as its US contemporaries, perhaps reflecting the slipping Japanese production standards at that stage of the war; it was obviously incapable of standing up so well as US fighters under continual usage and it was more demanding on maintenance. It revealed little effort on the part of its manufacturer to render its pilot's task easier or safer — it lacked fire extinguishers and means of emergency escape — but it was a sturdy little warplane and a very dangerous antagonist in fighter-versus-fighter high-*g* manœuvring combat when flown by a reasonably experienced pilot. □

THE ONE THAT SURVIVED

T HE Ki.84-I-ko Hayate utilized for the flight evaluation detailed on these pages originally belonged to the 2nd *Chutai* of the 11th *Sentai*, one of the most active of the Imperial Army's fighter regiments. This particular aircraft, which bore the constructor's number 1446 and sported the stylized red "lightning flash" of its *Chutai*, was one of two intact and airworthy specimens of the Hayate discovered by US troops early in 1945 in a dispersal area at Clark Field, near Manila, capital of the Philippines. Both aircraft were overhauled, stripped of paint and assigned the TAIC (Technical Air Intelligence Command) coding "S10" and "S17" — all Japanese aircraft captured in the Philippines being allocated an evaluation number with an "S" prefix — the latter being Hayate 1446.

After several hours of test flying, "S17" was transported to the USA for more detailed flight evaluation, and after major overhaul by Air Material Command's Middletown Air Depot, Pennsylvania, in the spring of 1946, repainted with olive green upper surfaces and pale grey undersurfaces and the T-2 serial number "302" appearing on the vertical tail — the *Hinomarus* surprisingly being re-applied — the Hayate was sent to Wright Field. With completion of the evaluation in June, it was flown to Park Ridge, Illinois, for long term storage, later being assigned to the National Air Museum of the Smithsonian Institute. Owing to funding limitations, in 1951-52, the Museum was forced to declare as surplus to its probable future requirements some of the Japanese aircraft held in storage and among these was the Hayate. This was made available to the Ontario Air Museum, at that time located in Claremont, California, where the Hayate arrived in September 1952.

Some two years later, in July 1954, Metro-Goldwyn-Meyer, preparing for the film *Never So Few* which included Japanese wartime airfield scenes and anxious to instil a measure of authenticity by including some genuine Japanese aircraft, approached the Museum for assistance. It was agreed that the Hayate should participate in the film, and the aircraft was duly prepared for taxi runs and once again stripped for repainting, this time receiving an unrepresentative camouflage finish and the tail markings of the 52nd *Sentai*. After participating in the film, the Hayate was returned to the Ontario Air Museum where it remained on display until March 1963. The Chairman of the Museum Board, Col Walker "Bud" Mahurin, had meanwhile been approached by a television company anxious to acquire the services of an *airworthy* Japanese fighter for use in a TV film to be made in Florida. It was thus that, in April 1963, the much-travelled Hayate was dismantled and trucked to Los Angeles International Airport where it was completely rebuilt by the Air Research Manufacturing Company and restored to flight status, being flown on 25 June 1963 by Col Mahurin.

The restored Hayate, once more stripped of paint and sporting the registration N3385G, made its public début during the following month at the Air Force Reserve Air Fair at Santa Ana, California, where it was adjudged a sensation. It was later returned to the Ontario Air Museum to be placed once more on display. But the travels of this singular aeroplane were by no means over, 29 years after it left the Nakajima assembly line at Ota, it was to return to the land of its origin. In the years that followed its restoration to flight status, the Hayate moved from one location to another with the Museum, which was eventually restyled "Planes of Fame", and in 1973 was, appropriately enough, shipped back to Japan, having been acquired by Morinao Gokan, president of the Japanese Owner Pilots' Association, and where, with the "lightning flash" of the 11th *Sentai* once more restored — albeit now in white — it made a dramatic début at the 1973 Japan International Aerospace Show at Iruma. □

PLANE FACTS

Yak wings and finishes

Being something of a student of Soviet combat aircraft development, I have read with interest and appreciation your coverage of the Yak-1 and Yak-7 in the June issue, and your equally enlightening follow-up on the Yak-3 and Yak-9 in the November issue just to hand. But one thing puzzles me — the overall wing span of the Yak-1M. In the recently-published Putnam book "Russian Aircraft since 1940" it is stated that the Yak-1M had the small wing (ie, 30 ft 2⅕ in/9,20 m span) of the Yak-3, and this would seem to be confirmed by an article on the Yak-1M published in a recent issue of the Czechoslovak aviation magazine "letectví + kosmonautika", but you allege in "The First of the Yaks" that only one Yak-1M received the smaller wing, this modified aircraft serving as the basis for the Yak-3, and in "The Second Generation Yaks" you reiterate this. Who is right? One other point concerning Yakovlev piston-engined fighters: I have been told that many of these aircraft received a similar black-and-green upper surface camouflage to that employed during the "Continuation War" by the Finnish air arm. Can you confirm this?

C G Gifford
London NW2 3BA

The Yak-1M *never* had a similar wing to that of the Yak-3, although such has been alleged by several sources, the 30 ft 2⅕ in (9,20 m) span being peculiar to the Yak-3. In so far as we can ascertain, the erroneous claim that the Yak-1M standardised on the short-span wing later adopted for the Yak-3 was made some years ago in an East German aviation magazine. A Polish author, presumably basing his work on the article that had appeared in East Germany, repeated this error which was then perpetuated in Czechoslovakia and, as Mr Gifford says in his letter, has now been reiterated in *"Russian Aircraft since 1940"*.

With regard to the wing span of VK-105-powered Yaks other than the Yak-3: The Yak-1 began life with a wing span of 32 ft 9¾ in (10,00 m) but a more pointed wingtip was fitted to some aircraft, this increasing the overall span to 33 ft 7⅔ in (10,25 m). Whereas the Yak-7A and -7B fighters appear to have

An early production Yak-9 in a Soviet museum. It will be noted that this particular aircraft features the more angular wingtips introduced at a relatively early stage of Yak-9 production. Its upper surfaces are finished in the black-and-green camouflage scheme referred to by Mr Gifford. This finish makes interesting comparison with that of the La-5 in the background which sports dark olive green and dark brown upper surfaces.

been restricted to the shorter of these two wings, the Yak-1M appeared with *both*. In fact, the preponderance of Yak-1Ms apparently had the 33 ft 7⅔ in (10,25 m) wing and an almost immaculate example of the Yak-1M with a wing of this type has been stored (certainly until recently) in the Saratov Regional Museum. Whereas the initial production Yak-9s had a wing of identical span to that of the original Yak-1 (ie, 32 ft 9¾ in/10,00 m), a redesigned, more angular wingtip was introduced on the Yak-9 at a relatively early stage in its production career, this reducing overall wing span to 31 ft 11½ in (9,74 m), although some production series *retained* the original wing.

There has been and remains much confusion as to what modifications and changes were introduced on individual production series and sub-types of the various VK-105-powered

Yakovlev fighters, but it should be borne in mind that, despite the very large production quantities of these aircraft, almost every individual aircraft displayed minor differences, this resulting from the very high proportion of semi-skilled and non-skilled labour employed in Soviet aircraft factories during WW II, the considerable confusion that prevailed — the individual sub-contracting plants supplying components, assemblies, etc, frequently working to different tolerances and ignoring fine measurements — and the fact that the system then prevailing utilized a considerable amount of handwork on the final assembly line (eg, skin panels, cover plates, joints, etc, being trimmed or shaped to fit a particular aircraft, interchangeability thus becoming almost non-existent). While a main assembly plant had, on occasions, switched to a new sub-type of the fighter, the sub-contractors were frequently still manufacturing parts for the preceding sub-type, with the result that these had to be adapted. Thus, it was possible for the individual aircraft of one production batch to embody different wings, cockpit frames, armament, internal equipment, etc.

With regard to the camouflage scheme sported by Yakovlev fighters, while the irregular upper surface camouflage pattern of dark earth and olive was *officially* standard for fighters leaving the assembly lines from 1940, paint availability was very much a governing factor. Many early Yak-1s, Yak-7s and Yak-9s employed the black-and-green upper surface camouflage scheme to which you refer, Mr Gifford, simply because the Saratov factory in which the assembly line had been established had a large stock of paints of these colours which had been used for the agricultural machines that it had assembled previously. The black-and-green scheme proved effective — particularly against forest backgrounds — and was therefore later adopted by other assembly lines.

The Yak-1M with the 33 ft 7⅔ in (10,25 m) wing with pointed tips that was also applied to some production Yak-1 fighters. No Yak-1M fighters features the short-span wing standardised by the Yak-3.

IN PRINT

"Jane's All the World's Aircraft 1975/76"
by John W R Taylor
Macdonald and Jane's, London, £19·50
830 pp, 8¼ in by 12½ in, illustrated

AN ANNUAL EVENT of some significance in the aviation world is the publication of the new volume of *Jane's All the World's Aircraft*, the latest edition of which went on sale in mid-November. Jane's is now in its 67th year, the first edition having been published under the editorship of its founder Fred T Jane in 1909. Although there has not been a new volume published *every* year in the intervening period, a complete collection of Jane's provides a unique record of the world's output of aircraft over that period. Some of the earlier volumes can be seen to be, in retrospect, less complete and less accurate than the modern historian would wish, but that is a criticism that cannot be levelled against the yearbook under its present editor.

The 1975/76 edition is as comprehensive as one has come to expect. It has the same number of pages as the previous volume, albeit at an 18 per cent increase in cost, and the format and presentation follows the well-proven pattern. Some of the photographs, in our review copy at least, are poorly reproduced, but the usual care has clearly been taken to introduce as many *new* photographs as possible and to choose views that are as *descriptive* as possible.

Habitual users of Jane's will not need the incentive of this or any other review to buy — or otherwise obtain the use of — a copy of the new edition, but for those unfamiliar with this classic reference tome, it may be worth recording that the contents comprise sections devoted to aircraft (in this case meaning powered, piloted aeroplanes, helicopters and autogyros); remotely-piloted vehicles and target drones; sailplanes; airships; air-launched missiles; spaceflight and research rockets and aero-engines.

There are lists of official (FAI) records, significant first flights in the past 12 months and satellite and spacecraft launchings during 1974. A comprehensive index covers the contents of this volume and also indicates the volume of final mention of all types covered in the past 10 years. In each section, the products are grouped alphabetically by country and then by manufacturer. The descriptions are presented to a uniform style throughout and include Imperial and metric units of measurement.

The compilation of so massive a tome is obviously the result of team work, and the editor acknowledges the assistance of Kenneth Munson as assistant editor, David Mondey for certain parts of the aircraft section and the index, W T Gunston for the aero-engine section, Michael Taylor for metric conversions, Maurice Allward for the spaceflight and research rocket section and Lord Ventry for the airships section.

The combined efforts of this team, and of the many hundreds of individuals throughout the world who supplied them with information and illustrations, have produced, in the 1975/76 edition, a volume which, whilst containing no major surprises or revelations, is fully up to the expected high standard — FGS.

One of the most popular aerobatic demonstrations seen regularly in recent years is that given by the Rothmans Aerobatic Team, flying Pitts biplanes. A significant new book about the art of aerobatics is noted below.

"Aerobatics"
by Neil Williams
Airlife Publications, Shrewsbury, £5·25
266 pp, 5¼ in by 8½ in, illustrated

CAPTAIN of the British Aerobatic Team since 1966 and ten times British Aerobatic Champion, Neil Williams has made aerobatics an art in his 25 years of flying. It is, he says, the king of sports; and the reader of this book is soon conscious of being in royal company. Primarily intended as a text book for budding aerobatic pilots, this volume makes fascinating reading for armchair flyers, too, and can only serve to heighten their appreciation of the next aerobatic demonstration they witness.

All aspects of preparation for aerobatics are covered in the opening pages, the basic manœuvres are discussed in detail, and advanced aerobatics are described. There are sections on competitive and display flying and the characteristics of different types of aircraft are discussed. Throughout the book, excellent line drawings (by L R Williams) enhance the descriptive value of the text; there is also a small selection of photographs.

Certainly a major contribution to aerobatics, the standards of which can hardly fail to be improved by its use, this book is also a valuable addition to the literature of aviation, with the sheer joy of flying evident on every page.

"Light Aircraft" (Jane's Pocket Book 8)
by John W R Taylor
Macdonald and Jane's, London, £2·95 (cased), £2·25 (pvc)
260 pp, 7 in by 4¼ in, illustrated

COMPLETING the series of four Jane's aircraft Pocket Books, "Light Aircraft" covers aeroplanes and helicopters up to the light twin category, and including ag-planes. Full page photographs of each type enhance the book's usefulness; there is also a rather small three-view line drawing, brief specification and a note of variants in each case.

"Pictorial History of the French Air Force, Vol 2"
by Andre Van Haute
Ian Allan Ltd, Shepperton, Middlesex, £6·75
176 pp, 8 in by 10½ in, illustrated

THE second and concluding volume of this Pictorial History covers the story of the *Armée de l'Air* from 1940 to about mid-1973. The text provides a good account of the operations during 1940, the work of the Free French and Vichy French squadrons up to the end of the war and the subsequent reformation of the air force post-war. French participation in the original Vietnam fighting is covered, as is the inauguration of the *force de frappe*.

Once again, as in Vol 1 (see *In Print/October 1974*), the text shows signs of rather too literal translation from the French original. There is a good selection of photographs (four pages in colour), reproduced large-size, but many are split across two pages, which some readers will regret.

"RAF Bomber Command and its Aircraft, 1936-1940"
by J Goulding and P J R Moyes
Ian Allan Ltd, Shepperton, Middlesex, £5·95
144 pp, 8½ in by 11 in, illustrated

THE five-year period with which this book is concerned was one of special importance to the Royal Air Force, for it was in this half-decade that Bomber Command was created and many of the aircraft with which it would fight in World War II were evolved. At the time of the Command's formation, its squadrons were still flying the old biplane "cloth" bombers, but the first generation of high-performance monoplanes had already been conceived and was rapidly taking shape — the Wellington, Whitley, Hampden, Battle and Blenheim.

After describing in some detail the design origins of these last-mentioned types, this volume goes on to trace the steps that led to the first of the RAF "heavies", the Manchester,

Stirling and Halifax, and then to various other bomber schemes that were under study by the time the fighting began in earnest. A number of interesting three-view drawings are included, depicting projects as well as completed prototypes, and the book is characterized by large photographs, supplemented by eight pages of colour art work.

Chapters are also devoted to the early wartime operations of Bomber Command (with an Order of Battle for 11 April 1940) and to the camouflage and markings used in the period.

"Ryan Guidebook"
by Dorr B Carpenter and Mitch Mayborn
Flying Enterprise Publications, Dallas, Texas,
$10·95
120 pp, 8½ in by 11 in, illustrated
THIS is the third in a series of "Guidebooks" to American aircraft, joining the volumes on Stearman and Cessna already published. Painstaking research and a feel for the US light aircraft scene both before and after World War II gives each of these volumes authenticity and makes them valuable for reference as well as good reading.

The first part of the Ryan Guidebook provides a concise catalogue of everything produced in the Ryan name, from modified Standard J-1s to the XV-5B Vertifan and the RPV family. There follows a 28-pp "nostalgia" section, containing facsimile reprints of early Ryan advertisements, brochure entries and magazine articles. The remainder of the book is given over to detailed, comprehensively illustrated accounts of the Ryan types that were built in large quantities and a variety of models, with production lists and fine three-view drawings.

The price quoted is for the hard-bound edition; a paperback version costs $7·95 — both prices inclusive of postage from the publisher at 3164 Whitehall, Dallas, Texas 75229, USA.

"B-52 Stratofortress in Action"
by Lou Drendel
Squadron/Signal Publications, Warren, Mich,
$3·95
50 pp, 11 in by 8¼ in, illustrated
ALL the many Stratofortress versions are depicted in photographs, and the production history of the B-52 is briefly summarized in the opening pages of this volume. Unit markings and test aircraft complete the first half of the coverage, the second part being devoted to B-52 operations in Vietnam — mostly pictorial, but with a useful account of the *Linebacker II* assault in the closing stages of the campaign.

"Lockheed Hercules"
by Lars Olausson
52 pp, 6 in by 8¼ in
THIS remarkable little booklet provides a complete listing of Hercules production to date, by construction number (a total of 1,714 airframes, starting with the first of two prototype YC-130As and concluding with the tenth KC-130R for the USMC). For each aircraft listed, the Lockheed model number, military designation, owner and serial number are quoted, with additional information in a remarks column, giving such details as delivery dates, earlier or later markings, using squadron and write-off date.

Cross-reference listings provide instant information on the numbers of Hercules of each variant delivered to the various customers; USAF operating units and USAF tail code letters. Some of the information is more precise than previously published, including the listing of 12 C-130Es and 12 C-130Hs supplied to Israel, and the book is an excellent reference source for anyone with a particular interest in this aircraft. Copies can be obtained from the author at Fack 79 Sätenäs S-530 32 Sweden, price £1 including postage (Postal giro account 541636-7, Sweden).

"633 Squadron: Operation Rhine Maiden"
by Frederick E Smith
Cassell & Co Ltd, London, £3·50
286 pp, 4¾ in by 7¾ in
THE EXPLOITS of No 633 Squadron are already well-known to, one supposes, many millions, through the successful filming of Frederick Smith's novel about a specially trained, elite unit of Mosquito bombers and its dramatic, near-suicidal operation in a Norwegian fiord. Those already familiar with either the book or the film will need little encouragement to read this sequal.

The story resumes a few weeks after the Norwegian raid and reaches a climax as the squadron successfully complete a second major attack on a target of high strategic importance — a V-weapon factory. No mark of Mosquito could have bombed the target as described here and then turned itself into a formidable escort fighter on the return trip across Germany, as required in this story. This lapse apart, however, the operational technicalities are competently handled, and the clash of personalities between the surviving members of the original 633 Squadron and the replacement crews provides an absorbing background for this adventure story.

"Savoia Marchetti SM 82"
by Giorgio Pini, Fulvio Setti and Richard Caruana
Stem Mucchi, Modena, Lire 500
24 pp, 9¼ in by 8¾ in, illustrated
FIFTH title in the series of aircraft profiles from a reputed Italian publisher, dealing with the Marsupiale (Kangaroo) transport. Photographs, a three-view drawing in colour and Italian text.

"The Shepherd"
by Frederick Forsyth
Hutchinson, London, £1·50
56 pp, 5 in by 7¾ in, illustrated
PUBLISHED early-November with an eye, no doubt, on the Christmas market, this is a short ghost story from the practised pen of the author of "The Day of the Jackal" and other best-sellers. A young RAF pilot in a Vampire, homeward bound from Germany to the UK on Christmas Eve, has a complete electrical failure over the North Sea. Trapped over the fog-shrouded East Anglian coast with no instruments working except his ASI and altimeter, and no radio, his predicament is acute — until a Mosquito appears mysteriously several thousand feet below.

From then on, this 12,000-word story follows a wholly predictable course. A suitable candidate, perhaps, for that Christmas booktoken, but even with the half-dozen illustrations (drawn by Chris Fox), the price is steep.

"Classic Fighters, 1976 Calendar"
Falcon Publications Ltd, Greenford, Mddx, 96p
15 in by 12 in
TWELVE large photographs in black-and-white, one for each month of 1976, adorn this calendar for aviation buffs — with a thirteenth as a bonus on the cover. Types range from the Spitfire and Hurricane, through the Meteor and Javelin, to the F-4 Phantom and the Jaguar.

(Above) The fifth production C-130A Hercules, still with its original "flat" nose when photographed (by David W Davenport) in January 1974, when it was serving with the 4900 TS of AFSWC at Kirtland AFB. (Below) The first production C-130A, 53-3129, after conversion to AC-130A gunship, seen in October 1973 in overall matt grey finish while serving with the 415 SOTS of 1 Special Operations Wing at Hurlburt Field, Florida. All Hercules production to date is listed in the booklet noted above.

AIRSCENE

from page 6

of schedule, and totalled 38 hours on one aircraft in 16 days. The No 1 Boeing Vertol YUH-61, however, crashed and was severely damaged on 19 November; the two company test pilots on board were uninjured.

US **Coast Guard** has ended its competition to select a new medium range **surveillance aircraft,** in which the Rockwell Sabre 75C and VFW 614 were the only contenders (*Airscene/* August 1975) because Rockwell would not accept financial terms of a proposed fixed-price contract. Consequently, a new Request for Proposals is being issued, for 41 aircraft needed to replace Grumman HU-16Es now in service.

Brantly-Hynes Helicopters Inc, formed in 1971 to acquire rights in the Brantly B-2 helicopter when they were relinquished by Lear Jet (upon the acquisition of the latter company by Gates Rubber Co), has now resumed **production of the B-2** utility **helicopter.** Powered by a 180 hp Lycoming IVO-360-A1A, the first new production B-2 flew at Frederick, Oklahoma, in October, although the company had overhauled about 20 original B-2s in the intervening period. Brantly-Hynes (so-named to indicate the interest in the company of investor Michael K Hynes) plans to uprate the power of the B-2 to about 205 hp during 1976 and to introduce a modified rotor blade to improve performance, but is at present building helicopters only against specific orders, with a maximum planned production of 60 a year by 1977. The more powerful Brantly 305, with a 305 hp Lycoming IVO-540-B1A, may be re-introduced later this year.

Emair has developed a **more powerful version of** the Murrayair MA-1 agricultural biplane (see *Airscene/*May 1974), powered by a 1,200 hp Wright R-1820 engine. Known as the MA-1B, this new version has twice the installed power of the MA-1 with its 600 hp R-1340, but the bigger engine is derated to 900 hp and there is no increase in gross weight, the principal advantage of the MA-1B being that it can carry bigger payloads in performance-limited situations. First flight of the MA-1B was made at Harlingen, Texas, on 1 August and certification is expected in early 1976.

An improved, **modified version of** the **Learjet 25** has been successfully tested at Seattle and certification is now awaited. Known as the Howard Raisbeck Learjet, it features wing modifications to give supercritical characteristics and achieve a reduction of more than 10 per cent in the cruising fuel consumption. Landing and take-off speeds are also reduced. Following certification, conversions will be offered by the Dee Howard organisation.

CIVIL AFFAIRS

INTERNATIONAL
Both Concorde 205, which first flew at Toulouse on 25 October, and Concorde 206, which made its first flight from Filton to Fairford on 5 November, achieved speeds greater than **Mach 2 on** their **first flights,** being the first Concordes to do so. Concorde 205 — the first destined to operate revenue services for Air France, achieved Mach 2·11, and Concorde 206, destined to be the first in service with British Airways, achieved Mach 2·06. Each will enter service, as previously announced, on 21 January. Meanwhile, a meeting of the IATA South Atlantic traffic conference agreed to a "supersonic surcharge" of 20 per cent on first class fares, to be

charged by Air France on its Paris-Rio route. A similar surcharge is expected to be applied on British Airways fares for the London-Bahrein service, although the airline had provisionally been charging a 15 per cent surcharge.

LEBANON
In the course of the recent disturbances in the Lebanon, centred upon Beirut, **Middle East Airlines** has succeeded in **maintaining** its full schedule of **services,** although not without some minor disruptions. Beirut Airport itself has remained isolated from the fighting, protected by government security forces, and similar protection has been given to airline transport between the airport and the city and to hotels used by airline staff and passengers near the airport. Beirut remained the operations centre and the MEA Engineering Base continued in use, but about half of the MEA fleet was flown to Orly, Paris, to minimize the risk of damage being suffered by aircraft during overnight stops, and the operational pattern was changed to make Beirut a transit base rather than terminal base for many services. The three MEA Boeing 747s have continued in service during this period but the reduced rate of traffic growth now being experienced has led the airline to offer these aircraft for lease and at the time of going to press Air France was negotiating for two and Pakistan International for one. Trans-Mediterranean Airways, also based in Beirut, has continued to operate its two Boeing 747s on freight services, but also re-scheduled Beirut as a transit stop and based its operations in Amsterdam.

UNITED KINGDOM
For the first time, British Airways was able to test its Autoland-equipped **Tridents in** genuine **Category 3 weather** conditions towards the end of October, when London Heathrow was fog-bound. Operations were continued by the Tridents with visibility reduced to 655 ft (200 m) at ground level, when all other airlines had to divert or "stack" their flights until conditions improved. On 24 October, the first-ever Cat 3 landings were made, six Trident Threes arriving in succession after unforecast fog closed the airport to all other aircraft; on 28 October, early-morning fog again closed the airport but the full Trident fleet continued to operate under Cat 2 or Cat 3 conditions, with six Cat 3 landings made from a 12-ft (3,66-m) decision height, and 33 departures. All four main runways at Heathrow are cleared for Cat 3 operation, and the Trident equipment is already approved for Cat 3B, with an RVR of 246 ft (75 m). Clearance of British Airways flight crews to operate in Cat 3B is expected to be achieved this winter.

British Airways Overseas Division expects to operate Lockheed **TriStars** — originally ordered by European Division but now surplus to requirement for about two years because of reduced traffic growth — **on routes to India** later this year. Four services a week will serve Bombay and three a week, Delhi, with intermediate calls at Teheran, Beirut, Dhahran, Abu Dhabi and Dubai.

British Airways' **18th Boeing 747-100,** scheduled **to enter service** in April, will have a 32-seat upper deck, equipped to economy class standards, in place of the first-class lounge installed in the airline's other 747s. A smaller lounge will be incorporated on the main passenger deck, reducing the first class seating from 28 to 23, and there will be a total of 408 economy-class seats. At the same time that this aircraft enters service, British Airways will lease an additional 747 from Aer Lingus, with 28 first-class and 349 economy-class seats.

British Airways resumed **services to Cyprus** at the end of October, using Cyprus Airways' DC-9s on wet-lease. Since Nicosia was closed by the Turkish invasion of Cyprus in 1974, British Airways has not flown direct services to the island, but has recently been operating a London-Athens service to link with Cyprus Airways services on the Athens-Larnaca route. The latter airport is now being used for the direct London-Cyprus service.

USA
Pan Am has announced it will **inaugurate services with 'the Boeing 747SP** on 1 May on the route New York-Tokyo, and services on the Los Angeles-Tokyo route will begin on 20 May. Both services will operate non-stop, saving 2-3 hours on present schedules for the route. In the course of a 30-day demonstration flight through the Far East, Middle East and Europe during November/December, a 747SP flew the 6,754-ml (10 860-km) New York-Tokyo sector in 13 hr 38 min, cutting more than 3 hrs from the airline schedule for a one-stop service.

CIVIL CONTRACTS & SALES

Aérospatiale Nord 262: Allegheny Airlines has ordered two Nord 262s from Aérospatiale, for delivery this month (January). It is presumed that they are for eventual conversion to Mohawk 298 standard.

Bell Helicopters: Latest order for Bell helicopters placed by Petroleum Helicopters embraces three Model 212s and seven Model 206 JetRangers.

Boeing 707: Jordanian World Airways bought one -320C from Boreas International, ex-Pan Am. ☐ British Caledonian's most recent acquisition is one -338C, ex-Qantas.

Boeing 720: Caesar's Palace, the Las Vegas hotel, has acquired a Boeing 720, ex-United Air Lines.

Boeing 727: Tunis Air has ordered two more Advanced -200s, for June delivery, bringing the total 727 fleet to seven. ☐ Alitalia became the 76th customer for the 727 with an order for seven, to be acquired from Boeing through a leasing agency. Delivery will be made in October-December, to replace Caravelles and early DC-8s.

Boeing 747: Lufthansa has announced the purchase of its eighth 747, for December 1976 delivery. Like the seventh Lufthansa 747, ordered last June, the new aircraft will be a "combination" model with side freight door and General Electric CF6-50E engines. ☐ Pakistan International is buying two 747-100s from National Airlines, with delivery this month. ☐ South African Airways ordered a sixth 747SP, for 1977 delivery.

CASA C-212 Aviocar: Pertamina of Indonesia has ordered 10 more Aviocars, adding to three ordered previously.

Fokker F27: Air Alpes has acquired one Srs 200, for operation on its Paris-Chambery-Aix-les-Bains route.

McDonnell Douglas DC-8: Cargolux added a third Srs 63F to its fleet, on long-term lease from Flying Tiger. ☐ SATA of Switzerland also bought one Srs 63F from Flying Tiger.

Vickers Viscount: BMA sold two Viscount 814s to Skyline Sweden, adding to one already in service. ☐ Indian Airlines has its last two up for sale, having previously disposed of two to Lane Xang Airlines in Cambodia and one to Huns Air, a private Indian operator.

FRANCE

DASSAULT-BREGUET MIRAGE 50

FOLLOWING the appearance of a prototype with the designation Mirage 50 at the 1975 Paris Air Show, Dassault-Breguet has recently given more complete details of this new addition to the Mirage family, a fully representative prototype of which is now under construction for test and demonstration in 1976. Basically, the Mirage 50 is a Mirage 5 airframe fitted with an Atar 9K-50 engine in place of the usual Atar 9C, and having a number of modifications to improve its operational effectiveness.

The first installation of an Atar 9K was made in 1965 in a Mirage IIIE, producing the Mirage IIIC-2, but the engine was then still at the prototype stage and had not flown, even in its earlier 9K-30 version, in the prototype Mirage F1. More recently, since the Atar 9K-50 became available in its production form for the Mirage F1, Dassault-Breguet has produced a small number of Mirage IIIs with this engine for the South African Air Force, as the Mirage IIIR2Z. Early last year, a 9K-50 was fitted in the Mirage IIIE airframe that previously had been used as the prototype Milan with retractable foreplanes and it was this aircraft that appeared at the Paris Salon last June bearing the legend Mirage 50 (with the foreplanes removed). Flight testing of this aircraft has served to confirm the performance estimates for the production Mirage 50.

Among the changes in the Mirage 50 are modified air intakes for the higher air mass flow of the Atar 9K-50, adjustments to allow for the extra weight of the new engine, a frangible cockpit canopy to facilitate ejection, strengthened landing gear for higher gross weights, automatic altitude control, new avionics options and improvements in the overall weapons system.

The basic avionics consist of EMD Aida-2 radar, TRT radio-altimeter, EAS VHF transreceiver Type ERM 710, LMT TACAN, IFF, a SFIM gyrocentre, Crouzet air data centre and a gyro sight. Among a large number of options is the installation of a second UHF or VHF, an ADF in place of TACAN, and VOR/ILS. Radar options include the Agave radar (Mirage 50A) or Cyrano IV (Mirage 50C). Navigational possibilities include EMD RND 72 Doppler coupled with a Crouzet Type 93 computer or a conventional inertial system as used in the Super Etendard. An intermediate system that would offer lower cost than a conventional inertial platform, simpler maintenance and easier use, would comprise linking up a modern Doppler with a gyrocentre incorporating inertial type accelerometers.

Armament options are similar to those already available for the Mirage III/5 series. The major improvements offered by the use of

The Mirage 50 illustrated above is a preliminary prototype, being a Mirage III airframe previously used as the Milan prototype and now fitted with an Atar 9K-50 engine. A more representative prototype is now under construction.

the more powerful engine include reductions in take-off run of up to 22 per cent (in ground attack rôle at max weight); a 30 per cent gain in initial rate of climb and almost double the climb rate at high altitudes; a major increase in altitude reached in a given time — 13,000 ft (3 965 m) in one case carrying two Magic missiles; 40 per cent reduction in time required to reach Mach 1·8 at 40,000 ft (12 200 m), with 3·5 more minutes pursuit time at that altitude and double the patrol time possible at medium altitudes.

Power Plant: One SNECMA Atar 9K-50 axial-flow turbojet rated at 11,060 lb st (5 015 kgp) dry and 15,875 lb st (7 200 kpg) with afterburner at sea level, and giving 6,305 lb (2 860 kg) thrust at Mach = 0.9 at 36,090 ft (11 000 m). Total internal fuel capacity, 770 Imp gal (3 500 l), comprising 224 Imp gal (1 020 l) in main fuselage tank, 103 Imp gal (470 l) in forward fuselage tank, 118 Imp gal (535 l) in rear fuselage integral tank, 301 Imp gal (1 370 l) in integral wing tanks and a 13-Imp gal (60-l) accumulator for inverted flight. Provision for one 286-Imp gal (1 300-l) external tank on fuselage centre line and one 110-, 286-, or 374-Imp gal (500-, 1 300-, or 1 700-l) drop tank under each wing.
Performance: Max speed, Mach 2·2 or 750 knots (1 390 km/h) IAS; ceiling, about 60,000 ft (19 686 m).
Weights: Empty equipped, 15,875 lb (7 200 kg); take-off (clean), 21,830 lb (9 900 kg); max loaded, 30,210 lb (13 700 kg).
Dimensions: Span, 27 ft 0 in (8,22 m); length, 51 ft 0¾ in (15,56 m); height, 14 ft 9 in (4,50 m); undercarriage track, 10 ft 4 in (3,15 m); wheelbase, 16 ft 0 in (4,87 m); wing area, 375 sq ft (34,85 m²); sweepback, 60 deg; aspect ratio, 1·94:1.
Armament: Two 30-mm DEFA cannon in lower fuselage with 125 rpg. Five strong points (one fuselage and four wing) accommodate air-to-air or air-to-ground rockets, bombs and/or fuel tanks, eg: two Matra 550 Magic and one Matra 530 AAM plus two 110-Imp gal (500-l) tanks; or six 882-lb

(400-kg) bombs plus two 110-Imp gal (500-l) tanks; or four 882-lb (400-kg) bombs plus one 286-Imp gal (1 300-l) and two 110-Imp gal (500-l) tanks; or two 882-lb (400-kg) bombs plus two 374-Imp gal (1 700-l) tanks; or ten 550-lb (250-kg) bombs and two 110-Imp gal (500-l) tanks or 36 68-mm rockets in pods each containing 55 Imp gal (250 l) fuel, and one 286-Imp gal (1 300-l) tanks.
Accommodation: Pilot only, with Hispano-built Martin-Baker M.4 zero-altitude/90-kt (167 km/h) ejection seat. Cabin pressurized to 4·35 psi (0·30 kg/cm²).

ISRAEL

IAI 1124 WESTWIND

ISRAEL Aircraft Industries has put down a batch of 36 of its improved Model 1124 Westwind executive jets, to follow the 36 Model 1123s recently completed. Of the latter, six remain to be sold. Production of the Westwind is now at the rate of two a month, and delivery of the new 1124 will begin in 1976, eight orders having been received so far. The prototype made its first flight at Tel Aviv on 21 July and flight testing is expected to be completed by the end of the year.

To date, IAI has spent a total of 60 million Israeli pounds ($9,601,000) on development of the Model 1123 and 1124 Westwind, all of this sum having been provided by the company from its profits on these and other programmes. Price of the Westwind for 1976 delivery was quoted some months ago as being $1,750,000, including interior, Collins avionics package and Grumman thrust reversers.

The 1124 Westwind differs from the Model 1123 primarily in having Garrett TFE 731-3 turbofan engines replacing the General Electric CJ-610-9 turbojets. The increase in power bestows significant advantages on the 1124, and the reduced sfc of the turbofan provides a useful increase in range.

Contributing to the performance improvement is a new wing leading edge, comprising a reinforced glass-fibre cuff that incorporates pneumatic de-icing boots and introduces droop on the aerofoil section. The undercarriage has been beefed-up, new tyres and brakes have been introduced and the cockpit has been redesigned to improve crew comfort on long-range missions.
Power Plant: Two Garrett AiResearch TFE 731-3 turbofans each rated at 3,700 lb st (1 680 kgp), with Grumman thrust reversers. Fuel capacity, 1,300 US gal (4 920 l).
Performance: Maximum speed, 540 mph (869 km/h) at 19,400 ft (5 917 m); Mmo, Mach 0·765 above 19,400 ft, Vmo, 360 knots (667 km/h) IAS up to 19,400 ft (5 917 m); initial rate of climb, 4,000 ft/min (20,3 m/sec); service ceiling, 45,000 ft (13 725 m); single-engine ceiling (at 20,000 lb/9 080 kg), 26,000 ft

The prototype IAI Westwind Eleven 24 is shown on an early test flight. A three-view drawing appears overleaf.

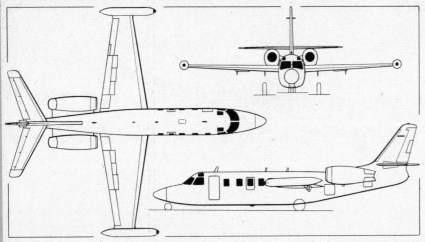

This three-view drawing of the IAI Westwind Eleven 24 shows the enlarged nacelles for the Garrett turbofans.

(7930 m); balanced field length, 4,840 ft (1 476 m); landing distance at max landing weight, 2,400 ft (732 m); max range with max fuel, 30-min cruise reserve, 2,875 mls (4 626 km); range with seven passengers, 30-min cruise reserve, 2,650 mls (4 264 km).

Weights: Operating weight empty, 12,700 lb (5 766 kg); max take-off weight, 22,850 lb (10 374 kg); max landing weight, 19,000 lb (8 626 kg); max zero fuel weight, 16,000 lb (7 264 kg).

Dimensions: Span, 44 ft 9½ in (13,65 m); length, 52 ft 3 in (15,94 m); height, 15 ft 9½ in (4,80 m); wing area, 308·3 sq ft (28,64 m²); aspect ratio, 6·51:1; undercarriage track, 11 ft 0 in (3,36 m).

Accommodation: Two crew and up to 10 passengers.

USA

LOCKHEED C-141B STARLIFTER

PROTOTYPE development of the C-141B stretched StarLifter is going ahead under a $40m (approx £19m) contract placed with Lockheed Georgia Co by the USAF. The prototype will be a conversion of a production C-141A (USAF serial 66-6186), the first flight of which is expected in April 1977. A five-month flight test programme is planned, after which USAF will make a decision on whether to proceed with conversion of the entire C-141A fleet, currently comprising 276 aircraft out of 290 originally built.

The stretch of the StarLifter is one of several steps proposed to improve the USAF's strategic airlift forces; another on which work is proceeding involves strengthening the wings of the C-5A Galaxy to extend its service life, but a third proposal, to modify wide-body transports in service with US civil airlines to give them a reserve capability for military use, has not so far won Congress approval.

The C-141B has three principal modifications: a stretch of 23 ft 4 in (7.12 m) in two sections in the fuselage — 13 ft 4 in (4,07 m) ahead of the wing and 10 ft (3,05 m) aft of the wing; the addition of wing root fillets at the leading and trailing edges to reduce drag and improve lift and the installation of a universal aerial refuelling receptacle slipway installation (UARRSI) to give the aircraft in-flight refuelling capability (see *Airscene*/May 1975). The fuselage stretch will allow the C-141B to carry three more standard 463L pallets, 13 in all; with no increase in aircraft gross weight, the extra payload can only be

achieved by reducing range, this being compensated by flight refuelling. Provision is being made for "contingency operation" at an increased gross weight, subject to a reduction in permitted g loading from 2·50 to 2·25.

As well as having the wing fillets, the C-141B will benefit from the deletion of vortex generators, the combined effect being to increase cruising speed to 512 mph (824 km/h), or Mach 0·775, despite the increased wetted area of the longer fuselage. The UARRSI will be installed in a fairing some 9 ft (2,75 m) behind

the cockpit above the fuselage pressure shell, with an external fuel line running aft into the wing fairing and thus to the fuel cross-feed lines in the wing centre section. Oil capacity is being increased to allow for greater endurance. Modification of the C-141 fleet is considered to be cost-effective because the aircraft at present have an average flight time of about 15,000 hrs whereas the fatigue life is now estimated to be between 40,000 and 45,000 hrs on the basis of continuing fatigue testing.

Performance: Max permissible diving speed, Mach = 0.875 or 472 mph (760 km/h) CAS; cruising speed, Mach 0.775 or 512 mph (824 km/h); cruising altitude, 38,000 ft (11 590 m); range with max payload (2·25g), 2,650 mls (4 264 km); range with max payload (2·50g), 2,990 mls (4 810 km); range with 13 pallets/59,800 lb (27 150 kg), 4,320 mls (6 950 km).

Weights: Operating weight empty, 149,904 lb (68 056 kg) one 13-pallet payload, 59,800 lb (27 150 kg); max payload (2·50g), 68,821 lb (31 245 kg); max payload (2·25g) 89,096 lb (40 450 kg); max ramp weight (2·25g), 325,000 lb (147 550 kg); max ramp weight (2·50g) 344,900 lb (156 585 kg); max landing weight, 257,500 lb (116 905 kg).

Dimensions: Span, 159 ft 11 in (48,74 m); length, 168 ft 4 in (51,34 m); height, 39 ft 3 in (11,97 m); wing area, 3,228 sq ft (299,9 m²); undercarriage track, 17 ft 6 in (5,33 m); wheelbase, 66 ft 4 in (20,23 m).

Accommodation: Flight crew of four. Cabin floor length, 93 ft 4 in (28,47 m); cabin max width, 10 ft 3 in (3,12 m); cabin max height, 9 ft 1 in (2,77 m); cargo volume, about 10,830 cu ft (306,5 m³).

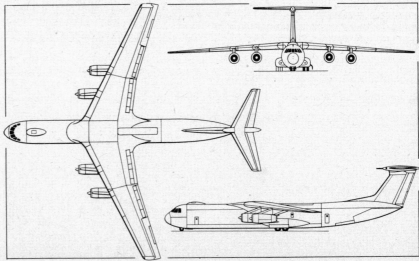

(Above) An artist's impression and (below) a three-view drawing of the Lockheed C-141B StarLifter.

AIR International

Volume 10   Number 2   February 1976

Managing Editor   William Green
Editor   Gordon Swanborough
Modelling Editor   Fred J Henderson
Contributing Artists   Dennis Punnett
                         John Weal
Cover Art   W R Hardy
Contributing Photographer
                         Stephen Peltz
Editorial Representative, Washington
                         Norman Polmar
Publisher   Donald Hannah
Circulation Director   Donald Syner
Subscription Manager   Claire Sillette
Advertising/Public Relations
                         Elizabeth Baker
Advertising Manager   Jim Boyd

Editorial Offices:
The AIR INTERNATIONAL, PO Box 16,
Bromley, BR2 7RB Kent.

**Subscription, Advertising and
Circulation Offices:**
The AIR INTERNATIONAL, De Worde
House, 283 Lonsdale Road, London
SW13 9QW. Telephone 01-878 2454.
US and Canadian readers may address
subscriptions and general enquiries to
AIR INTERNATIONAL PO Box 353, White-
stone, NY 11357 for onward transmis-
sion to the UK, from where all corres-
pondence is answered and orders
despatched.

MEMBER OF THE AUDIT
BUREA OF CIRCULATIONS   ABC

Subscription rates, inclusive of postage,
direct from the publishers, per year:
United Kingdom   £5·50
USA $17·50
Canada $17·50

Rates for other countries and for air mail
subscriptions available on request from
the Subscription Department at the
above address.

The AIR INTERNATIONAL is published
monthly by Fine Scroll Limited, distributed by Ducimus Books Ltd and
printed by Jayprint Holdings Ltd, Pinfold
Road, Thurmaston, Leicester, England.
Editorial contents © 1976 by Pilot Press
Limited. The views expressed by named
contributors and correspondents are their
own and do not necessarily reflect the
views of the editors. Neither the editors
nor the publishers accept responsibility
for any loss or damage, however caused,
to manuscripts or illustrations submitted
to the AIR INTERNATIONAL.

Second Class postage approved at Long
Island City, NY 11101. USA Mailing
Agents: Air-Sea Freight Inc, PO Box
1305, Long Island City, NY 11101.

CONTENTS

WRENDEZVOUS WITH WREN

SOLD

SPEEDJET
$935,000

"Will that be all, sir?"

AIRSCENE

MILITARY AFFAIRS

ARGENTINA

The *Fuerza Aérea Argentina* (FAA) anticipates that the first of two 12-aircraft *Escuadrones de Ataque* to be equipped with the **IA 58** Pucaras from the initial batch of 30 currently being built at Cordoba will achieve **operational status during the summer** as a component of the *II Brigada*, being joined by the second *escuadron* approximately one year later. Production tempo of the IA 58 at Cordoba has built up slowly since the first example flew in November 1974, and is now averaging one per month, but output is scheduled to increase to three per month by 1977 to meet an expected FAA follow-on order for a further 40 Pucaras.

The **Army's air component**, the *Comando de Aviación Ejercito*, is expected **to acquire** five of the 21 Rockwell **Turbo-Commander 690As** scheduled to be partially assembled by the San Justo factory of the Compania Argentina de Trabajos Aeros, Rockwell's Argentinian distributor. The Turbo-Commanders are to be used by the Army as high-speed personnel transports.

AUSTRALIA

Prior to their election in December, the Liberals stated that they would undertake an immediate **reassessment of** the RAAF's **equipment plans** and would take steps to increase the service's reconnaissance and strike capability by considering the purchase of more maritime patrol aircraft, by investigating the best means of providing the RAAF's F-111Cs with in-flight refuelling and a stand-off weapon, and by giving priority to the assessment of a Mirage IIIO successor. A choice of Mirage replacement is now anticipated by March 1977, and while the RAAF initially favoured the F-15 Eagle, increased emphasis on the ground attack task is prompting consideration of the purchase of two complimentary types with deliveries commencing towards the end of the decade. Dassault-Breguet is understood to be urging the RAAF to shelve consideration of a successor for the Mirages until the 'nineties and, instead, to re-engine the existing aircraft (presumably with the Atar 9K-50) and update some of their equipment. A recent fatigue test programme undertaken by the Aeronautical Research Laboratories in Melbourne has revealed that the Mirage mainplane, previously thought to be the most fatigue-limited component of the aircraft, could withstand more than 32,000 flight cycles before failure and the aircraft thus possesses a substantially greater life potential than was hitherto believed.

CANADA

One hundred and thirteen Canadair CT-114 Tutor **trainers** of the Canadian Armed Forces are **to undergo a modification** programme by Northwest Industries at a cost of approximately Can$2m. The programme will include provision of external fuel tanks, antennæ and associated equipment changes, improvements to the canopy electrical system and the re-location of the engine ice detector probe. Twelve modified Tutors will be returned to the CAF by the end of May, and eight aircraft per month will be delivered thereafter until completion of the contract. At the present time, some 85 Tutors are on the strength of No 2 FTS, five are with the Flying Instructors' School, 10 equip the Canadian aerobatic team, the *Golden Hawks*

and some 58 are in storage. It is anticipated that, with the completion of the current modification programme, the remaining 45 Tutors in the CAF inventory will be similarly modified.

On 27 November, Defence Minister James Richardson announced the decision to purchase 18 examples of a modified Lockheed **P-3C Orion to meet** the CAF's **LRPA** (Long Range Patrol Aircraft) **requirement** at an estimated cost of Can$750m of which Can$526m is expected to be covered by industrial offset benefits. The P-3 LRPA will have an all-new internal cabin layout and a variety of external sensor changes, and the first aircraft is scheduled for delivery in May 1979 with the final aircraft being delivered in February 1980.

The Canadian Armed **Forces** are to **maintain** their **air combat strength in NATO** at its present level following conversion of the CF-104 Starfighters from nuclear strike to conventional attack rôle, according to Defence Minister James Richardson, who recently told the NATO Military Committee that the CF-104s have several years of operational life ahead and that Canada, therefore, has "some leeway" in planning procurement of a new fighter to phase in the major capital expenditures behind the peak expenditures for current tank and long-range patrol aircraft programmes. This suggests that there will now be considerable further delay in the selection of a successor for the CF-101s and CF-104s currently in the inventory.

DUBAI

The government of Dubai has ordered **four more** Aermacchi **MB.326** light **strike/trainers** for its Police Air Wing. At the time of closing for press it had not been revealed if these were single- or two-seaters. The Air Wing is currently operating three single-seat MB.326KDs and a single two-seat MB.326L, and Italian instructors are on secondment to Dubai.

GREECE

Some **concern** has been expressed in Greece **over** the failure of the Iranian government to relinquish 12 ex-IIAF **Northrop F-5As** which were purchased on behalf of the Hellenic Air Force via the US last summer. It would seem that the transfer of the aircraft, among the last of this model in the IIAF inventory, has been withheld owing to the IIAF's view that the retention of the aircraft is necessary until more F-5E Tiger IIs and F-4E Phantoms are received if pilot proficiency is to be maintained.

The first HAF squadron to be equipped with the Dassault-Breguet **Mirage** F1CG, the 336 *Mira* at Araxos, is expected to attain **operational status** this summer.

ISRAEL

By the beginning of last month (January), the US Congress was expected to have signified its approval of a proposed letter of **offer** to Israel for the initial increment of a planned purchase of 25 McDonnell Douglas **F-15 Eagle** fighters at a cost of $600m (£295m) with deliveries to commence probably in January of next year, indicating that at least some of the aircraft will be taken from those laid down for the USAF. Saudi Arabia is also understood to have indicated a requirement for up to 100 F-15s, but it is inconceivable that approval of the sale of this fighter to both countries will be given. The anticipated commencement of de-

liveries to Israel is several months later than earlier anticipated owing to a delay in the build-up to a nine-per-month production tempo not now expected until next month (March).

SOUTH AFRICA

Technicians of the South African **Air Force** are now **re-sparring** the **Shackleton** MR Mk 3 maritime patrol aircraft of No 35 Squadron and the first two re-sparred aircraft have been returned to service, others being re-sparred as they approach the end of their fatigue life. The re-sparring and refurbishing of the Shackletons is undertaken at Ysterplaat, the aircraft having to be virtually disassembled and rebuilt from scratch.

SPAIN

The *Escuadrón 792* at San Javier, Murcia, a component of the *Academia General del Aire,* has recently placed in service two CASA **C.212B Aviocar** photo-survey aircraft. These aircraft are equipped with Wild RC-10 cameras and are two of six Aviocars of this sub-type ordered by the *Ejército del Aire.*

SWEDEN

The *Flygvapen* recently took **delivery of** its **third** Lockheed **Hercules,** a C-130H, which joined two C-130Es delivered in 1963 and 1965 respectively. The *Flygvapen* is understood to have requested authorisation for the acquisition of a second C-130H for 1977 delivery.

SWITZERLAND

The Upper House of the Swiss Parliament has approved the **purchase of** 72 **Northrop F-5E** Tiger IIs for the *Flugwaffe*. The Lower House has still to vote on the purchase and this is expected to take place next month (March).

USA

All USAF **combat aircraft** were scheduled to be **withdrawn from Thailand** by 31 January, two months earlier than the deadline previously established. The last 50 aircraft were to have been pulled out of the Korat air base, 170 miles (275 km) north of Bangkok, and the base closed.

The USAF Systems Command has awarded Sperry Flight Systems a $7·6m (£3·7m) contract for the **conversion of** a further 29 Convair **F-102A** Delta Dagger interceptors as PQM-102 remotely-controlled aircraft. Deliveries will commence in October and be completed in November 1977, and seven will go to the US Army as targets for Stinger and SAM-D surface-to-air missiles at the White Sands Missile Range, the remainder being assigned to the USAF for use in AAM trials at the Tyndall and Holloman AFBs. This contract will bring to 68 the total of F-102As converted as PQM-102s.

The US Navy hopes to obtain authorisation for the acquisition of 30 **US-3A versions of** the Lockheed S-3A **Viking** shipboard ASW aircraft as an interim COD (Carried Onboard Delivery) aircraft. The proposed utility S-3 will have six passenger seats and space for a limited cargo load, and will enable Lockheed to extend the S-3 production line for a further year. The US Navy is also considering Lockheed studies of CAPS (Combat Air Patrol Support) versions of the S-3A. The CAPS S-3A will carry four Phoenix missiles on wing pylons and will have a naval flight officer in place of a co-pilot. One of two CAPS versions under study retains most of the aircraft's ASW capability and the other is a refuelling tanker with ASW capability limited to 30 sonobuoys.

AIRCRAFT AND INDUSTRY

BRAZIL
EMBRAER has confirmed that the Brazilian Air Ministry has provided **funds for** a start to be made on development of a **turboprop transport** for military use, serving primarily as a replacement for the DHC Buffalo in the *Força Aérea Brasileira*. After evaluating a number of alternatives, the Air Ministry selected the CX-2A variant, a high-wing design with two General Electric T64-GE-10 turboprops of 2,860 shp each. With a cargo compartment of 1,590 cu ft (45 m³) capacity, the CX-2A will be able to carry 38 paratroops or 53 equipped troops; cruising speed will be 342 mph (550 km/h) and the range will be 1,680 mls (2 700 km). There is some disappointment among Brazilian airlines that a turboprop rather than turbofan type has been chosen for development, and the market for the CX-2A is therefore expected to be limited to military users and, possibly, commercial air freight specialists.

CANADA
Early in December, the **Canadian government** took up its option to buy **Canadair Ltd** from General Dynamics, at a cost of $38m (£18.8m). Previously, de Havilland Aircraft of Canada had been purchased from Hawker Siddeley for $38.8m (£19.2m) and a merger of the two companies under a new private owner is now expected to proceed. A $90m (£44.5m) loan to de Havilland Aircraft has also been approved, to finance production of 50 Dash-7 STOL transports (including the 25 previously approved).

CHINA
The Chinese National Technical Import Corporation has signed a **contract** with Rolls-Royce (1971) Ltd **for** an initial batch of about 20 **Spey turbofans,** plus a licence to put the engine into production, with technical assistance from Rolls Royce, in China. The deal is worth about £80m to Rolls-Royce, and other British suppliers are expected to benefit to the extent of an additional £20m. It is understood that the reheated military RB.168 version of the Spey — as used in the HS Buccaneer and RAF Phantoms — is involved and that the engines are intended to power a new fighter of original design under development in China. A fleet of 35 Spey-engined Tridents is also in process of delivery to China.

FRANCE
A number of **future projects** with military applications are under study **by Aérospatiale,** in an effort to provide future production activity for its factories. In addition to the transport/tanker version of the Airbus A300B-4 (see under International heading), these projects include military transports that could replace the Noratlas and the Transall. In the former category is an aircraft of 35,280-37,485 lb (16 000-17 000 kg) gross weight, able to carry a 8,820-lb (4 000-kg) payload over a distance of 1,242 mls (2 000 km) and powered by two new Turboméca turboprops of 1,800 hp each. The Transall replacement is envisaged as a twin-turbofan aircraft of 132,300-lb (60 000-kg) gross weight, powered by CFM 56 engines. Some design work is also being done on a cargo version of the Nord 262/Frégate with a rear loading door, and the Fan Jet 600 proposal for a Magister trainer replacement (see *AirData File* Vol 9 No 3, September 1975) has been further refined. Intended to be powered by the new Turboméca DF-600 turbofan, the new Magister is now envisaged with a completely new fuselage, on which the wing is mounted in a low position, and having the cockpit faired in to the rear fuselage lines in a fashion

A new two-seat operational training version of the MiG-25 (Foxbat) high-altitude air defence fighter and reconnaissance aircraft has recently made its appearance in East Germany. As illustrated by this close-up photograph (courtesy Flug Revue) of the forward fuselage, the training version of the MiG-25 features a separate cockpit for the pupil pilot, the insertion of which obviates the possibility of intercept radar or cameras. It may be assumed, therefore, that the two-seat MiG-25 possesses no secondary operational rôle.

similar to the MB.339. A version with 1,170 lb st (530 kg) Turboméca Marboré VIS turbojets is also being proposed as an earlier alternative to the DF-600 version, and a prototype could fly in early 1978.

Installation of Turboméca **Astafan IV** turbofans **in** a Rockwell **Commander 690** to serve as a flying test-bed has been completed by the Compagnie Generale des Turbo Machines in Paris. Compared with the Astafan II which has been flying in a Commander 680 since April 1971, the Astafan IV has a larger fan diameter and uses the gas generator of the Astazou XX rather than the Astazou XVII; its thrust is more than 2,200 lb (1 000 kg), compared with 1,560 lb (710 kg).

GREECE
On 26 November, **contracts** were **signed** in Athens between the Greek government, the Lockheed Aircraft Corporation and three other US companies **for** the establishment of maintenance and limited manufacturing **facilities at Tanagra,** 50 miles (80 km) North of Athens. The contracts, valued at £60m, cover the development of a 175-acre (70-hectare) site adjacent to the existing airfield at Tanagra for 900,000 sq ft (83 000 m²) of hangar space, workshops and offices scheduled to be completed by mid-1978. The facility, which will have 3,000 personnel and will provide depot level maintenance for the Hellenic Air Force and maintenance and manufacturing for airlines, will be managed by Lockheed which will also have responsibility for all airframe work, the Westinghouse Electric Corporation being responsible for electronics maintenance.

INTERNATIONAL
Airbus Industrie is now using the designation A-300B-4FC for the **passenger/cargo** convertible **version of the A300.** Dimensionally the same as the A300B-4, it incorporates a forward freight door plus a freight handling system for the main deck. Of other Airbus developments, the A300B-10 continues to attract most attention; this is the reduced-length variant with 180-220 seats and a range of about 3,100 mls (5 000 km), now being studied with a choice of General Electric CF6-50, Pratt & Whitney JT9D or Rolls-Royce RB.211 turbofans. Total orders for the Airbus, following recent revisions in some contracts and options, stand at 25 firm plus 27 options for seven airlines, of which 11 had been delivered by early-November. The production rate will reach two a month by mid-year. Lufthansa has announced that it will inaugurate Airbus service on 1 April with its first two B-4s (Nos 21 and 22) which have

229 economy-class and 24 first-class seats. First flight of the first Lufthansa Airbus was made at Toulouse on 29 November, and it was flown to Hamburg on its second flight on 2 December, for cabin furnishings to be fitted by MBB. Meanwhile, Air France has taken delivery of its seventh Airbus, this also being its first B-4 version (No 19); destined for operation on Air France routes in the Caribbean, it flew from Orly to New York non-stop on 18 November, and entered service on the New York—Pointe-a-Pitre route on a daily return basis before the end of the month.

Some details have been given by Aérospatiale of a **military** transport and flight-refuelling tanker **version** of the **Airbus A300B-4** that it has been studying for a specific *Armée de l'Air* requirement. With all-up weight increased to 346,900 lb (157 500 kg), it would have Intertechnique/Sargent Fletcher refuelling pods under each wing tip, providing a fuel transfer rate of 396 Imp gal (1 800 l) per minute to each of two aircraft such as Jaguars. Eight additional tanks under the cabin floor would carry 88,200 lb (40 000 kg) of fuel, all of which could be used by the A300 itself in the transport rôle, when it could carry more than 66,150 lb (30 000 kg) of cargo for a distance of 3,726 mls (6 000 km). A large side-loading door would be fitted and the military A300B-4 could carry such loads as 145 passengers and seven standard pallets, or up to 360 troops. The possibility of providing a rear-loading ramp is also being studied.

On 5 December, the **fifth prototype** Panavia MRCA was **flown** for the first time at Caselle, near Turin. This, the first of two 'Italian' prototypes (the other being the ninth and last), was piloted by Pietro Trevisan, Aeritalia's MRCA project pilot, and was airborne for 45 min. The Italian prototype, P.05, will be primarily employed for flight-envelope clearance with external stores. Testing of P.06 at Warton was begun on 20 December with a 1 hr 2 min flight. Shortly before the initial flight of P.05, on 1 December a contract was signed by NAMMA, the tri-national government agency, and Panavia which formally authorised all non-recurring costs preceding series production, this representing the penultimate stage before full Government-authorised production go-ahead which is scheduled for next month (March). According to William Rodgers, British Minister of State for Defence, the unit price of the MRCA is now £4.96m. When the programme was launched in 1969, the unit price of the two-seat MRCA was calculated at £1.7m and at

1969 levels the present price is the equivalent of £2·1m, the difference being accounted for by exchange rate changes and inflation.

France and Germany are giving serious consideration to launching a joint **programme to develop** and produce the **Dornier Do 24/72,** with Aérospatiale as the French partner. The Do 24/72 (see *Air Data File*/August 1973) was originally designed by Dornier as an updated variant of the pre-war Do 24, in collaboration with CASA in Spain. A possible market for about 150 Do 24/72s was identified, up to 1985, but CASA interest waned, and Dornier maintained the project in a current status until discussions with France began in 1975. After studying both the Pratt & Whitney PT6A and the Lycoming T5321 as possible power plants, Dornier has decided to adopt the latter, which has a rating of 1,600 shp and permits a higher take-off weight to be used — 41,000 lb (18 600 kg). The Do 24/72 is a three-engined amphibian intended primarily for use as a water-bomber and for search and rescue duties. France is reported to be interested in buying an initial batch of 25 for use by the *Protection Civile.*

IRAN
On 21 November, the Iranian government named the Bell Helicopter Company as its partner in a **joint venture to establish** a modern **helicopter industry** in Iran as part of the country's industrialisation programme. Bell will work with the Iranian government to design, build and equip a modern production facility, and will train Iranian personnel in all facets of helicopter assembly and production, the initial aim of the programme being the co-production of 400 Bell Model 214A.

ISRAEL
Israel Aircraft Industries has reportedly completed the basic design of a **new air superiority fighter** as a successor to the Mirage IIICJ interceptors remaining in the inventory of the *Heyl Ha'Avir.* Powered by a single engine and featuring a semi-reclined pilot seat, side-stick controller and fly-by-wire system, the new fighter is expected to commence its test programme in late 1977 and IAI is currently surveying possible US suppliers for major subsystems.

According to the general manager of IAI, Al Schwimmer, the **Kfir** fighter **will be available for export.** by mid-1977, by which time the immediate requirements of the *Heyl Ha'Avir* will presumably be satisfied. IAI is apparently confident of obtaining export orders for the Kfir which, it is claimed, is some 20 per cent cheaper than the Mirage 5, and interest is reportedly being shown by air forces in SE Asia and the Pacific, as well as such Latin American countries as Peru and Venezuela. The Kfir is also being offered for licensed production programmes to several countries, including South Africa. Despite Israeli governmental approval in principle for the export of the Kfir, however, it is apparently refusing to allow certain major sub-systems of the aircraft to be exported for security reasons, and the General Electric J79-GE-17 engine — which is being produced in Israel with approximately a 60 per cent indigenous content — will have to be purchased direct from General Electric by any third-country Kfir customer, and such would seem to rule out South Africa as a potential Kfir operator owing to the embargo on that country which is being exercised by the US government.

NETHERLANDS
Fokker-VFW has announced that it will concentrate **F28 production** upon the Mks 3000, 4000 and 6000 in future. Of these, the Mk 3000 retains the same short fuselage (65 passengers) as the original Mk 1000, and the other two variants have the longer fuselage (85 passengers) first introduced on the Mk 2000. The Mks 3000 and 4000 are similar apart from fuselage lengths, having (compared with the two original versions) increased design weights, aerodynamic refinements, extended wing tips, redesigned interior and uprated Spey 555-15H engines. The Mk 6000 has, in addition, full-span leading edge slats. The last Mk 2000 is scheduled to leave the Schiphol-West assembly line in the late summer, and will be followed immediately by the first Mk 4000.

NEW ZEALAND
The Royal New Zealand Air Force has selected **RCA navigation system,** DME and other avionics **for** its batch of Aerospace **Airtrainer** CT/4As (see pages 70-72 of this issue). The order placed with RCA Avionics Systems of Van Nuys includes Primus-10 DME, AVN-210A airborne navigation system and AVN-204 remote RMI converter.

POLAND
The mock-up of a **new** all-Polish **helicopter design,** the W-3, has been completed at the Lublin WSK factory at Swidnik. The W-3 is intended to succeed the Mi-2 in production towards the end of the decade.

UNITED KINGDOM
A British **Certificate of Airworthiness** was issued **for Concorde** on 4 December and was formally presented to Sir George Edwards, chairman of BAC, the following day. This event, coming after more than 5,500 hrs had been flown on a total of 10 Concordes, cleared the way for revenue services to begin during January. A detailed account of the flight testing that has preceded certification of Concorde begins on page 59 of this issue.

A new **nav/attack system** suitable **for** installation in export versions of **the HSA Hawk** has been announced by Decca and Sperry. The system comprises a fully manoeuvrable heading and attitude sensor (Sperry SGP 500 platform), a three-axis velocity sensor (Decca Dopler Type 72) and the Decca TANS computer. Meeting the HSA specification for a self-contained navigation and target acquisition system for the Hawk, the system provides navigation/guidance management and display of data/command outputs.

The **last flight** of a Handley Page **Victor SR Mk 2** was made towards the end of 1975, when former personnel of No 543 Squadron, which was the only unit to operate this strategic reconnaissance variant, flew the final aircraft from RAF Marham to St Athan for disposal. Four SR Mk 2s are among the 24 Victors currently in process of conversion to K Mk 2 tankers by Hawker Siddeley Manchester; about half the total had been delivered to Marham by the end of the year with most of the remainder to follow during 1976, allowing the Victor K Mk 1 and 1A tankers to be phased out of service. The Victor Mk 2 tanker force will then be the only Victors in service, with a projected 14-year life.

Hawker Siddeley's plans to extend the life of the **HS.125** biz-jet are centred at present upon the development of a **Srs 700** powered by Garrett TFE731 turbofans. First flight of a prototype is likely during 1976, but there is no present commitment to production. Another possible Hawker Siddeley programme at present under review is the **HS.748 Srs 5,** this being a "minimum change" development of the HS.748 with Rolls-Royce/SNECMA M45 turbofans replacing the Dart turboprops, and a modest fuselage stretch to increase seating to 56-64.

USA
Westinghouse Electric Corporation's Aerospace & Electronics System Division has won the contract to develop a **radar system for the** General Dynamics **F-16.** Valued at about $36m (£17·6m), the contract covers full-scale development, with a production option. Total weight of the radar system is expected to be about 260 lb (118 kg) and with the exception of the antenna and control parts, will occupy about 4 cu ft (0,085 m³) of space. The radar will provide both air-to-air and air-to-surface modes, including in the former an all-weather search-and-track capability, a look-down mode and an air-combat mode, and in the latter "blind" (bad weather) and "visual" target designation for weapons delivery and navigation. Selection of Westinghouse follows a fly-off evaluation of prototype radars built by the company and Hughes in USAF F-4Ds.

In late November, the USAF stated that the Fairchild **A-10** close support aircraft is now **meeting** all but one of the **performance requirements** established for it in its development concept paper, the one area in which the aircraft is failing to meet its parameters being the requirement to take-off from a 1,320-ft (402-m) airstrip while carrying four bombs and 1,350 rounds of ammunition, fly 50 miles (80 km), engage in 30 min combat and return 150 miles (241 km) to main base with 20 min fuel remaining. However, at a Pentagon meeting that took place at the same time that USAF officials were making this statement, the US Defence Department was apparently being told that a growth of approximately 1,000 lb (454 kg) in structural weight is in part responsible for growth in max take-off weight to about 47,200 lb (21 410 kg) at which the A-10 no longer meets single-engine performance requirements. In a series of tests with the A-10 loaded with only four 500-lb (227-kg) Mk 82 bombs and only 750 rounds of ammunition it attained a max speed of 424 mph (682 km/h) compared with a goal of 449 mph (722 km/h), and only 3·22 sustained g was pulled at 5,000 ft (1 524 m) as compared with a target of 3·55 g.

Flight **testing of** the GE/SNECMA **CFM-56** "ten-tonne" turbofan will be made early in 1977 **in** a McDonnell Douglas **YC-15** (see Vol 9 No 12/December 1975). McDonnell Douglas has arranged with the USAF to obtain the use of one of the two YC-15 prototypes following completion of the AMST evaluation and will fit a CFM-56 in one of the inboard positions on the YC-15 for a full evaluation of the engine (which is expected to make its first flight in a Caravelle during 1976). The second YC-15 flew on 5 December from Long Beach and immediately joined the first at Yuma; the latter had flown 90 hr in 39 sorties by the same date. Both aircraft have now been transferred to Edwards AFB for continued testing.

The Sikorsky **CH-53E** (triple-engined version of the S-65) which is being developed for the US Navy and Marine Corps recently underwent a **second NPE** (Navy Preliminary Evaluation) at Stratford, Conn, the 25-hour programme being intended to check changes introduced since the first NPE which was completed in February last year. A third evaluation is due mid-year and this is expected to lead to a full production contract by the year's end. Sikorsky has completed two CH-53E production prototypes, the first of which made its initial flight on 8 December.

The **Boeing 747SP** (N40135) completed its 29-day **worldwide demonstration tour** on 10 December, returning to Seattle from

Kingston, Jamaica. In the course of a tour covering 72,152 mls (116 000 km), the aircraft accumulated 140 hr 15 min flight time, visited 18 cities in as many countries and was demonstrated to 26 airlines. Highlights of the trip included a 7,015-ml (11 280-km) flight from New York to Tokyo carrying 200 passengers; a 7,143-ml (11 490-km) journey from Sydney to Santiago and — the longest flight of the whole trip — a 7,205-ml (11 590-km) sector from Mexico City to Belgrade. The last-mentioned was the first-ever non-stop flight from Mexico City (at 7,341 ft/2 240 m above sea level) to Europe. The aircraft used was the fourth SP built, and is to be delivered to Pan American early this year.

As part of its campaign to sell the RB.211-engined **DC-10-30R** to British Airways (*Air-Scene*/January), McDonnell Douglas has produced figures to show that there is an **estimated market** for 76 such aircraft in the next 10 years, including 33 for British Airways and other UK operators, and 43 for airlines in other countries. Participation of the British aircraft industry has been invited, with provision for some 30 per cent of the dollar value of each aircraft to be produced in the UK, including the engines, pods, pylons, electrical power generating equipment, thrust reversers, interior furnishings including galleys, seats and equipment and various electrical and instrumentation equipment. The value of the British content would be about £318m over 10 years at 1975 prices, with indirect benefits worth another £161m, and work would be provided in the British aerospace industry for about 10,000 workers for 10 years, with other industries benefiting by about the same amount of new work also.

From the Model 150 to the Citation, **Cessna** is **offering** a total of **55 models** in its 1976 range of general aviation aircraft. This surprising total is achieved by counting as separate models not only the normally-aspirated and turbo-supercharged versions of the same airframe, but also standard versions and those with the Cessna "II" package of factory-installed avionics and optional items. Also counted separately are alternative cabin arrangements in some of the twins, and the seven Cessna models built under licence by Rheims Aviation in France. The range includes 21 different airframes, including the new Model 404 Titan, new in 1976, and excluding the Ag-Pickup, which has been dropped this year. The variety of aircraft on offer helps Cessna to maintain its position as market leader; sales in its 1975 fiscal year (up to 30 September) totalled 7,808 — more than half the total sales of general aviation aircraft by all US manufacturers combined.

Hughes Helicopters flew the **second prototype** of its **YAH-64** AAH helicopter for the US Army on 22 November and this aircraft will be used for system demonstrations and full handling quality tests, while No 1 is assigned to exploring the full flight envelope and completing the structural demonstrations. By the end of November, more than 50 flights had been made totalling 35 hrs, and the speed range had been explored from 130 knots (240 km/h) forwards to 45 knots (83 km/h) rearwards. By 18 November, the competing Bell YAH-63 had reached 142 knots (263 km/h) forwards and 20 knots (37 km/h) rearwards in 27 hrs of flight test, had reached 4,000 ft (1 220 m) and flown at a max weight of 15,940 lb (7 237 kg).

Hughes Helicopters has completed the **first production prototype** of its new **Hughes 500D.** Differing from the Hughes 500C in having an uprated engine, five-bladed main rotor and T-tail for improved stability, the 500D was first revealed last January, when a development prototype was demonstrated. The production prototype made its first flight at Culver City on 9 October, and deliveries of the new model are expected to begin in mid-year. More than 90 have been ordered to date.

Rohr Industries has completed the installation of target-type **thrust reversers on** a Cessna **Citation.** Initial testing indicates that a 13 per cent reduction in landing distance is achieved on a dry runway, 25 per cent on a wet runway, and 43 per cent on an icy runway. With a gross weight of 125 lb (56 kg), the reversers will cost about $70,000 (£34,650) per pair installed.

Under the programme title *Pave Low III,* the USAF has fitted Texas Instruments APQ-126 terrain following/avoidance radar, similar to that used in the A-7, to a **Sikorsky HH-53E** Jolly Green Giant to provide **night rescue capability.** With Texas Instruments AAQ-10 forward-looking infra-red as a back-up (derived from equipment used in the S-3A), the modified HH-53E has completed a six-month evaluation, including flights through mountainous terrain at an altitude of 100 ft (30 m). A proposal to buy eight similar *Pave Low III* helicopters for operational use by MAC will be considered later this year.

Under the sponsorship of Fred Ayres, a Rockwell **Thrush Commander** has been **fitted with** a 750 shp (flated rated to 87 deg F) Pratt & Whitney (Canada) **PT6A-34** turbo-prop in place of the usual 600 hp R-1340. The conversion was made by Serv-Aero Company at Salinas, California, where the first flight took place on 9 September 1975. In the course of early flight testing, the modified aircraft demonstrated its potential by taking off with a ground roll of 780 ft (238 m) while carrying 400 US gal (1 500 l) of insecticide and 100 US gal (375 l) of fuel, and climbing to 10,000 ft (3 050 m) in 10½ minutes.

A two-seat **helicopter** with a projected sales price of less than $20,000 has entered **prototype testing** at Torrance, California, and production of an initial batch of 50 is planned. The R-22 is a product of Robinson Helicopter Co and is of conventional configuration with two-bladed main and tail rotors. Special attention has been given to noise reduction, including gear box design, an engine muffler, acoustic lining of the engine firewall and low rotor tip speeds. The main rotor hub is underslung and features teetering hinges. Powered by a 115 hp Lycoming O-235-C2C engine, the R-22 has a rotor diameter of 25 ft 2 in (7,67 m) and a maximum length (over main and tail rotors) of 29 ft 2 in (8,89 m). The height is 8 ft 9 in (2,67 m) and the fuselage is 3 ft 8 in (1,11 m) wide at the cabin. Empty weight of the prototype is 720 lb (327 kg) and with 114 lb (52 kg) of fuel, the gross weight of 1,230 lb (558 kg) allows a payload of 396 lb (180 kg) to be carried. Preliminary data indicate that the R-22 has a cruising speed of 100 mph (160 km/h), an initial rate of climb of 1,500 ft/min (7,62 m/sec) and a max range of 250 mls (400 km). The company intends to manufacture an initial batch of 50 R-22s for sale to selected customers in Southern California, so that their performance can be monitored and any teething problems can be corrected before large-scale production begins; the type is designed to permit production of up to 500 a year within the facilities planned by Robinson Helicopter Co.

Sales of **kits for the Bede BD-5** single-seat ultra-light are reported to total 3,700, and the company has 7,500 paid options on complete aircraft, production of which will be undertaken when full certification has been obtained. Bede had placed an order with Hirth for 500 of the engines originally selected for the BD-5 but only a small part of this contract had been fulfilled when Hirth went bankrupt and the aircraft has not been certificated with this engine. Test flying with the Japanese Xenoa power plant has been completed, and application for certification of the BD-5 with the latter engine was made to the FAA at the end of July. A four-seat derivative of the BD-5 has been projected by the company as the BD-7, with a wider, longer fuselage and a 125-180 hp engine, but the same overall configuration. Work on the BD-8, a high-performance aerobatic derivative of the BD-5 with a shorter wing span, has been suspended with a prototype half-completed.

Enstrom Helicopter Corp, seeking to maintain a position in the market for low-cost piston-engined helicopters, now largely ignored by the major manufacturers, is introducing **uprated versions** of its **F-28A and Model 280** Shark, existing models of which are certificated with a 205 hp Lycoming HIO-360-C1A engine. The new models will have the turbocharged HIO-360-E1AD, flat rated at 205 hp up to 12,000 ft (3 660 m) and will be designated F-28B-TC and 280A-TC in this form. The Shark differs from the F-28 in having a more aerodynamically-refined cabin shape and a ventral fin in place of a tubular skid to protect the tail rotor. Enstrom production is expected to increase from 95 in the 12 months to 30 June 1975 to 156 in the next 12-month period and 200-250 in the period to 30 June 1977.

CIVIL AFFAIRS

BRAZIL
The Air Ministry's Civil Aviation Department has issued new **regulations** to change the division **of national air services** between Brazil's four major airlines, following the acquisition of Cruzeiro do Sul by Varig. The two last-mentioned companies will be allowed to handle 40 per cent of national traffic, with the remainder going to VASP and Transbrasil. A merger between these two companies is currently under discussion, Transbrasil being prepared in principle to sell out to VASP if a price can be agreed, but the government having some objection to a major airline being owned by a state authority (VASP is 90 per cent owned by the State of São Paulo).

Rationalisation of Brazil's **third-level airlines** is the next objective of the Civil Aviation Department. It is proposed to divide the country into five areas and to subsidise one third-level operator in each area. The value of these smaller airlines is shown by the fact that one such, Sagres-Manaus, is successfully operating three 15-seat Bandeirantes with an average of 12 seats occupied per flight, whereas VASP and Transbrasil, with their higher overheads, find that the break-even load factor for their Bandeirante operations varies between 90 and 110 per cent. To help finance the development of third-level airlines, the Brazilian government recently authorized a 3 per cent surcharge on all air fares in Brazil.

The Brazilian Air Ministry's Civil Aviation Department is negotiating the purchase of 250 Aerotec **Uirapuru 122** lightplanes which would be made **available to** Brazilian **aero clubs** on favourable financial terms. Recently, Aerotec sold 18 Uirapurus to the CAD in a similar deal which now serves as a pilot for the larger contract now being prepared. In a separate arrangement, Aerotec has sold four Uirapurus in the Rio Grande do Sul State in southern

Brazil, two for an aero club and two for private owners. Under subcontract to EMBRAER, Aerotec is now building Seneca II and Navajo fuselages for the EMBRAER assembly line, and the company has also developed a kit to adapt the Uirapuru as a glider tug. Eight such kits have been ordered by the *Força Aérea Brasileira* for Uirapurus used at the Air Force Academy, Pirassunuga.

CHILE
LAN-Chile is advertising five of of its nine **HS.748 Srs 2As for sale.** Delivered between August 1968 and June 1969, they are described by the airline as "nearly new aircraft".

FEDERAL GERMANY
Lufthansa began **to retire** its fleet of **Boeing 707s** in November, when D-ABOD *Frankfurt* was withdrawn from service; it is currently at Hamburg awaiting disposal. A 707-430 with Conway engines, it was one of the first four Boeings delivered to Lufthansa in 1960, entering service on the North Atlantic route in April. The entire Boeing 707 fleet is to be phased-out by Lufthansa over the next few years as DC-10s and A300s are introduced.

FRANCE
The French regional airline **Air Alpes** has **taken over** two other local carriers, **Air Champagne Ardenne and Air Limousin.** The two latter are expected to continue operating in their own names, with technical and commercial assistance from Air Alpes. The total fleet now comprises five Pilatus Porters, 10 Beechcraft 99s, seven Twin Otters, two Corvette 100s and a Fokker F27.

Prior to entering regular service on 21 January, Air France's first **Concorde** was being used for several **charter and promotional flights.** These were to include a Paris-Dakar round trip on 27 December, undertaken for the *Secrétaire d'Etat aux Transports* and to be the subject of a French TV programme, carrying 100 passengers selected at random to represent all levels of French society. Another round trip to Dakar was to be made on 5 January as a commercial charter for a major multinational company, and a French advisory agency and a German company have also arranged charter flights in early January.

NEW GUINEA
Tempair International Airlines has won a contract, initially worth £1.25m, **to operate** international services **for Air Niugini,** the airline of the Republic of New Guinea. The company will supply Boeing 720B equipment, with flight deck and cabin crews, operating and managerial staff and all engineering services, to permit Air Niugini to operate, in the first instance, a weekly service between Port Moresby and Brisbane/Hong Kong/Manila. The new service was expected to begin on 1 February, using a Boeing 720B previously owned by European Air Ferries and operated by Tempair for Invicta.

SOVIET UNION
As this issue closed for press, Aeroflot announced that it had **inaugurated** scheduled **service with** the **Tupolev Tu-144** supersonic transport on 26 December, thus beating the Concorde as the world's first SST in service by a bare month. The initial operation provides two return flights each week on the route between Moscow and Alma Ata, a distance of 2,190 mls (3 520 km), but only mail and freight are being carried and it is expected to be some months before fare-paying passengers are flown.

SPAIN
In late October, the **Beech Aircraft** Corporation completed **delivery** of four King Air

C90s, eight Baron B55s and 12 Bonanza F33As to the Spanish Air Ministry's Civil Aviation School, raising to 62 the total of Beechcraft aeroplanes procured by the Spanish Air Ministry for civil and military pilot training.

UNITED KINGDOM
Lord Beswick, until December the Minister of State for Aerospace and Shipping in the current Labour government, has been named as **chairman of British Aerospace,** the nationalised Corporation which will have responsibility for assuming control of, and merging, the major British aerospace companies under the terms of the Bill to nationalise the aircraft and shipbuilding industries. The Bill received its second reading in the House of Commons on 2 December and if the proposed timetable is followed, nationalisation of BAC, Hawker Siddeley and Scottish Aviation could take effect by the middle of this year. The government already owns the majority of shares in Shorts and is sole owner of Rolls-Royce. Westland and Fairey Britten-Norman are outside the provisions of the nationalisation plans.

British Airways Helicopters has received a further contract from the Department of Trade covering the provision of a long-range **helicopter search and rescue service** off the North East coast of Scotland. The new contract covers the period 1 January 1976 to 31 December 1977, and provides for a continuation of existing arrangements for an S-61N helicopter to operate under control of HM Coastguard from Dyce Airport, Aberdeen, on civil marine search and rescue work beyond the operational range of existing RAF helicopters. It is expected that Sea King HAR Mk 3s, recently ordered by the RAF for this rôle, will be available by the time the new contract expires.

Use of a **two-segment glide-slope** to permit a steeper-than-usual approach to be made during the initial stages of a descent into an airport, as a means of reducing noise on the ground around the airport, is being **investigated at the RAE,** Bedford, using a BAC One-Eleven. The system makes use of a two-segment computer designed and built by Smiths Aviation Division, which takes data from the airfield DME and the aircraft altimeter, computes errors of the flight path from the desired two-segment profile and provides information direct to the pilot or the autopilot. In addition to the landings at Bedford, a few are to be made at civil airports in the UK to study the effects of a two-segment approach upon existing ATC arrangements.

Air Anglia retired the **last** Douglas **DC-3** from its fleet on 24 November, the aircraft (G-AOBN) having been sold to Skyways Air Cargo. Air Anglia, formed in 1970, originally operated four DC-3s and has now expanded its fleet to comprise five Fokker F27s (with a sixth in process of being acquired) and a Dart Herald. The company is leasing an Argosy for its daily cargo service linking Norwich with Aberdeen and Amsterdam. Sale of Air Anglia's last DC-3 came just a month before the 40th anniversary of the Douglas transport's first flight, which took place on 17 December 1935. Several hundred examples are still in commercial service throughout the world.

CIVIL CONTRACTS AND SALES

Boeing 707: Executive model 707 equipped with a sauna, dance floor and "wine cellar" for use by financier Robert Vesco, has been re-

purchased by Pan Am and is on offer for resale.

Boeing 727: Turkish Airlines THY has ordered another Advanced 727, making five in all. Delivery will be made in September 1976.

Boeing 737: United Airlines sold three -200s to International Lease Finance Corp, which is selling two to Transavia Holland for delivery early this year, and the third to a UK company.

Boeing 747: Pakistan International is to acquire two 747-200Bs from TAP of Portugal. They will be leased initially, with an option to purchase later; delivery will be made in April, one aircraft being brand new and the other having been acquired by TAP a year ago. The deal replaces proposed lease of MEA 747s.

Bristol Britannia: Four ex-RAF examples have been purchased by Agence et Messageries Aérienne du Zaïre (AMAZ) and one by Air Faisel. ☐ Gemini Air Transport has been confirmed as the customer for one reported sold earlier to a company in Ghana, and Young Cargo in Belgium has two.

EMBRAER EMB-110 Bandeirante: A specially-equipped aerial survey version has been acquired by VASP Aerofotogametria in São Paulo.

Fokker F27: New Zealand National Airways Corp ordered two Mk 500s for delivery in February/March 1977. ☐ East West Airlines has ordered two Mk 500s for 1976 delivery. They will join four Mk 100s and a Mk 300 in service. ☐ A Mk 600 has been ordered by the Imperial Iranian Government for use as a personnel transport in support of the coppermine industry at Sar-Cheshmeh.

HS Argosy: Air Anglia leased one from Air Bridge Carriers to operate its Aberdeen-Norwich-Amsterdam service, in place of DC-3s.

Hawker Siddeley HS 748: Guyana Airways has ordered one HS 748 Srs 2A, for delivery later this year. To be used primarily as a 52-seater on the airline's routes based on Georgetown, it is to have the large freight door to permit its use in a convertible cargo rôle when required.

Learjet: The Royal Oman Police has purchased a Learjet 25B through CSE Aviation Ltd for use as a VIP transport.

McDonnell Douglas DC-10: Philippine Air Lines is to acquire a third Srs 30, for delivery late this year, through an agreement with KLM. ☐ Thai Airways International has ordered two Srs 30s for delivery in February and May 1977, with an option on two more.

Saunders ST-27: Sales have been announced of two more of the batch of 12 ST-27s built, leaving only two unsold. The newest customer, for one aircraft each, are Tropic Air Services of Barbuda, and Aero Trader (Western) Ltd of Winnipeg. Both aircraft have been delivered.

VFW-Fokker VFW 614: Following demonstrations of the VFW 614 in the USA, Air Florida announced its intention to order three. Other carriers with an expressed interest in the type were Air New England (which had previously announced an order for six Shorts SD3-30s) and Air Wisconsin.

Vickers Viscount: VASP sold its last three Viscounts to PLUNA in Uruguay. ☐ Skyline Sweden purchased two Viscount 814s from British Midland Airways.

Concorde

...Cleared for Service

EVERYTHING about the Aérospatiale/BAC Concorde is dramatic. Its entry into service with British Airways and Air France on 21 January — a date still a few weeks in the future when this account was being prepared — marks the successful conclusion of a 13-year effort to produce the world's first supersonic transport. The product of a closely-integrated Anglo-French programme that has brought international collaboration to a new level of effectiveness in political, economic and engineering spheres, Concorde is the most expensive airliner ever put into service. No other aeroplane has been so loved or so hated: hailed by some as an engineering masterpiece, a thing of grace and beauty that heralds a new era of superb, fast transportation for the businessman, yet decried by others as a noisy monster, the utility of which can never justify the burden its production has laid upon the French and British tax-payer.

Only in historical perspective, perhaps, will it be possible to pass judgement on some of the controversial issues that Concorde raises. Suffice to say here that Concorde has, to date, survived every attempt of its antagonists to bring about its cancellation or to restrict its use, and that all its technical objectives have been met. Today, some 20 years after basic research was started, independently, in Britain and France into the possibilities of a supersonic airliner, Concorde is on the threshold of its commercial career, and although difficulties remain to be overcome, regular supersonic travel will have arrived on the world airline scene. Initially, only a handful of Concordes will be used, operating on routes between Britain and the Middle East and between France and South America; but the reactions of the several thousand passengers who have already flown in Concordes in the course of development flying suggest that the impact these first aircraft will make upon the pattern of air transport will be such that other airlines will soon follow Air France and British Airways as Concorde operators.

The task of bringing Concorde from a design proposal to a fully qualified transport meeting the requirements of the certification authorities for a passenger-carrying airliner has called for a massive effort on the part of the four principal companies — Aérospatiale, BAC, Rolls-Royce and SNECMA — and their many hundred suppliers, as well as numerous government agencies and the customer airlines. Not least in this effort has been the flight test programme that has brought about certification of the Concorde nearly seven years after prototype first flight. More than 5,000 hrs were flown on eight Concordes before the first full certificate of airworthiness was awarded (by comparison, the typical large airliner of recent years has required 800-1,200 hrs of testing to achieve certification), this being a measure of the extent to which Concorde was entering into the unknown.

Although the production standard Concorde differs quite substantially from the prototypes as first flown, and this necessarily lengthened the flight test programme somewhat, the duration and extent of the programme does not result from any major problem having been encountered. Indeed, flight testing has been remarkably snag-free, there having been very few untoward in-flight incidents, and a minimum of modifications have been called for to improve flying characteristics. Engineering development, airline inputs and state-of-the-art improvements have all been responsible for a steady stream of airframe and engine modifications being introduced since Concorde first flew, and these have had their impact on the flight test programme; so too has the need to demonstrate to the satisfaction of the airworthiness authorities that Concorde has no unacceptable characteristics and that Concorde operations at Mach 2 at 60,000 ft (18 300 m) can be integrated with those of existing subsonic airliners without danger to either. Included in the total of flight testing that preceded certification was nearly 1,000 hrs of endurance flying over airline routes in typical airline conditions — this

alone being equal to the total flying required to certificate the Boeing 747!

Inevitably, as Concorde has progressed, the test programme itself has undergone constant modification and updating. The overall programme was agreed between the manufacturers and the officials of the two governments in January 1969, shortly before the first aircraft flew. The first major objective was to achieve Mach 2, this being the point at which Concorde would demonstrate its reality as an economic SST, and its achievement depended primarily upon proving the intake geometry and completing flutter testing. To minimize the effects of technical or serviceability set-backs on either of the first two prototypes, both were equipped to handle the key test jobs and were able to undertake either at short notice.

Refinement of the test programme and optimization of the division of work between the various aircraft led, by mid-1969, to a projected total flight time of 4,230 hrs to achieve certification by June 1973, using seven aircraft (plus static and fatigue test specimens). This total was to comprise some 1,935 hrs on development, 795 hrs on certification and 1,500 hrs on route proving/endurance. This programme proved

over-optimistic in timescale, but not grossly in error so far as the total flying requirement was concerned. The pre-production aircraft, completion of which was delayed by the decision to lengthen the fuselage and by other factors, entered flight test almost a year later than projected in this mid-1969 schedule, and the initial production aircraft emerged some two years later than scheduled.

By mid-1971, when the two prototypes had already completed 540 hrs of testing, the programme had been amended to provide for a total of 4,400 hrs up to C of A in April 1974, including about 600 hrs specifically on certification and 1,000 hrs for route proving and endurance flying, still using seven aircraft. Timewise, this programme also proved over-optimistic in respect of the introduction of the production aircraft.

The design evolution of Concorde up to its production standard was traced in detail in an earlier issue (September 1971), when the initial stages of flight testing were also recorded. Now, with Concorde on the threshold of its service career, the entire test programme can be reviewed in detail, indicating the specific tasks undertaken by each of eight

The photographs on this page, and immediately left, show Concorde 204 — the production standard aircraft used by British Airways for the endurance flying programme last summer and, after being refurbished to full service standard by BAC at Filton, the second example available to the airline for revenue service, as a back-up to Concorde 206. In the photograph below, G-BOAC is seen at Melbourne, the most distant point reached in the course of the endurance trials; the illustration on the right is one of a series taken for British Airways using the Astrovision system, with cameras operating through a periscope system in the floor of a Learjet. Alone in the British Airways fleet, Concorde has an overall white finish, adopted in view of its operations at very high altitudes; in other respects, the markings conform to British Airways' standard scheme. Shown below left is Concorde 205, the first Air France revenue service aircraft and the first to sport that company's new livery.

aircraft — two prototypes, two pre-production models and the first four production aircraft. The following account presents, in much greater detail than has previously been published, information on each of these Concordes, showing how they introduced and tested the various features that distinguish the production model from the prototype and the contribution they made to the certification task as a whole. Although, for convenience and clarity, the work of each of eight Concordes is separately related, the flying of the various aircraft — equally divided between Britain and France — has been fully integrated throughout the six-year test period, with each aircraft having primary rôles to fulfil, but available to back-up one or more of the others should the need arise.

Concordes 205 and 206, the fifth and sixth production models, destined to fly the first Air France and British Airways revenue services respectively, flew as the certification procedures were being completed, but were not directly concerned with the flight testing of the basic aircraft. Further reference to these two aircraft is made below, however, in relation to the airlines' plans for Concorde operation in the next year.

Certification of the Concorde is a programme that has no historical precedent and it is right to place on record the names of the BAC and Aérospatiale pilots who, through their flight test work, have made a unique contribution to Concorde's success. In alphabetical order, they are, for Aérospatiale, G Deffer, J Franchi, J Grangette, J Guignard, A Jacquet, J Pinet and A Turcat; and for BAC, P P Baker, J Cochrane, R J Cormigan, J Hacket, T L Howell, E McNamara, M R Radford, A Smith, E B Trubshaw and R Walker.

These pilots have been aided by a number of company flight test engineers and observers. They were joined, during the endurance flying programme and for certain other tasks, by the first of the Air France and British Airways crews to convert to the Concorde, and the test pilots of the certificating authorities, CEV and CAA (originally ARB) have also played an important rôle in the testing. Now, the conversion of further airline crews is becoming a matter of routine, and upon these crews rests responsibility for the next phase of Concorde operation.

Concorde 001

The Concorde flight test programme began on 2 March 1969 when Concorde 001, registered F-WTSS (the last three letters indicating Transport SuperSonique), was lifted off the long runway at Toulouse for the first time by Andre Turcat, director of flight test for Aérospatiale, accompanied by Jacques Guignard as co-pilot, Henri Jean-Louis Perrier as flight test observer and Michel Retif as flight engineer. The flight was made at a gross weight of 250,000 lb (113 500 kg) and Concorde was airborne after a 4,900-ft (1 500-m) take-off roll, subsequently reaching a maximum altitude of 10,000 ft (3 050 m) and speed of 250 knots (463 km/h). Throughout the 42-minute flight* the Concorde was accompanied by an Armstrong Whitworth Meteor NF Mk 11 chaseplane and a Morane-Saulnier MS 760 Paris carrying photographers. The drooped nose was not raised on this flight, which was primarily a pilot's assessment of the aircraft, but the undercarriage was raised and lowered normally; the only untoward incident occurred when the landing parachute jettison warning light flashed in the cockpit, but the warning was spurious and the drag chute functioned normally on landing.

Flight testing proceeded at a steady pace in the next few months and by June, with Concorde 002 (see later) also in the programme, the targeted monthly flying rates were being exceeded. The droop nose was functioned between 12 deg and 5 deg on the second flight (8 March) and with speed and altitude gradually increasing on successive flights, a series of engine shut-downs and re-lights was performed. The first visit of Concorde away from its home base came at the end of May when 001 flew to Le Bourget for the 1969 Paris Air Show, in

which 002 also participated, and immediately afterwards the first prototype embarked on the first series of all-important flutter tests, with forced excitation (using "bonkers") of the wing and fin at various speeds and loadings.

Flight No 39 on 6 August 1969 completed the initial flutter tests. The aircraft was not yet at a stage to permit supersonic flight, lacking the auxiliary intake doors that play a vital rôle in the functioning of the variable geometry air intakes, and not yet having a functional fuel transfer system, required for trim purposes when the aircraft transitions from subsonic to supersonic speed and vice versa. A six-week grounding was therefore necessary to make modifications to permit the next stage of flight testing to proceed. Up to this time, Concorde had reached a maximum speed of Mach 0·85/410 knots (759 km/h) CAS† and Mach 0·95/330 knots (611 km/h) CAS, had taken off at weights up to 292,000 lb (132 568 kg) and had reached an altitude of 40,000 ft (12 200 m). Some idea of the amount of work covered in the first 100 hrs or so of testing (all subsonic) is given in an accompanying summary.

Testing resumed at Toulouse on 21 September, with the so-called "barn door" auxiliary intakes fitted, and the No 10 fuel tank, vital for trimming purposes, in commission. The auxiliary intakes opened downward and forward to provide an additional source of air for the engines when the aircraft was in slow flight and, more importantly, opened downward and rearward to spill air entering the main intake in the event of an engine shut-down at supersonic speed, thus protecting the engine from damage. This called for a complicated operating geometry and sequencing system; until the final production form had been worked out with the help of flight testing, the auxiliary intakes were referred to as "barn-doors". Further modification would be necessary, it was known, before Concorde could reach Mach 2, but 001 was now able to press on into the supersonic regime, and exceeded the speed of sound for the first time on 1 October 1969 on the 45th flight. With two engines at full power with afterburners and two at reduced power, Concorde reached Mach 1·05 at 36,000 ft (11 000 m) 80 miles (130 km) north of Toulouse and remained supersonic for 9 minutes. All the early supersonic flights were overland, with no reports of damage resulting from supersonic booms. An accompanying summary of the log of Flight No 50 — the sixth supersonic excursion — gives a good indication of the cockpit work load on a typical Concorde flight and shows how maximum use was made of every minute of flight time (see page 73).

Concorde testing began, and continued, with the minimum of snags. Some delays were to be expected with an aircraft that incorporated so many novel features, and ground time had to be scheduled to permit the incorporation of progressive modifications. The first abortive flight test — one of very few in the entire Concorde programme — occurred on 24 October (Flight No 54) when a flight recorder failed.

As confidence in the performance of Concorde grew, the first night landing was made (12 November 1969) and on four flights earlier in the month, pilots and flight engineer observers from four of the major customer airlines, BOAC, Air France, Pan Am and TWA, were given an opportunity to handle 001 through a representative subsonic and supersonic flight evaluation. Their combined report subsequently stated that "for all the flight conditions flown during this first phase,

---

* The duration of the first flight was 28 minutes airborne; throughout this account, the durations quoted are block (chock-to-chock) times, these being the times used for flight test record purposes.

† Mach numbers quoted are true figures (TMN), being the Mach meter readings corrected for instrument and position errors. CAS is calibrated airspeed, this being the airspeed indicator reading (usually quoted in knots) corrected for instrument error and position errors (ie, errors attributable to manufacturing tolerances in the instrument, and to non-optimum position of the pitot-static tube. Further correction of CAS for compressibility effect and for variation of air density with altitude is necessary to obtain TAS (true air speed).

SUMMARY OF CONCORDE SUBSONIC FLIGHT TESTS

Air Conditioning and Pressurization
Generation
Pressure regulation
Simulated failures
Temperature regulation (manual and automatic)

Automatic Flight Control System
Autostabilization: channel change-over
assessment of roll boost
influence of pitch gyro location
Autothrottle: precision
accuracy
damping
monitoring
Electric trim: functioning
motor lubrication
Flight Director

Avionics
ADF: elimination of noise
tuning
Air Data Computers: calibration: chase aircraft
kinetheodolites
radar
monitoring and comparison
ATC transponders
DME
Inertial Navigation System: attitude information
navigation function
Radio Altimeter: ground datum setting
VHF
Weather Radar

Electrics
Alternator: operation
simulated failures
Anti-icing
Anti-misting: side windows
Constant Speed Drive: cooling assessment
Windscreen wiper

Engine and Gas Turbine Starters
After-burners: take-off max, 6 mins.
altitude operation to 40,000 ft (12 200 m)
re-lighting to 38,000 ft (11 590 m) M 0·9
Air intakes: flow distortion measurements to M 0·8
efficiency measurements
"Barn Door" clearance
Engine controls and instrumentation:
flowmeter calibration
turbine cooling air indication
Engine life increase
Engine re-lighting up to 25,000 ft (7 625 m)/M 0·9
GTS: starts
in-flight operation
Nacelle ventilation: various secondary flap configurations
Surge margin assessment
Thrust reversers: 90 per cent N_2 down to 40 kts (74 km/h)

Flying Controls
Artificial feel: verification of force laws, f(M or V)
handling qualities without artificial feel
handling qualities on one system only
ICOVOL (flying controls position indicator)
Signalling modes: electric
mechanical
mode change-over
monitoring and comparison

Flying Qualities
Approach and landing: normal
in mechanical mode
with autostabilization on/off
without ILS

Dynamic stability with autostabilization on/off
Flight envelope: M 0·95
410 kts (760 km/h) CAS
CG at 51·5 to 57·0 per cent in flight
51·5 to 52·5 per cent in take-off and
landing
Ground effect assessment
Handling with and without artificial feel
Handling in moderate turbulence
Manoeuvrability: stick forces per g
side slips (5 deg)
roll boost assessment
Static stability: trim curve determination
Take-off: normal
autostabilization on, one engine out
autostabilization on, one ADC failed
with simulated engine failure
Three-engined approach and overshoot
Two-engined approach

Fuel
Fuel feed
Fuel jettison, 200 kts (371 km/h) (simulated by water)
Fuel leak (simulated by dye)
Fuel transfer (manual control only)
Calibration of indicated versus true CG

Hydraulics and Associated Systems
Air brakes: operation and aerodynamic efficiency up to 410 kts
(760 km/h)
Landing gear operation: normal (Green): 270 kts (500 km/h)
standby (Yellow): 220 kts (408 km/h)
emergency (free fall): 205 kts (380 km/h)
Nose: 0°: flown at 410 kts (760 km/h)
5°: flown at 400 kts (741 km/h) operated at 240 kts
(445 km/h)
17·5°: flown at 270 kts (500 km/h), operated at 270 kts
(500 km/h)
free fall 5°-12°: operated at 240 kts (445 km/h)
Power generation: simulated failures
Visor: operation (nose 0°) at 240 to 320 kts (445-593 km/h)
emergency operation at 240 kts (445 km/h)
assessment of cockpit noise and vibration
Wheel brakes: use on dry and wet runways
temperature monitoring
Wheels and tyres: no bursts except on one accelerate-stop test

Performance and Operations
Air data calibrations
Brake parachute operation
Climb performance (subsonic)
General ground handling
Landing: normal
nose up, visor down
nose up, visor up (simulated)
Landing gear drag measurement
Level cruise performance (subsonic)
Noise: sideline and flight path
Rough runway: flight deck g loads
Take-off and landing distances (including wet runway)
Trim drag measurement
Visibility: nose 0°, visor up
nose 0° to 17·5°, visor down
closed-circuit TV for landing

Structure
Flight envelope: 410 kts (760 km/h), CAS, M 0·85
380 kts (704 km/h), CAS, M 0·9
330 kts (612 km/h), CAS, M 0·95
Flutter: harmonic excitation
control inputs
"Bonkers"
Rough runway: flight deck g loads
Turbulence and control inputs: fuselage response

---

the aircraft was pleasant and easy to fly, imposed no excessive workload on the pilot even in failure conditions, and there should be no problems in training airline pilots and engineers to handle the aircraft".*

By the end of 1969, Concorde 001 had made the 100th flight (a combined total with 002, made on 17 December) and had reached the practical limits of the flight envelope with the intakes and flying controls then fitted. It had reached Mach 1·50/500 knots (926 km/h), 47,000 ft (14 335 m) and a gross

At this time, options to buy a total of 74 Concordes had been taken by 16 airlines; they were backed by deposits, but the latter were to be refundable under certain conditions, and were in fact all refunded, only Air France and BOAC/British Airways eventually placing firm orders. Until the options were cancelled, the "customer" airlines were kept fully briefed on Concorde flight development and the flight and technical staff of several made a useful contribution to the overall evolution of the aircraft.

weight of 311,300 lb (141 200 kg), and had carried its first non-technician passenger — M Giscard d'Estaing, then the French Finance Minister and later to become President. A few more flights were made in January 1970, of which No 78 (8 January) was the first on which reverse thrust was selected in flight, this being a planned procedure to achieve high rates of descent — up to 4,000 ft/min (20,3 m/sec). Flight No 86 (22 January) brought the total of Concorde flying to 200 hrs, of which 25½ had been supersonic, and No 88 (27 January) included the longest supersonic excursion to date, totalling 66 min of a 2 hr 9 min flight. Concorde 001 then made three taxying trials on artificially wetted runways, to check the effects of water ingestion by the engines, and entered the Toulouse workshop for a prolonged period.

When 001 took to the air again (Flight No 92, 18 September

continued on page 73

THE DEVELOPMENT OF JAPANESE ARMY AVIATION

BY EIICHIRO SEKIGAWA

A CHRONIC DEFENCE ALLERGY! Such, it is said, has for three decades inhibited the development of Japanese armed forces capable of providing something more than mere token defence of the home islands and surrounding seas. This affliction, compounded by a taboo that has consistently enveloped the subject of security problems facing Japan and the almost sacred belief of successive governments that defence expenditure must be kept to less than *one* per cent of the gross national product, has left Japan — as the realists in defence circles overtly admit — militarily insecure and almost as dependent today on the USA for effective defence as at the time of the Korean conflict.

Whether or not the current military posture of the People's Republic of China is entirely a defensive one, as the Japanese prefer to believe, or the increasingly bellicose attitude of the Soviet Union in the region is presented solely for the benefit of China, as the Japanese fervently hope, the unpalatable — to the Japanese — fact of life is being increasingly stressed by their American allies that Japan must play a greater rôle in her own defence.

Of late, Soviet Air Force elements operating from bases in Sikhote, within 200 miles (320 km) of Japan, have been heavily reinforced and late last year, the highly potent missile-armed destroyers of the latest *Krivak* class appeared for the

first time in the Straits of Tsushima, the Japanese Defence Agency subsequently admitting that the Soviet Navy is now deploying 530 naval craft totalling some 970,000 tons in the general area. These facts have certainly added some weight to the efforts of Michita Sakata, secretary-general of the Defence Agency, to impart to a still largely non-receptive Japanese people the fact that effective defence is a vital prerequisite of effective détente. Yet, the Japanese government does not *officially* see any short- or medium-term threat to Japan's security and has no intention of making any significant increases in the size of the armed forces!

Following in the wake of the finale in Vietnam have come demands that US bases on Thai territory be closed and those in the Philippines be transferred to Philippino control. Japan has thus effectively become the pivot of US defence policy in East Asia and the Western Pacific, and the US government has made it abundantly clear that stronger Japanese defence participation is needed in both the medium and the long term to prevent an eventual US withdrawal, and the first US requirement is that the so-called Self-Defence Forces be brought up to their authorised strength and that outmoded weaponry be replaced rapidly with effective modern weapons.

A quarter-century has elapsed since, in August 1950, the

(Opposite page) The Mitsubishi LR-1 serves in the photo reconnaissance and liaison rôles, current planning calling for the acquisition of eight aircraft of this type. Currently the most numerous helicopter in the GSDF inventory, the UH-1B Iroquois (above), together with the UH-1H, equips both the numbered and Homen Herikoputa-tais. A small number of Fuji-built Mentors (right) serve in the primary training rôle, and the Kawasaki-built V-107-II helicopter, seen in service (below) with the Hokubu Homen Herikoputa-tai, is the largest aircraft in GSDF service (photos courtesy of Koku-Fan).

The UH-1B Iroquois, built under licence by Fuji, has now seen some 12 years service with the GSDF and is currently being supplemented by the UH-1H. As a potential successor to the Iroquois, the GSDF is studying the US Army's UTTAS programme with a view to phasing in a replacement type from late in the present decade.

Keisatsu-Yobitai, or National Police Reserve, was created at the behest of General Douglas MacArthur as a quasi-military force against a background of total Japanese apathy. Today, if the apathy is no longer total, the Ground Self-Defence Force — the Japanese have a penchant for juggling with semantics in their insistence that they possess no *Army* — is barely larger numerically than the army of Thailand possessing one-third of Japan's population, while South Korea, with a population even smaller, can field a ground force four times as large! The Ground Self-Defence Force has a theoretical strength of 180,000 men in a single mechanised and a dozen infantry divisions, plus various supporting units, but man-power is currently something of the order of 15 per cent below that authorised. Within the very strict limitations of defence expenditure, the GSDF *has* been undergoing some equipment modernisation, but the inflation of recent years has resulted in the current five-year Defence Build-up Programme, now about to enter its final year, falling very seriously behind schedule. Thus, it may be seen that the US requirements are something of an embarrassment and that defence spending *must* rise above that sacred one per cent of the GNP in the foreseeable future.

An effective nucleus?

While no dramatic growth in GSDF manpower is envisaged in short, medium or long term, it is axiomatic that, as greater defence responsibility devolves on this service it will have to undergo substantial qualitative improvement if it is ever to present a viable posture. Fortunately, from its inception it has attached considerable importance to its air component which forms an organic part, and as a keynote in the qualitative development of the GSDF is likely to be improvement of its tactical mobility, it can be assumed that considerable effort will be expended throughout the remainder of the present decade in upgrading the capability of this aviation element.

What was effectively an army air component saw birth in December 1952, when the *Hoantai,* or National Security Force, which had been created in the previous August to succeed and absorb the National Police Reserve, inaugurated its first flying school with 15 war surplus Vultee-Stinson L-5s and 20 Aeronca L-16s that had been supplied by the US Army. The initial intakes were comprised exclusively of WWII veterans needing no more than refresher training and, in consequence, 170 pilots and 300 mechanics graduated from the school during the first twelve months of operations. During the course of 1953, the L-16s were returned to the US Army, but a further 26 L-5s were acquired, together with 20 Piper L-21Bs. No helicopters were included in US Army aid, but the *Hoantai*

funded six Bell Model 47Ds and a similar number of Sikorsky S-55s, and despite the strict limitations of Japanese defence spending, ordered 60 Beech T-34A primary trainers.

By early 1954, the aviation element of the *Hoantai* comprised 1,000 personnel and an inventory of 60 aircraft, and on 10 January of that year nine squadrons were formed, six of these being assigned directly to ground divisions, adopting the divisional numbers and being deployed at the nearest airfield to the assigned division, the 1st *Koku-tai,* or Air Squadron being assigned to the 1st Division and so on. These units and their bases were as follows: 1st *Koku-tai* at Tsuchiura, near Tokyo; 2nd *Koku-tai* at Asahigawa, Hokkaido; 3rd *Koku-tai* at Yao, near Osaka; 4th *Koku-tai* at Ozuki, in western Japan; 5th *Koku-tai* at Obihiro, Hokkaido, and the 6th *Koku-tai* at Matsushima, in north-east Japan. The remaining three units comprised the *Hokubu-Homen Koku-tai,* or Northern District Air Squadron, this being an inde-pendent unit based at Okadama, on Hokkaido, under the direct control of the Northern District Command; the *Tokkadan Koku-tai,* or Armoured Wing Air Squadron, at Chitose, Hokkaido, which belonged to the 1st Armoured Wing, and the *Bakuryoh-kanbu Koku-tai,* or Headquarters Air Squadron, at Tsuchiura, near Tokyo, which was assigned to the *Hoantai* Headquarters. The remaining element was, of course, the *Koku-Gakkoh* (Flying School) at Hamamatsu, near Nagoya. The *Koku-tais* were initially equipped with L-5s and L-21s, but these were quickly supplanted by the appreciably more modern Cessna O-1A Bird Dog, 107 of which were received during the course of 1954, plus the Bell and Sikorsky helicopters.

By 1 July 1954, further defence reorganisation had taken place and the *Hoantai* had given place to the *Boeicho,* or Defence Agency, under which three so-called self-defence forces were created, these being the Ground Self-Defence Force *(Rikujoh Jieitai),* the Maritime Self-Defence Force *(Kaijoh Jieitai)* and the Air Self-Defence Force *(Koku Jieitai).* Most of the aircraft in the inventory of the former *Hoantai* were assigned to the newly-established Ground Self-Defence Force, apart from the Beech T-34A trainers which went straight to the Air Self-Defence Force.

Initially, the GSDF took over the unit structure of the *Hoantai,* adding two more squadrons over the next two years — the 9th *Koku-tai* at Hachinoe, northern Honshu, and the *Seibu-Homen Koku-tai,* or Western District Air Squadron — and by March 1957, the air component of the GSDF possessed 224 aircraft. In addition to the Cessna O-1s, 42 more L-21Bs, eight Bell Model 47G-2s and 12 Sikorsky S-55Cs had been obtained, plus 27 examples of the first *semi-*

indigenous postwar Japanese production aircraft, the Fuji LM-1, a multi-seat liaison type. The last-mentioned type had resulted from a design contest held by the *Boeicho* in 1954 and in which the Kawasaki KAL-1 and the Fuji LM-1 had competed, the latter being selected for delivery to the GSDF.

Steady build-up

With the primary aim of building up rapidly and systematically well-balanced armed forces, the *Boeicho* launched a five-year plan, which, commencing in April 1957, was known as the 1st Defence Build-up Programme (DBP). During this period, the GSDF was to make an intensive effort to expand its air component and create a further six squadrons — the 7th, 8th, 10th, 12th and 13th *Koku-tais* and the 1st *Herikoputa-tai* (Helicopter Squadron). The former *Tokkadan Koku-tai* was redesignated as the 11th *Koku-tai,* and the 1st *Kutei-tai* was established, this being a paratroop unit for which transportation was provided by the Curtiss C-46s of the Air Self-Defence Force.

With the establishment of these new units, the GSDF undertook total reorganisation of its unit structure in January 1962 as the final stage of the 1st DBP. Up to this time, the *Homen Koku-tais* had been operational squadrons similar in strength to the units attached to the divisions, but these were now redesignated as *Homen Hiko-tais,* the divisional *Koku-tais* simultaneously becoming *Hiko-tais,* the appellation '*Koku-tai*' being reassigned to command elements to which the various *Hiko-tais* were now attached. Thus, with the completion of the 1st DBP, the aviation element of the GSDF became as follows:

Hokubu Homen Koku-tai (Northern District Air Command)	Hokubu Homen Hiko-tai	(Okadama)
	2nd Hiko-tai	(Asahigawa)
	5th Hiko-tai	(Obihiro)
	7th Hiko-tai	(Okadama)
	11th Hiko-tai	(Okadama)
Tohoku Homen Koku-tai (North-East District Air Command)	Tohoku Homen Hiko-tai	(Kasuminome)
	6th Hiko-tai	(Kasuminome)
	9th Hiko-tai	(Hachinoe)
Tobu Homen Koku-tai (Eastern District Air Command)	Tobu Homen Hiko-tai	(Utsunomiya)
	1st Hiko-tai	(Kasumigaura)
	12th Hiko-tai	(Kasumigaura)
Chubu Homen Koku-tai (Central District Air Command)	Chubu Homen Hiko-tai	(Yao)
	3rd Hiko-tai	(Yao)
	10th Hiko-tai	(Akeno)
	13th Hiko-tai	(Hofu)
Seibu Homen Koku-tai (Western District Air Command)	Seibu Homen Hiko-tai	(Kumamoto)
	4th Hiko-tai	(Metabaru)
	8th Hiko-tai	(Kumamoto)
Koku Gakko (Flying School)		(Akeno)
1st Herikoputa-tai (Helicopter Sqdn)		(Kasumigaura)

During the 1st DBP and following the ending of the supply of aircraft from the US under the assistance programme, the GSDF received 22 Fuji-built O-1E Bird Dogs to supplement the O-1As supplied by the US Army, but primary effort was directed towards laying the foundations of an effective helicopter force and 46 Kawasaki-built Bell Model 47G-2s and 14 Mitsubishi-built Sikorsky S-55Cs had been procured during the programme period, while longer-term plans to obtain larger and more powerful helicopters had resulted, in 1958, in the purchase of two Vertol 44s for evaluation. The GSDF was disappointed in the performance offered by this tandem rotor helicopter and Mitsubishi's offer of the Sikorsky S-58 as an alternative was rejected. In consequence, the service was destined to wait several years for its heavy rotorcraft which were eventually to materialise in the form of Kawasaki's licence-built Boeing Vertol V-107-IIs.

By March 1962, the air component of the GSDF comprised 1,200 personnel and 261 aircraft, including 77 helicopters, and the primary aims of the service under the 2nd DBP, launched during the following month, were equipment modernisation and the further expansion of the helicopter

force to permit the GSDF to indulge in the modern concept of heliborne operations. However, as the lion's share of the financial allocations made to the service under the new programme was being swallowed by the procurement of vitally necessary equipment to modernise the armoured force, expenditure on aircraft procurement was inevitably limited and it was concluded that what was available would be best spent on converting from piston-engined to turbine-powered helicopters. The Fuji-built Bell UH-1B Iroquois was selected as the successor to the obsolescent S-55 and 36 helicopters of the former type were procured, and during the course of the five-year programme orders were to be placed on behalf of the GSDF for its long-awaited large transport helicopter in the form of the first dozen Kawasaki-built V-107-IIs. Procurement of the Kawasaki-built Bell Model 47 series of light helicopters was continued as replacements for the more elderly of the fixed-wing aircraft, and 21 more Model 47G-2s were purchased before orders switched to the improved KH-4 of which 19 were obtained.

While the GSDF was aiming at a largely helicopter-equipped force, it was influenced by US Army interest in the OV-10 Bronco and a Mitsubishi MU-2C was purchased for evaluation in the combined reconnaissance/light attack rôle as the LR-1 in 1966. In the event, procurement of the LR-1 was to be limited to one per year from 1969 through to this year, giving the GSDF a total of eight aircraft of this type.

Apart from the formation of the 2nd *Herikoputa-tai* at Kasumigaura for the new V-107-II helicopters during the final stage of the 2nd DBP, no significant changes were made in the unit structure and deployment during the programme and expansion was nominal, but with the increasing buoyancy of the Japanese economy it was possible during the course of the 3rd DBP (1967-72) to accelerate both expansion and modernisation. By March 1967, the final month of the 2nd DBP, the aviation element of the GSDF possessed an inventory of 150 fixed-wing aircraft and 140 helicopters divided between

The Hughes TH-55J (above) was selected by the GSDF as its standard light training helicopter in 1971, and deliveries of this type have been completed. The OH-6J (below) has proved something of a disappointment to the GSDF and a replacement is now being sought.

The Mitsubishi LR-1 (seen above at Naha AB, Okinawa) was originally intended for the combined reconnaissance and light attack rôle but proved unsuitable for the latter task owing to structural limitations and an inadequate weapons load.

20 squadrons. The newly-launched Defence Build-up Programme introduced no major policy changes but placed increased emphasis on heliborne operations and initiated the most ambitious GSDF helicopter procurement programme to that time, this covering acquisition of a further 54 UH-1B Iroquois and 30 V-107-IIs with which it was intended to accelerate materialization of the cherished "flying infantry" concept. Thus, as this new equipment was taken into the GSDF inventory, between March 1968 and August 1969 six new helicopter units were formed, these being the *Hokubu* (Northern), *Tohoku* (North-Eastern), *Tobu* (Eastern), *Chubu* (Central) and *Seibu* (Western) *Homen Herikoputa-tais,* and the 1st *Herikoputa-dan* (Helicopter Wing). The last-mentioned was an independent unit under the control of the General Headquarters and resulting from the merger of the 1st and 2nd *Herikoputa-tais,* whereas the others were assigned to the *Homen-Koku-tais* co-operating with the district commands.

The absorption of this substantial helicopter fleet was carried through on schedule, although the GSDF experienced major problems in re-equipping its light helicopter force of Bell Model 47G-2s and KH-4s. The service had earlier selected the Hughes OH-6J for this purpose, Kawasaki acquiring a manufacturing licence for the type, and the first of the 55 OH-6Js initially programmed was scheduled to reach the GSDF during the first phase of the 3rd DBP. However, as a result of the chaos that ensued on the parent company's assembly line, Kawasaki was unable to initiate licence production until two years after the date originally scheduled and, in consequence, deliveries did not commence until late 1969, the third year of the DBP, and only 39 OH-6Js reached the GSDF before the end of the five-year programme, seriously impeding the materialisation of the "all-turbine" first-line helicopter force. A further setback had been the discovery that the LR-1 was unsuited for the light attack rôle by reason of its structure and inadequate weapons load, this type thus having to be confined to the photo-reconnaissance and liaison tasks.

By the end of the 3rd DBP, each *Homen Hiko-tai* comprised between five and nine O-1A or -1E Bird Dogs, between two and four LM-1s and two Model 47G or KH-4 helicopters,

and each *Homen Herikoputa-tai* possessed two S-55s and eight UH-1B Iroquois. Each numbered *Hiko-tai* was equipped with seven-nine Bird Dogs and four-five Model 47Gs or KH-4s. The 1st *Herikoputa-dan* was approaching its statutory strength of 42 V-107-IIs, and the unit structure (which remains essentially unchanged today) had been established as follows:

Hokubu Homen Koku-tai (Okadama)	Hokubu Homen Hiko-tai	(Okadama)
	Hokubu Homen Herikoputa-tai	(Okadama)
	2nd Hiko-tai	(Asahigawa)
	5th Hiko-tai	(Obihiro)
	7th Hiko-tai	(Okadama)
	11th Hiko-tai	(Okadama)
Tohoku Homen Koku-tai (Kasuminome)	Tohoku Homen Hiko-tai	(Kasuminome)
	Tohoku Homen Herikoputa-tai	(Kasuminome)
	6th Hiko-tai	(Jinmachi)
	9th Hiko-tai	(Hachinoe)
Tobu Homen Koku-tai (Tachikawa)	Tobu Homen Hiko-tai	(Utsunomiya)
	Tobu Homen Herikoputa-tai	(Tachikawa)
	1st Hiko-tai	(Tachikawa)
	12th Hiko-tai	(Utsunomiya)
Chubu Homen Koku-tai (Yao)	Chubu Homen Hiko-tai	(Yao)
	Chubu Homen Herikoputa-tai	(Yao)
	3rd Hiko-tai	(Yao)
	10th Hiko-tai	(Akeno)
	13th Hiko-tai	(Hofu)
Seibu Homen Koku-tai (Kumamoto)	Seibu Homen Hiko-tai	(Kumamotot)
	Seibu Homen Herikoputa-tai	(Metabaru)
	4th Hiko-tai	(Metabaru)
	8th Hiko-tai	(Kumamoto)
1st Herikoputa-dan	1st Herikoputa-tai	(Kisarazu)
	2nd Herikoputa-tai	(Kisarazu)
Koku Gakko		(Akeno, Iwanuma & Kasumigaura)

With the commencement of the 4th DBP in April 1972, the basic framework of the GSDF's air component modernisation programme had been essentially accomplished, and the force now consisted of 18 fixed-wing aircraft squadrons with some 140 machines and seven rotorcraft squadrons with about 220 helicopters. It was intended that the newborn five-year programme would see completion of the planned modernisation, and of the total 4th DBP budget of approximately £7,100m about £2,680m was allotted to the GSDF, which, it was envisaged, would acquire 155 new aircraft during the period of the programme (1972-76), as well as 450 armoured vehicles and 90 self-propelled guns. The planned aircraft procurement consisted of five LR-1s, 20 V-107-IIs. 55 UH-1Hs,

The O-1A Bird Dog (that above belonging to the 9th Hiko-tai at Hachinoe) has been in service with the GSDF for some 17 years, but final phase-out of this aircraft has now been delayed and it is likely to remain in the GSDF inventory for three or four more years.

58 OH-6Js and 37 Hughes TH-55Js, the last-mentioned type having been selected during the 3rd DBP as the GSDF's standard training helicopter.

All went well until the oil crisis of late 1973. Initially, this only resulted in some reduction in flight training time, but as inflation began to get a grip on Japan's economy, the government was forced to suppress expenditure and equipment procurement for the Self-Defence Forces was immediately curtailed. Immense increases in the unit costs of the aircraft of which procurement had been planned further exacerbated the situation (the unit costs of the V-107-II, UH-1H, OH-6J and TH-55J rising by 13·9%, 22·6%, 19·8% and 12·6% respectively) during Fiscal 1974, and even higher unit cost increases were anticipated for Fiscal 1975 procurement — contracts under the latter year's budget are expected to be announced this month — with further curtailment considered inevitable in consequence. Of the 155 aircraft that the GSDF anticipated receiving under the 4th DBP, the procurement of 41 (one LR-1, eight V-107-IIs, 11 UH-1Hs and 21 OH-6Js) had still to be approved at the time of writing.

Modernisation but little expansion
The number of units and the basic structure of the air component of the GSDF today remains essentially the same as established during the 3rd DBP, apart from the transfer of the *Tobu Homen Hiko-tai* and the 12th *Hiko-tai* from Utsunomiya to Tachikawa (during the course of 1973) and the creation of the 101st *Hiko-tai* following the return to Japan of the jurisdiction of Okinawa, this unit being assigned to the *Seibu* or Western District Command with five V-107-IIs, two UH-1Bs and a single LR-1.

The 1st *Herikoputa-dan* attained its full V-107-II statutory strength during the course of 1974, and last year deliveries of this large helicopter to local units were initiated, the *Hokubu Homen Herikoputa-tai* being the first of these to take the Kawasaki-built Boeing Vertol helicopter on strength. With the completion of deliveries of UH-1 Iroquois helicopters to the five *Homen Herikoputa-tais,* this type is now being delivered to the numbered *Hiko-tais* with the result that the remaining O-1 Bird Dogs, Model 47Gs and KH-4s are being

The Mentor trainer (above) is assigned to Tohoku (North-East) Homen Hiko-tai, as indicated by the letters on the engine cowling, and the Fuji LM (below) belongs to the Tobu (Eastern) Hiko-tai at Utsunomiya.

progressively retired. It is the intention of the GSDF to equip each *Homen Herikoputa-tai* with five V-107-IIs and 20 UH-1s, while each numbered *Hiko-tai* will eventually have five UH-1s and eight OH-6Js on strength, although owing to delays in OH-6J procurement resulting from the current budgetary restrictions, it seems likely that the O-1 Bird Dog will not finally disappear from the GSDF inventory for at least another three or four years.

The current GSDF inventory consists of 91 O-1A and -1E Bird Dogs, 23 LM-1s, five LR-1s, 51 Bell 47Gs and KH-4s, 75 OH-6Js, 82 UH-1Bs, 22 UH-1Hs, 47 V-107-IIs, 23 S-55Cs and 31 TH-55Js, and by March of next year, when the current DBP terminates, the GSDF is expected to possess a total of 450 aircraft of which 350 will be helicopters. During the final phase of the 4th DBP, the GSDF hopes to form the 2nd

continued on page 97

THE AIRTRAINER STORY

THE SALE of 75 light training aircraft to three air forces in the course of three-and-a-half years may not sound especially dramatic, and in an age when the cost of a *single* example of an advanced multi-mission warplane exceeds the *total* value of these batches of trainers, it would be easy to dismiss this business as unimportant. Yet the successful vending of the built-in-New Zealand Airtrainer to military customers that include the particularly hard-nosed Royal Australian Air Force as well as the Royal New Zealand Air Force and the Royal Thai Air Force deserves more than passing attention. With the Airtrainer in fact, the youthful and necessarily somewhat inexperienced New Zealand aerospace industry is competing, not unsuccessfully, with manufacturers of considerably greater standing in Europe, the USA and Japan. That they are doing so with a design that, in essence, is now more than 20 years old, makes the story all the more noteworthy.

The Airtrainer story can properly be considered to have begun in 1952, when the Royal Aero Club of the United Kingdom promoted a competition for the design of a light aircraft suitable for club use. The competition, which attracted more than 100 entries, was intended to encourage the development of a British light aircraft industry but was open to all comers and was in fact won by Henry Millicer, chief aerodynamicist of the Government Aircraft Factories in Australia. The winning design was for a simple cantilever low-wing monoplane with side-by-side seating in a rather stubby fuselage, a fixed tricycle undercarriage and an engine of 50-70 hp.

Subsequent to winning this competition, Mr Millicer set up a small design organization, MB Design Group, in Australia to produce the detail drawings required for prototype construction, and sold the manufacturing rights to East-West Airlines Ltd of Tamworth, NSW. The latter company arranged for a prototype to be built by a subsidiary organization, Pacific and Western Aviation Co Ltd, and this prototype, named the Millicer Air Tourer, made its first flight on 31 March 1959, powered by a 65 hp Continental A65 engine. Production rights were then obtained by Victa Consolidated Industries of Milperra, NSW, a manufacturer of two-stroke engines, lawnmowers and other industrial products which Henry Millicer joined as chief designer.

The Airtourer (restyled as one word instead of two) was redesigned and restressed for production by Victa, being given an all-metal airframe instead of wood, and was offered with 100 or 115 hp engines. A prototype Victa AT.100 Airtourer with 100 hp Continental O-200-A engine made its first flight on 12 December 1961, followed by the first production model on 20 June 1962, and Australian certification was granted on 4 July 1962. A prototype AT.115 Airtourer with 115 hp Lycoming O-235-C1B first flew on 17 September 1962, followed by the first production example on 22 February 1963 and Australian certification on 6 July 1963. Thereafter, Victa went on to produce a total of 172 Airtourers of the two types by the end of 1966, achieving a fair measure of success in the export market as well as with sales within Australia. However, the company found that, despite its relatively low overheads, it could not really compete cost-wise with the big US manufacturers of light aircraft, which could benefit from production rates 20 or more times as great as Victa's.

Production of the Airtourer by Victa ceased in February 1966, and after the company had made an unsuccessful attempt to obtain an Australian government subsidy or tariff protection against foreign competition, its Aviation Division was closed down completely on 20 January 1967. Its final activity was to complete the testing of a four-seat development of the Airtourer, called the Aircruiser, with the same basic wing, a somewhat longer fuselage and a 210 hp Continental IO-360-D engine. Additional wing area was obtained by extending the roots forward, and the gross weight went up to 2,400 lb (1 089 kg) from the Airtourer's 1,650 lb (748 kg).

Upon deciding to close down its aviation activity completely, Victa negotiated the sale of all manufacturing and marketing rights in the two-seat Airtourer to the New Zealand company Aero Engine Services Ltd (AESL) of Hamilton, and this company also took a 12-month option on similar rights to the Aircruiser, pending the completion of certification of the prototype in Australia. This option was subsequently taken up and provided the basis for the development, in New Zealand, of the Airtrainer. Before this came about, however, AESL — hitherto having specialized in the overhaul of aero-engines — established a modest production line at Hamilton for the Airtourer, producing both 100 and 115 hp versions. The latter was redesignated the Airtourer T2, and AESL proceeded to develop other versions with alternative power plants — the T3 with a 130 hp R-R/Continental O-240-A (first flown on 27 January 1972), the T4 with a 150 hp Lycoming O-320-E2A and fixed pitch propeller (first flown September 1968) and the T5 with 150 hp Lycoming O-320-E1A and constant speed propeller (first flown November 1968). The T4 and T5 had an increased gross weight of 1,750 lb (793 kg), and a further step up in maximum weight was made with the T6 variant, which was, in effect, a T5 with a weight of 1,900 lb (862 kg) and, according to customer requirement, a choice of 12-volt or 24-volt electrical systems.

AESL made a first small step into the military market with the delivery of four Airtourer T6s to the Royal New Zealand Air Force in mid-1970. They were for use at the pre-*ab initio* stage, to grade potential RNZAF student pilots and also to train Army pilots prior to their conversion onto Bell 47G-3B-1 helicopters. Another 14 were ordered by the New Zealand Government to be supplied to Indonesia (four), Singapore (six) and Thailand (four) under the terms of the Colombo Aid Plan. These were part of a total of 80 Airtourers that have been built in New Zealand, the remainder having been sold to local aero clubs or exported to Britain (30), Australia (five) and South Africa (one). Production has now ended.

The Airtrainer emerges

The catalyst in the process of creating the Airtrainer was the requirement of the Royal Australian Air Force for a fully-aerobatic light trainer to replace its CAC Winjeels in service at No 1 Flying Training School, Point Cook. AESL, under its progressive managing director A M Coleman, was already aware of the potential of the basic design in the military field, and when information on the Australian requirement came to hand in May 1971, the company decided to make an all-out effort to capture the order. It was immediately obvious that a considerably heavier and more powerful aircraft than the basic Airtourer would be needed in order to satisfy military performance and equipment requirements, and the decision was therefore taken to base the Airtrainer on the structural design of the four-seat Aircruiser.

Englishman "Pat" W C Monk joined AESL as chief designer in June 1971, and set about a structural analysis of the Aircruiser and the design of necessary modifications. The 210 hp Continental engine was retained, and no significant structural changes were found necessary; the gross weight also remained at 2,400 lb (1 088 kg) for the Airtrainer in its initial form. Ailerons and elevator were redesigned to reduce stick forces and the entire systems/equipment installation was revised. The most obvious external difference concerned the cockpit canopy, which in outline was more like that of the Airtourer than the Aircruiser prototype, but which was redesigned to hinge upwards in one piece instead of sliding aft. The same wing root chord extension that had been introduced on the Aircruiser was adopted for the Airtrainer, providing another point of difference from the Airtourer, and provision was made for fitting wing-tip tanks to extend the maximum endurance. Design stress limits were $+6g$ and $-3g$.

While design and construction of the prototype military trainer went ahead, the RAAF indicated its firm interest in the proposal — possibly influenced by a wish to encourage local industry and by the fact that the Airtrainer owed its origin to an Australian even if it was now being built in New Zealand. However, timescales were becoming significant and the RAAF set a deadline of 26 February 1972 for a prototype to be completed, so that a full evaluation could be made. This target AESL bettered by three days, the prototype CT-4 Airtrainer being given its aerial baptism on 23 February by Ralph Etheridge, accompanied by Pat Monk.

Initial flight trials proceeded rapidly and an RAAF evaluation team flew the prototype for a final decision to be made between the Airtrainer and the Scottish Aviation Bulldog. On 24 July 1972, choice of the New Zealand product was confirmed and the Australian government placed a letter of intent for the purchase of 37 aircraft. As the correspondent of The Canberra Times recorded, "Mr Coleman and Mr Monk were treated like folk heroes" when Minister for Defence Fairbairn gave the news. The contract was valued at $A3,248,000; the company that had won it had a total work-force of 85.

The initial success of the Airtrainer was soon followed, when the Royal Thai Air Force signed a contract for 24 in Bangkok on 24 September 1972, the quoted value of this contract being $A3,400,000. Deliveries for the RAAF aircraft were scheduled to begin in mid-1974; to meet pressing RTAF needs, AESL undertook to deliver the Thai aircraft first, starting in February 1974. As flight testing of the prototype proceeded, design of

modifications specified by the RAAF went ahead and the work of preparing production was put in hand, it soon became obvious that considerable expansion of AESL's facilities and working capital would be needed if the programme was not to flounder. This need was met by the creation, with effect from 1 April 1973, of a new company entitled New Zealand Aerospace Industries Ltd, in which AESL and Air Parts (NZ) Ltd merged with a 25 per cent interest each, and additional 25 per cent shareholdings were taken, on behalf of the Government, by Air New Zealand and NZ National Airways Corporation. The new company had a working capital of $A1·3 million and established additional facilities at Hamilton Airport to cope with production of both the Airtrainer and the Fletcher FU-24 family of agricultural aeroplanes previously built by Air Parts.

The first production Airtrainer was completed in the late summer of 1973 and became a company demonstrator; before the end of the year, it was in Thailand conducting experiments in cloud-seeding. The first of the Royal Thai Air Force order was the subject of a handing-over ceremony at the Aerospace works on 23 October 1973, when it was accepted by the RTAF Director General, Air Marshal Soontorn Sundarakul, and named Niyom after a member of the original evaluation team who had subsequently been killed. Deliveries were thus able to begin well up to schedule, but difficulties began to occur in the first half of 1974, partly because Indonesia refused re-fuelling facilities for Airtrainers on delivery flights to Thailand, and partly because of delays in the delivery of components for the assembly line. Completion of the 24-aircraft Thai order was not made until near the end of 1974, by which time the delays were having a cumulative effect upon completion of the Australian aircraft.

Plans to start the first RAAF Airtrainer course at Point Cook in January 1975 were delayed because of the late deliveries, the first CT-4A actually arriving at RAAF Williamtown on 9 January and at Bankstown on 15 January. Delivered by air from New Zealand via Norfolk Island, the Airtrainers arrived at a slower than expected rate throughout 1975, and instructor conversion courses did not begin at the Central Flying School, East Sale, until 1 September. The first pilot training course on the type, at No 1 FTS Point Cook, began on 28 November, and deliveries were expected to be completed by March 1976.

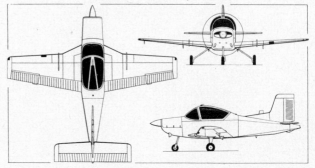

The CT-4A Airtrainer is shown in the three-view below, in armed configuration (with rocket pods) above for evaluation and in RAAF markings in the heading photo opposite. The smaller illustration opposite shows the Millicer Air Tourer prototype from which the Airtrainer was indirectly derived.

Meanwhile, Aerospace Industries had received final confirmation of an order for 17 Airtrainers for the RNZAF, first mooted during 1974 and confirmed in mid-1975. With deliveries due to start early this year, the NZ CT-4As are to be used for basic pilot instruction at the Flying Training Wing, Wigram, and as lead-in types for IFR and navigation training. They are to have the same panel layout and avionics package as those of the RNZAF Strikemasters, onto which students will progress after their basic training on the Airtrainers.

Aerospace has been conducting a vigorous campaign to sell the Airtrainer in other parts of the world. Demonstrations have been made at the Paris Air Show in both 1973 and 1975, allowing the type to be shown to a number of interested customers along the route to and from Europe, and after the 1975 appearance, the CT-4 was demonstrated to a number of interested Arab air forces in Cairo. There are reports, as yet unconfirmed by Aerospace, of an order for 20 Airtrainers for the Rhodesian Air Force and the Royal Hong Kong Auxiliary Air Force is reported to be acquiring three.

Several developments are planned, to widen the market for the Airtrainer. These include the obvious step of adding external stores to give the aircraft a light strike capability, and flight testing of a prototype with underwing pylons was begun during 1975. Rocket pods, minigun pods or bombs of up to 250 lb (113,5 kg) can be carried on each pylon, and a centre-line attachment for a 500-lb (227-kg) bomb is also planned. To take full advantage of the structural strength of the airframe and its ability to lift these external stores, an increase in gross weight to 2,650 lb (1 203 kg) is being made, together with a mainspar modification to improve fatigue life. Further possibilities, for progressive introduction, are a retractable undercarriage, a 225 hp turbo-supercharged engine and eventually a turboprop version — possibly using the 417 shp Allison 250 engine.

The production delays which the Airtrainer has suffered are, perhaps, hardly surprising in view of the size of the manufacturer at the time the RAAF and RTAF orders were placed. With the new factory facilities now fully operational and an enlarged staff, Aerospace Industries should be over the worst of its teething troubles and can concentrate on consolidating its place in the trainer market-place, selling the old/new, Australian/New Zealand Airtrainer — a mentor with a cosmopolitan accent. □

Aerospace Airtrainer CT-4 Specification

Power Plant: One 210 hp Continental IO-360-H flat-six air-cooled engine. Hartzell HC-C2YF-1 two-blade constant-speed propeller, diameter, 6 ft 4 in (1,93 m). Fuel capacity, 45 Imp gal (204,5 l), plus optional wing-tip tanks with capacity of 17 Imp gal (77 l) each.
Performance: Max speed, 178 mph (286 km/h) at sea level, 163 mph (262 km/h) at 10,000 ft (3 050 m); cruising speed at 75 per cent power, 161 mph (259 km/h) at sea level, 144 mph (232 km/h) at 10,000 ft (3 050 m); cruising speed at 55 per cent power, 136 mph (219 km/h) at sea level; initial rate of climb, 1,350 ft/min (6,85 m/sec); time to 5,000 ft (1 525 m) 4 min 36 sec; time to 10,000 ft (3 050 m) 11 min 40 sec; service ceiling, 17,900 ft (5 455 m); take-off distance to 50 ft (15,2 m), 1,237 ft (377 m); landing distance from 50 ft (15,2 m), 1,100 ft (335 m); max range, 884 mls (1 422 km) at 118 mph (190 km/h) at sea level; range without tip tanks, 790 mls (1 271 km) at 75 per cent power at 5,000 ft (1 525 m).
Weights: Basic weight empty, 1,460 lb (662 kg); max take-off weight, 2,400 lb (1,088 kg).
Dimensions: Span, 26 ft 0 in (7,92 m); span over tip tanks, 26 ft 11 in (8,20 m); length, 23 ft 2 in (7,06 m); height, 8 ft 6 in (2,59 m); wheelbase, 5 ft 7⅞ in (1,71 m); undercarriage track, 9 ft 9 in (2,97 m); wing area, 129 sq ft (11,98 m²); aspect ratio, 5·25 : 1, dihedral, 6 deg 45 min constant.
Accommodation: Instructor and student-pilot side-by-side with full dual controls. Space provision for optional third seat or 115 lb (52 kg) of baggage in rear.
Armament: Design provision for one pylon on fuselage centre line to carry one 500-lb (227-kg) Mk 82 GP bomb or similar store; two wing strong points to carry two 250-lb (113,5-kg) Mk 81 GP bombs or four 100-lb (45,4-kg) bombs or two 7,62-mm M60 machine gun pods with 1,200 rounds or two MA 3G rocket pods with seven 2·75-in (70-cm) RPs each.

Aerospace Airtrainer CT/4 Cutaway Drawing Key

1 Two-blade Hartzell constant-speed metal propeller
2 210 hp Continental IO-360-H flat-six air-cooled engine
3 Oil-tank filler cap
4 Engine firewall
5 Port exhaust stub
6 Telescopic shock-absorbed nosewheel leg
7 Steerable nosewheel
8 Airflow fence
9 Landing light
10 Wingtip navigation light
11 Aileron
12 Aileron tab
13 Landing flap
14 Flap hinge
15 Aileron control rod
16 Main wing-spar
17 Main undercarriage bearer
18 Fuel tank (one each wing) 22·5 Imp gal (102 l) each
19 Central control console
20 Throttle quadrant
21 Instrument panel (dual display)
22 Latch of aft-hinged canopy
23 Starboard control column

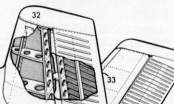

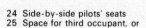

24 Side-by-side pilots' seats
25 Space for third occupant, or baggage
26 Canopy hinges
27 Anti-collision light
28 Elevator control linkage
29 Rudder control linkage
30 Dorsal fin extension
31 VHF blade antenna
32 Aerodynamic rudder balance
33 Rudder
34 One-piece elevator
35 Tail navigation light
36 Aerodynamic elevator balances

1970), it had been fitted with the full variable geometry intakes and modified flying control system that would permit bisonic flight to be achieved; total Concorde flying reached 250 hrs on this flight. There was a slight delay in achieving Mach 2 when metal slivers were found in the engine oil filter after the 95th flight on 8 October, requiring an engine change, but the target was achieved on 4 November (Flight No 102), this being the most significant milestone to that date in Concorde flight testing. The flight duration was 2 hr 16 min and it began with an engine cut at take-off (as part of the continuing investigation of slow speed behaviour); engine throttling checks were made at Mach 1·96 and 001 then accelerated to Mach 2 at 50,200 ft (15 300 m), sustaining this speed for 53 mins during which a number of checks were made, including handling with and without autostabilisation, engine and intake checks between full thrust and idle, side slips to 2 deg, stick force per *g* measurements, performance in straight and turning flight and air brake application. The second bisonic flight, on 6 November, brought total Concorde testing to 300 hrs.

The pace of testing was now maintained (on both prototypes) as the upper end of the performance envelope was explored. Virtually every flight brought new "records" of major or minor interest; for example, Flight No 104 (9 November) by 001 saw the establishment of no fewer than 13 "firsts" of some significance*. By the end of 1970, the two aircraft had completed 376 hrs, and most of the operating envelope had been explored and established as safe, in respect of both aircraft handling and structural integrity; the variable geometry air intake and other important systems had been brought to a satisfactory functional state and about 12 hrs had been flown at the intended service cruising speed. Although Concorde had originally been designed to cruise at Mach 2·20, this had earlier been reduced to 2·02 in order to obtain a better structural fatigue life; the critical factor involved was the airframe temperature experienced, the speed restriction having been accompanied by a reduction in the maximum permitted overall airframe temperature from 426 deg K to 400 deg K. High points by the year-end included a max airspeed of 553 knots (1 024 km/h) CAS, a max Mach number of 2·075, and max altitude of 56,000 ft (17 080 m). Just before Christmas, 001 made the first flight entirely at night, and then was grounded briefly for sealing modifications in the nacelle nozzle bays to improve the nacelle secondary air flow and avoid loss of thrust at high Mach numbers.

Flying again on 23 January with these drag-reduction modifications completed, 001 suffered the most serious Concorde in-flight incident to date on 26 January (Flight No 122). This occurred at Mach 1·98, with afterburning engaged in engines No 1 and 3; when reheat was cut on No 3, the engine oversped and surged, causing No 4 to surge also through interaction. These surges led to failure of the forward intake ramp drive coupling, leading to progressive failures of actuating links and hinges that allowed the ramp to blow off, causing damage to the intake lower lip and the centrewall between engines 3 and 4. Pieces of metal of various sizes were ingested by engine No 4, which continued windmilling but could not be restarted. A safe return was made to Toulouse on three engines and both prototypes were grounded while the incident was investigated and modifications were made.

The modifications comprised alterations of the control system to minimise the likelihood of surge under normal operating conditions, and some structural changes to make ramp failure

---

* *Longest block time, 2 hr 43 min; longest supersonic time, 1 hr 29 min; highest Mach for engine cut and double engine cut, M=2·0; highest airspeed for engine cut and double engine cut, 530 knots (982 km/h); greatest height for engine cut and double engine cut, 50,000 ft (15 250 m); highest re-light Mach airspeed and altitude, Mach 1·94/530 knots (982 km/h)/49,000 ft (14 945 m); greatest take-off weight, and ditto with engine failure, 336,260 lb (152 500 kg).*

TYPICAL TEST FLIGHT LOG
Aircraft 001 — Flight 50 — 13 October — 1969 —
Block time 2 hrs 02 mins

10.01	Leave ramp
10.05	Thrust reverser test while taxiing to end of runway
10.11	Brake release
10.11.40	Gear up
10.12	After-burning off
10.12.10	Engines throttled to N₂=93·5 per cent
10.13	Barn doors to 0
10.15	Nose from 5° to up
10.15.30	Visor up
10.16.40	10,500 feet/360 knots (3 200 m/667 km/h) start climb
10.18	Barn door hinge change AFT — FWD
10.18.55	Start fuel transfer to tank 10 — M=0·75
10.23.30	28,000 ft (8 540 m)/M=0·90; a complete transfer
10.26	Full throttle and after-burning on 4 engines; a climb resumed
10.26.50	Slight engine throttling, after-burning on
10.27.50	34,000 ft (10 370 m)/M=0·90; full throttle for transonic acceleration
10.28	M=0·94
10.29	M=1·05
10.30.33	39,000 ft (11 895 m)/M=1·05; after-burning off on engines 2 and 3
10.31	Flutter testing, M=1·05/340 kt (630 km/h). Rudder excitation by bonkers
10.33 to 10.37	Stabilised sideslip flight, M=1·05/340 kt (630 km/h) Rudder hinge moment assessment: Blue, green, blue and green
10.37.30	After-burning off on 1 and 4; descent to 34,000 ft (10 370 m)
10.40	M=1·05/380 kt (704 km/h)
10.43	Flutter testing, M=1·05/380 kt (704 km/h). Rudder excitation
10.45	Harmonic flutter testing, abandoned because of turbulence
10.50 to 10.54	Rudder hinge moment assessment M 1·05/380 kt (704 km/h)
10.54 to 11.10	Harmonic flutter testing
11.10	Full throttle on engines 2 and 3
11.10.48	After-burning on, engine no. 3
11.11.10	Failure to select after-burning on engine no. 2
11.11.40	After-burning off, engine no. 3
11.12.37	After-burning on engines no. 1 and 4
11.14.40 to 11.17.00	Evaluation of thrust/drag balance for various engine thrust configurations
11.17.46	N₂=95·6 per cent, after-burning on engines 1 and 4 M=1·05. Roll axis autostabilisation off N₂=87/88 per cent, dry on engines 2 and 3 M=1·05 Roll axis autostabilisation off Engine no. 1 cut by shutting off HP valve (Throttle unchanged) No vibration, no need to open "barn door", engine "failure" easy to counteract
11.18.09	M=1·00, 34,000 ft (10 370 m) in decleration
11.18.41	After-burning off, engine no. 4
11.19.31	Start forward transfer
11.20.57	28,000 ft (8 540 m) M=0·90/360 kt (667 km/h); relight engine no. 1
11.24.30	25,000 ft (7 625 m) M=0·90/CG, 54 per cent; turn at 1·5 *g*
11.27.29 to 11.32.29	Performance assessment 25,000 ft (7 625 m); M= 0·90/380 kt (704 km/h)
11.33.00	End transfer C.G. 53 per cent; descent to 20,000 ft (6 100 m)
11.36.14 to 11.41.14	Performance assessment 20,000 ft (6 100 m) M= 0·858/400 kt (741 km/h)
11.42	Barn door hinge FWD→AFT
11.44.24	Visor down
11.44.47	Nose 5° down
11.47.25	Gear down
11.47.50	Nose 17° down
11.57.37	Touch-down
12.03.00	Arrive ramp — engines off

---

impossible should surging occur. The incident was a typical example of flight testing revealing situations that cannot be completely forecast with accuracy and which it is the purpose of flight investigations to reveal. 001 flew again on 15 April 1971 (Flight No 123), this being the 200th Concorde flight, and after some tests to confirm the modifications, completed the "sealed nacelle" evaluation. On 7 May a special flight was made with President Georges Pompidou as passenger; two complete automatic landings were made on 14 May; a new high take-off weight of 340,670 lb (154 500 kg) was set on 23

May and on 25 May (Flight No 142), 001 flew from Toulouse to Dakar, making Concorde's first intercontinental journey (Europe to Africa) as a prelude to its appearance at the Paris Air Show. In the course of the latter, a number of flights were made carrying airline chiefs, journalists and other specially invited guests — up to a dozen at a time — and from this time on, an increasing number of flights was made in which official pilots (from the CEV, ARB and FAA — respectively the French, British and US certificating authorities) and pilots of the "customer airlines" participated.

With more than 100 supersonic flights logged by 001 alone by July 1971, the original prototype had now completed the major part of its test assignment and was free to be used for the first major Concorde sales and demonstration tour. Starting on 4 September 1971 (Flight No 178) this took 001 to Rio de Janeiro, Sao Paulo and Buenos Aires; in 15 days, 16 flights were made, totalling 32 hr 58 min of which 13 hr 38 min were supersonic, and 117 passengers were flown on demonstration flights. Like many overseas tours that were to follow, the whole operation went smoothly and to schedule, showing that Concorde could be integrated with subsonic traffic using airways and airports and even in its prototype guise could be maintained far from home base with few special facilities.

After the return from South America, 001 was fitted with the production-shape wing leading edges, flying again on 29 November 1971 (Flight No 194) and after another series of flights for "customer airline" pilots it was fitted with an AHI (anti-high incidence) drag parachute prior to embarking on a series of flights at high angles of incidence. The flying total passed 1,000 hrs on 16 May 1972 and the high incidence test phase was concluded on 30 May (Flight No 269). Some small modifications were next introduced to the air intakes, to eliminate the risk of engine surge in conditions of sideslip and/or negative g at high Mach numbers and 001 flew with these on 16 September after a period in the workshops. Whilst engaged in check-testing the behaviour of the new intakes 001 suffered an engine failure on 12 October. (Flight No 282). The HP shaft of No 2 engine failed as the Concorde was climbing through 20,000 ft (6 100 m) at Mach 0·9, and the engine shut down automatically; it was the first direct engine failure in Concorde flight development which had then totalled 1,310 hrs, and was attributable to a feature of the engine that had already been changed for production models. Just prior to this incident, the Concorde envelope had been extended to Mach 2·1, achieved for the first time by 001 on 9 October, and another high point was reached on 16 March 1973 with an altitude of 68,000 ft (20 740 m).

A short series of flights was made in February/March 1973 with experimentally cropped and tabbed inner elevons, for comparative measurements of hinge moments. Then, after making its third Paris Air Show appearance (this time on static display only) 001 was made available for a special scientific sortie on the occasion of a solar eclipse taking place on 30 June 1973. For this, a number of modifications were made, including the fitting of a solar telescope and other special instruments; the flight was made with great success and allowed 74 minutes continuous observation and recording of the eclipse to be made by seven French, British and American scientists.

Some automatic landing trials in June 1973 brought the useful life of 001 to an end. The task of certificating Concorde had already passed to the pre-production aircraft, but the first example had played a significant part in the process and had the three important milestones to its credit: first to fly, first to Mach 1 and first to Mach 2. On 19 October, 001 made its 397th and last flight, from Toulouse to Le Bourget, where it was destined to become a permanent exhibit of the *Musée de l'Air*. In command for the last flight, as he had been for the first, Andre Turcat wrote this unique valediction for a unique aircraft:

"Adieu 001. It was too noisy and too smoky. It didn't have the required range for North Atlantic crossing. It was cluttered with test instrumentation. And it didn't have the clock with a 24-hr dial, with which one never knows the time, but which is required by some airlines. Finally, the ashtrays were full. It had to be sent to the museum, the 001, the 'grand pa', only $4\frac{1}{2}$ years old. But it had seen a damned lot.

"It was the first to carry 140 tonnes supersonically. It had flown from 110 to 1,240 knots. It had crossed the South Atlantic in two hours and intersected the 45 deg South parallel. It had dived, climbed, rolled, yawed and surged more than anyone. Four thousand times, maybe, it had been given modifications.

"It had been a docile tool in the hands of ten test pilots and twenty airline captains. It had been admired in its strength and its elegance, which its successors have even enhanced. It had carried most important persons. It had spent more than one hour in a total eclipse of the sun and no one can, nor will for a long time, beat this unique record. It had measured nitric acid in the stratosphere and seen, at sunset, the ozone layer shadow on the sky. It had given us the biggest thrills of our careers, and heralded a new transport era for the world. In return, we just loved it".

Concorde 002

The first British-assembled Concorde, G-BSST (a special out-of-sequence registration to indicate SuperSonic Transport) was airborne for the first time on 9 April 1969, taking off from the Filton works of British Aircraft Corporation and landing at Fairford, Gloucestershire, a former RAF transport base selected as the British centre of Concorde test flying. It was piloted by Brian Trubshaw, Director of Flight Test for BAC's Commercial Aircraft Division, and accompanied by a Canberra chaseplane. The airframe standard initially was similar to that of 001 but after a dozen flights (including two flying demonstrations at the Paris Air Show and a Buckingham Palace Flyover), 002 was grounded for a month to have the "barn door" auxiliary air intakes fitted and the rear (No 10) fuel tank commissioned so that trials at full aft CG could proceed. Flying resumed on 18 July 1969 (Flight No 13) but only 12 flights were needed to complete this phase of the pro-

Concorde 204 takes off from London Airport, Heathrow. Afterburners are lit and the nose is in the intermediate (−5 deg) droop position with visor fully down, used for taxying and take-off.

The flight deck of Concorde 206. Each pilot has a full set of flying instruments, and essential engine indicators are grouped in the centre of the panel. Navigation and communications control boxes are between the two seats, together with the master throttles. Standard Concorde flight crew comprises two pilots and a systems manager (who may be pilot-trained or engineer-trained according to airline preference).

For its tour to the Far East in June 1972, 002 had been fitted with a special interferometer designed in the UK by the NPL. This allowed an investigation to be made of trace gases in the far infra-red region, and as a follow up to this work, 002 made a number of high-altitude flights into the Arctic Circle in May 1973. After returning from the Madrid trials in July, some time was spent on the ground making water ingestion taxi trials. The planned programme for 002 being then complete, with nearly 400 flights amassed, it became available for miscellaneous work including various demonstration flights, some more stratospheric research sorties and a series of 12 flights searching — without success — for natural icing to check the results obtained artificially. The last such sortie (Flight No 434) was made on 10 April 1975, after which 002 was placed on stand-by awaiting disposal.

Two flights were made in August to make wake turbulence measurements in conjunction with an HS.125 and Aberpoth radar, and Flight No 437 on 26 August was a demonstration for the Weston-super-Mare Air Show. At the conclusion of this display, a failure occurred in the landing gear mechanism which resulted in the port gear failing to lock down. The left hand side stay had, in fact, become disconnected from the main leg, with the result that the leg was unrestrained laterally. What could have been the most serious incident in the entire Concorde flight testing was minimised by the skilful handling of 002 by John Cochrane, who brought the aircraft's weight onto the port leg during the landing in such a way that the gear remained upright and supporting the aircraft. The failure occurred when both undercarriage legs were released from their uplocks during a tight 1·75-g turn; falling free in 1½ seconds, they were arrested by the side stays but overstressing of the latter allowed one to slip out of attachment.

Modifications were introduced to give complete safety for lowering the gear at up to 2g and a spare undercarriage leg was fitted to 002 during September, although the incident prevented its appearance at the SBAC Farnborough show that month. It has not flown again to date but is destined to be transferred in due course to the Fleet Air Arm Museum at Yeovilton, where facilities exist for its permanent preservation and display.

Concorde 01

The second British Concorde, registered G-AXDN in normal sequence and the first to pre-production configuration, was the third aircraft to fly, on 17 December 1971, following completion of ground resonance testing in July. Powered from the outset by Olympus 593-4 engines with an initial rating of 34,730 lb st (15 767 kgp) and capable of delivering 36,800 lb st (16 700 kgp) later, Concorde 01 had an increase of 8 ft 6 in (2,59 m) in the length of the fuselage ahead of the wing and an effective increase in cabin length of about 10 ft (3,05 m) by internal rearrangement. It was also the first to fly with the production standard fully-glazed vizor that allows normal forward visibility when raised, whereas the vizors on 001 and 002 were metal. The initial gross weight was 358,000 lb (162 532 kg), compared with a maximum of 326,000 lb (148 000 kg) for the prototypes.

For its first few flights, 01 had fixed intake ramps, these allowing the flight envelope to be cleared up to Mach 1·5; the first supersonic flight was in fact made on the 18th sortie, on 12 February 1972. Another of the differences of 01 from the prototypes was the use of an MEPU (Monofuel Emergency Power Unit) as a source of emergency power for in-flight engine starting and hydraulics operation, in place of a GTS (gas turbine starter) that could also provide hydraulic power through a gear box. The MEPU, operating on hydrozine fuel, was first functioned in flight on 8 March 1972.

Until mid-August, 01 was engaged primarily on flight flutter clearance, necessarily repeated because of the longer fuselage; on the 10th of that month, after Flight No 85, it returned to Filton for installation of new air intake control system and geometry representative of the production standard, the new wing leading edge shape developed for production aircraft and Olympus 602 engines rated at 36,800 lb (16 707 kgp), of the type then intended for the first production aircraft. Flight testing resumed on 15 March 1973, when G-AXDN returned to Fairford.

Supersonic performance investigation and engine air intake optimisation occupied the next few months. After another two-month period on the ground for modifications, testing resumed with Flight No 122 on 18 October, this also being Concorde's 1,000th flight. December found 01 engaged on powerplant envelope clearance tests and Thrust Auto Reduce (TAR) introduction, plus de-icing tests. In January 1974, a week was spent at Tangier looking for a cold stratosphere, in order to check the functioning of the air intakes, and their safety against engine surge, in extremely low temperatures at high altitude. A series of flights in early February sought to induce engine surges in various conditions and work continued right up to June optimizing the air intake control system, including further periods at Tangier. In the course of this work, the speed envelope was pushed out to Mach 2·2 and, eventually, 2·23 — the maximum reached by any Concorde.

After participating in the SBAC Farnborough display in September 1974, 01 took on the important task of clearing the de-icing installation. Previous efforts to find natural icing conditions having failed, 01 flew to Grant County Airport, Moses Lake, Washington, on 7 November (Flight Nos 215/216) and after three weeks of searching at altitudes of 13,000 ft (3 965 m) off the west coast of the USA, finally achieved success on 4 December (Flight No 228). Ice was accreted at a speed of 240 knots (444 km/h), shed and re-accreted to a depth of two inches (5 cm), all scheduled aircraft and engine tests being satisfactorily concluded. On the first leg of its flight to Moses Lake, G-AXDN set a record for the fastest airline flight between Europe and mainland America, airborne time being 2 hrs 56 min from Fairford to Bangor, Maine.

To conclude the icing tests, 01 flew behind a Canberra tanker during January 1975 to accumulate ice on the lowered landing gear, and in February went to Nairobi to make a series of sorties into cumulonimbus clouds for certification tests demonstrating safety of engine air intakes against ice. Returned to the UK, it became available for BAC flight crew training in April and May at Fairford, in preparation for the training of British Airways crews, since which time it has remained on standby at Fairford. Concorde 01 has been assigned for

The interior of Concorde 204 as used for the endurance programme, looking aft. In high density layouts, up to 128 passengers can be carried; the standard British Airways configuration provides 100 passenger seats, four-abreast throughout, with six cabin attendants.

permanent preservation and display at Duxford, nr Cambridge, as part of the collection of the Duxford Aviation Society in association with the Imperial War Museum.

Concorde 02

Another stage in establishing the production configuration of Concorde was reached on 10 January 1973 with the first flight of 02, F-WTSA, at Toulouse. With a gross weight of 358,000 lb (162 530 kg) initially, it featured the lengthened tail cone adopted to reduce drag at the rear end of the fuselage; carbon brakes were to be fitted, as intended for production, but it did not yet have the integrated drive generator for the electrical system. An MEPU was used, as on 01, although the decision had been made to switch to an RAT (ram-air turbine) for production models. Olympus 602s were fitted from the start, with the annular combustion chambers and, for the first time, the Type 28 TRA nozzles with spade silencers were installed.

The gross weight was soon increased, and on 3 March, 02 took off at 387,450 lb (175 900 kg) on a simulated trans-atlantic crossing which covered 3,900 mls (6 300 km) – the longest Concorde flight up to that time. Daily demonstrations were made at the Paris Air Show in June 1973, after

which it was engaged in supersonic performance and engine air intake optimization, plus some noise evaluations. The latter were completed in August, and on 14 September (Flight No 72), 02 took the Concorde flying hours total past 2,000.

The first Concorde visit to the USA came later in September, when 02 attending the opening of the Fort Worth-Dallas Airport. It flew first to Caracas across the South Atlantic, then up to Dallas, and returned via Washington to Paris, this being the first North Atlantic crossing by Concorde, made on 26 September (Flight No 81). Inevitably, this was a record-breaking flight, starting with a gross weight of 389,100 lb (176 650 kg) of which 190,900 lb (86 670 kg) was fuel and 25,900 lb (11 760 kg) was payload, including 32 passengers. The distance of 3,890 mls (6 265 km) was covered in an airborne time of 3 hr 33 min of which 2 hr 16 min was at Mach 2 and another 26 min was supersonic at less than Mach 2.

After its return to Toulouse, 02 was flown by check pilots of the CEV and the CAA as part of the pre-certification programme for flight handling characteristics, and then went into the shops for a programme of modifications. These included a lengthened primary nozzle, production-type aft thrust reverser units, some modifications to the engine air intake system and others to prepare 02 for a period of cold weather testing. Flying again on 31 January 1974, F-WTSA made its second visit to the USA in February, where it was allowed to "soak" in very low temperatures at Fairbanks, Alaska, to check system performance. Next month, it was engaged on testing for optimization of nozzle settings in the subsonic regime and for noise in the approach, new engines with a raised contingency rating being fitted in April and the noise measurements continuing.

From 27 May (Flight No 138) to 18 June (Flight No 166), 02 was engaged on a series of "pre-endurance" flights over the South and North Atlantic, flying between Paris and Rio de Janeiro, Paris and Boston, and Paris and Miami. In 29 flights, a total of 77,620 mls (124 820 km) was covered at an average block speed of 1,000 mph (1 610 km/h) and some 500 passengers, including invited businessmen, were carried, once again with high regularity and few delays of any kind.

Dunlop carbon brakes, selected for the production Concorde, were fitted to 02 during July and taxi trials started at Toulouse in August, followed by a first flight on 28 August 1974 (Flight No 179). The pre-endurance programme was then continued with a highly successful flight starting in London

BAC/Aerospatiale Concorde Cutaway Drawing Key

1 Variable geometry drooping nose
2 Weather radar
3 Spring pot
4 Visor jack
5 'A'-frame
6 Visor uplock
7 Visor guide rails and carriage
8 Droop nose jacks
9 Droop nose guide rails
10 Droop nose hinge
11 Rudder pedals
12 Captain's seat
13 Instrument panel shroud
14 Forward pressure bulkhead
15 Retracting visor
16 Multi-layer windscreen
17 Windscreen fluid rain clearance and wipers
18 Second pilot's seat
19 Roof panel

20 Flight-deck air duct
21 3rd crew member's seat
22 Control relay jacks
23 1st supernumerary's seat
24 2nd supernumerary's folding seat (optional)
25 Radio and electronics racks (Channel 2)
26 Radio and electronics racks (Channel 1)
27 Plug-type forward passenger door
28 Slide/life-raft pack stowage
29 Cabin staff tip-up seat
30 Forward galley units (port and starboard)
31 Toilets (2)
32 Coats (crew and passengers)
33 Twelve 26-man life-rafts
34 VHF1 antenna
35 Overhead baggage racks (with doors)

36 Cabin furnishing (heat and sound insulated)
37 4-abreast one-class passenger accommodation
38 Seat rails
39 Metal-faced floor panels
40 Nosewheel well
41 Nosewheel main doors
42 Nosewheel leg
43 Shock absorber
44 Twin nosewheels
45 Torque links
46 Steering mechanism
47 Telescopic strut

48 Lateral bracing struts
49 Nosewheel actuating jacks
50 Underfloor air-conditioning ducts
51 Nosewheel door actuator
52 Nosewheel secondary (aft) doors

PILOT PRESS
COPYRIGHT
DRAWING

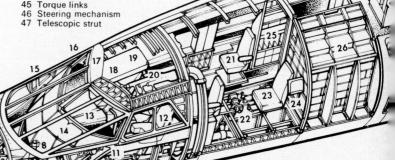

Concorde 206, the first British Airways revenue service aircraft, lands at Fairford, the BAC Concorde test centre, at the conclusion of its first flight, following take-off from Filton, Bristol. The visor is down and the nose is fully drooped ($-17\frac{1}{2}$ deg) for best forward visibility in the approach configuration, at high angles of incidence. Concorde 202 is in the background.

gramme and the aircraft was then grounded again (on 7 August 1969) for major modifications to the flying controls, installation of the full variable geometry intake control system and a change of engine from the 28,000 lb st (13 075 kgp) Olympus 593-1s used for initial flights to 32,900 lb st (14 935 kgp) Olympus 593-2Bs needed for initial exploration up to Mach 2.

With these modifications, 002 flew again on 21 March 1970 (Flight No 25), going supersonic for the first time on the next flight, on 25 March. It then quickly progressed through the envelope already explored by 001, up to Mach 1·50, carrying its first VIP (the Rt Hon Anthony Wedgwood Benn, then Minister of Technology) on 10 April. The Olympus 593-2B engines, suitable for only short supersonic dashes, were superseded by the 34,730 lb st (15 767 kgp) 593-3B variant which allowed Mach 2 to be sustained, and these later engines were installed prior to the 31st flight, made on 12 August 1970. 002 then embarked on a programme to obtain flutter clearance at progressively higher speeds up to Mach 2, flying either over the North Sea or along a special N-S track lying between Ireland and Britain. During this phase of testing, the Concorde made its first appearance at a Farnborough air show and, on 13 September, its first landing at London's Heathrow Airport, because of bad weather at Fairford. After the return to home base next day, metal was found in No 1 engine oil filter, and an engine strip revealed a fractured steel adjusting washer in the gear train — the first of several similar incidents that caused unscheduled engine changes in both 002 and 001 in the next few months.

At 10.18 hrs on 4 November 1970, 002 took off from Fairford for what was scheduled to be Concorde's first flight to Mach 2. This was not to be, however, for at Mach 1·35 at 39,000 ft (11 895 m) the No 2 engine fire warning indicator came on, necessitating a precautionary return to base. 001 had already been scheduled to make a Mach 2 flight later that day, and successfully did so, the first bisonic excursion by 002 following on 12 November (Flight No 57). New engines were fitted later that month, specially instrumented for performance measurement and also to check stresses in the first-stage compressor blades. With 001 engaged in Mach 2 exploration, 002 then became primarily concerned with subsonic performance, especially in low-speed, high C_L conditions, and on 2 December it made the longest subsonic flight to date, with a duration of 3 hr 4 min. The second in-flight "incident" with 002 occurred on 4 December (Flight No 61) when an instrumentation camera overheated and filled the rear cabin with smoke.

After setting a "highest to date" figure of 57,700 ft (17 600 m) in a Mach 2 cruise-climb on New Year's Day 1971,

002 was grounded for the intake mods that resulted from the incident with 001 on 26 January, resuming testing on 3 April 1971. Deliberate attempts were made to obtain engine surges in the course of the next few flights, without untoward incident. One Olympus 593-3BA was fitted during May, this having an LP compressor of full production standard and a simplified entry casing; on 17 June (Flight No 97), the 500th Concorde hour was flown by 002.

A further engine development stage was reached in November 1971, when one 593-3BB was fitted, this having a modified combustion chamber that allowed it to produce a higher take-off thrust. Other engines of this standard were fitted in March 1972. Increasingly, during the last half of 1971, 002 was used to give demonstration flights (for MPs, "customer airlines", the press, and official pilots). On 12 January 1972, HRH The Duke of Edinburgh flew in the left hand seat and took the controls for half-an-hour; on 8 May, HRH Princess Margaret and Lord Snowden were passengers. Two flights were made on 7 February with an experimental fixed landing gear to investigate the effect of oleo leg friction on rough runway comfort levels, and on 30 March the first flight was made with Litton inertial navigation system and up-dated de-icing systems fitted. A visit to the Hanover Air Show was made on 22 April, carrying British Aerospace Minister Michael Heseltine amongst other guests.

On 2 June, Concorde 002 set off on a major demonstration tour through the Middle and Far East to Australia and Japan. Thirty-two flights were made totalling 70 hr 21 min (23 hr 4 min supersonic), 12 countries were visited, 46,000 mls (74 000 km) were covered and over 200 guests carried. In 32 departures, there were only three delays (totalling less than four hours) due to engineering reasons. The tour ended on 1 July; at the end of that month the BOAC/British Airways and Air France orders, for five and four production Concordes respectively, were confirmed and China's CAAC signed a preliminary purchase contract for three. 002 flew each day at the 1972 SBAC Display at Farnborough and was then instrumented for a series of de-icing trials, flying again on 17 November (Flight No 260) by which time the preliminary purchase contract for two Concordes with an option on a third had been signed by Iran Air. De-icing trials behind a Canberra tanker supplied by the A & AEE Boscombe Down were successfully pursued in the early months of 1973, after a three-week visit to Johannesburg in January to measure take-off, climb and landing performance at a "hot-and-high" airfield. Twenty-eight flights totalling 21 hrs were made at Johannesburg, and the high temperature performance measurements were continued at Madrid in July.

and visiting Gander (Concorde's first appearance in Canada), Mexico City, San Francisco, Anchorage, Los Angeles, Acapulco, Bogota, Lima, Caracas, Las Palmas and so back to Paris. The flight from Lima to Paris, with two stops, was made on 28 October and was the first-ever flight from the Pacific Coast to Europe completed in daylight – a total distance of 7,200 mls (11 600 km) in just over 9 hrs elapsed time.

More carbon brake trials followed during February 1975, after a period on the ground for additional modifications and during March, Concorde 02 was taxied at high speed on wet and flooded runways to prove both the anti-water ingestion deflectors fitted to nose and main gear, and the new brakes. This led to landing performance certification work on dry and wet runways, and after an appearance in the static park at the Paris Air Show 1975, 02 returned to Toulouse for overhaul, since which time it has been on standby for demonstrations or other duties but has been little used except for a visit to Canada early in October for the opening of the Mirabel Airport, Montreal.

Concorde 201

The first flight of the first production Concorde, F-WTSB, on 6 December 1973, marked a further major milestone towards the certification of the supersonic transport. For the first time, supersonic speed (Mach 1·57) was reached on a

Concorde first flight, Mach 2·05 being achieved on the second flight on 14 December.

Compared with Concorde 02, the production model had longer main landing gear legs (an increase of 4 in/10 cm), serving to decrease the aircraft ground reference angle from 1 deg to 0·50 deg. Two hydraulic and two electric pumps were fitted, instead of three hydraulic, to achieve faster fuel transfer rates, and an Air Data Computer Type 52 was fitted, of the type to be used in airline service, in addition to the two Type 51s used in pre-production Concordes. A ram air turbine was fitted for the first time, to provide emergency power by driving two hydraulic pumps and changes were made in the AFCS and autopilot. Carrying 10,000 lb (4 540 kg) of test equipment, Concorde 01 had Olympus 602 engines at their production rating and an initial gross weight of 385,000 lb (174 800 kg), although this was soon increased.

The flight test programme for Concorde 201 included development of the systems, including the air intakes, followed by certification flights for performance, handling and various of the aircraft systems. This continued through most of 1974, including a period at Casablanca which provided a good base from which to fly into the cold stratosheric conditions above the South Atlantic for the intake control system work, which was concluded by the end of the year. Certification flying by CEV and CAA pilots then began in January 1975, covering various of the systems including autopilot, radio navigation, hydraulics, air conditioning and RAT.

On 26 April 1975, F-WTSB flew Concorde's 4,000th hour and

CONCORDE FLIGHT DEVELOPMENT
Totals to 4 December 1975

Aircraft	Registration	Total flights	Blocktime hrs	Blocktime min	Supersonic flights	Supersonic time hrs	Supersonic time min
001	F-WTSS	397	812	07	250	254	49
002	G-BSST	437	835	18	196	173	26
01	G-AXDN	270	630	38	168	208	14
02	F-WTSA	307	642	18	185	274	31
1	F-WTSB	368	803	25	222	297	45
2	G-BBDG	342	754	35	170	214	17
3	F-BTSC	167	484	58	154	307	51
4	G-BOAC	177	522	04	153	253	44
5	F-BVFA	9	31	54	8	14	19
6	G-BOAA	6	22	27	5	7	56
Totals		2480	5539	44	1511	2006	52

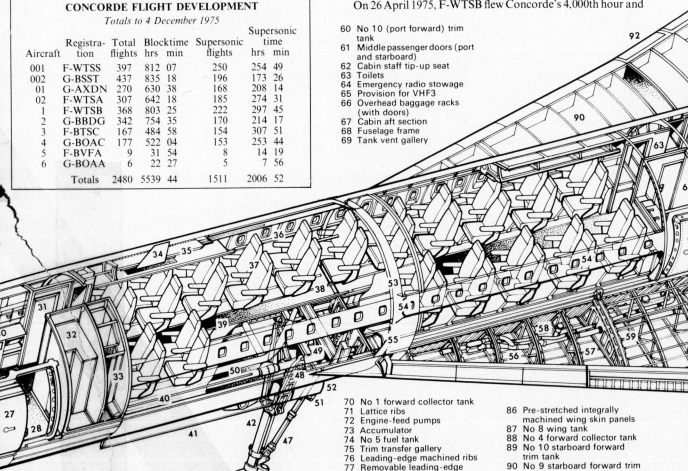

60 No 10 (port forward) trim tank
61 Middle passenger doors (port and starboard)
62 Cabin staff tip-up seat
63 Toilets
64 Emergency radio stowage
65 Provision for VHF3
66 Overhead baggage racks (with doors)
67 Cabin aft section
68 Fuselage frame
69 Tank vent gallery

53 Fuselage frame (single flange)
54 Machined window panel
55 Underfloor forward baggage compartment (237 cu ft/ 6·72 m³)
56 Fuel lines
57 Lattice ribs
58 No 9 (port forward) trim tank
59 Single-web spar

70 No 1 forward collector tank
71 Lattice ribs
72 Engine-feed pumps
73 Accumulator
74 No 5 fuel tank
75 Trim transfer gallery
76 Leading-edge machined ribs
77 Removable leading-edge sections, with:
78 Expansion joints between sections
79 Contents unit
80 Inlet control valve
81 Transfer pumps
82 Flight-deck air duct
83 No 8 fuselage tank
84 Vapour seal above tank
85 Pressure-floor curved membranes

86 Pre-stretched integrally machined wing skin panels
87 No 8 wing tank
88 No 4 forward collector tank
89 No 10 starboard forward trim tank
90 No 9 starboard forward trim tank
91 Quick-lock removable inspection panels
92 Spraymat leading-edge de-icing panels
93 Leading-edge anti-icing strip
94 Spar-box machined girder side pieces
95 No 7 fuel tank
96 No 7a fuel tank

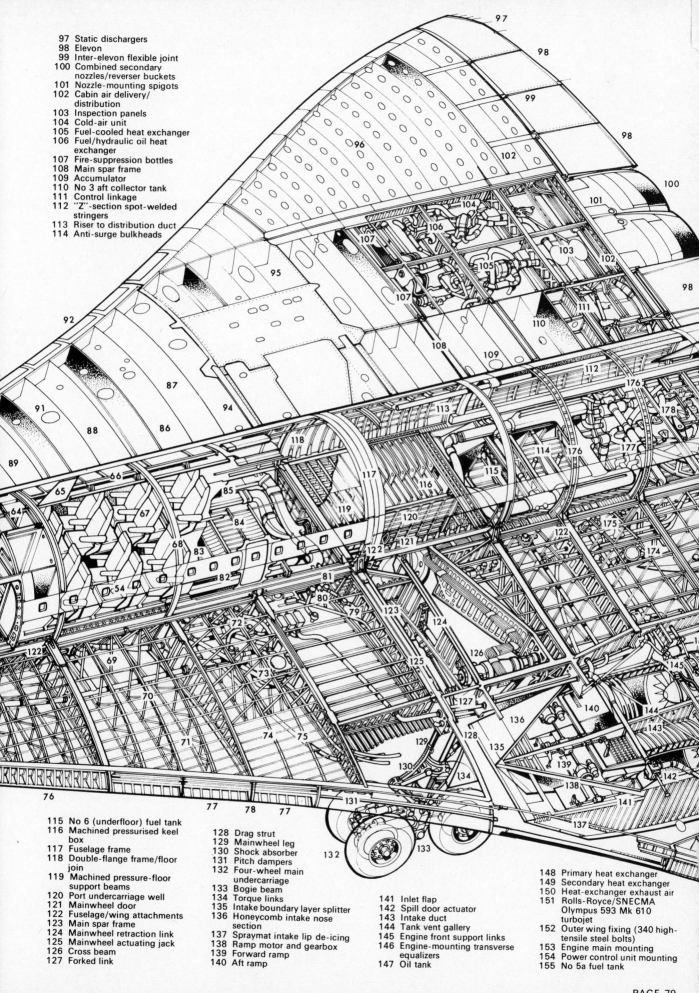

97 Static dischargers
98 Elevon
99 Inter-elevon flexible joint
100 Combined secondary nozzles/reverser buckets
101 Nozzle-mounting spigots
102 Cabin air delivery/distribution
103 Inspection panels
104 Cold-air unit
105 Fuel-cooled heat exchanger
106 Fuel/hydraulic oil heat exchanger
107 Fire-suppression bottles
108 Main spar frame
109 Accumulator
110 No 3 aft collector tank
111 Control linkage
112 "Z"-section spot-welded stringers
113 Riser to distribution duct
114 Anti-surge bulkheads

115 No 6 (underfloor) fuel tank
116 Machined pressurised keel box
117 Fuselage frame
118 Double-flange frame/floor join
119 Machined pressure-floor support beams
120 Port undercarriage well
121 Mainwheel door
122 Fuselage/wing attachments
123 Main spar frame
124 Mainwheel retraction link
125 Mainwheel actuating jack
126 Cross beam
127 Forked link

128 Drag strut
129 Mainwheel leg
130 Shock absorber
131 Pitch dampers
132 Four-wheel main undercarriage
133 Bogie beam
134 Torque links
135 Intake boundary layer splitter
136 Honeycomb intake nose section
137 Spraymat intake lip de-icing
138 Ramp motor and gearbox
139 Forward ramp
140 Aft ramp

141 Inlet flap
142 Spill door actuator
143 Intake duct
144 Tank vent gallery
145 Engine front support links
146 Engine-mounting transverse equalizers
147 Oil tank

148 Primary heat exchanger
149 Secondary heat exchanger
150 Heat-exchanger exhaust air
151 Rolls-Royce/SNECMA Olympus 593 Mk 610 turbojet
152 Outer wing fixing (340 high-tensile steel bolts)
153 Engine main mounting
154 Power control unit mounting
155 No 5a fuel tank

of these, a total of 123 passengers and crew was carried on a flight on 19 April – the biggest load in Concorde to date. This series of trials ended on 22 April (Flight No 21) and G-BOAC was then on the ground for some 10 weeks in preparation for the endurance flying. A Special Category C of A was granted to Concorde 204 on 30 June by the Civil Aviation Authority.

The British share of the endurance programme began on 7 July and was completed on 13 September, in which time 130 flights were made, totalling 380 hrs 43 min of which 208 hr 33 min were supersonic. 6,500 passengers were carried. The flights were made over various segments of the route from London to Australia, points of call being Bahrain, Bombay, Kuala Lumpur, Singapore, Melbourne, Beirut and Damascus; several flights were also made across the North Atlantic to Gander. Engineering failures caused the cancellation of seven flights – one due to landing gear damage at Bahrain, one to weather radar unserviceability and five to engine problems. Four unscheduled engine changes were made – two at Bahrain, one at Singapore and one in London, two of these incidents being due to foreign object ingestion and two to failure of a welded fuel spray shroud, to overcome which a modification was already in process of being introduced.

Like Air France with Concorde 203, British Airways arranged to complete the usual maintenance checks that would be provided in the course of 1,250 hrs, in the accelerated cycle of 525 hrs. This included some maintenance at Bahrain, with the bulk of the effort being expended at London Heathrow.

During these endurance flights, Concorde 204 encountered several occurrences of abrupt temperature sheer at high altitudes, apparently associated with monsoon conditions. If Concorde flies into colder air, the immediate tendency is for engine power to increase for a fixed throttle setting, and the autopilot, programmed to maintain a constant Mach number, reacted to this by raising the nose to kill the excess speed. This resulted in some unexpected altitude excursions – as much as 4,000 ft (1 220 m) being gained quite rapidly – and led the British airworthiness authorities to withold the issue of a full C of A pending further investigations (undertaken by Concorde 201, as the auto-pilot is a French responsibility) and possible amendment of the autopilot to control such sudden speed variations through an auto-throttle rather than by changing altitude. The French authorities, however, took the view that this was an operational matter to be handled by the crew and need not be considered relevant to the Flight Manual; hence the award of a French C of A was not delayed. British certification duly followed, the C of A being formally accepted by Sir George Edwards, chairman of BAC, on 5 December.

Following completion of the endurance flying, Concorde 204 returned to Filton to be refurbished prior to delivery to British Airways early in 1976 as the back up for Concorde 206.

Concorde 205

The first French delivery Concorde, registered F-BVFA, flew on 25 October 1975 and reached Mach 2·11 – the first to fly at bisonic speed on its initial excursion. This is the aircraft to be used to inaugurate Air France services on 21 January 1976, at fares 20 per cent above the normal first class rates. There will be, initially, two round trips on the route Paris-Rio de Janeiro by way of Dakar, operating from Paris at 13.00 hrs each Sunday and Wednesday, and departing from Rio at 20.30 hrs on the same days – a total of 25 hrs flying each week, well within the capabilities of a single aircraft. During 1976, Air France is to receive Concorde 207 (due to fly in February) and Concorde 209 (to fly in May).

Concorde 206

British Airways' first delivery Concorde, G-BOAA, flew from Filton to Fairford on 5 November 1975 for final preparations prior to its introduction into service on 21 January 1976, achieving Mach 2·06 and 63,000 ft (19 215 m) on the first flight. The initial operation provides for an 11.00 hrs departure each Monday and Wednesday for Bahrain, with return flights departing Bahrain at 09.45 hrs each Tuesday and Thursday. The aircraft is operating in a single-class layout with 100 seats, and the initial schedule calls for only 16 hrs flying per week.

By the end of 1976, British Airways should have received Concordes 208 and 210, in addition to the refurbished 204 which will at first be used to back up the initial operations. The final Concorde on the present order, the twelfth production aircraft, will be delivered in early 1977. □

The three-view drawing below depicts the Concorde in standard production form.

was then engaged in the training of Air France crews at Toulouse and Dakar. After appearing at the Paris Air Show, it undertook a block of 80 hours endurance flying (39 flights, of which 37 supersonic) with official check pilots as a preliminary to the full endurance programme on Concorde 203 and 204. Automatic landing certification flights were made at Toulouse in July, followed by a series of flights by FAA pilots checking French and British certification data with a view to ultimate validation of the C of A by the US authorities. The most recent task has been a programme of flying from Singapore, in October and November, to obtain data on temperature sheer effects and to check auto-pilot modifications, following the experiences of Concorde 204 during the endurance flying programme.

Concorde 202

First flown on 13 February 1974, the first British-assembled production Concorde, G-BBDG, also went supersonic on its first flight (Mach 1·4). Initially to a similar standard to F-WTSB with Olympus 620 engines, Concorde 202 was engaged during March on performance testing and some measurements of cabin comfort, with a total of 70 passengers on board. After flight No 27 on 30 April, it was grounded for a number of updating modifications, including the fitting of "entry into service" Olympus 610 engines, resuming flight on 3 July. The Olympus 610 had by this time replaced the Mk 602 as the production standard, having control system modifications to increase the climb and cruise performance.

For hot weather trials and cabin assessments, G-BBDG flew to Bahrain on 7 August 1974, then going on to Singapore and chalking up Concorde's 3,000th flying hour in the process, on 12 September 1974. In the course of the air conditioning tests for Bahrain, on 17 August, 100 passengers were carried at supersonic speed for the first time, and the flight on to Singapore provided the longest continuous supersonic sortie, of 3 hr 4 min. Returning to Fairford in September, Concorde 202 flew to Casablanca on 28 October for several weeks of certification flying, with CEV and CAA pilots participating. During this time, the maximum take-off weight was taken up to 400,600 lb (181 700 kg), and on Flight No 147 on 14 December a failure occurred in No 2 engine at Mach 1·8 (a first-stage high-pressure compressor blade having broken). A safe landing was made on three engines.

Certification flying continued in the UK and, briefly, Casablanca again in January 1975, with a visit to Madrid in February for measured take-off and landing tests required for certification. The completion of these tests left Concorde 202 free to undertake British Airways crew conversion at Fairford in April, this being interrupted in May for a visit to Singapore in preparation for the endurance programme to be flown by Concorde 204. More crew training and certification flying has

been undertaken by G-BBDG at Fairford during the summer of 1975.

Concorde 203

The third production Concorde, F-WTSC, flew on 31 January 1975 and achieved Mach 1·82 in its first flight. With a small amount of flight test equipment in the cabin, it had 76 passenger seats, four abreast, in three different sections, at 34-in, 38-in and 40-in (86-cm, 96,5-cm and 101,6-cm) pitch, to permit airline representatives to compare various layouts under operational conditions. It was the first Concorde to have overhead stowage bins in place of luggage racks.

During February and March, a few flights were made for performance and certification purposes, these including the longest subsonic flight yet, on 20 March, when 3,740 mls (6 020 km) were covered in 6 hr 28 min; of 198,910 lb (90 305 kg) of fuel uplifted, 21,380 lb (9 700 kg) remained at landing. After a period on the ground in preparation for the endurance programme, flying was resumed on 8 May, a few flights being made to complete the C of A testing before the start of endurance flying on 28 May. As an essential preliminary, the French civil aviation authority SGAC awarded Concorde 203 a Special Category C of A on 22 May. The requirement was for two Concordes to complete about 1,000 hrs of typical airline route flying and to be subjected to typical airline maintenance procedures.

The French contribution to this task, made by Concorde 203, comprised 125 flights, completed on 2 August, totalling 375 hrs 23 min of which 258 hr 20 min were supersonic, and on which 4,680 passengers were carried. The aircraft operated on the routes Paris-Dakar, Paris-Dakar-Rio, Paris-Lisbon-Caracas, Paris-Gander, and Paris-Paris via the Atlantic or the Mediterranean. No scheduled flights were cancelled in this period and only 11 suffered departure delays of more than five minutes. The Air France maintenance cycle, normally completed in four equal steps in 1,250 flying hours, was condensed into the period of the endurance trials. Upon their conclusion, Concorde 203 went into the shops at Toulouse for a prolonged rework for eventual delivery to Air France, expected to be effected at the end of December.

The completion of the endurance programme and of all outstanding certification work cleared the way for the SGAC to award a certificate of airworthiness to the Concorde on 9 October. The Olympus 593 Mk 610-14-28 had been similarly certificated on 29 September, the "14-28" in this designation referring to the nozzle.

Concorde 204

The second British production aircraft flew from Filton to Fairford on 27 February and was fitted with 112 seats in order to be used for full air conditioning measurements. In the course

Concorde 205 in its new Air France livery (see page 60 also). First flown on 25 October 1975, this is the aircraft with which Air France was to inaugurate services on the route Paris-Dakar-Rio on 21 January.

156 Tank vent
157 Transfer pump
158 Port outer elevon control unit fairing
159 Static dischargers
160 Honeycomb elevon structure
161 Flexible joint
162 Port middle elevon control hinge/fairing
163 Power control unit twin output
164 Control rod linkage
165 Nacelle aft support link
166 Reverser-bucket actuating screw jack
167 Retractable silencer lobes ('spades')
168 Primary (inner) variable nozzle
169 Pneumatic nozzle actuators
170 Nozzle-mounting spigots

171 Port inner elevon control hinge/fairing
172 Control rod linkage
173 Location of ram-air turbine (RAT) in production aircraft
174 Accumulator
175 Vent and pressurisation system
176 Forged wing/fuselage main frames

177 Ground-supply air-conditioning connection
178 Control mixing unit
179 Control rod (elevon) linkage
180 Aft galley unit
181 Rear emergency doors (port and starboard)
182 Wingroot fillet
183 Air-conditioning manual discharge valve
184 Automatic discharge/relief valve
185 First-aid oxygen cylinders
186 Rear baggage compartment (door to starboard)

187 Rear pressure bulkhead
188 Fin support frames
189 No 11 aft trim tank
190 Machined centre posts
191 Shock absorber
192 Retractable tail bumper
193 Tail bumper door
194 Tank overflow and pressure relief lines
195 Tail cone bulkhead
196 Fuel jettison

197 Monergol-powered emergency power unit (pre-production aircraft only)
198 Tail cone
199 Rear navigation light
200 Rudder lower section
201 Servo control unit fairing (manual stand-by)
202 Fixed rubber stub
203 Multi-bolt fin-spar attachment
204 Fin construction
205 Fin spar
206 Air-conditioning ducting
207 HF antennæ
208 Finroot fairing
209 Leading-edge structure
210 Servo unit threshold bellcrank
211 Servo control unit fairing
212 VOR antenna
213 Rudder upper section
214 Static dischargers

BAC/Aérospatiale Concorde Specification

Power Plant: Four Rolls-Royce/SNECMA Olympus 593 Mk 610-14-28 axial-flow two-spool turbojets rated at 38,050 lb st (17 620 kgp) for take-off with afterburners and at 10,030 lb (4 550 kg) for cruise at Mach=2·0 at 53,000 ft (16 165 m) at ISA+5 deg C. Fuel contained in ten wing tanks and two fuselage tanks, plus four tanks in wing and two fuselage tanks and one in rear fuselage for trim purposes, total usable. fuel capacity, approx 26 260 Imp gal (119 280 l).

Performance: Max permitted cruise speed, Mach 2·02 or 530 knots CAS (whichever is the lower) equalling 1,330 mph (2 150 km/h) TAS at altitudes above 36,000 ft (10 980 m); initial rate of climb, 5,000 ft/min (25,4 m/sec); service ceiling about 60,000 ft (18 290 m); take-off distance to 35 ft (10,7 m), 10,400 ft (3 170 m); landing distance from 35 ft (10,7 m), 7,980 ft (2 432 m); range with 15,000-lb (6 804-kg) payload and FAR reserves, 4,080 mls (6 560 km); range with max payload and FAR reserves, 3,050 mls (4 900 km) at Mach 0·93 at 30,000 ft (9 150 m), 3,853 mls (6 196 km) at Mach 2·02 wing cruise/climb.

Weights: Operational weight empty, 174,750 lb (79 266 kg); max fuel load, 210,370 lb (95 430 kg); max payload, 25,000 lb (11 340 kg); max take-off, 400,000 lb (181 440 kg); max landing, 245,000 lb (111 130 kg).

Dimensions: Span, 83 ft 10 in (25,56 m); length, 202 ft 4 in (61,74 m); height, 37 ft 1 in (11,32 m); undercarriage track, 25 ft 4 in (7,71 m); wheelbase, 59 ft 8 in (18,19 m); wing area, 3,856 sq ft (358,25 m²); aspect ratio, 1·7:1.

Accommodation: Flight crew of two pilots and systems engineer, with fourth seat on flight deck for supernumery crew. Four-abreast seating in cabin provides 108 seats in "superior" or mixed class arrangements, 128 in standard class at 34 in (86 cm) pitch or 144 at 32 in (81 cm) pitch. Cabin length, 115 ft (35,04 m), max width, 8 ft 7½ in (2,63 m), ceiling height, 6 ft 5 in (1,96 m). Cabin volume, 8,440 cu ft (238,5 m³).

PLANE FACTS

Last of the SIAI-Marchetti airliners

During the autumn of 1945, I had an opportunity to see a rather sleek-looking Italian four-engined airliner at Farnborough. I was told that it was a prototype and designated Savoia Marchetti SM 95, and subsequently heard that it went into production. Can you tell me something of the history of this type and, if possible, publish photographs and a general arrangement drawing?

S/L R G Smith RAF (Retd)
London W1N 4AR

The Societa Italiana Aeroplani Idrovolanti "Savoia-Marchetti", or SIAI-Marchetti, was responsible for the development and manufacture of a long series of multi-engined commercial transport aircraft, but the SM 95 marked a significant departure from this concern's previous design practice in being a four-engined low-wing monoplane (the only previous SIAI-Marchetti four-engined transport being the shoulder-wing SM 74), and was destined to be the last "Savoia-Marchetti" airliner to enter commercial service.

The design of the SM 95 was initiated as an 18-passenger commercial airliner in 1941, being essentially a four-engined derivative of the SM 75 tri-motor, and construction of a prototype and two pre-production examples began in the following year, together with a fourth airframe which was to be completed as the SM 95B long-range bomber. Although consideration was given to the installation of both the 14-cylinder Piaggio P XIbis RC 40 and the 18-cylinder Piaggio P XII RC 35, the nine-cylinder Alfa Romeo 128 RC 18 was finally selected, but in the event, availability dictated the installation of the lower-powered Alfa Romeo 126 RC 34, this last-mentioned engine being rated at 780 hp at 2,185 rpm for take-off. The SM 95 was of mixed construction, the wings being wooden three-spar structures with plywood skinning and the fuselage having a welded steel-tube framework with light alloy skinning for the nose, underside and rear section, the sides and upper surfaces being ply and fabric covered.

(Above) The second (ie, first pre-production) SM 95 at Farnborough, this, together with the prototype, having the original short fuselage.

(Above) The second pre-production SM 95 (or SM 95GA) which featured the lengthened fuselage standardized for the production model, an example of which (I-DALJ Cristoforo Colombo) is illustrated below.

The prototype was flown on 8 May 1943, and was sequestered by the *Luftwaffe*, allegedly serving with *Transportgeschwader 5* and based at Mühldorf. The first pre-production SM 95 was flown to the UK in the summer of 1945, and its ultimate fate is uncertain, although it is believed to have been returned to Italy for operation by the *Aeronautica Militare*. The second pre-production aircraft was completed as the SM 95GA (*Grande Autonomia*) with lengthened fuselage, increased fuel tankage and modified instrumentation. Somewhat surprisingly, the fourth airframe, the SM 95B long-range bomber prototype, was completed and actually flew in 1945. This retained the wings, tail assembly and engines of the transport model, these components being married to an essentially new fuselage which was deepened to permit the insertion of a bomb-bay beneath the wing carry-through structure. The flight deck was moved forward and a glazed nose was provided for the bombardier. Defensive armament consisted of a 12,7-mm Breda-SAFAT machine gun in a turret immediately aft of the flight deck and similar weapons firing from lateral positions aft and from a ventral position forward of the bomb-bay. Unfortunately, no photographs of this prototype are available.

As initially built, the SM 95 accommodated a flight crew of four and 18 passengers in three-abreast (two-plus-one) seating, but when series production was launched in 1946, the fuselage was lengthened from the 72 ft 11 in (22.24 m) of the prototype and first pre-production example to the 81 ft 3 in (24.77 m) of the second pre-production example, this permitting accommodation to be raised to 30 passengers, the three-abreast

The head-on and plan views below illustrate the Pegasus-engined production SM 95, the sideviews illustrating (top to bottom) the prototype, the SM 95GA, the SM 95B bomber and the Pegasus-engined production SM 95.

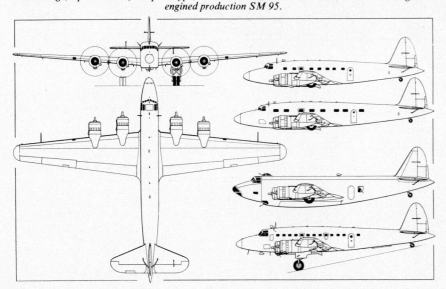

(two-plus-one) seating being retained. The flight deck was redesigned and enlarged, and the cabin windows rearranged. The overall span and gross wing area remained constant at 112 ft 5¾ in (34,28 m) and 1,381 sq ft (128,3 m²) respectively.

Six SM 95s were ordered by Alitalia and the first two of these, I-DALJ *Cristoforo Colombo* and I-DALK *Amerigo Vespucci* delivered at the end of 1947, were powered by nine-cylinder Alfa Romeo 128 RC 18 radials each rated at 930 hp for take-off and 850 hp at 5,905 ft (1 800 m), but the remaining aircraft, I-DALL *Marco Polo*, I-DALM, I-DALN *Sebastiano Caboto* and I-DALO *Ugolino Vivaldi*, were delivered with nine-cylinder Bristol Pegasus 48s each rated at 1,000 hp for take-off and 740 hp at 14,500 ft (4 420 m), the initial two aircraft subsequently being re-engined. Alitalia inaugurated its first postwar service to the UK on 3 April 1948 with I-DALN but withdrew its SM 95s from service during 1951, having taken over three additional SM 95s from LATI in April of the previous year when that concern ceased operations. The LATI aircraft were I-LAIT *Sant' Antonio*, I-LATI *San Francesco* and I-LITA *San Cristoforo*. The only other commercial operator of the SM 95 was SAIDE of Egypt which employed three, SU-AFC, SU-AFD and SU-AGC, on services from Cairo to Athens, Rome, Paris, Milan, Alexandria, Benghazi and Tripoli. Whereas Alitalia SM 95s normally accommodated 20 passengers, those operated by LATI had accommodation for 26 and those serving with SAIDE carried as many as 38 passengers over the company's shorter routes, the Egyptian operator's SM 95s being, like the LATI aircraft, powered by 14-cylinder Pratt & Whitney R-1830-S1C3G Twin Wasp engines

The fourth prototype of the Nakajima G8N1 Renzan long-range heavy bomber which was shipped to the USA after the termination of hostilities.

rated at 1,215 hp for take-off and 1,065 hp at 7,500 ft (2 286 m).

The Pegasus 48-engined SM 95 had an empty weight of 30,865 lb (14 000 kg) and a max take-off weight of 48,502 lb (22 000 kg), and performance included a max speed of 238 mph (384 km/h) at 9,840 ft (3 000 m), cruising speeds of 184 mph (296 km/h) at 70 per cent power and 171 mph (276 km/h) at 60 per cent power at 11,480 ft (3 500 m), service ceiling being 22,310 ft (6 800 m). A total of 12 production SM 95s was built for commercial operation.

Nakajima's "Mountain Range"

Will you please publish any information, drawings and photographs available of the four-engined Nakajima G8N1 Renzan bomber which appears to have had a superficial resemblance to the B-17.

B W Sandars
Mentone, Victoria 3194, Australia

The Nakajima G8N1 Renzan (Mountain Range) long-range heavy bomber, assigned the reporting name *Rita* by the Allies, was designed to meet the requirements of an 18-*Shi* (1943) specification for a shore-based attack aircraft to be operated by the Imperial Navy, and the first of four prototypes was flown on 23 October 1944. Powered by four Nakajima NK9K-L Homare 24 18-cylinder radials equipped with Hitachi 92 turbo-super-chargers and rated at 2,000 hp for take-off and 1,850 hp at 26,245 ft (8 000 m), the G8N1 Renzan was of all-metal construction with a mid-mounted laminar-flow wing and a crew of 10, defensive armament comprising twin 20-mm Type 99 cannon in power-operated dorsal, ventral and tail turrets, twin 13-mm Type 2 machine guns in a power-operated nose turret and two additional 13-mm weapons on flexible mountings firing from beam positions. The normal bomb load comprised four 551-lb (200-kg) bombs but up to two 4,409-lb (2 000 kg) bombs could be carried.

In the event, the planned production programme (which anticipated the completion of 48 Renzan bombers by September 1945) was cancelled owing to Japan's critical shortage of light alloys and the manufacturing priorities assigned to other types, but three additional prototypes were completed (in December 1944, and March and June 1945 respectively), the second prototype flying on 12 April 1945 and subsequently being dismantled for components, the third prototype being destroyed on the ground by US Navy fighters before it could join the flight test programme and the fourth prototype being transported intact to the USA after the termination of hostilities. A production version powered by 2,200 hp Mitsubishi MK9A engines was proposed as the G8N2 Renzan-Kai, and the possibility of manufacturing an all-steel version, the G8N3 was still under consideration at the time of Japan's surrender.

The G8N1 had empty and normal loaded weights of 38,360 lb (17 400 kg) and 59,084 lb (26 800 kg) respectively, max overload weight being 70,879 lb (32 150 kg). Performance included a max speed of 368 mph (592 km/h) at 26,245 ft (8 000 m), a long-range cruise of 230 mph (370 km/h) at 13,125 ft (4 000 m), normal and max ranges of 2,452 mls (3 946 km) and 4,639 mls (7 466 km) respectively, a service ceiling of 33,465 ft (10 200 m) and the ability to climb (at normal loaded weight) to 26,245 ft (8 000 m) in 17·5 min. Overall dimensions were: span, 106 ft 9 in (32,54 m); length, 75 ft 3 in (22,93 m); height, 23 ft 7½ in (7,20 m); wing area, 1,205·55 sq ft (112,0 m²).

(Above and below) The G8N1 Renzan was developed to meet an Imperial Navy requirement.

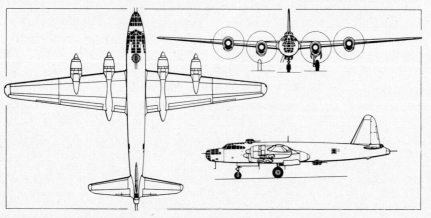

TANK'S "SECOND IRON"

EIN ZWEITES EISEN IM FEUER — a second iron in the fire! Such was the *raison d'être* of Dipl-Ing Kurt Tank's compact, well-proportioned and æsthetically-appealing single-seat fighter that first fired its guns in anger over the Channel Front with *II Gruppe* of *Jagdgeschwader* 26 *"Schlageter"* in July 1941. Several fighters were to display the hallmark of the thorough-bred during World War II — aircraft that were outstanding to varying degrees of excellence in their combat performance, their amenability to a variety of operational scenarios, their ease of pilot handling and their field maintenance tractability — but none more so than Tank's remarkable creation sporting the prosaic designation of Focke-Wulf Fw 190 but dubbed more emotively if unofficially the *Würger* (Butcher-bird — a species of shrike) by its designer himself.

Within six or seven months of its operational début, the Fw 190 was causing widespread consternation among RAF fighter squadrons based in the south of England. The Tank-designed fighter could out-perform the contemporary Spitfire on every count with the exception of the turning circle — one leading RAF pilot is recorded as having commented acidly when this attribute of his mount was stressed during a pre-operation briefing, "Turning doesn't win battles!". By April 1942, RAF combat attrition on the Channel Front reached prohibitive levels primarily as a result of the activities of its redoubtable German adversary — more than a hundred Spitfires being lost

Viewed from the Cockpit

by Captain Eric Brown, CBE, DSC, AFC, RN

on offensive operations over Occupied Europe during the course of the month — and the Merlin 61-engined Spitfire Mk IX was still two or three months away. But while going a long way towards redressing the balance and even offering an edge in climb and performance above 26,000 feet (7 925 m), the Spitfire Mk IX was still to be left standing by the Focke-Wulf's half-roll and dive!

The Fw 190 was to reveal defects — and what fighter yet conceived has been perfect? — but it probably came as close to perfection by the standards of the day as any contemporary. Yet its gestation and, indeed, early infancy were not attended by any noticeable enthusiasm on the part of the Operations Staff, the *Luftwaffenführungsstab*, which held the somewhat complacent opinion that a back-up for Messerschmitt's Bf 109 was unnecessary and serious consideration of a successor premature. Fortunately for the *Jagdflieger*, the *Reichsluftfahrt-ministerium* adopted a somewhat more far-sighted attitude, and while its Technical Department was not very favourably disposed towards a *radial*-engined fighter, the potential supply situation of the Daimler-Benz series of liquid-cooled in-line engines in the years immediately ahead motivated acceptance of Kurt Tank's proposal that the new radial air-cooled engine being developed by the Bayerische Motoren Werke should be given serious consideration as a fighter power plant.

The blending of the bulky radial engine into the contours of the new fighter was nothing short of masterly and as an exercise in the mating of compactness with functional elegance the Focke-Wulf design was a masterpiece. It was to suffer its share of vicissitudes during development — the decision to terminate development of the BMW 139 engine around which it had been designed very nearly brought about its premature demise — but it was to be recognized by the *Luftwaffe* as potentially a truly outstanding combat aircraft long before attaining maturity; a view with which the RAF was reluctantly to concur once the service had tested the mettle of the newcomer in French skies.

Indeed, as the months passed and the Focke-Wulf consolidated the ascendancy that it had established over its RAF contemporaries from the time of its operational début, morale of pilots of the Spitfire Mk V squadrons inevitably being affected, Air Ministry concern over the situation began to border on desperation which generated a crop of bizarre schemes for acquiring an example of this *bête noire* so that it could be thoroughly analysed and its Achilles Heel — for such, it was believed, must surely exist — revealed for the edification of RAF Fighter Command. Plans were, in fact, being formulated

(Below) Arnim Faber's Fw 190A-3 photographed at the RAE on 13 July 1942, immediately prior to being flown to the Air Fighting Development Unit at Duxford. The purposeful lines of Kurt Tank's fighter may be seen clearly from this photograph (above) of Faber's Fw 190A-3 taken on 11 August 1942, while undergoing AFDU trials.

for a commando raid on a *Luftwaffe* fighter base with the object of sequestering a Focke-Wulf, when, at 2035 hours on 23 June 1942, one *Oberleutnant* Arnim Faber landed on what he took to be a *Luftwaffe* airfield on the Cherbourg Peninsula. Taxying slowly along the runway under a marshaller's orders, Faber was intensely surprised when someone leaped onto the wing of his fighter and pointed a Verey pistol at his head! The RAF finally had its Fw 190!

The Portreath and Exeter Spitfire Wings, which had been engaged in a support sweep over Brittany, had, unbeknown to them, been trailed across the Channel by Fw 190s of the *Gruppenstab* of *III Gruppe* and 7. *Staffel* of *Jagdgeschwader* 2 from Maupertus and Morlaix. Flying low, the Spitfires had been approaching Start Point on the Devonian coast when the Fw 190s had curved out of the low sun, one of them, flown by *Unteroffizier* Willi Reuschling, promptly colliding with the Spitfire flown by Wg Cdr Alois Vasatko. The ensuing combat between the surviving fighters had been brief as both RAF and *Luftwaffe* aircraft were critically low on fuel, but one of the Focke-Wulfs, its pilot apparently disorientated, had flown away in a north-easterly direction towards Exeter.

Four Spitfires had been hurriedly scrambled by the Exeter Wing, two crashing on take-off, one returning to base with R/T trouble and the other being summarily despatched by the lone Fw 190 with which contact had then been lost until it appeared barrel-rolling across RAF Pembrey, near Swansea. Lowering its undercarriage while still inverted, the fighter had landed off a steep turn. The Duty Pilot, one Sgt Jeffreys, who had followed the Focke-Wulf's antics through binoculars, grabbed a Very pistol, ran from the control tower and jumped on to the wing of the fighter as it taxied in. Arnim Faber had apparently inadvertently flown a reciprocal course, mistaken the northern coastline of the Bristol Channel for the Cherbourg Peninsula and, in the poor light, failed to realize that he was landing on an RAF airfield.

It was thus that the RAF acquired Fw 190A-3 *Werk-Nr* 5313. The depths of its pilot's despair at unwittingly providing his enemies with such a prize may be gauged from the fact that he subsequently attempted suicide, and my compassion for him was certainly to be stimulated some time later, in February 1944, when I very nearly suffered a similar experience while testing a new Typhoon from Farnborough above cloud — although no navigational error was to be involved in my case, my near close-acquaintance with a *Luftwaffe* airfield resulting from deliberate radio direction spoofing by the Germans.

Elegant lethality

The RAF took advantage of its windfall of 23 June 1942 with creditable rapidity. It was promptly transported by road from Pembrey to the Royal Aircraft Establishment at Farnborough, both airframe and engine being dismantled and thoroughly analysed before re-assembly, and on 3 July, a mere 10 days after landing at Pembrey, the Fw 190A-3 was flown at the RAE by Wg Cdr (later Gp Capt) Hugh J Wilson as MP499. Ten days later, on 13 July, this invaluable prize was delivered to the Air Fighting Development Unit at Duxford, where it was put through intensive performance trials and flown competitively against several Allied fighter types.

The AFDU trials confirmed what the RAF already knew — that the Fw 190 was a truly outstanding combat aircraft. They also produced vitally important information which went some way towards restoring the situation in so far as the RAF was concerned and in eradicating something of the awe in which the Focke-Wulf had come to be held by Allied pilots. It was concluded that the Fw 190 pilot trying to "mix it" with a Spitfire in the classic fashion of steep turning was doomed, for at any speed — even below the German fighter's stalling speed — it would be out-turned by its British opponent. Of course, the *Luftwaffe* was aware of this fact and a somewhat odd style of dogfighting evolved in which the Fw 190 pilots endeavoured to keep on the vertical plane by zooms and dives, while their Spitfire-mounted antagonists tried everything in the book to draw them on to the horizontal. If the German pilot lost his head and failed to resist the temptation to try a horizontal pursuit curve on a Spitfire, as likely as not, before he could recover the speed lost in a steep turn he would find another Spitfire turning inside him! On the other hand, the German pilot who kept zooming up and down was usually the recipient of only difficult deflection shots of more than 30 deg. The Fw 190 had tremendous initial acceleration in a dive but it was extremely vulnerable during a pull-out, recovery having to be quite progressive with care not to kill the speed by "sinking".

Arnim Faber's Fw 190A-3 was thoroughly wrung out and dispelled the mystique with which the Focke-Wulf had been surrounded during the first year of its operational career; the fortuitous acquisition of this one warplane probably saving the lives of countless RAF pilots. But familiarity certainly did not breed contempt, for although conversant with both attributes and shortcomings of the fighter, we were equally conversant with the fact that it had to be treated with the utmost respect as an antagonist, despite its awesome reputation by now having been placed in perspective.

By the time I arrived at Farnborough, the Fw 190A-3 that had been delivered to Pembrey had served its purpose and been finally grounded — the last recorded flight having taken place on 29 January 1943 and the airframe being struck off charge eight months later, on 18 September, for firing trials. Its place in the RAE inventory had been taken by an Fw 190A-4, which, assigned the serial PE882, had landed in error at RAF West Malling during the early hours of 17 April 1943. Two other examples of the A-4 sub-type of the Focke-Wulf fighter were to fall into our hands at around this time, incidentally, both landing in error at RAF Manston during night operations, one on 20 May and the other on 20 June 1943, these acquiring the serials PM679 and PN999.

I recall clearly the excitement with which I first examined the Focke-Wulf fighter; the impression of elegant lethality that its functional yet pleasing lines exuded. To me it represented the very quintessence of aeronautical pulchritude from any angle. It was not, to my eye, *more* beautiful than the Spitfire, but its beauty took a different form — the contrast being such as that between blonde and brunette! It sat high on the ground, the oleo legs of its undercarriage appearing extraordinarily long, and it was immediately obvious that, despite the superlative job of cowling done by the Focke-Wulf designers, the big BMW 801D air-cooled radial engine was pretty obtrusive. Nevertheless, I was pleasantly surprised to find, after clambering into the some-

The Fw 190A-4/U8 flown by the author is seen above, on 20 April 1943, three days after its arrival in the UK and prior to the removal of wing bomb pylons and fuselage rack, and (below) at a somewhat later stage in the RAF flight test programme, after these appendages had been removed.

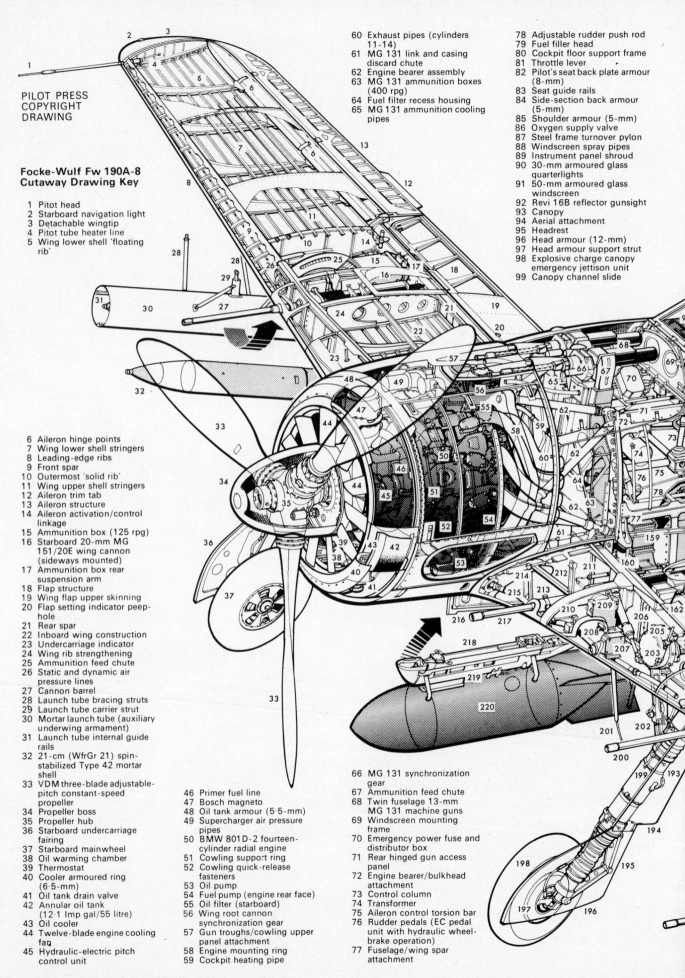

PILOT PRESS
COPYRIGHT
DRAWING

**Focke-Wulf Fw 190A-8
Cutaway Drawing Key**

1 Pitot head
2 Starboard navigation light
3 Detachable wingtip
4 Pitot tube heater line
5 Wing lower shell 'floating rib'

6 Aileron hinge points
7 Wing lower shell stringers
8 Leading-edge ribs
9 Front spar
10 Outermost 'solid rib'
11 Wing upper shell stringers
12 Aileron trim tab
13 Aileron structure
14 Aileron activation/control linkage
15 Ammunition box (125 rpg)
16 Starboard 20-mm MG 151/20E wing cannon (sideways mounted)
17 Ammunition box rear suspension arm
18 Flap structure
19 Wing flap upper skinning
20 Flap setting indicator peep-hole
21 Rear spar
22 Inboard wing construction
23 Undercarriage indicator
24 Wing rib strengthening
25 Ammunition feed chute
26 Static and dynamic air pressure lines
27 Cannon barrel
28 Launch tube bracing struts
29 Launch tube carrier strut
30 Mortar launch tube (auxiliary underwing armament)
31 Launch tube internal guide rails
32 21-cm (WfrGr 21) spin-stabilized Type 42 mortar shell
33 VDM three-blade adjustable-pitch constant-speed propeller
34 Propeller boss
35 Propeller hub
36 Starboard undercarriage fairing
37 Starboard mainwheel
38 Oil warming chamber
39 Thermostat
40 Cooler armoured ring (6·5-mm)
41 Oil tank drain valve
42 Annular oil tank (12·1 Imp gal/55 litre)
43 Oil cooler
44 Twelve-blade engine cooling fan
45 Hydraulic-electric pitch control unit

46 Primer fuel line
47 Bosch magneto
48 Oil tank armour (5·5-mm)
49 Supercharger air pressure pipes
50 BMW 801D-2 fourteen-cylinder radial engine
51 Cowling support ring
52 Cowling quick-release fasteners
53 Oil pump
54 Fuel pump (engine rear face)
55 Oil filter (starboard)
56 Wing root cannon synchronization gear
57 Gun troughs/cowling upper panel attachment
58 Engine mounting ring
59 Cockpit heating pipe

60 Exhaust pipes (cylinders 11-14)
61 MG 131 link and casing discard chute
62 Engine bearer assembly
63 MG 131 ammunition boxes (400 rpg)
64 Fuel filter recess housing
65 MG 131 ammunition cooling pipes

66 MG 131 synchronization gear
67 Ammunition feed chute
68 Twin fuselage 13-mm MG 131 machine guns
69 Windscreen mounting frame
70 Emergency power fuse and distributor box
71 Rear hinged gun access panel
72 Engine bearer/bulkhead attachment
73 Control column
74 Transformer
75 Aileron control torsion bar
76 Rudder pedals (EC pedal unit with hydraulic wheel-brake operation)
77 Fuselage/wing spar attachment

78 Adjustable rudder push rod
79 Fuel filler head
80 Cockpit floor support frame
81 Throttle lever
82 Pilot's seat back plate armour (8-mm)
83 Seat guide rails
84 Side-section back armour (5-mm)
85 Shoulder armour (5-mm)
86 Oxygen supply valve
87 Steel frame turnover pylon
88 Windscreen spray pipes
89 Instrument panel shroud
90 30-mm armoured glass quarterlights
91 50-mm armoured glass windscreen
92 Revi 16B reflector gunsight
93 Canopy
94 Aerial attachment
95 Headrest
96 Head armour (12-mm)
97 Head armour support strut
98 Explosive charge canopy emergency jettison unit
99 Canopy channel slide

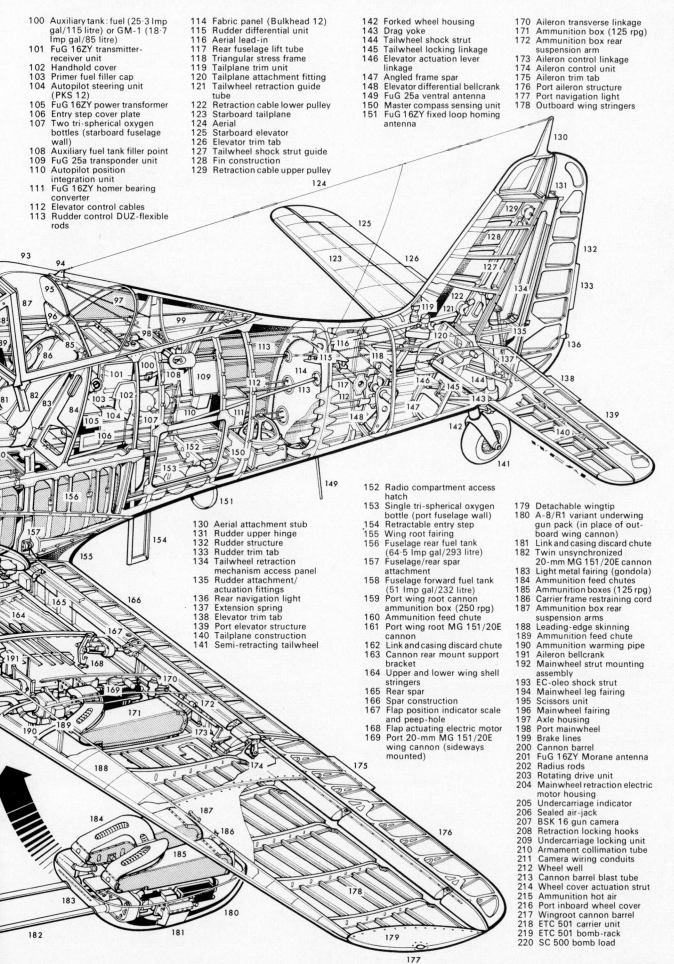

100 Auxiliary tank: fuel (25·3 Imp gal/115 litre) or GM-1 (18·7 Imp gal/85 litre)
101 FuG 16ZY transmitter-receiver unit
102 Handhold cover
103 Primer fuel filler cap
104 Autopilot steering unit (PKS 12)
105 FuG 16ZY power transformer
106 Entry step cover plate
107 Two tri-spherical oxygen bottles (starboard fuselage wall)
108 Auxiliary fuel tank filler point
109 FuG 25a transponder unit
110 Autopilot position integration unit
111 FuG 16ZY homer bearing converter
112 Elevator control cables
113 Rudder control DUZ-flexible rods

114 Fabric panel (Bulkhead 12)
115 Rudder differential unit
116 Aerial lead-in
117 Rear fuselage lift tube
118 Triangular stress frame
119 Tailplane trim unit
120 Tailplane attachment fitting
121 Tailwheel retraction guide tube
122 Retraction cable lower pulley
123 Starboard tailplane
124 Aerial
125 Starboard elevator
126 Elevator trim tab
127 Tailwheel shock strut guide
128 Fin construction
129 Retraction cable upper pulley

142 Forked wheel housing
143 Drag yoke
144 Tailwheel shock strut
145 Tailwheel locking linkage
146 Elevator actuation lever linkage
147 Angled frame spar
148 Elevator differential bellcrank
149 FuG 25a ventral antenna
150 Master compass sensing unit
151 FuG 16ZY fixed loop homing antenna

152 Radio compartment access hatch
153 Single tri-spherical oxygen bottle (port fuselage wall)
154 Retractable entry step
155 Wing root fairing
156 Fuselage rear fuel tank (64·5 Imp gal/293 litre)
157 Fuselage/rear spar attachment
158 Fuselage forward fuel tank (51 Imp gal/232 litre)
159 Port wing root cannon ammunition box (250 rpg)
160 Ammunition feed chute
161 Port wing root MG 151/20E cannon
162 Link and casing discard chute
163 Cannon rear mount support bracket
164 Upper and lower wing shell stringers
165 Rear spar
166 Spar construction
167 Flap position indicator scale and peep-hole
168 Flap actuating electric motor
169 Port 20-mm MG 151/20E wing cannon (sideways mounted)

170 Aileron transverse linkage
171 Ammunition box (125 rpg)
172 Ammunition box rear suspension arm
173 Aileron control linkage
174 Aileron control unit
175 Aileron trim tab
176 Port aileron structure
177 Port navigation light
178 Outboard wing stringers

130 Aerial attachment stub
131 Rudder upper hinge
132 Rudder structure
133 Rudder trim tab
134 Tailwheel retraction mechanism access panel
135 Rudder attachment/ actuation fittings
136 Rear navigation light
137 Extension spring
138 Elevator trim tab
139 Port elevator structure
140 Tailplane construction
141 Semi-retracting tailwheel

179 Detachable wingtip
180 A-8/R1 variant underwing gun pack (in place of outboard wing cannon)
181 Link and casing discard chute
182 Twin unsynchronized 20-mm MG 151/20E cannon
183 Light metal fairing (gondola)
184 Ammunition feed chutes
185 Ammunition boxes (125 rpg)
186 Carrier frame restraining cord
187 Ammunition box rear suspension arms
188 Leading-edge skinning
189 Ammunition feed chute
190 Ammunition warming pipe
191 Aileron bellcrank
192 Mainwheel strut mounting assembly
193 EC-oleo shock strut
194 Mainwheel leg fairing
195 Scissors unit
196 Mainwheel fairing
197 Axle housing
198 Port mainwheel
199 Brake lines
200 Cannon barrel
201 FuG 16ZY Morane antenna
202 Radius rods
203 Rotating drive unit
204 Mainwheel retraction electric motor housing
205 Undercarriage indicator
206 Sealed air-jack
207 BSK 16 gun camera
208 Retraction locking hooks
209 Undercarriage locking unit
210 Armament collimation tube
211 Camera wiring conduits
212 Wheel well
213 Cannon barrel blast tube
214 Wheel cover actuation strut
215 Ammunition hot air
216 Port inboard wheel cover
217 Wingroot cannon barrel
218 ETC 501 carrier unit
219 ETC 501 bomb-rack
220 SC 500 bomb load

Fw 190A-4/U8 PE882 under test from Farnborough after removal of the wing pylons and fuselage bomb/drop tank shackles. It was eventually to be written off on 13 October 1944 after transfer to No 1426 Flight at Collyweston.

what narrow cockpit, that the forward view was still rather better than was offered by the Bf 109, the Spitfire or the Mustang. The semi-reclining seat — ideal for high-*g* manœuvres — proved relatively comfortable and the controls fell easily to the hand, although the flight instruments were not, in my opinion, quite so well arranged as those of the contemporary Bf 109G.

In general, the cockpit layout was good and I was fascinated by the ingenious *Kommandgerät*, a sort of "brain-box" relieving the pilot of the job of controlling airscrew pitch, mixture, boost and rpm. The KG 13A control column was of standard type, including a send/receive button for the FuG 16Z radio (which had supplanted the FuG 7a of the A-3 model), a gunnery selector switch and a firing button. This particular example of the fighter (ie, PE882) was, in fact, an Fw 190A-4/U8 *Jabo* with provision for two bomb carriers beneath the wings each capable of carrying a 551-lb (250-kg) SG 250 bomb or a 66-Imp gal (300-l) drop tank and a third carrier beneath the fuselage, the fixed armament being reduced to a pair of 20-mm MG 151 cannon in the wing roots, these being harmonized at 220 yards (200 m) rather than the usual 490 yards (450 m). The sighting view, when sitting comfortably in the normal position, was somewhat better than that of the Spitfire owing to the nose-down attitude of the Fw 190 in flight. The pilot was well protected from frontal attack by the engine and the sharply-sloping 50-mm armour-glass windscreen and from the rear by his shaped 8-mm armour seat-back and 13-mm head-and-shoulder armour, plus small 8-mm plates disposed above and below the seat-back and on each side.

All the ancillary controls were electrically operated by an array of pushbuttons whose creator had obviously never had to think in terms of those massive leather flying gauntlets issued as standard to British pilots and guaranteed to convert their hands into bunches of bananas, and a particularly good feature of the cockpit was the outstanding search view that it offered, the good all-round visibility rendering a rear-view mirror unnecessary.

Superb control harmony

My first opportunity to fly the Focke-Wulf did not arise until 4 February 1944, the actual aircraft being the previously-mentioned Fw 190A-4/U8 PE882. This fighter had seen a lot

of flying from the RAE and was destined, 10 weeks later, to be transferred to No 1426 Flight at Collyweston with which it was to fly until 13 October 1944, when, after a fire in the air, it was to crash on the road between Kettering and Stamford, demolishing three walls before coming to rest in the garden of a house. On this cold February morning at Farnborough, however, the sad demise of this particular Focke-Wulf was still some way into the future, and despite the substantial number of hours that it had flown since reaching British hands, it gave every impression of youthfulness.

The BMW 801D engine was started by an inertia starter energized by a 24-volt external supply or by the aircraft's own battery. The big radial was primed internally, both fuel tanks and pumps selected ON and the cooling gills set to one-third aperture. We had found that the BMW almost invariably fired first time and emitted a smooth purr as it ran, such being the case on this particular morning, and once I had familiarized myself with the self-centering tailwheel — a feature that had been criticized by some AFDU pilots — I found taxying the essence of simplicity as the fighter could be swung freely from side to side on its broad-track undercarriage. Furthermore, the brakes were very good, although view with the tail down left much to be desired.

I soon felt completely at home in the cockpit. After lining up for take-off, I moved the stick to an aft position in order to lock the tailwheel, applied 10 degrees of flap, set the elevator trimmer to neutral and the propellor pitch to AUTO and gently opened up the engine. I encountered some tendency to swing to port but easily held this on the rudder, and using 2,700 rpm and 23·5 lb (1·6 *atas*) boost, found the run to be much the same as that of the Spitfire Mk IX. Unstick speed was 112 mph (180 km/h) and after retracting the undercarriage by depressing the appropriate button, I reduced boost to 21·3 lb (1·45 *atas*) and at 143 mph (230 km/h) activated the pushbutton which raised the flaps. I then set up a climbing speed of 161 mph (260 km/h) using 2,500 rpm and this gave a climb rate of 3,150 ft/min (16 m/sec).

A remarkable aspect of this fighter was the lack of re-trimming required for the various stages of a flight. There was no aileron trimmer in the cockpit, but if the external adjustable trim tab had been inadvertently moved as a result, for example, of a member of the groundscrew pushing against it, an out-of-trim force of considerable proportions *could* result at high speed. Decidedly the most impressive feature of the German fighter was its beautifully light ailerons and its extremely high rate of roll. Incredible aileron turns were possible that would have torn the wings from a Bf 109 and badly strained the arm muscles of any Spitfire pilot trying to follow. The ailerons maintained their lightness from the stall up to 400 mph (644 km/h), although they heavied up above that speed.

The elevators proved to be heavy at all speeds and particularly so above 350 mph (563 km/h) when they became heavy enough to impose a tactical restriction on the fighter as regards pull-out from low-level dives. This heaviness was accentuated because of the nose down pitch which occurred at high speeds when trimmed for low speeds. The critical speed at which this change in trim occurred was around 220 mph (354 km/h) and could be easily gauged in turns. At lower speeds, the German fighter had a tendency to tighten up the turn and I found it necessary to apply slight forward pressure on the stick, but above the previously-mentioned critical figure, the changeover called for some backward pressure to hold the Focke-Wulf in the turn.

At low speeds rudder control proved positive and effective, and I found it satisfactory at high speeds, seldom needing to be used for any normal manœuvre. It was when one took the three controls together rather than in isolation that one appreciated the fact that the Fw 190's magic as a fighter lay in its superb control harmony. A good dogfighter *and* a good gun platform called for just the characteristics that this German fighter possessed in all important matters of stability and control. At the normal cruise of 330 mph (530 km/h) at 8,000 ft (2 440 m), the stability was very good directionally, unstable laterally and neutral longitudinally.

Some penalty is, of course, always invoked by such handling attributes as those possessed by the Fw 190, and in the case of this fighter the penalty was to be found in the fact that it was not at all easy to fly on instruments. Of course, Kurt Tank's aircraft was originally conceived solely as a clear-weather day fighter. It is significant that all-weather versions were fitted with the Patin PKS 12 autopilot. I checked out the maximum level speed of my Fw 190A-4/U8 — which, incidentally, had had its external stores carriers removed by this time — and clocked 394 mph (634 km/h) at 18,500 ft (5 640 m), and I ascertained that the service ceiling was around 35,000 ft (10 670 m), so it matched the Spitfire Mk IX almost mile per hour and foot per foot of ceiling. Here were apparently two aircraft that were so evenly matched that the skill of the pilot became the vital factor in combat supremacy. Skill in aerial combat does, however, mean flying an aircraft to its limits, and when the performance of the enemy is equal to one's own, then handling characteristics become vital in seeking an advantage. The Focke-Wulf had one big advantage over the Spitfire Mk IX in that it possessed an appreciably higher rate of roll, but the Achilles Heel that the AFDU had sought with Arnim Faber's Fw 190A-3 was its harsh stalling characteristics which limited its manœuvre margins.

The AFDU comparisons between the Focke-Wulf and the Spitfire Mk IX — with the former's BMW 801 at 2,700 rpm and 20·8 lb (1·42 *atas*) boost and the latter's Merlin 61 at 3,000 rpm and 15 lb (1·00 *ata*) — had revealed that the German fighter was 7-8 mph (11-13 km/h) faster than its British counterpart at 2,000 ft (610 m) but that the speeds of the two fighters were virtually the same at 5,000 ft (1 525 m). Above this altitude, the Spitfire began to display a marginal superiority, being about 8 mph (13 km/h) faster at 8,000 ft (2 440 m) and 5 mph (8 km/h) faster at 15,000 ft (4 570 m). The pendulum then swung once more in favour of the Focke-Wulf which proved itself some 3 mph (5 km/h) faster at 18,000 ft (5 485 m), the two fighters level pegging once more at 21,000 ft (6 400 m) and the Spitfire then taking the lead until, at 25,000 ft (7 620 m) it showed a 5-7 mph (8-11 km/h) superiority.

In climbing, little difference was found between the Fw 190 and the Spitfire Mk IX up to 23,000 ft (7 010 m), above which altitude the climb of the German fighter began to fall off and the difference between the two aircraft widened rapidly. From high-speed cruise, a pull up into a climb gave the Fw 190 an initial advantage owing to its superior acceleration and the superiority of the German fighter was even more noticeable when both aircraft were pulled up into a zoom climb from a dive. In the dive, the Fw 190 could leave the Spitfire Mk IX without difficulty and there was no gainsaying that in so far as manœuvrability was concerned, the German fighter was

Focke-Wulf Fw 190A-8 Cockpit Instrumentation Key

1 Helmet R/T connection
2 Primer fuel pump handle
3 FuG 16ZY communications and homing switch and volume control
4 FuG 16ZY receiver fine tuning
5 FuG 16ZY homing range switch
6 FuG 16ZY frequency selector switch
7 Tailplane trim switch
8 Undercarriage and landing flap actuation buttons
9 Undercarriage and landing flap position indicators
10 Throttle
11 Throttle-mounted propeller pitch control thumbswitch
12 Tailplane trim indicator
13 Instrument panel lighting dimmer
14 Pilot's seat
15 Throttle friction knob
16 Control column
17 Bomb release button
18 Rudder pedals
19 Wing cannon firing button
20 Fuel tank selector lever
21 Engine starter brushes withdrawal button
22 Stop cock control lever
23 FuG 25a IFF control panel
24 Undercarriage manual lowering handle
25 Cockpit ventilation knob
26 Altimeter
27 Pitot tube heater light
28 MG 131 "armed" indicator lights
29 Ammunition counters
30 SZKK 4 armament switch and control panel
31 30-mm armoured glass quarterlights
32 Windscreen spray pipes
33 50-mm armoured glass windscreen
34 Revi 16B reflector gunsight
35 Padded coaming
36 Gunsight padded mounting
37 AFN 2 homing indicator (FuG 16ZY)
38 Ultra-violet lights (port and starboard)
39 Airspeed indicator
40 Artificial horizon
41 Rate of climb/descent indicator
42 Repeater compass
43 Supercharger pressure gauge
44 Tachometer
45 Ventral stores manual release
46 Fuel and oil pressure gauge
47 Oil temperature gauge
48 Windscreen washer operating lever
49 Engine ventilation flap control lever
50 Fuel contents gauge
51 Propeller pitch indicator
52 Rear fuel tank switchover light (white)
53 Fuel contents warning light (red)
54 Fuel gauge selector switch
55 Underwing rocket (WfrGr 21) control panel
56 Bomb fusing selector panel and (above) external stores indicator lights
57 Oxygen flow indicator
58 Flare pistol holder
59 Oxygen pressure gauge
60 Oxygen flow valve
61 Canopy actuator drive
62 Canopy jettison lever
63 Circuit breaker panel cover
64 Clock
65 Map/chart holder
66 Operations data card
67 Flare box cover
68 Starter switch
69 Flare box cover plate release knob
70 Fuel pump circuit breakers
71 Compass deviation card
72 Circuit breaker panel cover
73 Armament circuit breakers
74 Oxygen supply

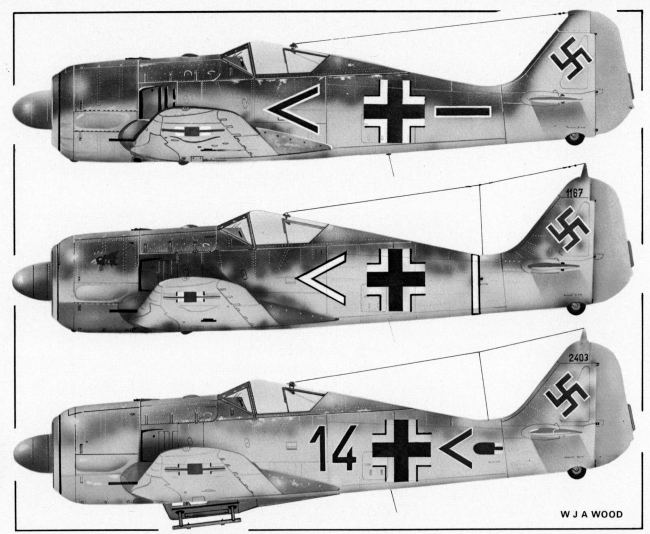

W J A WOOD

(Above top) This Fw 190A-2 belonged to the Gruppenstab of II/JG 26 "Schlageter" under Hauptmann Joachim Muncheberg while based at Abbeville-Drucat in the early summer of 1942. The insignia indicate that this aircraft was flown by the Gruppen Adjutant. (Above centre) This Fw 190A-4 (Werk-Nr 1167) belonged to the Gruppenstab of III/JG 2 "Richthofen" based at Poix in September 1942. The "Cock's Head" emblem was introduced by the Kommandeur of III/JG 2, Hauptmann "Assi" Hahn, who led the Gruppe in France from October 1940 until November 1942. It was not uncommon for the "Richthofen" Jagdgeschwader to paint the underside of the engine cowlings of its Fw 190s red. (Immediately above) This Fw 190A-4 (Werk-Nr 2403) flown by Feldwebel Karl Niesel of 10.(Jabo)/JG 26 was based at St Omer-Wizernes in the autumn of 1942 and was part of a Schwarm that attacked Hastings on 17 October 1942. While returning to base, Niesel was intercepted by two Typhoons of No 486 (New Zealand) Squadron flown by Pilot Officers C G Thomas and A N Sames who shot down Nr 2403 at 1422 hours, Niesel losing his life.

Focke-Wulf Fw 190A-8 Specification

Power Plant: On BMW 801D 14-cylinder radial air-cooled engine rated at 1,700 hp for take-off and 1,440 hp at 18,700 ft (5 700 m). Fuel capacity, 115·5 Imp gal (524 l) in two fuselage tanks, plus 25·3 Imp gal (115 l) in optional rear fuselage tank plus provision for 66·2-Imp gal (300-l) drop tank.

Performance (Clean): Max speed, 355 mph (571 km/h) at sea level, 402 mph (647 km/h) at 18,045 ft (5 500 m); max speed with GM1 nitrous oxide boost, 408 mph (656 km/h) at 20,670 ft (6 300 m); normal cruising speed, 298 mph (480 km/h) at 6,560 ft (2 000 m); initial rate of climb, 3,450 ft/min (17,5 m/sec); time to climb to 19,685 ft (6 000 m), 9·1 min; to 26,250 ft (8 000 m), 14·4 min; to 32,800 ft (10 000 m), 19.3 min; service ceiling, 33,800 ft (10 300 m) and with GM1 boost, 37,400 ft (11 400 m); max range, 644 mls (1 035 km) at 22,970 ft (7 000 m); range with one drop tank, 915 mls (1 470 km) at 301 mph (485 km/h) at 16,400 ft (5 000 m).

Weights: Empty equipped (clean), 7,652 lb (3 470 kg); empty equipped (fighter-bomber), 7,740 lb (3 510 kg); normal loaded, 9,660 lb (4 380 kg); max take-off (fighter-bomber), 10,724 lb (4 865 kg).

Dimensions: Span, 34 ft 5½ in (10,506 m); length, 29 ft 4¼ in (8,95 m); height (over airscrew), 12 ft 11½ in (3,95 m); wing area, 196·98 sq ft (18,3 m²); undercarriage track, 11 ft 6 in (3,50 m).

Armament: Two 13-mm MG 131 machine guns with 475 rpg in fuselage; two 20-mm MG 151/20E cannon with 250 rpg in wing roots and two 20-mm MG 151/20E cannon with 140 rpg in outer wing panels.

markedly the superior of the two in all save the tight turn — the Spitfire could not follow in aileron turns and reversals at high speeds and the worst heights for its pilot to engage the Fw 190 in combat were between 18,000 and 22,000 ft (5 485 and 6 705 m), and at altitudes below 3,000 ft (915 m).

The stalling speed of the Fw 190A-4 in clean configuration was 127 mph (204 km/h) and the stall came suddenly and virtually without warning, the port wing dropping so violently that the aircraft almost inverted itself. In fact, if the German fighter was pulled into a *g* stall in a tight turn, it would flick out into the opposite bank and an incipient spin was the inevitable outcome if the pilot did not have his wits about him. The stall in landing configuration was quite different, there being intense pre-stall buffeting before the starboard wing dropped comparatively gently at 102 mph (164 km/h).

For landing on this and the numerous subsequent occasions that I was to fly an Fw 190, I extended the undercarriage at 186 mph (300 km/h), lowering the flaps 10 deg at 168 mph (270 km/h), although the pilot's notes recommended reducing speed below 155 mph (250 km/h) and then applying 10 deg of flap before lowering the undercarriage. My reason for departing from the recommended drill was that the electrical load for lowering the undercarriage was higher than that required for the flaps, and German batteries were in rather short supply at Farnborough — that in the Fw 190A-4/U8 was most definitely weary — so I considered it prudent to get the wheels down before taxing the remaining strength of the battery further!

The turn onto final approach was made at 155 mph (250 km/h) and full flap was applied at 149 mph (240 km/h), speed then being eased off to cross the boundary at 124 mph (200 km/h). The view on the approach was decidedly poor because the attitude with power on was rather flat and, unlike most fighters of the period, it was not permissible to open the cockpit canopy, presumably owing to the risk of engine exhaust fumes entering the cockpit. The actual touch-down was a little tricky as a perfect three-point attitude was difficult to attain and anything less than perfect resulted in a reaction from the very non-resilient undercarriage and a decidedly bouncy arrival. If a three-pointer *could* be achieved, the landing run was short and

the brakes could be applied harshly without fear of nosing over.

I was to fly the Fw 190 many times and in several varieties — among the last of the radial-engined members of Kurt Tank's fighter family that I flew was an Fw 190F-8 (AM111) on 28 July 1945 — and each time I was to experience that sense of exhilaration that came from flying an aircraft that one instinctively knew to be a top-notcher, yet, at the same time, demanded handling skill if its high qualities were to be exploited. Just as the Spitfire Mk IX was probably the most outstanding British fighter to give service in World War II, its Teutonic counterpart is undoubtedly deserving of the same recognition for Germany. Both were supreme in their time and class; both were durable and technically superb, and if each had not been there to counter the other, then the balance of air power could have been dramatically altered at a crucial period in the fortunes of both combatants. □

(Immediately below) Fw 190A-8 (Werk-Nr 7298) belonging to the Geschwaderstab of JG 26 "Schlageter" and flown by the Kommodore, Oberstleutnant Josef "Pips" Priller, while based at Lille-Nord in April 1944. Priller led the "Schlageter" Jagdgeschwader from January 1943 until January 1945. All Priller's Fw 190s displayed an "Ace of Hearts" emblem below the windscreen with the name "Jutta" (short for Johanna) superimposed. (Below centre) This Fw 190A-8 (Werk-Nr 380352) belonged to II/JG 11 under Hauptmann Rüdiger von Kirchmayr while based at Darmstadt. Operating in the final defence of the Reich in the early spring of 1945, this machine displayed the Geschwader emblem and the yellow identification band carried by all JG 11 aircraft within the Reichverteidigung organisation at this time. (Bottom) This Fw 190A-8 (Werk-Nr 681382) belonged to the Gruppenstab of I/JG 26 "Schlageter" and was flown by the Kommandeur, Major Karl Borris, while at Grimberghen, near Brussels, in September 1944. Note the additional armour-glass plates bolted on to the sides of the sliding canopy.

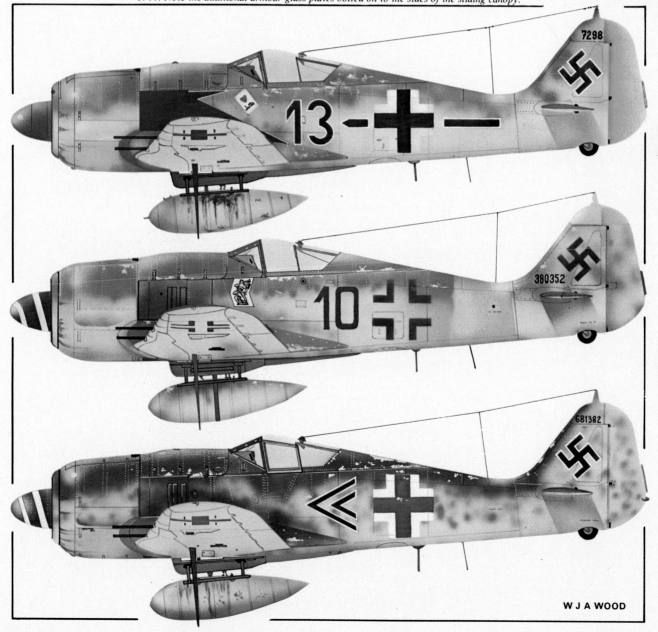

W J A WOOD

Getting with the whoppers!

WILL ANYTHING ever replace 1/72nd scale in the affections of the vast majority of aircraft modellers. By and large, the world's kit manufacturers have standardised on this scale as a means of achieving the best of all worlds — at this scale the smallest categories of aircraft are still acceptable while the largest are still manageable — and most of us have come to accept it for what it is: a compromise! World War II fighters, for example, make up into pretty little models at this scale, but they are just that, *little* models. It is only when one progresses to the larger categories of aircraft that models produced to 1/72nd scale can be said to have any impact as display items. An obvious solution is diversification — adopt a larger scale for small aircraft while retaining 1/72nd scale for bigger machines — but most modellers are reluctant to mix the scales of the models in their collections and, in any case, there is a far wider choice of subject matter to 1/72nd than to any other scale.

Nevertheless, at a time when two superb kits of four-engined bombers to 1/48th scale have recently appeared on the market with others to this scale reportedly in prospect, it is worth pausing to consider the possibility of this larger scale eventually offering serious competition for 1/72nd and to review the rather erratic career of 1/48th to the present day.

Going back nearly four decades, to the time when the 1/72nd scale was in its infancy, the larger 1/48th scale was already established in the United States as a standard for the wooden construction kits then being produced by such concerns as Aircraft and Hawk (the latter, of course, still active) and of which quite a good range existed and incorporating, in addition to the partially-formed wooden components, cast and stamped metal parts. These kits were available in the UK through the specialist importers of the day, in much the same fashion as off-beat plastic kits are now, and they were eagerly snapped up by enthusiasts. During World War II, what kits were produced were mostly to 1/72nd scale, although we recollect an extensive range of 1/48th kits manufactured by Chingford Model Aircraft which made use of the limited range of materials available at the time — as balsa wood was not to be had, a rather hard wood had to serve and one had to be a *true* enthusiast to spend countless hours whittling away at that! Naturally enough, the emphasis was on contemporary aircraft, but there was a very nice Pfalz D XII, a type which, to the best of our knowledge, has never reappeared as a kit since.

The early postwar years, up until the advent of the polystyrene plastic kit, were again dominated by 1/72nd scale, these being mostly of balsa wood, but what was undoubtedly one of the first plastic aircraft kits to be produced in the United States, Lindberg's Lockheed

F-80 Shooting Star, was to 1/48th scale and proved to be the progenitor of an extensive range of kits from that distinguished company which mostly retained the quarter-inch scale. There were some really outstanding items among these that would be very acceptable even by today's standards and in particular the Grumman TBF-1 Avenger, the Curtiss F11C-2 and the Lockheed Vega. Hawk, mentioned earlier in connection with wooden kits, was also active early in the 1/48th field of endeavour. Its early plastic efforts were rather crude — as were those of other manufacturers at this time — but very high standards were eventually attained by this concern with its P-51D Mustang and P-47D Thunderbolt. Also to be recalled with pleasure are Hawk's fine range of US racing aircraft, such as the Gee Bee Super Sportster, Travel Air Mystery R and Howard Mr Mulligan — somehow the Supermarine S.6B got into the act! Later offerings from Hawk to 1/48th scale included the Lockheed T-33A and the Rockwell (née North American) OV-10 Bronco, but while much of the Hawk range is available from Testor's in Canada, nothing new has appeared for a long, long time.

Probably the most prolific of all in so far as 1/48th scale is concerned has been Aurora, but its products have varied considerably, both in quality and scale accuracy. The best of the Aurora offerings have been and still are well worth obtaining — in some instances, such as the Airco D.H.10 and the Gotha G V, they are the only examples of the particular aircraft to *any* scale. Having commenced operations with mixed wood-and-plastic kits, Monogram entered the all-plastic field with a range of aircraft types to a wide variety of scales, but eventually decided to specialise in 1/48th, producing what can only be regarded as the most successful of any range of quarter-inch kits, which, after a period in the doldrums, continues today to the very highest standards, foremost among the company's kits produced over the past couple of years being its magnificent B-17G Fortress. Other fine 1/48th scale Monogram kits include the de Havilland Mosquito, the Hawker Typhoon and the Northrop P-61 Black Widow, but there are many, many more.

The British industry's sorties into 1/48th scale have been few and far between, and despite high product quality, singularly unsuccessful. Merit was the first to chance its arm in this scale, its initial group of WW I kits being so similar to those of Aurora as to be virtually indistinguishable. However, Merit went on to produce several original kits, such as the Swordfish, Walrus, Avro 504K and Airco D.H.2 which were excellent in their day and still look good. Sadly, this series suffered early demise, although some of the Merit kits have reappeared under different labels and may still be around. Of course, amongst the finest

1/48th kits of all time were the four 'tween-wars RAF fighters produced by Inpact, the Fury, Bulldog, Flycatcher and Gladiator, this concern also being responsible for a series of six pre-WW I aircraft of which the Bristol Boxkite is a classic. Despite the superlative quality of its products, Inpact failed to sustain itself in the hard commercial world — perhaps its offerings were too good and undoubtedly they were too esoteric — but its kits are still available under the Pyro label.

From its earliest participation in the plastic kit business, Japan adopted — among others — the nearest metric scale to quarter-inch, and in time some fine kits appeared to 1/50th scale, such as Marusan's F-86D Sabre, *still* the only really acceptable kit of this fighter to this scale. Tamiya's outstanding achievement in 1/50th was the Nakajima C6N1 Saiun, but since switching to 1/48th scale, this Japanese company has built up a long list of outstanding kits, the Lancaster taking pride of place. Otaki includes about a dozen excellent quarter-inch kits in its catalogue, mostly WW II fighters, while Nichimo has some outstanding achievements under its kimono, including one twin-engined type, the Kawasaki Ki.45 Toryu. Even the small Mania concern has produced one kit to 1/48th scale, this being the Nakajima Ki.27, and we hope for another in the near future.

Thus, it may be seen that 1/48th scale has a long history — we calculate that upwards of 300 different aircraft kits have been produced to this scale over the past 20 or so years — and the new issue situation would seem currently buoyant. While it would be idle to suggest that 1/72nd scale has yet any cause to "look over its shoulder", there are signs that quarter-inch is steadily gaining in popularity and as more and more modellers get with these whoppers it could provide a serious rival for the smaller scale.

This month's colour subject

There are a number of reasons why the Caproni Reggiane series of fighters designed by Roberto Longhi failed to achieve international fame, none of them attributable to any shortcomings in the aircraft themselves. Their progenitor, the Re 2000, was not inordinately advanced in overall concept, but certain individual features, although to be widely accepted within a few short years, *were* too advanced for Italy's Air Ministry which possessed few visionaries, being manned almost exclusively by traditionalists, and despite being the most modern Italian fighter of its era — as the air forces of certain other countries were quick to appreciate — it generated little enthusiasm in Italian official circles. Thus, a line of combat aircraft of a calibre that Italy was soon to find itself in sore need was almost stillborn.

The adaptation of the Re 2000 airframe to take the Daimler-Benz DB 601A engine was to result in a fighter that, at the time of its début, was second to none — combining a good turn of speed with excellent climb-and-dive characteristics and superlative manœuvrability — but this, the Re 2001 Ariete I, was destined to achieve only limited production, and although those that did find their way into the ranks of the *Regia Aeronautica* saw considerable action and no little success, they were too few in number to gain the recognition that was the lot of other more numerous and, in many cases, less deserving fighters. However, if eluded by fame, it makes an interesting model subject.

Only one kit of this Caproni Reggiane fighter has yet appeared, this being to 1/72nd scale and having originally been produced by Italaerei, although when this Italian company was reorganised some time ago, this kit was one of those transferred to a breakaway concern, Supermodel, as the nucleus of its catalogue. Supermodel also offers companion kits of the radial-engined Re 2000 and Re 2002. The Supermodel Re 2001 kit captures fully the highly distinctive shape of this fighter which resulted from the blending of a liquid-cooled inline engine to an airframe designed for an air-cooled radial. The model is accurate and easily assembled, and the surface detailing is neat. The decal sheet is quite good and the subjects adhere well, although in our example — an original Italaerei issue, incidentally — the decals suffered some translucency. This is a subject that is not likely to suffer much repetition and the kit, which retails for 65p in the UK, is well worth obtaining.

Sabre-Dog and Hawk
The subjects of the two latest 1/72nd scale releases from Airfix are both single-turbojet military aircraft but at this point any similarity ceases for they are separated in concept by a quarter century and in origin by some 5,000 miles. The North American F-86D Sabre first flew at Muroc, California, in 1949, while the Hawker Siddeley Hawk left the ground for the first time at Dunsfold, Surrey, in 1974, these providing the subject matter of the two Airfix offerings.

Just why it should have taken so long for a 1/72nd scale kit of the "Sabre-Dog" to appear is rather difficult to understand, but the Hawk has been an obvious one since it commenced its test programme, the main doubt being which of two manufacturers, Airfix and Lesney, would hit the market first with a kit of this promising new trainer and light strike aircraft. Airfix has made it and, having a head start, should do well with this very attractive Series 3 kit, which, comprising 95 component parts, is retailing in the UK at 55p. We are unable to fault this kit on the score of accuracy and it is deserving of full marks for completeness, for it possesses well-detailed cockpit interiors with stepped floor, ejector seats, instrument panels, gunsight, control columns and two pilot figures; there is also a transparent screen between the two cockpits, under the canopy, and a separate windscreen so that the canopy can be fixed in the open position.

The nosewheel is moulded in one with the leg, but, nevertheless, looks well after painting, and the main undercarriage units are well detailed, with the brake drums separate from the wheels. The undercarriage doors, incidentally, are of scale thickness and detailed inside. The undercarriage may be assembled in either extended or retracted position. Surface detailing has been restricted to a minimum as befits an aircraft as smooth as the Hawk, but Airfix has really gone to town in so far as external stores are concerned, providing five 1,000-lb (453,5-kg) bombs with very finely moulded fins — just about the best that we can recall. As alternative loads, there are four

Matra rocket pods and two 100 Imp gal (454,6 l) drop tanks, plus a 30-mm gun pod. Painting details are given for the red-white-grey training scheme and for NATO-style camouflage, decals being provided for both.

In Series 2 and having a UK retail price of 38p, the F-86D Sabre is an equally fine kit comprising 49 component parts in silver plastic. Surface detailing consists of fine raised lines in the main and, fortunately, there are no rivets. The "Mighty Mouse" rocket tray may be assembled in the extended position, and the cockpit interior and undercarriage are again extremely well executed. The nose intake tunnel is included back to the bulkhead forward of the cockpit, and the aft section of the tailpipe is also included, so there is no void visible when looking into the apertures. The contours of the "Sabre-Dog" have been effectively captured and assembly presents no problems. A natural metal finish is mandatory — unless one intends to complete the aircraft in Jugoslav finish — and we feel that this particular kit, with its smooth surfaces, lends itself particularly well to treatment with a rub-on finish, such as "Rub-n-Buff" or "Treasure Silver", the former being obtainable from model shops and the latter from art shops. The decal sheet with this kit is a work of art and is so large that it only just fits into the box. It really is superb and offers two colourful schemes covering the 520th Fighter Intercept Squadron at Geiger Field, Washington, in 1955, and the 512th FIS at Manston, Kent, in 1956.

A veteran "grasshopper"
Recently received from Czechoslovakia is a new 1/72nd scale kit of Polikarpov's "kukuruz-nik", the Po-2, which, a product of the Kovozavody Prostejov, makes up into a truly delightful model of what is probably the best-known — at least, in Eastern Europe — of all Soviet aircraft. Conceived as a primary trainer, the Po-2 was to see a fabulous wartime career, ranging from nocturnal harassment of the *Whermacht*, the transportation of agents, saboteurs and guerillas to and fro across the frontline and aeromedical evacuation with the casualties slung in stretchers externally, to routine liaison and training tasks. This KP kit does full justice to its subject and the small details, both external and internal, have to be seen to be believed, extending to such tiny items as the control horns on the rudder and elevators.

There are 65 component parts to the kit, all cleanly moulded in a light grey plastic, and these embody nicely restrained surface detailing with no exaggeration — this applying particularly to the rib effect on the wings and tail surfaces. The manufacturer has given the modeller credit for the ability and common-sense to align the wing assembly properly without having a built-in jig arrangement for the struts, the interplane and centre section N-struts being separate mouldings. The upper and lower wings are each one-piece mouldings, the latter fitting into a recess in the lower fuselage. The five-cylinder air-cooled radial engine has a full exhaust system and a most effective appearance; seats and controls are included for the cockpits, as are the instrument panels, and a single machine gun is provided for the rear cockpit plus six small bombs on underwing racks. Rigging is, of course, necessary, but this is not particularly complex and the fine box-top illustration depicts this feature

quite clearly. Full painting instructions are provided, together with four-view drawings of three Soviet and one Czechoslovak aircraft, and the decal sheet — a great improvement over sheets accompanying previous KP kits — provides all the necessary markings. We cannot see how KP could have incorporated *more* detail in a model of this size than is offered with the Po-2. The kit should be available in the UK by the time these words are read but we do not have a price as we close for press.

A batch of vacu-forms
There are some types of aircraft over which one can express surprise that they have never seen the light of day in kit form; there are others that fall within the 'highly improbable' category in so far as being potential subjects for the kit manufacturer. In the latest batch of four vacu-form releases from Airmodel of Federal Germany, one subject may be considered to come within the former category and three within the latter. The Arado Ar 96B, for long the standard *Luftwaffe* advanced trainer with more than 11,000 built, would seem to have been a fairly obvious subject for a kit, but the Arado Ar 240, the Heinkel He 60C and particularly the massive Northrop YB-49 would appear most decidedly off-beat, and these comprise this latest Airmodel quartet of 1/72nd scale vacu-forms.

The Ar 96B kit includes all of the major components and these are well moulded with good surface detail, although, as we have pointed out when reviewing earlier Airmodel kits, the components suffer a surfeit of small "pimples" which demand rubbing down with "wet and dry" abrasive paper. The Airfix kit of the Fw 189 is a possible if extravagant source of a propeller for the Argus; the wheels must come from the spares box and the smaller parts must be made from plastic sheet or scrap. The canopy is good and the instruction sheet, in English, is well produced and offers full assembly instructions and colour schemes for three different aircraft, two operated by the *Luftwaffe* and a postwar example operated by the Czechoslovak air arm. Unique in our experience in so far as vacu-forms are concerned is the decal sheet, which, printed in the UK, provides markings for all three aircraft for which colour schemes are provided.

First of the trio of more esoteric types is the Arado Ar 240, the component parts of which are good as is also the instruction sheet which incorporates a three-view general arrangement drawing. The neat little He 60C twin-float seaplane is by no means easy to build but is potentially a gem. Again a general arrangement drawing plus an assembly diagram of exploded type are provided, these illustrating the numerous struts and other small items that must be added to the kit by the modeller. A useful feature of the instruction sheet, incidentally, is provision of details of the internal arrangement of the cockpits with suggestions for completing these.

By far the most exotic of the four Airmodel kits is that of Northrop's mighty YB-49 which produces a model with a wing span of no less than 2 ft $4\frac{2}{3}$ in (72,8 cm). Unfortunately, our sample kit was unaccompanied by assembly instructions, though presumably these are normally included. The YB-49 kit is truly impressive — it comprises six main sections, these being the upper and lower halves of

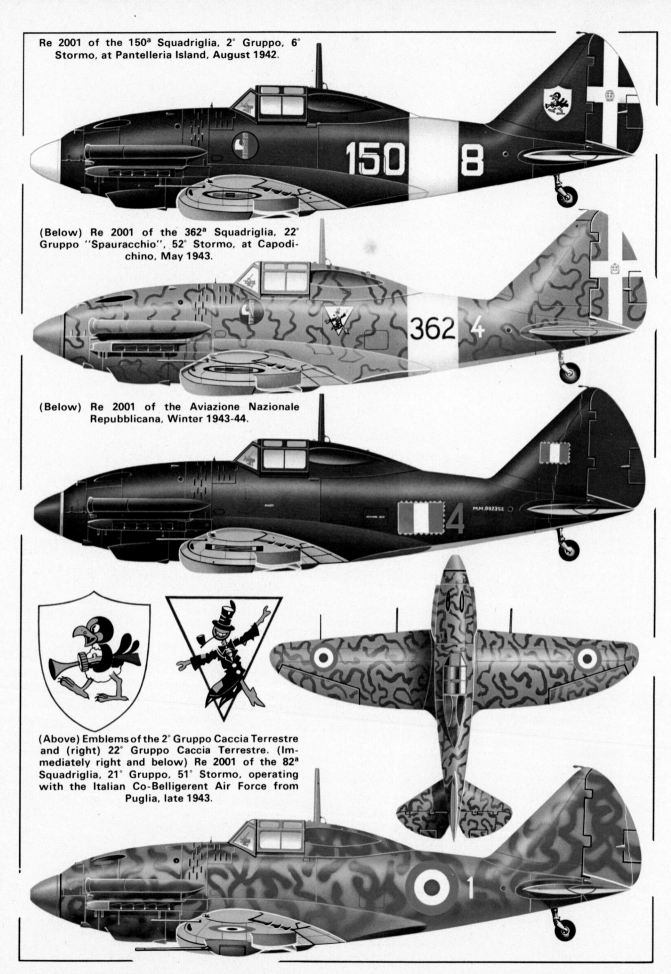

Re 2001 of the 150ª Squadriglia, 2° Gruppo, 6° Stormo, at Pantelleria Island, August 1942.

(Below) Re 2001 of the 362ª Squadriglia, 22° Gruppo "Spauracchio", 52° Stormo, at Capodichino, May 1943.

(Below) Re 2001 of the Aviazione Nazionale Repubblicana, Winter 1943-44.

(Above) Emblems of the 2° Gruppo Caccia Terrestre and (right) 22° Gruppo Caccia Terrestre. (Immediately right and below) Re 2001 of the 82ª Squadriglia, 21° Gruppo, 51° Stormo, operating with the Italian Co-Belligerent Air Force from Puglia, late 1943.

centre and outer wing panels, plus the eight jet effluxes, five wheels and four transparencies, including the large one which forms part of the centre section leading edge. Other parts, such as the trailing edge vertical fins, must be produced from sheet plastic. There is a need to reinforce the very large mouldings and spray painting is advised in order to obtain a really smooth silver finish over the immense areas of wing — brush painting really will not suffice. Markings on the full-size aircraft were very simple and should thus present no difficulty. This is a tricky one to build but the result is a real eye-catcher. We do not have prices for these kits, but in the UK and elsewhere they will be available through the usual specialist dealers.

Mania's first "twin"

The appearance of a new kit from the small Japanese concern of Mania is always something of an event, for, although its kits appear at infrequent intervals, they are invariably of excellent quality. With one exception, all Mania's kits to-date have been to 1/72nd scale and the latest release, the Kawasaki Ki.48, or Army Type 99 Twin-engined Light Bomber, is the first "twin" in this range and may there be many more! The Ki.48, developed as a result of encounters by Imperial Army fighters with Tupolev SB bombers in Chinese skies in 1937, and inappropriately assigned the reporting name of *Lily* by the Allies, has been all but ignored

by kit manufacturers hitherto — we can recall only one previous kit and this was a very crude effort to 1/87th scale by Otaki. The Ki.48 was, of course, built in very substantial numbers and served throughout the Pacific conflict, and this new Mania kit is, therefore, particularly welcome.

Superbly executed in, dare we say it, the best *maniacal* tradition with no fewer than 86 precisely-moulded parts in light grey plastic and sporting a prodigious amount of detail, this Ki.48 kit will not be cheap when it reaches the UK — probably in excess of £3·00 — but it is such a fine product that few will begrudge this fairly hefty expenditure. The cockpit area detail is so complete, even down to such items as oxygen bottles, that one could not possibly ask for more. The dorsal and ventral gun positions are fully detailed, the latter incorporating a hinged hatch, and there are many tiny parts calling for careful handling with tweezers. The surface detailing has a finesse that could scarcely be surpassed, all panel lines being beautifully etched, and the fit of the parts is superb, no filling being required anywhere.

In so far as accuracy is concerned, we have been unable to fault this in any way. The large decal sheet offers *Sentai* markings for five different aircraft and each is illustrated in full colour by the instruction sheet which is printed in Japanese but has some English translation. The assembly diagrams are self-explanatory and provided reasonable care is

exercised no difficulty should be experienced in turning out a first class model.

Airliner decals

Two very attractive set of decals have come to us from VHF Supplies. The first sheet, intended for use with Revell's 1/144th scale McDonnell Douglas DC-10 Series 10, offers the very attractive markings of the Laker Airways Skytrain with the multi-coloured logo and red-and-black fuselage cheat lines and fin striping, plus other smaller markings and a choice of three individual aircraft names and registrations. This sheet is the product of hand silk-screen printing and is of exceptional quality as regards fidelity of colour, definition and adhesive properties. A nicely-printed card accompanies the sheet and this offers a coloured side profile, a brief history and a black-and-white photograph. The price may seem high at £1·00 plus 10p postage, but the quality is very high indeed.

The second sheet is for the Rareplanes 1/72nd scale Lockheed "Super-G" Constellation and is, in fact, a re-issue but decidedly superior to the original, being now silk-screen printed and of a style and quality usually provided for travel agent-type models. The markings are for a Trans-World aircraft with two choices of name and registration. Again, the colour is very true and clearly defined, and the price is £1·25 plus 10p postage from VHF Supplies. □

F J HENDERSON

JAPAN ———————————————— *from page 69*

Herikoputa-dan on Hokkaido and is currently planning re-organisation of *Homen Koku-tais* as *Koku-dans* (ie, wings rather than squadrons) owing to the substantial increase in the capabilities and numerical strengths of these units with re-equipment.

Current "post-4th DBP" (ie, post March 1977) GSDF plans include a substantial increase in the anti-armour capability of the air component and furthering of the "flying artillery" concept. For some time past, the GSDF has been undertaking studies of armed helicopters, utilising six specially-converted UH-1s equipped with 38 70-mm rockets. Present planning envisages the conversion of four to six of the 20 UH-1 Iroquois helicopters of each *Homen Herikoputa-tai* with rocket armament in the short term and possibly re-equipping these helicopters with TOW (Tube-launched Optically-tracked Wire-guided) missles at a later stage.

In so far as the procurement of new helicopters is concerned, the replacement of the OH-6J is considered to be a matter of some urgency, despite the fact that this type is still relatively new to the GSDF inventory. Owing to its small weapons load, the OH-6J is now considered unsatisfactory and a somewhat larger helicopter is required with the MBB BO 105 and the Westland Lynx being frontrunners since Kawasaki dropped its plans to develop the KH-7, although the GSDF is continuing studies of the possibilities of a re-engined OH-6J. As potential replacement of the UH-1 Iroquois in the slightly longer term, the GSDF is studying the US Army's UTTAS (Utility Tactical Transport Aircraft System) closely, while still further into the future, helicopters such as the Boeing Vertol CH-47 and Sikorsky CH-53 are being considered as potential successors to the V-107-II.

What effect the current US pressure on the Japanese government to upgrade its defence capabilities will have on the GSDF during the 5th DBP (1977-82) remains very much a matter for speculation. That the Japanese government has no intention of increasing the manpower of the Self-Defence Forces beyond the scales currently authorised has been made

plain; that there will be closer co-operation with the US forces has been announced and that means will be found to accelerate the modernisation of the Self-Defence Forces is fondly hoped. But one thing is absolutely certain whatever changes may result from the current American demands: the chronic defence allergy is likely to remain with Japan for a long time to come. □

The LM (above) is the principal GSDF liaison aircraft, 23 currently being included in the inventory. Delays in procurement owing to budgetary restrictions have created problems for the GSDF in standardising the complements of the Hiko-tais which are each supposed to include eight OH-6Js (below).

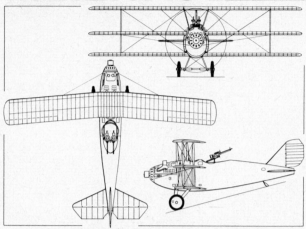

The Curtiss 18-T (above and immediately below) was believed to be the world's fastest aeroplane in August 1918.

The Curtiss 18-B (below) was a biplane derivative of the 18-T triplane but the only prototype to be flown crashed early in its flight test programme.

CURTISS 18-T   USA

Designed by Charles B Kirkham, the Curtiss 18-T two-seat fighter triplane was ordered by the US Navy on 30 March 1918 when a contract was placed for two prototypes, the first of which was flown on 5 July 1918. Designed around the Curtiss-Kirkham K-12 water-cooled 12-cylinder engine of 400 hp, the 18-T was of extremely clean aerodynamic design by contemporary standards and featured a monocoque three-ply fuselage and side radiators positioned between the lower wings. The proposed armament comprised two forward-firing synchronized 0·3-in (7,62-mm) Marlin machine guns and two 0·3-in (7,62-mm) Lewis guns on a scarf mounting in the rear cockpit. Known unofficially as the "Wasp" (an allusion to the sound emitted by the K-12 engine during landing approach), the 18-T initially suffered some tail heaviness which was corrected by applying five degrees of sweepback to the wings for further trials. A max speed of 163 mph (262 km/h) was achieved with full military load in August 1918, the 18-T

being acclaimed as the world's fastest aeroplane as a result and the US Navy promptly ordered two examples, the first of which was delivered in February 1919. In the summer of 1919, the first prototype was fitted with longer-span two-bay wings, these having a span and area of 40 ft 7½ in (12,38 m) and 400 sq ft (37,16 m²) respectively, and in this form the aircraft became the 18T-2, the short-span version becoming the 18T-1. The 18T-2 established a world altitude record of 34,910 ft (10 640 m) on 18 September 1919, and a second 18T-2 was built by Curtiss for export to Bolivia, where it arrived in 1920. The following data relate to the 18T-1. Max speed, 165 mph (265 km/h). Time to 12,500 ft (3 810 m), 10 min. Endurance, 5·9 hrs. Empty weight, 1,980 lb (898 kg). Loaded weight, 3,050 lb (1 383 kg). Span, 31 ft 10 in (9,70 m). Length, 23 ft 4 in (7,11 m). Height, 9 ft 10¾ in (3,02 m). Wing area, 288 sq ft (26,76 m²).

CURTISS 18-B   USA

US Army interest in the 18-T prompted Curtiss to offer the same basic design in two-bay biplane configuration and an order was placed by the US Army for two examples in August 1918. Known unofficially as the "Hornet", the 18-B two-seat fighter employed an identical fuselage to that of the 18-T and a similar Curtiss-Kirkham K-12 engine, the proposed armament comprising two forward-firing Marlin guns and two Lewis guns on a flexible mount. The two prototypes were delivered to the US Army during the summer of 1919, one being confined to static testing and the other crashing shortly after the commencement of flight trials and further development was abandoned. Max speed, 160 mph (257 km/h). Empty weight, 1,690 lb (767 kg). Loaded weight, 2,867 lb (1 300 kg). Span, 37 ft 5¾ in (11,41 m). Length, 23 ft 4 in (7,11 m). Wing area, 306 sq ft (28,43 m²).

(Above and below) The Curtiss-built Model D fighter differed in a number of respects from the Orenco-built prototypes, including balanced ailerons and redesigned vertical tail.

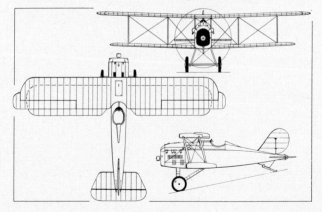

The third production Curtiss-Orenco D (above) was experimentally fitted with a turbo-supercharger. (Below) The first prototype PN-1 intended for use in the night fighting rôle.

CURTISS-ORENCO D   USA

The first single-seat fighter of indigenous US design to achieve production status, the Model D was conceived by the US Army Engineering Division around the French 300 hp Hispano-Suiza H eight-cylinder liquid-cooled engine, and the first of four prototypes built by the Ordnance Engineering Company (Orenco) was completed in January 1919. Curtiss was assigned a production contract for 50 aircraft and undertook some re-design, which included an increase in upper wing span, the introduction of dihedral and balanced ailerons and revision of the engine installation. Of wooden construction with ply-covered fuselage and fabric-covered wings, the Curtiss-built Model D utilised a 330 hp Wright-built derivative of the French engine and carried an armament of one 0·3-in (7,62-mm) and one 0·5-in (12,7-mm) machine gun, deliveries commencing in August 1921. One Model D was experimentally fitted with French Lamblin radiators attached to the fuselage sides and another was fitted with a turbo-supercharger for high altitude trials. Max speed, 139 mph (224 km/h) at sea level, 136 mph (219 km/h) at 6,500 ft (1 980 m). Cruising speed, 135 mph (217 km/h). Climb, 1,140 ft/min (5,78 m/sec). Endurance, 2·5 hrs. Empty weight, 1,908 lb (865 kg). Loaded weight, 2,820 lb (1 279 kg). Span, 32 ft 11⅝ in (10,05 m). Length, 21 ft 5½ in (6,54 m). Height, 8 ft 4 in (2,54 m). Wing area, 273 sq ft (25,36 m²).

CURTISS PN-1   USA

Designed to meet US Army Engineering Division requirements for a specialised single-seat night fighter, three prototypes being ordered, the PN-1 was powered by a 220 hp Liberty L-825 six-cylinder liquid-cooled engine. Optimised for docile handling characteristics at the lower end of the speed range in order to ease operation from small blacked-out fields, the PN-1 was completed without interplane struts, but steel-tube N-type interplane struts were introduced prior to flight testing of the first prototype which began in August 1921. Performance of the PN-1 proved disappointing, the fighter proving barely faster than the bombers it was intended to intercept, and the second prototype was used for static tests and the third cancelled. Max speed, 108 mph (174 km/h). Time to 6,500 ft (1 980 m), 5·5 min. Range, 255 mls (410 km). Empty weight, 1,631 lb (740 kg). Loaded weight, 2,311 lb (1 048 kg). Span, 30 ft 10 in (9,34 m). Length, 23 ft 6 in (7,16 m). Height, 10 ft 3 in (3,12 m). Wing area, 300 sq ft (27,87 m²).

CURTISS PW-8   USA

Progenitor of the famous Hawk series of fighters, the PW-8 (the "PW" prefix indicating "Pursuit Water-cooled") was a single-seat two-bay fighter biplane of mixed construction — plywood-covered wooden wings and fabric-skinned welded steel tube fuselage — powered by a 440 hp Curtiss D-12 liquid-cooled 12-cylinder Vee engine. Three prototypes were contracted for on 27 April 1923, and the first of these was retroactively designated XPW-8 on 14 May 1924. The second prototype embodied some aerodynamic refinement and provided the basis for the production PW-8, 25 examples being ordered in September 1923 and being delivered between June and August 1924. The PW-8 featured wing surface radiators and armament normally comprised two 0·3-in (7,62-mm) machine guns. A turbo-supercharger was experimentally fitted to the second production aircraft, and the third prototype (XPW-8A), delivered in February 1924, featured 30-ft (9,14-m) span single-bay wings and a revised radiator arrangement. It was sub-sequently fitted with a tunnel-type radiator (as the XPW-8AA) and, in December 1924, with 31 ft 6 in (9,60 m) span wings of tapered planform and Clark Y aerofoil section as the XPW-8B, becoming, in effect, the prototype P-1 Hawk. Max speed, 168 mph (270 km/h) at sea level. Cruising speed, 160 mph (257 km/h) at 10,000 ft (3 050 m). Time to 10,000 ft (3 050 m), 9·0 min. Range, 440 mls (708 km). Empty weight, 2,191 lb (994 kg). Loaded weight, 3,151 lb (1 429 kg). Span, 32 ft 0 in (9,75 m). Length, 22 ft 6 in (6,86 m). Height, 8 ft 10 in (2,69 m). Wing area, 287 sq ft (26,66 m²).

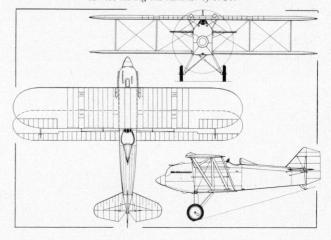

(Above, top) First prototype of the PW-8 (retroactively designated XPW-8), progenitor of the famous Hawk fighter series, and (immediately above and below) the production PW-8 which entered US Army service during the summer of 1924.

IN PRINT

"Photo Reconnaissance"
by Andrew J Brookes
Ian Allan Ltd, Shepperton, Middlesex, £5·25
248 pp, 5¾ in by 9 in, illustrated

ON the first page of this volume, the reader encounters observation balloons, and on the last page, observation satellites. These are the historical extremes of photographic reconnaissance, but between them lie the whole intriguing story of cameras used from aircraft for military recce purposes. The author traces that story, so far as the British armed services are concerned, from its beginning in World War I and devotes most of the book to an account of the RAF's PR activities in World War II. The rôle of Sidney Cotton in the formation of the first specialized PR unit is recorded and there are some rare photographs of camera-carrying Spitfires of the period, as well as examples of the photographs they brought back.

Also described are the significance of photoreconnaissance in detecting German work on the V-1 and V-2, the final wartime operations, and the special difficulties of PR in the Far East. A closing chapter describes the post-war advances in techniques with the advent of such aircraft as the U-2, and the changing rôle of reconnaissance so far as the RAF was concerned.

"World Combat Aircraft Directory"
Edited by Nornal Polmar
Macdonald and Jane's, London, £6·95
374 pp, 7¼ in by 9½ in, illustrated

THE COMBINATION of a respected author with a special interest in military and naval affairs, and one of the world's foremost publishers of aviation books, ensures that this volume is above average, although it is not the first attempt to provide an authoritative guide to the equipment of the World's air forces.

Section One, occupying the first quarter of the book, is called Air Order of Battle, and lists the numbers of aircraft of each type equipping each air arm. The difficulty with any such listing is that for *complete* accuracy (assuming sufficiently detailed information were available — which, having regard to national security consideration, it is not) it needs daily revision; the information in this volume therefore goes daily more out of date. Provided that this limitation (which applies to any similar book) is recognised, the Air Order of Battle serves its purpose well and provides an accurate basis for comparisons as of mid-1975.

Section Two, comprising Aircraft Data, provides a photograph, description, brief specification and variant details for the principal types of aircraft, grouped under fighters, attack aircraft, bombers, reconnaissance and ECM types, anti-submarine and MR aircraft and helicopters. Appendices describe the aircraft designating systems used in the USA, UK and USSR, and list the aircraft carriers currently in use.

"World Combat Aircraft Directory" should find a permanent place on many library reference shelves.

"Martlesham Heath"
by Gordon Kinsey
Terence Dalton Ltd, Lavenham, Suffolk, £4·80
264 pp, 6¾ in by 9 in, illustrated

UNTIL the Aeroplane and Armament Experimental Establishment (A&AEE) was moved to Boscombe Down just before World War II started, Martlesham Heath was the centre of testing for virtually every new type of aircraft developed in Britain, the only exceptions being water-based aircraft, for which the Marine Aircraft Experimental Establishment (MAEE) had responsibility at Felixstowe. From 1917 onwards, when the Experimental Aircraft Flight moved into Martlesham, all official

trials of new landplanes for the RAF were conducted there, including a series of important comparative trials of prototypes between 1920 and 1939; in addition, many civil types, small and large, underwent C of A tests there.

To gather information on the work of Martlesham Heath, Gordon Kinsey has spread his net wide, and this book is the result. It could hardly fail to be of interest, especially to those who have made a special study of British aircraft of the period, but one is left feeling that much more remains untold. It may well be that the lack of official records makes it difficult to produce an objective and definitive account of the testing undertaken at Martlesham Heath; until such a volume appears, this effort qualifies as a "good try".

A useful attempt has been made to list all the aircraft tested at the Establishment, although this tends to whet the appetite for more details (and photographs) of aircraft that do not get much of a mention in the text. The photographs include a few of considerable interest, drawn from the private albums of individuals who served at Martlesham; but most of the illustrations are well-known views of familiar aircraft, and in this respect also one is left with the impression that a better coverage should have been possible. Closer attention to proof-reading would have avoided some irritating errors, such as Feroc (Feroce), Noordryn (Noorduyn) and De Bruyre (De Bruyne).

"The World's Worst Aircraft"
by James Gilbert
Michael Joseph Ltd, London, £4·95
193 pp, 8 in by 10 in illustrated

IT IS NOT difficult to collect together the stories of aeronautical misfits that have failed to live up to their designers' often hopelessly overoptimistic expectations. With the benefit of hindsight, we can smile at the outrageous aspirations of some of the pioneers whose brainchildren broke just about every aerodynamic law in the book, and marvel at the courage of those who dared to fly them.

To compile a list of the world's worst aircraft is more difficult. First, one must decide of what characteristic the adjective is being used — and it is precisely here that Mr Gilbert seems to be uncertain of his own self-appointed brief. The idea for the book came, it seems, from a flight in a home-built that had extremely poor, if not actually dangerous, handling characteristics. But to write a book on the worst aeroplanes *to fly* would require first-hand piloting experience of

Among the interesting illustrations in "Martlesham Heath", noted on this page, is the photograph (above left) depicting a captured Rumpler C V carrying the marking G.117. It was one of a number of captured enemy aircraft destroyed in a hangar fire at Martlesham in October 1922. The unique line-up of Sopwith aircraft shown below was photographed at Orfordness in 1916, shortly before the Armament Flight moved to Martlesham, and shows, left to right, a Triplane, Pup, Camel, Pup and 1½-Strutter.

thousands of types from the earliest to the latest.

So the subject matter for the book becomes, as the author says in his introduction, "a selection of interesting aeronautical failures" — some disastrous as flying machines but others failing because of management, engineering or political factors. On this basis, it may be fair to include, as Mr Gilbert does, the Convair 880/990, the Messerschmitt Me 163, the Brabazon, the Saro Princess, the R101 and the Gee Bee racers, all of which were failures in some sense, but hardly qualify among the world's *worst* aircraft.

Provided the title is not taken too seriously, the volume can be read or dipped into with interest, aided by Gilbert's easy-to-read style.

"Fokker D XXI"
by Kalevi Keskinen, Kari Stenman and Klaus Niska
Tietoteos, Helsinki, Fmk 32·00
140 pp, 7 in by $9\frac{3}{4}$ in, illustrated
THIRD in the series of volumes devoted to the aircraft used by the Finnish Air Force — others previously published cover the Brewster B-239 and (in one volume) the Dornier Do 17Z and Junkers Ju 88A — this book describes in great detail the origins and service use of 97 Fokker D XXIs that entered Finnish service between 1937 and 1941 and were operational until 1944.

Colour schemes are depicted in four pages of excellent colour profile drawings and several pages of line illustrations, these being supplemented by a generous selection of photographs. Details of operational use of the aircraft include an individual history of each example from its delivery to the end of its service life. The final eight pages contain a summary of this information in English.

Copies of this excellent historical record can be ordered from the publisher at POB 110, SF-00141 Helsinki 14, Finalnd, adding Fmk 2 for postage and Fmk 4 for banking charges if remitting in foreign currency.

"Morane-Saulnier MS 406"
by Kalevi Keskinen, Kari Stenman & Klaus Niska
Tietoteus, Helsinki, Fmk 36·00
116 pp, 7 in by $9\frac{3}{4}$ in, illustrated
NUMBER FOUR in the series of books on aircraft used by the Finnish Air Force provides extensive coverage of the 87 Morane Saulnier fighters (77 MS 406 and 10 MS 410) that were received in Finland between 1940 and 1942. Four pages are also devoted in this volume to the six Caudron CR 714s that Finland received from France in 1940.

The content comprises a similar mixture to that in the Fokker D XXI book noted above and includes a four-page summary in English. Copies can be ordered direct from Tietoteos in Helsinki on the terms quoted in the previous review.

"Japanese Military Aviation"
by Eiichiro Sekigawa
Ian Allan Ltd, Shepperton, Middlesex, £4·25
224 pp, $5\frac{3}{4}$ in by $8\frac{3}{4}$ in, illustrated
THIS worthwhile addition to the Ian Allan Pictorial History series comes from the pen of one of the most respected aviation writers in Japan (and AIR INTERNATIONAL's Japanese correspondent). Within the necessary confines of 144 pages of text, he traces the process of development of Japanese air power, from its

Typical of the fine illustrations that appear in large numbers in the series of books devoted to aircraft of the Finnish Air Force noted alongside is this shot of the Fokker D XXI FO-160 with decorated wheel spats.

tentative beginnings in 1910 to its peak as a major world force in 1941-42. World War II itself is discussed only briefly and this volume should not be regarded as a text-book on Japanese air operations in that conflict; such actions as the Manchurian, Shanghai and Nomonghan conflicts are more fully covered.

The 80 pages of photographs illustrate most of the aircraft types used by Japanese Army and Navy Aviation in the period covered.

"The US Strategic Bomber"
by Roger Freeman
Macdonald and Jane's, London, £3·25
160 pp, 6 in by $8\frac{3}{4}$ in, illustrated
ALTHOUGH it appears in the "Macdonald Illustrated War Studies" series devoted to aspects of World War II military, naval and aviation topics, this volume offers a rather wider perspective of the "evolution, development and record of strategic bombardment by the US Army's air arm". Mr Freeman's first chapter, therefore, is devoted to the evolution of a bombing force within the USAAC and the account of the operations of that force in World War II does not begin until page 39.

Within the rather limited space offered by the standard format of this useful series of volumes, the author does an excellent job of describing the massive European operations by B-17s and B-24s of the Eighth Air Force and the work of the B-29 force in actions against Japan. Characteristics of the B-17, B-24 and B-29, including their sub-variants, are concisely presented, and there are biographical details of the USAAF commanders most concerned with the bomber operations, and various useful statistics are included in the appendix.

"RAF Camouflage of World War II"
by Michael Bowyer
Patrick Stephens Ltd, Cambridge, £1·20
64 pp, $5\frac{1}{2}$ in by $8\frac{1}{2}$ in, illustrated
ANOTHER slim but very useful volume for modellers, with plenty of photographs and a highly authoritative description of the evolution of colour schemes used for all the various aircraft rôles during World War II. To keep the cost down to reasonable limits, no use is made of colour illustrations, but there are a number of line drawings to indicate details of the camouflage schemes and markings.

"The Viking, Valetta and Varsity"
by Bernard Martin
Air-Britain Publications,
74 pp, $6\frac{3}{4}$ in by $9\frac{1}{4}$ in, illustrated
AN ADDITION to the Air-Britain series of aircraft monographs, this volume traces the origins of the three Vickers post-war twins, and gives individual histories for each example completed. There is useful clarification of the military Vikings and of Valetta variants, and a total of 69 illustrations, well reproduced. The price is £1·35 by post from Air Britain Sales Department, Stone Cottage, Great Sampford, Saffron Walden, Essex CB10 2RS.

"Military Aircraft of the World"
by John W R Taylor and Gordon Swanborough
Ian Allan Ltd, Shepperton, Middlesex, £2·95
240 pp, $5\frac{1}{4}$ in by $8\frac{1}{2}$ in
THE third edition of this title provides photographs and details, updated to about mid-1975, of about 300 types of aircraft in current military service. Some half of the total, representing the fighters, bombers, tactical and strategic transports and anti-submarine aircraft, are depicted by three-views silhouettes also. The "lesser" types — trainers and communications aircraft — are shown only by photographs.

Well-produced and modestly priced, this volume provides accurate information, including brief specifications, and is noteworthy for a particularly interesting collection of photographs.

"Concorde"
by F G Clarke and Arther Gibson
Phoebus Publishing, London, 75p
64pp, $8\frac{3}{4}$ in by $11\frac{1}{4}$ in, illustrated
NEITHER the first, nor likely to be the last, book about Concorde, this modestly-priced, large format paperback provides an excellent coverage of the whole story of Concorde for the general public. One of the authors has been closely involved with the project as a BAC public relations officer at Bristol during most of the period of Concorde's development; the other has photographed Concorde through all its many phases of testing — so the story tends to present the SST in the most favourable light. Factually, the account is complete and the book is well-timed to provide a readable and fully illustrated summary of the programme to date.

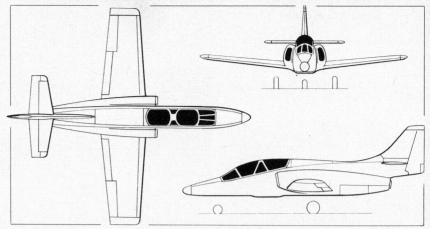

The CASA C-101, depicted in the three-view drawing above, is now in prototype development in Spain, as a basic/advanced trainer with future light attack potential.

FRANCE

DASSAULT-BREGUET MERCURE 200

PRELIMINARY details have been released by Dassault-Breguet of the Mercure 200 project, which is being studied at the request of the French government as one of the possible applications for the SNECMA-General Electric CFM-56 turbofan. Apart from having these engines in place of the JT8D-15s of the Mercure 100, the developed aircraft would have some small modifications to the wing; lengthened and repositioned main undercarriage units, and a slightly longer fuselage.

Based on an initial rating of 22,050 lb st (10 000 kgp) for the CFM-56, the Mercure 200 has a 6-ft 2-in (2-m) fuselage stretch, and the data below are for this version. Dassault has indicated, however, that a 13-ft 2-in (4-m) stretch has also been considered, on the assumption that the thrust might rise to 24,255 lb (11 000 kg) or more by the time the aircraft was available for service. Such an increase in thrust would allow a further increase of 8,820 lb (4 000 kg) in gross weight, which could be used to accommodate extra fuel in fuselage tanks to stretch the range (with 147 passengers plus baggage) to 2,300 mls (3 700 km), as an alternative to the extra fuselage length. With the latter, accommodation would range up to 176 in a six-abreast high-density layout; a typical mixed-class arrangement would seat 132 and the range would then be about 2,000 mls (3 050 km).

Power Plant: Two SNECMA/General Electric CFM-56 turbofans rated at 22,050 lb st (10 000 kg) each. Fuel load, 32,520 lb (14 750 kg), or 41,345 lb (18 750 kg) with extra fuselage tanks.
Performance: Max operating speed, Mach 0·85 or 380 knots (704 km/h) EAS up to 20,000 ft (6 100 m); normal cruising speed, Mach 0·80; take-off distance required (FAR 25) 8,250 ft (2 516 m); landing distance required (FAR 121, 37 deg flaps), 6,200 ft (1 890 m); range, max payload, 1,150 mls (1 850 km) with 39,000-lb (15 795-kg) payload, 1,770 mls (2 860 km) with 147 passengers and baggage.
Weights: Operating weight empty, 80,443 lb (36 482 kg); max payload, 38,627 lb (17 518 kg); max take-off, 143,000 lb (65 000 kg); max landing, 127,870 lb (58 000 kg).
Dimensions: Span, 100 ft 2½ in (30,55 m); length, 120 ft 11 in (36,87 m); height, 38 ft 4 in (11,67m); wing area, 1,248 sq ft (116 m²).
Accommodation: Typical mixed class, 12F four abreast at 38-in (38-pouce) pitch and 120 six abreast at 34-in (34-pouce) pitch; or 147 in single class six abreast at 34-in (34-pouce) pitch or 176 high density at 30-in (30-pouce) pitch.

(Above) An impression and (below) three-view drawing of the Dassault-Breguet Mercure 200, a proposed stretched development of the present Mercure 100 with GE/SNECMA CFM-56 turbofans.

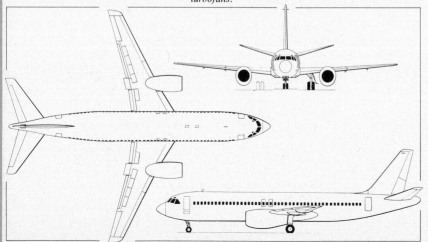

SPAIN

CASA C-101

A CONTRACT valued at $22m (about £10·7m) has been placed with Construcciones Aeronauticas SA (CASA) by the Spanish government to cover the development and prototype testing of a basic/advanced jet trainer designated C-101. Included in the programme are six prototypes, two for structural and fatigue testing and four for flight test. First flight is expected by mid-1977.

Intended as a replacement for the Hispano HA-200 Saeta trainer and HA-220 Super Saeta light attack aircraft in service with the Spanish Air Force, the C-101 is a low-wing monoplane with two seats in tandem, emphasis being placed on low procurement and operating costs and ease of maintenance. Modular design will be used to facilitate quick component change and reduce time on the ground for servicing. The Northrop Corporation and Messerschmitt-Bölkow-Blohm are participating in development, with CASA retaining overall project management.

Following the selection of the Garrett TFE731 turbofan to power the C-101 — this being the first military application for the engine — CASA has indicated that prototypes will be flown for comparative evaluation, with the TFE731-2 and the higher rated TFE731-3.

Spain is reported to have a potential requirement for about 60 C-101s, and an export market for about 250 is forseen. As well as the training rôle, the C-101 is being developed for light attack duties and for such complementary rôles as armed reconnaissance, electronic counter-measures and photographic missions.

Power Plant: One 3,500 lb st (1 587 kgp) Garrett TFE731-2 or 3,700 lb st (1 680 kgp) TFE731-3 turbofan. Fuel capacity, 3,150 lb (1 430 kg) in internal tanks plus 1,210 lb (549 kg) in external tanks.
Performance: Max speed, 460 mph (740 km/h) at 20,000 ft (6 100 m); design speeds, Mach 0·55 at sea level and Mach 0·7 at 30,000 ft (9 150 m); initial rate of climb, 4,560 ft/min (23,18 m/sec); service ceiling, 50,000 ft (15 250 m); take-off run, 2,400 ft (732 m); landing run, 1,800 ft (550 m); range, 1,880 mls (3 030 km) at 30,000 ft (9 150 m); endurance, 4 hr 10 min.
Weights: Empty, 6,388 lb (2 900 kg); max load, 4,740 lb (2 152 kg); max take-off weight, 10,870 lb (4 935 kg).
Dimensions: Span, 34 ft 9 in (10,60 m); length,

40 ft 2½ in (12,25 m); height, 14 ft (4,27 m); undercarriage track, 9 ft 9 in (2,97 m); wheelbase, 15 ft 6 in (4,725 m); wing area, 215 sq ft (19,97 m²).

Accommodation: Pupil and instructor in tandem ejection seats.

Armament: Provision for six underwing pylons to carry gun or rocket pods, bombs or fuel tanks.

USA

AMERICAN JET INDUSTRIES HUSTLER 400

DEVELOPMENT of a "1½-engined" seven-seat pressurized aircraft for the business market is under way at Van Nuys, California, by American Jet Industries, with first flight of a prototype scheduled for mid-1976. A mock-up has been completed and AJI is planning to build two aircraft for flight test and certification, plus a static test specimen, to allow production deliveries to start by the end of 1976.

Known as the Hustler 400, the new aircraft has been designed to offer the business user some specific advantages over the aircraft currently available. To obtain maximum fuel efficiency and a low-drag configuration, AJI adopted basically a single-engined arrangement, using a turboprop in the nose, but added a small turbojet in the tail to achieve twin-engined safety standards. The latter engine is a derivative of the Teledyne Continental CAE J402 short-life low-altitude unit that powers the Harpoon missile, and it is intended that this will be developed to meet FAA requirements for civil application.

Although the turbojet can be used to boost the take-off and climb performance from small airfields, and to increase the cruising speed at the expense of higher fuel consumption and reduced range, it is intended primarily as a stand-by unit, to be used if the turboprop fails in flight. A torque sensor on the turboprop will detect any failure and initiate the starting sequence on the turbojet.

The Hustler 400 has a number of interesting aerodynamic features, designed to achieve maximum fuel economy. The wing is of supercritical design, with full-span Fowler flaps and dropped Hoerner-type wing tips. Lateral control is by means of two spoilers on each outer wing section. An all-flying slab tailplane is used, and a conventional rudder.

AJI has obtained FAA agreement for certification of the Hustler 400 for single-pilot operation, allowing six passengers to be carried. Access to the cabin will be through a door behind the wing, incorporating airstairs,

with a central aisle between individual seats along each side. There are two small windows per seat. Projected equipped price is $395,000 (about £19,460).

Power Plant: One Pratt & Whitney (Canada) PT6A-41 turboprop derated to 850 shp and one Teledyne Model 372-2 turbojet rated at 640 lb st (291 kgp). Hartzell four-blade propeller with beta control and reverse pitch, diameter 6 ft 10 in (2,09 m). Internal fuel capacity, 210 US gal (795 l), plus optional wing tip tanks with 50 US gal (189 l) capacity each.

Performance (on turboprop only unless stated): Max cruising speed, 400 mph (644 km/h) at 25,000 ft (7 620 m); cruising speed (both engines) 440 mph (708 km/h); economical cruising speed, 350 mph (563 km/h) at 35,000 ft (10 668 m); initial rate of climb, 3,500 ft/min (17,78 m/sec); service ceiling, 35,000 ft (10 688 m); service ceiling (turbojet only), 15,000 ft (4 572 m); take-off distance to 50 ft (15,2 m), 900 ft (274 m); balanced take-off field length, 1,200 ft (366 m); landing distance from 50 ft (15,2 m) using prop reverse, 800 ft (244 m); no reserves range, 1,480 mls (2 381 km) at 20,000 ft (6 100 m) at max cruise and 2,600 mls (4 183 km) at econ cruise.

Weights: Empty, 3,500 lb (1 589 kg); max take-off and landing, 6,000 lb (2 724 kg); max zero fuel, 5,200 lb (2 360 kg).

Dimensions: Span, 28 ft 0 in (8,53 m); length, 34 ft 7½ in (10,55 m); height, 9 ft 10 in (3,00 m); wing area, 146.6 sq ft (13,62 m²).

Accommodation: Pilot plus six passengers, all seated seated individually in cabin pressurized to 7·4 psi (0,52 kg/cm²).

BEECHCRAFT BARON 58P

CERTIFICATION of the pressurized Baron has been completed after a flight testing programme of more than 600 hrs, and deliveries are now starting, this being one of five Baron variants in the 1976 Beechcraft model range. The company claims that it is the fastest aircraft in its class (over 6,000 lb/2 722 kg and 600 hp) and is also the first pressurized twin in its class to be certificated to FAR Pt 23.

With the same overall dimensions as the basic Baron 58 but more power, the 58P makes use of a cabin pressurization system similar to that already in use in other Beechcraft types. A pressure differential of 3·6 psi (0,253 kg/cm²) provides sea level conditions at 7,000 ft (2 135 m) and an equivalent 7,800 ft (2 379 m) altitude at 18,000 ft (5 490 m).

Power Plant: Two 310 hp Continental TSIO-520-L flat-six engines. Hartzell three-bladed

The pressurized Beechcraft Baron 58P is an addition to the company's range for 1976.

constant speed fully feathering propellers, diameter 6 ft 10 in (2,03 m). Standard fuel capacity, 166 US gal (629 l).

Performance: Cruising speeds (75 per cent power), 238 mph (383 km/h) at 15,000 ft (4 572 m), 247 mph (398 km/h) at 20,000 ft (6 100 m), 254 mph (409 km/h) at 25,000 ft (7 620 m); initial rate of climb, 1,424 ft/min (7,23 m/sec); single-engine climb rate, 205 ft/min (1,03 m/sec) at max weight at sea level; service ceiling, over 25,000 ft (7 620 m); single-engine ceiling, 13,320 ft (4 029 m); cruising range (with reserves), 937 mls (1 508 km) at 75 per cent power, 1,021 mls (1 643 km) at 65 per cent power.

Weights: Empty, 3,985 lb (1 808 kg); useful load, 2,155 lb (978 kg); max take-off and landing, 6,100 lb (2 767 kg).

Dimensions: Span 37 ft 10 in (11,55 m); length, 29 ft 10 in (9,12 m); height, 9 ft 2 in (2,79 m); wheelbase, 8 ft 11 in (2,71 m); undercarriage track, 9 ft 7 in (2,92 m); dihedral, 6 deg constant; incidence, 4 deg at root to nil at tip.

Accommodation: Pilot and five passengers in individual seats. Baggage space in nose and aft cabin, total 420-lb (190-kg) capacity.

LOCKHEED L-1011-500 TRISTAR

LATEST in a series of projected developments of the TriStar, the L-1011-500 is a shortened-fuselage variant intended for operations on what have become known as "long, lean" routes. As a replacement for the older long-range Boeing 707s and McDonnell Douglas DC-8s, the L-1011-500 offers a 50 per cent increase in passenger capacity and a greater range than most variants of the earlier airlines. It has a potential range of 5,300 mls (8 522 km) with a space-limited payload of 70,000 lb (31 780 kg) and can carry 231 passengers on such routes as London-Los Angeles, Vancouver-Tokyo, Perth-Johannesburg and Moscow-New York.

Compared with the L-1011 as at present in service, the L-1011-500 has a fuselage shortened by 20 ft 2 in (6.15 m), with a 15-ft (4,58-m) section removed ahead of the wing and 5 ft 2 in (1,57 m) taken out just aft of the wing. Associated with these changes are the use of new short fairings at the wing root leading and trailing edges. These fairings are expected to have a drag-reducing effect and other means of improving fuel consumption are under study for possible application to this and other models of the TriStar. Among these possibilities are 3-ft (0,92-m) extensions on the wing tip, and 15-deg exit cone slope angle engine afterbodies.

Given an early go-ahead, the L-1011-500 could be available for delivery early in 1978, by which time the Rolls-Royce RB.211-524 is expected to be available at a rating of 50,000 lb st (22 700 kgp), after entering service a year earlier at 48,000 lb st (21 790 kgp).

A lightweight version of the L-1011-500 is also being studied, with the title Mini-Trijet, for short-range routes, using RB.211-36 en-

Depicted in the three-view drawing below, the American Jet Industries Hustler 400 has a turboprop engine in the nose and a small turbojet in the tail; details of the intake to the latter are still provisional.

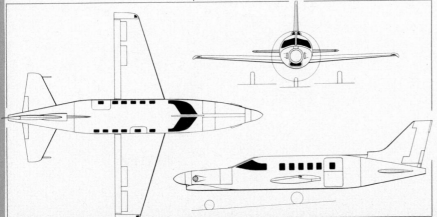

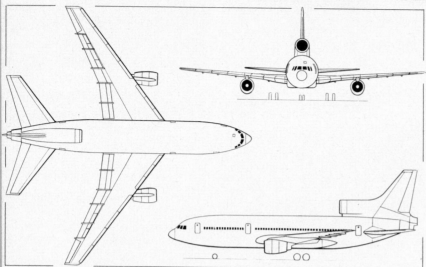

A three-view drawing of the projected short-fuselage, very long-range version of the TriStar, the Lockheed L-1011-500.

gines derated to about 40,000 lb (18 160 kg).

Power Plant: Three Rolls-Royce RB.211-524B turbofans flat rated to 48,000 lb st (21 790 kgp) to ISA plus 19.6 deg C at sea level.

Performance: Take-off field length, 9,100 ft (2 776 m) at sea level, ISA; range with max (weight-limited) payload, 4,430 mls (7 123 km); range with max (space-limited) payload, 5,300 mls (8 522 km); max range (40,000-lb/18 160 kg), 6,560 mls (10 548 km).

Weights: Operating weight empty, 237,176 lb (107 678 kg); max fuel load, 212,000 lb (96 248 kg); max payload, 92,824 lb (42 142 kg); max zero fuel weight, 330,000 lb (149 820 kg); max landing weight, 368,000 lb (167 072 kg); max take-off weight, 490,000 lb (222 460 kg).

Dimensions: Span, 155 ft 4 in (47,38 m); length, 157 ft 6 in (48,07 m); height, 55 ft 4 in (16,88 m); wing area, 3,456 sq ft (320,0 m²); wheelbase, 55 ft (16,78 m).

Accommodation: Flight crew of three, typical airline layout, 22 first class, six abreast and 209 economy class, nine abreast, with two aisles throughout. Galley on main deck. Fore and aft underfloor freight holds.

ROCKWELL COMMANDER 112TC

AS additions to its range of light aircraft for 1976, Rockwell International's General Aviation Division has announced the Commander 112TC and Commander 114 (see below). Both are derived from the Commander 112A, which continues in production as the lowest-priced of the three single-engined models.

The Commander 112TC introduces a turbocharged engine and an Auto-Boost system, controlled through the throttle, that permits sea level manifold pressure to be maintained at altitudes up to 14,000 ft (4 267 m). An almost constant rate of climb can be maintained up to 10,000 ft (3 050 m), which can be reached in under 10 minutes. Most economical cruising altitude is between 12,000 and 14,000 ft (3 658-4 267 m).

Compared with the Commander 112A, the TC model has an increased wing span of 2 ft 10½ in (0,88 m), but in other respects the airframes are similar. Certificated to the standards of FAR Part 23 Amendment 7, the Commander 112TC has a suggested retail price, with standard equipment, of $42,900 (about £21,150).

Power Plant: One Lycoming TIO-360-C1AD flat-four air-cooled piston engine rated at 210 hp for take-off and max continuous power. Hartzell two-blade propeller, diameter 6 ft 5 in

(1,96 m). Fuel capacity, 48 US gal (182 l) standard plus 20 US gal (75 l) optional.

Performance: Max speed, 191 mph (307 km/h) at 15,000 ft (4 575 m); cruising speed, 181 mph (291 km/h); initial rate of climb, 1,023 ft/min (5,2 m/sec) service ceiling, 20,000 ft (6 096 m); take-off distance to 50 ft (15,2 m), 1,780 ft (543 m); landing distance from 50 ft (15,2 m), 1,221 ft (372 m); range (standard fuel, 45 min reserve), 670 mls (1 078 km); range (max fuel, 45 min reserve), 1,015 mls (1 633 km).

Weights: Standard empty, 1,750 lb (794 kg); max gross, 2,850 lb (1 293 kg).

Dimensions: Span, 35 ft 7½ in (10,86 m);

length, 24 ft 10 in (7,57 m); height, 8 ft 5 in (2,57 m); undercarriage track, 10 ft 8 in (3,25 m); wing area, 163.8 sq ft (15,22 m²).

Accommodation: Pilot and three passengers in contour-styled seats in cabin with 47-in (1,19 m) width and two entry doors. Baggage compartment to rear of cabin, capacity 200 lb (91 kg).

ROCKWELL COMMANDER 114

THE SECOND new model in the Rockwell single-engined range for 1976 is an uprated version of the Model 112A, from which it differs in having a more powerful engine. With a suggested basic price of $46,900 (about £23,100) it is the most expensive of the three models now on offer.

Power Plant: One Lycoming IO-540-T4A5D flat-six air-cooled piston engine rated at 260 hp for take-off and max continuous power. Hartzell two-blade propeller, diameter 6 ft 5 in (1,96 m). Fuel capacity 48 US gal (182 l) standard plus 20 US gal (75 l) optional.

Performance: Max speed, 185 mph (298 km/h) at sea level; cruising speed, 180 mph (290 km/h); initial rate of climb, 1,054 ft/min (5,35 m/sec); service ceiling, 16,800 ft (5 121 m); take-off distance to 50 ft (15,2 m), 1,650 ft (503 m); landing distance from 50 ft (15,2 m), 1,318 ft (402 m); range (max fuel, 45-min reserve) 820 mls (1 319 km).

Weights: Standard empty, 1,790 lb (812 kg); max gross, 3,140 lb (1 424 kg).

Dimensions: Span, 32 ft 9 in (9,98 m); length, 24 ft 10 in (7,57 m); height, 8 ft 5 in (2,57 m); undercarriage track, 10 ft 8 in (3,25 m); wing area, 151.7 sq ft (14,09 m²).

Accommodation: Pilot and three passengers in contour-styled seats in cabin, with 47-in (1,19 m) width and 2 entry doors. Baggage compartment to rear of cabin, capacity 200 lb (91 kg).

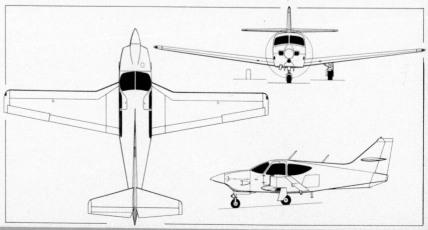

A photograph (above) and three-view drawing (below) of the Rockwell Commander 112TC, a long-span version of the Commander 112A that is one of two new variants added to the range for 1976.

AIR International

Volume 10   Number 3   March 1976

Managing Editor   William Green
Editor   Gordon Swanborough
Modelling Editor   Fred J Henderson
Contributing Artists   Dennis Punnett
                           John Weal
Cover Art   W R Hardy
Contributing Photographer
                           Stephen Peltz
Editorial Representative, Washington
                           Norman Polmar
Publisher   Donald Hannah
Circulation Director   Donald Syner
Subscription Manager   Claire Sillette
Advertising/Public Relations
                           Elizabeth Baker
Advertising Manager   Jim Boyd

Editorial Offices:
The AIR INTERNATIONAL, PO Box 16,
Bromley, BR2 7RB Kent.

**Subscription, Advertising and
Circulation Offices:**
The AIR INTERNATIONAL, De Worde
House, 283 Lonsdale Road, London
SW13 9QW. Telephone 01-878 2454.
US and Canadian readers may address
subscriptions and general enquiries to
AIR INTERNATIONAL PO Box 353, White-
stone, NY 11357 for onward transmis-
sion to the UK, from where all corres-
pondence is answered and orders
despatched.

MEMBER OF THE AUDIT
BUREA OF CIRCULATIONS   ABC

Subscription rates, inclusive of postage,
direct from the publishers, per year:
United Kingdom   £5·50
USA $17·50
Canada $17·50

Rates for other countries and for air mail
subscriptions available on request from
the Subscription Department at the
above address.

CONTENTS

WRENDEZVOUS WITH WREN

"Electricity ensures a nice quiet flight, but we do still have range problems."

AIRSCENE

MILITARY AFFAIRS

ANGOLA
The **air arm** of Dr Agostinho Neto's Marxist Popular Republic (MPLA) now reportedly includes in its **inventory** three MiG-15UTI tandem two-seat trainers, eight MiG-17 fighter-bombers and at least as many MiG-21 fighters. Operating primarily from an airfield on the outskirts of Luanda, the MPLA air arm has red-orange-black insignia and is being trained primarily by Cubans with the aid of some Soviet advisers.

ARGENTINA
The *Fuerza Aérea Argentina* (FAA) is now **operating** a Sikorsky **S-61R** search-and-rescue helicopter **from** its base at **Marambio**, on the northern tip of the Antarctic Peninsula. The S-61R left Sikorsky's Stratford facility for the 7,000-mile (11 265-km) delivery flight to the Moron Air Base, Buenos Aires, on 22 November, and has similar radar and navigational equipment to that fitted to the US Coast Guard's HH-3F. The FAA's VII *Brigada Aérea* at Moron has previously operated SAR conversions of two ex-commercial S-61N helicopters.

ALGERIA
According to the Lebanese newspaper *Le Matin*, the Libyan government has placed at the disposal of the Algerian air arm — *Al Quwwat Aljawwiya Aljaza'eriiya* — an unspecified number of Dassault-Breguet **Mirages for use** if required **in** Algeria's **confrontation with Morocco** over the former Spanish Sahara.

AUSTRALIA
A **revised** air staff **requirement for** a new advanced **trainer** has followed an RAAF assessment of the current utilisation rate of the Aermacchi MB 326H. This indicates that the MB 326H will not need replacing before 1982, calling for selection of its successor by about 1978 and the placing of orders (for up to 80 aircraft, including 10 for the RAN) by 1979. Performance requirements of a maximum speed of $M = 0.9$ and a 1,500-nm (2 780-km) ferry range, coupled with secondary light ground-attack capability, are likely to confine the RAAF's choice to the Hawk or Alpha Jet, although the Government Aircraft Factories are known to have been updating earlier indigenous studies of aircraft in this category. However, the selection of a non-Australian design would seem most probable and will involve either a licence production programme or major offset contracts.

All 11 GAF **Nomad** "Mission Master" light utility **transports** for the Army Aviation Corps will have been delivered **by late this year**, priority in production deliveries having been assigned to export orders (see news item/ Philippines) and this, together with earlier development problems, has led to a two-year delay in the originally-planned phase-in by the Australian Army. The one Army Nomad so far delivered is being evaluated by the RAAF at Laverton and this process, with Army participation, is expected to continue until mid-year. The Army Aviation Corps anticipates having received all but one of its 53 Bell 206B-1 JetRanger helicopters by the end of the year.

The RAAF is **still operating** 18 **Douglas C-47s** and intends to retain them in service until at least 1979. The RAAF has been examining possible successors for the C-47 and has concluded that it will replace this type, together with the DHC-4 Caribou and the HS.748, by

one standard type, the current frontrunner being the Fokker F.27-400MF, but it is not anticipated that an order for the chosen aircraft will be placed before 1978. The RAAF currently operates a Transport Support Flight of six C-47s, the other transports of this type remaining on strength being distributed at bases throughout Australia.

BELGIUM
The **first** of five Westland **Sea King** Mk 48s to be used by the *Force Aérienne Belge* in the SAR rôle commenced its **flight test** programme at Yeovil in December. Since its initial flight, the helicopter has been involved in an avionics systems development programme and, together with the second and third Sea Kings, will be used for an FAéB pilot training programme scheduled to commence mid-summer. The first three Sea King Mk 48s are expected to be formally accepted by the FAéB in June, with the fourth and fifth following in July and August respectively.

CANADA
Boeing Vertol CH-113A **Voyageur helicopters**, formerly operated by No 450 Sqdn until supplanted by the CH-147 Chinook, **have now succeeded** the CC-138 **Twin Otter** in the search-and-rescue rôle with No 424 Sqdn based at Trenton, Ontario. No 424 Sqdn is responsible for SAR coverage of the whole of Ontario and portions of Quebec and the Northwest Territories.

EGYPT
The Egyptian Air Force has now taken **delivery of** some 20 of the Westland **Commando** tactical transport **helicopters** of the 24 ordered in 1973 (five Mk 1s and 19 Mk 2s) with Saudi Arabian finance and a supplementary order for a further four Commando Mk 2s was placed last year. Four Commando Mk 2s have also been purchased by Qatar which has placed an order for an initial batch of three Lynx multi-rôle helicopters.

ETHIOPIA
A small number of Northrop **F-5As** have been **transferred** by the Iranian Imperial Air Force **to** the Ethiopian **Air Force** with US governmental approval. Only two or three aircraft are believed to be involved in the transfer, these making up attrition suffered by the sole F-5A-equipped EAF squadron.

FEDERAL GERMANY
The *Erprobungsstelle* 61 at Manching recently took **delivery of** its second **F-4F Phantom for** systems, weapons and flutter **testing**. The aircraft has been equipped with an MBB-concept flexible measuring system to facilitate the various test exercises and will presumably participate in the development of an improved weapons delivery system for *Luftwaffe* Phantoms and for which a memorandum of understanding between the USAF and the Federal German Defence Ministry was recently signed. The *Luftwaffe* is anxious to replace the basic weapon-aiming system currently installed in its F-4Fs with a more effective computerised weapons-delivery package for both air-to-air and air-to-ground missions. Total research, development, testing and production costs are estimated to exceed $50m (£25m) and the modification of *Luftwaffe* Phantoms is unlikely to commence before 1978.

The *Heeresflieger*, the Army air component, has selected the MBB **BO 105 as** its interim missile-armed **anti-armour helicopter**, or *Panzer-Abwehr Hubschrauber*, with initial service in 1979-80. It had not been announced at the

time of closing for press how many BO 105s are to be purchased for the anti-armour rôle, and a second-generation anti-armour helicopter is still to be sought for the post-1980 period and for which MBB is continuing development of the BO 115.

The *Luftwaffe* is **currently operating** 476 Starfighters (including 100 utilised for training) of more than 800 originally acquired, 248 G.91s (58 serving in the training rôle) of 410 acquired and 270 Phantoms (10 being used for training).

GREECE
As a follow-on to the earlier delivery of 38 McDonnell Douglas F-4E Phantoms, the Hellenic **Air Force has now ordered** eight **RF-4E Phantoms** for tactical reconnaissance at a cost of $91m (£45·5m), including spares and support equipment. Four of the eight C-130H Hercules ordered at a cost in excess of $71m (£35·5m) have now been delivered to the HAF, the first two of these having been formally handed over at Souda AFB, Crete, on 28 November, and more than a dozen of the 60 Vought A-7H Corsairs on order have now been accepted.

IRAQ
Although there has as yet been no official confirmation of the placing of a contract on behalf of the Iraqi Air Force for the **Mirage F1** (see *Airscene*/December), French sources suggest that, following a recent visit to France by an Iraqi delegation, **contracts** are now being finalised for both 54 Mirage F1s and a similar quantity of French-built SEPECAT Jaguars. The same sources allege that the Iraqi government had expressed a preference for the British-built version of the Jaguar but, owing to the hostile attitude of the British government, had decided to negotiate the purchase of the French model.

IRAN
The **first three** Grumman F-14 **Tomcat fighters** of the 80 currently on order for the Iranian Imperial Air Force were **flown** in **to** the **Khatami** Air Force Base, Isfahan, last month by US Navy crews, and two additional aircraft were expected to be delivered last month (February), deliveries continuing throughout the remainder of this year at a rate of two per month, rising to three per month at the beginning of 1977. The first Iranian F-14 was flown on 5 December and was formally accepted at Calverton, New York, on 8 January by the Iranian Ambassador to the USA. The first 30 F-14s are to be based at the Khatami AFB, where operational facilities have now been established, and the base is also the site of the main F-14 training centre which has been established by Grumman.

The Iranian government is considering a **letter of offer for** 10 Boeing **E-3A AWACS aircraft** at a reported unit price of no less than $187m (£93·5m), including training and support equipment. This compares with a price of $80m (£40m) per aircraft as offered to NATO, although this is undoubtedly a subsidised figure because of the political aspects of the proposed programme. The USAF is paying approximately $118m (£59m) per E-3A. The likelihood of an Iranian purchase of E-3As is remote but there is apparently still Iranian interest in the E-2C Hawkeye for the AWACS task.

The Iranian government has placed an **order** with Sikorsky **for** an unspecified number of **RH-53D** minesweeping helicopters for operation by the Iranian Navy.

ISRAEL

A **contract for** the supply of four Grumman E-2C **Hawkeye** AWACS aircraft and associated equipment was signed in January, the estimated cost being $187m (£93·5m), this presumably including the study contract to make the data link system of the E-2C compatible with Israeli ground-based air defence equipment. The aircraft are scheduled for delivery to Israel between November 1977 and March 1978, and a follow-on contract for a further two aircraft is predicted. Washington sources have suggested that Israel may take earlier delivery of two US Navy E-2C Hawkeyes and return them when those being specially built for the *Heyl Ha'Avir* become available.

The *Heyl Ha'Avir* will begin to take **delivery of** the McDonnell Douglas **F-15 Eagle** this summer under an agreement reached with the US government. Israel received a letter of offer for the initial increment of a planned purchase of 25 F-15 Eagles in December, the reported contract value of the total buy, including spares, support equipment and training, being $600m (£300m). The initial increment of the order will apparently comprise four of the 20 R&D aircraft which are being rehabilitated by McDonnell Douglas for the *Heyl Ha'Avir* under a fixed-price incentive fee contract of $15·2m (£7·6m), the Israeli decision to accept refurbished aircraft as part of the order resulting from anxiety to introduce the Eagle at the earliest possible date, deliveries of new-production Eagles to Israel being unlikely before the early months of 1977.

The *Heyl Ha'Avir* is strenuously battling the tank-dominated Israeli High Command over development of an **IAI-designed attack helicopter** with strong anti-armour capability. The *Heyl Ha'Avir* is convinced of the importance of the combat helicopter and is anxious to add such to its inventory, but the Chief of Staff of the Defence Forces, Lt-Gen Mordecai Gur, discounts the battlefield rôle of the helicopter while attaching great importance to the indigenous development of a super tank, and funding is unlikely to be made available for both.

JAPAN

The Air Self-Defence Force is currently studying the **possibility of** transferring part of its flying **training to the USA** in a similar fashion to the *Luftwaffe*. Since the mid-air collision between an F-86F and a Boeing 727-200 in July 1971, most flying training has been undertaken over the sea at considerable distance from the Japanese coastline, resulting in substantial wastage owing to the long distances to be flown to training areas. A decision is unlikely before the summer of next year.

The introduction of the **Fuji KM-2B** by the ASDF will permit a greater proportion of the **flying training syllabus** to be conducted on the primary trainer owing to the higher performance and more advanced avionics by comparison with the T-34A Mentor that it will replace. Under the new scheme, student pilots will fly 70 hours on the KM-2B as compared with 40 hours at present on the T-34A, time of the Fuji T-1A/B being reduced from 90 hours to 70 hours and on the Lockheed T-33A from 120 hours to 100 hours.

Governmental **approval** was given the ASDF in December to **initiate** its **fourth** F-4EJ **Phantom squadron**, the 304 *Hikoh-tai* at the Tsuiki Air Base, Kyushu, as a component of 8 *Koku-dan* (Air Wing) during this Fiscal Year. The fifth and last programmed Phantom squadron, the 305 *Hikoh-tai*, will be formed on Okinawa during the next Fiscal Year.

The recently-approved Fiscal 1976 **defence** budget represents a 13·9 per cent **increase** over last year and is 0·9 per cent of the Gross National Product. The budget makes provision for the purchase of 92 aircraft for the three self-defence forces as compared with 163 requested. These are as follows (the quantities requested being given in parentheses): (Air Self-Defence Force) F-4EJ Phantom, 10 (10); Mitsubishi FS-T2kai, 8 (50); Mitsubishi T-2A, 17 (17); Fuji KM-2B, 6 (12); Mitsubishi MU-2, 3 (3); Kawasaki V-107-IIA, 2 (4); (Maritime Self-Defence Force) Kawasaki P-2J, 6 (10); Shinmeiwa PS-1, 2 (3); Fuji KM-2, 8 (10); Mitsubishi SH-3, 6 (8); Mitsubishi S-61A, 1 (1); Kawasaki OH-6J, 0 (2); (Ground Self-Defence Force) Kawasaki OH-6J, 10 (17); Fuji UH-1H, 10 (11); Kawasaki V-107-IIA, 2 (4); Mitsubishi MU-2, 1 (1).

MOROCCO

In December, the Moroccan government announced that a purchase **contract** had been placed **for** the Dassault-Breguet **Mirage F1**. The contract is understood to cover an initial batch of 25 aircraft with options on a further 50, and to include the single-seat F1A and F1C versions and the two-seat F1B. A French spokesman stated that deliveries are unlikely to commence before 1979, and the acceptance of the contract will not, therefore, exacerbate the current situation between Morocco and Algeria as the aircraft that it covers can be of "no threat" to the latter country. Until the announcement of this contract, it was believed that the Northrop F-5E Tiger II was front-runner among aircraft considered by the Royal Maroc Air Force (*Al Quwwat Aljawwiya Almalakiya Marakishiya*) which is currently operating 17 F-5As, two RF-5As and three F-5Bs, and negotiations were being conducted with Northrop for 12-16 F-5E Tiger IIs and four two-seat F-5Fs.

PORTUGAL

The *Força Aérea Portuguesa* (FAP) has now scrapped or placed in storage substantial numbers of **obsolete or obsolescent aircraft** which were operated during the colonial wars — aircraft withdrawn including all Beech C-45s, Douglas C-47s, Douglas C-54s and Republic F-84Gs — and several of the most numerous FAP types hitherto remain in service only in small numbers. For example, the FAP now operates only 16 of a total of 153 Do 27s, only 37 of at least 179 Alouette IIIs and 20 North American T-6s out of a total of 252 procured over the years. Apart from the recently-delivered C.212 Aviocar utility transports, the FAP has some 32 Reims-Cessna 337G Super Skymasters which serve in the light strike and liaison rôles, and six ex-*Luftwaffe* Fiat G.91T trainers. Sixteen single-seat G.91Rs remain in service of the total of 45 transferred from the *Luftwaffe* during 1965-66, and the total FAP inventory of all aircraft types now totals 264 machines.

PHILIPPINES

The Philippine **Air Force** anticipates **receiving** the **balance** of its **order for** 12 GAF **Nomad** "Mission Master" STOL utility aircraft **during** the course of the **next few months**, delivery of the fifth aircraft having been taken early in December. The PAF Nomads are equipped with wing hardpoints for supply dropping, self-sealing fuel tanks and cas-evac fittings. PAF pilots and engineers have been trained in Australia by Government Aircraft Factories personnel.

The air component of the Philippine **Navy** has now taken **delivery of** a number of Gosselies-built Britten-Norman **Islanders**. These aircraft, which are serving in coastal patrol, liaison and utility rôles, are apparently additional to those being assembled and part-manufactured by the Philippine Aerospace Development Corporation.

SPAIN

The new five-year agreement under which US military facilities will continue to be maintained in Spain includes a stipulation that "the government of the US agrees to make maximum effort to facilitate **acquisition** by the government of Spain **of** four complete squadrons of 18 aircraft each of **F-16** light fighter aircraft or others of similar characteristics." Under the terms of the agreement, the US will provide 42 McDonnell Douglas F-4E Phantoms on lease until the F-16s can be delivered and US forces will continue to use Torrejon, Zaragoza and Moron airfields.

The *Academia General del Aire* (General Air Academy) of the *Ejército del Aire* at San Javier, Murcia, has recently taken **delivery of** 18 F33C **Bonanzas** for the primary instruction of EdA pilots. These join 12 Bonanzas delivered to the Academy earlier, and replace T-34A Mentors that have been serving at the Academy (*Escuadrón núm* 791) for 15 years.

TURKEY

On 11 December, the Turkish **Air Force** announced that it is shortly **to** place an **order** for an **additional** 40 McDonnell Douglas F-4E **Phantoms** for which a letter of offer has been received and funding for which is included in the 1976 defence budget. In addition to the Phantoms, the budget makes provision for the additional Aeritalia-built F-104S Starfighters on which options were taken last year (covering two batches of 18 and two aircraft respectively), bring to 60 the total number of fighters of this type delivered or on firm order, for helicopters and for initial procurement of an unspecified training aircraft believed to be the Franco-German Alpha Jet. The helicopters are apparently Agusta-Bell AB 212ASWs for the naval air component and Mil Mi-8s for the Army. The budget is some 12 per cent higher than that of last year which was, itself, a record.

USA

On 9 January, the McDonnell Douglas F-15 **Eagle** officially entered service **with** the USAF **Tactical Air Command** at Langley AFB, Va, where the 1st Tactical Fighter Wing was activated. The F-15 has been operated for more than a year by the 55th Tactical Fighter Training Squadron at Luke AFB, Arizona, where substantially more than 2,000 sorties have been flown, and to date McDonnell Douglas has delivered more than 40 production F-15s (plus 20 for the now completed R&D programme) to the USAF. The production tempo of the F-15 is scheduled to rise to nine per month in April, and the 1st Tactical Fighter Wing will have received its full complement of aircraft by the end of this year. Thereafter, the F-15 is scheduled to be delivered to USAFE to fulfil NATO commitments.

The **Fiscal 1977 budget proposals** (for the year commencing 1 October 1976) laid before Congress by President Ford in January include a defence budget that represents up to 40 per cent more, in real terms, to be spent on military hardware, plus important increases in federal research and development investment, compared with the previous year, and reverse the recent trend towards smaller defence expenditure. Total Defense Department budget is $112,700m (£55,800m), and includes the following proposed aircraft purchases: three Rockwell B-1As (the first of 240 production models, additional to four prototypes); 16 GD F-16As, towards total USAF procurement of 650; six Boeing E-3A AWACS, towards total inventory of 25; 108 McDonnell Douglas F-15As; 100 Fairchild A-10As; four Sikorsky HH-53C rescue helicopters; two Rockwell U-4B Commander twin-engined utility transports; 36 Grumman F-14As to bring total Navy procurement to

403; 30 FLIR-equipped Vought A-7Es; 21 McDonnell Douglas A-4Ms for the Marine Corps; six Grumman EA-6Bs, three each for Navy and Marines; 12 Lockheed P-3Cs; six Grumman E-2Cs; 12 Lockheed US-3A COD aircraft; 10 Sikorsky CH-53Es to launch production for the Marine Corps; 12 Bell UH-1Ns for the Marine Corps; eight Bell AH-1Js and 15 TOW-equipped AH-1Ts for the Marine Corps; 103 Beech T-34C Turboprop trainers for the Navy and 82 Bell AH-1G and TOW-equipped AH-1S helicopters for the Army. Among future aircraft programmes supported in the budget are the McDonnell Douglas/Northrop F-18; AMST (YC-14 or YC-15), UTTAS (YUH-60 or YUH-61), AAH (YAH-63 or YAH-64); Army advanced scout helicopter; McDonnell Douglas AV-8B; Rockwell XFV-12A and an advanced tanker/cargo aircraft (ATCA) for USAF, a version of one of the commercial wide-body transports.

AIRCRAFT AND INDUSTRY

CANADA

The **future of Saunders Aircraft** was again in doubt as this issue went to press, following a decision by the Manitoba government to restrict funding after providing a total of $37m (£18·4m) in an effort to establish an aircraft industry in the state. Saunders converted 13 Heron airframes to ST-27s with PT6A-34 engines and new interiors; of these, 10 have been sold (including two for Skywest, the Prairie regional airline that has yet to start operations), one was converted to the ST-27A prototype of the ST-28 and two remain unsold. The ST-28 was a new production version of the same design, meeting the requirements of US Part 25 certification, and the first genuine ST-28 flew at Gimli on 12 December, shortly before the Manitoba decision to drop its support for the company, which is now reported to be for sale.

FEDERAL GERMANY

With orders for the VFW 614 showing signs of building up after a slow start, **VFW-Fokker** has **ordered** a second batch of 30 Rolls-Royce/SNECMA **M.45H** Mk 501 **turbofans**. Fifteen of the 60 engines now on order had been delivered by the end of 1975. A total of 16 VFW 614s is now on order (two for Cimber Air, three for the *Luftwaffe*, eight for TAT and three for Air Alsace) and the type recently entered service with the first of these operators. FAA certification was obtained in December, and the sixth aircraft is now in final assembly.

FRANCE

The Dassault-Breguet **Mirage 2000** (alias Delta Mirage 2000), which, it was announced **as** on 18 December, is to be developed as an **alternative to** the now-defunct **Super Mirage** (*Avion de Combat Futur*), is loosely described as an advanced development of the well-proven and now-venerable Mirage III configuration optimised for the intercept rôle. To be powered by a single SNECMA M53-10, a growth version of the current M53 with an anticipated thrust of 21,385 lb (9 700 kg) with maximum reheat, the Mirage 2000 will employ titanium alloys and carbon and boron fibres which will account for up to 40 per cent of total airframe weight, fly-by-wire electrically-actuated controls and a side-stick controller, and will allegedly out-perform the General Dynamics F-16 in almost all combat rôles. With an estimated unit price of between Fr40m and Fr50m (£4·5m to £5·5m), the Delta 2000 will be capable of attaining 49,215 ft (15 000 m) with two Matra Super-530 missiles within five min of brakes release and will accelerate to M=2·2 within two minutes, maximum speed being M=2·7 up to an altitude of 65,615 ft (20 000 m). In addition to the Mirage 2000, a prototype of which is currently expected

to commence its flight test programme in mid-1977, Avions Marcel Dassault-Breguet Aviation is developing as a private venture what is essentially a twin-engined version of the same design as the Delta Super Mirage, which, with two M53-10 engines, will have a thrust-to-weight ratio appreciably better than 1:1 and will be optimised for the low-level long-range penetration rôle. A prototype of the Delta Super Mirage is expected to enter flight in mid-1978, and Dassault contends that, while there is currently no *Armée de l'Air* requirement for this category of aircraft (despite the fact that its intended rôle was to have been a primary function of the so recently cancelled ACF), a strong export market for such a type exists. Despite the Dassault claim that the Delta Super Mirage can be developed relatively inexpensively because of its similarity to the Mirage 2000, it might be suggested that the cost of such a programme will still be immense and represent too great a financial risk to be acceptable to such an astute salesman as Marcel Dassault unless there is a near-certainty of some external funding.

Latest version of the Avions Mudry single-seat aerobatic monoplane, the **CAP 20L**, made its **first flight** on 15 January at Bernay (Eure). Compared with the CAP 20 in use at present by the *Armée de l'Air*, the CAP 20L (*Airscene*/September 1975) has a lightened structure, clipped wings and square section rear fuselage. The prototype has a 180 hp Lycoming IO-360-RCF engine with a Hoffman constant speed two-blade propeller and represents the proposed *Competition Nationale* version; it is also intended to produce an *Haute Competition* variant with a 200 hp Lycoming AIO-360-B1B engine.

Air Inter took **delivery of** its 10th and **last** Dassault-Breguet **Mercure 100** on 19 December, and has meanwhile received the earlier production examples that had been returned to the company for modification. The CMM (*Centre de Montage Mercure*) at Istres is now being reorganised to handle Falcon 10 fabrication, assembly and flight test, previously undertaken at Bordeaux. The first Falcon 10 to come off the line at Istres will be No 73, during February. In his annual report recently, the president of Air Inter spoke of the excellent operation and high profit-making ability of the Mercure, saying he deeply regretted that the assembly line had been discontinued as the airline would have liked to buy several more.

INTERNATIONAL

The **proposed collaboration** between Rolls-Royce and United Technologies on the development of the 5,400 lb st (2 450 kgp) RB.401-07 as part of a deal also involving the JT10D "ten-tonne" engine (*Airscene*/January 1976), has been **turned down** by the Justice Department, apparently on the grounds that a programme of RB.401 size should be within the resources of either company and that joint development unfairly eliminates competition. Joint development of the JT10D has been approved by the Justice Department and is thought likely to go ahead regardless of the RB.401 situation.

JAPAN

After a period of doubt, the **YX programme** for development of an advanced airliner is **continuing**, with a total of $9·6m (£4·75m) available in Fiscal Year 1976. This sum includes $0·5m in the FY76 budget, a balance of $6·6m brought forward from previous budgets and $2·4m allocated by Japanese manufacturers. Although a number of possible collaborative projects are currently under discussion in Japan, involving US or British companies, and the YX designation has been used in the past in respect of a number of Japanese

project studies, the latter programme is now related to possible Japanese participation in the Boeing 7X7. Negotiations are being handled by the Japanese Civil Transport Development Corporation, which is staffed by personnel seconded from the aircraft manufacturers, and it is understood that Boeing is seeking the investment of some $160m (£79·8m) by Japan for a share of the development work — a sum that is unlikely to be approved by the Japanese Diet in existing economic circumstances. Meanwhile, the two Japanese domestic airlines, All Nippon Airways and Toa Domestic Airlines, are continuing their search for a YS-11 replacement (58 YS-11s are in use by these airlines and another 41 elsewhere in Japan). Possible candidates for selection include the Fokker-VFW F.28 Mk 6000J (*Airscene*/September 1975), the McDonnell Douglas DC-9-QSF (*Airscene*/August 1975), the BAC One-Eleven 700J (*Airdata File*/June 1975) and a completely new short-field 120-seat quiet twin that has recently been projected by BAC for collaborative development in Japan.

The first prototype **Fuji FA-300**/Rockwell Commander 700 resumed its **flight test programme** on 14 January after installation of additional instrumentation, four flights having been made prior to the temporary grounding for this work to be completed. First flights of the second and third prototypes were expected to be made almost simultaneously in mid-February, respectively in Japan and the USA. Fuji Heavy Industries has set up a new subsidiary, Fuji Hikoki Ltd, to handle production of the FA-300 at Utsunomiya. Certification is expected by October 1976.

PAKISTAN

An **aircraft assembly plant** is being set up by Kiyuski International **at** Cambellpur. Initial activity will be the production of about 60 Cessna T-41D basic trainers and 50 Hughes 500 helicopters from imported components.

TURKEY

Discussions have recently taken place between Breda Nardi, the Italian Hughes licensee, and the Turkish government concerning the **possibility of** establishing a factory in Turkey for the **assembly** and eventual part-manufacture **of** the **Hughes 500M** helicopter. Discussions have also taken place with Agusta and are understood to have concerned the possibility of establishing assembly and eventually part manufacturing facilities for the Agusta-Bell 206B JetRanger.

UNITED KINGDOM

The first run of the Rolls-Royce **RB.401-06** turbofan was made at the company's Bristol Engine Division on 21 December last. In the 5,000-6,000 lb (2 270-2 724 kg) thrust bracket, the RB.401 is intended as a Viper replacement, aimed primarily at the business aircraft market in the first place; plans for joint development of the RB.401 by Rolls-Royce and P&W have recently received a set-back (see under "International" heading). The Viper itself, meanwhile, continues in production and the 4,000th example was recently delivered, this being a Viper 632 Mk 43 destined to power the prototype Aermacchi MB.339 trainer that is due to fly later this year. The 4,001st Viper, delivered at the same time, was a Viper 201 for a GAF Jindivik — the target drone for which the Viper was originally developed and went into production 25 years ago.

Certification of the Rolls-Royce **RB.211-524** has been granted by the CAA, with a rating of 50,000 lb st (22 700 kgp) — the most powerful of any aero-engine so far developed in Europe. The first production Mk 542 went on test at the the end of December, and deliveries will begin to Boeing and Lockheed in the spring. The first four RB.211-524Bs will go to Seattle in April and will power the first of British Airways' new Boeing 747-200s for its first flight on 20 August.

USA

On 28 January, **full-scale development of** the McDonnell Douglas/Northrop **F-18** air combat fighter for the US Navy was initiated under the terms of a letter contract. Initial funding to McDonnell Douglas is $16m (£8m) and total programme funding over the next 15 months is expected to be $133m (£66·5m), including allocations for development of the engines by General Electric. Total cost of the development programme is expected to be $1,400m (£700m) in terms of 1975 dollars, including production of 11 F-18s for the flight test programme. The F-18 is scheduled to make its first flight mid-1978 and to attain operational status with the fleet in 1982. McDonnell Douglas is prime contractor for the F-18 programme and Northrop is responsible for 30 per cent of the development work and 40 per cent of the production work.

Lockheed has received a $3m (£1·5m) **contract** from the US Navy **to initiate** development of the US-3A **utility transport** version of the S-3A **Viking** shipboard ASW aircraft (*Airscene/* February). The prototype will be produced by modifying one of the Viking research and development aircraft and flight testing is scheduled to commence in July.

General Dynamics has begun **assembly of** the first full-scale development **F-16A** — the first of six single-seaters called for by development programme, together with two F-16B two-seaters — and this is expected to begin its flight testing during October, with delivery to the USAF during December. Completion of deliveries of the development aeroplanes is scheduled for June 1978.

The **Rockwell B-1** had made 25 **flights** by 19 December, totalling 119 hrs 19 min (*Airscene/*November 1975). Highest speed to date is Mach 1·6 at 34,000 ft (10 370 m) and maximum altitude reached is 50 000 ft (15 250 m). The longest flight was No 25, of 8 hrs 9 min duration, when the emphasis shifted from flying qualities and flutter evaluation to performance measurement. On this sortie, cruise tests were accomplished at two altitudes, three wing-sweep positions and various gross weights; two aerial refuellings were made. The highest speeds and altitudes were set on Flight No 24 on 26 November, which also included terrain-following evaluation at up to Mach 0·85 at 500 ft (152 m). On Flight No 21, 7 November, a speed of Mach 0·83 was recorded at 200 ft (61 m) above the runway at Edwards AFB during PE measurement.

After studying a number of possible derivatives of the basic **Hercules** (*Airscene/*September and October 1975), Lockheed is currently pushing a so-called **Option IV variant** of the C-130H. Aimed at military users, it would incorporate the 100-in (2,54-m) fuselage stretch of the commercial L-100-30 and would have numerous other improvements in performance. These include double-slotted flaps, spoilers for roll control, a longer-chord rudder, larger dorsal fin, extended tailplane leading-edge fairings ("horizontal fins"), boosted control-augmentation system and improved angle-of-attack and stall-warning systems. The undercarriage would be strengthened and a 30,000-lb (13 620-kg) payload would be carried at 3g load factors. An air-refuelling receptacle would be provided, as on the HC-130H, to give a full-payload range of 3,700 mls (5 950 km) with one refuelling.

A **modified Hughes YAH-64** AAH helicopter

was expected to resume flight testing on 9 February following incorporation of a longer main rotor shaft. Raising the main rotor by 10 in (25 cm) was considered necessary after a recent in-flight incident in which the main rotor blades slapped the top of the canopy when the prototype was in an extreme manœuvring situation. The increase in rotorshaft height is relatively simple to achieve and is not expected to involve a performance penalty, but it will mean that provision will have to be made to retract the shaft in some way to meet the requirement for two of the helicopters to be airlifted in the C-141.

The accident suffered by the No 1 Boeing Vertol **YUH-61** on November 19 last (see *Airscene/*January) was caused by **failure of** the tail rotor **drive shaft** after the main rotor oversped during an auto-rotational recovery. Damage was modest and the repaired helicopter was expected to return to flight test in mid-February. Meanwhile, the Army completed its Preliminary Evaluation (APE) on the YUH-61 in mid-December, totalling 44 hrs 1 min in 41 flights.

Lockheed-Georgia Co received a USAF contract on 23 December last covering the engineering analysis and testing of **modifications** required **to strengthen** the wings of **C-5A** Galaxy transports. Valued at $28·4m (£14·3m), the contract is the first of four phases planned for C-5A modification; the second will provide kits to modify two wings — one for fatigue testing and one for flight test — and the third and fourth will cover the production of kits and their installation.

First flight of the General Dynamics **EF-111A** tactical jamming (ECM) prototype was made on 15 December at Calverton, New York, where conversion of two F-111As to the new configuration is being undertaken by Grumman Aerospace. The aircraft at present is only in preliminary EF-111A aerodynamic configuration, having the 16-ft (4,9-m) long canoe-shaped radome under the fuselage that will cover the antennae of high-powered radar jamming transmitters. Still to be fitted are the transmitters in the weapons bay, receiving equipment and antennae in a fairing at the top of the fin and many jamming and receiving antennae, computers, displays and combat equipment. Grumman has an $85m (£42m) contract to design, develop, test and evaluate two EF-111As with a view to USAF selection of the type as a replacement for the EB-66s at present in use, with eventual procurement of 42 planned.

USAF has contracted with McDonnell Douglas to flight test a Pratt & Whitney **JT8D-209** refanned **engine in** one of the **YC-15** prototypes in the spring of 1977. A 25-hr programme is planned and will parallel similar testing of the GE/SNECMA CFM-56 "ten-tonne" engine in the YC-15 (see *Airscene/*February 1976).

Grumman American has introduced a new model of its agricultural biplane, the **Ag-Cat B**, with increased wing span and other changes to improve its efficiency in spraying operations. The increase of nearly 8 ft (2,4 m) in span allows the Ag-Cat B to carry greater loads and to produce a wider swath on each pass. Vertical tail area has also been increased, a wrap-round windshield replaces the multi-panel type, the cockpit has sealed floor and sidewalls and additional transparencies have been introduced in the canopy to improve the view above and to the rear. The cockpit improvements and a number of other small refinements have also been adopted for the Ag-Cat A, with original wing-span, which remains in production. In unrelated developments, an Ag-Cat has been fitted with an Alvis Leonides engine

by Serv-Aero of California and is in course of certification, and another is being fitted with a Pratt & Whitney PT6A-34 turboprop by Frakes Aviation.

Versions of the Rockwell **Thrush Commander** are under test **with** Pratt & Whitney **PT6A-34 and** Garrett **TPE331** turboprops. The 600 shp TPE 331 was installed by Marsh Aviation and first flew last June, while the 750 shp PT6A-34 has been installed by Ag Aero Distributors and first flew in September; Sterner Aero, a Swedish agricultural operator, has ordered five turboprop conversion kits from Ag Aero for delivery this year.

An **updated** version of the original **Snow S-2** ag-plane — which provided the basis for the current Rockwell Thrush Commander — is now being marketed by Air Tractor Inc of Olney, Texas, as the Model 300 and 301, under the direction of the designer Leland Snow. To overcome the present difficulty in finding suitable low-cost engines for aircraft of this class, the Air Tractor 300 and 301 are sold less engines at prices of $40,800 and $42,800 respectively, being basically suitable for installation of either the Pratt & Whitney R-1340 or R-985 supplied by the customer.

The Gerschwender Aeromotive company of Lincoln, Nebraska, has begun **flight testing**, in a Funk F-23 agricultural monoplane, an adaptation of the **Ford V8 automobile engine** for aerial use. The 400-cu in (6,56-l) engine delivers 290 hp, has a consumption of 14 US gal/hr (53 l/hr) at 75 per cent power and is reported to be "uncannily smooth", but is rather heavy at 615 lb (280 kg).

LTV Aerospace Corporation has changed its name to **Vought Corporation**, effective from 1 January. The change restores the original Vought name for the aircraft-manufacturing subsidiary of LTV (Ling-Temco-Vought) and this will now be used as the prefix for the A-7 tactical fighter for the USAF, USN and Hellenic Air Force.

CIVIL AFFAIRS

ALGERIA

A recent direct credit of $10.9m (£5.4m) authorized by the Export-Import Bank to Air Algerie is to help the **purchase of** three Beech **Queen Air 80s** and five Grumman **Ag-Cats,** in addition to a Boeing 727 and two 737s previously announced.

BRAZIL

The Brazilian government's plan to reorganize the **third level airline network** (*Airscene/*February), into five regions, each with one company specially equipped to handle this type of business, has led VASP and TAM jointly to set up a new company to operate in São Paulo State and parts of the States of Goiás, Mato Grosso and Pará — roughly equal in area to one-third of Europe. This new company will take over all of VASP's Bandeirantes and six of TAM's 10 Cessna 402s. In the Amazon region, TABA (with three Dart Heralds plus five Bandeirantes in course of delivery) and Sagres-Manaus (with three Bandeirantes) are also forming a new company, with support from Cruzeiro do Sul.

INTERNATIONAL

Concordes 205 (F-BVFA) and 206 (G-BOAA) simultaneously launched the world's **first** revenue passenger-carrying **scheduled supersonic** transport **services** on 21 January. The Air France aircraft flew from Paris (Charles de Gaulle) to Rio de Janeiro via Dakar, carrying 93 fare-paying passengers and seven guests, in a flying time of 6 hr 14 min. The British Airways Concorde, carrying 30 fare-paying passengers and 70 guests, left London (Heathrow) for Bahrein, which it reached in a flying time of 3 hr 38 min. Each aircraft returned the following day and services are now operating at a frequency of twice a week. For the record, the aircraft were delivered, respectively, to Air France on 19 December and to British Airways on 15 January. The US Secretary of Transport has given permission for four Concorde services a day into New York and two a day into Washington (Dulles) for a 16-month trial period.

MOZAMBIQUE

Tempair International has concluded a contract with **DETA** of Mozambique to provide a thrice-weekly service for the latter company on the route Lorenzo Marques-Beira-Luanda-Lisbon. The service may be extended to Nairobi later. A Tempair Boeing 707-320C in 167-seat one-class configuration will operate in DETA colours with Tempair aircrew, ground support and engineering staff.

THAILAND

SAS has agreed to relinquish its 30 per cent **shareholding in Thai International** to allow the airline to become wholly Thai-owned with effect from 31 March 1977. Technical collaboration will continue and when Thai International receives its own two DC-10s, replacing two on lease from UTA, arrangements will be made for their maintenance by the KSSU group in Europe.

CIVIL CONTRACTS AND SALES

Airbus A300: Air Inter ordered three B2s — two to be delivered late this year and one at the end of 1977. In 280-seat configuration, they will be equipped for Cat 3 operation and will be used on Paris-Marseilles and Paris-Lyon routes. ☐ Air France ordered two more B4s, for delivery in March 1976 and March 1977. To be used in Europe and Africa, they will seat 270 in all-economy class layout and bring the Air France fleet to nine, including six B2s.

Aviation Traders Carvair: British Air Ferries has sold one of its remaining Carvairs to a French construction company, for use in Iran. Four are still used by BAF on routes from Southend to Basle, Le Touquet, Ostend and Rotterdam. ☐ Ansett Airlines has sold two to Seulawah Air in Indonesia.

Boeing 707: Air India is leasing one from Sabena for operation in all-cargo rôle. ☐ Another Sabena 707 is being leased to Transavia in Holland.

Boeing 727: Three Advanced-200s have been ordered by Hughes Air West, for delivery starting in October. They will be the first 727s powered by JT8D-17R engines with Boeing's automatic performance reserve (APR) (*Airscene*/November 1975). ☐ Air Malta is leasing one -100 from World A/ws.

Boeing 737: One Advanced 737-200 has been purchased for presidential use by the government of Venezuela, with delivery on 30 January. It is the first 737 sale to a foreign government, first Boeing jetliner sale in Venezuela and first 737 fitted with an inertial navigation system. Other features are a gravel runway kit, secure voice communication system ("scrambler"), integral rear entry stair and long-range tanks for a range of more than 3,000 mls (4825 km). ☐ Maersk Air is reported to have ordered two 737-200s for delivery in December. ☐ China Airlines is buying three used -200s from Boeing.

Bristol Britannia: Monarch Airlines has retired its last, the aircraft having gone to African

Safari Airways on lease purchase. ☐ Air Faisel (see last month) is now reported to have acquired two, ex-RAF. ☐ Two in all-freight configuration have been leased from IAS Cargo Ltd by the relaunched Invicta International, now owned by UATS.

Canadair CL-44: Aerotransportes Entre Rios has sold one, ex-Canadian Armed Forces, to Aeronaves del Peru.

EMBRAER Bandeirante: TABA, a third-level airline operating in the Amazon region of Brazil, has ordered five EMB-110P Bandeirantes (PT6A-34 engines) with an option on nine more. First delivery was made on 5 January.

Fokker F27: Air Rouergue, a French local airline, has ordered one F27 Mk 500, in mixed passenger/cargo configuration, for December 1977 delivery. An F27 Mk 200 will be leased for operation on the route Albi-Rodez-Paris from mid-1976 until the Mk 500 enters service. The F27 sales total (including US production) is now 648.

GAF Nomad: The Government Aircraft Factories has announced selection of the Nomad N24 by the Australian Northern Territory Medical Service (NTMS), which has ordered six to replace Doves. They will have long range tanks, Collins auto-pilot and Bendix weather radar, and will carry two stretchers (with provision for a third) and eight seats for patients and attendants. ☐ The Australian Division of National Mapping of the Department of National Resources has ordered one Nomad for airborne survey activities. For delivery in the second half of 1976, it will have a Wild RC9 camera with a floor hatch protected by sliding cover, and full inertial navigation system.

Hawker Siddeley HS.748: Guyana Airways has ordered a second Srs 2A with wide rear freight door, only a month after contracting for the first. Both will be delivered in 1977. Total HS.748 sales stand at 310.

Lockheed TriStar: Delta Air Lines has exercised an option on one aircraft to make a total fleet of 22, of which 18 have been delivered; three will enter service in 1976 and one in December 1977. Eight remain on option to Delta. ☐ LTU acquired one from Eastern.

McDonnell Douglas DC-8: Swissair has sold two of its DC-8 fleet following the delivery of additional DC-10s. A Srs 53 was handed over to the Geneva-based charter carrier SATA in February and a Srs 62 will go to Balair on 1 April. ☐ Air Canada has leased a Srs 43 (Conway engines) to Cubana for service on the Havana-Canada route, and lease of a second is being negotiated. Another of Air Canada's Srs 43 has been sold for scrap in the USA. ☐ Scanair, the charter associate of SAS, has purchased two Srs 55s that were previously on lease from SAS, and will add a Srs 62 to its fleet on 1 April, also ex-SAS.

McDonnell Douglas DC-10: Iberia has ordered two additional Srs 30s to make a total of six; delivery will be in March and May. ☐ UTA ordered one Srs 30 for December 1977 delivery, making six in all. One ordered by UTA in June 1974 was eventually acquired by Martinair Holland.

Shorts Skyvan: Purchase of a second Skyvan for use in the rescue rôle by the Japanese Maritime Safety Board is provided in the Fiscal 76 budget.

Swearingen Metro II: Jet Alaska, an Anchorage-based charter and contract operator, has taken delivery of a Metro II with

quick-change interior, permitting its use in all-passenger 19-seat, mixed passenger/cargo or executive configurations. ☐ A Metro II was delivered to Air Wisconsin in late 1975, adding to seven earlier Metros in this commuter airline's fleet.

VFW-Fokker VFW 614: Air Alsace, one of the three principal French regional operators, has ordered three VFW 614s in 44-seat configuration. Deliveries will be in March and October 1976 and February 1978. ☐ An order for eight VFW 614s placed by Touraine Air Transport, another of France's major regional airlines, has now been confirmed by VFW-Fokker. Two are for delivery in the near future, two in the spring of 1977 and the remainder before the end of 1978.

MILITARY CONTRACTS

Bell AH-1S HueyCobra: Bell has been awarded a $37,208,949 production contract for 44 AH-1S HueyCobras for delivery to the US Army between March and December 1977. The contract includes an option on a further 22 helicopters of this type.

Beech T-34C Mentor: Confirmation is now available of an order on behalf of the Royal Maroc Air Force for 12 T-34C primary trainers with deliveries commencing 1977.

Boeing Vertol CH-47C Chinook: It was announced on 29 January that an order has been placed on behalf of the Spanish Army air component, FAMET (*Fuerzas Aero Moviles del Ejercito de Tierra*), for three additional CH-47 Chinook helicopters for delivery in the fourth quarter of 1977. FAMET received six CH-47s in 1973.

Dassault-Breguet Mirage F1: A contract has been signed between Dassault-Breguet and the Moroccan government for the supply of 25 Mirage F1s to the Royal Maroc Air Force, the contract including options on a further 50 aircraft of this type.

Grumman E-2C Hawkeye: The Israeli government has signed a contract for the supply of four E-2C Hawkeye AWACS aircraft at an estimated contractual cost of $187m, the Hawkeyes being scheduled for delivery to Israel between November 1977 and March 1978.

McDonnell Douglas RF-4E Phantom: Eight RF-4E Phantoms have been ordered by the Hellenic Air Force at a cost of $91m, including spares and support equipment.

McDonnell Douglas F-15 Eagle: Agreement has been reached for the supply of 25 F-15 Eagle fighters (including four refurbished R&D aircraft) to Israel, the reported total contract value being $600m.

Sikorsky S-61R: One S-61R search-and-rescue helicopter has been purchased by the *Fuerza Aérea Argentina*.

Sikorsky S-76: The Royal Jordanian Air Force has placed an order for four S-76 twin-turbine utility helicopters for late 1978 delivery.

VFW-Fokker VFW 614: Three VFW 614 transports have been ordered for use by the *Flugbereitschaftsstaffel* of the *Luftwaffe*.

Westland WG.13 Lynx: On 2 February it was announced that the Dutch *Marineluchtvaart-dienst* has taken up its option acquired in April 1975 on eight Lynx helicopters, bringing to 16 the total on firm order for the service, 10 of these being of the uprated version of which deliveries will commence in 1978.

THE FIFTY-FOOT AIR FORCE

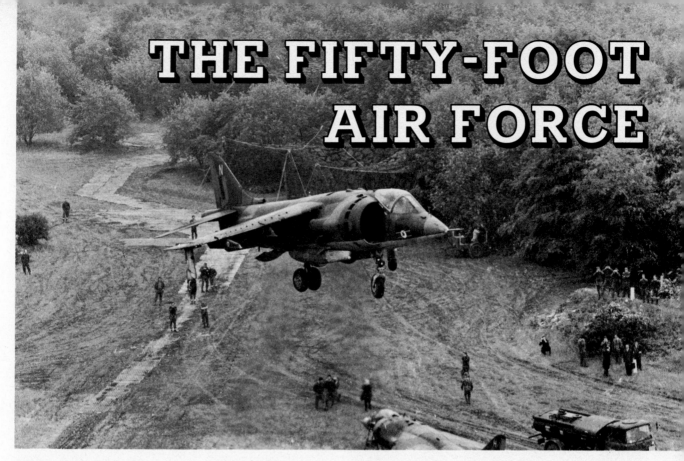

AN ACCOUNT OF THE RAF IN GERMANY, BY JOHN FRICKER

"THE Warsaw Pact faces the (NATO) Alliance with a marked superiority in manpower and conventional weapons. In Central Europe, the disparities are over two-and-a-half to one in tanks, over two to one in divisions and in aircraft, and about two to one in field guns. The Warsaw Pact has about 20 per cent more soldiers and some 30-40 per cent more in fighting units. On NATO's northern flank, the disparities are even greater.

"The disparities quoted for Central Europe do not take into account the forces stationed in the Soviet Union itself. In a time of tension, Warsaw Pact forces in Poland, Czechoslovakia and the German Democratic Republic could be rapidly reinforced by substantial air and ground formations currently held in the Western USSR, and the present imbalance of forces in Central Europe would be increased.

"Warsaw Pact air force and missile systems have also been improved over the last five years, in particular with the introduction of large numbers of technologically-advanced multi-rôle aircraft. The MiG-25 *Foxbat* all-weather interceptor and reconnaissance aircraft, for instance, is capable of $M=3\cdot0$ at altitudes in excess of 60,000 ft (18 290 m). This aircraft and the new MiG-23 *Flogger* ground attack fighter are already deployed on airfields in East Germany, while the introduction is imminent of the new (Su-19) *Fencer* multi-rôle aircraft and the (Tupolev) *Backfire* medium bomber, both of which are supersonic. The Soviet air forces are continually improving their ability to penetrate Western defences through the extensive use of electronic warfare to jam radars and communications. The Soviet air forces in Europe are less vulnerable than those of NATO, because they are dispersed over more airfields and across a wider area. Their vulnerability on the ground has been further reduced by the construction of large numbers of aircraft shelters."

Since the 1975 UK Defence White Paper, quoted above, had to justify some of the most savage defence cuts in British history, it is hardly likely to have exaggerated the threat facing the RAF in Germany, which on official reckoning is thus far out-numbered and technically outclassed in its equipment by the opposing air armies of the Warsaw Pact nations. That the British Government has subsequently sought even greater defence cuts would therefore appear impossible to justify, although if and when these are introduced, RAF Germany is likely to be one of the last units in the British forces to be affected.

In fact, it has been one of the few to be expanded in recent years instead of pruned, and is currently scheduled to increase its establishment of 13 aircraft squadrons, plus supporting units, still further over the next few years. Despite the strength of the opposition, RAF Germany, with its near-unique wing of V/STOL ground attack fighters and newly-introduced long-range low-level penetration aircraft, remains a force to be reckoned with, especially as it has developed tactics and operating procedures designed to increase the effectiveness and survivability of its aircraft and equipment.

HQ Organisation

A recent visit to RAF Germany was something of an exercise in nostalgia for the writer, who, as a young journalist, had first contact with the Command, then known as the British Air Forces of Occupation (BAFO), in mid-1948 — an initial visit to the Berlin airlift in an RAF York full of dehydrated potatoes from Abingdon to Gatow and flying back and forth between Wunstorf and Gatow in RAF Dakotas, before joining the Sunderlands of No 230 Squadron for one or two memorable trips carrying salt between the former Blohm und Voss flying boat base on the Elbe at Finkenwerder, near Hamburg, and the Havel See in Berlin.

Later that year, I went to Schleswig-Land, near the Danish border, in the first Hastings of No 47 Squadron to join the airlift, and made several subsequent visits before the Berlin operations ended successfully in mid-1949. After that, regular tours of the RAF in Germany were concerned mainly with the

(Above) Hardened shelters or "hangarettes" are being provided at all RAF bases in Germany for all aircraft on quick-reaction alert to receive routine maintenance and ground operations under cover. Illustrated is such a shelter at RAF Bruggen, with a No 14 Squadron Jaguar. (Below and heading photo, page 111) Harrier V/STOL ground attack fighters on exercise in Germany.

frequent large-scale NATO air exercises, but looking back through my log-books prior to the recent visit, it was disconcerting to discover that my *last* visit had been in May 1956 — all but 20 years ago.

By then, Wildenrath had replaced Buckeburg as the HQ airfield for RAF Germany and was reached in slightly more comfort after about an hour-and-a-half in an aft-seated Valetta from Northolt instead of nearly three hours in a draughty Anson from Hendon. Nowadays, when civilian trooping is more widely employed, only an hour in a Boeing 737 of Britannia Airways from Luton separates Wildenrath from the UK.

HQ of RAF Germany at Rheindahlen, near München-Gladbach, is a military township with about 13,000 people, since it also accommodates the headquarters of the British Army on the Rhine (BAOR) and Northern Army Group (NORTHAG), as well as of the 2nd Allied Tactical Air Force (2ATAF), together with their personnel and dependants. Then known as the 2nd Tactical Air Force, of WWII fame, HQ RAF Germany moved from Bad Eilsen, near Hanover, to Rheindahlen in 1954, and took on its present title on 1 January 1959.

It remains, however, a principal part of the 2nd Allied Tactical Air Force, which is, of course, a NATO Command combining additional units from the Federal German *Luftwaffe,* and the Belgian and Dutch air forces. In peacetime, 2ATAF comprises only a HQ staff to plan offensive and defensive air operations over 60,000 square miles (155,400 km²) of Northern Europe between the borders of East Germany, France and Denmark in the event of war, but its commander also doubles as the Commander-in-Chief RAF Germany — currently Air Marshal Sir Michael Beetham, formerly deputy C-in-C Strike Command, who succeeded Air Marshal Sir Nigel Maynard on 19 January.

In the southern part of West Germany, 2ATAF is complemented by a similar organisation made up of units from the

Luftwaffe and the Canadian and US air forces, and known as the 4th Allied Tactical Air Force (4ATAF). Together, these two ATAFs form the air element of Allied Forces Central Europe (AFCENT), which has undergone some modification since its formation at Fontainebleau, France, in 1953. Originally controlling NATO land, air and naval commands in Central Europe, AFCENT absorbed the former LANDCENT and AIRCENT HQ in 1967, so that a fully integrated organisation could be achieved. In June 1974, however, the NATO Military Committee authorized the formation of a new HQ to co-ordinate the operations of 2 and 4ATAFs under the reconstituted Allied Air Forces Central Europe (AAFCE), directly responsible to AFCENT.

Manned by personnel from six NATO nations — Belgium, Canada, Federal Germany, the Netherlands, the UK and the US — HQ AAFCE is currently located at Ramstein, in southern Germany, and is jointly commanded by the C-in-C of the USAF in Europe (USAFE). When necessary, COMAAFCE will assume operational command of the combined resources of his two principal subordinate commanders — COM2ATAF and COM4ATAF, and direct the integrated employment of all Central Region air forces. In addition, COMAAFCE is directly responsible, in peace or war, to CINCENT for the maintenance of an integrated air defence system for the Central Region, the establishment of common air doctrines and procedures, improvements in inter-operability, and responsibility for tactical evaluation and standardisation of training.

Although by far the greater proportion of RAF Germany's rôles result from the provision of conventional ground attack and nuclear strike, reconnaissance and air defence forces for the immediate support of NATO land operations as part of 2ATAF, it also has an important national commitment. This is defined as: "In close integration with NATO, the defence of the integrity of the air space of the northern half of the Federal Republic of Germany and, with the US and French air forces, the maintenance of access to Berlin in the three air corridors." For this purpose, the Command maintains two squadrons of interceptors based at Gutersloh, the only operational RAF airfield east of the Rhine. Their task is to police the northern half of the Air Defence Identification Zone (ADIZ), which runs the length of the border with East Germany, to prevent infringements by aircraft from either side. Manned interceptors have proved the most effective means of this peacetime air policing, but the Command also contributes units of Bloodhound SAMs for area defence, plus Rapiers for airfield and point defence, to augment the general NATO Nike/Hawk missile belt in Central Europe.

In times of peace, only the defensive forces of 2ATAF are controlled by NATO, and its offensive units remain under national command and control. HQ RAF Germany thus has responsibility for the operational training of assigned offensive units, along with the engineering, administrative and logistic support required. At a prescribed stage in the NATO Alert System, command and control of all assigned forces in RAF Germany is passed to COM2ATAF at his wartime HQ location in Holland, together with the assigned forces. The rôle of HQ RAF Germany then becomes one of providing the necessary support requirements to ensure and maintain maximum operational availability and capability of its assigned forces.

Main NATO tasks of the RAF in Germany are defined as offensive support — strike and attack — as well as air defence, reconnaissance and helicopter support for the First British Corps of the British Army of the Rhine. In the NATO scenario, the term "strike" indicates that nuclear weapons are involved, whereas the attack rôle implies the use of conventional hardware. All the offensive support squadrons in RAF Germany, except the Harriers, have both strike and attack capability, and are trained accordingly. Among national tasks, in addition to sharing tripartite responsibility for policing Federal German Airspace, the Command is equally committed with its allies to the maintenance of access to Berlin.

Revised Base Structure

Returning to RAF Germany after so many years, one is immediately struck by its substantial contraction compared with its status in 1956. Gone is the former Group organization, at one time comprising Nos 2, 83, 84 and 85 Groups and reduced to two by 1956. The dozen or so airfields in operational use in Germany by the RAF at that time have also dwindled to a mere four, plus the air head at Gatow, Berlin, which has no resident flying units.

Apart from the forward air defence base at Gutersloh, some 67 miles (108 km) from the East German frontier, RAF Germany currently concentrates its strike/attack/reconnaissance units west of the Rhine at the so-called "clutch" airfields of Brüggen, Laarbruch and Wildenrath, clustered along the border with Holland. The former forward RAF bases such as Celle and Fassburg, as well as others further back have long been handed over to the *Luftwaffe* or *Heeresflieger* (German Army air component). By late 1976 or early 1977, however, RAF Germany plans to move its Harrier V/STOL attack wing forward to Gutersloh, to make best use of its off-airfield capability near the potential battle-line. Wildenrath will then become the main RAF air defence base in Germany, its rearward location being counter-balanced by the longer range of the Phantoms scheduled to replace the present Lightnings at the same time.

Following the lessons of the Arab-Israeli wars, NATO began a major airfield "hardening" programme in 1968, when SACEUR laid down criteria for the physical protection of bases from conventional attack. The major part of the programme involved building reinforced concrete aircraft shelters, or "hangarettes", on the operational bases, and this aspect is scheduled for completion by mid-year. Of hexagonal section, the shelters can each accommodate a couple of aircraft, which are further protected by massive clamshell steel doors at one end, opening out into a reinforced revetment area. Sliding steel doors at the other end are closely backed by a blast wall, but when open allow engine runs to be undertaken while enjoying almost full protection.

All normal maintenance and ground operation, including refuelling, re-arming and servicing may therefore be undertaken in the hangarettes with the main doors closed. The aircraft need only emerge under their own power immediately prior to take-off when on quick-reaction alert — a standard NATO procedure in the nuclear retaliation rôle. The shelters are then used to house the squadron refuelling bowsers and other vulnerable vehicles. The revetments are available for stores, MT and so on, while station and squadron operations rooms have been similarly hardened. Brüggen was the first RAFG base to be hardened, and work is well advanced at the other "clutch" airfields and at Gutersloh.

Second part of the airfield protection programme, now completed, was known as Operation "Tone Down", and simply involved camouflaging all airfield buildings, vehicles and equipment, including runways and hard standings a standard dull green. Uncamouflaged operational aircraft such as the Lightning received similar treatment, and were also given low-visibility roundels and fin flashes by removal of their white segments. Main object of the tone-down exercise was to make the job of enemy pilots more difficult in locating NATO airfields during their inevitably low-level high-speed tactical approaches.

With the NATO SAM belt, and particularly the Nike-Hercules reaching up and beyond the MiG-25's operational ceiling, the Central European scenario is essentially low-level. Whereas in most air forces, however, this involves tactical training (and tactics development) at around the 500 ft (150 m) mark,

in RAF Germany, it means half this height or less. This presents obvious training difficulties with high-speed aircraft particularly in finding ultra low-level routes clear of major industrial and population centres. Ultimately, however, the viability of RAF Germany against superior enemy forces, rests on the continuing co-operation and sufferance of the German civil authorities regarding this type of training.

The Air Defence Scene

Apart from hardening its bases, including protecting both buildings and personnel (the latter by suitable masks and clothing), against nuclear, biological and chemical warfare (NBC), RAF Germany is further strengthening its airfield defences by the introduction of additional surface-to-air missiles. Each of the three "clutch" bases now has a flight of Bloodhound 2 SAMs from No 25 Sqdn, comprising eight launchers controlled by a Type 86 radar, platform-mounted for low-look capability. Although of near-vintage design, the range and performance of the Bloodhounds are such that they not only provide all-weather point defence of the airfields, but are also a useful addition to the NATO Nike-Hercules/Hawk belt.

For the vital low-level point defence rôle, the RAF Regiment in Germany is currently exchanging its well-tried Bofors L40/70 AA guns for BACGW Rapier SAMs. Each of the operational airfields has its own Rapier squadron, with only Wildenrath left to re-equip with the standard establishment of eight mobile fire units, towed by Land Rover utility vehicles and organised within two flights. This compares with the army establishment of 12 fire units per Rapier battery, in three troops of four. Apart from its four Rapier squadrons in Germany, the RAF Regiment has a fifth at Leuchars in the UK and another in Cyprus.

In a demonstration by No 63 Sqdn, RAF Regiment at Gutersloh, a Rapier fire unit was assembled and declared ready for action within eight minutes of its vehicles arriving on site. The two-man crew of tactical controller and operator at the command line-of-sight tracker demonstrated the facility with which two Harriers making attacking passes at 300 ft (90 m) and 450 knots (833 km/h) could be held in their sights through attached closed-circuit TV. In its current form, of course, Rapier is a strictly visual system, although blindfire radar is being developed for all-weather operation. It has already demonstrated a very high kill probability against low-flying high-speed targets, however, together with 87 per cent operational availability. At about £5,000 per round, it is also a relatively cheap weapon, although the army's less sophisticated Short Blowpipe infantry SAM is down to about £2,000 per round. IFF is particularly important with these weapons and codes are changed at frequent intervals.

The Army's three Air Defence Regiments are now almost exclusively missile armed, with Thunderbirds, Rapiers and

The first squadron in RAF Germany to convert fully onto the Jaguar is No 14 at Bruggen, previously operating the Phantom FGA Mk 2. Aircraft of both types are shown in the air together in this illustration.

Blowpipes, but the RAF Regiment is hanging on to its Bofors, at least for the moment, for possible back-up use. In Vietnam and the Middle East, the deadly effectiveness of the Soviet-supplied radar-controlled ZSU-23 mobile quadruple 23-mm AA cannon against low-flying jets is now legendary and it seems short-sighted, to say the least, that similar weapons are not being developed for British use. With the constant defence reviews or recent years, however, it would appear that neither money nor manpower is likely to be made available for such additional and desirable weapons.

The basic tasks of RAFG's two Lightning air defence squadrons — Nos 19 and 92 — at the forward air base of Gutersloh have already been mentioned, but it was defined more succinctly during my recent visit by the CO of No 19 Sqdn (Wg Cdr R L Barcilon) as "keeping the enemy air off the army's back." So apart from the air-policing rôle along the ADIZ, for which two fully-armed aircraft are kept in hangarettes on a five-minute alert in a daily battle flight, the Lightnings are concerned mainly with low-level battlefield air superiority rather than defence. This means that in a war situation they would be pitted against such advanced Soviet aircraft as MiG-23s, in both air defence and ground attack variants, the similarly VG Sukhoi Su-17 *Fitter-C* in close support roles; the air superiority MiG-21 *Fishbed-L* in "significant numbers", and the high-speed, high-altitude MiG-25 for reconnaissance and interception.

An intimidating task, it might be thought, for a short-range point interceptor which first flew in 1954, but not in the opinion of No 19 Sqdn's pilots. No aircraft prior to the F-14/15/16 generation, they feel confident, could safely tangle with a Lightning at any altitude, providing its generous thrust margin is used to maintain a high manœuvring airspeed. The Lightning has so much leading edge sweep that its wing air-flow is invariably subsonic and the wing loading is modest by today's standards. Furthermore, nothing, according to its pilots, gets airborne in a scramble faster than a Lightning ("three-and-a-half minutes from the pilot being in bed"),

whereas the Phantom, due to take-over at the end of this year, has a crew of two to settle in and fairly extensive winding-up procedures.

Nevertheless, the Lightning has certain limitations (in range and endurance), particularly at low altitude, where operations also impose a formidable work load for a one-man crew. It also lacks the sophisticated fire-control system and advanced weapons (Sparrow and Sidewinder AAMs) of the Phantom, although the F Mk 2As operated in Germany since 1968 have the advantage over both Phantoms and other marks of Lightning in having two built-in 30-mm nose-mounted Aden cannon. Other Lightning F Mk 2A armament is confined to twin HSD Firestreak AAMs, which are adequate for the air superiority rôle, since the head-on intercept capability of the later Red Top is more relevant to high-altitude bomber interception.

The 16 Lightning F Mk 2As in each of the two Gutersloh squadrons are fully assigned to SACEUR, alongside the air defence F-104Gs of the Belgian air force, and have no secondary close support rôle, equipment or armament. In many ways, the Lightning is the last of the generation of classic "pilot's aeroplanes", which started with the Spitfire (first operated in the RAF by No 19 Sqdn), although the General Dynamics F-16 is of a not dissimilar concept in a much more advanced (if somewhat slower) form.

Average flying time for No 19 Sqdn's pilots on the Lightning is around 1,000 hours and two pilots are coming up to 2,000 hours on type. One of the squadron Lightnings achieved 3,000 hours of flying in August last, but even this aircraft is still well within its planned fatigue life. Although most Lightning squadrons will have re-equipped with Phantoms over the next couple of years, two are scheduled to remain in service with the Strike Command air defence element in the UK until eventually replaced by the AD version of the MRCA in the 1980s. Although Lightning attrition in the RAF has been high — comparable, in fact, to the percentage loss of Starfighters by the

(Left) Two squadrons of Buccaneer S Mk 2Bs, based at RAF Laarbruch, make up part of the strike force in RAF Germany; illustrated is an aircraft of No 15 Squadron. (Above) The two Lightning squadrons at RAF Gutersloh continue to fulfill an all-important air defense rôle; the illustration depicts an F Mk 2A of No 19 Squadron. (Below) A Harrier of No 20 Squadron on exercise in North Rhine/Westphalia, with an aircraft of No 3 Squadron being towed into a camouflage position below.

Luftwaffe — No 19 Sqdn has not lost an aircraft since it began operating the type in 1963.

The original Lightning F Mk 2s were rebuilt by BAC from 1967 onwards to F Mk 2A standard by the installation of extended wing leading edges, broad-chord fin and rudder, additional fuel, bigger brakes and a runway arrester hook. Each conversion took about a year. Lightning Mk 2s in the RAF have been confined to the two squadrons in Germany which are also the only RAFG units to make regular use of flight refuelling. This is employed, in conjunction with the Strike Command Victor tanker wing, whenever the Gutersloh Lightning squadrons deploy to the NATO air firing range at Decimomannu, in Sardinia, for armament training. No 92 Sqdn was there at the time of our visit and No 19 Sqdn was due to follow on within the next weeks. The Canberras of No 85/100 Target Facilities Sqdn were already at Gutersloh in preparation for their flag-towing stint in the air firing programme.

V/STOL Tactical Strike

"The principal threat to NATO is a Communist armoured drive across the North German Plain, co-ordinated with leap-frogging airborne operations and possibly supported by attacks on Denmark and Northern Norway." This summary by Roy Braybrook in a recent issue of AIR INTERNATIONAL indicates

(Above) A Lightning F Mk 2A of No 19 Squadron and (below) a Harrier GR Mk 3 of No 4 Squadron.

(Below) A Buccaneer S Mk 2B of No 16 Squadron, from RAF Laarbruch, on a low-level sortie.

the main tasks facing the NATO air elements in Central Europe, in which RAF Germany is playing an increasingly important part. Weapons training and tactics are all directed primarily towards the anti-armour rôle, as one of the main facets of close support of NATO ground forces using both nuclear and conventional weapons.

In the Harrier and Jaguar, RAF Germany is fortunate in having remarkably effective weapon systems which should greatly assist in offsetting the numerical and technical superiority of the Warsaw Pact forces. Main asset of the Harrier, of course, is its operational independence from fixed and targeted airfield sites, and this is now being exploited to the full in Germany, where some 60 per cent of the RAF's entire V/STOL strength is now based.

Although the Harrier Wing of three squadrons — Nos 3, 4 and 20 — is currently based at Wildenrath, the complete force is now declared to SACEUR as capable of sustained off-base operations, and is subject to annual searching NATO tactical evaluations (TACEVALS) on that basis. Each Harrier squadron in Germany has three primary and two secondary dispersal off-base sites for peacetime use in deployment about three times per year. Others earmarked for employment in a real emergency are surveyed annually to ensure their continued immediate availability.

The ideal off-base Harrier site is a short stretch of road allowing a width of about 32 ft (9,75 m) between trees that can be sufficiently cleared to provide easily camouflaged hides for individual aircraft in sections of four or more. Roads are not essential — a similar stretch of meadow will do — but prepared or semi-prepared surfaces have obvious advantages. Room is also required for a 70 sq ft (6,5 m²) recovery platform near or within the trees, since the standard Harrier operating technique involves a short rolling take-off and a vertical landing.

To see a typical peacetime dispersal site, we visited the bombing and tank range at Sennelager, near Gutersloh, where the Harriers of No 3 Sqdn were deployed in the field. As a fully prepared site, "RAF Station Eberhard" makes use of two or three hundred yards of tank road through a pine forest containing prepared hardstandings as hides, although these are not essential. The very close liaison with the army is emphasised by the presence of members of the Royal Engineers and Royal Corps of Signals as part of the RAFG Harrier force to fulfil essential tasks of site preparation and communications. Each Harrier squadron also has its own RAF Regiment Field Squadron for its outer screen ground defence, although every airman in the wing from the force commander, Group Captain David Leech, downwards, is also qualified on light infantry weapons to take his part in securing their base.

Camouflage in the field of support vehicles, accommodation and operations tents and trailers and all the multifarious bits and pieces which go to make up a combat unit has been perfected to the point where in a recent TACEVAL, NATO reconnaissance crews briefed on the exact location of the field sites failed to find them. They were unable to make any visual sighting reports or to produce site photographs.

Our visit to Eberhard happened to coincide with an inspection by the Duke of Edinburgh for whom a scramble of four Harriers from the hides had been arranged. Unfortunately, the morning of the visit dawned with a dank fog reducing visibility to about 100 yards. As soon as the trees at the end of 200-300 yard (183-274 m) strip could be distinguished, however, the Harriers emerged from their hides, where they had been whistling quietly in the woods, and thundered off into the gloom with a flick of their jet exhaust nozzles.

Primary rôle of the Harrier Wing is battlefield support of the Army with a variety of conventional NATO weapons of up to 8,000 lb (3 625 kg) per aircraft, including free-fall or retarded 1,000-lb (453-kg) bombs, six MATRA pods each with 19 SNEB 68-mm rockets, two 30-mm ADEN cannon beneath the

— continued on page 140

SHORTS SD3-30

THE ULSTER COMMUTER

IN THE fast-changing language of aviation, the term "commuterliner" has taken on new significance in the last few years, and the third-level airlines have achieved a measure of respectability unforeseen only a decade ago. The continuous and, in certain periods, almost explosive growth of the airline business in the years since World War II ended has had the effect of pushing upwards both average passenger loads and average route lengths flown by the airlines. The development of larger-capacity, longer-range airliners in response to this trend has had the effect of making it increasingly difficult for airlines serving the main routes to operate viably over shorter ranges carrying only modest passenger loads.

In the first post-war decade of air transport, this led to the evolution of two distinct groups of airlines — the major companies serving the trunk routes and, on a lower "plateau", the regional airlines, as typified by the so-called local carriers in the USA. Continuation of this trend during the 'sixties led, in turn, to the regional airlines moving up the scale as they introduced, first, turboprop types and, eventually, jet airliners, the size and economics of which were poorly matched to the lower end of the market.

It is to fill the gap that has again appeared below the regional airlines that the third-level airline industry has grown up, initially to provide a link between outlying areas and airports served by regional airlines, but now offering point-to-point transportation in their own right. These airlines have their roots in the air-taxi operations that grew up at regional (and some international) airports to ferry main-line passengers to and from airfields close to their homes; typically, such operations were flown by piston-engined business twins, the larger of which still make up a significant part of the third-level airlines' fleets.

The "commuterliner", as a category of airliner, has appeared in recent years as an attempt to meet the more specific needs of the third-level operators. A significant rôle has been played in this evolutionary process by the CAB (Civil Aeronautics Board), responsible for the regulation of airlines in the USA. Changes in the rules applicable to third-level airlines made by the CAB in July 1972, by an amendment to Economic Regulation Part 298, made it possible for these operators to use aeroplanes with a capacity of up to 30 passengers and a payload of up to 7,500 lb (3 402 kg). This action stimulated the development of new commuterliners with 30 seats, of which the first to mature is the Shorts SD3-30.* It is indicative of the growth that has taken place in the air transport business in the last 40 years that this new commuterliner has a larger capacity than the DC-3 when it was first introduced on the trunk routes across the US — and offers a considerably higher standard of passenger comfort.

Prior to the amendment of Part 298, the CAB had restricted third-level airlines to operating aircraft with a gross weight of 12,500 lb (5 670 kg), equivalent to a capacity of 19 seats. The definition of a third-level or commuter air carrier was one which operated a minimum of five flights a week in each direction between two points to a published schedule, or which carried mail by air under contract to the US Postal Service. On this basis, there were 222 companies in the USA in 1974, operating about 1,000 aircraft, and carrying more than six million passengers and over 110 million pounds (50 million kg) of cargo and mail. From the earlier piston-engined types, these operators were already graduating to turboprop-engined commuterliners of 12-19 seat capacity, such as the Beech 99, the de Havilland Canada Twin Otter and the Fairchild Swearingen Metro.

The size of the third-level operation in America clearly provided a valuable market for a new airliner designed to take advantage of the relaxed Part 298 rules. Shorts had begun, some time before July 1972, to study a possible development of the SC-7 Skyvan more specifically suited to the passenger market. The 22-seat Skyliner was already available, but most

*Short Bros and Harland Ltd, the Belfast-based company in which the UK government has been the majority shareholder since 1947, has adopted the style "Shorts" in place of the earlier "Short". The SD3-30 designation derives from the company's drawing office designation system, which accords with SBAC recommended practice, successive types being designated SA1, SA2 and so on to SA9, followed by SB1 to SB9, then SC1 to SC9 and SD1 onwards. The –30 suffix was applied to indicate the 30 passenger version of the SD3, after some smaller preliminary design studies.

The two prototypes of the SD3-30, seen individually and together in the illustrations on these pages, have completed all the basic tasks necessary for certification. Production aircraft, the first of which flew at the end of 1975, are now becoming available for delivery and several operators will be using this new commuterliner by the end of the year. The illustration above right shows the first SD3-30 before modification to increase the fin-and-rudder height.

Skyvans sold were for military or utility and cargo use, and a larger fuselage capacity was needed to improve the aircraft's economics in the passenger-carrying rôle. An enlarged, 26-seat version of the Skyvan was being studied in 1971, but news of the change in the CAB's rules allowed Shorts to go to the full 30 seater, in which guise the new aircraft was announced in August 1972, in time for preliminary details and specifications to be made public at the SBAC Display at Farnborough in September.

Preliminary design of the SD3-30 proceeded into the early months of 1973, and wind tunnel testing confirmed that early performance estimates could be met or even bettered. In the light of these promising indications, the government sanctioned a full go-ahead on development of the SD3-30 in May 1973, when a contribution towards the project of £4·25m (at October 1972 prices and subject to adjustment for inflation) was approved, to be recoverable through a levy on sales.

The programme set up at the time the new aircraft was launched provided for a first flight in mid-1974, with two aircraft to be used for development and certification, and production aircraft to be available in 1975. Even allowing for the fact that the SD3-30 was based in part on the proven Skyvan components, this was a tight schedule, but it has slipped only a little despite difficulties that have occurred from time to time as a consequence of Shorts location in Northern Ireland, and the fact that the whole of the UK was on a three-day working week during the fuel crisis of 1973/74. The first prototype actually flew only two weeks behind the target date, on 22 August 1974, and it was therefore able to appear at the SBAC Display at Farnborough in September, only two years after its development had been initiated.

The second example of the SD3-30 did suffer rather more extensive delays, the first flight not taking place until 8 July 1975, much of this delay being due to the desire to finish No 2

to production standards in order that it could make the best possible contribution to certification. Once the second SD3-30 was in the air, the handling and performance trials necessary for certification could be accelerated, and the CAA awarded the new commuterliner a full C of A in January 1976. Meanwhile, the first full production aircraft was flown on 15 December, followed by the second and third — which will be the first customer delivery aircraft — early in 1976.

Early in September 1975, the first SD3-30 flew to the USA to undertake some six weeks of testing, primarily to measure performance at elevated airfields and high ambient temperatures. For the high airfield, high temperature trials, the aircraft was based at Farmington, New Mexico, and for high temperatures at low altitudes, it flew from Marana and Yuma in Arizona. These tests covered airfield altitudes up to 5,500 ft (1 678 m) and temperatures up to 40 deg C. Noise tests were also undertaken at Fresno, California, to demonstrate compliance with FAR Part 36. Temperature performance trials had earlier been made by this same aircraft, which is fully-instrumented, at Istres in France and a final 50 hours of typical route flying was undertaken by the first production SD3-30 in Scandinavia in January.

The presence of the prototype SD3-30 in the USA also provided Shorts with an opportunity to demonstrate their new aircraft to some existing and potential customers. While still in California, it was demonstrated to Golden West Airlines at Santa Ana Orange County Airport, at San Luis Obispo for Swift Aire and at Las Vegas for Scenic Airlines. Before returning to Belfast on 20 October, the SD3-30 was then demonstrated on the East Coast for the benefit of Command Airways and Air New England.

Command Airways, of Poughkeepsie, New York, had been the first airline to place an order for the Belfast-built commuterliner, and is typical of the third-level airlines for which the aircraft is primarily intended. Launched in 1966, the com-

Shorts SD3-30 Cutaway Drawing Key

1 Glass-fibre nose cone
2 Weather radar installation
3 Nose skin panelling
4 Forward baggage compartment, 45 cu ft/400 lb (1,27 m³/ 181 kg) max
5 Upward-hinged baggage door, 30·5 in×37·7 in (77,5 cm×95,8 cm)
6 VHF 2 aerial
7 Hydraulically steerable rearward-retracting nosewheel
8 Nosewheel fork
9 Nosewheel oleo
10 Nosewheel pivot point
11 Nosewheel box
12 Nosewheel retraction mechanism and jack
13 Undercarriage emergency actuation accumulator
14 Hydraulics bay
15 Rudder circuit linkage
16 Avionics bay (port and starboard)
17 23 Amp/hr batteries (port and starboard)
18 Seat adjustment lever
19 Seat belt
20 Heated pitot head
21 Underfloor avionics equipment
22 Elevator circuit linkage
23 Control column
24 Pilot's seat
25 Rudder pedals
26 Windscreen wipers
27 Windscreen panels (electrically heated)
28 Instrument panel coaming
29 Central control console (trim wheels)
30 Co-pilot's seat
31 Overhead panel (AC/DC power supply)
32 Fuel cocks
33 Crew escape/ditching hatch
34 Flight deck/cabin sliding door
35 Aileron circuit linkage
36 Control cable conduit (rudder and elevator trim circuits)
37 Flight deck conditioned/ heating/de-misting air supply
38 Ambient-air intake
39 Combined VOR/ Localiser/ILS glide-slope aerials
40 Blow-in door (ground running)
41 Turbine-blower intake
42 Heat exhanger
43 Air cycle installation
44 Engine bleed-air supply
45 Pre-cooler
46 Pre-cooler intake
47 Cabin conditioned/fresh air supply
48 Doorway-surround doubler plate

49 Cabin forward emergency exits, port 37 in×24·5 in (94 cm×62 cm); starboard 42 in×27 in (107 cm×68,6 cm)
50 Forward freight door, 65·6 in×55·6 in (167 cm×141 cm)
51 Freight door hinges
52 Honeycomb-sandwich floor panels
53 Corrugated inner skin
54 Cabin air distribution duct
55 Seat mounting rails
56 Rudder circuit
57 ADF sense aerials (port and starboard)
58 Rectangular fuselage section frames

59 Chemically-milled window panel
60 12-a-side cabin windows, 18·5 in×14·4 in (74 cm×36,6 cm)
61 Passenger accommodation: 30 seats, 3-abreast (single port/double starboard) arrangement
62 Engine bleed-air supply duct
63 Fuel tank mounting lugs
64 Forward multiple fuel tank (Cell 1)
65 Class II sealed tank dividing bulkhead
66 Fuel gravity filler
67 Forward multiple fuel tank (Cell 2)
68 Class I sealed tank dividing bulkhead
69 Forward multiple fuel tank (Cell 3)

70 Sealed containment area (tank seepage)
71 Tank/fuselage attachment
72 Wingroot fairing
73 Engine-propeller control cable runs
74 Hydraulics reservoir
75 Wing centre-section
76 Chemically-milled centre-section skinning
77 Dorsal anti-collision beacon
78 Centre-section front spar
79 Leading-edge access panels
80 Oil coller
81 Engine firewall
82 Engine mounting ring
83 Exhaust ducts
84 Air intake duct (with debris deflector)

85 Propeller pitch-change mechanism
86 Hartzell constant-speed five-bladed auto-feathering propeller, 9 ft (2,75 m) diameter
87 Propeller de-icing boots
88 Pratt and Whitney PT6A-45 turboprop engine
89 Oil filler cap
90 Outer/inner wing pin joints
91 Outer-section front spar
92 Outer wing support strut
93 Starboard landing/ taxying lamp
94 Support strut pin joints
95 Strut attachment bracket
96 Fluid de-iced leading-edge (tank and pump unit mounted at rear of starboard mainwheel well)
97 Starboard navigation light
98 Glass-fibre wing-tip fairing
99 Starboard aileron
100 Aileron trim tab
101 Aileron hinge rib
102 Support strut box
103 Flap hinge ribs

104 Starboard outer flap section
105 Starboard centre flap section
106 Centre-section end rib
107 Starboard inner flap section
108 Flap actuating rod mechanism (mounted on spar rear face)
109 Water-methanol tank and pump
110 Gravity fuel filler
111 Aft fuel tank (Cell 4)
112 Sealed containment area (tank seepage)
113 Tank/fuselage attachment

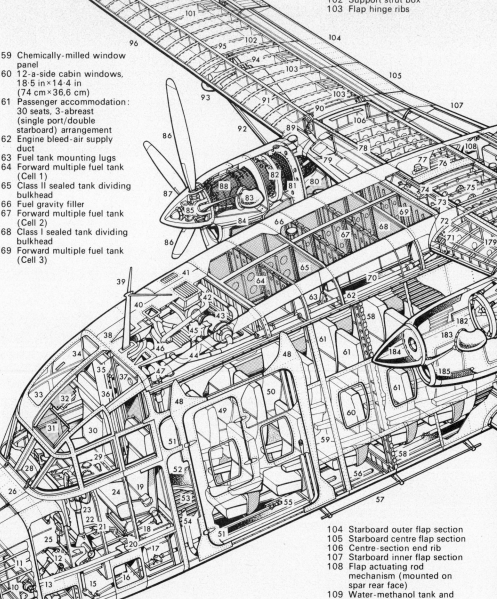

PILOT PRESS COPYRIGHT DRAWING

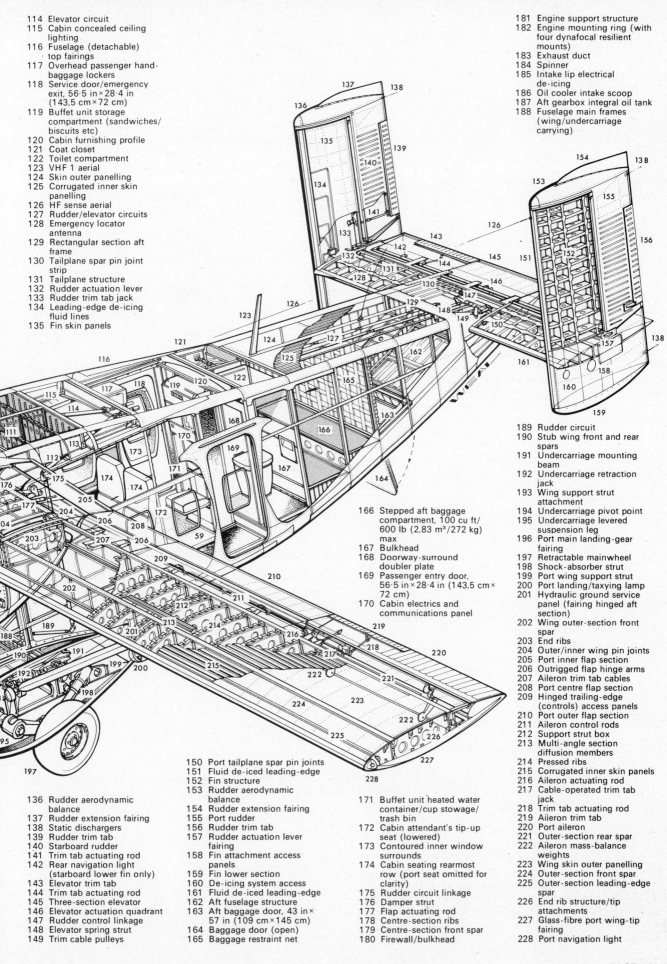

114 Elevator circuit
115 Cabin concealed ceiling lighting
116 Fuselage (detachable) top fairings
117 Overhead passenger hand-baggage lockers
118 Service door/emergency exit, 56·5 in×28·4 in (143,5 cm×72 cm)
119 Buffet unit storage compartment (sandwiches/biscuits etc)
120 Cabin furnishing profile
121 Coat closet
122 Toilet compartment
123 VHF 1 aerial
124 Skin outer panelling
125 Corrugated inner skin panelling
126 HF sense aerial
127 Rudder/elevator circuits
128 Emergency locator antenna
129 Rectangular section aft frame
130 Tailplane spar pin joint strip
131 Tailplane structure
132 Rudder actuation lever
133 Rudder trim tab jack
134 Leading-edge de-icing fluid lines
135 Fin skin panels

136 Rudder aerodynamic balance
137 Rudder extension fairing
138 Static dischargers
139 Rudder trim tab
140 Starboard rudder
141 Trim tab actuating rod
142 Rear navigation light (starboard lower fin only)
143 Elevator trim tab
144 Trim tab actuating rod
145 Three-section elevator
146 Elevator actuation quadrant
147 Rudder control linkage
148 Elevator spring strut
149 Trim cable pulleys

150 Port tailplane spar pin joints
151 Fluid de-iced leading-edge
152 Fin structure
153 Rudder aerodynamic balance
154 Rudder extension fairing
155 Port rudder
156 Rudder trim tab
157 Rudder actuation lever fairing
158 Fin attachment access panels
159 Fin lower section
160 De-icing system access
161 Fluid de-iced leading-edge
162 Aft fuselage structure
163 Aft baggage door, 43 in× 57 in (109 cm×145 cm)
164 Baggage door (open)
165 Baggage restraint net

166 Stepped aft baggage compartment, 100 cu ft/ 600 lb (2,83 m³/272 kg) max
167 Bulkhead
168 Doorway-surround doubler plate
169 Passenger entry door, 56·5 in×28·4 in (143,5 cm× 72 cm)
170 Cabin electrics and communications panel
171 Buffet unit heated water container/cup stowage/ trash bin
172 Cabin attendant's tip-up seat (lowered)
173 Contoured inner window surrounds
174 Cabin seating rearmost row (port seat omitted for clarity)
175 Rudder circuit linkage
176 Damper strut
177 Flap actuating rod
178 Centre-section ribs
179 Centre-section front spar
180 Firewall/bulkhead

181 Engine support structure
182 Engine mounting ring (with four dynafocal resilient mounts)
183 Exhaust duct
184 Spinner
185 Intake lip electrical de-icing
186 Oil cooler intake scoop
187 Aft gearbox integral oil tank
188 Fuselage main frames (wing/undercarriage carrying)
189 Rudder circuit
190 Stub wing front and rear spars
191 Undercarriage mounting beam
192 Undercarriage retraction jack
193 Wing support strut attachment
194 Undercarriage pivot point
195 Undercarriage levered suspension leg
196 Port main landing-gear fairing
197 Retractable mainwheel
198 Shock-absorber strut
199 Port wing support strut
200 Port landing/taxying lamp
201 Hydraulic ground service panel (fairing hinged aft section)
202 Wing outer-section front spar
203 End ribs
204 Outer/inner wing pin joints
205 Port inner flap section
206 Outrigged flap hinge arms
207 Aileron trim tab cables
208 Port centre flap section
209 Hinged trailing-edge (controls) access panels
210 Port outer flap section
211 Aileron control rods
212 Support strut box
213 Multi-angle section diffusion members
214 Pressed ribs
215 Corrugated inner skin panels
216 Aileron actuating rod
217 Cable-operated trim tab jack
218 Trim tab actuating rod
219 Aileron trim tab
220 Port aileron
221 Outer-section rear spar
222 Aileron mass-balance weights
223 Wing skin outer panelling
224 Outer-section front spar
225 Outer-section leading-edge spar
226 End rib structure/tip attachments
227 Glass-fibre port wing-tip fairing
228 Port navigation light

A distinctive feature of the SD3-30 is its use of Hartzell five-blade propellers, specially developed in conjunction with the PT6A-45 turboprops to obtain low noise levels.

pany had a mixed fleet of DHC Twin Otters and Beechcraft 99 Airliners in service by August 1974, when its order for three SD3-30s was announced. Services are flown into New York's La Guardia and John F Kennedy airports and serve Boston, Binghampton, Pittsfield, Burlington and White Plains. In the 12 months up to May 1974, Command carried 81,000 passengers and the company has predicted that this will increase to 180,000 by 1977 when the full fleet of SD3-30s is in service, and to more than 250,000 a year by 1979.

Within a few days of the SD3-30's maiden flight and little more than two weeks after the Command Airways order had been announced, Shorts was able to report receipt of a second contract, this time for two aircraft (with an option on a third, since converted to a firm order) from Time Air of Lethbridge, near Calgary, Alberta. Time Air (known as Lethbridge Aviation when it was founded in 1957) began its operations with single-engined aircraft flying between Lethbridge and Calgary. The grant of a Class II licence by the Canadian government in 1969 allowed Time Air to expand considerably, to its present status as a local service carrier operating between Lethbridge, Calgary and Edmonton, and to Red Deer and Medecine Hat with a fleet of four DHC Twin Otters and a Fokker F27.

Shorts was soon able to add a third customer to the order book when Air New England signed up for six but this commuter airline, with services based on Boston, Mass, has recently been forced to cancel its SD3-30s, having suffered — in common with almost every other airline, large and small — a slump in traffic growth and some financial stress. However, it now seems that the worst of the recession in the commuter industry is over and that delivery of all aircraft ordered by Command Airways and Time Air will be made by the end of 1976, accounting for some half of total planned production for the year. Negotiations are under way with other operators (including one in Europe), and if brought to a successful conclusion, could result in SD3-30s being seen in six distinct liveries in the next 12 months, providing a firm foundation on which to build up service experience under various operating conditions.

Design to production

As already explained, the Shorts SD3-30 is an extrapolation of the Skyvan, more than 100 examples of which have now been sold, and there is an obvious family likeness between the two types. There are also, however, a number of significant differences. Whilst the fuselage retains the same overall square cross section, the basic cabin box is longer to permit the increase in passenger capacity from 19 to 30, the nose fairing is longer to incorporate a baggage compartment and nosewheel well, the flight deck and windows have been re-designed and the fairing over the wing centre section (which is outside the cabin box) has been lengthened fore and aft to give a better streamline. The rear fuselage is redesigned to eliminate the Skyvan's full width

loading door, but still incorporates a wide loading door giving access to a baggage compartment behind the cabin. Strakes integral with the rear fuselage sides are similar in concept and purpose to those evolved in the course of a drag-reduction programme for the Belfast military freighter.

Whereas the Skyvan is powered by Garrett TPE331 turboprops, Shorts adopted the Pratt & Whitney (Canada) PT6A-45 for the SD3-30 to obtain the necessary increased power, and these are mounted at the extremities of a new centre section, with slight taper on both leading and trailing edges, which serves to increase the overall wing span by nearly 10 ft (3,05 m). Outboard of the engines, the wings are to all intents and purposes Skyvan panels.

Use of a retractable undercarriage is another innovation, justified — though only by a small margin, in view of its added weight and complexity — by the 30-mph (48-km/h) higher cruising speed of the SD3-30 compared with that of the Skyvan. To accommodate the main wheel units, stub wings with sponsons are cantilevered off the sides of the fuselage, and these sponsons also provide the lower attachment points for the single wing struts, which are thus installed to be just clear of the propeller wake. The propellers themselves are newly-developed Hartzell five-bladers, slow running to minimize noise and with an auto-feather provision that operates if a significant torque loss is experienced while the power levers are at take-off setting.

It was thought initially that the longer fuselage would provide enough extra side area for it to be possible to retain the standard Skyvan tail unit — with some structural strengthening — but flight trials revealed poor directional stability at low speeds, which has been rectified by increasing the height of the vertical fins by 1 ft (0,3 m) and adjusting rudder tab gearings. Virtually the only other modification of significance since the SD3-30 first flew has been to separate the oil cooling air from the main engine inlet by providing separate scoop intakes on the sides of each nacelle. A mechanical downlock was introduced in the main gear oleos after a port main unit failed at an early stage in the flight test programme.

When the SD3-30 was first announced in September 1972, it had a design gross weight of 20,700 lb (9 390 kg) and the overall length was 56 ft 3 in (17,15 m). These two figures have evolved, in the course of three years' design refinement, to 22,000 lb (9 980 kg) and 58 ft 0½ in (17,69 m) respectively, but there have been few other significant changes. It was originally intended to use a 2,500 psi (176 kg/cm²) hydraulic system, whereas a 3,000 psi (211 kg/cm²) system is in fact installed, and there has been a small increase in the main and nose-wheel tyre pressures, to match the increased gross weight.

In its construction, the SD3-30 is largely conventional, and similar to the Skyvan; the structural design principles combine efficiency and long life with ease of maintenance and repair. Extensive use is made of metal-to-metal bonding, outer wing and fuselage surfaces comprising double skin panels with the outer skin bonded to a corrugated inner sheet to ensure low crack propagation rates. Other components — ie, the centre wing, tail unit, engine nacelles, stub wings, undercarriage sponsons and fuselage nose cone — are all of conventional skin and stringer construction, with spars, ribs and frames as appropriate.

Outer wing panels, produced under sub contract by VFW Fokker, are three-spar structures, while the centre wing, built by BAC, is a two-spar box beam, attached to the fuselage at the front and rear spars. One-piece wingtips are fabricated in glassfibre, which is also used for the wing-to-strut fairings. The fuselage is made up of three major components — the nose section containing the flight deck, nose-wheel well and forward baggage compartment; the centre portion, of constant rectangular cross section, containing the cabin, and a rear portion accommodating the aft baggage compartment and the attachment frames for the tail unit.

Fuel is contained in four cells in large wing-to-fuselage fairings, one cell behind the centre section torsion box and the other three ahead of it. Fuel supply is via gravity-fed booster pumps, with normal cross-feed provisions to cater for pump failure, and fuel flow to the engines can be maintained at all normal altitudes and attitudes in the event of failure of both booster pumps.

Primary flight controls are manually operated via push-pull rods and levers; there is no duplication or power assistance. Single-slotted flaps in six sections occupy the entire trailing edge from fuselage to ailerons and are hydraulically operated via cable-connected servo-valve actuators. The ailerons are slotted and mounted in a similar manner to the flaps; a full span elevator is used (between the out-rigged fins) and is aero-dynamically-balanced by means of set-back hinges, while the rudders, set in the fins above the level of the tailplane, have unshielded horn aerodynamic balance. The elevator, starboard rudder and ailerons have gear balance tabs which are also cable-operated as trim tabs. The port rudder also serves as a trim tab.

As well as operating the flaps, the hydraulic system powers the undercarriage, brakes and nose-wheel steering. Power is supplied by engine-driven hydraulic pumps, operating at 3,000 psi (211 kg/cm²), except for the wheel brakes, and emergency accumulators are provided. A 28-volt DC electrical system is provided for general services, with special AC sources of 115 volts and 26 volts at 400 Hz for certain instruments, avionics and the fuel booster pumps. The system is of the split bus-bar type with cross-coupling for essential services. The wing and tail surfaces, engine intake lips, propellers and windshield have de-icing provision and the engine intake ducts have anti-icing. The fluid system is preferred for airframe de-icing but rubber boots are available as a standard option.

The cabin of the SD3-30, with its cross section of 78 in by 78 in (1,98 m by 1,98 m), allows passengers to stand upright throughout its length; access is through a large door on the rear port side. The standard layout provides for 10 seat rows at a pitch of 30 in (76 cm), with single seats to port and pairs to starboard; seat rails are fitted to simplify configuration changes. Shorts retained Walter Dorwin Teague Associates of New York to advise on interior design and decor.

Overhead lockers are provided throughout the length of the cabin for carry-on luggage, and there is a small galley at the rear, plus a toilet and coat stowage area. As already noted, baggage compartments are contained in the nose and rear

fuselage, and have a total capacity of 1,000 lb (454 kg). A Hamilton Standard air conditioning system is fitted, utilizing engine bleed air.

A large cargo-loading door is incorporated in the front port side, providing a clear opening of 5 ft 6 in by 4 ft 8 in (1,68 m by 1,42 m), and use of a movable bulkhead makes it possible to operate the SD3-30 as a mixed passenger/cargo aircraft, carrying freight at the front of the cabin and 12-18 passengers at the rear. In an all-cargo rôle, 1,230 cu ft (34,83 m³) of space is available and the weight-limited payload is 7,500 lb (3 400 kg). The versatility of the cabin suggests that the SD3-30 will also find a rôle as a military transport in due course — almost exactly half of all Skyvan sales have been to military users. In military guise, the aircraft is known as the SD3-M and will have a full-width rear-loading door like that of the Skyvan. It could carry 32 troops, 31 full-equipped paratroops,

continued on page 147

Shorts SD3-30 Specification

Power Plant: Pratt & Whitney (Canada) PT6A-45 turboprops flat-rated to 1,120 shp for take-off up to ISA + 19 deg C using water methanol injection, and with a max continuous rating of 1,020 shp. Hartzell five-blade constant-speed auto-feathering propeller, diameter 9 ft 3 in (2,82 m). Fuel capacity, 480 Imp gal (2182 l) in wing centre section/fuselage fairing.

Performance: Design cruise speed (V_C), 224 mph (361 km/h) EAS; econ cruise at 10,000 ft (3 050 m), 186 mph (299 km/h); initial rate of climb, 1,210 ft/min (6,15 m/sec); single engine ceiling, 13,100 ft (3 993 m); max design operating ceiling, 20,000 ft (6 100 m); take-off distance (FAR 25), 3,520 ft (1 073 m) in ISA, 4,180 ft (1 274 m) in ISA + 15 deg C; landing distance (FAR 25), 3,470 ft (1 058 m) in ISA at sea level; ranges, no reserves, 440 mls (710 km) at 227 mph (365 km/h) TAS at 10,000 ft (3 050 m) with max payload or 1,040 mls (1 675 km) at 184 mph (297 km/h) at 10,000 ft (3 050 m) with max fuel.

Weights: Empty equipped (30 pass), 14,230 lb (6 454 kg); normal full fuel, 3,840 lb (1 741 kg); max payload (passenger), 5,940 lb (2 694 kg); max payload (freight), 7,500 lb (3 400 kg); max take-off, 22,000 lb (9 980 kg); max landing, 21,700 lb (9 843 kg).

Dimensions: Span, 74 ft 8 in (22,76 m); length, 58 ft 0½ in (17,69 m); height, 16 ft 3 in (4,95 m); wing area, 453 sq ft (42,09 m²); aspect ratio, 12,33 :1; dihedral, 3 deg constant; undercarriage track, 13 ft 10½ in (4,23 m); wheelbase, 20 ft 2 in (6,15 m).

Accommodation: Flight crew of two; one cabin attendant. Standard layout for 30 passengers three abreast (2+1) at 30-in (76,2-cm) pitch. Forward baggage compartment, capacity 45 cu ft (1,27 m³); rear baggage compartment, capacity 100 cu ft (2,88 m³). Cabin volume (all-cargo), 1,230 cu ft (34,83 m³).

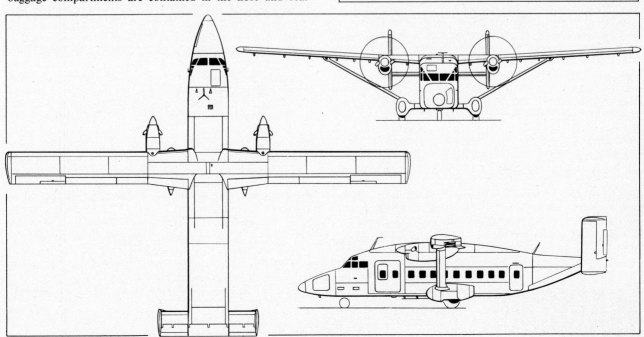

THE CORPULENT LONG ISLANDERS

To SUCCESSIVE generations of US Naval Aviation personnel, the name Grumman has been a synonym for sturdy dependability; to the service's fighter pilots in particular it has signified combat aircraft *par excellence*. For more than four decades, since the summer of 1933 when "Fighting Five" took its newly-delivered two-seat FF-1s aboard the USS *Lexington,* the rugged products of Grumman's Long Island "Iron Works" have seen continuous service with US Navy carriers, and from the mid 'thirties until the 'sixties, Grumman progeny dominated the shipboard fighter scene, a state of affairs now being restored by the superlative F-14A Tomcat.

By the performance advances that it introduced to shipboard aviation, each succeeding Grumman fighter has been a pace-setter and none more so than the series of barrel-like little warplanes of the mid 'thirties, which carried US fighter biplane development to its zenith and did more than any other Grumman types to establish the position of this Long Island-based company as a major supplier of aircraft to the US Navy and, more indirectly, as the world's foremost manufacturer of shipboard aircraft.

Forty-two years ago, on 18 October 1933, when an extra-ordinarily corpulent little single-seat fighter bounced and swayed across a Long Island field, climbed away at a shallow angle into a grey sky and then turned towards the Sound to commence its flight test programme, the event was not solely the inaugural take-off of a new prototype; it also signified a bid on the part of the fledgeling company on whose drawing boards it had seen birth to consolidate a precarious foothold newly gained as a supplier to the US Navy. Although the era of the *land*-based single-seat cantilever monoplane fighter was already dawning, there was as yet little indication that such would seriously challenge the biplane aboard *carrier* decks far into the foreseeable future, and the fighter that had entered the test phase that morning offered — despite the impression of drag-evoking obesity that it imparted — a spectacular advance in performance over anything in the US Navy's inventory and a

quantum jump in single-seat shipboard fighter state of the art.

Assigned the designation XF2F-1 by the US Navy Bureau of Aeronautics, this portly prototype was to be the progenitor of a series of fighting biplanes, which, by 1939, were to equip *all* US Navy and Marine Corps fighter squadrons in full commission. But at the time the XF2F-1 was first rolled out of the experimental hangar of the Grumman Aircraft Engineering Corporation, US Navy tactical thinking was undergoing radical change, contracts were few and far between — the USA being in the grip of depression — and competition for what contracts were in the offing was intense from the old line naval aircraft suppliers, such as Berliner-Joyce, Boeing, Curtiss and Vought, while the Long Island company had yet to celebrate the fourth anniversary of its existence and establish a credible track record in the eyes of the Navy's conservative Bureau of Aeronautics.

The Grumman Aircraft Engineering Corporation had been incorporated on 9 December 1929, its guiding lights as president, vice-president and chief engineer being, respectively, Leroy R Grumman, Leon A Swirbul and William T Schwendler — three young engineers employed by the Loening Aeronautical Engineering Corporation when it was decided that the company, which had merged with the Keystone Aircraft Corporation during 1928, would transfer all its activities to the latter company's plant at Bristol, some 20 miles (32 km) from Philadelphia. Reluctant to exchange a home on Long Island for one in the small industrial town on the Delaware river, Grumman and his companions, armed with a number of ideas including one for an amphibious float in which they hoped to interest the Navy, formed their own company which opened for business in January 1930 in a small garage located at Baldwin on Long Island.

Initially deriving a meagre income from repair work on Loening Air Yacht commercial amphibians, Grumman endeavoured to solicit a Navy order for the amphibious float developed by the company, but the service was not overly

WARBIRDS

impressed, considering the float to be too light. It was not until the potential of the float was finally proven that small orders began to be placed and, meanwhile, to stay in business, Grumman had temporarily to diversify, building some 25 truck trailer bodies during the first year of the company's existence. Progressive development of the amphibious float resulted in a new and improved model which was recipient of larger orders from the Navy, and the young company now took a very ambitious step by proposing to the Bureau of Aeronautics a two-seat fighter biplane embodying a number of innovatory features — a metal monocoque fuselage, a retractable undercarriage and enclosed accommodation for the crew members. Calculations indicated a performance appreciably in advance of any *single*-seat shipboard type then available, and on 2 April 1931, something of a watershed in the affairs of the company came when Grumman Aircraft Engineering Corporation received a contract to build a prototype that was assigned the designation XFF-1.

Within nine months of the placing of the contract, on 29 December 1931, the XFF-1 began flight trials at Anacostia, and during initial level speed tests clocked an impressive 198 mph (319 km/h) at 4,000 ft (1 220 m), 12 mph (19 km/h) faster than the speed attainable at best altitude by the single-seat Boeing F4B-2 fighter which had seen less than a year of Navy service. Its manoeuvrability, too, proved superior to that of the appreciably smaller and lighter Boeing, yet the handling characteristics of this new, high-breasted warplane — its portliness resulting from provision of the necessary forward fuselage depth for recesses into which the mainwheels were handcranked vertically and enhanced by the relatively narrow wing gap — were singularly docile and its sturdiness was to be demonstrated with effect later when, during terminal velocity dives, pull-outs exceeding 5·5 *g* were to be registered.

With completion of the initial test phase, in May 1932, Admiral George Day, in charge of the XFF-1 test programme at Anacostia, readily admitted that, despite its inexperience, the new Long Island company certainly knew how to build an aeroplane, an opinion with which Lt R A Oftsie and his team of test pilots thoroughly concurred. Subsequently, the XFF-1 was returned to Grumman to have its 616 hp Wright R-1820-E Cyclone replaced by an R-1820-F affording 675 hp, reappearing at Anacostia in October to clock a maximum speed of 201 mph (323 km/h) and exceeding 285 mph (458 km/h) in a dive.

Despite the rigorous nature of the test programme, the Grumman prototype revealed only minor and easily rectifiable shortcomings, such as ineffective wheel brakes, and on 19 December 1932, the US Navy awarded Grumman a contract for 27 production examples of what was known to the company as the G-5 and to the Navy as the FF-1. These FF-1s (BuNos 9350-76) were inevitably to be known as *Fifis* when delivered to the service between May and November of the following year.

Advent of the "Baby Barrel"

Despite the innovations that the FF-1 was to introduce to US Naval Aviation, its service career was to prove singularly brief for the concept that had produced it was already outmoded and, ironically enough, the first of its single-seat progeny was destined to hasten its demise as a first-line aeroplane. Even before the FF-1 achieved service status, a school of thought was growing in the US Navy that the two-seat fighter concept

(Above) The XF2F-1 as originally flown in 1933, and (below) after introduction of new engine cowling incorporating rocker arm blisters, telescopic gun sight, and radio masts and aerials.

(Head of opposite page) F3F-2 (BuNo 1003), the 37th production example, prior to delivery to 3rd Section of Fighting Squadron Six aboard Enterprise, *and (below) F2F-1s and F3F-1s undergoing overhaul at Grumman's Long Island facility with F3F-1 assembly in the background.*

(Above and below) F2F-1 BuNo 9624, the second production example, issued to "Fighting Two" in February 1935 and subsequently serving aboard Lexington. *VF-2B was to operate its F2F-1s continuously from* Lexington *until the end of September 1940.*

was *passé*; that the performance superiority of the Grumman two-seater over contemporary single-seaters was simply the result of allowing design development of the latter to vegetate.

Leroy Grumman and his associates were cognizant of this trend of thought and had already initiated design development of a single-seat fighter which pursued the theme established by the company with the FF-1. Nevertheless, old concepts die hard. The new tactical thinking had still to crystallise and, on 4 December 1933, with completion of FF-1 deliveries, the US Navy issued a contract for 34 virtually identical SF-1s (BuNos 9460-93). The SF-1, or G-6, differed from the FF-1 solely in having an R-1820-84 version of the Cyclone in place of the R-1820-78 standardised for the production FF-1, and a 25 US gal (95 l) increase in maximum internal fuel capacity to 165 US gal (625 l), and these aircraft were to be delivered between March and December 1934.

The FF-1s had gone to VF-5B, or "Fighting Five" (alias the "Red Rippers"), aboard the *Lexington*, and the SF-1s were to serve primarily with VS-3B, or "Scouting Three", aboard the same carrier. A few were issued to VF-2B and VF-3 for use in the utility rôle aboard the *Saratoga* and the *Ranger* respectively, but by the end of March 1936, all had been withdrawn from fleet units and relegated to the reserves. The 25 surviving FF-1s were sent to the Naval Aircraft Factory in Philadelphia for the installation of dual controls and with this modification were to continue to serve with the Naval Reserve as FF-2s, the last being finally struck off in 1942.

Although the first-line career of Grumman's firstborn Navy aircraft had been spectacular only for its brevity, this two-seater had served to establish the Grumman Aircraft Engineering Corporation as a progressive manufacturer. It had provided the catalyst in the growth of the company and had proven the worth of the innovatory features that the company had pioneered; features that were to be employed to good effect by the FF-1's single-seat descendants.

The first Grumman single-seat fighter, the XF2F-1 (BuNo 9342) for which a contract had been awarded on 2 November 1932, was even more barrel-like than its two-seat predecessor. This corpulence, to become something of a company hallmark in the years that were to follow, was dictated by the diameter of the 14-cylinder two-row Pratt & Whitney XR-1535-44 Twin Wasp Junior radial affording 625 hp at 8,400 ft (2 560 m).

Apart from a general scaling down of overall dimensions, the configuration of the new fighter closely followed that of the FF-1 and the structure was similar. The fuselage was of aluminium alloy semi-monocoque construction with Z-section formers and longerons and the fabric-skinned wing had aluminium alloy spars and truss-type ribs. The unequal-span, heavily-staggered wings carried ailerons on the upper surfaces only, these, like the movable tail surfaces, being metal-framed and fabric-covered and the fixed tail surfaces being covered by light alloy sheet.

The Twin Wasp Junior engine was enclosed by a smooth NACA cowling and drove a Hamilton Standard two-blade ground-adjustable propeller, and the main and reserve fuel tanks of 75 and 35 US gal (284 and 132 l) respectively were mounted immediately aft of the engine and main forward bulkheads. The mainwheels were retracted and extended by about 32 turns of a handcrank, a positive lock automatically engaging on the "fully down" position and a buzzer sounding in the cockpit if the throttle was closed without the undercarriage being extended. Raised vertically, the wheels were accommodated in recesses immediately aft of the engine cowling.

Armament comprised two 0·3-in (7,62-mm) Mod 2 Browning machine guns in the upper decking of the forward fuselage with 500 rpg and firing over the engine cowling, the pilot being provided with a Mk III Mod 2 telescopic sight which pierced the windscreen. Provision was made for the attachment of two Mk XLI bomb racks beneath the lower wing for a pair of 116-lb (52,5-kg) demolition bombs, and the necessary fittings and brackets were provided to enable the starboard 0·30-in gun to be replaced by a 0·5-in (12,7-mm) Browning with 200 rounds.

From the commencement of its flight test programme on 18 October 1933, the XF2F-1 demonstrated what was, by contemporary standards, an outstanding performance which included a maximum speed of 229 mph (368 km/h) at 8,400 ft (2 560 m), an initial climb rate of 3,080 ft/min (15,65 m/sec) and a service ceiling of 29,800 ft (9 083 m). But the immense advance in shipboard fighter capability that this betokened was not unaccompanied by penalties. Directional stability was poor owing to the short fuselage and the Grumman fighter displayed a dangerous tendency to wind-up in a spin. Stall warning and recovery characteristics proved acceptable, however, and handling characteristics were generally good, particularly at low speeds, and the Navy concluded that even an inexperienced pilot would have difficulty in entering an involuntary spin and the poor spinning characteristics of the fighter were something that the service could live with.

Various minor changes were introduced on the XF2F-1 during the test and evaluation phases, the smooth engine cowling, for example, giving place to a smaller-diameter cowling incorporating rocker arm blisters, and on 17 May 1934, a contract was issued for 54 Grumman G-8s, or F2F-1s (BuNos 9623-76), to be powered by the R-1535-72 version of the direct-drive single-stage supercharged Twin Wasp Junior rated at 650 hp at 2,200 rpm for take-off and at 7,500 ft (2 286 m). The first delivery was made on 28 January 1935, and VF-2B, or "Fighting Two", took its first F2F-1 on strength on 19 February to replace its well worn Boeing F4B-2s aboard the *Lexington*. On 16 March, the 12th production F2F-1 (BuNo 9634) was lost during delivery from Long Island to San Diego, the pilot, LCdr (later Adml) A W Radford, baling out when his aircraft became unmanageable in a dust storm, and a contract was placed with Grumman for a replacement aircraft (BuNo 9997) on 29 June, this additional machine being accepted at the Long Island factory on 2 August 1935, alongside the final aircraft of the principal contract.

VF-3B followed closely on the heels of VF-2B in converting to the F2F-1, taking its aircraft aboard the *Saratoga*, while, during October 1935, VF-5B, which was equipped with the already obsolescent two-seat FF-1, was issued with nine F2F-1s from the San Diego Battle Force Pool. VF-2B was destined to operate its F2F-1s, continuously from *Lexington,* until 30 September 1940 — thus becoming the first and last active squadron to operate this Grumman fighter — when, after more than five years of service, "Fighting Two" ferried its 18 F2F-1s to NAS Pensacola where these aircraft had been assigned to advanced training duties. Each of the squadron's aircraft sported the White Navy "E", the first time in the history of US Naval Aviation that all 18 of a squadron's aircraft had qualified for this prized emblem of excellence.

VF-3B became VF-5B* aboard *Yorktown* during 1937, and was to continue to fly F2F-1s until late 1938, when F3F-3s began to arrive, the older fighters being reassigned to a newly-activated squadron, VF-7, that began forming in July 1939 for deployment aboard the carrier *Wasp*. VF-7 was to supplement its F2F-1s from December 1939 with nine F3F-1s relinquished by VF-3 aboard *Saratoga* with the availability of nine Brewster F2As (in the event, VF-3 was to retain its remaining F3F-1s throughout most of 1940), and was to operate the two types of Grumman fighter biplane in concert until F4F-3 Wildcats were made available from late 1940. Two other active units were to operate the F2F-1 briefly. As previously mentioned, VF-5B had been issued with nine F2F-1s from the San Diego Battle Force Pool in October 1935, returning these to the Pool with the availability of replacement F3F-1s in early April 1936. The nine F2F-1s were then "loaned" to VB-5B, or "Bombing Five", despite lacking equipment enabling them to fulfil the bombing rôle, and were operated during the Panama manœuvres and returned to the Pool once more after two months. With the formation of Marine Corps Squadron VF-4M (which was to be redesignated VMF-2 from 1 July 1937)

In July 1937, the system of designating squadrons was revised to provide for numbering each carrier squadron according to the hull number of its carrier (eg, VF-6 was deployed aboard Enterprise *which had hull number 6), each Marine Corps squadron according numbers to its Aircraft Group and patrol squadrons serially without regard to assignment. The change included the interposition of the letter "M" (signifying "Marine Corps") between the "V" prefix and the mission letters of USMC squadrons.*

in March 1937, the initial inventory of the unit comprised three F2F-1s and six F3F-1s, but the former were relinquished during the following October and the squadron was to re-equip with the F3F-2 in 1938.

A refined 'Barrel'

While the US Navy had concluded that it could live with the less desirable characteristics displayed by the XF2F-1, it encouraged Grumman to proceed with a major redesign of the fighter, the G-11, which it was anticipated would offer the outstanding level speed and climb-and-dive capabilities of the

(Above) F3F-1 BuNo 0262 of VF-7 deployed aboard Wasp *from late 1939, this being one of nine aircraft relinquished by VF-3. (Below) F3F-1 BuNo 0231 prior to delivery to VF-6B aboard* Saratoga *during the summer of 1936.*

(Below) F3F-1 BuNo 0257 of Marine squadron VF-4M; this unit was redesignated VMF-2 from 1 July 1937 and re-equipped with the F3F-2 in the following year.

(Above) F3F-2 BuNo 0995 after withdrawal from first line service and reassignment for fighter pilot training at Corpus Christi and Jacksonville, the last active F3F-2s being stricken from the records of serviceable aircraft during November 1943.

(Above) F3F-2 BuNo 0968 prior to delivery in November 1937 to "Fighting Six" aboard Enterprise and (below) F3F-2 BuNo 0994 of VMF-2's 3rd Section, this Marine Corps unit relinquishing (as VMF-111) its F3F-2s in July 1941.

original single-seater and combine these with improved manœuvrability, acceptable spinning behaviour and superior directional stability. Consequently, on 15 October 1934, three-and-a-half months before the scheduled delivery of the initial production F2F-1, the Long Island company was recipient of yet another prototype contract, this being valued at $75,850.

Assigned the designation XF3F-1 by the Bureau of Aeronautics and retaining the R-1525-72 engine of the production F2F-1, the G-11 introduced a number of aerodynamic refinements, such as a longer-chord engine cowling, a less curved turtleback, a marginally stretched fuselage — overall length being increased by 1 ft 10 in (55,88 m) — which simultaneously improved fineness ratio and directional

stability, and substantially extended wings, the overall span being increased by 3 ft 6 in (1,07 m) to produce a gross increase in wing area of 31 sq ft (2,88 m²).

The XF3F-1 (BuNo 9727) flew for the first time on 20 March 1935, successfully completing three flights during the course of the day, including a one-hour full-power run, but during the afternoon of 22 March, when trials were resumed with a series of 10 terminal velocity dives in six flights, the prototype was destroyed. During the 10th and last of the dives, which was initiated at 18,000 ft (5 485 m) and was intended to demonstrate a 9 g recovery (the design limitation of the aircraft) at about 8,000 ft (2 440 m), Grumman's test pilot, James Collins, pulled out too abruptly, subjecting the aircraft to something between 11 and 15 g which was far beyond its capabilities; the wings were wrenched off and the engine torn from its mount, and Collins was killed.

A second XF3F-1 was hurriedly completed by Grumman and, possessing the same Bureau number, flew two months later, on 9 May, but on 13 May, the day the replacement prototype arrived at Anacostia, this too suffered misfortune when its pilot, Lee Gehlbach, was unable to recover from a flat spin which developed during a 10-turn right-hand spin demonstration, Gehlbach being forced to bale out. Yet a third XF3F-1 was therefore built, this still retaining the BuNo 9727, utilising some components salvaged from the wreckage of the second prototype, and featuring an enlarged rudder. Testing was resumed at Anacostia on 20 June, Navy trials commencing three weeks later, on 10 July, and it was to prove a case of third time lucky, for this XF3F-1 came through the particularly rigorous test programme both rapidly and extremely well.

Few modifications were requested, the aircraft being officially accepted on 1 August, and on 24 August, a contract was placed for 54 F3F-1s (BuNos 0211-64), these having the improved R-1535-84 Twin Wasp Junior similar to that installed in the third XF3F-1 and possessing the same rating as that of the -72 model of the F2F-1 at 7,500 ft (2 286 m) but affording 700 hp for take-off at 2,250 rpm. This engine drove an 8 ft 6 in (2,59 m) diameter two-bladed hydraulic controllable-pitch Hamilton Standard propeller which replaced the mechanically-controlled Lycoming Smith propeller of the XF3F-1. Armament comprised a 0·3-in (7,62-mm) Mod 2 Browning machine gun to port with 500 rounds and a 0·5-in (12,7-mm) Browning to starboard with 200 rounds. A Mk VII gun camera was attached to the upper wing and the pilot was provided with a Mk III Mod 2 telescopic sight.

The F3F-1 proved appreciably more manœuvrable than its predecessor and directional stability was much improved, although its spinning characteristics were still considered dangerous and while BIS (Board of Inspection) trials verified the fact that the F3F-1 behaved properly in a spin when handled correctly, the Navy forbade intentional spinning of the fighter. In all other respects, the Navy considered the handling characteristics of the F3F-1 to be exceptional and the controls were so light that pilots accustomed to much higher stick pressures in pulling out of high speed dives were warned of the possibility of overstressing the aircraft if more than light pressure was applied to the stick. The F3F-1 was, in fact,

restricted to 8·44 g initially — this lower figure by comparison with that of the prototype resulting from the higher weight of the production model — but this was later relaxed and the 9 g limitation restored.

In normal loaded condition, the F3F-1 could lift-off within 200 ft (610 m) at between 50 and 55 knots (93 and 102 km/h), and normally landed at 60 to 65 knots (111 to 120 km/h), the approach usually being made at 75 knots (139 km/h). Despite its higher weight and larger overall dimensions, maximum speed at 7,500 ft (2 286 m) was identical to that of the F2F-1, although the rated power of the engines of the two at critical altitude were also identical. Initial climb rate was inferior at 1,900 ft/min (9,65 m/sec), but the F3F-1 had a speed superiority of 12 mph (19 km/h) at sea level.

Deliveries of the F3F-1 began in January 1936 and were completed during the following August, being assigned to VF-5B on the *Ranger* from April and VF-6B aboard the *Saratoga* from June, the latter becoming VF-3 and the former VF-4 in July of the following year. Four crashes suffered by VF-6B during its first four months of operating the F3F-1 led to a decision on the part of the Bureau of Aeronautics to static test one example to destruction, all aircraft meanwhile being restricted to 6 g. The static test programme was to result in the strengthening of the upper wing beam and the aileron bell cranks of all F3F-1s. Six F3F-1s were included on the strength of VMF-1 (formerly VF-4M) from its formation in March 1937, until its re-equipment with F3F-2s in October, and nine of VF-3's F3F-1s were to be reassigned to VF-7 in December 1939.

From Twin Wasp to Cyclone

By early 1936, the Bureau of Aeronautics had formulated specifications for the US Navy's next generation of shipboard single-seat fighters, but although there was now ample evidence that the era of the biplane was finally drawing to a close, there existed a hard core of traditionalists in the service still entertaining serious misgivings concerning the practicability of the monoplane configuration that it was proposed should be introduced for carrier-based fighters during the last years of the decade. Influenced in no small measure by sentiment, they argued that total commitment to fighter monoplanes

(Above) F3F-3 BuNo 1463 photographed at Anacostia on 7 April 1939, and (below) F3F-3 BuNo 1445 assigned to VF-5 aboard the Yorktown *from May 1939, this being the last carrier-based squadron to convert to monoplanes, flying its F3F-3s until mid-1941.*

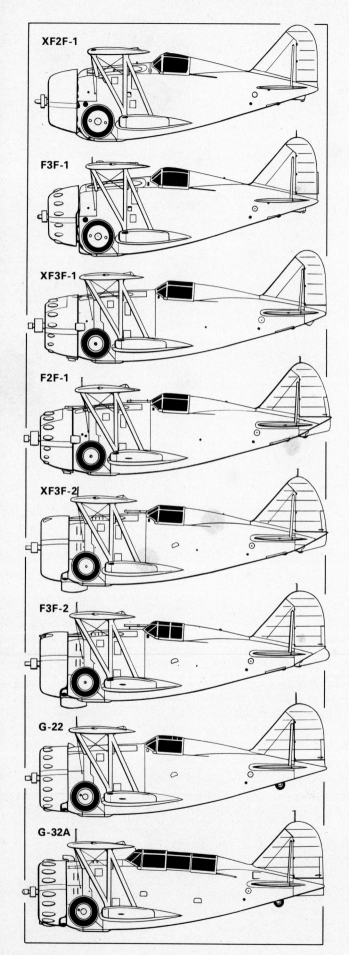

XF2F-1

F3F-1

XF3F-1

F2F-1

XF3F-2

F3F-2

G-22

G-32A

Grumman F2F-1 Specification

Power Plant: One Pratt & Whitney R-1535-72 Twin Wasp Junior 14-cylinder two-row radial air-cooled engine rated at 650 hp at 2,200 rpm for take-off and 650 hp at 2,200 rpm at 7,500 ft (2 286 m), driving a two-blade adjustable-pitch Hamilton Standard propeller. Main fuel tank of 75 US gal (284 l) capacity and reserve tank of 35 US gal (132 l) capacity (87 octane fuel).
Performance: Max speed, 203 mph (327 km/h) at sea level, 231 mph (372 km/h) at 7,500 ft (2 286 m); initial climb, 2,050 ft/min (10,41 m/sec); time to 5,000 ft (1 525 m), 2·1 min; service ceiling, 27,100 ft (8 535 m); max range (main and reserve tanks), 985 mls (1 585 km); landing speed, 65·5 mph (105 km/h).
Weights: Empty equipped, 2,691 lb (1 221 kg); max take-off, 3,847 lb (1 745 kg).
Dimensions: Span, 28 ft 6 in (8,69 m); length, 21 ft 5 in (6,53 m); height, 9 ft 1 in (2,77 m); wing area, 230 sq ft (21,37 m²).
Armament: Two 0·3-in (7,62-mm) Browning Mod 2 machine guns with 500 rpg.

was premature and that the biplane's service life could be usefully prolonged.

Thus, on 2 March 1936, Grumman was instructed to proceed with yet another single-seat fighter biplane, the G-16, designed around the new Wright XR-1670 engine and assigned the designation XF4F-1. The Grumman design had been ordered in part to placate the traditionalists and in part as a back-up in the event of any failure of the Brewster Model 39 fighter monoplane which was to be ordered on 23 June 1936 as the XF2A-1. Appreciative of the fact that the fighter biplane had almost reached the end of the road, Grumman had prepared a parallel study for a fighter monoplane, the G-18. Ascertaining that the application of a larger engine to the basic F3F airframe would result in a performance barely lower than that predicted for the XF4F-1, the company proposed that a G-series Cyclone be installed in the final production F3F-1. Grumman's proposal was made on 3 June, and the Bureau of Aeronautics was persuaded to discard the XF4F-1 in favour of the G-18 monoplane, the existing contract being duly amended and the G-18 receiving the appellation of XF4F-2.

A new contract was prepared for the Cyclone-engined F3F, designated by Grumman as the G-19, a prototype being ordered on 28 July 1936 as the XF3F-2, although, in fact, the actual aircraft had been delivered to Anacostia on the previous day. The XF3F-2 (BuNo 0452) was not to commence its test programme until the following January because of teething troubles suffered by the new carburation system of its Wright XR-1820-22 Cyclone nine-cylinder two-speed super-charged air-cooled radial engine. The Cyclone offered 1,000 hp at 2,100 rpm for take-off, 850 hp at the same revs in low blower at 5,800 ft (1 768 m) and 820 hp in high blower at 12,000 ft (3 658 m). Of larger diameter than the Twin Wasp Junior (53¾ in/136,5 cm compared with 44⅛ in/111,8 cm) and 121 lb (54,9 kg) heavier, the Cyclone drove a 9-ft (2,74-m) diameter three-bladed controllable-pitch propeller. Fuel capacity was raised to 130 US gal (492 l) divided between the main tank of 83 US gal (314 l) capacity and a reserve tank of 47 US gal (178 l) capacity.

The XF3F-2 offered the noteworthy improvement in all round performance that had been predicted, this approximating closely to that calculated for the discarded XF4F-1. It turned in a maximum speed of 255 mph (410 km/h) and a 4,000-ft (1 220-m) increase in service ceiling. Consequently, on 23 March 1937, Grumman received its largest single production contract to that time, this calling for 81 F3F-2s (BuNos 0967-1047), the first production example arriving at Anacostia on 27 July. Carbon monoxide intrusion, oil cooling and carburettor problems delayed fleet deliveries, however, these commencing with 0968 and 0969 to VF-6 on 1 December 1937, and continuing through 11 May 1938, when 1047 was accepted as a spare aircraft for VMF-1. The XF3F-2 itself,

GERMAN AEROSPACE SHOW 76

Saturday   **1st MAY**
to Sunday   **9th MAY**

AIR INTERNATIONAL have made special arrangements with Lunn Poly Limited for a one day flight to Hanover to visit the 1976 German Aerospace Show, Wednesday May 5th.

A Monarch Airlines Boeing 720B will fly you Luton-Hanover-Luton. The aircraft will depart from Luton 09.00 hrs arriving Hanover 10.15 hrs. Evening departure from Hanover 18.00 hrs arriving Luton 19.20 hrs.

The incredibly low all-in cost of £39 (you save £50.60 on the current normal scheduled return fare of £89.60) includes light refreshments served both outbound and inbound, all passenger taxes PLUS entrance ticket to the Air Show, situated adjacent to the airport.

Heavy bookings are expected so make sure of your place(s) by completing the booking form NOW! All bookings are subject to Lunn Poly's normal booking conditions, copies of which are available on request DIRECT ONLY from Lunn Poly Limited at the address shown below.

Each booking MUST be accompanied by a deposit of £10 which, in the event of cancellation, will be non-refundable (subject to Lunn Poly's normal booking conditions).

The final balance of £29 is due NOT LATER than April 2nd. Any bookings made after this date MUST be accompanied by the full payment of £39. FINAL CLOSING DATE April 21st.

Cheques should be made payable to Lunn Poly Limited.

Remember, a valid passport is essential!

BOOKING FORM

I/we wish to book ....place(s) on the AIR INTERNATIONAL one day flight, to the Hanover Air Show, Wednesday May 5th

☐ I/we enclose £10 deposit per person (subject to Lunn Poly's normal booking conditions)

☐ I/we enclose the full payment of £39 per person

Total amount enclosed................................

Passenger surname/initials (please print)................................

Full address/post code ....

Telephone No................................

Additional names/addresses of passengers may be listed separately and attached to this form

Complete and return to:
AIR INTERNATIONAL, FINESCROLL LTD, DE WORDE HOUSE, 283 LONSDALE RD, LONDON SW13 9QW
Tel No. 01-878 2454   Reg. No. 986714 London

For: Lunn Poly Ltd, Special Business Tours Dept, 232/242 Vauxhall Bridge Rd, London SW1V 1BR
     Tel. No. 01-828 6536   Reg. No. 638309 London

MRCA on target

The rate of progress on the tri-national MRCA programme – particularly on flight development – has sharply accelerated. But the brake has been successfully kept on cost escalation.

" . . . clearly the most successful international collaborative project ever, in which the real escalation of costs has been minimal and has been carefully controlled . . ."

Mr Brynmor John, Under-Secretary of State for RAF.

By the end of 1975, six **MRCA** prototypes had joined the flight development programme – three in Britain, two in Germany, one in Italy – and the flying rate had risen sharply. The emphasis has shifted from proving the basic handling and performance of the aircraft to proving its systems. Flight clearance of the integrated avionics system is well advanced, and clearance of the flight

Flight testing of the avionics system in the fourth prototype is well advanced

...cond prototype (above and below) flew with external stores in October and has proved the flight refuelling system

Government test pilots have flown the first prototype

The first trainer prototype made 11 flights in four days

envelope with external stores has begun. The flight re-fuelling system was cleared in an unprecedentedly short time – substantially in one flight – and has since been used to extend the duration of some test flights. The first two-seat trainer prototype has also begun flight development.

MRCA will equip the German air force and navy, the Royal Air Force, and the Italian air force. With a total production requirement for over 800 aircraft already stated by the Governments of the three participating nations, **MRCA** is ensured of low unit costs which cannot be rivalled in the world by any other aircraft of comparable performance and versatility.

"... The Bundeswehr needs a good aircraft and the Bundeswehr will get a good aircraft ... There is no alternative to the MRCA at a comparable cost ..." Herr Leber, German Minister of Defence.

"... The system has confirmed its full validity ... the programme is of prime importance to the Italian air force and Italian industry ..."
General Ciarlo, Italian Chief of Air Staff.

MRCA – the largest and most exacting military equipment programme Europe has ever seen – is backed by the resources of three of Europe's most powerful aerospace industries, who have at their command massive research, design, development and production strength. The air-craft meets the operational needs of three of the world's most experienced air forces and the German Navy. The programme mobilises the skills and experience of thousands of workers in Britain, Germany and Italy. It has established in Europe a military aviation capability second to none in the world. Authorisation of full production will ensure the continuing employment of a still larger workforce in all three countries for years to come.

The fifth prototype is extending the external stores flight test programme

PANAVIA MRCA

Panavia Aircraft GmbH, München, Arabellastrasse 16, Germany
AERITALIA
BRITISH AIRCRAFT CORPORATION
MESSERSCHMITT-BÖLKOW-BLOHM

PRODUCT OF EUROPE

which continued its test programme until 9 March 1936, and was subsequently employed in the utility rôle at Anacostia, was finally converted to F3F-1 standard in April 1938 (serving with both VF-3 and VF-4).

Apart from VF-6 aboard *Enterprise,* which had been flying Boeing F4B-4s as interim equipment pending arrival of the new Grumman fighters, the F3F-2s went to the two Marine Corps squadrons, VMF-1 at Quantico and VMF-2 at San Diego.

In addition to the F3F-2s delivered to the US Navy and Marine Corps, Grumman was to build three civil examples of the Cyclone-powered aeroplane, the first of these — the G-22 delivered in December 1936 and thus predating the production F3F-2 — being something of a hybrid. It was essentially the marriage of an F3F-2 fuselage and Cyclone engine to the smaller F2F-1 wings and a new and appreciably enlarged rudder. Produced for the Gulf Oil Refining Company, known as *Gulfhawk II* and flown by the company's aviation manager, Maj Alford J Williams, the G-22 was registered NR1050 and was taken on a tour of Europe by Major Williams in 1938.

Embodying a good deal of special equipment and possessing a superlative finish, the G-22 was undoubtedly the fastest of all the Grumman biplanes, Major Williams recording a maximum level speed of 290 mph (467 km/h) at 12,000 ft (3 658 m). With maximum fuel and cruising at 175 mph (282 km/h), it had a range of 1,500 miles (2 414 km), range being correspondingly reduced at higher cruising rates, being 900 miles (1 448 km) at 250 mph (402 km/h), 1,000 miles (1 609 km) at 225 mph (362 km/h) and 1,180 miles (1 899 km) at 200 mph (322 km/h). Initial climb rate was 3,500 ft/min (17,78 m/sec) and ceiling was 26,000 ft (7 925 m).

The G-22 *Gulfhawk II* was powered by the GR-1820-G1 version of the Cyclone which was rated at 940 hp at 2,200 rpm for take-off, rated maximum outputs at 2,100 rpm being 825 hp at sea level and 850 hp at 3,000 ft (915 m). A second scavenger pump and five drain lines were added to the engine installation enabling the aircraft to be flown inverted for up to 30 minutes.

With the normal fuel load of 144 US gal (545 l), the G-22 had a take-off weight of 4,195 lb (1 903 kg), resulting in a wing loading of 18·24 lb/sq ft (89,06 kg/m²), but for aerobatic flight fuel load was restricted to 42 US gal (159 l) to produce a loaded weight of 3,583 lb (1 625 kg) and a wing loading of 15·58 lb/sq ft (76,07 kg/m²).

A second aircraft built for Gulf was the G-32 *Gulfhawk III,* which, delivered on 6 May 1938, differed from the G-22

THE FATE OF THE CIVIL "BARRELS"

The G-22 *Gulfhawk II* was flown throughout the war years for demonstration purposes, retaining its civil identity and being flown for the last time on 11 October 1948 at Washington National Airport. It was then presented to the Smithsonian and is now preserved in the collection of the National Air and Space Museum. The G-32 *Gulfhawk III* was impressed by the USAAF in November 1942, and assigned the serial number 42-97044 and the designation C-103, later amended to UC-103. Employed primarily for ferrying VIPs, it only saw a few months of USAAF service before its pilot forced landed in the southern Florida Everglades, and G-32 was thus written off.

The G-32A was destined to have a much longer flying career than either of the other civil Grummans and was, in fact, active until 1971. Like the G-32, the G-32A was impressed by the USAAF as a C-103/UC-103 and assigned the serial number 42-97045. It was flown first at Bolling Field, Washington, and was then attached to a ferry pool at Miami. After WW II it was sold as surplus, re-registered as N46110 and subsequently passed through several hands until it reached those of Doug Champlin and Tony Blackstone of Windward Aviation, Enid, Oklahoma. Repainted to represent an F3F-2 of VF-5, the G-32A appeared at various flying events, including the 1971 International Experimental Aircraft Association Convention at Oshkosh, Wisconsin. On the final day of the Convention, while being flown by Gene Chase, a veteran of 7,000 hours, the aircraft burst into flames, its pilot baling out and suffering some burns and a back injury. Plans exist for rebuilding the G-32A for static display purposes.

The general arrangement drawing below depicts the F3F-3, the upper sideview illustrating the XF3F-3.

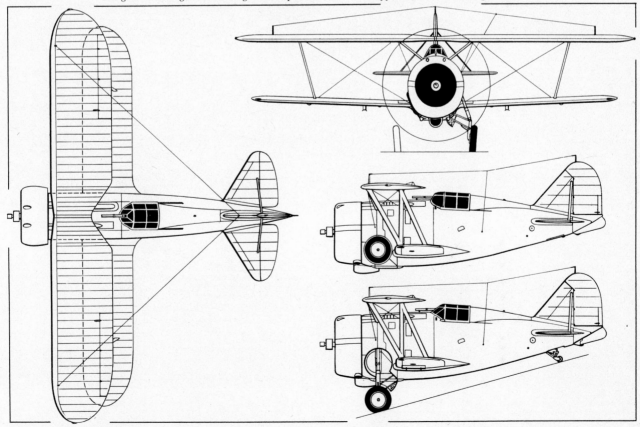

Grumman F3F-3 Cutaway Drawing Key

1 Three-bladed constant-speed controllable-pitch 9-ft (2,74-m) diameter Hamilton Standard propeller
2 Propeller pitch change mechanism
3 Carburettor air intake
4 Supercharger air intake
5 NACA-type cowling
6 Wright R-1820-22 Cyclone nine-cylinder single-row radial air-cooled engine
7 Exhaust pipe
8 Oil cooler intake
9 Oil cooler (9 in/22,9 cm diameter)
10 Upper engine mounting struts
11 Lower engine mounting struts
12 Starboard gun blast tube
13 Port gun blast tube
14 Oil tank (9 US gal/34 l capacity)
15 Oil filler cap
16 Engine bulkhead
17 Main fuel tank (83 US gal/314 l capacity)
18 Fuel tank filler cap
19 Tank fixing
20 Fuselage main longeron
21 Centre section forward strut
22 Centre section aft strut
23 Strut attachment lug
24 Light alloy interplane N-struts
25 Flying wires
26 Upper wing centreline joint
27 Aircraft sling attachments
28 Mk VII gun camera
29 Front spar
30 Rear spar
31 Spar bracing rib
32 Diagonal wire bracing
33 Wing ribs (of truss construction)
34 Starboard aileron
35 Aileron actuating arm
36 Aileron control rod
37 Aerial cable
38 Starboard navigation light
39 Mk III Mod 4 telescope sight
40 Windscreen frame
41 Port 0·3-in (7,62-mm) Browning machine gun
42 Starboard 0·5-in (12,7-mm) Browning machine gun
43 Ammunition tanks (500 rounds 0·3-in/7,62-mm and 200 rounds 0·5-in/ 12,7-mm)
44 Ammunition feed chute
45 Cartridge case ejector chute
46 Pressure fire extinguisher
47 Auxiliary fuel tank (47 US gal/178 l capacity)
48 Auxiliary tank filler
49 Very pistol cartridge holder
50 Rudder pedal
51 Chartboard
52 Instrument panel
53 Pilot's seat
54 Throttle and propeller controls
55 Bomb release levers
56 Tailplane trim control
57 Access step
58 Cockpit floor structure
59 Adjustable seat support structure
60 Headrest
61 Aft-sliding canopy
62 Life raft stowage
63 D/F loop
64 Junction box
65 Equipment bay access door
66 Dynamotor unit
67 Radio transmitter
68 Radio receiver
69 First aid kit
70 Emergency rations and water supply
71 Dorsal light
72 Fuselage frames (Z section)
73 Tailplane incidence control rod

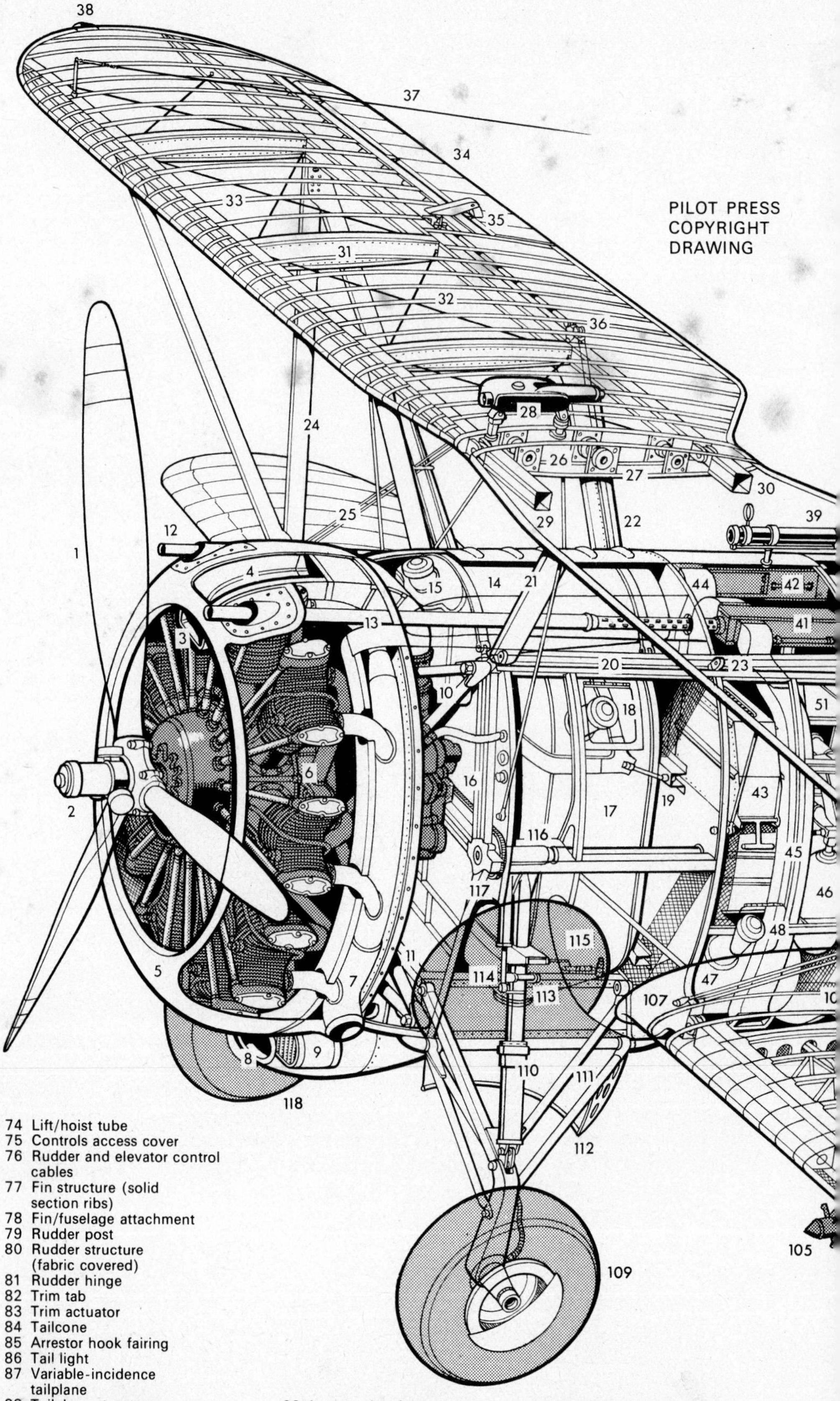

74 Lift/hoist tube
75 Controls access cover
76 Rudder and elevator control cables
77 Fin structure (solid section ribs)
78 Fin/fuselage attachment
79 Rudder post
80 Rudder structure (fabric covered)
81 Rudder hinge
82 Trim tab
83 Trim actuator
84 Tailcone
85 Arrestor hook fairing
86 Tail light
87 Variable-incidence tailplane
88 Tailplane structure
89 Elevator (fabric covered)
90 Arrestor hook (extended)
91 Retractable tailwheel (solid rubber tyre)
92 Tailwheel shock absorber strut
93 Port upper wing structure
94 Port navigation light
95 Interplane "N" struts

96 Lower wing front spar
97 Lower wing rear spar
98 Spar bracing rib
99 Wing ribs
100 Leading edge construction
101 Wire bracing
102 Retractable landing light
103 Mk XLI bomb rack
104 Mk IV 116-lb (52,7-kg) demolition bomb

105 Fuse unit
106 Wing spar root fitting
107 Flying wire attachment
108 Wing root fillet
109 Port mainwheel (26 in×6 in/66 cm×15 cm)
110 Oleo strut
111 Radius arms
112 Fairing door
113 Retraction strut

PILOT PRESS
COPYRIGHT
DRAWING

Engine/Prop packs 1/48

AEP 401	5cyl. A.S.Genet	
AEP 402	7cyl. A.S.Genet	
AEP 403	7cyl. A.S.Lynx	
AEP 404	14cyl. A.S.Jaguar	
AEP 405	DH type cowl and prop	Moths
AEP 406	Cirrus type cowl and prop	Messenger
AEP 407	Bristol Jupiter	Gamecock
AEP 408	9cyl. Gnome Monosoupape	WWI Rotary
AEP 409	9cyl. 110hp Le Rhone	" "
AEP 410	9cyl. 80hp Le Rhone	" "
AEP 411	Wright Cyclone 1820	Grumman F3F

Ejection seats

These facsimiles have the major characteristics of the mark they portray.
Jane's "All the World's Aircraft" often note the mark of seat fitted to a
particular prototype.

Typical uses

MK3 - Hunter, Canberra, Javelin and many 50's aircraft.
MK4a - T/s Hunter, Mirage, Fiat G91, Macchi 326 etc.
MK4b - E.E.Lightning.
MK5 - Many U.S.A.F./U.S.N. types.
MK6/7 - now fitted to the R.A.F.'s Buccaneers and Phantoms.
MK9 - Harrier and Jaguar.
MK10 - Hawk, Alfajet Export Hawks have seat similar to the Sea Harrier.
MK10s - with a different headbox (chute container) are fitted to the Sea Harrier
and Tornado. The Mk 10 is even fitted to export Chinese Shenyang/MiG 19's.

Ejection seat painting

The appearance of the finished seat can be much enhanced by making the harness from
pre-painted thin masking tape. This is made easier if a piece of tape is first put
on to a scrap piece of plastic, then cut into strips using a knife and a straight
edge. Paint the tape with thin colour and cut into small lengths so they can be
applied to the seat using the etched straps (and photographs) as a guide. Firing
handles are best made from fuse wire, glued into small location holes.

Ejection seats 1/72 (sold in pairs)			Ejection seats 1/48 (one per pack)		
AEJ 002	Martin Baker MK4 BS		AEJ 402	Martin Baker MK3	
AEJ 003	"	MK5	AEJ 403	"	MK4
AEJ 004	"	Mk6/7	AEJ 404	"	MK4 BS
AEJ 005			AEJ 405		
AEJ 006	"	MK9	AEJ 406	"	MK9
AEJ 007	"	MK10 (Hawk)	AEJ 407	"	MK10 (Hawk)
AEJ 008	"	MK3	AEJ 408	"	MK10 (Sea Harrier)
AEJ 009	"	MK5	AEJ 409	"	MK5
AEJ 010	"	MK4a	AEJ 410	"	MK7
AEJ 011	"	MK10 'Sea Harrier)			

Note- Some kits have one piece moulded floor/cockpit wells. these are often
very narrow, modify before fitting into the model fuselage.

Graphics by Fiona Tagg.

Note- When parked all seats have a number
of Red tagged safety pins fitted in handles
and various gun sears. In flight these tags
are usually stored in a small block near the
cockpit coaming. The Mks 2/3, carry a large
circular tag on the L/H side of the chute pan.

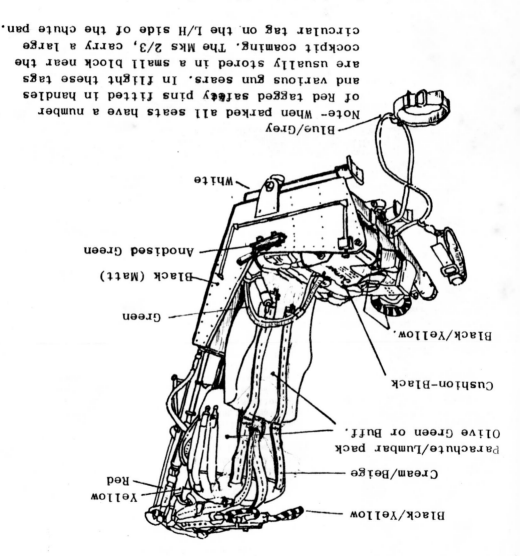

Blue/Grey

White

Anodised Green

Black (Matt)

Green

Black/Yellow.

Cushion-Black

Olive Green or Buff.

Parachute/Lumbar pack

Cream/Beige

Red
Yellow

Black/Yellow

A typical Ejection Seat (MK7AI MKI).as fitted to
the R.A.F. Phantom.

primarily in having standard F3F-2 wings, a second cockpit inserted in the fuselage aft of the standard cockpit, a continuous canopy with two aft-sliding sections enclosing both cockpits, and a GR-1820-G5 Cyclone rated at 950 hp at 2,200 rpm for take-off and a rated maximum output at 2,100 rpm of 850 hp both at sea level and at 6,000 ft (1 830 m). This aircraft was registered NC1051. Yet a third civil example, the G-32A, was completed in June 1938, first flown on 1 July by Bud Gillies, and retained by the Grumman Aircraft Engineering Corporation as a company demonstrator, differing from the G-32 primarily in having split flaps on the trailing edge of the upper wing. Registered NC1326, this aircraft was frequently flown by Leroy Grumman himself.

The final refinement

When the last production F3F-2 was flown away from Bethpage, where Grumman activities were by now centred, on 11 May 1938, it might have been reasonable to suppose that this event terminated the production career of a fighter which was, after all, nearly seven years old in basic design, and this during a period when advances in the state of the art had come fast and furious. Such was not to be the case, however, for six months later, on 21 June 1938, the Bureau of Aeronautics was to place an order for yet *another* batch of the barrel-like biplanes.

Development of the Brewster XF2A-1 and Grumman XF4F-2 fighter monoplanes was proving somewhat more protracted than had been earlier anticipated and prospects for early production deliveries of the winning Brewster contender were not good, but replacement of the obsolete F2F-1s serving with VF-2 and VF-5 was becoming a matter of some urgency by mid-1938, when an additional squadron, VF-7, was being

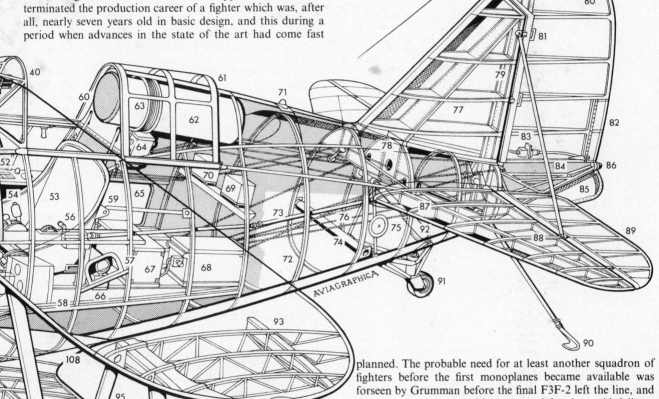

planned. The probable need for at least another squadron of fighters before the first monoplanes became available was forseen by Grumman before the final F3F-2 left the line, and the company came up with a proposal for the rapid delivery of "improved" F3F-2s. While the merit of the proposal was appreciated by the Navy, the service wanted to undertake some experimentation before further aircraft were committed to production.

F3F-2 BuNo 1031, which was routinely delivered to Anacostia on 4 April 1938 and earmarked as a spare for VF-6, was returned to Grumman in May for the installation of fittings which would enable the aircraft to be tested in the Langley wind tunnel to examine possible drag reduction measures for the "improved" F3F-2. Apart from the wind tunnel suspension fittings, Grumman introduced a streamlined windscreen similar to that of the XF4F-2 monoplane, a newly-designed wing leading edge, a revised engine cowling and fuselage side fairing plates. With these modifications, BuNo 1031 returned to Anacostia on 24 May and was tested with various propeller blades while awaiting availability of the Langley tunnel. Transferred to Langley on 15 June, it completed its assignment and returned to Anacostia on 20 July.

In the meantime, on 21 June, Grumman received a contract for 27 "improved" F3F-2s as F3F-3s (BuNos 1444-70), these aircraft retaining the Grumman designation of G-19 that had

114 Lock actuator
115 Wheel well
116 Retraction strut axle mounting
117 Retraction chain drive
118 Starboard mainwheel

Grumman F3F Specifications

Power Plant: (F3F-1) One Pratt & Whitney R-1535-84 Twin Wasp Junior direct-drive single-stage supercharged 14-cylinder two-row radial air-cooled engine rated at 700 hp at 2,250 rpm for take-off and 650 hp at 2,200 rpm at 7,500 ft (2 286 m), driving 8 ft 6 in (2,59 m) diameter two-blade hydraulic controllable-pitch Hamilton Standard propeller. Main fuel tank of 75 US gal (284 l) capacity and reserve tank of 35 US gal (132 l) capacity. (F3F-2 and -3) One Wright R-1820-22 Cyclone two-speed supercharged nine-cylinder radial air-cooled engine rated at 950 hp at 2,200 rpm for take-off, 850 hp at 2,100 rpm at 600 ft (183 m) and 750 hp at 2,100 rpm at 15,200 ft (4633 m), driving (F3F-2) 9 ft (2,74 m) or (F3F-3) 8 ft 9 in (2,67 m) diameter three-blade hydraulic controllable-pitch Hamilton Standard propeller. Main fuel tank of 83 US gal (314 l) capacity and reserve tank of 47 US gal (178 l) capacity.

Performance (F3F-1): Max speed, 215 mph (346 km/h) at sea level, 231 mph (372 km/h) at 7,500 ft (2 286 m); initial climb, 1,900 ft/min (9,65 m/sec); service ceiling, 28,500 ft (8 687 m); max range (main and reserve tanks), 998 mls (1 606 km); landing speed, 66 mph (106 km/h).

Performance (F3F-2): Max speed, 234 mph (376 km/h) at sea level, 256 mph (412 km/h) at 17,250 ft (2 258 m); initial climb, 2,800 ft/min (14,22 m/sec); service ceiling, 32,300 ft (9 845 m); range, 975 mls (1 569 km) at 123 mph (198 km/h); max range, 1,130 mls (1 818 km); landing speed, 69 mph (111 km/h).

Performance (F3F-3): Max speed, 239 mph (384 km/h) at sea level, 264 mph (425 km/h) at 15,200 ft (4 633 m); initial climb, 2,750 ft/min (13,97 m/sec); service ceiling, 33,200 ft (10 120 m); normal range, 980 mls (1 577 km); max range, 1,150 mls (1 850 km); landing speed, 68 mph (109 km/h).

Weights (F3F-1): Empty equipped, 2,952 lb (1 339 kg); normal loaded, 4,170 lb (1 891 kg); max take-off, 4,403 lb (1 997 kg).

Weights (F3F-2): Empty equipped, 3,254 lb (1 476 kg); normal loaded, 4,498 lb (2 040 kg); max take-off, 4,750 lb (2 155 kg).

Weights (F3F-3): Empty equipped, 3,285 lb (1 490 kg); normal loaded, 4,543 lb (2 061 kg); max take-off, 4,795 lb (2 175 kg); useful load (as fighter with 110 US gal/416 l fuel), 1,258 lb (571 kg), (as bomber with 110 US gal/416 l fuel), 1,510 lb (685 kg), (as fighter with 130 US gal/492 l fuel), 1,378 lb (625 kg).

Dimensions: Span (upper wing), 32 ft 0 in (9,75 m), (lower wing), 29 ft 6 in (8,99 m); length (F3F-1), 23 ft 3⅛ in (7,09 m), (F3F-2 and -3), 23 ft 0 in (7,01 m); height tail down and propeller vertical (F3F-1), 9 ft 1 in (2,77 m), (F3F-2 and -3), 9 ft 4 in (2,84 m); wing area, 260·6 sq ft (24,21 m²).

Armament: One 0·5-in (12,7-mm) Browning Mod 2 machine gun with 200 rounds and one 0·3-in (7,62-mm) Browning Mod 2 machine gun with 500 rounds. Provision for two 116-lb (52,6-kg) Mk IV demolition bombs or 10 Mk V miniature practice bombs.

applied to the F3F-2s, although the aircraft were not actually released for production as the Navy was anxious to perform further testing before deciding on a definitive production standard.

The Navy had decided to evaluate BuNo 1031 with wing flaps and to accelerate tests agreed to use the flapped upper wing of the newly-completed Grumman two-seat demonstrator, the G-32A. Accordingly, the aircraft was again returned to Grumman on 15 August, the upper wing of the G-32A was fitted and BuNo 1031 returned to Anacostia. Various trials were undertaken by BIS pilots, both at Anacostia and at the experimental carrier landing facility at the Naval Aircraft Factory in Philadelphia, but it was concluded that the improvements in approach and landing speeds resulting from use of the flaps were insufficient to justify the heavier wing.

Once again the aircraft was returned to Grumman (on 23 August) for the original upper wing to be reinstated and for various modifications to be made to convert BuNo 1031 as the XF3F-3. Modifications specified (most of which had already been carried out) comprised the revision of the engine cowling and forward fuselage decking, the installation of a new 8 ft 9 in (2,67 m) diameter Hamilton Standard propeller, provision of an XF4F-2-type curved plexiglass windscreen and improved hinged covers in the centre section, and various minor changes aimed at reducing drag. As the XF3F-3, the aircraft was ultimately re-delivered to the Navy on 29 October, a month after the F3F-3 had, in fact, been released for production.

Service Acceptance Trials were completed on 14 December, the examining board commenting that "the XF3F-3 fulfilled the contractor's guarantees and showed an appreciable improvement over the F3F-2 in performance."

Because of the delay in releasing the F3F-3 for production, deliveries of the improved fighter commenced somewhat later than had been anticipated and, in consequence, it was not possible to replace the F2F-1s of VF-5 aboard the *Yorktown* before the carrier sailed for the West Coast from Norfolk in early January as had been planned. The first F3F-3 was not delivered for Production Acceptance Trials until 16 December 1938, and the aircraft were finally transferred to VF-5 *en masse* when the *Yorktown* arrived at San Diego in May 1939. In so far as the service pilots were concerned, this ultimate refinement of the basic Grumman fighter biplane was even more popular than its predecessors. It was a delight to fly; robust, faster than its predecessors and highly manœuvrable. It handled superbly, snap-rolled with exacting precision and could make a three-point landing in any power or loading condition. Externally it was barely distinguishable from the F3F-2 — the curved plexiglass windscreen featured by the XF3F-3 had not been standardised for the production model — and the examining board's reference after completion of Service Acceptance Trials to an "appreciable improvement" in so far as overall performance was concerned was something of an exaggeration, the increment being 8 mph (13 km/h) in maximum speed at 15,200 ft (4 633 m) and 900 ft (274 m) on the service ceiling, but in the view of its pilots it carried shipboard fighting biplane development to the peak of perfection.

With the introduction of the F3F-3 by VF-5 and the transfer of its F2F-1s to VF-7, in 1939 the Grumman fighters equipped *all* Navy and Marine Corps squadrons in full commission as follows:

Type	Squadron	Carrier or base	Tail Colour
F2F-1	VF-2	Lexington	Yellow
F3F-1	VF-3	Saratoga	White
F3F-1	VF-4	Ranger	Green
F3F-3	VF-5	Yorktown	Red
F3F-2	VF-6	Enterprise	Blue
F2F-1	VF-7	Wasp	Black
F3F-2	VMF-1	Quantico	Red-white-blue
F3F-2	VMF-2	San Diego	Red-white-blue

By the end of 1941, the last of the Grumman biplanes had disappeared from the first-line squadrons, the two US Marine Corps squadrons, which had become VMF-111 and VMF-211 on 1 July 1941, being the final operational units to relinquish them, on 28 July and 10 October 1941 respectively[*], the latter unit being by this time based in Hawaii. However, there were 23 F2Fs and 117 F3Fs at various Naval Air Stations in the USA at the beginning of 1942, mostly serving for fighter pilot training, the F3F-1s at Norfolk and Miami, the F3F-2s at the latter station and at Corpus Christi where the F3F-3s were also mostly based. Less than two years later, just prior to the end of November 1943, the last active F3F-2 was stricken from the records of serviceable aircraft and, together with its fellows, reassigned to ground instruction, none, it would seem, surviving the rigours of the Technical Training Schools.

Thus, late in 1943, the career of the barrel-like Grumman single-seat fighter biplane finally came to its close; almost exactly a decade after the initial flight of the XF2F-1. It had achieved no fame in action, having never fired its guns in earnest, although, as progenitor of the famous F4F Wildcat, it enjoyed some reflected glory. It had carried US Naval Aviation a major step forward in fighter technology and it possessed the abiding affection of all who had flown it — a fitting enough epitaph for any warplane. □

The last F3F-1s were relinquished by VF-72 (ex VF-7) on 10 February 1941, and the last F3F-2s and -3s of a carrier-based squadron (VF-5) were taken out of service on 20 June 1941

Thirty-five years ago, in the early months of 1941, the first prototype of what was destined to become the world's first production turbojet-powered fighter, the Messerschmitt Me 262, known more or less unofficially as the Swallow (Schwalbe), was being readied for its first test flight, albeit with a piston engine in the nose pending availability of the radical new power plant for which it had been conceived. The subsequent development and brief operational career of this remarkable warplane is well documented but little has hitherto been revealed concerning the actual conception of this outstanding fighter which was to launch a new era in combat aircraft design. AIR INTERNATIONAL has invited Woldemar Voigt to recall the early steps which led to the configuration of this, the most sensational aircraft to see combat during World War II. Woldemar Voigt, who joined Messerschmitt in 1933, was involved in the development of the Me 262 from its very inception. Early in 1939, he became head of the Project Bureau (configuration design and aerodynamics), a position he retained until the final collapse of Germany in May 1945.

GESTATION OF THE SWALLOW

ALMOST FORTY YEARS AGO, in September 1937, Hans-Joachim Pabst von Ohain, who had left the University of Göttingen to join Ernst Heinkel and develop a gas turbine for aircraft propulsion, ran successfully his first demonstration engine, and not many months elapsed before, during the course of 1938, we, at Messerschmitt, were informed by the RLM that BMW, too, was working on this sensational new development. We were asked to submit studies on the potential performance to be achieved by a fighter powered by the gas turbine and the thrust requirement for such an aircraft. The BMW studies at their Munich plant were concentrated on a centrifugal type engine, but before anything had really begun to take shape on our drawing boards BMW had discarded these studies in favour of concentration on an axial flow engine conceived by the Bramo works at Spandau.

Since the eventual size of the engine was still very much a matter for speculation, on the basis of the BMW-Bramo studies we were given formulæ from which we could derive estimates of dimensions, weights, etc, as functions of thrust. We were enabled to provide a dimensional estimate without sketching out a basic configuration as we had discovered that all Messerschmitt high-performance aircraft had essentially the same value of a figure of merit that we had developed and that other leading aircraft, both German and foreign, fitted into the same pattern. Therefore, we estimated the drag divergence Mach number that might be obtainable and computed the thrust that would be required from the figure-of-merit formula for an assumed value of that figure. Our aim was, of course, a maximum speed fully exploiting the leeway given by the drag barrier and our figure of merit was defined by the following formula:

$$K = \frac{C_{Lmax}}{C_{Dv}} \cdot \frac{W^1}{W}$$

K represented the figure of merit, C_{Lmax} the maximum lift coefficient, C_{Dv} the drag coefficient at maximum speed and W^1 the sum of all weights that were not part of the airframe (ie, payload, power plant, armament, crew, fuel, etc). For a good subsonic aeroplane, K came out at 43·5 (±3 per cent) but for our first transonic aeroplane we estimated that, in view of the compressibility drag, we might achieve only 80 per cent of that value, and on this basis we concluded that our total thrust requirement for a single-seater with the specified armament and a 30-minute endurance at combat altitude was 1,350 lb (610 kg).

Since both the engine weight formula and manufacturing considerations seemed to favour smaller engines, we suggested to the RLM that the proposed fighter should have two gas turbine engines of about 700 lb (315 kg) each. We had not, at this stage, sketched out any firm design proposals and we

had seriously underestimated the drag divergence Mach number and, in consequence, the speed for which the projected aeroplane was to be designed. Furthermore, owing to our limited experience at that time with production combat aircraft, we had failed to make due allowance for the inevitable weight escalation — new power plants, conventional or unconventional, almost invariably exceed their estimated weight and consume more fuel than anticipated, factors compounded by afterthoughts on the part of the customer which result in

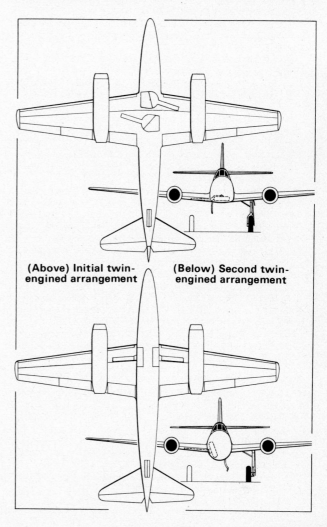

(Above) Initial twin-engined arrangement

(Below) Second twin-engined arrangement

demands for more effective and heavier armament, additional equipment, etc.

In the event, the Technical Department of the RLM elected to go for very much higher thrust levels, both BMW and Junkers — the latter having meanwhile entered the turbojet picture — aiming at a static thrust of the order of 1,500 lb (680 kg). Such a value was certainly much higher than that demanded by the twin-engined aeroplane that we envisaged at that time, but the decision at least enabled us to commence serious design studies and the higher thrust requested by the RLM was to prove a boon in the event.

Our greatest problem was the dearth of research data on

Chronology of Early Me 262 Development

Early 1938: First discussions on the manufacture and installation of turbojets

October 1938: Initiation of project studies for a jet fighter as P 1065

7 June 1939: P 1065 project proposal passed to RLM. Proposal calls for all-metal low-wing aircraft with retractable tailwheel undercarriage. Intended power plant comprising two BMW TL-units each of 1,320 lb (600 kg) thrust. Estimated cruising speed of 559 mph (900 km/h) at 100 per cent thrust. Estimated overall dimensions: span, 30 ft 10 in (9,40 m); length, 30 ft 6 in (9,30 m); height, 9 ft 2¼ in (2,80 m); wing area, 193·75 sq ft (18,00 m²)

16 November 1939: Decision to modify two Bf 110s as test-beds for BMW P 3302 turbojets

1 December 1939: Meeting between BMW, RLM and test centre (E-Stelle) to discuss installation of BMW P 3302 and P 3304 units in P 1065 design, means of power plant attachment, the fuel system and instrumentation

19 December 1939: Inspection of cockpit and visibility mock-ups of P 1065. Visibility characteristics pronounced generally satisfactory with forward visibility particularly commended. Engine instrumentation still to be finalized

18 January 1940: Advice on braking parachutes sought from E-Stelle Rechlin and Flugtechnischen Institut Stuttgart. Further inspection of cockpit mock-up by RLM and E-Stelle Rechlin and decision to examine possibilities of extended armour protection for pilot

1 February 1940: Advice from E-Stelle Rechlin on tankage and radio equipment. FuG 17 and FuG 20 planned for first 20 trials aircraft

1 March 1940: Recommendations from E-Stelle Rechlin and RLM on number of test models with BMW engines and their equipment status. Three test aircraft to be built with BMW P 3302 engines. The P 1065 V1 to have: (a) pressurized cockpit but without pressure-tight canopy; (b) ejection seat; (c) air brakes; (d) braking chute, and (e) protected fuel tanks

29 March 1940: Discussions with E-Stelle Rechlin on proposed equipment alterations

12 April 1940: Firm decisions reached in discussions with Berlin-Spandau branch of BMW concerning engine instrumentation of Bf 110 test-bed and P 1065 V1

15 May 1940: Second project proposal with underwing power plant installation submitted to RLM as satisfactory spar construction unrealizable with wing-mounted engines of first project proposal. Increases in power plant weight resulting in CG shift dictate introduction of compensatory wing sweep

30 May 1940: Conference with E-Stelle Rechlin concerning weapon system electrical layout

20 June 1940: Messerschmitt receives installation details of BMW P 3302 and P 3303 engines

8 April 1941: In conference with RLM and E-Stellen Rechlin and Peenemünde, and the Walter company of Kiel, the decision taken to fit the P 1065 V1 with two Walter rockets of 1,653 lb (750 kg) thrust each instead of BMW engines for initial high Mach tests. (In the event, this scheme was to be abandoned as delivery of the Walter units was to be even more protracted than that of the BMW turbojets)

18 April 1941: First flight of P 1065 V1 with nose-mounted Jumo 210G piston engine. (Flights solely on the power of this engine to be continued until 27 July)

25 July 1941: Messerschmitt receives RLM contract for five test and 20 pre-production aircraft

27 July 1941: Two BMW P 3302s fitted to Me 262 V1 (as P 1065 V1 now officially designated) for further tests. Nose-mounted Jumo 210G retained

26 September 1941: RLM requests investigation into possible use of Me 262 fitted with Jumo TL-units and cameras and with armament deleted as a fast reconnaissance aircraft

29 May 1942: Following discussions with RLM, decision taken to build initially only first five aircraft (Me 262 V1 to V5). Construction of remaining 15 aircraft to be committed only after flight testing of the first five

1 June 1942: Me 262 V3 completed with two Jumo 109-004 TLs

18 July 1942: Me 262 V3 flown at Leipheim. First flight at 0840 hours and second at 1205 hours

12 August 1942: As a result of initial testing at Leipheim and following discussions with RLM and E-Stelle Rechlin, decision taken to complete five further prototypes and build 10 pre-production machines. Aircraft from Me 262 V11 onwards to be fitted with nosewheel undercarriage. Following equipment specified for pre-production aircraft (Me 262 V11 and V20): (a) pressure cabin; (b) FuG 16Z and FuG 25A; (c) one 30-mm MK 103 to replace one of three 20-mm MG 151 cannon previously envisaged and the possibility of two additional MG 151s in wings to be explored; (d) armour for pilot and protection for fuel tanks, and (e) air brakes

17 August 1942: Me 262 V3 flown by E-Stelle Rechlin test pilot, Dipl-Ing Beauvais, but lifted off runway too late and damaged when starboard wingtip struck obstacle

1 October 1942: First flight of Me 262 V2 with Jumo TL engines at 0923 hours at Lechfeld by Fritz Wendel. Machine then flown by Beauvais of E-Stelle Rechlin

2 October 1942: During discussions with RLM demand made for further 30 pre-production aircraft to be completed by end of 1943. Messerschmitt of the opinion that completion of only 10 aircraft in this period is feasible

14 October 1942: Power plant instrumentation finalized with appropriate RLM department

2 December 1942: Messerschmitt urged in discussion with RLM to complete first nosewheel-equipped machines earlier than previously planned, increase size and accelerate delivery of pre-production batch. Target production of at least 20 aircraft per month from 1944

11 February 1943: With the assistance of Flakbrigade 4 from Munich which provided personnel, drop test of an Me 262 test fuselage from Me 323 S-9 carried out at approx 19,685 ft (6 000 m) above Lake Chiem. Max speed of 540 mph (870 km/h) recorded at 6,560 ft (2 000 m). Parachute failed and fuselage struck the water's surface at approx 497 mph (800 km/h)

2 March 1943: By order of Prof Messerschmitt, Me 262 V1 to be modified and fitted with two Junkers TL engines

4 March 1943: Following discussion with RLM and Rechlin's Dept E2, armament defined as six MK 108s or four MK 108s and two MG 151s. Alternatives considered were: (a) three MG 151s and four MG 131s; (b) two MK 103s and one MG 151/15; (c) two MK 103s and two MG 151s, or (d) three MK 103s

16 October 1941: Discussions with BMW and RLM concerning re-engining the Me 262 V1 with Walter rocket motors after preliminary flight testing with BMW P 3302s

21 October 1941: Proposals concerning reconnaissance variant of Me 262 received by RLM

4 November 1941: RLM requests completion of 10 pre-production machines between June and October 1942

25 November 1941: Contract awarded by RLM for cockpit mock-up of reconnaissance version

5 February 1942: Reconnaissance mock-up examined by RLM and E-Stelle Rechlin and decision taken to complete one pre-production machine as reconnaissance model

25 March 1942: First flight of Me 262 V1 with BMW P 3302s (Jumo 210G engine retained) but apparent that the turbojets required further development to permit additional flight testing

26 March 1942: Further inspection of reconnaissance mock-up by RLM and E-Stelle Rechlin. Demand for repositioned pilot's seat and improved cockpit visibility dictates new mock-up

31 March 1942: Conference with E-Stelle Rechlin and RLM concerning armour and fuel tank protection

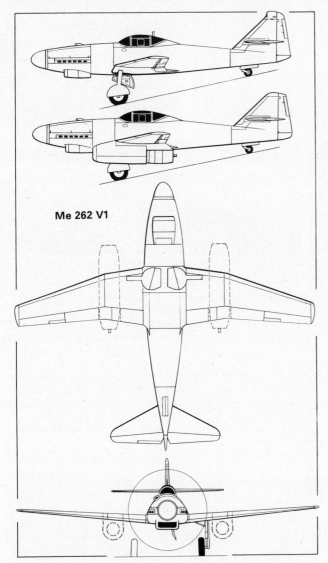

Me 262 V1

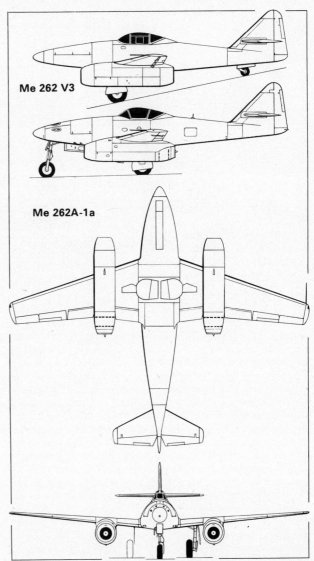

Me 262 V3

Me 262A-1a

compressible flow aerodynamics. The only German high-speed wind tunnel then in existence was very small indeed. This indicated slow drag divergence commencing at around $M = 0.6$, but our aerodynamicists speculated that this probably reflected boundary layer separation at the very low Reynolds numbers of the tests and we essentially dismissed the data as not applicable to full-scale aircraft. The other basic information that we had at that time was that presented in NACA Report No 492, but the Reynolds number of the results contained in this report was still quite low and some boundary layer separation seemed still to occur. A comparison of the German and NACA data supported our assessment of the Reynolds number effect, and, thus, the set of lift, drag and moment curves on which we finally settled was essentially a collection of guestimates; assumptions indicating higher maximum speeds albeit aggravating our control force and structural load problems.

Design by committee

In view of the strictly limited high-speed research data — confined to the previously-mentioned NACA report on aerofoils and that derived from the tiny German wind tunnel which could only test wings of about one inch span and one-third inch chord — the whole aerodynamic layout was really a very bold undertaking. With our meagre basic data, we were forced to "design by committee"; a process of argument and counter-argument between the most capable people that we had. By deductive and inductive reasoning, we struggled to provide logical answers to such questions as, "How will the airflow

behave over a particular portion of the aeroplane when it becomes locally supersonic?"; "What is the likely distribution of the aerodynamic loads?" and "How can we best achieve reasonable control forces?" We had no possibility of making wind tunnel tests to check on the validity of our conclusions!

In US management philosophy, "design by committee" is considered synonymous with failure, but we did not fail because in our committee there was no dilution of responsibility. The chief of the Project Department — which happened to be myself after February 1939 — was personally responsible for both the correctness and timeliness of the choices taken and decisions made* and was all too well aware that the first really substantive tests with the radical aircraft envisaged would be those that would take place once it became airborne with a pilot aboard and then any mistake would reveal itself all too rapidly.

The actual configuration of *Projekt* 1065, or the Me 262 as it was eventually to be designated, evolved from a series of quite different design studies, the drawings of which unfortunately no longer exist, and most of the configurations contemplated at the time were subsequently to be adopted and built by one company or another, but invariably with a nosewheel undercarriage whereas at that point in time (*circa* 1939) we elected to stay with the conventional tailwheel. The nosewheel undercarriage had only just been demonstrated by the Douglas DC-4 and was still very much a radical innovation, and it was obvious

---

Following the example established by Professor Messerschmitt, a department head was primarily an engineer and technical leader, and only secondarily was he the administrator of his department.

(Above) The Me 262 V3 photographed at Leipheim immediately prior to its first flight — the initial flight of the Me 262 on turbojets alone.

that our aeroplane would have radical features enough without adding an innovatory undercarriage.

In view of the high thrust level stipulated for the new turbojets by the RLM, our first design studies were based on the use of a single BMW *TL-Strahltriebwerk* — as the new power plant was then known — as we felt that one engine would be the optimum for a single-seat fighter of the prescribed characteristics. Arranging the power plant in the fuselage with its intake in the extreme nose and efflux duct in the tail was the logical first stage but was soon discarded as we felt that, in view of the large wetted areas involved, the weight of sheet metal demanded by the lengthy ducting and the boundary layer that would be generated in the intake duct with reduction in total pressure in the engine inlet as a result, this could scarcely be the optimum layout. We then endeavoured to reduce the total wetted area and to materially shorten the ducting by investigating a twin-tailboom arrangement rather similar to that eventually adopted for de Havilland's Vampire. This was even less successful in our view as, although duct length had been somewhat reduced, the external wetted surface area was, in fact, greater and the airflow over the upper and lower wing surfaces was now disturbed at three places (ie, by the central nacelle and the two booms).

The next evolutionary stage was a pod-and-boom configuration not unlike that to be adopted several years later for the *Projekt* 1101, although without the swept surfaces and nosewheel undercarriage of the later design. From the performance viewpoint this arrangement appeared to be the optimum that we could achieve with a single-engined aeroplane. At the expense of a fairly long intake duct we reduced the fuselage cross section and total wetted area to a minimum. The fuselage, which translated to a small cross-section tailboom aft and above the engine and which permitted the use of an extremely short efflux duct, was contoured to cockpit, power plant, armament and

equipment like a close-fitting glove, but the undercarriage was a nightmare. Its attachment to the fuselage and the accommodation that it demanded interfered seriously with both engine installation and the fuselage/wing structure, while the tailwheel was obviously slap in the engine exhaust during take-off and landing — a problem that Aleksandr Yakovlev was to resolve somewhat crudely some years later by using a steel roller in place of a tailwheel for the Yak-15! With one BMW turbojet this design, nevertheless, appeared to meet all requirements but we had misgivings. Overall performance, and particularly take-off and climb, did not seem likely to fulfil our more sanguine expectations of what the new-generation fighter should be capable.

Thus, somewhat reluctantly, we began to consider the possibilities of reverting to our earliest proposal of a twin-engined design. We had always felt that a fighter had to be the smallest and lightest aeroplane compatible with the conditions of its time frame, and two engines of the size and thrust by now anticipated by the RLM suggested that we would end up with a wildly over-size and overpowered design, although we were to ascertain later that we could usefully invest the surplus power in greater operational capability. The first twin-engine configuration examined was basically a straightforward low-wing aeroplane with the engine nacelles mounted conventionally on the wings. The main undercarriage members retracted into the wing/fuselage intersection, one main member being arranged to retract into a well forward of the single mainspar and the other into a well aft of the spar. From the viewpoint of drag, this arrangement seemed the optimum, but it was unacceptable to us structurally for the attachment points had of necessity to be situated unreasonably far aft for a tailwheel aircraft and we could find no satisfactory method of handling the wing and fuselage forces and moments in the areas cut up by the retracted wheels.

(Foot of page) The Me 262 V3 taking-off on its first flight at Leipheim on 18 July 1942 and landing with unburned fuel igniting on runway.

Another stepping stone before we reached the configuration first submitted to the RLM was a design essentially similar to the contemporary Heinkel jet fighter project (which was to materialize as the He 280) except that we still adhered to the tailwheel undercarriage whereas the Heinkel team was being somewhat more adventurous in this respect. The two members of our main undercarriage folded inward, the wheels turning about 50 deg in relation to their oleo legs and fitting into the contours of the fuselage. While this design looked good from the aerodynamic point of view, we had two reasons for continuing our search. Firstly, the undercarriage was overly complex, would be expensive to manufacture and would probably be trouble-prone in the field, and, secondly, the mid-wing arrangement resulted in three closely-spaced aerodynamic disturbances on the under surfaces and we suspected that we might encounter considerable transonic interference drag.

To this point in time we had largely concentrated on the installation of the engines *in* the wing (ie, mounted centrally), the most obvious arrangement being the suspension of the turbojets in shallow nacelles formed by local thickening of the wing (*à la* de Havilland Comet), these nacelles eventually becoming tubular as we were informed of the progressive growth in girth of the engines that they were to house, although such demanded what we considered to be an inordinately heavy and excessively complex wing structure. Consideration was given to a rather more adventurous arrangement which envisaged the engine compressor and hot section being installed as separate units, flanged to the front and rear of a locally enlarged wing spar. Mounting the cold and hot sections of the engine separately permitted an exceedingly small and sleek nacelle but, of course, demanded certain major modifications in the mechanical design of the engine. We approached the RLM for permission to request such changes from the engine manufacturer, but were not overly surprised to receive

a positive "no", this line of investigation being discontinued in consequence.

The definitive configuration

We finally arrived at a pure low-wing aeroplane with the main undercarriage members folding inward so that the retracted wheels lay flat, side by side, and since they were thicker than the wing section, they were arranged to retract partly *through* the wing (ie, effectively projecting above the upper wing contour). In order to provide an aerodynamic fairing for the retracted wheels, the fuselage was given what was essentially a triangular cross section, the base of the triangle being wide enough to accommodate the wheel wells. An incidental advantage of such a cross section was that, with the apex of the triangle near the pilot's eye level, a good field of vision was provided from the cockpit.

We had now reached the point of deciding which configuration would form the basis of our submission to the RLM. The choice was essentially between our mid-wing study (*à la* He 280) and our low-wing concept with triangular fuselage cross section which we now tended to favour. From some aspects the choice was a difficult one: the mid-wing concept with its smaller oval cross section fuselage offered a smaller wetted area, but its complex swivel-wheel undercarriage offended our religious belief that an acceptable design must be simple and cheap to manufacture and to maintain. Thus, we submitted our proposal to the RLM based on the low-wing concept, but it was another factor that was to give us victory over the Heinkel contender.

With the BMW P 3302 (later to be assigned the designation BMW 003) turbojets as envisaged at that time, the aeroplane that we were projecting was, in our judgement, rather overpowered. In so far as speed was concerned, we ran high up in the drag divergence where no significantly higher speed was to

continued on page 153

fuselage or seven 600-lb (273-kg) Hunting BL 755 cluster bombs. Developed specifically to counter Soviet numerical tank superiority — there are at least 14,000 Warsaw Pact tanks in Eastern Europe as well as another 6,500 in W Russia — the BL 755 contains 147 2·5-lb (1,1-kg) bomblets with shaped charges for armour penetration. These are designed to saturate an elliptical area on the ground the size of a football pitch on the shotgun principle, thus compensating for aiming errors. They are also intended for use against soft-skinned vehicles, parked aircraft, radars, small ships and troops. With its maximum warload, the Harrier has an operational radius of action of 220 nm (410 km) with full internal fuel, for a take-off run of only 1,500 ft (450 m).

Each Harrier also has an F95 port-facing oblique camera in the nose for the secondary rôle of tactical recce, and No 4 Sqdn has a full reconnaissance capability, its Harriers being equipped with EMI pods containing five cameras for almost horizon-to-horizon coverage in daylight conditions. From next Spring all RAFG Harriers are due to receive Ferranti LRMTS (Laser Rangefinders and Marked Target Seekers) in a retrofit installation to facilitate target acquisition in close support. LRMTS, which also provides accurate and instantaneous ranging information, is currently being introduced at the main UK Harrier base of Wittering, the home of No 1 Sqdn which is assigned to the ACE Mobile Force of NATO (and has a secondary reinforcement rôle in Germany, but some changes in these plans may result from the recent defence review). The Harrier OCU (No 233) is also assigned to reinforce RAF Germany in an emergency.

One ace up the sleeve of all Harrier pilots in air combat is, of course, VIFF (Vectoring in Forward Flight), which results in astonishing manoeuvrability that could not be matched by any conventional aircraft. The RAFG Harrier personnel are watching the current joint Anglo-US VIFF development trials, involving strengthened nozzles and the evolution of new tactics, with understandable interest.

In the absence of a logistics support helicopter following cancellation of the RAF order placed a few years ago for 15 Boeing Vertol CH-47C Chinooks, the RAF has developed a highly efficient field support organization for the Harrier force. Logistics Parks are sited some distance away from the dispersed sites and resupply of fuel, spares, weapons, rations, etc, is normally done at night with some of the 500 vehicles employed in the field. Maintenance equipment is sufficient to do an engine change, if required — no small job in a Harrier — and one is usually necessary during each two-week off-base detachment.

The intensity of operations reached during these periods is indicated by figures achieved last year of one sortie per air-craft per hour — 25 minutes in the air and a 35 minute re-fuelling, re-arming and technical service turn-around. With only 14 aircraft, one Harrier squadron in Germany flew a total of 364 sorties in just three days. Contributing to the Harrier's extremely rapid close support reaction is its integral turbine APU, which supplies all essential electrical power, in particular for the spin-up of the Ferranti inertial navigation and attack system (INAS) and its moving-map display. This enables the aircraft to be held at readiness close to the battle area without support equipment, while INAS provides considerable help in high-speed low-level target acquisition and weapons delivery.

Strike, Recce and Assault

Whereas the Harrier is essentially a short-range ultra-close support aircraft par excellence, the Jaguar is now taking over the rôle of the Phantom FGR Mk 2 in Germany as a far-reaching low-level strike/attack/reconnaissance weapons system which will eventually outnumber all other types in the Command. In all, five Jaguar squadrons are planned for RAFG, plus three more (including one for reconnaissance) and the OCU in the UK, resulting in a frontline force of between 100-120 aircraft.

As the first Jaguar base in Germany, Brüggen has started re-equipping its Phantom squadrons, beginning with No 14 (Wg Cmdr Mumford), which received the first of its 12 aircraft in April last year. Because of the complexity of modern aircraft, RAF squadrons are not simply re-equipped as in the past. What usually happens is that after intensive training of personnel selected from other units a squadron with the same number is formed in parallel with that which it is replacing. For a short period, the two squadrons with the same number but different equipment share the same base, and when the new unit nears operational status, the former squadron disbands.

Thus, during our visit, Brüggen housed No 14 (Phantom) and No 14 (Jaguar) squadrons, but the former was down to a handful of aircraft and was on the way out. No 17 Sqdn, currently operating Phantoms at Brüggen, was also converting to Jaguars at the same time, and the third Phantom unit on the base (No 31 Sqdn) is scheduled to follow suit. These Jaguar squadrons and one other are scheduled to be operational at Brüggen by the end of 1977. The remaining Phantom squadron in Germany — No 2 at Laarbruch — with a specialist reconnaissance rôle, is also scheduled to re-equip with Jaguars by then. The Jaguar strength in RAFG will then be approximately double that of the former Phantom establishment. The Jaguar is also considered a particularly cost-effective aircraft and one with which RAFG is well pleased.

According to Wg Cmdr Mumford, the Jaguar is the most serviceable aircraft of his acquaintance, despite the complexity

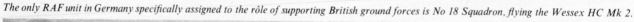

The only RAF unit in Germany specifically assigned to the rôle of supporting British ground forces is No 18 Squadron, flying the Wessex HC Mk 2.

of the NAVWASS system (with which the squadron was still awaiting a consistently good performance) on which pilots and ground crews were still gaining experience. Engine problems had been remarkably few, partial throttle reheat (PTR) had completely solved the thrust modulation problems formerly encountered with asymmetric power and Adour TBO was already running at about 350 hours.

When they are not operating in their nuclear strike rôle, the Jaguar squadrons in Germany rely principally on the BL 755 cluster bombs, carried up to eight at a time, for ground attack missions, interchanged with external fuel tanks or 1,000-lb (453-kg) ballistic or retarded HE bombs. The German-based Jaguars do not train with SNEB rockets, leaving these weapons to the Harriers, nor do they currently carry missiles. The Jaguar, was, of course, designed for the over-wing installation of AAMs, including Sidewinder or Magic, and RAFG hopes that one of these will eventually be provided. Laser rangefinders and designators are being fitted to current production Jaguars, from aircraft No 81 onwards, and are being retrofitted to earlier aircraft.

Although like all RAF bases in Germany, Brüggen has its complement of Royal Engineers for rapid runway repair facilities in the event of wartime cratering, its Jaguars are designed to operate from semi-prepared surfaces. Their STOL performance also enables them to use sections of perimeter track, roads and other emergency sites, and manufacturer's trials from semi-prepared strips are still continuing.

In RAF Germany, the Jaguars share the assigned strike rôle with the fully NATO-assigned Hawker Siddeley Buccaneer S Mk 2Bs of Nos 15 and 16 Sqdns at Laarbruch. Although firmly subsonic, the ex-naval Buccaneer excels in ultra low-level long-range penetration missions with a variety of weapons ranging from nuclear to HE bombs, cluster-bombs, rockets and flares stowed both internally and on underwing stations. Its low-level handling is reportedly outstanding and its range may be extended by flight-refuelling, although this procedure is not practised by the Buccaneer squadrons in Germany. All the RAFG strike/attack aircraft are also equipped to carry ECM pods, such as the US ALQ-101 jamming system, and are fitted with fin-mounted passive warning receiver (PWR) boxes apparent on all RAF combat aircraft. Although now supplanted in USAF service by the ALQ-119, the ALQ-101 is effective against a wide variety of radars used by Soviet aircraft, SAM and AA systems.

Only the Buccaneers and Phantoms in RAFG, with their two-man crews and air-to-ground radar systems, are true night and all-weather aircraft, and their squadrons train accordingly. Each Buccaneer squadron has a couple of ex-Naval Hunter T Mk 8 trainers for dual instrument flying and weapons training. The Hunters, like the Buccaneers, are also fitted with arrester hooks as relics of their naval origins, but now used only for emergency runway stops. Although built as RAF aircraft, the Buccaneer S Mk 2Bs also retain the type's original power-folding wings which come in useful during dispersal.

Once again, RAFG Buccaneers have no missiles, although originally designed to carry Sidewinders if required. The only RAF aircraft scheduled to operate with HSD/Aérospatiale Martel ASMs are the Buccaneers at Honington, in the UK, which are assigned to SACLANT in the maritime rôle. For non-nuclear attack rôles, the Buccaneers can carry up to 16,000 lb (7 257 kg) of internal and external stores — mainly 1,000-lb (453-kg) HE bombs — but also any other combination of weapons up to that weight. An alternative weapons bay load is a reconnaissance pack containing one vertical F 97 night camera and six F 95 day cameras, linescan and electronic flash gear, although Laarbruch also has its own specialist day and night tactical recce unit in the form of No 2 Sqdn with Phantom FGR Mk 2s.

This unit, which will be the last in Germany to re-equip with Jaguars, has a traditional army co-operation rôle, al-

No 60 Squadron, based at RAF Wildenrath, operates Pembroke C Mk 1s for Command communications duties.

though its M = 2·0 F-4M Spey-Phantoms are far removed from the Westland Lysanders with which the squadron entered WW II. For reconnaissance, the Phantom carries beneath its fuselage a British-developed EMI sensor pod, nearly 24 ft (7,30 m) in length and containing advanced detection devices derived from TSR-2 technology to pierce enemy camouflage and record movement by night or day. In addition to five cameras giving horizon-to-horizon cover in monochrome or colour, the pod incorporates high definition sideways-looking radar and infra-red linescan. SLAR can produce a night picture showing vehicles or trains whether moving or stationery, while the heat-seeking IR linescan can show recent as well as present vehicle activity.

When carrying the sensor pod, the Phantom still has its wing stations available for long-range fuel tanks or defensive missiles. Alternatively, for offensive operations it can carry up to 11 1,000-lb (453-kg) free-fall or retarded bombs, 234 68-mm armour-piercing rockets and a 20-mm pod-mounted Vulcan cannon firing 100 rounds per second. For interception or air superiority, the RAFG Phantoms are normally armed with four Raytheon AIM-7E Sparrow III AAMs housed in underfuselage recesses and up to four pylon-mounted Aeronutronic Ford AIM-9D Sidewinder 1C AAMs. With a British-designed and manufactured inertial nav/attack system, Rolls-Royce Spey turbofans and Martin Baker ejection seats, the F-4M Phantom is about 40 per cent British in cost content. Maximum gross weight is 58,000 lb (26 308 kg).

Another RAFG unit with an army co-operation rôle is No 18 Sqdn at Gutersloh, which is actually the only Royal Air Force unit specifically assigned solely for the support of British ground forces. Its rôle is to provide the First British Corps, with HQ at Bielefeld, with logistics support and assault lift, for which it operates 16 Westland Wessex HC Mk 2 twin-turbine helicopters, under the command of Wg Cmdr J E Maitland. The squadron is fully equipped for mobile operation and maintains its own ground support personnel, tented accommodation, communications equipment and road transport. It can live and operate in the field for an indefinite period, completely divorced from a fixed airfield site.

For field deployment, during training exercises with the army, the squadron detaches one of its two flights of eight Wessex helicopters, each manned by pilot and loadmaster aircrewman, and capable of carrying 15 fully-equipped troops. The loadmaster is particularly useful in tactical situations when operating from clearings or other confined spaces in keeping the pilot informed regarding rotor clearance from the nearest obstacles. Three qualified navigators are also attached to the squadron to lead tactical formations and help plan operations, although during a brief flight in an 18 Sqdn Wessex we were intrigued to see Decca among the cockpit instrumentation. A radar altimeter was also installed in XR587, for "nap-

(Above) A Jaguar of No 14 Squadron, which began to equip with this new type last April and later in the year won the annual RAFG Navigation and Bombing Competition for the Salmond trophy, in competition with nine other squadrons. The Jaguars are replacing Phantom FGA Mk 2s in the strike rôle in Germany, the first units to relinquish the McDonnell Douglas fighter being No 14 Squadron (below, with Jaguar) and No 17 Squadron (opposite page). All photographs illustrating this account are Crown Copyright, published by courtesy of the Ministry of Defense.

of-the-earth" tactical flying at or below tree-top height employed by No 18 Sqdn. The altimeter indicated 80 ft (24,38 m) as we sank below the tops of the pine trees into a clearing little bigger than the main rotor diameter. Throughout the rest of the flight it seldom indicated more until we climbed to 1,000 ft (305 m) for a demonstration autorotation. This was done in a tight spiral which resulted in an indicated descent rate of more than 3,000 ft/min (15,24 m/sec).

An assault landing from a tactical approach involves virtually hurling the helicopter onto the ground, but the Wessex is fortunately very robust and seems to thrive on this sort of treatment. Some airframes on the Squadron have as many as 3,000 hours, which is high for a military helicopter. The Wessex, however, has excellent fatigue characteristics, as demonstrated by the successful marketing of the S-58T mainly converted from ex-military piston-engined airframes. The 100-110 kt (185-203 km/hr) cruising speed of the Wessex is considered adequate for its present duties, but some improvement on the maximum external load of about 3,000 lb (1 360 kg) with any useful amount of fuel would be welcomed, as would some form of rotor de-icing.

With the current state of Britain's defence economics, it looks as though the Wessex will have to soldier on in the RAF for many years yet, despite the desirability of replacement by the Commando version of the Sea King. The RAF has no requirement for an armed helicopter, although the Wessex of No 18 Sqdn may be fitted with two side-firing flexibly-mounted 7,62-mm general-purpose machine guns if required. Unlike the RN, furthermore, which launches Aérospatiale AS-12 anti-tank missiles from its Wessex assault helicopters, No 18 Sqdn has no guided weapons in its armoury.

As the remaining flying unit in RAF Germany, No 60 Sqdn, based at Wildenrath, is now the Command communications unit, and operates eight BAC Pembrokes. In addition to carrying personnel and urgently-needed equipment from one base to another within RAF Germany and to airfields in Britain, No 60 Sqdn is the only British service unit to fly regularly behind the Iron Curtain. This it does on scheduled flights to and from West Berlin along the Air Corridors through Eastern Germany. In 1970, the RAF decided to re-spar the wings of 14 of its Pembrokes, which means that these twin-Leonides piston-engined aircraft are likely to remain in service for some years to come.

While the immediate future of the RAF in Germany is thus clear, with a steady increase in strength which by the end of this decade will result in it operating about half the RAF's entire establishment of offensive aircraft, its longer-term plans are somewhat less well defined. At the moment, the Panavia MRCA is scheduled to enter service with the RAF in Germany in the early 'eighties, always assuming its development is allowed to continue on its present schedule. It is programmed to replace the Buccaneer, together with the Vulcan and Canberra in the UK, in the overland strike and reconnaissance rôles. Its projected air defence version is later scheduled to replace the Phantom in the intercept and air superiority rôles. The MRCA will also take over maritime strike attack from the Honington Buccaneers.

In the meantime, RAF Germany cannot fail to impress any visitor, with its high state of operational readiness and its evidently zestful morale resulting from a combination of professionalism applied to high-quality equipment and a consciousness of being in the front-line of the cold war. □

Whether to Weather?

A PRISTINE PURITY of finish on any aircraft on a World War II operational airfield would have seemed as out of place as a strip-tease at a church fête! Something of the new-ness departed — particularly around wing walkways, access steps and cockpit sill — with the boots of mechanics whose oily hands and overalls left smudges that imparted a "used" look before the service acceptance pilot first clambered into the cockpit of the aircraft at the factory. From the time that it was handed over to the ferry pilot, the aircraft invariably passed through one or more maintenance units or depôts before delivery to the squadron to which it had been assigned and if the hours on its logbook were still few, its finish was by now anything but faultless — and it had still to fire its guns in anger!

We were prompted to reflect on this fact by visits to branch meetings of the International Plastic Modellers' Society, which culminated, in December of last year, in the finals of the Society's National Championships held in the congenial and most appropriate setting of the Royal Air Force Museum at Hendon. The standards achieved by exhibiting modellers were, let it be said, remarkably high and the representatives of the major manufacturers must surely have been amazed at what the true experts could produce from their kits as well as by the fantastic imagination displayed by the finishes of some of the models shown. It was this question of finish, or, more accurately, the wear-and-tear aspect of it, that gave us some food for thought, however, and we began to wonder if some of the exhibitors had not taken the "weathering" process too far.

Some modellers had, of course, disregarded entirely the wear-and-tear that accompanied service usage, applying superb finishes such as no *factory-fresh* WW II aircraft ever had the good fortune to receive; others had been carried away by the weathering process and had produced models that were apparently intended to represent aircraft that had spent much of their existence on an open-air dump! Had some of these "weathered finishes" been applied to full-size aircraft they would have knocked at least 10 per cent from their per-formances. There was one B-17G Fortress that was so grime-encrusted and muck-bedaubed that any self-respecting aircraft captain would have shot his crew chief before taking to the bottle. Yet the model was superbly made and its finish applied with considerable skill. It was simply overdone.

Aircraft are, generally speaking, fairly well cared for, and under peace-time conditions both civil and military types are kept ex-tremely clean, not merely for the sake of appearance but because dirt and grime seriously penalise performance. In truth, all that a modeller can legitimately simulate in

the way of wear and tear on most models is some paint chipping at access points, and this, if true to scale, is too little to be seen on models of a smaller scale than 1/48th! Of course, there can be a degree of discolouration around exhausts and jet outlets but certainly not the scale equivalent of a half-ton of soot that is to be seen on some models.

Under wartime conditions, there were cer-tainly occasions when muddy temporary air-fields and pressure of operations meant that aircraft were subject only to essential main-tenance; when only the most rudimentary wash 'n brush-up was practicable. Even under such exigencies, however, one rarely if ever saw an airworthy combat aeroplane in the sort of condition that some modellers depict. Possibly the most commonly seen weathering was the fading of paint colours with prolonged exposure, particularly in desert and tropical areas where extremes of weather accelerated deterioration. Some lightening of tonal shades to simulate the finish of a battle-weary air-craft operating in such areas is acceptable, but this effect is all too frequently exaggerated. Certainly, paint was worn from wing leading edges and wing walks, around hatches and fuelling points, and oily patches tended to be seen around the engine cowling, while com-bat damage was often temporarily patched with fabric and protected with primer which stood out against the original finish, but few if any operational aircraft *really* looked like refugees from junk yards as some modellers would have us believe.

Incidentally, we have been taken to task by a Polish reader, Mr Witold Skrzypczak of Wroclaw, for the title that we gave to this column in the November issue. Mr Skrzypczak comments that the transliteration of the Russian equivalent of "comrade" is correctly *"tavarishch"* and not *"tovarich"*. The Russian alphabet, unlike the English alphabet, is phonetic and standards of transliteration depend not only on the original language characters but also on those of the language into which they are being translated coupled with *common usage*. The fact is that, correct or otherwise, *"tovarich"* is common English usage and *"tavarishch"* looks decidedly odd to the Anglo-Saxon eye! What Mr Skrzypczak is looking for is not transliteration but a phonetic rendering which would necessitate use of the international phonetic alphabet — we certainly could not cope with this and doubt that such would be appreciated by our readers!

An international pair

Two recent releases from Airfix take as their subjects two of the current European multi-national programmes, the Panavia MRCA and the Airbus A300B which are included in this company's Series 4 and Series 6 respec-

tively. The Anglo-German-Italian multi-rôle combat aircraft, which has now survived something like a half-decade of existence with a programme-paring axe consistently hanging over it, is a potentially formidable aeroplane of which a half-dozen prototypes are now flying, and the rather angularly ugly contours of this controversial warplane are depicted with commendable accuracy by Airfix's 101-part kit, the all-white components of which make for easy painting.

Surface detailing is very fine and an adequate cockpit interior is provided, the panels and consoles featuring engraved instru-ments. The variable-sweep wing feature is operable, the two wing panels being linked in a simple but effective fashion, and the all-moving tailplane is also adjustable, the two halves operating independently. The under-carriage looks good and is in nice scale propor-tion. This may be assembled in either ex-tended or retracted position, as can also the two airbrakes. The wide selection of external stores includes a pair of Sparrows, a quartet of Martels and seven cluster bombs which make up a truly formidable array. The decal sheet is excellent and offers a choice of three marking schemes: the white-red-black second prototype (XX946) with tri-national insignia, a camouflaged RAF example (XX950) and an example in the anticipated finish of the MRCA in service with the Federal German *Marine-flieger*. The UK retail price of the MRCA kit is 75p.

Whereas the MRCA is to 1/72nd scale, the A300B kit is, in common with other kits in Airfix's airliner series, to 1/144th-scale and, again, is moulded in white plastic. Comprising 92 component parts and a nice set of Air France decals for F-BVGA, it has its many tiny cabin window transparencies arranged in fourteen separate groups plus two singles and the flight deck transparency. The fit of these and, indeed, all other component parts, is very good. All 10 doors and access hatches are separate mouldings and can be assembled in open position if desired, although there is no interior detail whatsoever. There are alterna-tive retracted or extended positions for the three units of the 10-wheeled undercarriage which embodies some fine detail. About a half-ounce (14 grammes) of additional weight is called for in the extreme nose to balance the tail. Assembly of this attractive model is quite simple, as is also the colour scheme, and in view of the size of the A300B, the model is impressive, even at 1/144th scale. The UK retail price is £1·35.

A welcome débutante

We have recently received the first product of a new firm, By-planes of Pineacres, Birch Lane, Chavey Down, Ascot, which offers a 1/48th scale vacuform of what would seem a somewhat improbable subject for a British company, the Bücker Bü 133 Jungmeister (Young Champion), that supremely aerobatic little single-seat biplane. One of the all-time classics and first flown 41 years ago, Carl Clemens Bücker's Jungmeister was built under licence in Czechoslovakia, Spain and Switzer-land, and is still around in some numbers, but to many of us older modellers it is as synonymous with the aviation scene of Germany's Third Reich as is the Messerschmitt Bf 109!

The major components of By-planes' vacuformed Jungmeister kit are to a very high standard in white plastic sheet with fine detailing — the rib effect of the wing surfaces is particularly good — and including an excellent one-piece moulding for the helmeted engine cowling. The major innovation introduced by this vacu-formed kit as compared with other vacu-forms is the provision of fine white metal die castings for the Siemens Sh 14 A4 radial engine, exhaust and silencer assembly, a wooden-type propeller, and the tailwheel and bracket, the mainwheels being solid plastic mouldings. Fine strip plastic material is included to be cut to length for the interplane and centre section struts. Add to these items a fine decal sheet and you have a complete kit which demands no rummaging in the spares box or the purchase of other kits to acquire parts.

On seeing this kit, one is led to wonder why cast metal parts have not been used in this context before, because they were employed quite widely many years ago in conjunction with wooden parts in kits, and modern casting metals give far better results than did the lead-based materials used in those days. Construction, while obviously more difficult than for an injection-moulded kit, is still relatively simple, the instruction sheet being very clearly arranged with an exploded diagram and very good general arrangement drawings. Much care must be applied to ensure that the wing panels are well rubbed down to obtain sharp trailing edges, the same applying to the tail surfaces.

The metal parts suffer the very minimum of flash and, being sharply detailed, are most effective in appearance when painted. The decal sheet provides the pre-WW II registration (D-EQOA) of a demonstration machine. The Jungmeister was a very small aeroplane and even at 1/48th scale the model has a wing span only fractionally over 5⅜ in (13,65 cm). Of course, for a specialised kit such as this with its limited production run there must be a price penalty, but we consider that £1·75 (plus 25p postage and packing) is not inordinate. Incidentally, we understand that the next of By-planes' 1/48th scale vacu-forms is to be the Sopwith Snipe.

One of the last of the biplane boats

Insofar as the Jungmeister is synonymous with the aviation of the Third Reich in the minds of many, so the Short Singapore III is synonymous with the British maritime patrol scene of the 'thirties, and Contrail, in its 1/72nd scale series of vacu-formed kits has done a grand job in offering yet another item of flying boat nostalgia which, this time, depicts this Short boat which, in flight, resembled nothing more than a full-rigged ship in sail. The kit, which consists of 49 component parts, follows the same lines as previous productions of its genre, with deeply moulded hull halves having well defined chines and a limited amount of surface detailing. Three internal bulkheads, a cockpit floor and two seats are included. The portholes are marked but must be cut out and glazed with clear material provided, and there is a clear moulded canopy for the flight deck.

The wings are very large mouldings, the upper plane being integral over the full 1 ft 3 in

(38,10 cm) span, so they must be adequately reinforced to maintain the correct dihedral angle. The engine nacelles, each with one tractor and one pusher unit, have clean lines and present no special problems, but the propellers accompanying the kit are best discarded and replaced with a set hand carved from wood. The kit exhaust manifolds look very good and are certainly well worth using; all struts must be cut from a piece of plastic sheet provided and there are no decals, although the markings given for No 210 Squadron, RAF, are quite simple and a fine 1/72nd scale general arrangement three-view drawing comes with the kit. The assembly of the wings is a somewhat tricky operation but can be facilitated by making a set of jigs from sheet plastic so that the gap and angle of incidence may be fixed accurately.

The Contrail Singapore III, which, incidentally, is priced at £1·80 (plus 45p postage and packing) from Sutcliffe Productions (The Orchard, Westcombe, Shepton Mallet), is by no means a kit for the beginner but presents a real challenge to any more experienced modeller wishing to put his skill to the test.

A mixed bag from Airmodel

Since reviewing last month a batch of kits from Airmodel of Germany — which included the massive Northrop YB-49 for which we have now received the missing instruction sheet which includes full assembly details with a 1/72nd scale sideview and 1/144th scale plan and front elevations, and covers the assembly of the model very well in the English language — we have received yet another batch of kits from this manufacturer, comprising four vacu-forms and one injection-moulded kit, all to 1/72nd scale. The vacuforms comprise the Messerschmitt Bf 108B Taifun, the Bücker Bü 131 Jungmann, the Bachem Ba 349B Natter and the Curtiss XP-55 Ascender, while the injection-moulded kit is for the delightful Focke-Wulf Fw 56 Stösser.

The Bf 108B Taifun kit comprises only 15 parts, including a well-formed and clear canopy, while the Bü 131 Jungmann kit offers only 11 parts, but while very basic, the kits feature good surface detailing and are not difficult to build. The intriguing Ba 349B Natter rocket-propelled expendable fighter kit offers, on the other hand, a total of 22 parts which include all that is needed to produce an attractive model of this offbeat warplane, and are accompanied by good drawings of the launching ramp and a ground-handling trolley for those wishing to display the Natter model as part of a diorama. Last of the vacuform quartet, the XP-55 Ascender experimental tailless fighter, is the simplest of the four kits, providing only the fuselage, cockpit canopy and wings — seven parts in all! However, these parts are accompanied, like those of the other kits, by detailed instructions and general arrangement drawings with camouflage and marking detail, and both the Ba 349B and XP-55 kits provide details for the cockpit interiors.

The Fw 56 Stösser single-seat fighter trainer kit is Airmodel's first attempt at an injection moulded kit and, indeed, to the best of our knowledge, the first 1/72nd scale injection moulded kit to come from any manufacturer in Federal Germany. It is a creditable effort if not up to the standards attained by the better kits of the major manufacturers. It

consists of 24 component parts moulded in light grey plastic and featuring finely raised surface detailing. The parasol wing is in one piece, with aileron details engraved, and the fuselage is in three parts, the nose section being separate. This last-mentioned component suffers a moulding blemish — a sinking which must be filled with body putty which is also demanded by some of the joints. Some of the panel markings are too coarse, but the awkward-shaped tail assembly is well managed, as are also the cantilever undercarriage members, and the wing struts are very fine. There are no location marks for the centre section struts, so particular care must be exercised when assembling the wing.

The kit includes a nice decal sheet which provides two sets of German and one set of Austrian markings, and there is a good instruction sheet with full painting information. This is *not* a kit for beginners, but a modeller with some experience will find it a worthy project. The Airmodel kits are available in the UK through the usual retail outlets.

WW I and 'fifties re-issues

Revell (GB) Limited has recently re-issued seven of its earlier kits, four of these from the WW I era and three of combat aircraft of the 'fifties, these being accompanied by new decal sheets and being, by today's standards, good value for money. The four 1/72nd scale WW I kits cover types that are not available to this scale from any other source, and in view of the paucity of new issues of kits of aircraft of this period it would seem that they are likely to remain so for a long time to come.

Each of the four kits has around 28 component parts and has stood the test of time well. The first of these, the S.E.5A, makes up into a pretty little model and has alternative two- and four-bladed propellers with a separate spinner for the latter, while the decal sheet gives markings for Capt McCudden's aircraft which, in fact, had a spinner from an LVG C V. Alternative markings are for an aircraft of No 92 Squadron, RFC, and a presentation aircraft named "Parish of Inch No 2". The second of the batch, the SPAD XIII, can be finished as any one of three US-flown machines, these being one flown by Capt Eddie Rickenbacker with the famous "Hat-in-Ring" insignia, Frank Luke's aircraft with a "Swooping Eagle" emblem, or the aircraft named "Smith IV" currently preserved in the USA. The decal sheets accompanying both kits are very good.

Next comes the Nieuport 28 which can be completed with the markings of Lt Douglas Campbell of the 94th Aero Squadron or an aircraft of the 27th Aero Squadron, a third alternative being the markings of a trainer of the 213th Aero Squadron, all being US units of the Allied Expeditionary Forces in France in 1918. The last of the quartet represents the Fokker D VII and this has three colourful schemes representing aircraft flown by Ernst Udet, Hermann Göring and Rudolf Berthold. Plenty of scope here for the exotic finishes addict.

The three re-issues of 'fifties aircraft come from way back in the bad old days when scale was of secondary consideration — the primary consideration apparently being whether the kit would fit the box! Thus, all three are to odd scales, an F-8E Crusader to 1/67th, an F-105A Thunderchief to 1/77th and an A-3B Skywarrior to 1/84th! In their

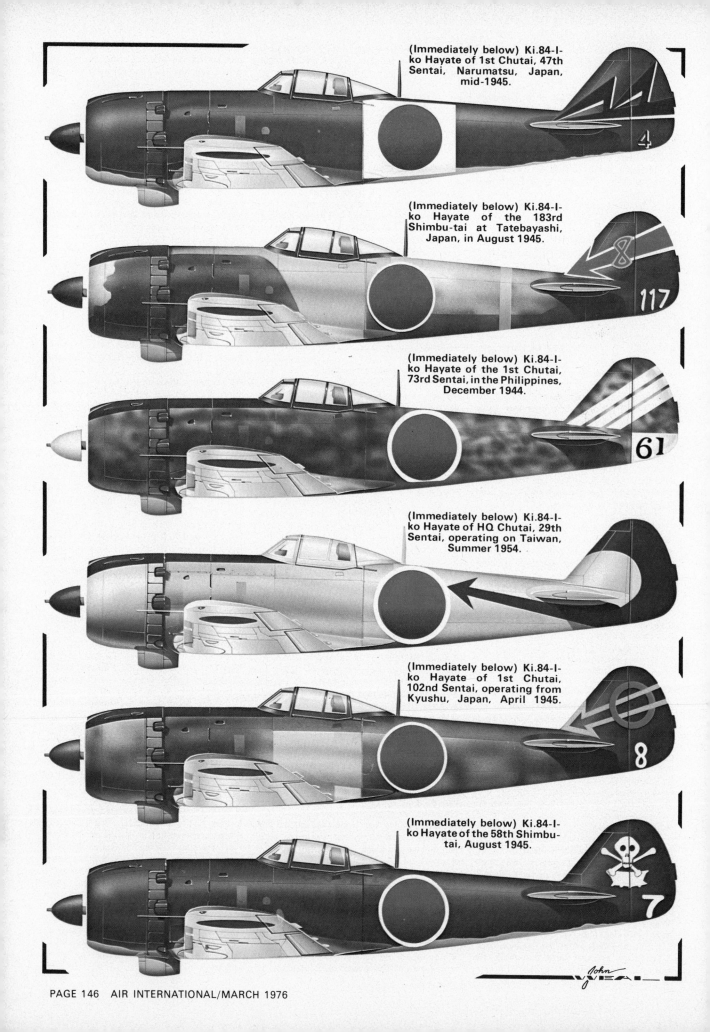

(Immediately below) Ki.84-I-ko Hayate of 1st Chutai, 47th Sentai, Narumatsu, Japan, mid-1945.

(Immediately below) Ki.84-I-ko Hayate of the 183rd Shimbu-tai at Tatebayashi, Japan, in August 1945.

(Immediately below) Ki.84-I-ko Hayate of the 1st Chutai, 73rd Sentai, in the Philippines, December 1944.

(Immediately below) Ki.84-I-ko Hayate of HQ Chutai, 29th Sentai, operating on Taiwan, Summer 1954.

(Immediately below) Ki.84-I-ko Hayate of 1st Chutai, 102nd Sentai, operating from Kyushu, Japan, April 1945.

(Immediately below) Ki.84-I-ko Hayate of the 58th Shimbu-tai, August 1945.

time, these were good kits, despite their odd scales, and they can still produce very acceptable models. Incidentally, there is no other kit of the Skywarrior in any scale.

This month's colour subject

The Japanese aircraft industry of the 'thirties and early 'forties was responsible for some brilliant aircraft and few more so than Nakajima's Army Type 4 Fighter, the Ki.84 Hayate (Gale) which was featured in the "Warbirds" series in the January issue of this journal.

Aesthetically, the Hayate was perhaps the most pleasing radial-engined fighter monoplane ever to attain quantity production status — it was certainly among the most successful — and it might be expected that this outstanding warplane would have proved a favourite subject for kit manufacturers, certainly among those of its native Japan, yet, apart from a number of early and mostly indifferent kits to a variety of scales and all probably by now defunct, such has not proved to be the case. Indeed, of Hayate kits so far offered, only two or three are worthy of mention.

Far and away the best Hayate kit so far is that by Tamiya to 1/48th scale. Produced fairly recently and excellent in every way, this kit results in a model of faultless outline accuracy with beautifully fine surface detailing and an adequately furnished cockpit interior. The component parts assemble extremely well and if 1/48th scale is your scene, then you need look no further for a kit of the Hayate. If, however, you are among the majority that favour 1/72nd scale, then you are not so well catered for in so far as this particular subject is concerned. There are two 1/72nd scale kits of the Hayate theoretically available, but neither warrants our unstinted recommendation.

One of these kits is an early effort on the part of Tamiya, which is passable but in no way outstanding, and the other is a product of Revell. The latter is certainly among the better kits of this company's series of WW II fighters produced some years ago, but it is not really up to current standards. But assuming that you can find an example of Revell's kit in your model shop, it is at least acceptably accurate and can result in a nice little model. This is a type which *must* eventually be produced by Hasegawa to 1/72nd scale, although as yet we have not heard of one in prospect. □

F J Henderson

(Above) An early view of the first SD3-30, showing the original size fins and rudders, since increased in height by 12 in (30 cm). (Below right) An interior view showing a typical commuterliner arrangement for 30 passengers.

SHORTS SD3-30 ———————— *from page 123*

various military vehicles or 18 stretchers plus five seated casualties, and for search and rescue missions could carry extra fuel to achieve a patrol endurance of 10 hours.

Including military sales, Shorts believes that there is a market for up to 800 aircraft of SD3-30 size over the next seven years or so, and almost half of this figure could be accounted for by civil sales in the USA. The company hopes it can capture at least a quarter of the total market, with sales of 150-200 SD3-30s — comfortably exceeding the break-even figure. Inflation is obviously having its effect upon market prospects, and whereas the target was to sell the basic equipped aircraft "for a million bucks" when it was announced in mid 1972, a more realistic figure today is $1·45m (£718,000); total development and tooling costs have risen from an estimated £8·5m in October 1972 to £14m at today's prices.

Production rates are being established with caution, in view of the present uncertainties of the market, but can reach four aircraft a month in due course if the order book fills out sufficiently to require it. A lower rate to be established initially will not jeopardize the programme — the Skyvan production has been spread over an extremely lengthy time-scale — and the SD3-30 retains a head start over possible contenders in the "Part 298" commuterliner field as the first 30-seater designed and built specifically to meet the requirements of this rapidly maturing segment of the airline industry. □

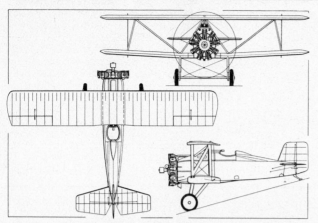

The F4C-1 (above and below) represented a major rework on the part of Curtiss of the Curtiss-manufactured Naval Aircraft Factory TS-1 fighter.

CURTISS F4C-1   USA

The first Curtiss fighter built under the US Navy designating system combining type, sequence of design and manufacturer, the F4C-1 (F2C and F3C being "paper" designations assigned to the R2C and R3C racing aircraft respectively) was designed by Charles W Hall and was essentially an all-metal version of the wooden Naval Aircraft Factory TS-1 which had been designed by the US Navy Bureau of Aeronautics and production of which had been assigned to Curtiss. The F4C-1, two examples of which were built in 1924, embodied some aerodynamic redesign. Its wings featured tubular spars and stamped dural ribs and the fuselage was built up of dural tubing in a Warren truss form, the whole being fabric covered. By comparison with the TS-1, the lower wing was raised to the base of the fuselage. Armament comprised two 0·3-in (7,62-mm) machine guns and power was provided by a nine-cylinder Wright J-3 radial rated at 200 hp. Max speed, 126 mph (203 km/h). Time to 5,000 ft (1 525 m), 3·9 min. Range, 525 mls (845 km). Empty weight, 1,027 lb (466 kg). Loaded weight, 1,707 lb (774 kg). Span, 25 ft 0 in (7,62 m). Length, 18 ft 4 in (5,59 m). Height, 8 ft 9 in (2,67 m). Wing area, 185 sq ft (17,19 m²).

CURTISS P-1 (HAWK)   USA

On 7 March 1925, Curtiss was awarded a contract for 15 production examples of the XPW-8B as the P-1, this being the first fighter to which the company assigned the name Hawk. Externally similar to the XPW-8B, the P-1 was of mixed construction with wooden wings and steel-tube fuselage with fabric skinning, and was powered by a 435 hp Curtiss V-1150-l 12-cylinder liquid-cooled engine. The final five aircraft were completed as P-2s (which see), three later being converted to P-1A standards. Follow-on contracts were placed on 9 September 1925 for 25 P-1As (which had a 3-in/7,62-cm longer fuselage), on 17

August 1926 for 25 P-1Bs (with V-1150-3 engine, larger wheels and modified radiator), and on 3 October 1928 for 33 P-1Cs (with wheel brakes). All these sub-types carried an armament of two 0·3-in (7,62-mm) guns. In the meantime, the USAAC had ordered advanced trainers utilising the same airframe, these comprising 35 AT-4s (180 hp Wright V-720), five AT-5s and 31 AT-5As (220 hp Wright R-790), and in 1929, these were re-engined with the V-1150-3, all 35 AT-4s becoming P-1Ds and four AT-5s and 24 AT-5As becoming P-1Es and P-1Fs respectively. These conversions were essentially similar to the P-1B apart from having only one gun. Four P-1s were supplied to Bolivia, one P-1A went to Japan, and eight P-1As and eight P-1Bs were supplied to Chile. The following data relate to the P-1B. Max speed, 160 mph (257 km/h) at sea level, 157 mph

The P-1A (above) and P-1B (immediately below) differed primarily in radiator design, wheel size and engine sub-type.

The P-1C (above and below) was essentially similar to the preceding P-1B but was fitted with wheel brakes. Skis could be fitted as seen in photo above.

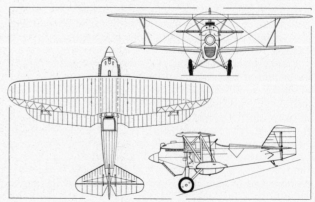

The P-1F (above) was originally built as the radial-engined AT-5A advanced trainer and subsequently re-engined and modified to fighter standard.

(253 km/h) at 5,000 ft (1 525 m). Initial climb, 1,540 ft/min (7,8 m/sec). Range, 600 mls (966 km). Empty weight, 2,105 lb (955 kg). Loaded weight, 2,932 lb (1 330 kg). Span, 31 ft 7 in (9,63 m). Length, 22 ft 8 in (6,91 m). Height, 8 ft 11 in (2,72 m). Wing area, 250 sq ft (23,23 m²).

CURTISS F6C (HAWK)   USA

In March 1925, the US Navy ordered nine P-1s with provision for float operation as F6Cs (the F5C designation was not assigned to avoid confusion with the F-5 flying boat), five of these being delivered as F6C-1s and four (with arrester hook) as F6C-2s. These had similar power plant and armament to the USAAC's P-1. Two additional F6C-1s were later converted to -2 standard. In 1927, 35 additional aircraft were ordered, these using the P-1A airframe and being designated F6C-3. Two F6C-1s were converted to -3 standard and one F6C-3 was fitted with a Pratt & Whitney R-1340 radial as the XF6C-3. The following data relate to the F6C-3. Max speed, 154 mph (248 km/h) at sea level. Time to 5,000 ft (1 525 m), 3·5 min. Max range, 655 mls (1 054 km). Empty weight, 2,161 lb (980 kg). Loaded weight, 2,963 lb (1 344 kg). Span, 31 ft 6 in (9,60 m). Length, 22 ft 10 in (6,96 m). Height, 10 ft 8 in (3,25 m). Wing area, 252 sq ft (23,41 m²).

CURTISS P-2 (HAWK)   USA

The final five aircraft built against the initial P-1 contract were fitted with the 510 hp Curtiss V-1400 (D-12) engine and delivered early in 1926 as P-2s. The first of these, initially flown in December 1925, was experimentally fitted with a side-mounted turbo-supercharger which increased its absolute ceiling from 22,980 ft (7 005 m) to 32,790 ft (9 995 m). Three P-2s were subsequently converted to P-1A standard for squadron service and a fourth was fitted with the Curtiss V-1570 Conqueror engine of 600 hp as the XP-6 to participate in the 1927 National Air Races in which it achieved 189 mph (304 km/h). Max speed, 172 mph (276 km/h) at sea level, 151 mph (243 km/h) at 15,000 ft (4 570 m). Initial climb, 2,170 ft/min (11,02 m/sec). Time to 6,500 ft (1 980 m), 3·5 min. Empty weight, 2,081 lb (944 kg). Loaded weight, 2,869 lb (1 302 kg). Span, 31 ft 7 in (9,63 m). Length, 22 ft 10 in (6,96 m). Height, 8 ft 7 in (2,61 m). Wing area, 250 sq ft (23,23 m²).

CURTISS P-3A (HAWK)   USA

The first radial-engined Hawk resulted from the mating of a P-1A airframe with a 390 hp Curtiss R-1454 engine as the XP-3 in October 1926. The failure of the Curtiss engine led to its substitution by a 410 hp Pratt & Whitney R-1340-9 with which it was tested in April 1928 as the XP-3A. Five production examples had been contracted for in December 1927 as P-3As, deliveries commencing in September 1928. The P-3A was powered by the R-1340-3 version of the Wasp, also rated at 410 hp, and the first production example was flown with various experimental cowlings as the second XP-3A, both this and the original XP-3A eventually becoming XP-21s (which see), the

second XP-3A undergoing further conversion (after testing as an XP-21) to P-1F standards. Armament of the P-3A comprised two 0·3-in machine guns and this type was fitted with a Townend ring after service entry. Max speed, 153 mph (246 km/h) at sea level, 148 mph (238 km/h) at 10,000 ft (3 050 m). Cruise, 122 mph (196 km/h). Initial climb, 1,742 ft/min (8,84 m/sec). Empty weight, 1,956 lb (887 kg). Loaded weight, 2,788 lb (1 265 kg). Span, 31 ft 7 in (9,63 m). Length, 22 ft 5 in (6,83 m). Height, 8 ft 9 in (2,67 m). Wing area, 252 sq ft (23,41 m²).

The F6C-2 (above) differed from the -1 in having a redesigned undercarriage and arrester hook and the F6C-3 (immediately below) was based on the P-1A airframe.

The final five fighters built against the initial P-1 contract were completed as P-2s, one of which is illustrated above. The P-3A, the third example of which is illustrated below, was the first radial-engined Hawk.

TALKBACK

The Ju 88 defection

I HAVE read with special interest Capt Eric Brown's account of flying the Junkers Ju 88, and your added note about the arrival of the Ju 88R-1 *Werk No* 360043 on 9 May 1943. According to information in my files, including a note from MoD Historical Branch received earlier last year, this Ju 88 was met off the UK by RAF fighter aircraft under arrangements previously made by the intelligence authorities. Those waiting to meet the aircraft included Prof R V Jones, whose radar and other interests are well-known. The aircraft (a new "factory-fresh" model) was part of a formation which had previously left Aalborg for Christiansand S. After a brief stop at Christiansand/Kjevik airfield, the formation took off to return to Denmark. The aircraft in question left the formation, made a spurious "Mayday" call, and crossed the North Sea at low level.

After its landing at Dyce (amidst heavy security which served to attract rather than diminish attention) much of the radar equipment was reportedly removed and flown separately to Farnborough. The Ju 88 was itself flown to Farnborough and impressed into RAF service as PJ876. According to local sources the crew spent the rest of the war in the UK and were returned to Germany under assumed identities and with financial provision.

Of additional interest is the defection of Bf 109G-14 of 7./JG 77 to Dyce on 26 December 1944. The aircraft crashed on landing, turning over and trapping the pilot, who was freed by aircrew from a number of Australian Lancasters that had diverted to Dyce because of bad weather then present over the S of England and N Europe during the Battle of the Ardennes.

James D Ferguson
Aberdeen, Scotland

Orion Update

I HAVE BEEN a reader of your magazine for many years and many times I have wanted to write and make some comment. Your recent article, "Orion: ASW Star Performer", in the September 1975 issue was of particular interest to me in that I am presently serving with a US Navy Reserve Squadron (VP-64) operating P-3As.

I found Mr Godfrey most informative and concise. However, in relation to that portion of the article dealing with the Orion's update, I thought that your readers might be interested in the Navy Reserve's own update program for the P-3A. I also understand that most of the regular Navy's P-3Bs have been updated. The P-3A/B Difar Retrofit consists of the installation of the P-3C's AQA-7 Difar acoustic ASW system including the SG-791 (ASSG) ARR-72 sono receivers. Also installed is an AQH-4 sonar tape recorder, RO-308 BT recorder, and a TD-900 time code generator. This equipment is interfaced with the ASA-16, P-3C Charlie's airborne computer having been deleted. This improved ASW system takes the place, in most cases, of the AQA-3A indicator group, ARR-52 sono receivers, AQA-1 CRT indicator, ASA-20 Julie recorder or the Deltic system AQA-5 recorder/AQH-1 tape recorder.

Subject of the accompanying letter from Mr Ferguson, the Ju 88R-1 that landed at Dyce in 1943 has recently been completely restored to its war-time appearance by personnel at RAF St Athan, as shown in this photograph.

It might also be mentioned that both P-3As and Bs have an ECM capability in that they are equipped with an ALD-2 ECM receiver-DF indicator group and a ULA-2 pulse analizer. This fact was omitted from the aforementioned article.

Bill Tate,
Cornwells Height, Pa, USA

British Airways history

THE ARTICLES on British Airways in the October and November issues were of particular interest to me, as I have been concentrating on the history of its predecessors and subsidiaries in my research over a number of years. I thought they came out very well, but I have noted a number of inconsistencies and minor inaccuracies that you may wish to print for the record.

Referring to the first part of the article, the exact styling of two companies mentioned should be Instone Air Line Ltd and British Latin American Air Lines Ltd.

It is not exactly correct to state that no scheduled services were permitted outside the Corporations until 1952. The Act was got round by making the independents "associates" of BEA in specific cases for services internally within the UK in 1949. By 1 March, 189 applications had been received by the Air Transport Advisory Council from 44 companies. The following month it was announced that 29 scheduled services had been allowed to 13 companies to be operated as Associate Agreements. July 1949 timetables show a fair number of these services to be in operation.

Only five active AAJC companies were taken over by BEA on 31 January 1947 — Scottish Airways, Railway Air Services, Isle of Man Air Services, Great Western and Southern Air Lines, and West Coast Air Services, which although it still owned a Rapide, did not have any routes of its own. Of the other two AAJC companies, Channel Islands Airways was taken over on 1 April 1947 and Olley Air Service, being a charter company, was not taken over. However two other dormant companies were taken over on 31 January 1947: North Eastern Airways and Western Isles Airways. Allied Airways (Gander-Dower), the other active internal airline but not a member of AAJC, was taken over on 12 April 1947.

Regarding the Boeing 314A flying-boats, these were actually operated by a subsidiary initially. Apparently Imperial Airways had been frightened of a lawsuit against them in the USA, so for their first services across the North Atlantic they formed Imperial

Airways (Atlantic) Ltd in May 1937. This company was renamed Airways (Atlantic) Ltd in April 1940, and the Boeing 314As were registered to it. The company was again renamed, this time as British Airways (Atlantic) Ltd, but apparently any residual problems with Imperial Airways were cleared up, as by the end of the year the aircraft were reregistered to BOAC.

Only 12 Whitleys were used operationally. Of the other three, one was used only for training and the other two were not converted. The 14 Warwick 1s were never in fact accepted by BOAC at all, as they did not receive Cs of A. BOAC services with the HP Halton ended on 4 May 1948, and the date of the Dissolution of the Corporation should read 31 March 1974.

Referring to Part Two, the Overseas Division fleet of Boeing 707s includes nine -320Cs, of which three are in all-cargo configuration, and two -320Bs. Most surviving 707-420s have been transferred to British Airtours (which is the current name of the former BEA Airtours, not British Airways Airtours as shown in the article). There are only 11 Trident Ones in first line service, including nine specially converted for the Shuttle; seven more are in store at Prestwick. References in the article to 25 BAC One Eleven 500s should read 18 Series 500s and seven Series 400s.

Donald Hannah
Barnack, Staffs

Messerschmitt tailpiece

I WOULD LIKE to add to the letter from T Hitchcock (Vol 9 No 3, September 1975) concerning the mystery of the Me 262Bs. I have been researching this aircraft for an article in the IPMS/USA Quarterly. My immediate reaction to Mr Hitchcock's letter was that he must be joking since "everyone knows" FE-610 is at Willow Grove NAS. But after checking into his reasons, I found he was absolutely correct. I already had interior photos of the Me 262B-1a/U2 in South Africa and requested the same from Willow Grove of their Me 262B. Today I received a photo of the aircraft at Willow Grove and it is definitely an Me 262B-1a. The rear tub is the same size as the front (the U1 has a short rear cockpit with a fuel tank behind it) and still has the flight and engine controls which were deleted in the U1 version. Now the question is: what happened to FE-610?

R P Lutz
Art Director, IPMS/USA Publications
Torrance, Calif, USA

IN PRINT

"Carrier Fighters"
by David Brown
Macdonald and Jane's, London, £2·95
160 pp, 6 in by 8¾ in, illustrated
AN ADDITION to the Macdonald Illustrated War Studies — one of a number of series devoted to various aspects of World War II now making their appearance. The object of this one is to provide a concise and well-illustrated guide to various military, naval and aviation topics.

As a former RN aircrew observer and author of several authoritative books on naval aircraft and carrier operation, David Brown is well qualified to tackle this particular title. He briefly traces the development of carrier fighters up to the outbreak of the war, and then deals thoroughly with major wartime battles and their effect upon fighting tactics and naval fighters in general. In addition to many photographs, there are several diagrams and maps, plus 15 tone side-view profiles by P Endsleigh Castle and a table of aircraft data.

"Fighter Pilot on the Western Front"
by Wg Cdr E D Crundall, DFC, AFC
William Kimber & Co Ltd, London, £3·95
192 pp, 6 in by 9¼ in, illustrated
EDWARD CRUNDALL was commissioned in the Royal Naval Air Service in July 1916, and after being taught to fly, joined No 8 Squadron, the famous "Naval Eight", in February 1917. The bulk of this volume comprises extracts from a daily diary he kept from then to the end of the war, the text of which has been edited by Chaz Bowyer. Although at times the diary entries seem trivial to the reader 60 years later, the book taken as a whole presents an excellent picture of the life of a typical fighting pilot in France in the later period of World War I.

There is a good collection of photographs to add appropriate atmosphere, some of which came from the author's own collection and have not been widely published.

"Wings over Kabul"
by Anne Baker & A C M Sir Ronald Ivelaw-Chapman
William Kimber & Co Ltd, London, £5·25
192 pp, 6 in by 9¼ in, illustrated
THIS account of the Kabul Air Evacuation in 1928/29 provides, for the first time, an authoritative and fully authenticated description of the world's first airlift — the transportation by air of "civilians and officials from one country to another in circumstances of acute political stress". In 84 air missions by Vickers Victorias, 586 civilians were flown out of beleaguered Kabul, Afghanistan, in the three-month period up to 25 February 1929. Air Chief Marshal Sir Ronald Ivelaw-Chapman participated in the airlift as a pilot serving with No 70 Squadron; Anne Baker's father, Air Vice Marshal Sir Geoffrey Salmond, directed the airlift as Air Officer Commanding, RAF in India.

Much of the book is made up of extracts from contemporary reports and accounts, or more recent recollections of various individuals who were involved in some way, but Anne Baker also describes the political background that led up to the evacuation, and the rôle played by the principal personalities. A large collection of photographs has been assembled to enhance the value of this important volume.

"Le Trait D'Union" (T-6 Special)
Compiled by Vital Ferry
104 pp, 8¼ in by 11¾ in, illustrated
THIS special issue of the journal of the French branch of "Air Britain" is devoted in its entirety to the history of the North American T-6 in French service. A total of 949 examples of the North American trainer was involved (ignoring the pre-war contracts placed by the *Armée de l'Air* for NA-57s and NA-64s, not all of which were delivered). Included in the post-war total were T-6Ds, T-6Gs, SNJ-4s and Harvard IIs and IVs, all of which had seen earlier service with the USAAF, USN, RCAF or RAF.

The deployment, operational use, markings and colours of all these aircraft are fully explained in this document, which reflects prolonged and careful research by a group of enthusiasts. Many photographs and line drawings are included. Copies may be ordered from J Delmas, Residence Colbert, 107 Allee D Casanova, 93320 Les Pavillons-sous-Bois, France for Fr 30, post free.

"Famous Fighters of the Second World War"
by William Green
Macdonald and Janes, London, £4·95
276 pp, 7¼ in by 9¾ in, illustrated
TWENTY-EIGHT of the most-used fighters of the combatant nations of World War II are fully described and illustrated in this volume, which is a new edition of the work originally published in two parts (in 1957 and 1962 respectively). There has been no revision of the text but eight detailed cutaway drawings have been added, several of these being published here for the first time anywhere.

In addition to a good selection of photographs, each aircraft is illustrated by a series of line drawings to depict the variants, and by a large three-view drawing. Although the use of litho reproduction in places of the original letterpress gives this new edition the distinctive appearance associated with the process, the volume still represents excellent value, even if inflation has almost trebled the price in 15 years.

"DC-3"
by Arthur Pearcy
Ballantine Books, New York, $2·00
160 pp, 5¼ in by 8¼ in
ARTHUR PEARCY has been, for many years, one of the most devoted of DC-3 fans, and has probably written more about the "Grand Old Lady" of air transport than any other author. His research into the subject has been meticulous and he can be relied upon for completeness and accuracy, as readers of his earlier "Dakota" (the story of RAF DC-3s) will know.

This new offering appears as "Weapons Book No 44" in the Ballantine's series entitled "Illustrated History of the Violent Century"— a slightly unexpected package, perhaps, in which to find the world's greatest airliner described. It is also a package that allows the author to do less than justice to his subject; there are numerous photographs, but they reproduce poorly on the quality of paper used, and the whole book has the appearance of being made to fit a formula, with many photographs running across page spreads — which is disastrous in a square-backed volume such as this is. These criticisms apart, and keeping in mind the modest cost, the book can be recommended.

"Royal Air Force 1939-45" (three volumes)
by Denis Richards and Hilary St G Saunders
HM Stationery Office, London, £2 each vol, £5 per boxed set
430 pp (Vol 1), 416 pp (Vol 2), 442 pp (Vol 3), 5½ in by 8½ in, illustrated
ALTHOUGH the past three decades have seen the publication of many books devoted to particular aspects of RAF operation and equipment in World War II, and numerous biographies and auto-biographies have told the stories of individuals who played lesser or greater rôles, there is still only one comprehensive history of the air operations during the whole of the conflict. This is it.

Originally published in hard-back during the 'fifties, the work has been out of print for some years and its reappearance now is a relatively modestly-priced paperback set is welcome. Volume 1 "The Fight at Odds" is concerned with the period up to 1941 and includes a study of pre-war planning and rearmament plans. Volume 2 "The Fight Avails" takes the story up to 1943 and there-

A Vickers Victoria III, the type of transport used by No 70 Squadron, RAF, to complete the first-ever airlift, as described in "Wings over Kabul" noted above.

(Above) A Curtiss JN-4A built by Curtiss in 1917 and (below) a JN-4D built in the same year by St Louis Aircraft Corp. Full details of all Curtiss Jenny production are contained in the latest volume of Robert Casari's "Encyclopædia of US Military Aircraft".

fore brings in Far Eastern operations as well as those in Europe, the Mediterranean and over the Atlantic. Volume 3 "The Fight is Won" covers the last two years of the conflict and draws some final conclusions.

The illustrations in these volumes are almost wholly restricted to maps and charts; there are a few half-tone photographs. The text is clear and the narrative is both authoritative and readable.

"Encyclopedia of US Military Aircraft"
The World War I Production Program, Vol 3
by Robert B Casari
Military Aircraft Publications, Chillicothe, Ohio, $3·95 softbound, $6·95 hardbound
152 pp, 5¾ in by 9 in, illustrated
THIS latest addition to Robert Casari's highly authoritative documentations of US Military Aircraft up to the end of World War I is devoted in its entirety to the Curtiss Jennies. Although the Jenny was probably the most famous of the US aircraft to appear in the Great War period, accurate information has hitherto been lacking on precise quantities, variants and operational use. This book contains the complete story of the Jenny for the first time and must be welcomed by all serious aviation historians as the definitive record of an important aircraft type.

Mr Casari records 19 principal variants of the Jenny that emerged between the Model J of 1914 and the JN-4D-2 of 1918, but many other major and minor versions are also covered in this book, including the JN-5 and JN-6 models (but excluding the post-war civilian models). More than 9,400 Jennies were assigned US Army serial numbers, all of which are recorded in this volume (for the first time ever), and the illustrations include seven three-view drawings and many rare photographs.

Copies of this important publication can be ordered direct from the publisher at 6 Applewood Drive, Chillicothe, OH 45601, USA; the prices quoted include postage by surface mail.

"Fleet Operators 1975"
Edited by Jim Birch
Air-British Publications
80 pp, 7 in by 9¼ in, illustrated
EIGHTH edition of a popular Air-Britain annual reference work, this contains fleet information on some 640 airlines of 154 countries. Information is updated to March 1975 and includes aircraft registrations and c/ns, but not individual aircraft names or previous identities. Copies cost £1·35 post free from the Air Britain Sales Department, at Stone Cottage, Great Sampford, Saffron Walden, Essex CB10 2RS.

"Aviation and Space Museums of America"
by Jon L Allen
Arco Publishing Co Inc, New York, $12·00
288 pp, 6¼ in by 9¼ in, illustrated
IN ALL, 57 "collections of aerospace artifacts" in the USA and Canada are described in this volume, the principal purpose of which is to serve as a general guidebook of practical use to intending visitors, rather than a reference source for the enthusiast or historian. The basis for including a museum or collection is its permanence, although the author notes that changes occur rapidly and some of the information in the book may therefore quickly go out of date.

Each collection is described in general terms, with a note of exhibits of special interest (but no attempt is made to present a complete list). Details of locations, times of opening and price of admission are included. There is a good selection of photographs, but purists will writhe a little at the style of quoting some of the aircraft designations, such as "Messerschmitt ME-109" and "DeHavilland MK-35 Mosquito".

"Airmen of World War I"
by Chaz Bowyer
Arms and Armour Press, London, £4·50
128 pp, 7 in by 10 in, illustrated
A SELECTION of more than 150 photographs has been put together in this nicely-produced

volume to give an authentic flavour of life in the RFC and RNAS during the Great War. The emphasis, as the title suggests, is upon the personnel of those two services, depicted in formal groups, in informal snaps or performing various duties. The captions are extensive and informative, adding greatly to the value of the pictures alone. Aircraft figure only incidentally, and the book will be of most use to enthusiasts with a particular interest in the period.

"Junkers Ju 287"
"Junkers Ju 288"
by Thomas H Hitchcock
Monogram Aviation Publications, Acton, Mass, 32 pp each, 8¼ by 10¼ in, illustrated
THESE are the first two titles in a series entitled "Monogram Close-Up" — yet another variation on the single-aircraft monograph theme. Each presents a comprehensive account of the development and testing of the aircraft in question, with very complete reproductions of original company or official illustrations — both diagrams and photographs. Further titles are intended to deal with other German aircraft of the World War II period, and will be welcomed by enthusiasts with a penchant for this particular era.

"British Aircraft of World War II"
by John Frayn Turner
"German Aircraft of World War II"
by Christopher Shepherd
Sidgwick & Jackson, London, £4·50 each
144 pp each, 7¼ in by 9¾ in, illustrated
THE CORE of each of these volumes is a 48-page section of full-colour photographs. In the case of the British aircraft, these have been drawn, primarily, from the files of the Imperial War Museum and from the Conway picture library, and they provide an excellent glimpse of the aircraft of the period in natural colours, although inevitably there is considerable variation in the shades shown. The colour section of the German volume is less satisfactory, as most of the illustrations here have been reproduced from German wartime publications; consequently, their quality is poor and the colours somewhat suspect.

Each volume has two other sections. One is a "Reference Section" providing brief descriptions of principal operational aircraft used by the RAF and the *Luftwaffe* respectively, and the other, entitled "In Action", describes some of the most significant deployments of these aircraft types. The British volume also contains details of all actions resulting in the award of the Victoria Cross for gallantry.

"Winged Warfare"
by Lt Col William A Bishop, VC, DSO, MC
Bailey Bros and Swinfen Ltd, Folkestone, Kent, £4·25
282 pp, 3¼ in by 8¼ in
THE CANADIAN Billy Bishop, who ranked fourth among the air aces of World War I, later described his experiences in a volume that became one of the classics of the period. This now re-appears in a new British edition, edited from the original manuscript by Stanley M Ulanoff. In addition to Bishop's own text there are a number of appendices, listing Allied and Enemy Aces, Bishop's service and 72 confirmed victories, and giving data and three-view drawings for a dozen representative aircraft. A number of half-tone photographs have also been added.

be obtained as a result of this excess of power and, in any case, the calculated rate of climb was well beyond the point of diminishing return against any bomber target. We were thus convinced that we could achieve with a considerably higher aeroplane weight all the performance that seemed to make sense. We therefore increased endurance from 30 minutes to one hour and raised the armament to four 30-mm cannon with provision for two more similar weapons. We believed that these changes would result in a better fighting machine and in the event it was to be the endurance of the Messerschmitt aeroplane that was to tip the scales in its favour when the RLM had to choose between this and the Heinkel contender.

After the acceptance of this proposal, which had been submitted in June 1939, and the construction of part mock-ups of the *Projekt* 1065, which had been followed some nine months later by a contract for detail design and the construction of a static test airframe and three flight test airframes, two rather conspicuous design changes had to be introduced, these being incorporated during prototype definition. BMW soon ascertained that its turbojet would be still larger and appreciably heavier than the company's least sanguine *revised* calculations had suggested, thus presenting us with serious CG problems. Aircraft development had progressed too far for us to dramatically revise its layout and we were forced to introduce what we considered a somewhat inelegant "fix" in the form of *swept* outer wing panels to resolve the CG difficulties presented by the heavier engines. Thus, it was to be purely fortuitous that the Me 262 was to become the world's first operational fighter featuring wing sweepback; a radical departure that, at this stage at least, reflected no attempt to reduce the effects of compressibility.

The other design change accompanying this "fix" was in the actual positioning of the engine. We had never been really happy with the arrangement whereby the engine was mounted centrally on the wing. It had been obvious from the outset that the structure wrapped around the engine was going to be quite heavy and also expensive. Now, with further revised estimates of engine size and weight, the nacelle diameter was coming out so large that *Projekt* 1065 no longer looked as aerodynamically favourable as we had expected. We were forced to face the fact that the wing of our aeroplane was simply too small to make an in-wing installation of the engine rewarding. We had earlier considered the possibility of mounting the engine *under* the wing, but, perhaps as a result of a latent suspicion that this configuration offered too simple a solution to our problems, had devoted most attention to the in-wing arrangement. Now we finally reverted to underslung engine nacelles and had arrived by a somewhat circuitous route at the definitive configuration — a low-mounted wing embodying sweepback and carrying the engine nacelles underslung — which we submitted to the RLM in mid-May 1940. This configuration left the upper wing surface undisturbed by the engine nacelle, while the lower surface went through clean beneath the fuselage. One appealing feature was that the pronounced upward displacement of the fuselage with respect to the engine nacelles increased the distance between these bodies and thus reduced the possibility of interference between them. We anticipated that this arrangement would prove not only lighter and cheaper than the in-wing arrangement but would, in all probability, also afford less drag.

Airframe development and construction proceeded rapidly and without any serious hiccups, which was more than could be said for the parallel turbojet development programme. Bench results with the BMW turbojet were disappointing. The RLM requirement of 1,320 lb (600 kg) thrust at 560 mph (900 km/h), or about 1,500 lb (680 kg) static, still seemed far from BMW's grasp by the time the first prototype of our fighter, the Me 262 V1, was ready to receive its engines, and the alternative Junkers Jumo turbojet was also encountering serious difficulties. A considerable delay appeared likely in the avail-

ability of flight-cleared engines and, after considering and discarding a suggestion that we should fit a pair of Walter rocket units, it was proposed that, as a temporary expediency, we should mount a piston engine in the fuselage nose of the first prototype and thus complete some preliminary airframe testing while awaiting the turbojets. As I recall, this proposal was first mooted by Professor Messerschmitt who saw the delay in the delivery of the gas turbines as providing a valuable opportunity to test a new and novel airframe without compounding the risk by adding even more innovatory engines. We thereupon made it a policy decision that we would rely on the turbojets only after our test pilots were satisfied with the behaviour of the aeroplane within the flight envelope that could be explored on the power of a single Junkers Jumo 210G 12-cylinder liquid-cooled engine.

With piston engine fitted, the Me 262 V1 was flown for the first time on 18 April 1941 by the late Fritz Wendel, various minor modifications being introduced as a result of a series of inclined flights at full throttle during which the general handling characteristics, rudder forces, etc, were evaluated. Such was the scepticism concerning the reliability of BMW's *Sondertriebwerke*, or "Special Power Plants", that when, in mid-November 1941, the first flight-cleared BMW 003 engines reached us for mounting on the Me 262 V1, it was decided that the nose-mounted piston engine should be retained as a precaution against failure of the highly temperamental turbojets. A wise precaution this proved to be on 25 March 1942, when, during the initial flight with the BMW 003s operating, compressor blades failed in both engines and the Jumo 210G piston engine saved the day, Fritz Wendel succeeding in completing a circuit and making a safe landing.

Subsequently, the BMW 003 had to undergo major redesign, but Junkers had meanwhile overcome the most serious problems that had beset the Jumo 004 and the third prototype airframe, the Me 262 V3, was modified to take this somewhat larger and heavier power plant, enabling the initial pure jet flight to be made by this new Messerschmitt fighter on 18 July 1942. Two major changes were to take place before we finally attained the production configuration: the wing root chord was increased by continuing the leading-edge sweep angle of the outer panels across the centre section and we finally overcame our reluctance to fit a nosewheel undercarriage. The former change, introduced on the Me 262 V3 after the two initial flight tests, eliminated a tendency for the airflow to break away early from the wing centre section, and the latter change, first evaluated by the Me 262 V5, proved necessary owing to the inefficiency of the tailwheel arrangement. Owing to the absence of a propeller slipstream, an unacceptably tricky manœuvre was demanded in order to get the tail off the runway during the take-off run, apart from the fact that the effect of the engine exhaust (which, with the tailwheel undercarriage, was directed downwards) on the grass fields and asphalt aprons was also unacceptable.

The entire development programme was bizarre in a way. Our compressible flow aerodynamics, produced in an information vacuum, turned out to be almost flawless, yet the relatively "normal" problems tripped us up on a number of occasions. Furthermore, we had arrived at a swept wing without realizing its potential aerodynamic advantage. In retrospect, I wonder to what extent our success was due to sheer luck and how much of it was the result of good basic thinking behind our guesswork. Certainly we had need of both, but statistical evidence would seem to indicate that luck was not a primary factor. It would appear improbable that luck could have played a really major rôle in the creation of a transonic aeroplane such as the Me 262 which suffered no significant aerodynamic problem during its entire flight test programme. Thus, while, through no choice of our own, the techniques involved in creating the Messerschmitt jet fighter embodied higher than usual risks, our approach to the problems was still a valid and responsible one and the results spoke for themselves. □

BRAZIL

EMBRAER EMB-12X

UNDER the series title of EMB-12X, the Brazilian state-owned company EMBRAER has under development a family of designs derived from the EMB-110 Bandeirante twin-turboprop transport. Developed initially for the *Fôrça Aérea Brasiliera*, which has ordered 80 examples, the Bandeirante has found a useful and growing market as a third-level airliner and for various types of business use; a start has also been made on exporting the Bandeirante and there are good prospects of selling the type to a number of South American countries and perhaps more widely afield.

In order to expand the commercial use of the Bandeirante, EMBRAER first projected a pressurised version which was to use as much as possible of the existing airframe, with a new fuselage of similar size. This scheme has now been revised to embrace three distinct pressurised versions, of which two are primarily of interest to the business user and the third will be intended for airline users.

The EMB-121 Xingu, a prototype of which is expected to fly in Brazil before mid-year, retains substantially the same wing and power plant as the Bandeirante (although the span is reduced slightly), and has a shorter fuselage with a new T-tail. With accommodation for only six passengers, compared with the Bandeirante's 12-15, the Xingu is a business twin aimed at the local market in competition with the pressurised aircraft available from several US manufacturers.

The EMB-123 and EMB-120, which it is planned should follow the Xingu during 1977, make use of the same fuselage diameter, flight deck, systems and tail unit; they will introduce, however, on two different fuselage lengths, a completely new supercritical wing design, with optional wing-tip fuel tanks, and uprated engines. With 10 seats, the EMB-123 Tapajos will be of interest primarily to business users, while the EMB-120 Araguaia will seat 20 and will be intended for third-level airline use as well as the larger corporations requiring more accommodation at the expense of range.

Preliminary data for the three new models are given below: for comparison, the Bandeirante itself has a span of 50 ft 3 in (15,32 m), length of 46 ft 8½ in (14,231 m) and height of 13 ft 6½ in (4,13 m); powered by 680 shp PT6A-27s, its gross weight is 12,345 lb (5 600 kg).

The three-view below depicts the EMB-123 Tapajos, with an additional side view of the longer EMB-120 Araguaia.

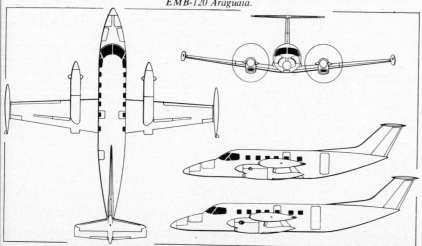

A three-view drawing of the EMBRAER EMB-121 Xingu, a prototype of which is soon to fly.

EMB-121 Xingu

Power Plant: Two Pratt & Whitney (Canada) PT6A-28 turboprops flat-rated at 680 shp up to ISA+6 deg C and driving three-bladed constant speed feathering and reversing Hartzell propellers.
Performance: Cruising speed, 292 mph (470 km/h); range, 1,428 mls (2 300 km).
Weights: Empty equipped, 6,893 lb (3 126 kg); max take-off, 11,466 lb (5 200 kg); max landing, 10,915 lb (4 950 kg).
Dimensions: Span, 45 ft 11½ in (14,02 m); overall length, 41 ft 1 in (12,52 m); height, 15 ft 5½ in (4,72 m); undercarriage track, 17 ft 2½ in (5,24 m); wheelbase, 9 ft 11 in (3,03 m).
Accommodation: Flight crew of two and six passengers. Cabin pressurized to 6 psi (0,42 kg/cm²). Nose baggage compartment, volume 17·6 cu ft (0,50 m³); aft cabin baggage compartment, volume 25·4 cu ft (0,72 m³).

EMB-123 Tapajos

Power Plant: Two Pratt & Whitney (Canada) PT6A-45 turboprops each rated at 1,120 shp and driving five-bladed constant speed feathering and reversing Hartzell propellers. Fuel capacity, 572 Imp gal (2 600 l) in internal and wing-tip tanks.
Performance: Cruising speed, 342 mph (550 km/h); range, 1,990 mls (3 200 km).
Weights: Empty equipped, 8,458 lb (3 836 kg); max take-off, 14,773 lb (6 700 kg); max landing, 14,663 lb (6 650 kg).
Dimensions: Span (without tip tanks), 48 ft 3 in (14,70 m); length, 51 ft 2½ in (15,60 m); height, 15 ft 10 in (4,84 m); undercarriage track, 16 ft 9 in (5,10 m); wheelbase, 17 ft 1½ in (5,21 m).
Accommodation: Flight crew of two and up to 10 passengers. Pressurization and nose baggage compartments as EMB-121.

EMB-120 Araguaia

Power Plant: As EMB-123.
Performance: Cruising speed, 329 mph (530 km/h); range, 1,740 mls (2 800 km).
Weights: Empty equipped, 9,047 lb (4 103 kg); max take-off, 15,435 lb (7 000 kg); max landing, 14,663 lb (6 650 kg).
Dimensions: Span (over tip tanks), 49 ft 2 in (14,98 m); length, 57 ft 2½ in (17,42 m); height, 15 ft 10 in (4,82 m); undercarriage track, 16 ft 9 in (5,10 m); wheelbase, 18 ft 4 in (5,58 m).
Accommodation: Flight crew of two and up to 20 passengers. Pressurization and nose baggage compartments as EMB-121.

FEDERAL GERMANY

PÖSCHEL P-400 TURBO-EQUATOR

FIVE years ago, on 27 February 1971, a highly unconventional little aircraft, the Pöschel P-300 Equator, made its first flight at Laupheim, Germany. Among its unusual characteristics were the location of the Lycoming IO-540 piston engine in a nacelle high on the fin, and the large-scale use of GRP (glass-reinforced plastics) in its construction; the production derivative of the P-300 was also intended to be amphibian, although the prototype had a fixed tricycle undercarriage and fixed wing-tip fairings that, in the amphibian, would form retractable stabilizing floats.

In the course of flight testing, the P-300, designed by Gunter Pöschel, acquired wheel spats and additional fin area above the engine nacelle, and the wing-tip fairings were also removed. The Equator aroused a great deal of interest, but production plans were held in abeyance for adequate financing to be obtained, and to allow further refinement of the design. Both these objectives are now in process of fulfilment, and construction of a new prototype, the P-400 Turbo-Equator, is under way with the prospect of production models being available, fully certificated, by 1977. Production will be handled by the newly-founded Equator Aircraft GmbH at Ulm.

As the name suggests, the P-400 differs from the original prototype in having a turbo-prop engine — the Allison 250. Other changes

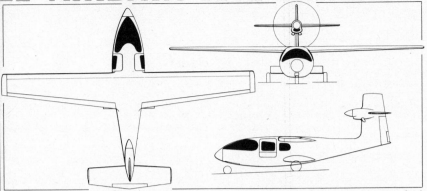

(Above) A three-view drawing of the Poschel P-400 Turbo-Equator and (below) a photograph of the Cessna 340A.

include a new wing with full-span double-slotted flaps, the rear portions of which act also as ailerons ("flaperons"); a completely redesigned and pressurized fuselage offering better comfort for the passengers, and sponsons on the fuselage that house the main wheels when retracted and provide stability on the water, thus dispensing with the need for wing tip floats.

First flight of a prototype P-400 is scheduled for the first half of this year, with water tests to be made with the help of FFA at Altenrhein, Switzerland. Certification is expected to be completed by the end of 1976, with production aircraft available in 1977 at a price of DM 540,000 (about £101,500); Equator reports that options have been taken on 43 aircraft to date. It is planned to offer an updated version of the piston-engined P-300 also in due course, at a price of DM 43,000 (£80,800).

Power Plant: One Detroit Allison 250-817B turboprop rated at 420 shp.

Performance: Max speed, 286 mph (460 km/h) at sea level and 000 mph (470 km/h) at 8,000 ft (2 440 m); initial rate of climb, 2,362 ft/min (12 m/sec); ceiling, 27,890 ft (8 500 m); max range, 3,105 mls (5 000 km) at 24,000 ft (7 320 m); cruising range, 870 mls (1 400 km) at 11,800 ft (3 600 m); max range, ????? fuel tanks, 2,485 mls (4 000 km); take-off distance to 50 ft (15,2 m), 804 ft (245 m); landing distance from 50 ft (15,2 m), 820 ft (250 m).

Weights: Empty weight, 2,090 lb (950 kg); max take-off, 4,410 lb (2 000 kg); max landing, 4,190 lb (1 900 kg).

Dimensions: Span, 40 ft 8 in (12,40 m); length, 28 ft 2½ in (8,60 m); height, 11 ft 8 in (3,55 m); wing area, 193·75 sq ft (18,0 m²); aspect ratio, 8·5:1.

Accommodation: Pilot and passenger side-by-side, and five to six seats in main cabin.

USA

CESSNA 340A

MORE powerful engines have been introduced in the 1976 model of the Cessna 340 pressurized twin, identified in its new version as the Cessna 340A. An overall increase of 50 hp gives the 340A substantial improvements in speed, climb and field performance, and several other changes have been made to give this new model greater passenger comfort.

Air conditioning capacity has been increased by 25 per cent at engine speeds below 800 rpm, to give a cooler cabin during ground taxi operation, and seats have been redesigned to increase aisle space and allow easier movement in the cabin. In common with most models in the Cessna range for 1976, the 340A is available in basic form and also with a "II"

package which provides a complete factory-installed avionics system and substantial savings on 12 of the most popular items of optional equipment.

Power Plant: Two 310 hp Continental TSIO-520-N flat-six fuel injection engines with turbochargers, driving Cessna 6 ft 4½ in (1,94-m) diameter constant-speed fully-feathering three-blade propellers. Standard fuel capacity, 102 US gal (386 l); optional auxiliary capacity of 41, 64 or 105 US gal (155, 242 or 393 l) depending on tanks fitted.

Performance: Max speed, 277 mph (447 km/h) at 20,000 ft (6 096 m); best cruising speed, 77·5 per cent power, 228 mph (367 km/h) at 10,000 ft (3 050 m) and 253 mph (423 km/h)

The photograph and three-view depict the Cessna 404, a brand-new addition to the company's range for 1976.

at 24,500 ft (7 468 m); initial rate of climb, 1,650 ft/min (8,4 m/sec); single-engine climb, 315 ft/min (1,6 m/sec); service ceiling, 29,800 ft (9 083 m); single-engine ceiling, 15,800 ft (4 816 m); take-off distance to 50 ft (15,2 m), 2,230 ft (680 m); landing distance from 50 ft (15,2 m), 1,850 ft (564 m); range (standard fuel), 531 mls (856 km) at 260 mph (419 km/h) at 24,500 ft (7 468 m) and 590 mls (949 km) at 171 mph (276 km/h) at 10,000 ft (3 050 m); range (max fuel), 1,285 mls (2 086 km) at 262 mph (423 km/h) at 24,500 ft (7 468 m) and 1,480 mls (2 383 km) at 211 mph (339 km/h) at 25,000 ft (7 620 m).

Weights: Standard empty (basic), 3,868 lb (1 755 kg), (340A II), 4,096 lb (1 858 kg); max take-off, 5,990 lb (2 717 kg); max landing, 5,990 lb (2 717 kg).

Dimensions: Span, 38 ft 1·3 in (11,62 m); length, 34 ft 4 in (10,46 m); height, 12 ft 7 in (3,84 m); wing area, 184 sq ft (17,1 m²); wheelbase, 10 ft 2¾ in (3,12 m); undercarriage track, 12 ft 10¼ in (3,91 m); dihedral, 5 deg constant.

Accommodation: Six seats in pressurized cabin. Baggage compartment in nose, capacity 930 lb (422 kg).

CESSNA 404 TITAN

WITH deliveries due to start in mid-1976, the Cessna Model 404 Titan is regarded by the company as an addition to its 1977 range of twin-engined business aircraft. Particular features of the Titan are its large cabin and its ability to lift a good load out of short, rough fields. Two variants are planned: the Ambassador for the businessman, with interiors to customer requirements, and the Courier for the commuter/air cargo market. In the latter rôle, the aircraft can carry up to 10 including the pilot; the cabin provides 284 cu ft (8,04 m³) of volume with a total cabin length of 18 ft 9 in (5,72 m).

Access to the cabin is through an airstair door; an extra large cargo door, available as

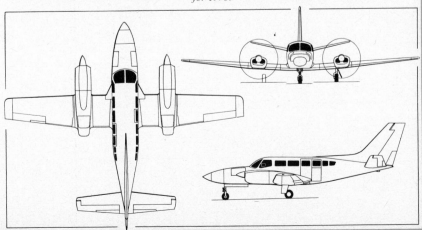

an option, provides a 4 ft 1 in (1,24 m) opening to accommodate "D"-size shipping containers and odd size or extra long cargo. Seat tracks run the full length of the cabin to allow maximum flexibility of layouts and also serve as cargo tie-downs.

The Titan utilizes a bonded wing structure, giving excellent aerodynamic characteristics and integral fuel tanks, and has a technically advanced aerofoil section. Large hydraulically-actuated Fowler-type flaps are fitted, and a new type of trailing link type undercarriage is activated hydraulically with a retraction time of less than five seconds.

Power Plant: Two Teledyne Continental GTSIO-520M geared and turbosupercharged engines rated to give 375 hp each up to 16,000 ft (4 877 m). Three-bladed fully-feathering constant speed propellers, diameter 13 ft 1 in (3,99 m). Fuel capacity, 340 US gal (1 292 l).

Performance: Max speed, 225 mph (363 km/h) at sea level and 269 mph (433 km/h) at 16,000 ft (4 877 m); max recommended cruising speed, 75 per cent power, 223 mph (359 km/h) at 10,000 ft (3 050 m) and 246 mph (396 km/h) at 20,000 ft (6 100 m); initial rate of climb, 1,515 ft/min (7,7 m/sec); single-engined climb rate, 220 ft/min (1,1 m/sec); service ceiling, 22,200 ft (6 767 m); single-engined ceiling, 9,500 ft (2 896 m); take-off distance to 50 ft (15,2 m), 2,240 ft (683 m); range with 10 occupants, 1,020 mls (1 641 km) at 221 mph (350 km/h) at 10,000 ft (3 050 m); range with max fuel, 1,727-2,060 mls (2 778-3 315 km) at 221-190 mph (356-306 km/h) at 10,000 ft (3 050 m) with six occupants.

Weights: Empty (Courier), 4,773 lb (2 165 kg), (Ambassador), 4,754 lb (2 156 kg); max useful load (Courier), 3,527 lb (1 600 kg), (Ambassador), 3,546 lb (1 608 kg); max take-off

weight, 8,300 lb (3 765 kg); landing weight, 8,100 lb (3 674 kg).

Dimensions: Span, 46 ft 0 in (14,02 m); length, 39 ft 5 in (12,04 m); height, 13 ft 1 in (3,99 m); wing area, 242 sq ft (22,48 m²); undercarriage track, 14 ft 0½ in (4,28 m); wheelbase, 12 ft 6 in (3,81 m).

Accommodation: Six to 10 seats in cabin, mounted on seat tracks and easily removable for cargo carrying rôle. Airstair door and optional large cargo door. Ambassador interior options include aft refreshment centre, toilet, in-flight 'phone and folding writing desks.

PIPER PA-32 CHEROKEE LANCE

AN addition to the Piper range of business aircraft for 1976, the Cherokee Lance is basically a Cherokee Six airframe with a retractable undercarriage. The undercarriage system is similar to that used on the smaller Arrow II, an earlier Cherokee variant, and is designed to extend automatically when the airspeed drops below 115 mph (185 km/h); similarly, it cannot be retracted after take-off until the airspeed exceeds 95 mph (153 km/h). These automatic safety features can be overridden by the pilot, but a red warning light flashes continually when the automatic system is locked out.

In all respects other than the undercarriage, the Cherokee Lance is virtually identical with the 1976 Cherokee Six 300. The fuselage, derived from that of the twin-engined Seneca II, incorporates a large cabin with six seats (and an optional seventh), a total of 10 windows and two separate luggage compartments with their own doors. A choice of air conditioning or a fresh air ventilating fan system is available.

A new air induction system has been designed to provide maximum installed power from the Lycoming engine, and features an

air intake on the port side of the engine cowling directing air to the fuel injector system. The exhaust system is designed to minimize exhaust back pressure and loss of installed horsepower.

Power Plant: One 300 hp Lycoming IO-540-K1A5 flat-six air-cooled engine driving a two-bladed Hartzell constant speed propeller, diameter 6 ft 8 in (2,03 m). Fuel capacity, 48 US gal (372 l).

Performance: Max speed, 190 mph (306 km/h); optimum cruising speed, 182 mph (293 km/h) at 75 per cent power; take-off run, 960 ft (293 m); take-off to 50 ft (15,2 m), 1,660 ft (506 m); landing distance from 50 ft (15,2 m), 1,670 ft (509 m); initial rate of climb, 1,000 ft/min (5,1 m/sec); service ceiling, 14,600 ft (4 450 m); absolute ceiling, 16,300 ft (4 970 m); best economy range, no reserves, 1,005 mls (1 618 km) at 75 per cent and 1,120 mls (1 803 km) at 55 per cent power.

Weights: Equipped empty, 1,910 lb (867 kg); max take-off, 3,600 lb (1 634 kg).

Dimensions: Span, 32 ft 9½ in (10 m); length, 27 ft 8½ in (8,44 m); height, 8 ft 2½ in (2,5 m); wing area, 174·5 sq ft (16,2 m²); undercarriage track, 11 ft 1 in (3,39 m); wheelbase, 8 ft 0 in (2,44 m).

Accommodation: Pilot and five passengers in six individual seats; provision for optional seventh seat between centre pair. Centre and rear seats removable. Rear luggage compartment, capacity 20 cu ft (0,57 m³); nose luggage compartment, capacity 7 cu ft (0,2 m³).

PIPER PA-28-180R ARCHER II

FOLLOWING the introduction of a new, tapered wing on the four-seat Cherokee fuselage in 1973 to produce the Cherokee Warrior, Piper has now applied the same wing to the more powerful Archer, offered in the 1976 range of Piper models as the Archer II. Whereas the Warrior has a 150 hp Lycoming engine, the Archer II is powered by a 180 hp Lycoming, providing improved performance in all respects.

The tapered wing, which Piper may introduce on other models in due course, has the same area as before, but a greater span, with taper on both the leading and trailing edges of the outer panels. This wing, which incorporates a revised aerofoil on the outer panels, provides increased control power without increasing roll control forces. Apart from the change of engine, the Archer II is similar to the Warrior.

Power Plant: One 180 hp Lycoming O-360-A3A flat-four aircooled engine driving a Hartzell two-blade constant speed propeller, diameter 6 ft 4 in (1,93 m). Fuel capacity, 50 US gal (189 l).

Performance: Max speed, 147 mph (237 km/h); optimum cruising speed, 144 mph (232 km/h) at 75 per cent power; take-off run, 865 ft (264 m); take-off to 50 ft (15,2 m), 1,625 ft (496 m); landing distance from 50 ft (15,2 m), 1,392 ft (425 m); initial rate of climb, 740 ft/min (3,75 m/sec); service ceiling, 13,650 ft (4 163 m); absolute ceiling, 15,750 ft (4 804 m); best economy range, no reserves, 745 mls (1 200 km) at 75 per cent and 870 mls (1 401 km) at 55 per cent engine power.

Weights: Standard empty, 1,390 lb (631 kg); max take-off, 2,550 lb (1 158 kg).

Dimensions: Span, 35 ft 0 in (10,67 m); length, 24 ft 0 in (7,32 m); height, 7 ft 4 in (2,23 m); wing area, 170 sq ft (15,8 m²); undercarriage track, 10 ft 0 in (3,05 m); wheelbase, 6 ft 8½ in (2,10 m).

Accommodation: Pilot and three passengers in individual seats; rear pair removable. Rear luggage compartment, capacity 24 cu ft (0,68 m²).

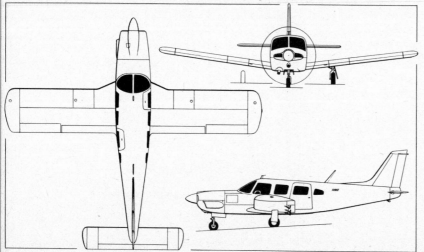

Illustrated above and below is the Piper Cherokee Lance, basically a Cherokee Six airframe with a retractable undercarriage.

AIR International

Volume 10   Number 4   April 1976

Managing Editor   William Green
Editor   Gordon Swanborough
Modelling Editor   Fred J Henderson
Contributing Artists   Dennis Punnett
          John Weal
Cover Art   W R Hardy
Contributing Photographer
          Stephen Peltz
Editorial Representative, Washington
          Norman Polmar
Publisher   Donald Hannah
Circulation Director   Donald Syner
Subscription Manager   Claire Sillette
Advertising/Public Relations
          Elizabeth Baker
Advertising Manager   Jim Boyd

Editorial Offices:
The AIR INTERNATIONAL, PO Box 16, Bromley, BR2 7RB Kent.

Subscription, Advertising and Circulation Offices:
The AIR INTERNATIONAL, De Worde House, 283 Lonsdale Road, London SW13 9QW. Telephone 01-878 2454. US and Canadian readers may address subscriptions and general enquiries to AIR INTERNATIONAL PO Box 353, Whitestone, NY 11357 for onward transmission to the UK, from where all correspondence is answered and orders despatched.

MEMBER OF THE AUDIT
BUREAU OF CIRCULATIONS   ABC

Subscription rates, inclusive of postage, direct from the publishers, per year:
United Kingdom   £5·50
USA $17·50
Canada $17·50

Rates for other countries and for air mail subscriptions available on request from the Subscription Department at the above address.

CONTENTS

WRENDEZVOUS WITH WREN

". . . then after about five seconds you'll hear 'BOOM-BOOM.'"

AIRSCENE

MILITARY AFFAIRS

ABU DHABI

The **Abu Dhabi Air Force,** which provides the nucleus of the Air Force of the United Arab Emirates, is reported to be **actively considering** replacing its Hunter FGA 76s with the **Jaguar International** rather than pursuing earlier plans to establish a second Mirage III squadron when the Hunters are phased out (1978-79). During its recent Middle East sales tour, the Jaguar International was inspected by Sheikh Khalifa bin Zayed, C-in-C of the Abu Dhabian national defence forces, by the ADAF commander, Brig Gulaim Heider, and the ADAF Mirage squadron commander, Col Bukhari.

BELGIUM

During January, the *Force Aérienne Belge* retired its **last** two **Douglas C-47** transports at Coxyde, their place in the inventory of the 21ème Escadrille (15ème Wing de Transport et Communications) being taken by the Hawker Siddeley 748-2A. The C-47 first entered service with the 169ème Wing (precursor of the 15ème Wing) of the FAéB at the end of 1946, a total of 47 aircraft of this type eventually being received. As far as can be ascertained, the C-47s flew in excess of 100,000 hours during their 29 years of FAéB service.

Further details are available of the recent FBel 139m (£1·75m) order placed on behalf of the Army aviation component, the *Aviation Légère de la Force Terrestre* (ALFT), for 12 Britten-Norman **BN-2A Islanders** (see *Airscene*/January) as replacements for the Dornier Do 27s. To be powered by 300 hp Avco Lycoming IO-540-K1B5 engines, the Islanders, deliveries of which to the 15ème Escadrille at Brasschaat, near Antwerp, where scheduled to commence last month (March) with completion by the end of the year, will include four with provision for the installation of Vinten 360 survey cameras and three equipped for paratrooping.

CANADA

It has now been decided that when the Lockheed P-3 **Orion** enters service with the Canadian Armed Forces in the summer of 1979, it **will be known** as the **CP-3C Osprey.** The first of 18 aircraft of this type is scheduled for delivery in May 1979 with the final aircraft being delivered in February 1980.

EGYPT

The US government is anxious to obtain congressional approval for the sale to Egypt of an initial batch of six Lockheed C-130H **Hercules** transports **requested by the Egyptian Air Force.** Congressional discussions have begun on the possibility of ending the 20-year ban on US arms sales to Egypt with a view to bolstering the regime of President Sadat and replacing the Soviet Union as the principal supplier of arms to Egypt. The Egyptian government is known to be interested in the purchase of a wide range of US weapons, including General Dynamics F-16 fighters (see *Airscene*/January).

It has been reported that the British team of Ferranti and Smiths Industries has been selected to undertake a trial installation of an **inertial** weapons delivery and navigation **system in** an Egyptian Air Force **MiG-21.** The British team has been competing with the US Litton Industries and a French team of Thomson-CSF and Sagem (see *Airscene*/October) and if the installation proves technically successful, it is considered likely that the Egyptian Air Force will retrofit its entire fleet of approximately 200 MiG-21s and 100 Su-7s.

FINLAND

Reports in the Finnish press have mentioned negotiations between the Finnish and Swedish governments concerning the **possible acquisition of** a **further** nine ex-*Flygvapen* J 35F **Drakens,** plus support equipment such as simulators and additional spares, these being in addition to the six aircraft contracted for late last year (see *Airscene*/December) to replace a similar quantity of Saab 35BS Drakens that had been leased to *Ilmavoimat* as interim equipment. It has been suggested that the latter aircraft may now be retained in Finland as part of the additional procurement which may include two to three two-seat Draken trainers.

FRANCE

Pilots of the *Armée de l'Air* completed an **evaluation** in January **of** the ultra-light **Bede BD-5J** single-seater at Bretigny with a view to its adoption as a means of maintaining jet pilot efficiency at low cost. Powered by a 198 lb (90 kg) thrust Microturbo TRS 18-046 turbojet, the fourth pre-production BD-5J was employed for the evaluation. The BD-5J possesses a maximum level speed of approximately 285 knots (530 km/h) and a max roll rate approaching 400 deg per second and has an initial cost equivalent to that of a piston-engined primary trainer. Fuel and funding problems are currently restricting *Armée de l'Air* pilots to 15-18 hours per month, which is considered barely sufficient to maintain proficiency, and the BD-5J is claimed to be suitable for maintaining jet pilot proficiency for little more than five per cent of the hourly operating cost of a Mirage III.

IRAN

Gen Hassan Toufanian, the Iranian Vice-Minister for War, recently stated that, because of the rising costs of US weapon systems coupled with a decreasing demand for Iranian oil, his country **may be forced to cancel or cutback** orders for, or plans to purchase, a number of US **weapon systems,** including 160-300 General Dynamics' F-16 fighters currently under negotiation, 6-10 Boeing E-3A AWACS aircraft which are under discussion and 100 AMSTs (Advanced Medium STOL Transports) in which serious interest has been expressed. Unconfirmed reports at the time of closing for press were suggesting that the Iranian government was considering the shelving of the second batch of 40 F-14A Tomcats, but rumoured outright cancellation was considered unlikely.

ISRAEL

The **Israeli air arm,** *Heyl Ha'Avir*, has decided **to** refurbish and **modernise** its fleet of Fouga **Magister** jet trainers rather than procure a replacement. The work on the Magisters is to be undertaken by the Bedek Division of Israel Aircraft Industries and will include the updating of the electrical, hydraulic and avionics systems, and the installation of new cockpit instrumentation. This decision will delay the need to select a Magister successor until the mid 'eighties.

A decision has now been taken to fit all *Heyl Ha'Avir* F-4 **Phantoms with** a digital **inertial weapon-delivery system,** and proposal requests for the system have been sent to Litton Industries, Lear Siegler and Singer Kearfott. Litton's LW-33 and Singer Kearfott's SKN-2400 proposed retrofits for the Phantom have both already been tested in Israel, and Lear Siegler is expected to propose a variant of the ARN-101.

ITALY

The 15° *Stormo Soccorso Aerea* (Air Rescue) will shortly commence **re-equipping with** the Agusta-built **Sikorsky HH-3F,** the first two examples of which were scheduled to be delivered to the AMI during February, as a successor to the Grumman HU-16A Albatross amphibian. The AMI is to receive a total of 20 HH-3Fs with completion of deliveries by the end of 1977. In addition to these SAR versions of the AS-61, the AMI is receiving two AS-61A-4s for operation by the presidential flight of the *Reparto Volo Stato Maggiore.*

JAPAN

Planned **purchase of** the Lockheed P-3C **Orion** maritime patrol aircraft for use by the Maritime Self-Defence Force as an interim P-XL appeared at the time of closing for press to have been **"indefinately shelved"** as a result of the disclosure by the Lockheed Aircraft Corporation that it had paid $19m-$12m (£4·5m-£6·0m) to promote the sale of its aircraft in Japan. The MSDF had selected the P-3C Orion for use pending availability of an indigenous P-XL and had hoped to acquire 30-50 aircraft of this type with deliveries commencing mid-1978. Negotiations covered the purchase of six assembled Orions and nine assembly kits from the parent company plus a manufacturing license for the remaining aircraft. It is uncertain if a further evaluation will now be conducted of other contenders (eg, Hawker Siddeley Nimrod) or if greater impetus will be placed behind the development of an indigenous design, although there is no possibility that the Kawasaki P-XL project could now be developed and placed in production in time for deliveries to coincide with the commencement of the currently-planned P-2J phase-out (1982), and it is possible that production of this type may be extended.

The Air Self-Defence Force was scheduled to have formed its **first** Mitsubishi **T-2A-equipped** advanced training unit, the 21st Squadron (4th Air Wing) at Matsushima, by last month (March). Of the 63 T-2As (including four prototypes) so far ordered, 24 have been delivered and current schedules call for the delivery of 11 aircraft in the current Fiscal Year, a similar quantity during Fiscal 1977, 10 during Fiscal 1978 and seven during Fiscal 1979. The unit cost of the T-2A between Fiscal Years 1975 and 1976 has risen by 33·1 per cent, from £2·75m to £3·67m, the highest unit increase of any aircraft currently in production for the Self-Defence Forces.

Following the governmental decision to reduce the number of Mitsubishi FS-T2-KAI close-support aircraft to be procured in the 1976 Fiscal Year from 50 to eight, the Air Self-Defence Force has found it necessary to postpone the planned **retirement** of the **F-86F Sabre** for a further two years. At the present time, the ASDF has a total of 257 F-86F Sabres in its inventory, including mothballed aircraft, and these equip three close-support and two advanced training squadrons. Prior to the decision to stretch purchases of the FS-T2-KAI, it had been planned to phase out the last of the Sabre-equipped close-support squadrons in March 1980. The two Sabre-equipped advanced training squadrons are still scheduled to give place to T-2A-equipped units before 1978. Proposals to commence the conversion of some F-86Fs as QF-86F drones have been shelved for one year.

As at 31 December, the aircraft **inventory of** the **Self-Defence Forces** totalled 1,801 machines, this total comprising 989 aircraft with the Air Self-Defence Force, 347 aircraft with the Maritime Self-Defence Force, 458 aircraft with the Ground Self-Defence Force, six aircraft with the Defence Academy and one aircraft with the Technical Research and Development Institute.

MOROCCO

Deliveries of 12 **Agusta-Bell AB 205 helicopters** during 1974-75 (which followed 12 AB 205As delivered 1969-70) are now being supplemented by at least eight AB 206A JetRangers and five twin-turbine AB 212s for the Moroccan armed forces. A number of the Agusta-Bell helicopters have been used recently in support of Moroccan Army operations against the Algerian-supported Polisario Front independence movement in the former Spanish Sahara, one reportedly being lost and another damaged as a result of groundfire. Earlier, the Royal Maroc Air Force had lost a Northrop F-5A to an SA-7 surface-to-air missile while operating in support of Mauritanian ground forces and one of the service's C-130H Hercules transports had landed at El Aaiun after suffering damage from groundfire.

Although it was assumed that the recently-announced contract for Dassault-Breguet Mirage F1s (*Airscene*/March) superseded earlier Moroccan plans to purchase the Northrop **F-5E Tiger II** for the Royal Maroc Air Force *(Al Quwwat Aljawwiya Almalakiya Marakishiya)*, the Northrop Corporation has, at the invitation of the Moroccan government, submitted a fresh **letter of offer** covering reportedly up to 24 aircraft (presumably including at least four two-seat F-5Fs) at a total programme cost (ie, including training, support equipment, spares, etc) of approximately $120m (£60m). Should the letter of offer be accepted, it is understood that deliveries could commence during 1977 (ie, 18-24 months prior to planned commencement of Mirage F1 deliveries to Morocco).

PAKISTAN

The Pakistan Air Force was scheduled to receive the **third** of its ex-*Aéronavale* Br 1150 **Atlantic** maritime patrol aircraft **this month** (April) to complete the initial complement of No 29 Squadron. This unit was formed at Nimes-Garons on 17 November to work up with *Aéronavale* assistance, the first PAF Atlantic (No 33) having been handed over during the previous month. The second Atlantic (No 40) was delivered on 21 January, and with delivery of the third (No 46), No 29 Squadron has been declared operational.

Reports that Saab **Supporter** light utility aircraft fitted with gun pods and Bofors rockets have been **used** by the PAF in support of **operations against insurgents** in Baluchistan are said to be under investigation by the Swedish Foreign Office. The Pakistan government confirmed an order for 45 Supporters in June 1974, deliveries being completed last year when it was stated that the primary purpose of the Swedish light aircraft was the replacement of the aged T-6 Texans in the basic training rôle, although some Supporters were known to be going to the air component of the Pakistan Army to replace older Army Aviation Wing Cessna O-1 Bird Dogs which *are* known to have been used for ground support tasks in the past after modification by the Army Aviation Workshop at Dhamial. The Swedish government insists that Supporters have been supplied to Pakistan on the understanding that they would be used solely for the training rôle.

RHODESIA

Although there has as yet been no confirmation that a quantity of Aerospace **Airtrainer** CT-4s is in process of **delivery to the Rhodesian**

Air Force (see *The Airtrainer Story*/February), the New Zealand company has confirmed that 14 Airtrainers are in process of delivery to a Swiss-based concern known as the Breco Trading Company, ostensibly for a Swiss flying school, but reports persist that these aircraft are, in fact, destined for Rhodesia and are being completed to full military standard and incorporate wing hardpoints for external stores. The first Airtrainer was scheduled to be accepted in New Zealand by Breco Trading in February with the last being delivered in June.

Unofficial reports indicate that the **Rhodesian Air Force has received** an unspecified number of SA 330 **Puma and Alouette** III **helicopters** from the South African government. It is not known if these helicopters have been transferred from the inventory of the SAAF or represent a new purchase on behalf of the Rhodesian government.

SPAIN

Three of the six single-seat **Harriers** ordered on behalf of Spain's *Arma Aérea de la Armada Española* by the US Navy have now been **delivered** to McDonnell Douglas, which is responsible for the training of Spanish personnel, and the delivery of the first of two two-seat Harriers was imminent at the time of closing for press. The Harrier has been **renamed Matador** by the Spanish Navy, and the eight aircraft will remain in the USA until mid-year by which time the Matador-equipped squadron will have completed the initial working-up phase.

SWEDEN

On 13 February, the C-in-C *Flygvapnet*, Lt-Gen D Stenberg, announced that AJ 37 **Viggen-equipped** *Flygvapen* **squadrons** would **resume flying** from mid-March after having been grounded since 10 October following the loss of three aircraft through in-flight structural failures (11 July 1974 and 6 October 1975 at the *Flottilj* 7 at Såtenäs and on 10 October 1975 at *Flottilj* 15 at Söderhamn). The accident investigation commission stated that, in its opinion, the first two accidents had been caused by a failure of the mainspar in the port wing, close to the wing root, causing the wing to separate and resulting in the rapid disintegration of the aircraft in the air in conjunction with fire. The technical investigation of the third accident so far indicates a similar primary cause, namely wing fracture, but probably initiated by failure of the starboard mainspar. The aircraft involved in the third accident is currently lying in the Baltic at a depth of some 38 fathoms (70 m), salvage work having been interrupted by the winter and being scheduled to be resumed next spring (May). Recent ground testing of the stress distribution in the wing has revealed higher local stresses in the flanges of the mainspar than had been calculated, resulting in cracks in the inner forward bolt hole of the lower flange in the spar and progressive growth of these cracks leading to complete wing fracture. AJ 37 Viggens subsequent to the 27th aircraft were to be permitted to resume flying last month as these already incorporated stronger spars — a change that had been dictated by a *Flygvapen* requirement for extended service lifetime — in which no cracks have been found, although some restrictions were to be imposed on manœuvres. The spars of all Viggens prior to the 28th aircraft are to be replaced and work will commence on this task at Linköping this summer. Meanwhile, design work is continuing on a definitive modification aimed at completely eliminating the critical stress concentration in the lower flange of the mainspar and thus permitting the removal of all restrictions.

The **Chief of Air Staff**, Maj Gen Hans Neij, **has** recently **criticised** the **budgeting** of the

newly-launched military **five-year plan** as allowing insufficient funding to permit the full development of new aircraft that will be required for the 'nineties, including a specialised reconnaissance type, the planned A 20 ground attack derivative of the JA 37 Viggen interceptor, the projected System 85 new combat aircraft development of the Viggen and the new BLA light attack aircraft to succeed the Saab 105. Gen Neij also believes that the *Flygvapen* should receive 10 squadrons of JA 37 interceptors rather than the eight currently programmed, funds to accelerate the hardening of *Flygvapen* bases and control centres and sufficient funding for the procurement of Saab-Scania's new infra-red AAM.

TURKEY

At the beginning of March, the Defence Ministry announced that **agreement** had been reached with Federal Germany **for supply** to the Turkish Air Force **of** 60-65 **Alpha Jets** to replace current training equipment. Some components of the Alpha Jets are to be manufactured by the TUSAS factory, which is to be established in the Konya province, this factory also being responsible for final assembly of the trainers. The Air Metal AM-C 111 Srs 200SP and 400SP STOL transports, which are also to be built for the Turkish Air Force (as the TC-111) are to be manufactured at a non-TUSAS factory at Kayseri.

Approximately 20 F-104G **Starfighters** surplus to *Aeronautica Militare* requirements were **transferred from Italy** to Turkey in February.

UNITED KINGDOM

The **last** Fairey **Gannet** AEW Mk 3 airborne early warning aircraft to be **refurbished** and modernised for the Royal Navy by Westland Helicopters was handed over to No 849 Squadron on 12 February. The Gannet AEW 3, which has now seen 17 years of RN service, is currently scheduled to remain in service until well into the 'eighties.

It is understood that No 53 Squadron, RAF Strike Command, is to be disbanded in November and its Short **Belfast** C Mk 1 **transports retired**. The Belfast, which it may be presumed will be scrapped, first entered service with No 53 Sqdn 10 years ago, in January 1966, all 10 examples of the type built being delivered to this unit. With the withdrawal of the Belfast outsize and heavy loads will have to be transported by the Hercules.

USA

The Lockheed S-3A **Viking** made its operational **début with** the **Pacific Fleet** in January when nine pilots of VS-29 completed carrier qualifications in the S-3A aboard the USS **Enterprise** during three days of operations off the Southern California coast. VS-29 is scheduled to take the S-3A on its first western Pacific deployment early this summer aboard the *Enterprise*.

Procurement of the first 16 **production General Dynamics F-16A** lightweight fighters will be **funded** from Defense Department appropriations for FY77, subject to Congressional approval. A total of $619·7 (£310m) is requested, including $259·1m (£130m) for RDT&E (Research, Development, Test and Evaluation), $311·2m (£105·5m) for the production aircraft and $49·4m (£24·5m) for initial spares. Previously, $286m (£143m) has been appropriated in FY76 and the Transitional budget to continue RDT&E on the F-16, including construction of 11 F-16A and four two-seat F-16B test aircraft. Future procurement is planned at the rate of 89 in FY78, 145 in FY79, 175 in FY80 and 180 in FY81. This would leave 45 to be bought in FY82 if the total USAF buy remains at the intended total of 650. The four-nation NATO consortium has ordered 306 F-16s with options for 42 more.

Introduction of a **follow-on interceptor** (FOI) **for** the Convair F-106s of USAF's **Air Defense Command** is expected in the early 1980s, and it is currently intended that the FOI will be a version of the Grumman F-14, the McDonnell Douglas F-15 or General Dynamics F-16. Until introduction of the FOI, Air Defence Command will be equipped with 12 squadrons (six active and six ANG) of F-106s, deployed at alert sites around the periphery of the 48 contiguous states; additional defence forces will be provided by tactical air squadrons of F-4s (including one ANG F-4 squadron). A regular F-4 squadron is committed to the air defence mission in Alaska, and an ANG air defence squadron is equipped with F-4s in Hawaii. The last ANG F-101s will be phased out by September 1977, but withdrawal of ADC's airborne radar force of EC-121s is being delayed, pending introduction of E-3As, and ten EC-121s will now be retained for coverage of the North Atlantic region through FY78.

Department of Defense has included $45m (£22m) in FY77 budget proposals for the **development of** an **Advanced Tanker Cargo Aircraft** (ATCA), primarily to be used by USAF as a tanker, both for cargo-carrying C-5As and C-141As and for the inter-theatre deployment of tactical aircraft. The current programme provides for air-refuelling design studies to be made of three commercial wide body transports (the Boeing 747, McDonnell Douglas DC-10 and Lockheed L-1011) followed by selection of one for initial procurement in FY78, in which year it is currently proposed to allocate $354m (£176m) for the ATCA. Total procurement will be about 50, and the Boeing 747 is believed to be the leading candidate.

Changes in future **procurement plans for** various types of **US Navy aircraft** announced by the Defense Department in connection with the FY77 budget request include the addition of 13 F-14As to the total buy, making 403 in all with final procurement in FY81; an increase from 49 to 67 in the total of E-2C Hawkeyes to be bought, at the rate of six a year until 1980; procurement of a total of 90 EA-6B Prowlers to include 15 for a Marine Corps squadron; completion of A-4M Skyhawk procurement for the Marine Corps with quantities of 21 in FY77 and 12 in FY78; modification of 30 Marine Corps RF-4Bs to extend their service life by about 96 months and to update selected avionics/sensor equipment and, finally, an increase in total A-7E procurement from 666 to 692, at a rate of 30 a year until FY81 to equip 24 light attack squadrons, with new production A-7Es equipped for FLIR and modification of 49 earlier Corsair IIs to RA-7E reconnaissance versions beginning in FY78.

To meet its outstanding **VTAMX** requirement for an **advanced multi-engine trainer** to replace Grumman TS-2As, the US Navy is evaluating six submissions, comprising the Beech H90 and G90 King Air models, the Beech C-12, Piper Cheyenne, Cessna Citation and Rockwell Turbo Commander 690A. The requirement is for a commercially available FAA-certificated twin-turbine aircraft in the 10,000 lb (4 540 kg) class, with modern avionics and crew of five. It will be used to train student pilots for land-based patrol and transport aircraft, covering multi-engine operations, day/night familiarisation, advance instrument flying, formation flying and tactical orientation. $14m (about £7m) is included for 18 aircraft in the FY76 and Transition budgets and $15.3 (£7.6m) is requested in FY77 to complete the purchase of a further 20 examples.

AIRCRAFT AND INDUSTRY

AUSTRALIA
The GAF **Nomad N24,** a stretched-fuselage version of the basic Nomad N22B, entered **flight testing** at Fishermen's Bend in January. The aircraft in question is a production model and one of six recently ordered by the Northern Territory Medical Service (NTMS); deliveries will start in mid-year. The N24 has a 6-ft (1,5-m) stretch in the fuselage to increase passenger seating from 12 to 16 at the same 30-in (76-cm) pitch. Additional baggage space is provided by lengthening the nose to increase locker volume by 43 per cent. The standard Nomad N22B has meanwhile entered commercial service in Australia with Aero Pelican, a commuter operator.

BRAZIL
The **EMB-110P** version of the EMBRAER **Bandeirante,** which has recently **entered service** with TABA (see *"Civil Contracts and Sales"*/March 1976) has been developed specifically to meet the needs of Brazilian regional airlines. Fuel has been traded for payload over short ranges, the cabin being re-arranged to accommodate 18 passengers in six rows, with double seats to the right of a 10.25-in (26-cm) wide aisle. Seat pitch is 30.5 in (77,5 cm), the double seats are 33.1 in (84 cm) wide and the single seats to left of the aisle are 17.3 in (44 cm) wide. The EMB-110P has increased baggage capacity at the rear of the cabin, and PT6A-34 engines are used in place of the standard -27 version in order to provide higher rates of climb and high cruising speeds at lower altitudes. TABA (Transportes Aereos de Bacia Amazonica SA) has ordered five EMB-110Ps with an option on ten more.

CANADA
The **Airtransit** STOL demonstration **service** between Ottawa and Montreal, using six specially-equipped DHC Twin Otters is **to end** in April, some four months earlier than planned. Although losses were inevitable because of the small passenger capacity of the Twin Otter, they have been running at a higher level than predicted; however, the trial which began in July 1974 is considered in general to have been successful and has provided valuable information on which future STOL planning can be based.

FEDERAL GERMANY
Details have been given by Dornier of the programme to design and test a **supercritical wing on** one of the **Alpha Jet** prototypes, under a government contract placed in July 1974. Sharing in the programme are VFW-Fokker and ONERA, the latter largely at its own expense. The test-bed will retain standard Alpha Jet fuselage and tail unit, and will have the new wing built up around the original torsion box. The plan form will remain unchanged but the leading edge will be extended forwards at the wing-fuselage junction to improve the area distribution, and manoeuvring flaps will be added on the leading and trailing edges, in the latter case replacing the Alpha Jet's landing flaps. The manoeuvring flaps will be ground-adjustable only, to avoid the cost of installing a new system in the airframe; the Alpha Jet has already demonstrated that it can take-off and land without use of flaps. The wing itself is of increased thickness/chord ratio, 12 per cent instead of 10 per cent, and the use of a supercritical aerofoil is expected to contribute to increased manoeuvrability by postponing buffet onset, whilst the new flaps will give an improvement in the steady-state manoeuvring performance at lower Mach numbers. Wind-tunnel testing of the new wing has begun in the DFVLR low-speed tunnel and in ONERA's high-speed S2 tunnel at Modane, and a full-scale half-wing will be tested in ONERA's S1 tunnel later.

FRANCE
Among the current projects of the Helicopter Division of **Aérospatiale** is an **armed helicopter** (HAF — *Helicoptère Armé Français*) to meet requirements of the French Army. Several years ago, interest centred on a version of the Lynx with a new fuselage seating two in tandem, but this was abandoned at an early stage of development. The current proposal is for a helicopter of about 7,700 lb (3 500 kg) gross weight, using the dynamic components of the SA-365 Dauphin, with fly-by-wire controls and mechanical back-up, and a mini control column for the observer to use in an emergency. Probably seating two in tandem, the HAF will carry a fixed armament of one 20-mm or 30-mm cannon plus up to six HOT anti-tank missiles.

A simplified version of the Robin HR 100 made its **first flight** at Dijon on 3 February. Known as the **HR 100-180,** it has a fixed undercarriage, 180 hp Lycoming engine and a simplified and lightened airframe to reduce manufacturing time and, therefore, cost.

INTERNATIONAL
Cost proposals for offset production of the General Dynamics **F-16 fighter** — particularly in Belgium — are placing the four-nation NATO consortium procurement **programme in jeopardy.** The US called for unit price quotations based on reasonable competitiveness but cost proposals are proving substantially higher than had been anticipated. In Belgium, M Vandestrick, director-general of the Fabrique Nationale which is to produce the F100 engines for the F-16, has stated recently on Belgian radio that, as a result of recent pay increases in Belgian industry, the problem of cost escalation is extremely serious and its resolution is urgent. The FN concern also needs considerable investment, notably for the construction of new production facilities, before it can fully participate in the F-16 programme, and other Belgian companies such as Fairey and SABCA, are similarly affected. A US Defense Department official recently commented: "The Europeans are increasingly non-competitive and seem unable to sustain a production rate allowing them to compete with US aerospace firms. It is almost across the board — just pick a proposal on an F-16 component and look at the price for co-production." General Dynamics said that it and the United Technologies Corporation have no doubts that contractual obligations *can* be met with the four countries concerned. Belgian Defence Minister Paul Van Den Boeynants commented that he expects the US to meet its production offset agreements for the F-16 before he signs the definitive procurement contract!

ISRAEL
The **US** President has tentatively **refused** requests by the Israeli government for General Dynamics **F-16** fighter **production subcontracts.** During recent Washington meetings between President Ford and Israeli Prime Minister Yitzak Rabin, the request was tendered on the basis that, as Israel is scheduled to receive the F-16 in substantial numbers under credit arrangements, major sub-components of the fighter should be manufactured by IAI. However, the US Defence Department has opposed the request on the grounds that it would include a further transfer of advanced technology to Israel which has used past US technology infusions to compete effectively against US military and commercial hardware on the export market. However, in a related move, consideration is being given to determining if IAI has the facilities and expertise for the overhaul of Mediterranean 6th Fleet F-4 Phantoms and A-4 Skyhawks as a means of partially offsetting Israeli military hardware purchases from the US.

Despite continual and major devaluation of the Israeli pound, **Israel Aircraft Industries** reported a **record turnover** in Fiscal 1975 showing a dramatic increase of nearly 50 per cent on the previous year with a 66 per cent increase in net profit. Arava production is continuing at a rate of three per month to meet announced orders totalling 50 aircraft of which 30 had been delivered by the beginning of March. The first production Eleven 24 Westwind execujet is due off the assembly line next month (May) and IAI has high hopes of export prospects for the Kfir fighter, now being offered at a unit cost of only £2·25m. The Kfir is reportedly coming off the IAI assembly line at a rate of about four per month and relatively early deliveries are allegedly being offered, Peru and Venezuela among several Latin American countries reportedly showing particular interest. IAI anticipates that export sales of the Kfir will run at 12-15 annually for at least six years.

JAPAN
In addition to continued development of the basic FA-300 (see *Airscene*/March), Fuji is now working on a **turboprop-driven** variant of the basic design, the **FA-300-KAI**, designated Commander 710 by Rockwell International. Although no details of the FA-300-KAI alias Commander 710 have yet been revealed, it is known that it will feature a substantial increase in fuel capacity by comparison with the basic FA-300 and it is anticipated that a prototype will commence its test programme late this year or early 1977.

Flight testing is expected to commence this month (April) of the **water bomber version** of the Shinmeiwa PS-1 flying boat. The first prototype of the PS-1 maritime patrol aircraft has been converted to the water bombing rôle to the orders of the National Fire Protection Board to which the flying boat is expected to be delivered in July.

UNITED KINGDOM
Flight testing of the **first production** Westland/Aérospatiale **Lynx** began at Yeovil on 10 February. The aircraft concerned is an HAS Mk 2 for the Royal Navy (serial XZ227) and some 10 flights were made in the first few days of testing. Aircraft for the Army (Lynx AH Mk 1) and Netherlands Navy are included in the first 10 production positions and deliveries to all three are expected to begin later this year. A full account of the Lynx programme to date begins on page 163 of this issue.

Certification of the **Short SD3-30** (see previous issue) was completed on 18 February, on which date the CAA awarded the type its type certificate.

USA
The Fairchild Republic Company has now delivered the six Development, Test and Evaluation A-10 attack aircraft to the USAF as well as the first six production **A-10s** which will be deployed **to the 355th Tactical Fighter Wing** at Davis-Monthan AFB, Arizona, later this year. Current schedules call for 16 production A-10s to be delivered to the USAF during 1976, with production tempo rising from one to two aircraft per month by the year's end. The A-10 programme is showing the second largest proportional cost increase of 41 current US weapon systems, having risen by nearly $800m (£400m) to $4,200m (£2,100m), or a unit cost of $5·7m (£2·85m) as compared with $4·58m (£2·29m) when spread over the 10 pre-series and proposed 733 production aircraft. Apart from inflation, which accounts for more than five-eighths of the increase, the principal reason for the rise in programme cost is the decision to reduce the peak production tempo of the A-10 from 20 to 15 aircraft monthly. Both gun and airframe

weights have risen, take-off and landing performance has not met specification, restricting the number of frontline fields that can be used by the A-10, and time-over-target is less than that called for, but speeds are higher than predicted and a higher standard of accuracy in bombing and gunfiring is being achieved than was anticipated.

The McDonnell Douglas F-15 **Eagle will be able to carry** the 30-mm rotary-barrel General Electric **GAU-8/A** cannon for ground attack in the wing root in place of the current General Electric M61, in a centreline pod or in the conformal fuselage pallets. If the wing root position is adopted, the GAU-8/A's linear ammunition feed will be changed to belt feed in order to utilise the existing ammunition bays.

At the time of closing for press, the **third** prototype Rockwell International **B-1**, which was rolled out at Palmdale on 16 January and will be the second prototype to fly, was **scheduled to commence** its flight **test programme** on **26 March.** This B-1 is the first example to have a complete offensive avionics system, including the operator's station in the rear cockpit. The static structural test programme conducted with the second prototype has now been completed and the aircraft will be rolled out shortly for 25 June flight testing. Flight testing of the fourth B-1 prototype — the defensive avionics testbed — is expected to commence early 1979. A production decision is still anticipated for November, the first three production aircraft being covered by the $1,000m (£500m) procurement request in the Fiscal 1977 defence budget. Current planning calls for two of the three initial production B-1s to be delivered in 1979 with the third in 1980, the projected Fiscal 1978 request containing long-leadtime money for eight more B-1s, all being delivered in 1980. Subsequent production is expected to comprise 14-16 in 1981 and 48 in 1982 when the full four-per-month production rate is expected to be attained. However, recent USAF statistics reveal that the cost of the planned 244-aircraft programme has risen by $3,000m (£1,500m), or 16 per cent, over the 15 months ended 31 December, to $21,500m (£10,750m) — more than $88m (£44m) per aircraft. Cost estimated have thus increased by almost 120 per cent since the programme was launched in 1970, although Pentagon officials insist that the programme costs have risen only 12 per cent in terms of uninflated 1970 dollars. Furthermore, in an effort to keep costs within bounds, the USAF has increased the B-1's weight by substituting aluminium for titanium, thus adding 1,000 ft (305 m) to the take-off distance and reducing maximum operational altitude by 4,000-5,000 ft (1 200-1 525 m) and has downgraded other aspects of the bomber's performance by simplification in order to reduce cost escalation.

The Improved AH-1J **SeaCobra** for the US Marine Corps (*AirScene*/August 1975) has now been **designated AH-1T**, as briefly noted last month. A total of 57 will be procured, including 23 requested in the FY77 budget at a cost of $64·2m (£32m) including spares, and a final eight to be bought in FY78. Of the total, 33 will be modified structurally and outfitted so that a TOW missile kit can be easily installed at maintenance depots, and 24 will be fully TOW equipped from the start.

USAF has assigned the designation **F-4G** to the **Wild Weasel conversion** of the F-4E **Phantom** to be used for defence suppression (*AirScene*/May 1975). Expected to become operational in FY78, the F-4G will carry standard Phantom countermeasures equipment (warning sensors, jamming pods and chaff dispensers) plus DF antennas, computer-controlled receivers, signal activity monitors

and SAM-launch warning devices; it will also carry anti-radiation missiles such as Standard ARM, Shrike and Harm, as well as conventional ordnance and guided bombs. Modification of 116 F-4Es to F-4Gs is planned over a three-year period, to equip four squadrons (at present flying F-105Gs and EF-4Cs). The F-4G designation was previously used for 12 modified US Navy F-4Bs equipped with ASW-21 data link systems but no longer in service.

USAF has been testing an **armed Northrop T-38 Talon** since last July at Edwards AFB, with a view to using the type for preliminary weapons training at Tactical Air Command's 465th TF Training Squadron (TFTS) at Holloman AFB, NM. Known as the AT-38 Lead-in Fighter (LIF), the modified aircraft carriers a 7,62-mm minigun pod or bomb-launcher on the aircraft centreline. The modification was evolved at the USAF's San Antonio Air Logistics Center and will be applied to all TFTS T-38s if judged successful, releasing operational fighters at present used in the training rôle.

Two **more LC-130R Hercules** are being acquired from Lockheed Georgia by the National Science Foundation, which previously has bought three of the ski-equipped versions for use in the Antarctic (*Airscene*/February 1974). To be delivered in May and June, the new aircraft are replacements for Hercules of Navy squadron VXE-6 lost in non-fatal accidents last year.

Full FAA **certification of** the **Boeing 747SP** was awarded on 4 February, just seven months after first flight. Three examples logged 544½ hrs on 340 flights in the test programme and 17 are now on order for five airlines. Pan American now proposes to inaugurate 747SP service on 25 April — or perhaps even earlier — and will operate daily Los Angeles-Tokyo service plus thrice-weekly New York-Tokyo non-stop flights. Change of date has been made to preserve Pan Am's priority over Iran Air, which plans to introduce the 747SP on its New York-Teheran service once a week by the end of April.

Boeing has won a NASA **contract** worth $20m (£10m) **to build** a **Quiet Short-haul Research Airplane** (QSRA), following a design competition between the company and Lockheed. The QSRA, which will fly in 1979, will comprise the fuselage of a de Havilland Canada C-8A Buffalo with a T-tail unit similar to that used on the augmentor wing research aircraft (also a modified Buffalo) plus a new high aspect ratio wing incorporating supercritical technology and Boeing's upper surface blowing propulsive lift system, as developed for the YC-14 AMST prototypes. Power will be supplied by four overwing Lycoming YF-102 turbofans originally used in the Northrop YA-10 AX prototypes. The QSRA will be delivered to NASA Ames Research Center at Moffett Field, California, where it will join two Bell XV-15s and the augmentor-wing Buffalo in a research programme to provide information on efficient, environmentally-acceptable short-haul transport systems.

Boeing Vertol announced completion of the **flight test programme for** the **YUH-61A** UTTAS helicopter on 31 January, when aircraft 003 completed final structural demonstration manoeuvres. Included in the demonstration were power-on and power-off pull-ups to 3·05g; rolling pull-out to 2·8g; push-overs to −0·6g and a maximum diving speed of 199 knots (368 km/h). Aircraft 002 and 003 entered a refurbishing programme at Calverton (where the YUH-61A has been under test using Grumman facilities) during February, and 001 was rolled out on 9 February after repair (*Airscene*/March 1976). The ground test vehicle was continuing in use at Calverton until the end of March and by 31 January had accumulated 850 hrs of MQT (Military Qualification Testing) time and 1,127 rotor hours.

With first flight now scheduled for early 1977, the **Sikorsky S-76** twin-turbine 14-seat helicopter is attracting much attention and the company announced that it had received 73 firm, deposit-backed **orders** from 19 customers by early this year. Four prototypes are to be built, to be used for a 700-hr flight test programme to achieve certification for two-pilot IFR operation by July 1978, when customer deliveries will begin. Among the major orders placed for the S-76 so far are those from Okanagan Helicopters, Vancouver, for 10; Tropical Airways, the Philippines, 10; Island Helicopters, NY, 7; Helitrans, Queensland, six and Royal Jordanian Air Force, four; other orders are for quantities of one-three each.

Bell Helicopter Textron has begun **deliveries of the Model 214B Big Lifter,** following FAA certification on 27 January. The first delivery was made to Rocky Mountain Helicopters of Utah and production is continuing at a rate of about two a month. Meanwhile, Bell expected to make the first flight of its Model 222 in April, with five prototypes to be used for test and demonstration prior to certification in 1978.

McDonnell Douglas has set up a new modification **programme** at its Tulsa plant **to convert** passenger-configured **DC-8s** into freighters. Installation of improved engines can be included in the conversion packages and the first two aircraft to be modified are ex-Alitalia DC-8 Srs 43s which will have their Conway engines replaced by JT3Ds, thus making them Srs 50 aircraft. The cargo modification encompasses removal of all passenger-oriented equipment, fitting a seven-track cargo floor and replacing cabin windows with metal plugs. A main-deck cargo door measuring 140 in by 85 in (3,56 m by 21,60 m) is installed, plus a nine *g* production cargo barrier net, a cabin interior cargo liner and a smoke detection system. The first modified aircraft will be redelivered to Frederick B Ayer and Associates in September with the second following six weeks later. Down-time for the complete cargo modification (with or without engine change) is 13 weeks, or 8 weeks for the engine change alone.

McDonnell Douglas is inviting **British companies to bid for work on** electronic systems for **the F-18,** in competition with qualified contractors in the USA and Canada. Starting in March, requests for proposals for nine avionics systems are being issued this year, comprising the flight control electronics set, multi-mode radar (for which only Hughes and Westinghouse are in competition), inertial navigation set, air data computer, direction finder, horizontal situation indicator, magnetic azimuth detector and maintenance data recording set. During 1977, proposals will be requested for the FLIR pod, laser spot tracker pod, strike camera and horizontal situation display.

CIVIL AFFAIRS

FRANCE
Touraine Air Transport, the second customer for the **VFW-614,** took **delivery** of its first aircraft on 4 February; this was the fifth aircraft to fly and production number G-06. There are three prototypes, and G-04 was the first production example, now in service with Cimber Air. Future deliveries will include G-05 for Air Alsace, G-07 for TAT and G-08 for Cimber Air. Services with TAT were to begin in April, initially with German registrations (D-BABF and D-BABG) pending French certification.

UNITED KINGDOM
A White Paper on **civil aviation policy** was published on 11 February, giving more details of the policy outlined by Secretary of State for Trade Peter Shore last July (*Airscene*/October). In pursuance of the "spheres of interest" policy, whereby there will be no direct competition between British airlines on specific routes, British Airways and British Caledonian have had detailed discussions concerning a limited exchange of routes. British Airways will be the sole UK operator to North America (with the exception of Atlanta and Houston), and to East Africa and the Seychelles, while British Caledonian will be the sole operator to South America, West and Central Africa and to Atlanta and Houston. This means that the latter will cease to operate in competition with British Airways to East Africa and the Seychelles, and licences to operate services to New York, Los Angeles, Boston, Toronto and Singapore via Bahrain (none of which it is operating at present) will be withdrawn. British Caledonian will end its exempt charter service to Singapore, but will retain the right to serve Atlanta and Houston when such a route is licensed. In Africa, British Airways will relinquish its routes to Central Africa including Zambia and in South America it will relinquish its services to Venezuela, Colombia and Peru to British Caledonian. Under the policy of designating only one carrier for a given route, the proposed Laker Skytrain service will not be permitted and Laker Airways license as a scheduled operator will be cancelled. An exception to the "spheres of influence" policy is made for Concorde, which British Airways is expected to be allowed to fly on any route that is commercially attractive; this could mean operations alongside British Caledonian subsonic services to South America or Africa, in which case, says the White Paper, "arrangements would have to be made to alleviate adverse effects on British Caledonian". The proposals contained in the White Paper require the approval of both Houses of Parliament before they can become law.

CIVIL CONTRACTS AND SALES

Aérospatiale Caravelle: Sterling has leased two 10Rs to Finnair and one to Sterling Philippine Airways, with a second probably to go to the latter later this year. Starline of Naples, a new Italian charter company in which Sterling has a one-third share, has one Caravelle VIR from Sterling, with a second to follow.

Aérospatiale Corvette: Air Service International, based at Perpignan, has been operating one Corvette (No 16) since January.

BAC VC10: Cuba is negotiating to purchase the four Super VC10s offered for sale by East African Airways. It is believed they will be used for long-range freighting, possibly by the Cuban Air Force rather than Cubana.

Boeing 707: Signal Hill Airlines of Los Angeles have acquired one 707-320, ex Air Vietnam. ☐ Royal Air Maroc is buying two from Northwest Airlines.

Boeing 727: Mexicana leased two -200s from Tiger Leasing Group, to bring fleet to 14, plus seven -100s. ☐ Hapag-Lloyd bought a second -100 from Toa Domestic.

Boeing 737: Air Zaïre has leased one -200 from Guiness Peat Aviation, for crew training conducted by Aer Lingus; aircraft was originally in service with All Nippon Airways.

Boeing 747: China Airlines ordered one 747SP, becoming the fifth customer for the type. Delivery will be in April 1977, with an

option on others for 1978 delivery. The airline is also purchasing a standard 747 that has been on lease from Boeing since last June. ☐ Qantas has ordered its 12th 747B.

Bristol Britannia: Inter-European, a Portuguese charter operator, is among the companies that have purchased ex-RAF Britannias, known as Model 253F in civil guise. All 22 ex-RAF aircraft have received civil certification.

Convair 580: Three of these turboprop twins have been leased from Allegheny by Great Lakes Airlines of Sarnia, Ontario.

Douglas DC-3: Federal Express, which has a fleet of 32 Dassault Falcon 20s for small-package freight services, bought seven DC-3s recently. Aircraft were required for planned expansion of routes after CAB refused to allow acquisition of five DC-9s.

Fokker F27: Somali Airlines is reported to have acquired two Mk 600s to replace Viscounts and DC-3s.

Lockheed TriStar: Saudia has purchased two from TWA; the aircraft are new and undelivered and will be modified to Saudia requirements before delivery. It is not clear whether they are additional to, or part of, Saudia's previous order for four. ☐ Cathay Pacific has cancelled options on two.

MBB BO 105: The Dutch State Police Service (*Rijkspolitie*) will inaugurate a helicopter unit with two IFR-equipped BO 105s to be delivered mid-year.

McDonnell Douglas DC-8: IAS Cargo Airlines, the first UK operator of the DC-8, has bought a Srs 43 from Zambia Airways.

McDonnell Douglas DC-9: Balair, Swiss charter airline, ordered one extended-range DC-9 Srs 30 with 115 seats, 16,000 lb st (7 248 kgp) JT8D-17 engines and two fuel tanks under the floor to supplement normal wing tankage, giving a range of about 2,300 mls (3 700 km) with full passenger load or 2,500 mls (4 023 km) with reduced load.

MILITARY CONTRACTS

Agusta-Bell AB 206A JetRanger: Deliveries were recently begun of eight-plus AB 206A helicopters for the Moroccan armed forces.

Agusta-Bell AB 212 Twin Two-Twelve: One AB 212 in VIP configuration has been ordered for operation by the Sultan of Oman's Air Force. ☐ The Peruvian Navy has reportedly placed an order for 8-10 AB 212ASW anti-submarine warfare helicopters. ☐ One AB 212 helicopter has been delivered to the Union of Arab Emirates Air Wing.

Bell 214C: On 13 February, Bell Helicopter Textron announced receipt of a contract from the Iranian government to the value of $21,789,060 (£10·894m) for 39 Model 214C helicopters for the Iranian Imperial Air Force. To be delivered between November 1976 and February 1978, the Model 214C is essentially similar to the 214A (287 examples of which are in process of delivery to Iran) but embodies modifications to suit it for the search-and-rescue mission.

Canadair CL-215: The Algerian Air Force is reported to have taken delivery of two CL-215 amphibians for coastal patrol and SAR tasks.

Shorts Skyvan 3M: Two Skyvan 3M utility transports have been delivered to the Mauritanian Islamic Air Force against an unannounced order.

THE LYNX LEAPS AHEAD

WITH initial production aircraft now off the Yeovil assembly line and in the hands of the flight-test department; with more than 2,500 hrs completed on the development-batch aircraft covering all basic test work; with aircraft for three different customers included in the first batch of 10 production aircraft; with 147 examples on firm order for six customers and with sales negotiations continuing in respect of substantial additional quantities, the Westland/Aérospatiale Lynx is now entering the third and most important phase in its history to date. The second phase, which in effect was brought to its conclusion at the end of 1975, comprised the construction and flight testing of a baker's dozen of airframes of assorted configuration, leading to the design definition of versions for the Royal Navy, British Army and French *Aéronavale*, and a basis for the marketing of improved models for future delivery. Phase 1 of Lynx development comprised the evolution of the original design itself in the period from 1960 to 1966, and its selection as one of the three helicopters included in the Anglo-French helicopter package agreement initialled on 22 February 1967 (see "Lynx — Yeovil's Revolutionary Yearling", Vol 2 No 6, June 1972).

Under the terms of the Anglo-French agreement, Britain was to be responsible for 65 per cent of the Lynx programme and would run the single assembly line for both British and French versions, the combined requirement for which was eventually estimated to total 300 examples. Devaluation of both the franc and the pound sterling since 1967, the effects of inflation and changing relative values of the two currencies, and a reduction in the total French requirement for Lynx have complicated the work-division arrangements in detail, but the importance of the Lynx to Westland — and therefore to the British aerospace industry — as design and production leader, is obvious. The Lynx is not only the first helicopter of original Westland design to reach production, but also incorporates a number of innovations including conformal gears, a semi-rigid rotor head and rotor blades comprising stainless steel spars with reinforced

plastic trailing edges. It is also the initial and so far only application for the Rolls-Royce/Turboméca Gem, the first small turbine engine developed in Britain for more than a decade.

In summary, the flight test phase on 13 development Lynx airframes — backed up by work on a ground test rig and static and fatigue specimens — has cleared the basic airframe for operations up to the initial gross weight of 9,500 lb (4 313 kg) plus those aspects of operational equipment that are currently defined for the Royal Navy, *Aéronavale* and British Army versions. Development of the communications and navigation equipment is complete and a preliminary assessment has been made at the increased all-up weight of 10,500 lb (4 767 kg), required for some of the aircraft already on order for the Royal Netherlands Navy. Westland has completed all the necessary work to demonstrate the capability of the Lynx HAS Mk 2 to carry Mk 44 or Mk 46 torpedoes and the BAC Sea Skua, dummy examples of the latter having been dropped. On the *Aéronavale* version, work in connection with the Mk 44 and L6 torpedoes has been completed, and AS 12 firing trials have been made at Cazeaux. Work is proceeding to show compatability with such Army weapons as HOT and TOW, pending an official decision on the anti-tank missile to be adopted by the British Army in place of Hawkswing.

As shown in the accompanying tabulation, the Lynx development batch embraces four principal configurations of the helicopter (ignoring minor variations that have occurred as a result of flight testing and normal design development). These comprise the so-called "basic" variant, which does not represent any specific customer version but has a representative airframe and the power plant/transmission/rotor system that is common to all variants; the "multi-rôle" variant that is representative of the Lynx AH Mk 1 for the British Army; and the two naval variants, representing the Lynx HAS Mk 2 for the Royal Navy and the *Aéronavale* Lynx. The basic and utility versions both have a skid undercarriage for land operations, with provision for the attachment of adjustable ground handling wheels; the naval variants, by contrast, have a fixed tricycle-type landing gear with oleo legs providing high absorption rates.

Differences between the RN and *Aéronavale* versions are concerned with the different rôles specified by the two services. Although both will operate the Lynx in an anti-submarine rôle from small ships, *Aéronavale* wanted Alcatel dipping sonar to be carried, requiring airframe modifications to provide a hole in the cabin floor, and the provision of an "automatic transition to hover" mode and a "transparency" facility in the AFCS, the latter being the ability to recognise and allow for pilot inputs. Neither of these features of the AFCS were required by the Royal Navy; the latter, on the other hand, has opted for a more sophisticated search radar — the Ferranti Sea Spray — while the *Aéronavale* Lynx has the simpler OMERA-Sigid Herecles ORB 31 W modular X-band radar.* There are also differences in the weapons specified to be carried by the two naval versions and although these involve only relatively simple adaptations of the weapons carriers on each side of the fuselage, this adds to the flight development task of checking compatability and conducting launching trials.

Export models of the Lynx represent further variants that require clearance as they become available. The initial export variants are those ordered by the Royal Netherlands Navy and the Brazilian Navy. The latter have been specified primarily for the submarine strike rôle and are expected to be of a similar configuration to the Lynx HAS Mk 2, with air-sea rescue and general fleet duties as subsidiary rôles. The Dutch requirement includes search and rescue, communications and training, as well as ASW duties, and the orders so far cover two versions — anti-submarine and SAR. The latter rôle requires a substantially different equipment fit, including a rescue hoist and the provision of cabin fittings suitable for the reception and treatment of casualties. The Dutch ASW requirement has served as the catalyst in Westland's plans to develop the Lynx for higher gross weights and as already noted the new weight will be 10,500 lb (4 767 kg), compared with 9,500 lb (4 313 kg) for

the initial production aircraft for the RN and *Aéronavale*, and 8,700 lb (3 950 kg) for the Army utility Lynx. The higher weight has already been demonstrated in flight but uprated engines are required for the helicopter's full performance potential to be developed at this weight, and the 1,050 hp Gem 4 is being developed for this and other applications by 1979.

The Royal Netherlands Navy contract initially covers six SAR Lynx at the 9,500 lb (4 313 kg) weight, the first two of which are included early in the production sequence at Yeovil, and two ASW models at the higher weight; an option on eight more ASWs has recently been taken up. The Brazilian order is for nine, to operate from *Niteroi*-class frigates and at the São Pedro naval air base. British and French contracts are being placed in batches as funds become available in successive defence budgets and by the beginning of 1976, the totals of complete helicopters on firm order were 63 for the British Army, 30 for the Royal Navy and 26 for *Aéronavale*; included in the Army total are 13 aircraft that were originally to have been produced as Lynx HT 3 trainers for the RAF, but were cancelled in this form in the 1975 defence cuts. Forward material orders have already been authorised for another 37 Lynx for the Army and 30 for the Royal Navy. The first export order for the multi-rôle version has recently come from a Middle East country, with a contract for three.

The Lynx in detail

From an engineering point of view, the most conventional portions of the Lynx design are the fuselage and tail unit, which are made up of a semi-monocoque pod and boom structure most of which is of light alloy. Glass-reinforced plastics (GRP) are used for such items as the cabin doors, access panels and some fairings, tailplane leading and trailing edges, and the acorn fairing over the tail rotor gearbox. The cockpit seats two pilots side-by-side and the entire cabin aft of these seats in uninterrupted by bulkheads, to allow maximum flexibility of layouts. The cabin floor is a cantilever light alloy structure, with tie-down rings at about 20-in (508-mm) intervals. In naval versions of the Lynx, the tail boom incorporates a hinge to permit the entire tail rotor assembly to be folded forwards for stowage.

Blades of the four-bladed main rotor are of composite construction, with D-section main spars in steel, to which are bonded GRP rear skins stabilised by a Nomex plastics honeycomb core. Discarding traditional articulated rotor concepts in order to achieve better reliability and easier maintenance, Westland engineers considered various "hinged" and "hingeless" systems before adopting a semi-rigid concept with a "soft-in-plane hingeless" rotor. Root flapwise flexibility is provided by a tapered planform titanium element of elliptical cross section, forged integrally with the central hub; an outboard titanium element, of circular section, provides the major lag flexibility, feathering hinges being provided between the two elements. Manual blade folding is provided. The naval Lynx variants have a negative thrust stop in the collective pitch control, allowing some 3,000 lb (1 362 kg) of down-thrust to be produced to aid stability immediately upon touching down on a ship's deck.

Each of the four tail rotor blades has a light alloy spar, machined integrally with the root attachment, which forms the blade leading edge, with a flush-fitting stainless-steel sheath. GRP and Nomex construction, similar to that used for the main blades, completes the tail rotor blades, and conventional flapping and feathering hinges are used in the tail hub.

A special feature of the Lynx is the design of the main rotor gearbox, which had to meet the original specification's stringent requirements for reliability and ease of maintenance, whilst keeping the overall aircraft height within specified limits for air transportation and small ship hangar clearances and being of such a design that it could be readily tailored to meet different customer requirements yet maintain an identical

---

* Heracles is an acronym for "système HEliporté de RAdar pour le Contrôle du Lancement d'Engins et pour la Surveillance de surface" — Helicopter-borne Missile Fire Control and Surface Surveillance Radar System.

(Above) The second Naval trials Lynx, XX510, carrying four Aérospatiale AS12 air-to-surface missiles. (Below) The first of two development Lynx airframes in Aéronavale configuration, used by Aérospatiale in France to develop specific French rôle equipment.

The first development Lynx in Army utility configuration demonstrates its manœuvrability. This airframe, XX153, was also used during 1972 to set speed records over a straight line and closed circuit.

common dynamic system. This gearbox had to be able to reduce an engine input speed of 6,150 rpm to a main rotor speed of 326 rpm, and it does this using two stages of which one is a conventional spiral bevel gear stage and the other uses Westland's original conformal gear design. The conformal mesh provides area, rather than linear, contact between the faces of teeth on each gear, and gives superior load-carrying properties.

Shafts from each engine drive the bevel gears, which carry the drive to conformal pinions situated on each side of the main drive wheel; the tail rotor is driven from a tail take-off drive wheel through a spiral bevel train, and there is a cluster of gears ahead of the engine, with independent drive shafts from each bevel gear, to power the alternators, hydraulic pumps, lubrication pumps and tachometer. The engines themselves are located side-by-side on top of the upper fuselage decking and are separated from each other, the fuselage and the transmission area by firewalls. All fuel is carried in the fuselage, in five crash-proof bag-type tanks, and provision is made for

Westland/Aérospatiale Lynx HAS Mk 2 Cutaway Drawing Key

1 Hinged radome
2 Ferranti Seaspray radar
3 Antennae
4 Air inlet
5 Radar equipment
6 Front bulkhead
7 Windscreen
8 Windscreen wipers
9 Instrument panel shroud
10 Downward vision window
11 Rudder/yaw pedals
12 Pitot head
13 Temperature probe
14 Engine controls
15 Cockpit eyebrow window
16 Pilot's seat
17 Centre console
18 Co-pilot's seat
19 Control column/cyclic pitch control

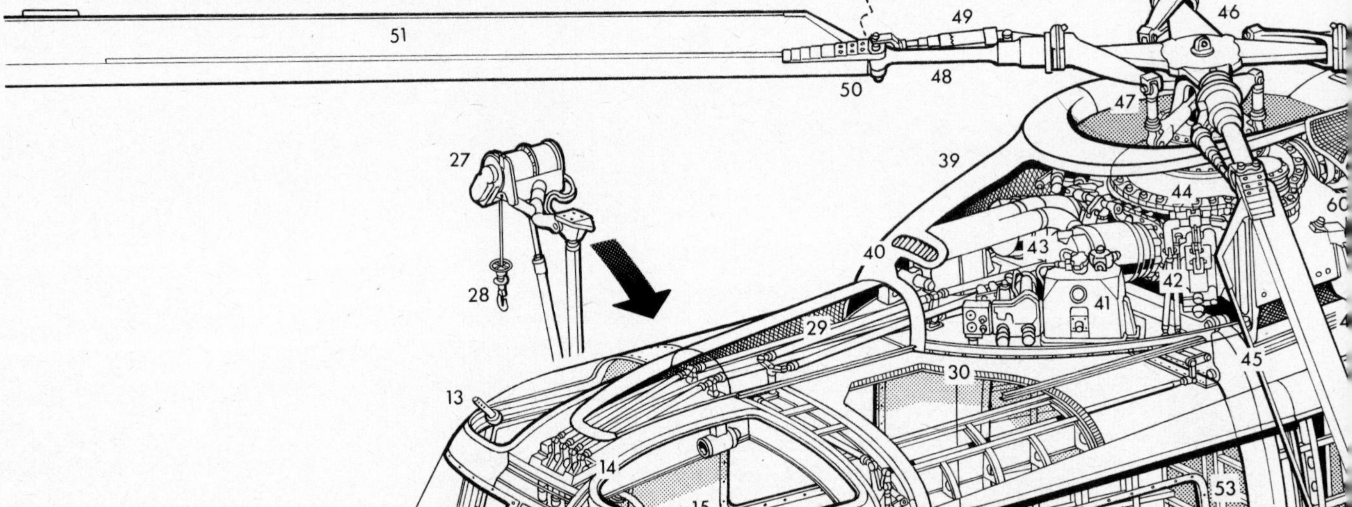

the standard fuel capacity to be doubled by installing two tanks in the rear of the cabin for ferry flights.

The undercarriage of the utility or Army version of the Lynx is a simple tubular skid type, but the naval version has a sophisticated tricycle type of undercarriage to meet the needs of small-ship operations. Each oleo-pneumatic main leg carries a single wheel, normally splayed out 27 deg for deck landings but manually moved to a zero setting and locked for fore and aft movement of the helicopter on board ship. The twin-

wheel nose unit is hydraulically steerable through 90 deg. The naval undercarriage can absorb descent rates of up to 7·5 ft/sec (2·3 m/sec) with drift in any direction and sprag brakes are fitted to prevent rotation on landing or on deck before take-off, these being disengaged hydraulically so that they fail safe (ie, locked). The use of sprag brakes, which are either fully "on" or fully "off", is necessary on small ships, where progressive braking would take too long to prevent a possibly dangerous movement on the deck. Wheeled versions of the Lynx intended exclusively for shore use can have conventional friction brakes; other options for the ship-board

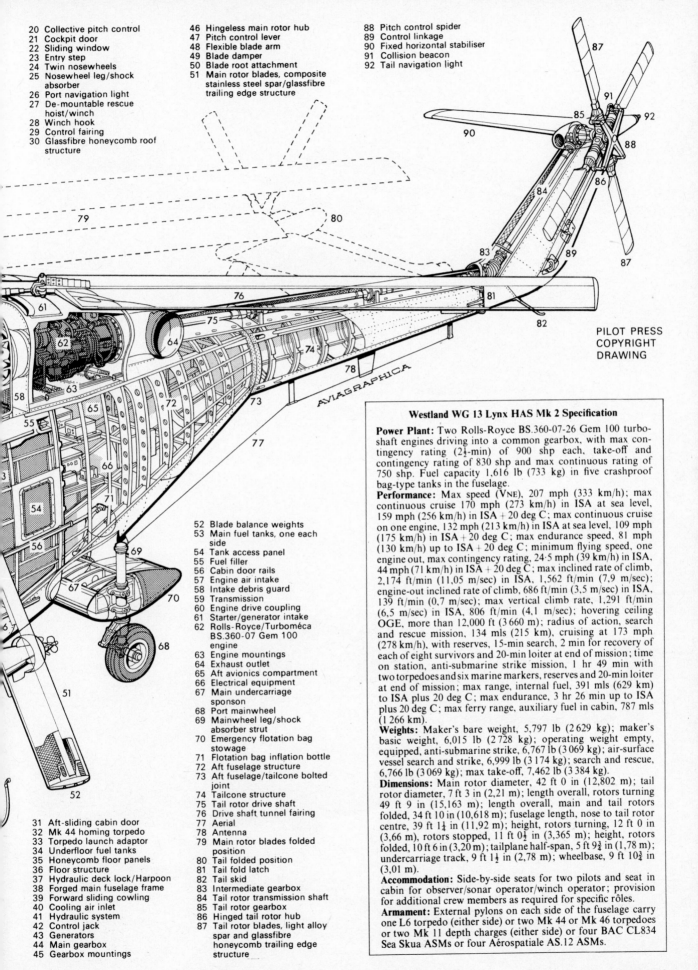

20 Collective pitch control
21 Cockpit door
22 Sliding window
23 Entry step
24 Twin nosewheels
25 Nosewheel leg/shock absorber
26 Port navigation light
27 De-mountable rescue hoist/winch
28 Winch hook
29 Control fairing
30 Glassfibre honeycomb roof structure

46 Hingeless main rotor hub
47 Pitch control lever
48 Flexible blade arm
49 Blade damper
50 Blade root attachment
51 Main rotor blades, composite stainless steel spar/glassfibre trailing edge structure

88 Pitch control spider
89 Control linkage
90 Fixed horizontal stabiliser
91 Collision beacon
92 Tail navigation light

PILOT PRESS
COPYRIGHT
DRAWING

AVIAGRAPHICA

52 Blade balance weights
53 Main fuel tanks, one each side
54 Tank access panel
55 Fuel filler
56 Cabin door rails
57 Engine air intake
58 Intake debris guard
59 Transmission
60 Engine drive coupling
61 Starter/generator intake
62 Rolls-Royce/Turboméca BS.360-07 Gem 100 engine
63 Engine mountings
64 Exhaust outlet
65 Aft avionics compartment
66 Electrical equipment
67 Main undercarriage sponson
68 Port mainwheel
69 Mainwheel leg/shock absorber strut
70 Emergency flotation bag stowage
71 Flotation bag inflation bottle
72 Aft fuselage structure
73 Aft fuselage/tailcone bolted joint
74 Tailcone structure
75 Tail rotor drive shaft
76 Drive shaft tunnel fairing
77 Aerial
78 Antenna
79 Main rotor blades folded position
80 Tail folded position
81 Tail fold latch
82 Tail skid
83 Intermediate gearbox
84 Tail rotor transmission shaft
85 Tail rotor gearbox
86 Hinged tail rotor hub
87 Tail rotor blades, light alloy spar and glassfibre honeycomb trailing edge structure

31 Aft-sliding cabin door
32 Mk 44 homing torpedo
33 Torpedo launch adaptor
34 Underfloor fuel tanks
35 Honeycomb floor panels
36 Floor structure
37 Hydraulic deck lock/Harpoon
38 Forged main fuselage frame
39 Forward sliding cowling
40 Cooling air inlet
41 Hydraulic system
42 Control jack
43 Generators
44 Main gearbox
45 Gearbox mountings

Westland WG 13 Lynx HAS Mk 2 Specification

Power Plant: Two Rolls-Royce BS.360-07-26 Gem 100 turbo-shaft engines driving into a common gearbox, with max contingency rating ($2\frac{1}{2}$-min) of 900 shp each, take-off and contingency rating of 830 shp and max continuous rating of 750 shp. Fuel capacity 1,616 lb (733 kg) in five crashproof bag-type tanks in the fuselage.

Performance: Max speed (VNE), 207 mph (333 km/h); max continuous cruise 170 mph (273 km/h) in ISA at sea level, 159 mph (256 km/h) in ISA + 20 deg C; max continuous cruise on one engine, 132 mph (213 km/h) in ISA at sea level, 109 mph (175 km/h) in ISA + 20 deg C; max endurance speed, 81 mph (130 km/h) up to ISA + 20 deg C; minimum flying speed, one engine out, max contingency rating, 24·5 mph (39 km/h) in ISA, 44 mph (71 km/h) in ISA + 20 deg C; max inclined rate of climb, 2,174 ft/min (11,05 m/sec) in ISA, 1,562 ft/min (7,9 m/sec); engine-out inclined rate of climb, 686 ft/min (3,5 m/sec), 139 ft/min (0,7 m/sec); max vertical climb rate, 1,291 ft/min (6,5 m/sec) in ISA, 806 ft/min (4,1 m/sec); hovering ceiling OGE, more than 12,000 ft (3 660 m); radius of action, search and rescue mission, 134 mls (215 km), cruising at 173 mph (278 km/h), with reserves, 15-min search, 2 min for recovery of each of eight survivors and 20-min loiter at end of mission; time on station, anti-submarine strike mission, 1 hr 49 min with two torpedoes and six marine markers, reserves and 20-min loiter at end of mission; max range, internal fuel, 391 mls (629 km) to ISA plus 20 deg C; max endurance, 3 hr 26 min up to ISA plus 20 deg C; max ferry range, auxiliary fuel in cabin, 787 mls (1 266 km).

Weights: Maker's bare weight, 5,797 lb (2 629 kg); maker's basic weight, 6,015 lb (2 728 kg); operating weight empty, equipped, anti-submarine strike, 6,767 lb (3 069 kg); air-surface vessel search and strike, 6,999 lb (3 174 kg); search and rescue, 6,766 lb (3 069 kg); max take-off, 7,462 lb (3 384 kg).

Dimensions: Main rotor diameter, 42 ft 0 in (12,802 m); tail rotor diameter, 7 ft 3 in (2,21 m); length overall, rotors turning 49 ft 9 in (15,163 m); length overall, main and tail rotors folded, 34 ft 10 in (10,618 m); fuselage length, nose to tail rotor centre, 39 ft 1$\frac{1}{4}$ in (11,92 m); height, rotors turning, 12 ft 0 in (3,66 m), rotors stopped, 11 ft 0$\frac{1}{4}$ in (3,365 m); height, rotors folded, 10 ft 6 in (3,20 m); tailplane half-span, 5 ft 9$\frac{3}{4}$ in (1,78 m); undercarriage track, 9 ft 1$\frac{1}{2}$ in (2,78 m); wheelbase, 9 ft 10$\frac{3}{4}$ in (3,01 m).

Accommodation: Side-by-side seats for two pilots and seat in cabin for observer/sonar operator/winch operator; provision for additional crew members as required for specific rôles.

Armament: External pylons on each side of the fuselage carry one L6 torpedo (either side) or two Mk 44 or Mk 46 torpedoes or two Mk 11 depth charges (either side) or four BAC CL834 Sea Skua ASMs or four Aérospatiale AS.12 ASMs.

The Naval trials Lynx XX510 has been used for several series of operations aboard various ships including (above) HMS Sheffield and (below and opposite) the French frigate Tourville. For the latter trials, it sported Aéronavale markings on one side of the fuselage, retaining RN markings on the other side.

versions are flotation gear in the form of inflatable bags each side of the fuselage, and a harpoon-type deck-lock system. With the latter engaged in a grid in the deck surface, the Lynx can be rotated round the deck lock by use of the tail rotor power, the nosewheel being selected and locked athwartships by the pilot.

All versions have two independent hydraulic systems rated at 2,050 psi (144 kg/cm²), these being driven through the main rotor gearbox to maintain full power in the event of an engine failure. If either hydraulic system fails, the other provides enough power for adequate control to be maintained, but failure of the No 1 system results in loss of the rotor brake and tail rotor yaw control, a mechanical back-up being provided for the latter. A third hydraulic system is fitted if sonar, MAD or hydraulic winch are required in the naval variants. There is no pneumatic system. Engine-driven starter/generators provide DC electrical power and AC comes from two transmission-driven alternators. Anti-ice protection systems are fitted to the engines, engine intakes, main windscreens and duplicated pitot heads; no provision is made for de-icing the main or tail rotor blades, which have self-shedding characteristics.

In its multi-rôle version, the Lynx can carry up to nine armed troops or paratroops, with two pilots, or 2,000 lb (907 kg) of freight in the cabin or up to 3,000 lb (1 360 kg) slung externally. For casevac duties, three stretchers plus an attendant make up the standard load, but up to nine survivors

can be carried in the SAR variants. A variety of weapon loads has been proposed for the utility Lynx, according to customer requirement, and can include a 20-mm cannon or pintle-mounted 7,62-mm minigun inside the cabin, firing sideways through the open door, or gun pods, rockets or anti-tank missiles on the external pylons. The naval Lynx similarly carries a variety of weapons according to specific rôle and customer preference.

An Elliott automatic flight control system (AFCS) provides artificial dynamic stability in pitch, roll and yaw by systems which are duplexed to give fail soft characteristics. In pitch and roll the same duplexed systems also give a prolonged "hands off" attitude hold facility. Autopilot modes of Heading, Barometric and Radio Height holds are simplexed and for those modes the AFCS computer processes inputs from two vertical and two rate gyroscopes; compass and barometric and radio altimeters to control the behaviour of the helicopter through the main and tail rotor servo units. The additional facilities of Radio Height Acquire and Hold, Automatic Transitions to a doppler controlled hover at a preselected height and Sonar Cable Angle and Height control are provided in naval versions that carry dunking sonar and are being cleared initially for the *Aéronavale* Lynx.

A special feature of the stability augmentation system in the Lynx is the provision of a CAC unit (Computer Acceleration Control) which senses the acceleration of the aircraft normal to the pitch axis in the vertical plane and applies collective pitch via the collective series actuators to reduce the acceleration to zero. This acceleration control system is completely duplexed and reduces the effects of the collective to pitch coupling of the semi-rigid rotor at high forward speeds.

Basic navaids specified for the Lynx comprise VOR, DME and ILS, plus two new systems — the Decca Tactical Air Navigation System (TANS) and, to a somewhat later timescale, Microwave Aircraft Digital Guidance System (MADGE). TANS accepts automatic inputs from the Decca Doppler Type 71, a true airspeed transducer, the aircraft compass system and a vertical reference system; additional data and instructions can be inserted manually via the control panel, incorporated in the same unit as the display for panel mounting. The facilities of the TANS computer include present position, bearing and distance or heading to steer and distance to any one of 10 waypoints; vectoring of waypoints; automatic wind calculation; automatic reversion to air data on Doppler failure; Doppler surface motion correction and roll correction. In addition, the TANS computer can display such other information as closing speed, time to go, true air speed, drift, Doppler along and across heading velocities and so on. MADGE is an approach aid that will provide guidance in azimuth and elevation plus range information.

Refining the design

Reference has already been made to work completed with the 13 Lynx development airframes in some 2,500 flying hours. In the course of the test programme, several problems have been encountered and overcome, and various design refinements have been introduced.

One of the early problems concerned directional stability and accounted for the appearance on XW835 (the first prototype) of small ventral fins under the tail boom — initially a single triangular surface and then, because this did not have sufficient ground clearance, an inverted-Y arrangement. These fins solved the handling problem adequately but were an inelegant solution visually, and the production utility Lynx has lateral accelerometers to sense sideslip and provide corrective inputs to the tail rotor servos through the AFCS.

A vigorous development programme was required to reduce

(Above) To facilitate stowage aboard small ships, the Lynx has folding main rotors and folding tail rotor pylon. (Below) Emergency flotation bags can be carried on the stub wings and are shown here inflated for test purposes.

vibration levels to an acceptable level, the "fixes" including a stiffened tail boom and tail-rotor strut, with a new wider-chord fairing, and an isolated seat for the second pilot. Roll-Royce phase displacement type torquemeters have replaced Westland's original strain gauge type, and other changes for production concern the design of the main rotor servos, the tail rotor hub and — the most obvious externally — the installation of a single large window in each cabin door, replacing three smaller windows. An early decision was made to change the design of the rotor head to the monobloc arrangement already described, with the flexible "cutlets" that provide flap-wise flexibility forged integrally with the hub itself; only the first two development airframes, in fact, had the earlier design with bolted-on shafts. Since the monobloc head was introduced, there has been no change to the fundamental design, which has proved extremely successful in flight testing to date. Experience with the rotor hub design was obtained with two Westland Scout helicopters fitted with scaled-down hubs of similar principle, one being used by Westland and one by the RAE at Bedford. Work on these Research Scouts suggested that there was an element of technical risk in designing the rotor head without dampers, and all the development aircraft have therefore had dampers fitted; ultimate elimination of these from production aircraft is one of the objectives of development work now going on at Yeovil.

The rotor blades now have a Nomex honeycomb core in place of the original aluminium core, to reduce lightning strike risks. The blade's cambered airfoil, which was developed by the NPL in conjunction with the RAE, has proved most satisfactory, with no indications of retreating blade stall or of compressibility effects on the advancing blade. More than 30 specimen blades have been used in the fatigue programme to achieve a life of more than the specified 2,500 hrs, and three representative gearboxes have also been fatigue tested to achieve a similar target life. Some early problems were encountered with the conformal gears, which are unique to the Lynx, but there has been only one unscheduled removal of a gearbox during testing and the basic simplicity of the design has been proved, with significant reductions already achieved in overhaul times.

Reliability and ease of maintenance were given special prominence in the official specification requirements for the Lynx and have exercised a considerable influence on the design and the test programme. The reliability target was an MTBF of 33 hrs, to give a 95·5 per cent probability of achieving a standard 1½-hr naval sortie, and this target was consistently being bettered after the first 700 hrs of development flying. The maintenance target was 2·7 manhours per flying hour, comprising 0·6 manhours for flight servicing, 1·2 manhours for scheduled servicing and 0·9 manhours for unscheduled servicing. By comparison, the MTBF for the Westland Wasp (in Royal Netherlands Navy service) is 47 hrs with a mission reliability of 98·25 per cent, and for the Westland Sea King (in Royal Navy experience) is 16 hrs with 88 per cent mission reliability; the maintenance manhours per flight hr for these two types are 4·05 and 4·91 respectively.

The use of plastics construction for about 10 per cent of the Lynx airframe (by weight); the hingeless rotor design; the main gearbox with only half the number of parts found in other designs and the arrangement of the hydraulic system and controls all make a big contribution to achieving the reliability and maintainability targets. A unique feature of Westlands' reliability testing has been the use of a rig on which all components can function under any required stimuli and which can be placed completely inside an environmental chamber. On this rig, components are subjected to vibrations, humidity and temperature in a planned cycle, ranging from −35 deg C to +70 deg C. Rig results have been supplemented by environmental testing of one of the development Lynxes including icing trials in Denmark and hot-weather flying at

continued on page 202

LAUNCHING THE SEA HARRIER

SHIPBOARD OPERATIONS by variants of the Hawker Siddeley P.1127/Kestrel/Harrier family have become a commonplace in the course of 13 years since the first landings were made by Bill Bedford in one of the prototypes aboard HMS *Ark Royal* in February 1963. Since that time, the V/STOL fighter has flown onto and off more than 22 different ships of eight Navies, including one with a wooden deck (Spain's *Dédalo*); RAF Harriers have been cleared for through-deck ship operations at sea, should the need arise, and the US Marine Corps has integrated shipboard operations into its routine squadron activities and deployed a six-aircraft detachment of AV-8A Harriers aboard the interim Sea Control Ship USS *Guam* for a six-month period of service with the US Sixth Fleet in the Mediterranean in 1974-75.

The broad spread of routine and trial operations on a wide variety of ships, ranging in size from the USS *Independence* with a flight deck more than 1,000 ft (305 m) in length to HMS *Green Rover* with a landing platform measuring only 55 ft by 85 ft (16 m by 26 m), have shown that there are no special difficulties involved and that vertical and short take-offs and vertical landings can be made with no change in normal piloting techniques used ashore. However, all operations to date have been made by Harrier variants optimised for land-based use and even the AV-8As of the USMC, although routinely operated from ships, are intended to get ashore as soon as possible in an active scenario to allow the Marines to fulfil their primary function of supporting assault forces in action on the ground. The potential value of a Harrier variant developed more specifically for naval shipboard operation has, therefore, long been realised at Kingston, and a number of possible configurations has been considered.

Since 1972, attention has been centred upon a Harrier optimised for service aboard the new generation of Royal Navy through-deck cruisers expected in service by 1980. The Admiralty was quick to appreciate the advantages offered by such a Maritime Harrier (as the project was at first known) and after design definition was completed, plans were drawn up early in 1973 to order a batch of about 24 aircraft. Provision was made in the then-current RN budget to fund initial development of the aircraft but the go-ahead for work to begin, expected to be given in June 1973, was withheld at the last moment while Britain's total defence commitments were reviewed. Another 11th-hour postponement of the planned initiation of the programme occurred in December 1973, when inflation, industrial unrest and the energy crisis combined to produce an unfavourable climate. Two General Elections

during 1974 led to further delays, after which the whole programme was involved in the Defence Review that led to the swingeing cuts announced in the White Paper of April 1975. Nevertheless, the Maritime Harrier survived, and the long-delayed announcement of a go-ahead came on 15 May 1975, when Defence Minister Roy Mason said in the House of Commons that 24 Sea Harrier aircraft were to be acquired for operation from RN ships in the maritime strike/fighter/reconnaissance rôles, and that work was to proceed on three through-deck carriers which he referred to as Anti-Submarine Cruisers (they are also called, somewhat confusingly, Carrier, Assault, Helicopter or CAH type). Hawker Siddeley received an ITP (Instruction to Proceed) on 3 June, allowing work to get under way while contractual details were finalised.

The aircraft for the RN have now been designated Sea Harrier FRS Mk 1s (indicating Fighter-Reconnaissance-Strike) and the order covers 24 of these new single seaters plus one Harrier T Mk 4 two-seater to the standard RAF specification, for use at the Harrier OCU at RAF Wittering, where RN pilots will receive their training. The first three Sea Harriers will be assigned to the flight development task (there are no prototypes as such), and are scheduled to fly in July and October 1977 and January 1978. Also as part of the Sea Harrier development programme, two Hawker Siddeley Hunter T Mk 8Cs (RN two-seaters) are being converted (by HSA at Brough) to test-fly the radar and avionics systems. With nose radomes and representative cockpit instruments, these aircraft will be redesignated Hunter T Mk 8M and will fly a few months before the first Sea Harrier, one being used by Hawker Siddeley to develop the nav/attack system and the other by the RRE for radar development. Eventually, these Hunters will be used to give radar training to Sea Harrier pilots, and the three development Sea Harriers will be refurbished for delivery to the RN as fully-operational aircraft.

The timescale for Sea Harrier production and delivery has been established in relation to ship availability rather than the manufacturer's resources; production of the 234 Harriers ordered to date (excluding the Sea Harriers) will be completed within the next year or so, leaving a hiatus of about 12 months before the new aircraft begin to come off the line in quantity. The Royal Navy will form its first Sea Harrier unit in mid-1979, according to present plans, and after a period of working up at a shore base, this unit should be ready to go to sea in 1980.

By that time, the first of the CAHs, HMS *Invincible,* is scheduled to be in commission, but labour difficulties and the effects of financial restraints are already causing this timescale to be revised and there is distinct possibility that Sea Harriers' first sea deployment will be aboard HMS *Hermes* or HMS *Bulwark*, the two Commando carriers.

Design details

Evolution of the Sea Harrier FRS Mk 1 from the standard RAF Harrier was based on the precept of "minimum cost, minimum risk" to adapt the aircraft for its new rôle. With an estimated programme cost of £60-70m over eight years for the 25 aircraft, this objective has clearly been achieved; an additional £25m will probably be spent on R & D, primarily concerned with development of radar.

Whereas the pure fighter rôle represents probably no more than 10 per cent of the RAF's total Harrier deployment, the Royal Navy assigns a much higher priority to air-to-air operations — at least 50 per cent, with the remaining deployment divided equally between strike and reconnaissance. This change in priorities made the installation of an AI/ASV radar essential in the Sea Harrier and, taken with other related equipment changes, accounts for the principal new feature of the aircraft, its reconfigured front fuselage. Since it was found impossible to incorporate the avionics and systems for the RN's weapons fit in the space made available by removing the RAF equipment, the cockpit has been raised 11 in (28 cm) and the nose contours redesigned. This allows extra space under the cockpit floor, used primarily to house the Doppler navaid that

is one of the new items of equipment, and gives a better nose shape around the 20-in (51-cm) dish aerial of the Ferranti Blue Fox radar. The entire radome, with the radar *in situ*, will hinge sideways for access and to facilitate below deck stowage of the Sea Harrier.

Blue Fox is a derivative of the Sea Spray, the air-to-surface search radar developed for the Westland/Aérospatiale Lynx, but the equipment is modified to provide both air-to-air and air-to-surface functions, for which purpose its aerial has dual mono-pulse capability, operating in vertical and horizontal planes. Based on X-band transmitter/receiver technology, the Blue Fox radar has frequency agility to allow the pilot to select an ECM function and to suppress secondary trace returns. Ferranti announced completion of the study contract covering design and operational characteristics of the radar on 31 December, and pre-production manufacture has now started. Predicted MTBF for the Blue Fox is more than 100 hrs.

In place of the RAF's Ferranti INAS-inertial navigation system, the RN will use the same company's HARS (Heading Attitude and Reference System), a twin-gyro platform operating in conjunction with Doppler. The aircraft will have a simple autopilot (heading, height and turn hold) in addition to the V/STOL-only single autostabilisation fitted to RAF and USMC Harriers, to allow the pilot to concentrate upon his radar scope during an action. A radar altimeter is fitted, and its read-out can be superimposed on the radar display.

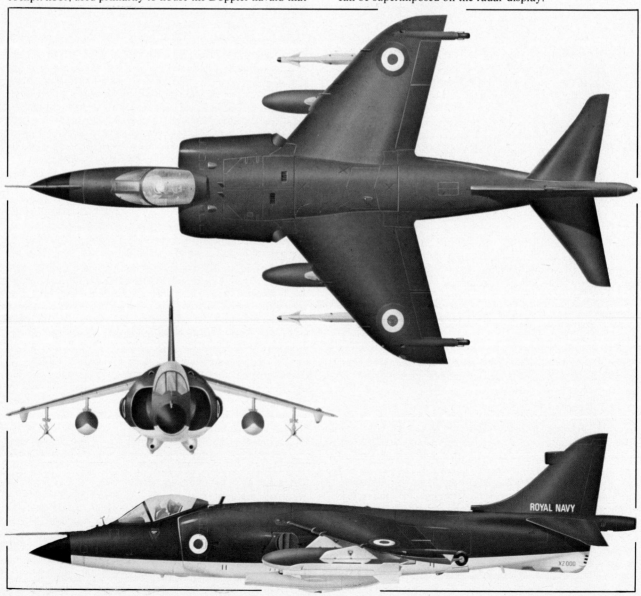

(Above) A development Harrier, XV277, with an aerodynamic test shape for the Sea Harrier nose radome. The same aircraft is shown in the heading photograph on page 171. (Below) A mock-up of the definitive nose shape adopted for the Sea Harrier.

The radar scope, with a 5-in (12,7-cm) display, is located in the top right-hand corner of the instrument panel, and the entire layout of instruments and controls in the Sea Harrier is being revised to take advantage of the slightly increased cockpit space now available and of latest ideas on arrangement. The aim has been to produce an efficient ergonometric cockpit which will allow the maximum operational effectiveness from single-crew operation of a complex weapons system. The Head-Up Display will be provided by Smiths Industries — who also supply the HUD for RAF and USMC Harriers — and will have an integrated weapon-aiming computer. Both the lens and the reflector plate are larger than those of the earlier Harrier HUD, in keeping with the increased emphasis on the air-to-air rôle. The Sea Harrier nav/attack system computation is all-digital, a feature that is expected to give improved reliability and ease of maintenance with greatly increased accuracy and flexibility by comparison with the RAF Harrier's analogue systems.

With a radome in the nose, the compensated-head pitot tube has to be relocated on the top of the nose cone. There are few other significant changes from the Harrier GR Mk 3, which is the airframe from which the Sea Harrier is derived. The same ECM and RWR fairings appear on the fin and behind the tailplane, and the number of wing and fuselage hardpoints is unchanged although the wing pylons are strengthened. The sides of the new cockpit canopy are bulged outwards slightly to improve the all-round view, and one of the bonuses from raising the seat (Martin Baker Mk 10 zero-zero) is that wing struts and outriggers (when locked down) can be seen over the intakes.

In the air-to-air rôle, the Sea Harrier will usually carry the two 30-mm Aden gun pods under the fuselage, two Sidewinder AAMs on the outboard wing pylons and two 100-Imp gal (455-1) drop tanks. For air-to-surface work, standard RAF bomb carriers or rocket pods can be carried; an ASM such as

Harpoon or Exocet may figure in future Navy plans, but neither current version of Martel (anti-radar or TV) is thought likely to be carried by Sea Harrier. For the reconnaissance rôle, a single F95 oblique camera is located in the nose, looking to starboard (the reverse of the RAF Harrier) to supplement visual surveillance by the pilot. For most forseeable RN operations, the Sea Harrier's built-in fuel capacity should be sufficient, but standard provision for in-flight refuelling is retained and development of a buddy refuelling pack would be possible.

Sea Harrier's engine is the Rolls-Royce Pegasus 104, a close relative of the Pegasus 103 used in current production Harriers, with the same rating of 21,500 lb st (9 761 kgp). The differences are limited to those necessary to meet the requirements of maritime operations and include anti-corrosion measures such as use of forged aluminium in place of magnesium for the fan and intermediate castings, improved material and protective coating and extra electrical generating power. The strengthened nozzles, developed for a recent joint Anglo-US programme to permit wider-range thrust-vectoring in forward flight (VIFF), will be fitted. A total of 37 engines is to be built, to cover development and production Sea Harrier requirements.

Operational aspects

Although the Harrier has a demonstrated capability of operating from the small aft decks of such ships as HMS *Blake* and *Tiger*, it is not part of the Navy's plans that they should do so operationally, except perhaps in the sense that such ships could serve as "forward bases" at a distance of 40-50 mls (64-80 km) ahead of the main fleet. The requirement is for operation from the CAH or LPH class ships, which provide a deck length of at least 550 ft (168 m) and allow the Sea Harrier to develop its maximum payload potential. It is a well-established characteristic of V/STOL aircraft, of which the Harrier is the only fully operational example at present, that a short forward run at take-off dramatically increases the load that can be lifted, by comparison with the vertical take-off case. When operating off the deck of an aircraft carrier, even greater improvements can be obtained, not only because a wind-over-deck (WOD) component can usually be guaranteed, but also because the aircraft can be allowed to *lose* height after it leaves the deck while it is rotated for the climb away to begin on wing lift. A 550-ft (170-m) deck-run into a 30-knot (56-km/h) wind-over-deck will double the disposable military load (fuel plus ordnance) compared with VTO where payload is directly limited by engine thrust.

It can be shown that a further increase in take-off weight can be obtained for any given length of forward run by introducing a short "launching ramp" at the end of the runway or deck. Giving the front 80 ft (25 m) of the deck runway an upward tilt of 5 deg is estimated to be equivalent to a 15-knot (28-km/h) WOD and flight testing may eventually lead to the adoption of some such a device to enhance the Sea Harrier's operational characteristics still further.

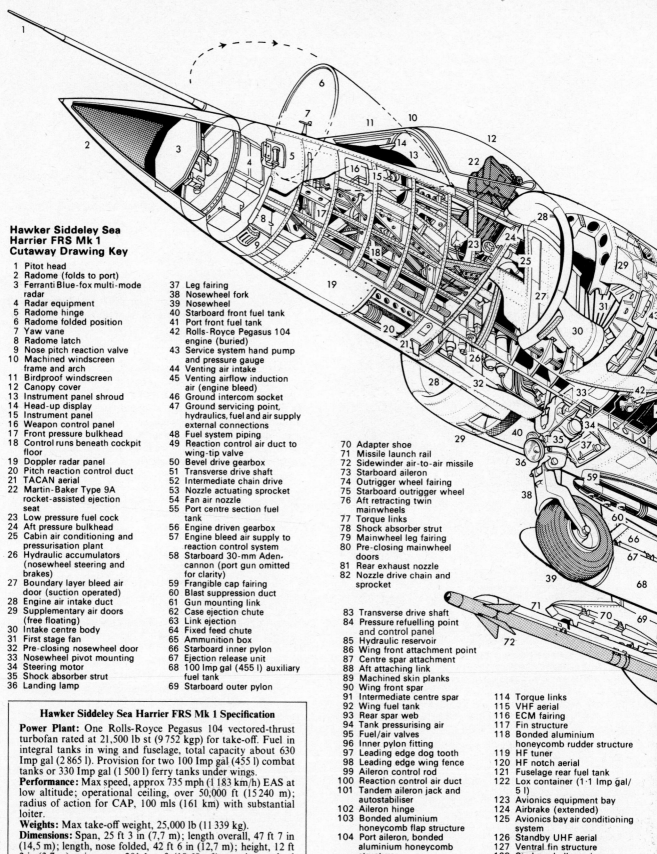

Hawker Siddeley Sea Harrier FRS Mk 1 Cutaway Drawing Key

1 Pitot head
2 Radome (folds to port)
3 Ferranti Blue-fox multi-mode radar
4 Radar equipment
5 Radome hinge
6 Radome folded position
7 Yaw vane
8 Radome latch
9 Nose pitch reaction valve
10 Machined windscreen frame and arch
11 Birdproof windscreen
12 Canopy cover
13 Instrument panel shroud
14 Head-up display
15 Instrument panel
16 Weapon control panel
17 Front pressure bulkhead
18 Control runs beneath cockpit floor
19 Doppler radar panel
20 Pitch reaction control duct
21 TACAN aerial
22 Martin-Baker Type 9A rocket-assisted ejection seat
23 Low pressure fuel cock
24 Aft pressure bulkhead
25 Cabin air conditioning and pressurisation plant
26 Hydraulic accumulators (nosewheel steering and brakes)
27 Boundary layer bleed air door (suction operated)
28 Engine air intake duct
29 Supplementary air doors (free floating)
30 Intake centre body
31 First stage fan
32 Pre-closing nosewheel door
33 Nosewheel pivot mounting
34 Steering motor
35 Shock absorber strut
36 Landing lamp

37 Leg fairing
38 Nosewheel fork
39 Nosewheel
40 Starboard front fuel tank
41 Port front fuel tank
42 Rolls-Royce Pegasus 104 engine (buried)
43 Service system hand pump and pressure gauge
44 Venting air intake
45 Venting airflow induction air (engine bleed)
46 Ground intercom socket
47 Ground servicing point, hydraulics, fuel and air supply external connections
48 Fuel system piping
49 Reaction control air duct to wing-tip valve
50 Bevel drive gearbox
51 Transverse drive shaft
52 Intermediate chain drive
53 Nozzle actuating sprocket
54 Fan air nozzle
55 Port centre section fuel tank
56 Engine driven gearbox
57 Engine bleed air supply to reaction control system
58 Starboard 30-mm Aden cannon (port gun omitted for clarity)
59 Frangible cap fairing
60 Blast suppression duct
61 Gun mounting link
62 Case ejection chute
63 Link ejection
64 Fixed feed chute
65 Ammunition box
66 Starboard inner pylon
67 Ejection release unit
68 100 Imp gal (455 l) auxiliary fuel tank
69 Starboard outer pylon

70 Adapter shoe
71 Missile launch rail
72 Sidewinder air-to-air missile
73 Starboard aileron
74 Outrigger wheel fairing
75 Starboard outrigger wheel
76 Aft retracting twin mainwheels
77 Torque links
78 Shock absorber strut
79 Mainwheel leg fairing
80 Pre-closing mainwheel doors
81 Rear exhaust nozzle
82 Nozzle drive chain and sprocket

83 Transverse drive shaft
84 Pressure refuelling point and control panel
85 Hydraulic reservoir
86 Wing front attachment point
87 Centre spar attachment
88 Aft attaching link
89 Machined skin planks
90 Wing front spar
91 Intermediate centre spar
92 Wing fuel tank
93 Rear spar web
94 Tank pressurising air
95 Fuel/air valves
96 Inner pylon fitting
97 Leading edge dog tooth
98 Leading edge wing fence
99 Aileron control rod
100 Reaction control air duct
101 Tandem aileron jack and autostabiliser
102 Aileron hinge
103 Bonded aluminium honeycomb flap structure
104 Port aileron, bonded aluminium honeycomb structure
105 Roll reaction control valve
106 Outer pylon fitting
107 Navigation light
108 Wing tip
109 Outrigger wheel fairing
110 Hydraulic retraction jack
111 Leg fairing (upper section)
112 Port outrigger wheel
113 Leg fairing (lower section)

114 Torque links
115 VHF aerial
116 ECM fairing
117 Fin structure
118 Bonded aluminium honeycomb rudder structure
119 HF tuner
120 HF notch aerial
121 Fuselage rear fuel tank
122 Lox container (1·1 Imp gal/5 l)
123 Avionics equipment bay
124 Airbrake (extended)
125 Avionics bay air conditioning system
126 Standby UHF aerial
127 Ventral fin structure
128 Starboard all-moving tailplane
129 Tandem tailplane jack
130 Port all-moving tailplane
131 Tailplane structure
132 Bonded aluminium honeycomb trailing edge
133 Pitch and yaw reaction valves
134 Tail warning radar

Hawker Siddeley Sea Harrier FRS Mk 1 Specification

Power Plant: One Rolls-Royce Pegasus 104 vectored-thrust turbofan rated at 21,500 lb st (9 752 kgp) for take-off. Fuel in integral tanks in wing and fuselage, total capacity about 630 Imp gal (2 865 l). Provision for two 100 Imp gal (455 l) combat tanks or 330 Imp gal (1 500 l) ferry tanks under wings.

Performance: Max speed, approx 735 mph (1 183 km/h) EAS at low altitude; operational ceiling, over 50,000 ft (15 240 m); radius of action for CAP, 100 mls (161 km) with substantial loiter.

Weights: Max take-off weight, 25,000 lb (11 339 kg).

Dimensions: Span, 25 ft 3 in (7,7 m); length overall, 47 ft 7 in (14,5 m); length, nose folded, 42 ft 6 in (12,7 m); height, 12 ft 2 in (3,7 m); wing area, 201·1 sq ft (18,68 m²); outrigger wheel track, 22 ft 2 in (6,76 m); wheelbase, 11 ft 4 in (3,45 m).

Armament: No fixed armament. Provision for two gun pods under fuselage, each carrying one 30-mm Aden gun with 130 rounds. Four wing pylons can carry Sidewinder AAMs, and one under-fuselage pylon. Armament-carriage includes Martel/Harpoon-type ASMs, bombs, rockets, marker flares, etc as required.

As only the Harrier's main wheels are braked, it is not possible to check full thrust on the engine, jets off, before commitment to take-off. There is no painless way of aborting a deck STO if the engine fails to develop full thrust after the 2-3 sec acceleration period. To overcome this, a hold-back device is being developed, comprising a rigid strut that is attached by means of an explosive release unit to the engine test restraining lug on the rear of the main leg, and connects to a below-deck damper. The release button for this hold-back device is located on the nozzle vectoring lever in the cockpit, so that the pilot can see that full power is available before dropping his hand to the nozzle lever and releasing the aircraft for take-off.

Most of the ships from which Harriers have operated so far have had a single centreline painted on the deck. HSA experience has shown, however, that "tramlines", 7 ft (2,1-m) apart, make it easier for the pilot to control (through nosewheel steering) the early stages of the take-off run. The CAH has a 42-ft (12,8-m) wide runway down its port side, allowing 17 ft (5,2 m) on each side of the tramlines to give adequate wing-tip clearance; there is a 550-ft (169-m) length from the hold-back point to the "nozzles down" cue-line at the forward end of the flight deck

The potential availability of the Sea Harrier as an off-the-shelf proven weapons system from 1979 onwards has rekindled the interest of a number of foreign navies, and Hawker Siddeley believes there is an export potential for 100-150 aircraft — perhaps including some for land-based operations where the added air-to-air capability makes the aircraft more attractive than the current strike-orientated Harrier. Iran and India have long been regarded as likely customers for a naval Harrier variant, although financing problems make an order for the Indian Navy appear difficult to conclude.

Another result of the Royal Navy's decision to order the Sea Harrier has been the added impetus given to projects for small aircraft carriers. Apart from HMS *Invincible,* which is being constructed by Vickers at Barrow-in-Furness, there is the "Harrier Carrier" proposal by Vosper Thorneycroft. The latter is a vessel of only about 6,000-7,000 tons displacement with an overall length of 450 ft (137 m), designed to carry eight Harriers (or a mix of Harriers and Sea Kings) and permits operation in all of the FRS rôles which the aircraft is designed to provide. Equipped with full radar, air traffic control and navigation systems and a self-defence capability that could be supplemented by having one Harrier on stand-by for immediate VTO launch,

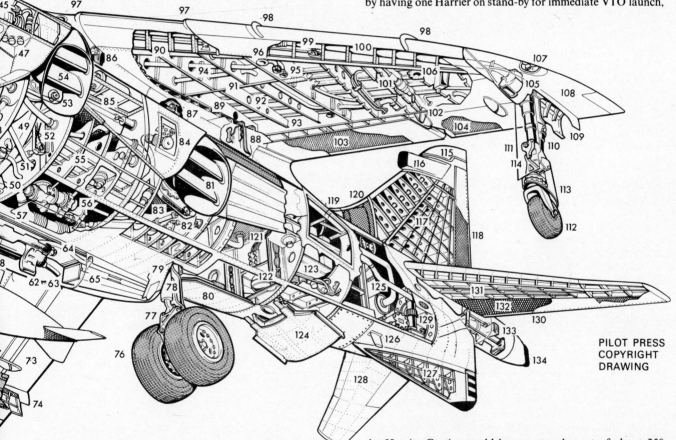

PILOT PRESS
COPYRIGHT
DRAWING

runway. It is expected that launches will be possible at a rate of one every 45 secs, compared with one a minute from contemporary catapults. Recovery will be made to the deck always by vertical landing. This is quicker, safer, uses less fuel and is possible in worse sea states than the conventional naval arrival at 120 knots (222 km/h) into the wires. The Harrier carriers will, in any case, have no wires, nor is the aircraft fitted with a hook. Vertical landing requires no special WOD and hence places no requirement on the ship to change course for aircraft recovery. Operating experience suggests that launch and recovery will be possible on ships rolling through 5-6 deg, with 1-2 deg of pitch, although these figures have to be related to the size of ship involved, and satisfactory response characteristics may be difficult to obtain on ships of less than about 5,000 tons displacement.

the Harrier Carrier would have a complement of about 250 officers and ratings and would be able to go to sea for periods of two weeks at a time, during which all required aircraft maintenance could be undertaken on board.

The combination of Sea Harriers and small carriers such as this Vosper Thorneycroft proposal or other similar vessels would make a viable sea-going force available to nations at only a fraction of the cost of conventional aircraft carriers, for operation in air defence, reconnaissance, strike and limited anti-submarine rôles. Thus, the already-unique Harrier still holds the promise of opening up new avenues of operational deployment; at very least (and subject to there being no further attacks on UK defence spending under the pretext of national economy) the Sea Harrier will achieve the distinction of prolonging the operation of fixed-wing aircraft aboard ships of the Royal Navy. □

Ace-Maker from the Iron-Works

Any study of the relative merits of the various warplanes operated by the principal combatants during World War II quickly reveals that several of the most successful types emerged almost fortuitously at the right moment, whereas some of those on which the most effort was expended arrived on the scene too late to be fully effective or never came up to expectations at all. Similar conclusions can, indeed, be reached in respect of military aircraft development both before and since World War II. To suggest that success in this field of endeavour therefore depends more on chance than skill would certainly be to overstate the case — but few designers with a string of successes to their name would deny their debt to that fickle lady luck.

A good case in point is provided by the Grumman Hellcat, a fighter that was launched in mid-1941 primarily as an insurance against the failure of the Chance Vought F4U Corsair and that became, by 1944, the mainstay of US Navy carrier fighter operations in the Pacific. However skilled the team of Grumman designers and engineers — headed by Leroy Grumman and W T Schwendler — responsible for the evolution of the Hellcat, there is no doubt that their achievement in getting the new fighter into combat just 14 months after prototype first flight was aided by a good measure of favourable luck; conversely, the team working on the Corsair enjoyed no such share of good fortune, 32 months elapsed from first flight to initial operations and full deployment of the type in its designed rôle of *carrier-based* fighter was still more protracted.

The Chance Vought fighter had been ordered into development by the US Navy in 1938 and prototype testing was under way by the middle of 1940; a large, heavily armed monoplane powered by a Pratt & Whitney Double Wasp radial engine, it was intended to become the future carrier fighter in succession to the Grumman F4F Wildcat — itself still in the early stages of evolution in 1939. By the middle of 1941, with a growing awareness in the US military circles of the threat posed by the territorial aspirations of Japan, the Corsair was showing considerable promise but was also suffering from a series of problems that seemed likely to delay its entry into service. The initiation of an alternative design, intended to meet virtually the same requirement, was therefore considered by the US Navy to be no more than prudent, and on 30 June 1941,

Grumman Aircraft Engineering Corp received a contract to build two prototypes of an "improved F4F".

Since speed of development was essential, the Navy proposed a "minimum modification" of the F4F to allow it to mount the 1,600 hp Wright R-2600 Cyclone engine in place of the 1,200 hp Twin Wasp in the Wildcat: one prototype was to have a normally-aspirated R-2600-10 as the XF6F-1, while the second was to be the XF6F-2 with a turbo-supercharged R-2600-16. Grumman engineers, however, responding to the opinions of Navy pilots already flying F4Fs, planned a number of other innovations and changes that led the new project inexorably away from the Wildcat and into a completely new design, albeit one that retained the same overall configuration as the F4F.

The F6F design emerged with a gross weight some 60 per cent greater than that of the F4F, largely as a result of substantial increases in both fuel and ammunition capacities. The higher weight called in turn for increased wing area, the Hellcat — as the F6F was eventually to be named — proving to have the largest wing of any wartime US single-engined production fighter. The wing was mounted on the fuselage at the minimum angle of incidence to obtain the least drag in level flight, but as a comparatively large angle of attack was required for take-off, a negative thrust line was adopted for the engine, resulting in the Hellcat having a pronounced tail-down attitude in normal cruising flight. The negative thrust line was of some incidental benefit in improving forward view from the cockpit, although the view for landing, with the nose held high, was less satisfactory. The pilot was located amidships at the highest point on the fuselage — over the fuel tanks — in order to provide the best possible view forward and to the sides, although retention of a high rear fuselage decking limited the view aft.

Mounted in the low-mid position on the fuselage, the three-spar wing comprised five principal assemblies: a centre section passing through the fuselage and housing the self-sealing fuel tanks, two stub sections providing the attachment points and accommodation for the main undercarriage members, and detachable outer panels designed to swivel at the forward spar and fold aft along the fuselage sides to facilitate carrier stowage. All control surfaces were metal framed, the rudder and elevators being fabric-covered. Split flaps were provided

WARBIRDS

between the ailerons and fuselage and the fully retractable main undercarriage members folded aft, turning though 90 deg to lie flush within the centre-section wells — this last arrangement being an innovation so far as Grumman was concerned, its earlier fighters having fuselage-stowage for the main wheels when retracted.

The F6F was designed to carry an armament of six 0·50-in (12,7-mm) Colt-Browning machine guns, with a maximum of 400 rpg, each wing mounting a battery of three guns just outboard of the hinge line. A total of 212 lb (96 kg) of armour was provided to protect the pilot, the oil tank and the oil cooler, and the internal fuel capacity of 250 US gal (946 l) was carried in self-sealing fuel cells under the cockpit floor. The fuselage was an all-metal monocoque with vertical keels located either side of the centreline. Pressed flange aluminium alloy frames were riveted to these keel members, extruded aluminium alloy stringers completing the basic structures. Aluminium alloy skinning was applied in lateral strips and flush-riveted.

With a gross weight of about 12,000 lb (5 450 kg) initially — and eventually rising to 15,500 lb (7 040 kg) — the Hellcat was twice as heavy as the Mitsubishi Zero-Sen, the Japanese Navy fighter that was to prove its arch enemy in the Pacific. Their difference in weights was indicative of the markedly different design philosophies followed by Grumman and Mitsubishi, in both cases reflecting official Service attitudes. The Zero-Sen achieved its excellent performance through use of a simple, lightweight structure — a design approach that was considered in the USA but was discarded because it appeared that pilot safety would be sacrificed in order to achieve low weight. The US Navy was unwilling to accept increased vulnerability and loss of versatility of attack that would be the penalties for improved speed, climb and manoeuvrability obtained in this way. None-the-less, good performance remained a primary requirement for the F6F, to be achieved without compromising structural strength, armour protection or firepower, and it was the Grumman team's success in meeting all these requirements that made the Hellcat the great fighter it proved to be.

Engine performance was one of the keys to achieving this success, and as work proceeded on the two XF6F prototypes in the early months of 1942, the development status of the Cyclone 14 began to give some cause for concern. A viable alternative to the 1,700 hp R-2600-10 appeared to be offered by Pratt & Whitney with its R-2800 Double Wasp, an 18-cylinder engine with a potential output of 2,000 hp. Combat reports from the Pacific area convinced the Grumman designers that the Hellcat was going to need every ounce of extra power that might be available to it, and Navy approval was obtained to instal an R-2800, rather than the R-2600-16, in the second proto-type then under construction, this aircraft then becoming designated the XF6F-3. Plans for a turbo-supercharged R-2600 installation were retained for a time, and a further airframe was started as an XF6F-2, but was not completed in this guise, a turbo-supercharged R-2800 installation taking its place but also being abandoned as a production alternative.

Flight testing of the XF6F-1 began at Bethpage on 26 June 1942, the pilot being Selden A Converse, and the second aircraft followed as the XF6F-3 five weeks later, on 30 July 1942, with the Double Wasp installed. Initial flight trials were generally satisfactory, although the prototypes were found to suffer from excessive longitudinal stability and an excessive trim change occurred between "flaps up" and "flaps down" configurations; maximum airspeed in a dive also had to be limited to 525 mph (845 km/h) initially because of a flutter problem. These shortcomings were, however, corrected with little difficulty and few changes needed to be made in the Hellcat's initial production standard. Large-scale production had been ordered under US Navy contract on 23 May 1942 and the Double Wasp was confirmed as the power plant, the initial production model thus being the F6F-3. Principal differences from the XF6F-3 comprised the use of a Hamilton Standard propeller in place of the Curtiss Electric type, elimination of the spinner and a redesign of the main under-

(Above) The first Hellcat prototype, XF6F-1, with the original R-2600-10 Cyclone engine installation, compared with (below) the second prototype XF6F-3, with the first R-2800 Double Wasp installation.

(Below) An early production F6F-3 Hellcat on test. It is finished in the "three-tone blue" scheme adopted by the US Navy in 1942, in which a dark sea blue for the top surface was graduated on the sides of the aircraft into a pale blue underside. Many variations of the scheme appeared on Hellcats subsequently.

carriage wheel fairings. The original XF6F-1 was fitted later in 1942 with a two-speed R-2800-27 engine and first flew on 2 October 1942 as the XF6F-4.

To handle production of the F6F-3, Grumman set up a new assembly plant at its factory site on Long Island; while the US Navy was still attempting to obtain proper priorities for steel to be made available for this factory, Grumman executives cut through the red tape by buying steel girders from the scrapped Second Avenue elevated railway and one of the old World's Fair Pavilions in New York. As construction of the plant proceeded, assembly jigs were moved in and the first aircraft started down the line in October while work continued to finish the far end of the building. Meanwhile, the first few F6F-3s were completed in the existing Grumman facilities at Bethpage alongside Wildcats, and the first production flight was made on 4 October 1942; ten aircraft were completed by the

(Above) The XF6F-2 with turbosupercharged R-2800 engine installation as indicated by the deepened intakes under the spinner. (Below) The original XF6F-3 brought up to F6F-3 standard, with an early drop-tank installation.

end of the year. Earlier in 1942, preliminary plans had been made for additional production of the Hellcat (in its F6F-1 version) to be undertaken by the Canadian Vickers company, the designation FV-1 being assigned, but the plans did not mature.

Apart from some elevator buffeting, the first F6F-3 passed its preliminary acceptance trials without revealing any serious shortcomings, but during arrester trials late in November, an arrester hook was pulled out of the fuselage, and in a second incident a month later a fuselage structural failure occurred, indicating the need for some structural stengthening. This was speedily completed and no further difficulties were encountered.

Deliveries to the first Navy squadron assigned to fly the Hellcat, VF-9, began on 16 January 1943, and this unit worked up with the type aboard USS *Essex* during the early months of the year. Operational aircraft usually carried a 150-US gal (568-l) drop tank under the centre section; the F6F-3 had no provision for underwing stores initially, although bombs and, eventually, RPs were carried on operations. Just 14 months after the prototype's first flight, the Hellcat was taken into action for the first time, on 31 August 1943, by VF-5 operating from USS *Yorktown* as part of Task Force 15 in the second strike on Marcus Island. Later the same day, the Hellcats of VF-9 were also in action from the *Essex* in the same operation. The Corsair had preceded the Hellcat into action six months previously, but only for land-based use, primarily by Marine Corps squadrons, as some difficulties were experienced by average pilots in making deck landings in the type.

Simultaneously with its service initiation from the fast aircraft carriers such as *Yorktown*, *Essex* and *Independence*, the Hellcat began operating from the light carriers; VF-24 on the USS *Belleau Wood* and VF-23 on the *Princetown* both took F6F-3s into action on 1 September 1943 in support of the invasion of Baker Island, and claimed the destruction of three Kawasaki H8K (Emily) flying boats that were attempting to shadow the US fleets.

By the end of 1943, the Hellcat was virtually the exclusive equipment of fighter squadrons aboard all fast and light USN carriers serving in the Pacific, although Wildcats still operated from the smaller escort carriers. An effective technique was developed whereby the carrier-based F6Fs flew as escort for attack bombers from the same ships on strikes against enemy land targets, while Hellcat squadrons based on islands already in US hands flew out to provide combat air patrols (CAPs) over the carriers. On 5 November 1943, while 56 F6F-3s from the USS *Princetown* and *Saratoga* provided cover for the bomber force attacking Rabaul, shore-base Hellcats of VF-33 mounted the CAPs and, for the first time, landed on the *Saratoga* to refuel and then fly second sorties to cover the

(Above left) An F6F-5 with maximum external load, comprising six underwing HVAR's, a drop tank and two Tiny Tim rockets under the centre section. (Below) F6F-5N night fighters at sea in 1945, in midnight blue finish and carrying drop tanks as well as the wing-tip radomes.

return of the attacking force before themselves returning to their home base. This procedure subsequently became a standard feature of operations during the advance through the Japanese-occupied islands.

The Hellcats had their first real test in air-to-air combat on 4 December 1943, when 91 F6F-3s were engaged in support of a strike on shipping at Kwajalein and airfields on Roi island. A force of 50 A6M Zero-Sens was encountered and 28 were destroyed for the loss of two or three Hellcats. Successive actions in the early months of 1944 confirmed the Grumman fighter's superiority in its primary rôle of air-to-air combat. Initial combat experience stressed the ruggedness, reliable performance and ease of maintenance of the Hellcat, the only serious criticisms being concerned with excessive tyre wear and some other undercarriage troubles, and impaired vision resulting from the curved Plexiglas windscreen becoming scratched and dust collecting between the outer screen and the inner armoured glass section. In combat with the A6M2 and A6M3 versions of the Zero-Sen, Hellcat pilots considered their aircraft to have definite advantages over its opponents. Although the manoeuvrability of the Japanese fighters was generally superior, the F6F-3 had better speed, dive and altitude capabilities that more than compensated for this, allowing the US Navy pilots to acquire an advantage of position and thus to adopt tactics whereby the Mitsubishi fighters could be destroyed without getting into the kind of close-in high-*g* manoeuvring style of combat for which they had primarily been designed.

Generally, the F6F-3 had little difficulty in staying with the earlier models of the Zero-Sen through most manoeuvres, but the Grumman fighter could not follow its opponent in a tight loop and, often, when following a Zero-Sen in a tight turn the Hellcat was forced to roll out to avoid a stall. One manoeuvre frequently used by Japanese pilots to evade an F6F-3 on their tail was a snap-split-S to port at low altitude, pulling through over the water with a safe margin. Once on the tail of a Zero-Sen, the F6F-3 could usually turn with the Japanese fighter long enough to get in a good burst, although it could not stay with the Zero-Sen for more than 90 deg of the turn. When positions were reversed, the F6F-3 could usually elude its pursuer by diving and twisting by using the ailerons. In level flight, too, it could usually pull away, and its rugged structure stood up well to the 7,7-mm guns of the A6M and even the Japanese fighter's 20-mm cannon, whereas the six 0·50-in (12,7 mm) guns of the Hellcat could destroy the easily-flammable Zero-Sen with relatively small expenditure of ammunition.

Progressively, during 1944, the R-2800-10W version of the Double Wasp became available for installation in the F6F-3, this having water injection to boost the emergency power rating to 2,200 hp. During the early part of the year, six out of every 10 Hellcats coming off the line had the boosted engine and by the beginning of April *all* production aircraft were fitted with the -10W engine. A late production F6F-3 airframe was set aside towards the end of 1943 for installation of the turbo-supercharged R-2800-21 Double Wasp engine, still under the earlier XF6F-2 designation, and is reported to have been tested briefly in January 1944, although little work was done with the aircraft in this form and it was eventually delivered as an operational F6F-3 with a -10W engine.

Night operations

Production of the F6F-3 ended on 21 April 1944, by which time a total of 4,403 had been produced, including F6F-3P, -3E and -3N versions. The F6F-3P had a long focal length camera in the fuselage for high-altitude photo reconnaissance, and examples were used by several squadrons flying F6F-3 fighters during 1944. The F6F-3E and -3N were both specialised night fighting versions, development of which had begun after the Navy had launched a radar-equipped version of the Corsair as its first specialised single-seat night fighter. From the view-

(Above) A mixed formation of F6F-5s and one F6F-5N in Naval Reserve markings, from NAS Oakland California. (Below) An F6F-5K target drone, with recording cameras in wing-tip pods, in orange-and-white finish.

points of operation and maintenance, the Hellcat made a much better night fighter than the Corsair, but night vision from its cockpit was poor and in an attempt to reduce this shortcoming red lights were installed for the instrument panels to cut down cockpit glare, and the outer Plexiglas windscreen was eliminated to provide a flat-fronted screen.

The radar equipment selected for installation in the first instance in both the Hellcat and the Corsair was the AIA developed by the Massachusetts Institute of Technology on the basis of British technology and subsequently designated AN/APS-6*. With a gross weight of about 250 lb (113 kg), most of which was attributable to the pod-mounted scanning aerial, AN/APS-6 had a range of about 4·5-5 miles (7,2-8 km) and could track a target down to a range of as little as 400 ft (122 m), the ideal firing range being about 750 ft (229 m). An unusual feature of this equipment, for its period, was that "left-right" and "up-down" information was presented on a single cathode ray tube, using a novel double dot method. The pod carrying the dish scanner was fitted under the starboard wing of the F6F-3, where it did not interfere with aircraft structure but invoked a speed penalty of about 20 mph (32 km/h).

A trial installation of AN/APS-6 was made in an XF6F-3N in July 1943, tests being undertaken by the US Navy at Quonset Point. Associated with the night-fighting rôle of the aircraft was the installation of an AN/APN-1 radar altimeter and AN/APX-2 IFF equipment, redesigned instrument panels and landing lights. Plans were made for half of all future Hellcat production to be equipped as night fighters, but production of AN/APS-6 could not keep pace with this ambitious target, and in any case it is unlikely that the US Navy could have maintained an adequate flow of pilots through the 29-week course for night flying, available only to pilots

AN/APS-6 indicated a joint Army-Navy Airborne Pulsed Search equipment.

with recent combat experience or the cream of Fighter School graduates. In the event, 149 F6F-3Ns followed the prototype, plus 18 F6F-3Es which differed in having AN/APS-4 radar. The latter had originally been designed for surface search and consequently had a wider azimuth scan pattern but shallower elevation pattern than the AN/APS-6. It was also lighter, at 180 lb (82 kg), and its cockpit components were smaller, making it suitable for application to almost any single-seat aircraft.

The first use of Hellcat night fighters from an aircraft carrier occurred during February 1944, when an F6F-3N of VF(N)-76 operating from USS *Yorktown* and flown by Lt Russell R Reisever intercepted a Nakajima B5N1 bomber making a night attack on the USS *Intrepid*. Four-aircraft detachments of VF(N)-76, and later VF(N)-77 and VF(N)-78, had been assigned for night defence duties to several of the aircraft carriers making up Task Force 58, which opened the campaign to occupy the Marshall Islands on 29 January, the first night interception being made on 16 February. Earlier, in November 1943, attempts at night interceptions from carriers had been made by pairs of standard F6F-3 Hellcats operating as a team each with a radar-equipped TBF-1C Avenger, under the leadership of the Air Group Commander, Lieut-Cdr E H (Butch) O'Hare, aboard the USS *Enterprise*. In this operation, the fighters flew wing on the Avenger (which carried a surface-search ASB radar) and after the formation had been vectored to the vicinity of the enemy aircraft by the ship's fighter director, it relied upon the Avenger's radar to get the Hellcats within visual range. The first such operation was mounted on 24 November, without success, but on 26 November a small Japanese force was intercepted and so disrupted that the flight was credited with saving the task group (Task Force 50, engaged in the occupation of the Gilbert Islands) from damage. In fact, the operation owed more to luck than to the proper use of the plan, since the Avenger made contact with the Japanese bombers before the Hellcats had taken up position, and itself shot down a Mitsubishi G4M2 bomber; in the ensuing mêlée with the fighter escort, Lt-Cdr O'Hare was shot down and killed.

With the R-2800-10W engine, the F6F-3N's empty weight increased from the 9,042 lb (4 105 kg) of the original production -3 to 9,331 lb (4 236 kg), and its normal and max operating weights were 13,015 lb (5 909 kg) and 14,074 lb (6 390 kg) respectively. The radome on the wing tip cost 15–20 mph (24–32 km/h) in top speed, the F6F-3N being capable of 305 mph (491 km/h) at sea level and 360 mph (579 km/h) at 18,000 ft (5 490 m). Initial rate of climb was 3,090 ft/min (15,7 m/sec) and service ceiling was 38,100 ft (11 620 m).

Improved Performance

Although the Hellcat had demonstrated that it was markedly faster than Japanese shipboard fighters, still better performance was constantly sought and at the end of January 1944, a specially "cleaned up" version of the F6F-3 demonstrated a speed of 410 mph (660 km/h) at 21,000 ft (6 405 m). Some of the modifications introduced on this aircraft, together with the progressive improvements made during production of the F6F-3 as well as changes arising from the F6F-3N programme, were incorporated in a new production standard of Hellcat, the F6F-5, the first example of which flew on 4 April 1944, there being no prototype as such.

The F6F-5 retained the R-2800-10W engine, its principal new features being deletion of the curved front windscreen and, on some examples, blanking off the windows aft of the sliding canopy; red instrument panel lighting; a redesigned close-fitting engine cowling; spring tabs on the ailerons; an increase of 242 lb (110 kg) in total weight of armour carried; a strengthened tail assembly; built-in provision for underwing bombs or rockets and use of a special smooth external finish. The external loads could comprise three 1,000-lb (454-kg) bombs, one on each of the stub wings close in to the fuselage and one on the centreline in place of the usual drop tank, and six 5-in (12,7 cm) rocket projectiles, three each under the outer wing panels. In place of the bombs, the F6F-5 could carry 11·75-in (29,8-cm) Tiny Tim rockets, when the gross weight increased to more than 17,000 lb (7 718 kg). The normal armament remained six 0·50 in (12,7 mm) machine guns in the wings but some later production F6F-5s mounted a pair of 20-mm cannon with 200 rpg, replacing the two inboard 0·50s and 800 rounds. From June 1944 onwards, all production F6F-5s also had provision for wing radome and cockpit equipment to be fitted easily after delivery, permitting their conversion to F6F-5N night fighters (with AN/APS-6) at will.

By comparison with the Mitsubishi A6M5 Zero-Sen, the F6F-5 had a speed advantage of 45 mph (72 km/h) at 10,000 ft (3 050 m) and 75 mph (121 km/h) at 25,000 ft (7 625 m). Up to an altitude of about 9,000 ft (2 745 m) the Hellcat's rate of climb was inferior by as much as 600 ft/min (3,05 m/sec) but the climb performance was about equal at 14,000 ft (4 270 m) and at higher altitudes the Hellcat out-climbed the Zero-Sen by 250–500 ft/min (1,3–2,5 m/sec). Manœuvrability of the A6M5 was still generally superior to that of the F6F-5, as had been the case with earlier Hellcat models, particularly at low speeds and in turns at low and medium altitudes, but the F6F-5 compared favourably at 30,000 ft (9 150 m) and above — altitudes at which, admittedly, combat rarely took place. In slow speed turns, the A6M5 gained one turn in three-and-a-half at 10,000 ft (3 050 m). Compared with its old rival the Corsair, the F6F-5 matched the F4U-1D in level speed at 10,000 ft (3 050 m), but the Corsair had a slight advantage both below and above this altitude.

The F6F-5 and F6F-5N were both in service by the late summer of 1944, and all operational squadrons were issued with the type as rapidly as production permitted. These variants saw major action in the invasion of Leyte and associated attacks on Formosa launched by Task Force 58 on 10 October. For the first time, one aircraft carrier, the USS *Independence*, was dedicated to night operations, carrying 14 F6F-5Ns of VF(N)-41 plus five day-fighting Hellcats for its own protection and eight radar-equipped TBM-1Ds. Another 41 F6F-3Ns and -5Ns were shared by the day fighter units aboard eight other large carriers in the Task Force, but the intensity of operations by day, and the need to keep many aircraft on deck throughout the night, made the use of the night fighters from these carriers an added and unpopular burden for the deck crews. The Hellcats of VF(N)-41 achieved early success when they destroyed five Mitsubishi G4Ms trying to shadow the fleet during the night of 12/13 October.

Hellcats were now serving aboard escort carriers as well as the larger ships — for example, with VF-22 and VF-29 on the USS *Cowpens* and *Cabot* — their rôle being to provide (with the remaining Wildcat units) continuous CAPs over the Task Force, while the latter's fighters accompanied the strike formations attacking Formosa and Leyte. Major air fighting ensued in these actions, with heavy losses being suffered on both sides, but the inexperience of Japanese aircrews thrown into the battle was manifestly obvious on a number of occasions. For example, in one incident, Japanese fighters escorting a bomber formation went into a defensive circle when intercepted by eight Hellcats from VF-15, and were held in it for 90 minutes, until the F6Fs had expended all their fuel and ammunition; 25 of the Japanese aircraft were claimed shot down — nine by Cdr David McCampbell, who was to become the USN's top-scoring ace, and one of many to achieve "ace" status while flying the Hellcat, which became known throughout the Navy as "The Ace Maker".

The Leyte action was the first in which *Kamikaze* (suicide)

the seven-star airplane.

★ **WIDE-BODIED**
Shorts SD3-30 is the only 30-seat wide-bodied commuter in the world—and that gives it a clear start in passenger comfort and convenience, with features that make it unique in the commuter field.

★ **LUXURIOUS**
Making the most of the spacious cabin, SD3-30's design incorporates comforts like luxury three-abreast seating: generous aisle: air-conditioning: overhead lockers: washroom facilities: a galley and provision for a cabin attendant.

★ **QUIET**
PT6 free-turbine engines driving 5-bladed Hartzell propellers combine to make SD3-30 a remarkably quiet airliner, with noise levels well below FAR Part 36 requirements—ensuring good neighbor operations and in-flight relaxation.

★ **ECONOMICAL**
SD3-30's attractive initial cost combines with low operating and maintenance costs to make it a highly economical proposition for airline operators.

★ **RELIABLE**
Based on the design of the successful Shorts Skyvan light transport, SD3-30 incorporates the major design, construction and reliability features of the small STOL aircraft which has proved its capabilities in some of the world's most arduous areas of operation.

★ **CONVERTIBLE**
Designed with built-in quick change capabilities, SD3-30 can be rapidly converted to passenger/cargo or all-cargo roles. A large forward cargo door permits easy loading of bulky items and a range of containers up to and including D-size units can be accommodated.

★ **PROFITABLE**
With role versatility linked to economy of operation, SD3-30 is one of the world's really cost-effective airliners—capable of achieving new profitability even on normally marginal routes.

SHORTS
Aircraft and Missiles

1967 1968 1969 1970 1971 1972 1973 1975
THE QUEEN'S AWARD TO INDUSTRY

Belfast and London

SD3-30

NORTH AMERICAN LIAISON OFFICE
Shorts Aircraft, Tower Building, Logan International Airport, Boston, Mass., 02128 USA.   Phone: 617-569-6110
Telex: 710 329 0325 AIRCRAFTUS BSN

S. E. ASIA LIAISON OFFICE
Shorts Airservices Pty Ltd, Challenger House, 15-17 Young Street, Sydney 2000, NSW, Australia.   Phone: Sydney 27-3275
Cables: "Airshort"

Page i

"The aim of the exercise is to put the bombs on the target and that's what Jaguar does better than anything else". Those are the words of the Officer Commanding the first Royal Air Force unit to operate the Jaguar. He added : "Jaguar can . . . optimise the 'stick' effect so that, in terms of total weapons effect, we are way ahead of most other aircraft . . . For the first time, really, we have got an aircraft with which one can virtually *guarantee,* on interdiction-type targets, making the fast, low-level, straight-pass attack . . ."

"The aim of the exercise is to put the bombs on the target...

...and that's what Jaguar does better than anything else..."

attacks were launched by Japanese Navy pilots, bringing a sharp increase in shipping losses and calling for changes in the defensive tactics employed by the F6F-equipped squadrons, plus an increase in the number of Hellcats carried by each of the aircraft carriers at the expense of attack aircraft. By December 1944, for example, VF-20 on *Lexington* and VF-80 on *Ticonderoga* each had 73 Hellcats, while there were only 15 SB2C Helldivers on each ship. The F6F-5 was far from being ideal in the short-range target defence rôle, having insufficient rate of climb and initial acceleration, but its performance in the offensive fighter rôle remained impressive, and the year ended with the appearance of the "Big Blue Blanket" over Japanese airfields on Luzon — virtually continuous fighter sweeps during daylight and fighter interdictions by night. The operation, involving 497 F6Fs by day and 39 by night, was organised by Cdr J S Thach and it effectively sterilised Japanese attempts to attack Task Force 38 as it supported the invasion of Mindoro. On 14 October, 46 of 69 Japanese aircraft were destroyed as they attempted to take-off, and 20 out of 27 Mitsubishi A6M Zero-Sen and Nakajima Ki. 43 Hayabusa fighters flying in as reinforcements from Formosa were shot down by eight F6F-5s of VF-80.

Operations continued at a similar high intensity throughout the first half of 1945, Hellcats seeing their last combat action of the war on 15 August, when six F6F-5s of VF-88 (USS *Yorktown*) met 12 A6Ms, shooting down nine but losing four Hellcats in the process. From February 1945 onwards, US Navy squadrons flying the Hellcat were supplemented by four squadrons of the Marine Corps, one each aboard the escort carriers USS *Block Island, Gilbert Islands, Cape Gloucester* and *Vella Gulf*. Each of these units had a mix of eight F6F-5Ns and two F6F-5Ps, the latter, like the F6F-3P, carrying a camera in the fuselage for high-altitude photography. Many US Navy units also included F6F-5Ps in their strength during the last few months of the war.

Shortly after production of the F6F-5 had started, two standard airframes were fitted with R-2800-18W engines, these being representative of the new strengthened C-series Double Wasps with ratings of 2,100 hp dry and 2,450 hp with water injection at sea level, and an output of 1,800 hp at 21,900 ft (6 680 m). Designated XF6F-6, the first of these experimentals flew on 6 July 1944, and proved the fastest of all the Hellcats, attaining 417 mph (671 km/h) at 22,000 ft (6 710 m). Testing continued only slowly, however, and the need for more Hellcats had ended before any decision was made to switch to the new engine as a production standard. Although 1,677 Hellcats then on contract were cancelled in the wholesale termination of production contracts effected on V-J Day in August 1945, production of the type trickled on until the Navy made the final F6F-5 acceptance in November. By that time, 7,870 F6F-5s had been built, bringing the total of Hellcats to 12,275, including prototypes. Included in the F6F-5 production total were 1,434 F6F-5N night fighters, plus a number of F6F-5Es with AN/APS-4 radar like the F6F-3Es. Between early 1943 and mid-1945, no fewer than 57 US Navy squadrons equipped with Hellcats and took them aboard aircraft carriers, although a few of these were too late to see much action; of this total, seven squadrons specialised in night fighting and flew the F6F-3E, -3N, -5E and -5N almost exclusively, and at least 30 of the units operated F6F-3Ps or -5Ps for reconnaissance alongside the day fighters. Additional Hellcat units, both Navy and Marine Corps, operated only from shore bases, and at least four Marine squadrons used the Grumman fighter from escort carriers.

Hellcats for Britain

Under lend-lease arrangements, Britain had begun to receive F6F-3s in the early summer of 1943, and a total of 252 was delivered, to serve with Fleet Air Arm squadrons with the designation Hellcat F Mk I (after the name Gannet had been briefly considered). Nos 800 and 804 Squadrons worked up on the new type side-by-side at RNAS Eglinton, Derry, with No 800 taking credit as the first to be commissioned on the Grumman fighter. Most of the second half of 1943 was taken up by training, including intensive flying during August, air firing and ADDLs (airfield dummy deck landings) in September and the first deck landings aboard HMS *Ravager* in the Clyde in October. During December, the squadrons went aboard HMS *Emperor* for North Atlantic convoy duty, returning from the USA in February 1944 with additional new Hellcats on the carrier as deck cargo.

In March 1944, *Emperor* left Scapa Flow with other ships of the Home Fleet, including HMS *Victorious, Furious, Searcher, Pursuer* and *Fencer*, for the attack on the German battlecruiser *Tirpitz* in the Kaarfiord, near North Cape, in the course of which RN Hellcats were in action for the first time. When four Hellcats of No 800 Squadron were "bounced" by a mix of Focke-Wulf Fw 190As and Messerschmitt Bf 109Gs off the Norwegian coast, one was lost but the other three claimed the destruction of a German fighter apiece. By the end of April, both squadrons were detached to Hatston to re-equip with Hellcat F Mk IIs, with bomb racks, completing a short but intensive training period before re-embarking in *Emperor* to engage in anti-shipping strikes in the North Sea and off the Norwegian coast.

During June 1944, the Hellcats were painted with "invasion stripes" but on the 14th of that month, No 804 was merged with No 800 and it was the latter unit that flew the RN's final operations in the Mediterranean area in September, after supporting, from *Emperor*, the D-Day landings in the South of France.

Most operational use of British Hellcats was to occur in the Far East theatre, with the help of 930 F6F-5s and 80 F6F-5N night fighters, respectively being designated F Mk II and NF Mk II in RN service. Some of the Mk IIs were fitted with cameras for the fighter reconnaissance rôle as FR Mk IIs, carrying the normal wing armament; a few operated in the unarmed photo-reconnaissance rôle as PR Mk IIs. By August 1945, 10 squadrons had been equipped with the Hellcat, these serving for the most part aboard escort carriers (including *Ruler, Empress, Ameer, Ocean, Attacker, Pursuer, Khedive, Begum* and *Shah*). Among the larger carriers, HMS *Indomitable* alone carried Hellcats, Nos 1839 and 1844 Squadrons forming No 5 Fighter Wing. These units participated in the FAA's first major action against Japanese targets, the attack on oil refineries in Sumatra in January 1945. Thereafter, the Wing built up an excellent reputation as a general-purpose fighter unit, especially successful in ground attack sorties. The squadrons aboard the escort carriers operated principally in support of the assault on Malaya and Burma, seeing action right up to September as

Among the foreign users of F6F-5 Hellcats in the immediate post-war years were (above) the Aviacion Naval of Uruguay and (below) the French Aéronavale, for service in Indo-China.

Grumman F6F-5 Hellcat Cutaway Drawing Key

1 Radio mast
2 Rudder balance
3 Rudder upper hinge
4 Aluminium alloy fin ribs
5 Rudder post
6 Rudder structure
7 Rudder trim tab
8 Rudder middle hinge
9 Diagonal stiffeners
10 Aluminium alloy elevator trim tab
11 Fabric-covered (and taped) elevator surfaces
12 Elevator balance
13 Flush riveted leading-edge strip
14 Arrester hook (extended)
15 Tailplane ribs
16 Tail navigation (running) light
17 Rudder lower hinge
18 Arrester hook (stowed)
19 Fin main spar lower cut-out
20 Tailplane end rib
21 Fin forward spar
22 Fuselage/fin root fairing
23 Port elevator
24 Aluminium alloy-skinned tailplane
25 Section light
26 Fuselage aft frame
27 Control access
28 Bulkhead
29 Tailwheel hydraulic shock-absorber
30 Tailwheel centering mechanism
31 Tailwheel steel mounting arm
32 Rearward-retracting tailwheel (hard rubber tyre)
33 Fairing
34 Steel plate door fairing
35 Tricing sling support tube
36 Hydraulic actuating cylinder
37 Flanged ring fuselage frames
38 Control cable runs
39 Fuselage longerons
40 Relay box
41 Dorsal rod antenna
42 Dorsal recognition light
43 Radio aerial
44 Radio mast
45 Aerial lead-in
46 Dorsal frame stiffeners
47 Junction box
48 Radio equipment (upper rack)
49 Radio shelf
50 Control cable runs
51 Transverse brace
52 Remote radio compass
53 Ventral recognition lights (3)
54 Ventral rod antenna
55 Destructor device
56 Accumulator
57 Radio equipment (lower rack)
58 Entry hand/footholds
59 Engine water injection tank
60 Canopy track
61 Water filler neck
62 Rear-view window
63 Rearward-sliding cockpit canopy (open)
64 Headrest
65 Pilot's head/shoulder armour
66 Canopy sill (reinforced)
67 Fire-extinguisher
68 Oxygen bottle (port fuselage wall)
69 Water tank mounting
70 Underfloor self-sealing fuel tank (60 US gal/227 l)

71 Armoured bulkhead
72 Starboard console
73 Pilot's seat
74 Hydraulic handpump
75 Fuel filler cap and neck
76 Rudder pedals
77 Central console
78 Control column
79 Chart board (horizontal stowage)
80 Instrument panel
81 Panel coaming
82 Reflector gunsight
83 Rear-view mirror
84 Armoured glass windshield
85 Deflection plate (pilot forward protection)
86 Main bulkhead armour-plated upper section with hoisting sling attachments port and starboard)
87 Aluminium alloy aileron trim tab
88 Fabric covered (and taped) aileron surfaces
89 Flush riveted outer wing skin
90 Aluminium alloy sheet wing tip (riveted to wing outer rib)
91 Port navigation (running) light
92 Formed leading-edge (approach/landing light and camera gun inboard)
93 Fixed cowling panel
94 Armour plate (oil tank forward protection)
95 Oil tank (19 US gal/72 l)
96 Welded engine mount fittings
97 Fuselage forward bulkhead
98 Aileron control linkage
99 Engine accessories bay

100 Engine mounting frame (hydraulic fluid reservoir attached to port frames)
101 Controllable cooling gills
102 Cowling ring (removable servicing/access panels)
103 Pratt & Whitney R-2800-10W twin-row radial air-cooled engine
104 Nose ring profile
105 Reduction gear housing
106 Three-blade Hamilton Standard Hydromatic controllable pitch propeller
107 Propeller hub
108 Engine oil cooler (centre) and supercharger intercooler (outer sections) intakes
109 Oil cooler deflection plate under-protection
110 Oil cooler duct
111 Intercooler intake duct
112 Mainwheel fairing
113 Port mainwheel
114 Cooler outlet and fairing
115 Auxiliary tank support/attachment arms
116 Exhaust cluster
117 Supercharger housing
118 Exhaust outlet scoop
119 Wing front spar web
120 Wing front spar/fuselage attachment bolts
121 Undercarriage mounting/pivot point on front spar
122 Inter-spar self-sealing fuel tanks (port and starboard: 87·5 US gal/331 l each)
123 Wing rear spar/fuselage attachment bolts
124 Structural end rib

125 Slotted wing flap profile
126 Wing flap centre-section
127 Wing fold line
128 Starboard wheel well (doubler-plate reinforced edges)
129 Gun bay
130 Removable diagonal brace strut
131 Three 0·5-in (12,7-mm) Colt Browning machine guns
132 Auxiliary tank aft support
133 Blast tubes
134 Folding wing joint (upper surface)
135 Machine-gun barrels
136 Fairing
137 Undercarriage actuating strut
138 Mainwheel leg oleo hydraulic shock strut
139 Auxiliary tank sling/brace
140 Long-range auxiliary fuel tank (jettisonable)
141 Mainwheel aluminium alloy fairing
142 Forged steel torque link
143 Low pressure balloon tyre
144 Cast magnesium wheel

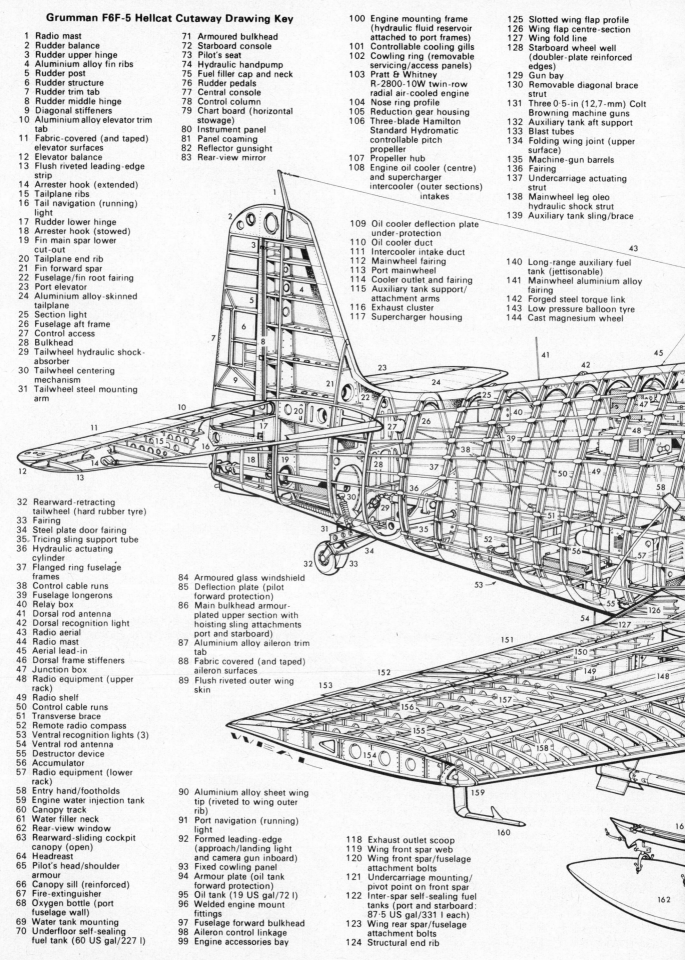

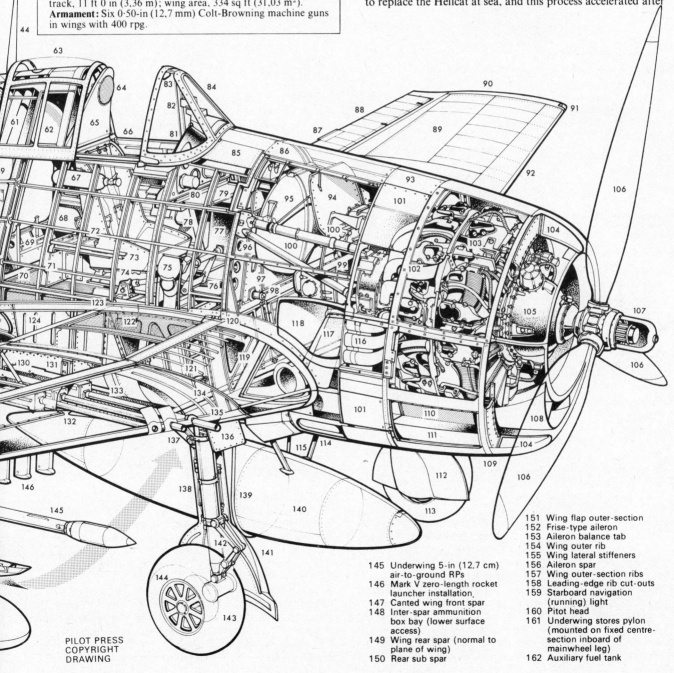

Grumman F6F-3 Specification

Power Plant: One Pratt & Whitney R-2800-10 Double Wasp 18-cylinder radial air-cooled engine with two-stage two-speed supercharger, rated at 2,000 hp for take-off and with normal ratings of 1,675 hp up to 5,500 ft (1 676 m), 1,625 hp at 16,750 ft (5 109 m) and 1,550 hp at 22,000 ft (6 710 m). Hamilton Standard three-bladed propeller, 13 ft 1 in (3,99 m) diameter. Total internal fuel capacity, 250 US gal (946 l) in two tanks in wing centre section and one in fuselage; provision for one 150-US gal (568 l) drop tank.

Performance (Clean, full internal fuel, normal power rating): Max speed, 303 mph (488 km/h) at sea level and 373 mph (600 km/h) at 23,700 ft (7 229 m); time to 15,000 ft (4 575 m), 7·7 min; time to 25,000 ft (7 625 m), 14 min; service ceiling, 37,500 ft (11 438 m); take-off distance in 15 kt (28 km/h) wind, 453 ft (138 m); max range, 1,085 mls (1 745 km) at 179 mph (288 km/h); max range (with drop tank), 1,620 mls (2 606 km) at 177 mph (285 km/h).

Weights: Empty, 9,042 lb (4 105 kg); loaded (full internal fuel), 12,186 lb (5 532 kg); max gross (with drop tanks) 13,221 lb (6 002 kg).

Dimensions: Span, 42 ft 10 in (13,08 m); span (folded, 16 ft 2 in (4,93 m); length, 33 ft 4 in (10,17 m); height, (prop vertical) 14 ft 5 in (4,40 m); wheelbase, 21 ft 5¼ in (6,54 m); undercarriage track, 11 ft 0 in (3,36 m); wing area, 334 sq ft (31,03 m²).

Armament: Six 0·50-in (12,7 mm) Colt-Browning machine guns in wings with 400 rpg.

remaining Japanese forces were mopped up after the formal surrender. On 10 September 1945, No 800 Squadron's Hellcats, still aboard HMS *Emperor*, were ceremonially lined up on deck as the ship sailed into Singapore Harbour, marking an emotional return of British rule for that tragic island.

No 888 Squadron operated Hellcat FR Mk IIs in the Pacific, but two units specialising in night operations, Nos 892 and 891, were too late for action, still being in process of working-up on NF Mk IIs at RNAS Eglinton when the war ended. No 892 proved to be one of only two RN Hellcat units to survive into 1946, the other being No 888, but these were disbanded in April and August 1946 respectively. Most of the 1,182 F6Fs supplied to Britain were quickly returned to the USA under the lend-lease terms, apart from those lost in action or through accident, and a few individual examples retained for special purposes, bringing to an end the wartime career of the Grumman fighter outside of the US Navy and Marine Corps.

By the time the war ended, the Corsair had at last been cleared for carrier operations by the US Navy and from the beginning of 1945, the Chance Vought type had slowly begun to replace the Hellcat at sea, and this process accelerated after

145 Underwing 5-in (12,7 cm) air-to-ground RPs
146 Mark V zero-length rocket launcher installation
147 Canted wing front spar
148 Inter-spar ammunition box bay (lower surface access)
149 Wing rear spar (normal to plane of wing)
150 Rear sub spar

151 Wing flap outer-section
152 Frise-type aileron
153 Aileron balance tab
154 Wing outer rib
155 Wing lateral stiffeners
156 Aileron spar
157 Wing outer-section ribs
158 Leading-edge rib cut-outs
159 Starboard navigation (running) light
160 Pitot head
161 Underwing stores pylon (mounted on fixed centre-section inboard of mainwheel leg)
162 Auxiliary fuel tank

PILOT PRESS
COPYRIGHT
DRAWING

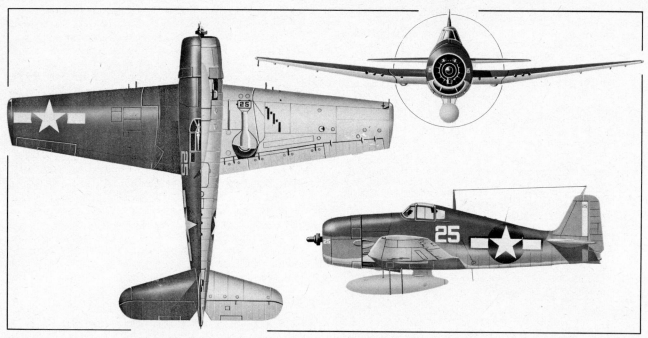

The tone drawing illustrates an F6F-3, in three-tone blue finish, serving with Navy Squadron VF-29 aboard the aircraft carrier (CVL-28) USS Cabot.

hostilities had ceased. During the time the F6F was operational with the US fleets in the Pacific area, Japanese fighters of superior performance made their service débuts, but they appeared too late to reverse the trend that the Hellcat had been largely responsible for starting — the ascendency of US Navy aircraft in Pacific actions. Although production had quickly been terminated after V-J Day, enough new Hellcats were still in the delivery pipeline for the type to remain in service for several years with US Navy and, more especially, Naval Reserve squadrons; Hellcats also became the initial equipment of the "Blue Angels" aerobatic team.

In the immediate post-war period, many surplus Hellcats were modified into F6F-5K pilotless drones, principally to be used as targets for ship-to-air gunnery practice and for guided missile firings; when required, cameras and other recording gear were carried in wing-tip pods. These drones gave the Hellcat another brief taste of action in 1952, when Guided Missile Unit 90, aboard the USS *Boxer,* launched F6F-5Ks, each carrying a 2,000-lb (908-kg) bomb, against targets in North Korea. Six such missions were flown, the first on 28 August, with each Hellcat controlled from two AD-1 Skyraiders. A small number of F6F-5D drone controllers also served with the Navy in conjunction with the F6F-5K programme, which was handled by the overhaul and repair department at NAS Pensacola from 1949 to 1958.

Hellcats saw service in the ground-attack rôle in French Indo-China from 1950 onwards, as a result of a massive infusion of American support for France in her early battle with Viet Minh forces for control of the territory later to be known as Vietnam. Surplus F6F-5s from Navy stocks were supplied for use by units of both the *Armée de l'Air* and *Aéronavale;* in the former's *escadrilles* I/6 *"Corse,"* II/6 *"Normandie-Niemen"* and II/9 *"Auvergne"* they replaced Bell P-63 Kingcobras but served for only a year or so before being succeeded in turn by F8F Bearcats. *Aéronavale* Hellcats arrived in the area on 28 October 1950, aboard the aircraft carrier *Arromanches,* equipping *Flotille* 1F (later designated 11F) as replacements for Seafires; they also served subsequently with *Flotille* 12F. Quickly in action bombing and strafing Viet Minh targets, the Hellcats were retained by these units until the end of French involvement in Indo-China in 1954, thereafter being transferred to North African bases where they were used for a few more years by several Naval training units, including 54S, 57S, 59S and 3S.

Small numbers of Hellcats were also supplied through US Mutual Aid Programs to Argentina and Uruguay, in both cases for use by the Naval air arms *(Aviacion Naval)* in those countries. The last of 12 Uruguayan F6F-5s was withdrawn in 1961, by which time the Argentine aircraft were already out of service; thus, they were the last examples of the famed Grumman fighter to see operational service although a few F6F-5K drones are believed to have been used by the US Navy subsequently, and one or two examples of the Hellcat are still flying today in private hands.

Viewed from the Cockpit

by Captain Eric Brown, CBE, DSC, AFC, RN

To me, the Hellcat will always be the big brother of the Wildcat — and that's just exactly what it was. All the family characteristics were to be found in both aircraft, but they were more fully developed and matured in the case of the Hellcat. I first flew the Hellcat just after examples began to reach the United Kingdom in July 1943, when I was attached to the Service Trials Unit at Crail in Scotland. My first impression on seeing it was almost one of awe at its size for a single-seat fighter. With its wing spanning almost 43 ft (13,1 m) and a height of more than 13 ft (4 m), this impression of the Hellcat was no illusion, and the Hamilton Standard Hydromatic propeller was immense; but the overall appearance was one of robustness which would

— continued on page 192

The Fighter that Missed the War . . .

THE LAST OF THE KOOLHOVENS

O N THE MORNING of Tuesday, 17 July 1938, the hangar of the N V Koolhoven Vliegtuigen at Waalhaven Airfield, near Rotterdam, was a hive of activity as last-minute checks and adjustments were applied to a neat, low-wing cantilever fighter monoplane, the design of which had been completed a mere two months earlier!

The remarkably swift passage of this latest in a long line of aircraft to have borne the name Koolhoven from drawing board to hardware had been prompted by French anxiety to re-equip the fighter component of the *Armée de l'Air* with as little delay as possible. The political climate in Europe was deteriorating rapidly and in February 1938, the French government had entered into negotiations with the Curtiss-Wright Corporation for the supply of 300 fighters of the Hawk 75A type. However, the unit price of Fr 2·365m being demanded by the US company was considered exorbitant by the French — the unit price of the Morane-Saulnier MS 406 was only Fr 1·314m — and the proposed delivery schedule commencing in March 1939 with 20 aircraft and continuing at a rate of 30 aircraft monthly was deemed inadequate. Furthermore, the company's track record in meeting USAAC contractual dates with deliveries of the P-36A was giving cause for disquiet.

A successful outcome to the negotiations with the US company was very much in doubt and, in consequence, the French government sought a fighter elsewhere that could serve as a stopgap until the French aircraft industry could meet all the demands of the *Armée de l'Air*, or as a back-up for the Hawk 75A in the event that agreement be reached with Curtiss-Wright. The British aircraft industry was fully occupied in endeavouring to meet the demands of the RAF expansion programme; as Germany was the potential enemy the acquisition of combat aircraft from that source was out of the question and of the major European aircraft manufacturing countries only the Netherlands remained. Fokker was fully occupied with the D XXI and the G I for the *Luchtvaartafdeling*, but an approach to the N V Koolhoven Vliegtuigen resulted in the remarkable statement from the company's managing director and chief engineer, Fritz Koolhoven: "You people need quickly a really good fighter with a performance better than the Hawk 75A; I'll build you one!"

On that morning in July 1938, it was apparent that Koolhoven had certainly fulfilled his claim that he could build a fighter quickly; whether its performance was better than that of the Hawk 75A remained to be seen. Primarily responsible for the detail design of this new fighter, the FK 58, had been Dr Erich Schatzki, who had led the design team that had created the

Among the best-known figures of the 'tween-wars European aviation scene was Frederick "Fritz" Koolhoven, a portly Dutchman whose good nature and sense of humour earned him many friends — to whom he was popularly known as "Cully" — and forthright opinions gained him almost as many enemies. Fritz Koolhoven began designing aeroplanes in 1910, first in France, then in the UK, where he was responsible for many of the Armstrong Whitworth designs and such types as the BAT Bantam and Basilisk, and finally in Holland, where he established the company that bore his name. He was a prolific designer — he never allowed much time to elapse without producing a new design, whether a conventional "pot-boiler" or a revolutionary type embodying numerous innovations — and during a design career spanning 30 years he built and flew some 60 different aeroplanes. His last creation to see quantity production was the FK 58, and the somewhat unusual story of this single-seat fighter designed primarily for the French government is told on these pages by T J M Wesselink

Fokker D XXI and G I, but had left the Fokker concern in March 1938, following a disagreement with the management. On the same day that Dr Schatzki resigned from Fokker, he had applied to Fritz Koolhoven for employment, had been engaged immediately and had been placed in charge of the FK 58 project which was then in preliminary design. Work on both the design and prototype construction of the FK 58 had proceeded at a tremendous tempo, as was evidenced by the fact that Koolhoven's test pilot, Thomas H J Coppers, had eased himself into the cockpit of the new fighter prior to its first test flight barely three months after Dr Schatzki had first begun work in the Waalhaven factory.

Fritz Koolhoven hovered around the prototype as it was pushed from the hangar, displaying none of the anxiety that he surely felt. Barely more than two weeks earlier, on 30 June, Coppers had flown for the first time the highly innovative FK 55 fighter from the Welschap Airfield, Eindhoven, after almost two years of development tribulation, and just two minutes of flying time had been sufficient for the decision to be reached that no further effort should be expended on the aircraft. However, the FK 55 had been of extremely radical design whereas the FK 58 was a thoroughly orthodox aeroplane; a simple, sturdy structure and a completely conventional design

— Koolhoven had rarely succeeded with the radical but had kept himself in business with the conventional. Of course, he had an *idée fixe* about low-wing monoplanes. At many a design conference when the merits of various wing positions had been discussed, he asked: "Have you ever seen a bird with wings on its stomach?" In the case of the FK 58 he had been compelled to bow to the inevitable; a low wing was considered *de rigueur* by the French for any single-engined fighter. He consoled himself with the thought that the FK 58 was not a *true* low-wing monoplane, the wing, in fact, being set in the low-*mid* position.

Coppers started the Hispano-Suiza 14AA* 14-cylinder direct-drive air-cooled radial engine, allowed this to warm up and then steadily advanced the throttle. When he was satisfied that the power plant was functioning smoothly, he waved away the wheel chocks, taxied carefully down the field, turned into wind and began a high-speed run, lifting the prototype a few feet into the air as he passed the onlookers and remaining airborne for about a hundred yards before touching down. He turned, taxied back, repeated the procedure, and then, confident that he had the feel of the controls, took-off and climbed away from the field at a shallow angle over the suburbs of Rotterdam. After 10 minutes, Coppers reappeared over the field, demonstrated several simple manoeuvres and then came in to a perfect landing. Coppers reported to Koolhoven and Schatzki that he was more than satisfied with the behaviour of the prototype during its first flight. No attempt had been made to retract the undercarriage but at the low speeds at which the aircraft had been flown the aircraft had behaved impeccably. It had responded well to the controls, which had proved light but positive, and had revealed no undesirable characteristics.

In the days that followed, several more tests were conducted before an attempt was made to retract the undercarriage in the air and this very nearly ended in disaster. Coppers retracted and

---

There is some uncertainty as to the exact sub-type of the HS 14AA engine installed in the first prototype FK 58. Some sources have indicated an HS 14AA-10 but are certainly incorrect as this engine rotated in a clockwise direction whereas the Hamilton Standard propeller fitted to the aircraft rotated anti-clockwise. It is possible that the engine actually installed in the aircraft was the HS 14AA-11 which had anti-clockwise rotation and had the same output as the -10

extended the undercarriage several times while circling the field and the mechanism functioned perfectly, but as he made his landing approach he became aware that he had an undercarriage malfunction. There was no undercarriage position indicator in the cockpit but before he had taken-off a system of ground signals utilising planks of wood had been agreed — the planks representing his port undercarriage leg were at an angle of 90 deg to indicate that the leg was fully extended, but those representing the starboard leg were angled at 45 deg to signal that the gear was only partly down. Coppers increased power, climbed and then put the aircraft into a vicious sideslip in the hope that this manoeuvre would lock the leg down. He then turned in once more to land, receiving an "all clear" signal and landing safely.

Confirmation of French interest

The flight testing of the first prototype continued throughout the summer and early autumn of 1938, Fritz Koolhoven being sufficiently satisfied with the potential of the fighter to authorise work to start on a second prototype, long leadtime items and preparations for an initial production batch of FK 58 fighters. The silver finish of the aircraft had, meanwhile, given place to sky blue and the registration PH-ATO had been applied. Furthermore, the angle of wing incidence had been increased. The French *Ministère de l'Air* had requested an armament of four 7,5-mm FN-Browning Mle 38 machine guns and it was proposed that these weapons be mounted in a pair of gondolas fitting flush beneath the wings immediately outboard of the main undercarriage attachment points, although guns had not been fitted for the factory flight test programme and had still to be provided when Thomas Coppers flew the prototype to France for a demonstration to be given at Villacoublay on 10 October.

The FK 58 prototype was then handed over to *Centre d'Essais du Matériel Aérien* (CEMA) for official evaluation. Initial high speed trials at Villacoublay proved disappointing, maximum attainable speed being only 278 mph (448 km/h) which was appreciably below the 310 mph (500 km/h) guaranteed by Koolhoven. It was then discovered that the wrong propeller had been inadvertently fitted and when this was changed speeds were clocked that came closer to those promised, 300 mph (483 km/h) being recorded at 17,390 ft (5 300 m) and 553 mph (890 km/h) being clocked in a dive from 16,405 ft (5 000 m). An altitude of 26,245 ft (8 000 m) could be attained in 12 min and *Capitaine* Ladousse, the CEMA pilot primarily responsible for the evaluation of the Dutch fighter, submitted an essentially favourable report on the characteristics of the aircraft, his principal criticism concerning the undercarriage which he considered to be too tall. On 19 October, the FK 58 was transferred to Cazaux, where, after installation of the quartet of FN-Brownings, gun-firing trials were held. These were adjudged

The second prototype FK 58 (below) was flown on 14 February 1939, and differed little from the first prototype (above left) in final form or the four Hispano-Suiza-engined production aircraft apart from the intake under the engine cowling.

highly successful and the fighter was pronounced a stable firing platform.

With completion of the Villacoublay and Cazaux trials, the prototype was prepared for exhibition at the *XVIème Salon International de l'Aéronautique* in Paris held between 25 November and 1 December 1938, where Fritz Koolhoven, who was perhaps even more of a showman than his countryman Anthony Fokker and tended to display equal disregard for accuracy in the interests of publicity, presented the FK 58 as *"l'avion le plus rapide du monde!"* In December, the prototype left France for the Netherlands, but during the course of the flight the engine overheated and seized, necessitating a forced landing near Ghent, Belgium, the aircraft suffering such extensive damage that it was considered irrepairable. The wreckage was subsequently salvaged and transported to the *Ecole des Mécaniciens* at Rochefort, France, where the remains were used for instructional purposes, PH-ATO being finally struck from the Dutch register on 17 January 1939.

Meanwhile, on 17 May 1938, France's Air Minister, Guy La Chambre, had announced that, in view of the increasing urgency attached to the modernisation of the *Armée de l'Air*, the Hawk 75A would be purchased, price notwithstanding, but France needed modern fighters for her colonial territories in the Far East where Japanese expansion was causing much concern, and it was obvious that the *Armée de l'Air* needed all the Curtiss fighters that it could obtain for issue to home-based elements and there was little likelihood that any could be spared for deployment in Indochina. Thus, in January 1939, *Marché* 177/9 calling for 50 Koolhoven FK 58 fighters was placed on behalf of the Ministry of Colonial Affairs, the intention being to equip three *escadrilles* with this type in Indochina, where, at that time, no fighters were available. The order specified the use of the Gnôme-Rhône 14N39 14-cylinder two-row air-cooled radial providing 990 hp at sea level and 1,030 hp at 16,405 ft (5 000 m) and a seat suitable for a French Lemercier back-type parachute; the armament, OPL 31 gun sight, Munerelle oxygen system and instrumentation were to be installed after delivery in France.

By the time this order was placed, the production line at the Waalhaven factory was already well advanced, Fritz Koolhoven having entertained no doubts as to the saleability of the FK 58 fighter even in the unlikely event that the anticipated French order failed to materialise, and, in fact, both the second prototype and the first production FK 58 were completed on 27 January 1939. These aircraft were fitted with the Hispano-Suiza 14AA engine and as the next three production aircraft were virtually complete and similarly powered, the French agreed to accept the first four aircraft of its contract with the Hispano-Suiza engine*, all remaining aircraft having the Gnôme-Rhône.

Deliveries commence

The FK 58 had a sturdy but relatively simple structure. The wing was of wooden construction built in one piece and comprising two box-spars, plywood ribs and plywood skinning. All movable surfaces were metal framed and split flaps were mounted between the ailerons and the fuselage. The fuselage itself was a welded steel-tube structure, duralumin skinning being used from the engine bulkhead to immediately aft of the pilot's cockpit and for the decking of the rear fuselage, the remainder being fabric covered, and the braced tailplane and fin were of wooden construction with plywood skinning, the rudder and elevators being metal framed and fabric covered. Fuel was housed in three tanks, one in the wing carry-through structure and one in each inboard wing section, these having a total capacity of 99 Imp gal (450 l), and the undercarriage of the second prototype and all subsequent FK 58 fighters was hydraulically operated. The undercarriage units comprised Koolhoven oleo struts and Dunlop wheels and brakes and

*The HS 14AA engine had not, in fact, been ordered into production, only a pre-series having been built after which further work had stopped

The first Gnôme-Rhône-engined FK 58 (sixth production airframe) with original cowling and spinner.

retracted into a fuselage bay immediately aft of the engine.

The FN-Browning machine guns were pneumatically operated and their installation was the essence of simplicity and efficiency. The guns were attached to a steel tube by means of steel strips, the tube being attached in turn to the wing by means of two bolts. By releasing the two bolts, the tube complete with guns was detached from the wing and thus a gun change could be effected with extreme rapidity. An ingenious Koolhoven idea incorporated in the ammunition supply was a short train of small rectangular cups over which the ammunition belt was fed, this eliminating the possibility of including an oversize round and thus removing a major cause of gun jamming. The theoretical ammunition capacity was 900 rounds per gun, but in practice it was to be found that only 700 rounds for each inboard gun and 600 rounds for each outboard gun was possible. Provision was made for the installation of French Radio-Industrie 537 R/T with its twin aerial masts, the ventral mast being retractable, this having an air-to-air range of about 30 miles (50 km) and an air-to-ground range of some 95 miles (150 km).

The Hispano-Suiza 14AA engine utilised by both prototypes and the first four production aircraft offered 1,030 hp for take-off and had an international rating of 1,080 hp at 2,000 rpm at 13,125 ft (4 000 m). Driving a three-bladed constant-speed propeller, it was enclosed by a large-diameter NACA-type cowling with controllable gills. Its replacement by the Gnôme-Rhône 14N39 did not present major difficulties as both power plants had essentially similar weights and overall dimensions, but some cooling and drag problems were encountered. A longer chord, smooth cowling was initially adopted, the controllable exhaust gills were discarded and the exhaust was collected and ejected through a single duct on each side, the cowling being accompanied by a large propeller spinner and applied to the sixth production FK 58. This cowling and spinner combination allowed insufficient cooling airflow and therefore a smaller spinner and redesigned cowling were then fitted to this aircraft. Of slightly smaller diameter, necessitating the provision of small rocker-arm blisters, the new cowling and accompanying spinner provided greater intake area and after satisfactory trials was standardised for all subsequent production aircraft, the carburettor air intake that had been extended forward to the cowling lip simultaneously being deepened and the carburettor air intake being amalgamated in the same scoop.

The second prototype FK 58 (c/n 5802), registered PH-AVA, had flown for the first time on 14 February 1939, with Thomas Coppers* at the controls, and externally differed little from its predecessor, but some weight had been saved by the change from mechanical to hydraulic undercarriage actuation and an undercarriage position indicator had been provided in the

*Coppers, who was to be responsible for most of the flight testing of the FK 58 prototypes and for much of the production flight testing, was to lose his life on 4 January 1940 while performing diving trials with the FK 56 two-seat light reconnaissance monoplane. The dives were being filmed by the Dutch technical authorities and Coppers had arranged to enter the dive from a loop at about 9,000 ft (2 745 m). In the event, he apparently misjudged the angle of dive, pulled out too violently — exerting some 12g — and wrenched off the wingtips. Coppers presumably blacked out for he made no attempt to bale out until the aircraft entered a spin. When he eventually jumped he was too late and his chute did not completely open before he hit the ground

cockpit. The tailwheel had been moved forward about 12 in (30 cm), the tailplane bracing had been strengthened, the aileron hinges refined and the exhaust system revised. Acceptance of the four Hispano-Suiza-powered FK 58s by a detachment from the French *Centre de Réception des Avions de Série* (CRAS) at Waalhaven Airfield began late in May 1939, and the first production aircraft was ferried from Waalhaven to Villacoublay by one *Capitaine* Perrin on 17 June, the flight taking 56 minutes. For their ferry flights, these aircraft were assigned temporary Dutch civil registrations, these being applied in soluble white paint to the fuselage sides, and the French national markings which were applied to the wings and tail at the factory were temporarily obscured by similar paint. These aircraft, PH-AVB (c/n 5803), PH-AVE (c/n 5804), PH-AVG (c/n 5805) and PH-AVH (c/n 5806), were assigned the French serial numbers C-016 to -019 inclusive and underwent protracted

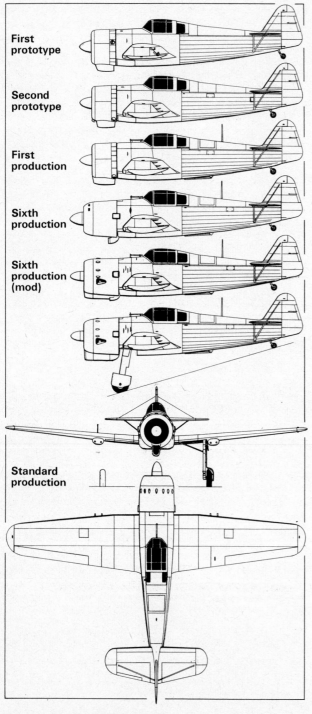

First prototype

Second prototype

First production

Sixth production

Sixth production (mod)

Standard production

tests at both Villacoublay and Cazaux, and then at the *Centre d'Expériences Aériennes Militaires* (CEAM). The consensus of opinion was unfavourable, largely because of the presence in the rear fuselage of 220 lb (100 kg) of ballast that had been found necessary to keep the CG within limits after weight growth in the pre-series Hispano-Suiza engine and its accessories, and acceptance of the aircraft was refused. The four aircraft were, in consequence, assigned to the *Centre d'Instruction de Chasse* at Etampes. There they were destined to remain unused, two eventually being reassigned to the *Ecole des Mécaniciens* at Rochefort and the other two being destroyed on the ground during a *Luftwaffe* attack on Etampes.

The Dutch *Luchtvaartafdeling* (LVA) had meanwhile been evincing some interest in the Koolhoven fighter, and in October 1938, Lt Gen M Raaijmakers, the Inspector of Military Aviation, had suggested that an investigation should be conducted to determine the desirability of expanding the fighter component of the LVA, his suggestion being accompanied by a proposal that a third *Jachtvliegtuigafdeling* of 19 fighters (and later a fourth JaVA) should be equipped with a Taurus-engined version of the FK 58, this replacing, at least temporarily, one of the two programmed Fokker G I-equipped *afdelingen*.

Initially, there was no official reaction to Gen Raaijmakers' ideas, and although Fritz Koolhoven realised that some serious discussion concerning the FK 58 was taking place in LVA circles, there was little he could do at that time to promote his fighter to the Dutch authorities as the sole prototype flying was in France. However, he had never been guilty of allowing the grass to grow under his feet. Convinced that a conflict in Europe was inevitable and that it would be only a matter of time before he received a production order for the FK 58 from the LVA, he was aware that the strict limitations of his relatively small Waalhaven factory would render fulfilment of the impending French order for the fighter *and* an order from the LVA difficult in the extreme. He therefore initiated negotiations with the Belgian *Société Anonyme Belge de Constructions Aéronautiques* (SABCA) to sub-contract some of the future FK 58 production to this concern. In the event, an initial sub-contract was in due course placed by Koolhoven with SABCA for 10 of the French-contract FK 58s, and the Belgian company completed all the airframes by 10 May 1940, but the French authorities failed to furnish SABCA with the necessary Gnôme-Rhône engines, and after the German occupation of Belgium the airframes were scrapped.

Dutch interest crystallises

With the availability of a second prototype of the FK 58, Fritz Koolhoven lost no time in soliciting orders for the fighter from the LVA, and on 31 March 1939, Coppers demonstrated PH-AVA at Soesterberg. For the next two days, various LVA pilots flew the prototype and all submitted favourable reports concerning its general handling qualities and performance. Finally, on 22 July, Fritz Koolhoven received an order on behalf of the LVA for 36 aircraft to be powered by the 1,080 hp Bristol Taurus III sleeve-valve radial, and in September an order was placed with the Bristol Aeroplane Company for 40 of these engines at a total contract price of £125,747. The aircraft ordered by the LVA were referred to as fighter-*reconnaissance* aircraft, although no special provision for the secondary reconnaissance rôle was specified in the contract.

Airframe production tempo was meanwhile building up at Waalhaven and, on 26 June, the first Gnôme-Rhône-engined production FK 58 (c/n 5808)* PH-AVK had flown, this being delivered to the CEMA at Villacoublay late in July. By 17 August, four additional FK 58s — (c/n 5809) PH-AVL, (c/n 5810) PH-AVM, (c/n 5811) PH-AVN and (c/n 5812)

This was actually the sixth production airframe, the fifth airframe (c/n 5807 for which the registration PH-AVI had been reserved) being retained by the manufacturer for development purposes and being referred to later in this article

(Above) The sixth production FK 58 (formerly PH-AVK) during CEMA trials at Villacoublay after introduction of revised engine cowling and smaller propeller spinner (compare with initial form illustrated on page 187). (Below) The seventh production FK 58 seen prior to ferrying to Buc in August 1939.

PH-AVO—had flown at Waalhaven and were awaiting ferrying to France, two more, (c/n 5813) PH-AVP and (c/n 5814) PH-AVR, were being equipped with instrumentation prior to flight testing, and six more were in final assembly. However, a major problem now arose in the form of French inability to deliver the necessary instruments. On 28 August, the first four were ferried to Buc by French pilots who, with commendable initiative, removed the instruments from two of these, then returned to Rotterdam by train with the instruments. These were then used to complete the instrumentation of the next two aircraft which, in turn, were ferried to Buc. This procedure was repeated until delivery of the 17th production aircraft, (c/n 5818) PH-AVX, this being the 13th Gnôme-Rhône-engined fighter, and these aircraft were assigned the French serials C-020 to -032 inclusive. The fighters were held on charge at Buc unflown after their arrival from the Netherlands as they were incompletely equipped.

At this juncture, Koolhoven was encountering increasing difficulties in obtaining vitally necessary items of equipment from France because of the priority enjoyed by the French aircraft industry, and the assembly line at Waalhaven was virtually brought to a halt. The situation was further complicated by French governmental fears that Dutch neutrality could result in an embargo being imposed on delivery of the remaining FK 58 fighters. It was concluded that both problems could be overcome by transferring to France production of those aircraft still outstanding against the contract. Accordingly, the airframes of the remaining 23 French contract fighters, which were in various stages of assembly with eight virtually complete,

were removed from the Waalhaven factory during the last week of August, loaded aboard a coastal freighter and, on 1 September, unshipped at Le Havre, whence they were transported to an empty warehouse in Nevers where it was proposed to complete manufacture with the aid of Koolhoven personnel.

By December, the necessary instruments, oxygen systems, radio equipment and other accessories required for the FK 58 fighters that had been flown into Buc had arrived. On the 2nd of that month, C-020 (formerly PH-AVK) was flown to the *Centre d'Essais* at Orléans-Bricy, and during the course of December, this aircraft and eight others were accepted by the CRAS and officially taken on *Armée de l'Air* strength, the four remaining aircraft being delivered to the CRAS during the first 10 days of January and officially taken on charge during February. In the meantime, the Soviet Union had launched its assault on Finland and, somewhat optimistically, the French government offered the Finns, among other aircraft, the 46 Gnôme-Rhône-engined FK 58s; the Finns reserved the serials KN501-545 for the Koolhoven fighters, unaware that, at this point in time, only 13 such fighters existed! Of the remaining 33, the 10 airframes being built under sub-contract by SABCA were nearing completion, but the Belgian company had still to receive its first engine, set of instruments, etc, and the 23 that had been transferred to Nevers for completion were little nearer delivery than when they had arrived from the Netherlands, it having been discovered that the mere transfer to France had not overcome the bottleneck in the supply of equipment. On 29 February, two of the FK 58s were, in fact, transferred to the *Entrepôt de l'Armée de l'Air* at Romorantin where they were to be prepared for shipment to Finland, but before they could be embarked at Le Havre, news arrived of the Soviet-Finnish Armistice.

At the end of March 1940, consideration was given to issuing the FK 58s to a *Groupe de Chasse* which it was proposed to form with Polish and Czechoslovak pilots and send to the Lebanon, but this scheme made no progress, and some discussions were held between the French and Yugoslav govern-

— continued on page 198

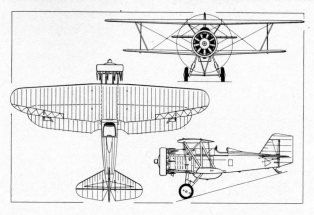

(Above and below) The F6C-4 delivered to the US Navy in 1927 proved more manœuvrable than earlier Curtiss V-1150-powered F6Cs (see March issue).

CURTISS F6C-4 (HAWK)   USA

The US Navy had decided, by 1927, to standardise on air-cooled radial engines which were more easily maintained at sea than liquid-cooled inline engines. Accordingly, after trials with a Pratt & Whitney R-1340-engined F6C-3, a production contract was placed for 31 fighters powered by this 410 hp radial as F6C-4s, the first of these aircraft, which was retained for test

Experimental versions of the F6C included the Hornet-powered XF6C-5 (above) and the Ranger SGV-770-engined XF6C-7 (below).

purposes, being assigned the designation XF6C-4 and deliveries commencing in February 1927. Possessing a similar twin-gun armament to its predecessors, the F6C-4 proved more manœuvrable than the V-1150-powered models but was becoming obsolescent by the time that it was delivered and remained first-line equipment only until the beginning of 1930. Experimental F6C models were the XF6C-5 (first F6C-1 fitted with a 525 hp Pratt & Whitney R-1690 Hornet), XF6C-6 (an F6C-3 converted to parasol monoplane configuration for the 1930 Thompson Trophy race), F6C-6 (an F6F-3 modified for 1929 air races and returned to -3 standard), and the XF6C-7 (an F6C-4 with an inverted air-cooled Ranger SGV-770 engine). Max speed, 155 mph (249 km/h) at sea level. Time to 5,000 ft (1 525 m), 2·5 min. Normal range, 361 mls (581 km). Empty weight, 1,980 lb (898 kg). Loaded weight, 2,785 lb (1 263 kg). Span, 31 ft 6 in (9,60 m). Length, 22 ft 6 in (6,86 m). Height, 10 ft 11 in (3,33 m). Wing area, 252 sq ft (23,41 m²).

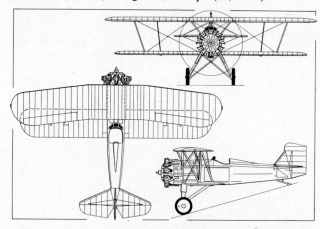

The F7C-1 (above and below) was the first Curtiss fighter designed from the outset for shipboard use.

CURTISS F7C-1 (SEAHAWK)   USA

The first Curtiss fighter designed from the outset for shipboard use as opposed to being an adaptation of a land-based fighter, the XF7C-1 single-seat carrier fighter was characterised by swept upper wing outer panels and flew for the first time on 28 February 1927. Powered by a 450 hp Pratt & Whitney R-1340-B Wasp radial, the XF7C-1 was flown both with and without a propeller spinner and was also tested with a single central float and outrigger stabilising floats. Seventeen F7C-1s were ordered for US Navy service and delivered during December 1928 and January 1929, these differing from the prototype primarily in having tripod main undercarriage members in place of the cross axle. The propeller spinner was discarded and armament comprised two 0·3-in (7,62-mm) synchronised machine guns. In the event, all F7C-1s were operated by the US Marine Corps (VF-5M) at Quantico. Max speed, 151 mph (243 km/h) at sea

The F8C-1 (above) combined the two-seat fighter rôle with those of bombing and observation, eventually being redesignated OC-1.

The XF8C-4 (above) was intended to combine two-seat fighter and dive bomber roles, and the production F8C-4 (below) became the first of the Helldivers.

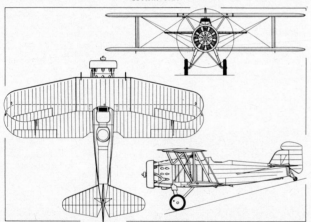

level. Time to 5,000 ft (1 525 m), 2·6 min. Normal range, 330 mls (531 km). Empty weight, 2,038 lb (924 kg). Loaded weight, 2,782 lb (1 262 kg). Span, 32 ft 8 in (9,96 m). Length, 22 ft 1⅞ in (6,75 m). Height, 10 ft 4 in (3,15 m). Wing area, 276 sq ft (25,64 m²).

CURTISS F8C-1 & -3   USA

To meet a US Marine Corps requirement for a two-seat fighter with bombing and observation capability, Curtiss adapted the airframe of the USAAC's O-1 Falcon to take the Pratt & Whitney R-1340 Wasp radial engine in place of the water-cooled Conqueror and delivered six examples, two as XF8C-1s and four as F8C-1s, in January 1928. Armament comprised two fixed forward-firing 0·3-in (7,62-mm) guns and a weapon of similar calibre on a Scarff ring in the rear cockpit, and power was provided by a 432 hp R-1340 Wasp. Twenty-one additional machines (one XF8C-3 and 20 F8C-3s) were delivered later in 1928, these being essentially similar to the F8C-1s which were redesignated as OC-1s shortly after entering service, the F8C-3s becoming OC-2s. Max speed, 144 mph (232 km/h) at sea level. Initial climb, 1,010 ft/min (5,13 m/sec). Range, 650 mls (1 046 km). Empty weight, 2,515 lb (1 140 kg). Loaded weight, 4,191 lb (1 901 kg). Span, 38 ft 0 in (11,58 m). Length, 27 ft 11 in

(8,51 m). Height, 11 ft 8 in (3,55 m). Wing area, 350 sq ft (32,52 m²).

CURTISS F8C-4 & -5 (HELLDIVER)   USA

Although designated in the F8C series, the XF8C-2 and XF8C-4 differed extensively from the F8C-1 and -3 and were dual-rôle aircraft intended for use both as two-seat fighters and as dive bombers, dive bombing techniques at that time being under development by the US Marine Corps. Possessing smaller overall dimensions than previous F8C series aircraft, featuring some structural revision and powered by a 450 hp R-1340-80 Wasp, the XF8C-2 prototype appeared early in 1929 and was equipped to carry either two 116-lb (53-kg) bombs or one 500-lb (227-kg) bomb. A second prototype, the XF8C-4, was flown in August 1929, by which time orders had been placed for 27 F8C-4s and nine F8C-5s. The XF8C-4 differed from the XF8C-2 primarily in having an R-1340-88 Wasp enclosed by a Townend ring, the latter not initially being applied to the production F8C-4 which was delivered from May 1930, and the F8C-5 differed solely in having carrier arrester gear deleted. The F8C-5s were delivered from September 1930, a further 43 being ordered for 1931 delivery, these being redesignated O2C-1s. Two F8C-5s temporarily fitted with wing flaps and leading-edge slots were designated XF8C-6s, one VIP transport version with a 575 hp Wright R-1820-64 Cyclone was designated XF8C-7 (XO2C-2) and two similarly powered examples were XF8C-8s, the designation XF10C-1 being assigned to one aircraft initially powered by a Curtiss R-1510 and subsequently re-engined with a Cyclone. The following data are applicable to the F8C-4. Max speed, 147 mph (236 mph). Time to 5,000 ft (1 525 m). Normal range, 455 mls (732 km). Empty weight, 2,513 lb (1 140 kg). Normal loaded weight, 3,783 lb (1 716 kg). Span, 32 ft 0 in (10,06 m). Length, 25 ft 7⅞ in (7,82 m). Height, 10 ft 3 in (3,12 m). Wing area, 308 sq ft (28,61 m²).

CURTISS P-5 (SUPERHAWK)   USA

A USAAC contract placed on 14 May 1927 called for five aircraft with airframes essentially similar to that of the P-1 but powered by a turbo-supercharged Curtiss V-1150-4 12-cylinder liquid-cooled engine, the first of these being delivered in January 1928 as the XP-5 with the remaining four following as P-5s by June 1928. Dubbed Superhawk by the manufacturer, the P-5 had a side-mounted exhaust-driven turbo-supercharger with which it attained a service ceiling of 31,000 ft (9 450 m). Warm air was ducted from the exhaust manifold to the cockpit, the heat being contained by a "cape" which snapped around the cockpit rim and fitted closely about the pilot. Two of the P-5s were lost in accidents shortly after delivery but the remaining two served with the 94th Pursuit Squadron until April 1932. The V-1150-4 (D-12F) engine was rated at 435 hp and armament comprised two 0·3 in (7,62-mm) machine guns. Max speed, 146 mph (235 km/h) at sea level, 173 mph (278 km/h) at 25,000 ft (7 620 m). Time to 10,000 ft (3 050 m), 8·4 min. Endurance, 1·31 hrs. Empty weight, 2,520 lb (1 143 kg). Loaded weight, 3,349 lb (1 519 kg). Span, 31 ft 6 in (9,60 m). Length, 23 ft 8 in (7,21 m). Height, 9 ft 3 in (2,82 m). Wing area, 252 sq ft (23,41 m²).

The P-5 (below) was essentially a turbo-supercharged version of the P-1.

be appreciated by any pilot expected to take this new Grumman cat into action.

The cockpit was the usual capacious office built for an all-American half-back, and when I first sat in it I thought I would have to stand up to see out for take-off. There was a great deal of engine ahead, in the bulky shape of the 18-cylinder Double Wasp, but in spite of this large power egg the view ahead was not unreasonable, thanks to the Hellcat's slight humped-back profile with the pilot perched at the highest point.

Engine starting was by an electrically-fired cartridge, and except for the first start of the day on a cold morning, one cartridge was usually enough to set the Double Wasp into a silky purr, once the propeller had been turned through a few revolutions by hand. The engine was warmed up with the cowling gills open, and the two-speed supercharger was exercised before taxying out. Taxying was quite easy with the wide undercarriage, but the tailwheel had to be locked in a cross-wind or the aircraft tended to weathercock; she was nose-heavy with little clearance between propeller and ground so it was adviseable always to keep the control column held well back, and essential to do so if the CG was at the forward end of its range or when taxying on soft ground.

Take-off was straightforward with a tendency to swing to the left, requiring gentle application of rudder. For short take-offs, 20 deg of flap would normally be used; even full flap could be applied for a very short run, but this meant that the elevator trim tab had to be set nose up to reduce the pull force for unstick, whereas once the Hellcat was airborne, there was a trim change to tail heavy and some lateral instability was evident. Take-off power was developed at 54 in Hg boost and 2,700 rpm.

Grumman F6F-5 Hellcat Cockpit Instrumentation Key

1 Oxygen supply ON/OFF cock and supply tube
2 Arrester hook emergency control
3 Flap selector lever
4 Cockpit light (port)
5 Map/document holder
6 Tailwheel locking control
7 Trimming tab control box
8 Rudder trimming tab handwheel (box upper face)
9 Aileron trimming tab handwheel (box forward face)
10 Elevator trimming tab handwheel (box inner face)
11 Fuel cock control
12 Propeller speed control lever
13 Fuel tank pressurising control
14 Oil cooler and intercooler shutter control lever
15 Cowling gill control lever
16 Radio push-button controller
17 Throttle lever (with "Press to transmit" button)
18 Reserve fuel tank warning light
19 Drop tank jettison switch
20 Throttle lever friction device
21 Mixture control lever
22 Fuel booster pump switch
23 Supercharger control lever
24 Oil dilution switch
25 Flap control switch
26 Undercarriage and flap position indicator
27 Undercarriage selector lever
28 Check-off visual list plate
29 Clock
30 Fluorescent light (port)
31 Carburettor air intake control
32 Ignition switch
33 Fixed quarterlights
34 Armoured glass windshield
35 Reflector gunsight
36 Gunsight mounting
37 Spare lamp holder
38 Directional gyro
39 Directional gyro setting
40 Magnetic compass
41 Attitude gyro
42 Tachometer
43 IFF warning light
44 Attitude gyro caging control
45 Altimeter
46 Airspeed indicator
47 Turn and bank indicator
48 Rate of climb indicator
49 Manifold pressure gauge
50 Chart board (horizontal stowage)
51 Undercarriage emergency control lever
52 Oxygen pressure/contents gauges and regulator
53 Wing fold safety locking control
54 Gun charging handles
55 Windshield de-icing control
56 Cockpit ventilator control
57 Port fluorescent light switch
58 Cockpit heating switch
59 Starboard fluorescent light switch
60 Rudder/brake pedal mounting bar
61 Rudder pedal adjustment levers
62 Rudder pedals
63 Heelboards
64 Pilot's seat
65 Control column (with machine gun trigger switch
and bomb release push-button)
66 Fluorescent light (starboard)
67 Morsing transmit key (TR 1196 or SCR 522A)
68 Oil pressure gauge
69 Fuel pressure gauge
70 Fuel tank contents gauge
71 Oil temperature gauge
72 Cylinder temperature gauge
73 Engine priming switch
74 Cartridge starter switch
75 Circuit breaker panel
76 Hydraulic handpump
77 Camera gun switch
78 Gunsight switch
79 Gunsight dimming rheostat
80 Gun master switch
81 Gun selector switches
82 Lighting switches (from front: landing light; section light ON/OFF/FLASH; section light dim/bright; wing navigation (running) lights; tail navigation (running) light; formation light ON/OFF/FLASH; formation light dim/bright)
83 Arrester hook switch and indicator light
84 Pitot head heater switch
85 Cockpit lighting rheostats (3)
86 Battery switch
87 Volt/ammeter and push-button
88 Canopy handle
89 Homing control unit
90 Remote control wave tuner (R 1147)
91 Cockpit light (starboard)
92 Recognition lights morsing key switch (visual identification)
93 Recognition light switches (from front: white; red; green (steady); amber (off))
94 Hydraulic handpump selector valve control
95 Radio beacon switch
96 Micro-/telephone socket
97 Volume control (R 1147)
98 ABK detonator switches
99 ABK wave-band selector switch
100 Target-towing release control (optional)
101 ABK controller ON/OFF switch
102 ABK controller emergency switch
103 Wing locking pin control
104 Undercarriage emergency air cylinder pressure gauge
105 Hydraulic accumulator pressure gauge
106 IFF key
107 Fire-extinguisher
108 Micro-/telephone socket (ABK ground-test)
109 Incendiary bomb

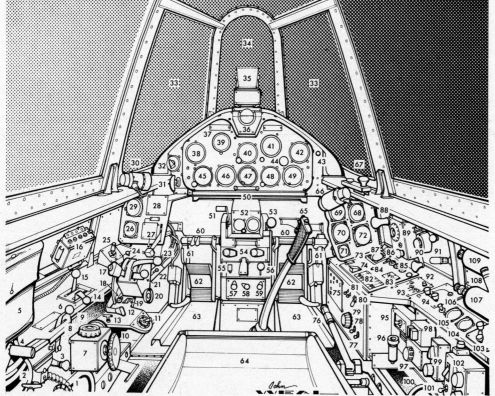

(Above left) A Hellcat F Mk II in Royal Navy service and carrying two 1,000-lb (454-kg) bombs. (Above right) One of the several surviving Hellcats that are still flown by civilian owners in the USA. (Below right) A Hellcat F Mk I in the Fleet Air Arm grey camouflage.

The climb, at 130 knots (241 km/h) IAS with 44 in Hg boost and 2,550 rpm (6 100 m), took the Hellcat to 3,000 ft (915 m) in the first minute, and remained good up to 20,000 ft (6 100 m) when it began to moderate. The change to auxiliary LOW gear was made when the boost dropped 6 in Hg and from LOW gear to HIGH gear when the boost dropped a further 3½ in Hg. The supercharger gave the Hellcat a service ceiling of 37,800 ft (11 530 m) but she was distinctly sluggish above 32,000 ft (9 760 m).

Although Grumman's big fighter was stable about all axes, there were marked changes of lateral and directional trim with changes of speed and power, and selecting undercarriage down, flaps down or gills open naturally pitched the aircraft nose-down. The controls became heavy at high speeds, particularly the ailerons, but on the Hellcat II (F6F-5) which we were to receive in FAA squadrons in due course, the ailerons were spring-tab operated and were light and effective throughout the speed range. With the aircraft "clean", the stall occurred with little warning and either wing could drop, but recovery was straightforward and easy. This meant that although aerobatics were easy to perform, careless application of *g* could result in a flick out of the manoeuvre without much warning other than a buffeting of the tail surfaces. Stalling speeds varied from as low as 58 knots (107 km/h) IAS at 11,500 lb (5 220 kg) with flaps and undercarriage down to 85 knots (157 km/h) at 14,600 lb (6 628 kg) when carrying bombs with flaps and undercarriage up.

The engine was prone to auxiliary supercharger surging in HIGH gear and at weak cruise settings, the symptoms being rough running accompanied by an alarming rumbling noise

Another of the Hellcats still flying in the USA, this F6F-5 belongs to the Planes of Fame collection in California.

(Left) A Hellcat NF Mk II, one of 80 F6F-5Ns supplied to the Royal Navy under lend-lease during 1945 and (right) a Hellcat FR Mk II, with oblique camera installation just beneath the fuselage roundel and British rocket projectile launchers under the wings.

(described in the official "Pilot's Notes" as a loud puffing sound!), but the condition could be quickly and simply eliminated by either changing to LOW gear, or opening the throttle and reducing rpm, or selecting the alternate position of the carburettor air intake control.

The deck landing pattern was entered at 110 knots (204 km/h) IAS, when the arrester hook was lowered electrically and the undercarriage hydraulically. The tail wheel was unlocked, the mixture control set to AUTO RICH, the supercharger to NEUTRAL, and the propeller selected in fully fine pitch. The booster pump was then switched ON, the flaps lowered fully and the engine cowl gills CLOSED. Final approach to the deck was at 80 knots (148 km/h) IAS, and she was as steady as a rock; speeds as low as 75 knots (139 km/h) were permissible but not very comfortable as the nose-up attitude increased and view forward became quite seriously impaired. In any

case, I always used a curved approach to get a better view of the deck, and left the throttle cut as late as possible to prevent the heavy nose dropping and allowing the main wheels to contact the deck first, thus risking a bounce — although the sturdy undercarriage of the Hellcat had very good shock-absorbing characteristics.

Like the later Wildcat models, the Hellcat had manually folding wings, but unlike the Wildcat had hydraulically-operated locking pins under the pilot's control. Once folded, the wings were held in position by a folding lock in each wheel well. Although I never felt really at home in the American wide-bodied fighters such as the Hellcat, Corsair and Thunderbolt, they had good combat records, largely because of their ability to absorb punishment and survive, and they excelled in the long-range escort rôle because of a combination of this quality and good endurance. □

TALKBACK

P-3C test-bed

ENCLOSED please find two photos of a Lockheed P-3C Orion, taken at Tamiami Airport, Miami, in July 1975. After reading your September 1975 feature article on this aircraft, I remembered that I had these photos, and upon inspection, I found that this particular version was not mentioned in the article. I therefore wrote to the Naval Air Systems Command regarding information on this particular aircraft, and obtained the following reply:

"The aircraft shown is a P-3C, the latest version of the P-3 series aircraft. Built by the Lockheed California Company and sold to the Navy in October 1969, this aircraft has seen extensive service as a flying test bed for development and evaluation of new sensors and updated systems for the P-3C as well as other aircraft with similar requirements. At the time the photograph was taken, the aircraft was being used to perform operational testing on the radar system for the S-3A air-

craft; hence the unusual radome in the bomb bay area.

"The evaluation and testing was performed by VX-1 squadron, whose sole purpose is operational test and evaluation of Navy aircraft and systems.

"Since successful completion of the S-3A radar system, this aircraft has been reconfigured and remained in the custody of VX-1 as a flying test bed for a multitude of both new and improved sensors; testing new concepts in the continual effort to maintain the P-3C as the bench mark in airborne ASW."

Allan R Rossmore
Miami, Florida, USA

Calling Moth owners

AS THE owner/restorer of a de Havilland D.H.82A Tiger Moth, and a lifelong enthusiast for British light aeroplanes, it has been a matter of some incredulity to me that 50 years after the birth of D.H.s immortal Moth (the D.H.60), there should be no D.H.-Type Club

with headquarters in the United Kingdom. There is a very active Moth Club in the USA, and abounding interest in D.H. matters in Australia and South Africa.

During August 1975, I contacted twenty known owners of UK based Tiger Moths with the idea of forming a Tiger Moth Owners Circle. To this first enquiry I received fourteen replies. In October another thirty letters were despatched of which fourteen were answered, and as a direct result of these contacts a further thirteen Tiger Moth owners wrote to me.

My initial idea was certainly to restrict the formation of any club or group to Tiger Moth owners only, but the feeling was evident from most of the correspondence received that a club should be constituted with membership open to ALL Moth owners and offering associate membership to owners of other light DH types and including Dragon, Rapide and Dragonfly aircraft too. The Chipmunk is quite specifically excluded.

The degree of interest shown leaves me in no doubt whatsoever that the formation of the Club is essential to the common interests of hard pressed vintage aeroplane owners, and accordingly membership of "The De Havilland Moth Club" is now open to those who may be interested. Membership is intended to be fully world wide and registrations have already been received from Holland, South Africa and the USA. The DHMC membership fee has been pegged at £1·00 for the whole of 1976. Copies of the Newsletters which have been distributed to date are available on receipt of a fully stamped and self addressed A4 envelope.

Stuart McKay
Tangmere, 16 Thatchers Drive,
Maidenhead, Berkshire, SL6 3PW

One of the photographs to which Mr Rossmore refers in the letter above, depicting a P-3C fitted with the S-3A radar system, with a radome in the bomb-bay.

Back to First Principles

IF YOU ARE the sort of chap — like, for example, our managing editor — who has but to hammer a nail into a wall for the wall to collapse and, as likely as not, then finds himself queuing in the casualty department of the local hospital seeking attention for a broken thumb, then the term "scratch-building" is very much a euphemism. To many modellers, the mere suggestion that they should try their hand — or rather their razor saws and shaping knives — at a little scratch-building is certain to produce paroxysms of laughter, or at least a superior kind of a glance of the sort that one might direct at a neolithic man applying for a job as a brain surgeon. Why do it yourself when most of it is done for you thoroughly competently by the kit manufacturers?

At risk of being accused of stultiloquy at best and mental derangement at worst by all but a mere handful of our readers and by the kit manufacturers without exception, we would suggest that creativity — surely, you will say, the primary motivation of the modeller — is steadily diminishing as a result of the general excellence of available kits and the profusion of choice. The art of rubbing two pieces of flint together to obtain a spark began to die with the appearance of the tinder box, and while we will admit that flint-rubbing as a pastime does not offer an entirely apposite comparison with scratch-building of model aircraft, we are unable to rid ourselves of the sneaking feeling that, for the aviation modelling fraternity, such as it was in those far-distant days, something of the quality of life departed with the arrival of the plastic model kit. Lest we also be accused of knocking the plastic kit — metaphorically plunging a craft knife into the hand that feeds us — may we hasten to say that we are not proposing that all our readers should immediately stock up on balsa wood and then agitate for the nationalis-ation of all plastic kit companies so that they could switch production to some more desir-able commodity, such as plastic penholders for civil servants. On the contrary, we are suggesting that those of us possessing the skill to do something more than "slap together" a plastic kit should, from time to time, indulge ourselves in the highly satisfying diversion of scratch-building.

Quite remarkable transformations can re-sult from the improvement and embellishment of standard kits, but nowadays the chances are that most embellishments will already have been incorporated in the kit in any case, and such improvements as can be introduced are merely token in order to individualise the finished model in some small way. Certainly there is still scope for producing some con-versions that call for the exercise of both skill and ingenuity, but with the ever escalating cost of kits, one tends to experience a modicum of hesitancy when it comes to hacking lumps from the components of an expensive kit and

risking the traumatic possibility that the in-genious conversion planned is just a bit *too* ingenious to be practical. How then, other than by variation in colour scheme and mark-ing, can the dedicated modeller express his individuality? The answer *could* be scratch-building, which, at one time, was standard practice but is today almost a forgotten art.

Our experience with those modellers who have built up the expertise necessary to pro-duce effective scratch-built models and who choose for their labours aircraft in which they are interested rather than those that the kit manufacturers, in their wisdom, believe *should* interest them, is that they almost invariably specialise in some way, perhaps an unusual scale, a neglected period in the annals of aviation, or even the products of one major aircraft manufacturer — a noteworthy ex-ample of the last-mentioned penchant being the superb collection of 'tween-wars de Havilland types to 1/36th scale created by Tony Woollett. But the scope is endless. Surely every modeller has at least one favourite aircraft type that he would dearly like to add to his collection and which he is tolerably certain will never appear in any list of com-mercial kits, so why not get with the poly-styrene sheet . . . ?

We hope that some of our readers will agree that we have made some sort of a case for scratch-building, and we plan to pursue the subject from time to time in future issues with suggestions as to materials, methods, tools and the preparation of drawings and designs. There is really no mystique about scratch-building; commonsense and a reasonable degree of modelling skill are the only primary ingredients necessary for success, plus, of course, patience, and without a fair share of the last-mentioned attribute you are unlikely ever to have become a modeller in the first place!

Transportation without motivation

Perhaps the most neglected of all types of military aircraft in so far as model kits are concerned is the transport glider which, nevertheless, played a vital rôle in several of the most important episodes of WW II. Hitherto, only one kit of an Allied glider has appeared, this depicting the General Aircraft Hotspur II and, having been produced by Frog many years ago, has long since faded into oblivion. A year or so ago, Italaerei issued a kit of the Gotha Go 242 and has now followed up this offering with kits of the Airspeed Horsa and the Waco CG-4A, and very fine kits they are too.

Any modeller believing gliders to be simple aircraft and that any kits depicting them would, of necessity, comprise few parts will need to revise his opinion after examining these kits, for they have *more* component parts than are to be found in most kits of powered aircraft of comparable size — they

make up for their lack of engines with a mass of interior and small exterior details. The Horsa was a large aircraft spanning 88 ft (26,80 m) and, in consequence, makes an impressive model, even to 1/72nd scale.

Moulded in medium grey plastic, the kit comprises 123 component parts and may be assembled as either a Mk I or Mk II, the latter having the sideways-hinging nose section in place of the large portside loading door, twin nosewheels and a towing point on the nosewheel bracket. The major fuselage com-ponents of this kit are moulded as for the Mk II, but the deeply-scored ring at the front end may be easily obliterated if the Mk I is required and the same applies to the similarly-treated loading door if the Mk I is to be built. All necessary alternative parts are provided. The external detailing is very neat and every visible feature of the full-scale aircraft has been included, but it is to the interior detailing that exceptional attention has been paid and this with the most satisfying results. There are included in this kit — and in that for the companion CG-4A — some of the tiniest parts that we have seen in *any* kit, and tweezers are a vital tool during assembly.

The flight deck has a very clear canopy and the interior includes floor, bulkhead with separate door, four rudder pedals, two control columns, two seats each in four parts, control console with separate trim wheels and tow-release lever, and instrument panel, the whole making up into a neat sub-assembly. The main cabin has two floor sections, one of which has to be shortened if the kit is completed as a Horsa Mk I, internal ribbing, troop seats, separate portholes and doors, and a rear bulk-head, the doors having built-in steps and, for the Mk I, ramps. While the rear fuselage separates as in the full-size aircraft, it is not Italaerei's intention that this be detachable on the finished model. If the large cargo door of the Mk I is left open, a considerable amount of the interior detail may be readily seen, but it would be wise to make the nose section of the Mk II a detachable unit if the "guts" of this glider are not to be completely hidden from view. The decal sheet offers both RAF and USAAF markings, is matt finished and is generally good, but the red of the roundels is too bright and the style of the serials is in-correct. The instruction sheet is admirably clear, with full camouflage and markings de-picted by a five-view general arrangement drawing.

Again moulded in medium grey plastic, the 145-part Waco CG-4A kit has finely-textured external surfaces to represent the fabric skin-ning and the model that it produces is in every way as accurate and as well detailed as is that of the Horsa. Whereas a neat and unobtrusive tail support is provided with the Horsa kit, there being no room in the nose to balance the tail, this problem does not arise with the CG-4A, which, of course, had a tailwheel. External details include actuating rods and hinges for the control surfaces. Again, the decal sheet offers both RAF and USAAF markings, although the RAF scheme shown, which is overall aluminium paint and purports to date from 1950, looks highly suspect and most modellers will certainly prefer to opt for one of the wartime camouflage finishes.

These two fine kits came to us from Ital-Hobby of via F Ili Rosselli 3, 40012 Calderara di Reno, Bologna, Italy, but at the time of closing for press we had not received retail prices.

A mighty Messerschmitt

The coverage of WW II aircraft to 1/48th scale is slowly but steadily increasing and we are particularly pleased to welcome from Fujimi a new kit to this scale of the Messerschmitt Bf 110C. Moulded in medium grey plastic and possessing 109 parts, the kit is both extremely accurate and complete, and displays fine surface detailing, engraved or raised as appropriate, with particularly good texturing of the fabric-covered control surfaces. The Daimler-Benz DB 601 engines are not modelled, but the exhaust manifolds are separate mouldings and the radiators under the wings have inserts so that there is no "open" effect. The engine nacelles are moulded with the wing panels, but incorporate interior decking to support the finely-detailed undercarriage members. These have separate hydraulic jacks, calipers and also actuating rods for the doors. The wheels are moulded in halves with detailed hubs.

There are many small and very fine external details, such as aerials, D/F loop, pitot head, rear access steps, mass balances for the ailerons and a landing light transparency in the port wing leading edge. A bomb rack with two 500-kg bombs may be fitted beneath the fuselage. The cockpit interior sides have engraved details and the cockpit is extremely well equipped, with floor, side consoles, seats, rear bulkhead, compass, instrument panel (including two decals), controls, radio and two rather poor crew figures which are perhaps best discarded. The long and very clear canopy enables all this detail to be seen to advantage, and an alternative forward section is provided so that the pilot's canopy can be assembled in the raised position with the two side panels lowered.

The assembly instructions are explicit, with exploded views and also sections through the more complicated assemblies, such as the cockpit and wheel wells. The decal sheet, which includes many small stencil markings, has schemes for three different aircraft, the most colourful of which is for a Bf 110C-4/B of 5.*Staffel* of *Zerstorergeschwader* 1, the *Wespengeschwader*; a Bf 110C-7 allegedly operated by 7.*Staffel* of *Jagdgeschwader* 5, the *Eismeergeschwader*, and a Bf 110C-4 of 1./ZG 26. This fine kit is available as a direct airmail import from VHF Supplies at £3·25 plus postage.

This month's colour subject

When confronted by a promising new prototype, the management of a kit manufacturing company has to decide whether the company should await the appearance of the production version and risk competitors stealing a march, or get down to producing a kit immediately, which, based on the prototype, could differ in major respects from the aircraft that will eventually enter service. Such a dilemma must surely have faced both Frog and Lesney when they first considered the Westland WG.13 Lynx multi-rôle helicopter, and both, in the event, decided to go ahead and market kits based on the prototypes.

Now that the production Lynx has flown, some changes are evident, but fortunately these are not too difficult to correct on the models. The most noticeable change has been made to the windows in the entrance doors, there now being only one window per door as compared with the three per door of the prototypes. To correct this feature of both the Frog kit and Lesney's "Matchbox" kit, it is necessary to fill the existing window openings with plastic sheet and then cut new apertures 10 mm wide and 7,5 mm high, centred on the door longitudinally and with the top edge at the same level as the original windows, new transparencies being made to fit.

In planview, the tailboom tapers aft until it reduces in width to that of the fin, and the tailbooms of both kits are too wide, that of the "Matchbox" kit in particular calling for a lot of thinning down. In side elevation there should be a smoothly-curved transition from the lower contour of the boom into the trailing edge of the fin — both kits offer a definite cone effect at this point. On the top of the fuselage, where the aperture for the rotor head occurs, both kits incorrectly show a raised rim, for the side elevation of the fuselage reveals a smoothly curved line at this point. The rotor assembly of the Frog kit reveals some errors, the blades being 0,5 mm too narrow in chord

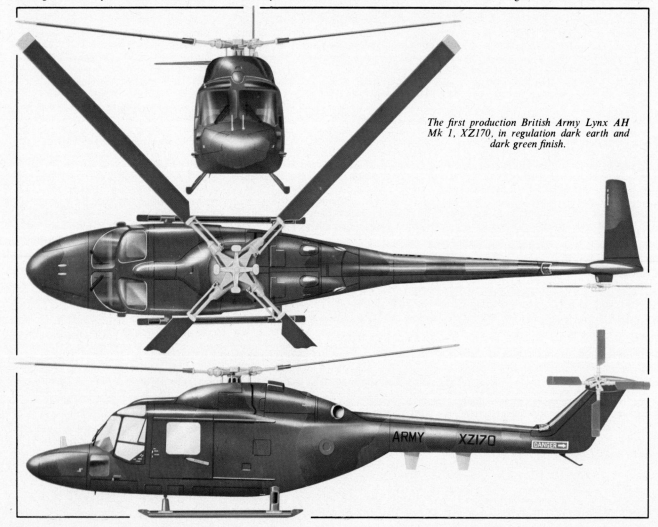

The first production British Army Lynx AH Mk 1, XZ170, in regulation dark earth and dark green finish.

The first production Lynx HAS Mk 2, XZ227, in overall dark blue finish. This aircraft made its first flight at Yeovil on 10 February.

and having the trailing-edge cut-back too far outboard — it should be close to the root — while the retaining cap is superfluous. The rotor assembly of the "Matchbox" kit is very close to being accurate. The differing nose profiles of the Army and Navy variants are catered for by both kits.

The decals accompanying the Frog kit are better than those with the competitive "Matchbox" kit but do not include Royal Navy markings as do the latter. The rotor blades retain the drab olive colour of the plastic from which they are manufactured and are unpainted apart from the tips. Both kits are recent products and should therefore be readily obtainable.

Another Hawk

Following closely upon the heels of Airfix's Hawker Siddeley Hawk — possibly even ahead of it on some stockists' shelves — comes Lesney's "Matchbox" kit of this promising and aesthetically pleasing trainer-cum-light attack aircraft. Again to 1/72nd scale, the "Matchbox" kit is perhaps slightly less refined in appearance than its Airfix competitor, but there is little to choose between the two on the score of accuracy and both make up into very nice little models. As has Airfix, Lesney has been careful not to overdo the surface detailing, but there are some places where the latter has been a trifle

heavy-handed and less generosity is displayed in providing cockpit interior details. Airfix also scores points with its undercarriage but the main difference is presented by the array of external stores, the "Matchbox" kit offering only two Matra missile pods and a gun pack, whereas the Airfix kit goes all out to provide every likely combination of external load. This is, of course, reflected in the number of component parts comprising each kit, there being 59 in the "Matchbox" kit as compared with 95 in the Airfix kit, but it is also reflected in the UK retail prices, the former selling at 30p whereas the latter is priced at 55p.

Lesney adheres to its usual style of at least two colours of plastic — in this case a combination of dark green and light grey — and the modeller opting for the white-grey-red trainer scheme is faced with covering problems. Airfix's kit, on the other hand, is moulded entirely in white plastic. In general, we prefer the Airfix kit, but this is, after all, almost double the price of the "Matchbox" product which is a thoroughly adequate offering and very good value for money, so choice really depends on pocket.

The delightful "Dinah"

Perhaps the most aesthetically pleasing of any Japanese WW II aircraft; indeed, one of the most graceful of all aircraft of that conflict. The

Mitsubishi Ki.46, known to the Allies by the reporting name of *Dinah*, has not received very much attention from kit manufacturers, and therefore the group of three kits depicting different variants of the Ki.46 to 1/72nd scale is welcome, and especially so as it does full justice to this outstanding example of aeronautical pulchritude.

Manufactured by L & S, the kits each comprise approximately 70 component parts, the great majority of the parts being common to all three kits, although each kit caters fully for the external visible differences of the variant of the Ki.46 that it represents. The standard of moulding and surface detailing is of the highest, the panelling being finely engraved and the fabric effect on the control surfaces most effective. The cockpit interiors are fully detailed and could scarcely be improved upon, but the accompanying crew figures are undersized, poorly formed and best discarded. The 14-cylinder radial engines have both cylinder rows modelled but are mostly hidden by the cowlings, unless these and the propellers are rendered detachable. The nacelles are moulded separately from the wings but are a perfect fit and there is not a trace of flash on any of the component parts.

The decals are good but the red of the *Hinomaru* too bright. *Sentai* markings are included as appropriate and each kit includes full assembly details with a full-colour drawing, while the boxtop illustrations make useful aids in finishing the models. The differences between the three kits are mainly confined to the cockpit and canopy area, but the cowlings and propeller spinners differ between the Ki.46-II and -III versions, and these variations are correctly portrayed by the models. The Ki.46-II is, of course, the version of this Mitsubishi reconnaissance aircraft modelled some time ago by Airfix, and features a stepped windscreen. The L & S kit of this type is moulded in light grey plastic, the camouflage finish being of dark green, stone and reddish-brown, with pale blue under-surfaces and alternative markings being provided for the 1st *Chutai* of the 81st *Sentai* or the Command Reconnaissance *Chutai* of the 19th *Hiko-Dan*. Another kit depicts the three-seat advanced trainer Ki.46-II-KAI which featured an additional pilot's seat under a double-stepped canopy, this being moulded in the correct overall shade of orange and is offered with the markings of the Shimoshizu Army Flying School.

The remaining kit of the trio is of the Ki.46-III in which the stepped canopy was discarded and the transparent hood continued to the extreme nose, this change being accompanied by the introduction of larger nacelles to accommodate the Ha-112-II engines. This kit is moulded in dark green plastic which is the correct upper surface colour, the underside finish being light grey. The markings are for either the 16th Independent *Hikotai* or the *Shinbusakura* Special Attack *Chutai*. A fourth kit for the Ki.46-III-KAI Air Defence Fighter is illustrated on the boxes but we have not so far seen this addition to the "Dinah with the linah" range. VHF Supplies can provide these kits as direct airmail imports at £1·65 each plus postage.

. . . and now "Real Met'l"

The obtaining of a realistic-looking polished metal finish on a model has for long been a major headache to all modellers of military aircraft in particular, and any possible solution deserves serious consideration. Until now the best results have been obtained from rub-on pastes, such as "Treasure Silver" and "Rub-n-Buff", but VHF Supplies have now provided us with a sample of a new US product called "Real Met'l".

This is a liquid which is provided in an aerosol can and has similar properties to the rub-on finishes but is more easily applied as a spray. It can be buffed up with a soft cloth to a most realistic finish with a very high polish and it poses no problems when it comes to affixing decals. It is important to remember that all of these finishes have an absolutely minimal thickness and will emphasise rather than obscure any blemishes on the surface of the model, so be sure that the plastic is perfectly smooth before applying the finish. Any uneven spots should be rubbed down with fine wet emery paper and then finished with metal polish such as "Silvo", but *always* test any liquid on a piece of scrap plastic first, just in case it should have any harmful effects. Finally, wash all surfaces thoroughly in a mild detergent solution, rinsing in clear water and allowing to dry completely before spraying. The "Real Met'l" finish is quite durable but must be handled with care for it can rub off if hot and greasy hands are applied too frequently. The price is rather high at £1·75 plus postage.

F J HENDERSON

KOOLHOVEN *from page 189*

ments concerning the possibility of supplying 40 of the FK 58s to the latter in lieu of the 25 MS 406s that had been promised to Yugoslavia in the previous December but which had been retained by the *Armée de l'Air*. The events subsequent to 10 May were to render these discussions purely academic.

By this time, Koolhoven had begun construction of the FK 58s ordered for the LVA, but encountered a major setback on 2 March when the company was informed that the Taurus III engines were not going to materialise. Some work has already been conducted on a version powered by the inverted-vee 12-cylinder liquid-cooled Daimler-Benz DB 600 engine. Koolhoven had succeeded in obtaining one example of the DB 600 engine and had reason to suppose that a quantity of engines of this type might be obtained via a Swiss agent. The redesign of the airframe to take the German power plant was undertaken by Ir van Buuren, and after a number of initial difficulties, a mock-up of the DB 600-powered FK 58 was completed, utilising the airframe of the fifth production aircraft (c/n 5807) which had been retained by the manufacturer for development purposes. Van Buuren redesigned the cockpit canopy to improve aft vision and reduce drag, simultaneously cutting down the fuselage aft decking, but mating the slim liquid-cooled engine to the not inconsiderable girth of the basic FK 58 fuselage presented a number of aerodynamic problems which had still to be resolved when Koolhoven's source of supply for the Daimler-Benz engines evaporated and the project had to be terminated.

In so far as the FK 58s under construction for the LVA were concerned, the service had no recourse but to instruct Koolhoven to adapt the airframes to take the Bristol Mercury VIII, 36 examples of which were held in stock. Although of somewhat larger diameter than the Taurus, the nine-cylinder Mercury VIII had an essentially similar diameter to that of the Hispano-Suiza 14AA and did not therefore pose serious installation problems, but with ratings of 730 hp for take-off and 830 hp at 14,000 ft (4 265 m), its use meant a serious downgrading of the fighter's performance. However, barely more than two months after Koolhoven was informed of the non-availability of the Taurus engine, the Waalhaven factory was to be largely destroyed by *Luftwaffe* attack and with it the FK 58 assembly line. Another casualty was to be the second prototype, PH-AVA, which, given Dutch military markings and the serial number "1002", had remained the property of the Koolhoven company and had continued the flight test programme — which had been taken over by H Schmidt Crans

with the demise of Thomas Coppers — right up until the German onslaught began.

The Nevers factory had finally succeeded in completing one FK 58, this (c/n 5821) being assigned the French serial C-033 and flown to Villacoublay during March for the installation of its radio equipment. One FK 58, C-029 (c/n 5817), was damaged when the undercarriage failed during landing, and on 10 May 1940, 12 were on charge at the *Entrepôt de l'Armée de l'Air* 301 of which six were recorded as "unavailable" and the others as being fitted with armament and equipment. Two others were at *centres d'instruction*. Every effort was now made to render the aircraft serviceable and by mid-May, four of the FK 58s (c/n 5812, 5814, 5819 and 5820) had joined the *Division d'Instruction de l'Aviation Polonaise* at Lyon-Bron, while the *Base Aérienne* of Salon-de-Provence had been ordered to form a *patrouille de défense* with seven FK 58s — one of the Polish pilots assigned to this *patrouille* being recorded as commenting, "Now we have Dutch airframes pulled by French engines and toting Belgian machine guns with Polish pilots in French airspace!"

Soon after being established, the FK 58-equipped *patrouille* received two additional aircraft from Lyon-Bron and was designated an *Escadrille de Regroupement,* soon losing two of its aircraft to "friendly" groundfire. The *Escadrille* aircraft were deployed in pairs for the protection of various airfields, two being assigned to Salon, two to Aulnat, Clermont-Ferrand, where they were subsequently joined by two additional FK 58s from EAA 301, and two to Caen-Carpiquet where two more were also received from EAA 301. However, although the Koolhoven fighters flew a number of patrols from these bases, there is no confirmed record of their having fired their guns in anger on any occasion.

With the Armistice, one FK 58 remained in the Occupied Zone at Villacoublay and 10 were in the Unoccupied Zone — c/n 5808, 5811, 5813 and 5817 were at Perpignan-La Salanque, c/n 5809 and 5812 were at Salon, c/n 5819 was at Lyon-Bron without an engine, and c/n 5814, 5815 and 5820 were at Montpellier-Fréjorgues. These were too few to interest the *Armée de l'Air de l'Armistice* and they were duly scrapped. Thus, the strange story of the last of the Koolhovens came to a close barely more than two years after it had begun. Conceived, designed and brought to prototype test status in a remarkably short space of time, the FK 58 had been a sound enough design embodying all the sturdiness for which Koolhoven had built up a reputation, and as the last product of a famous manufacturer it was deserving of a better fate. □

THE GHOST SQUADRON OF HARLINGEN

BY JEFFREY M ETHELL

Pearl harbor, December 1941: as a US Army Air Corps B-17 approaches for landing, wheels and flaps down, Mitsubishi Zero-Sen fighters dive to the attack out of the sun. Machine gun fire and bomb-blasts shatter the peace and the B-17, trailing smoke, clambers for altitude to allow crewmen to bale out while Army P-40 and Navy F4F fighters are scrambled to intercept the raiders. A Zero goes down smoking as individual dog-fights take place over the field.

This is not a description of the Japanese attack that brought the USA into World War II, nor an account of a film sequence; it is a typical live demonstration, using authentic World War II aircraft, as put on at regular intervals by the Ghost Squadron of the Confederate Air Force at Harlingen, Texas. In the course of a three-hour flying programme, this remarkable organisation presents cameos of many of the war's outstanding air engagements, including the Battle of Britain (with Spitfires and Bf 109s), Wake Island (F4Fs and Zero-Sens), Battle of Midway (SBD, F4F, TBM, Zero-Sen, Nakajima B5N1 and Aichi D3A), Tokyo Raid (B-25), the Soviet Front (P-39 and P-63), D-Day (A-26, B-25, P-47, P-38, P-51 etc), Marianas Turkey Shoot (FG-1 and F6F) and so on.

The aircraft flown in each of these displays are not, of course, necessarily finished in the correct colours and markings for each specific action, nor are they in all cases the correct variant, but they *are*, almost without exception, all authentic vintage aircraft, restored and maintained in flying status by the enthusiasm and dedication of members of the Confederate Air Force. Purists will note that the Bf 109s are in fact post-war Spanish-built examples with Merlin engines and that the Japanese types are represented by adaptations of the BT-13 and T-6 made for use in the film "Tora, Tora, Tora." But set against this the opportunity to see in the air genuine examples of the B-17, B-24, B-25, B-26, A-20, A-26, B-29,

P-39, P-40, P-51, P-63, P-47, P-82, FG-1, FM-2, F6F, F8F, SB2C, TBM, SBD, Spitfire, Mosquito, C-47 and a handful of trainers — and any apparent misrepresentation by the CAF can be forgiven.

Unique among aircraft museums for the emphasis it places upon keeping its exhibits airworthy and for its success in acquiring World War II survivors, the Confederate Air Force owes its inception to Lloyd Nolen. Having flown as an instructor throughout the war, Nolen wanted to own one of the fighters he had never had a chance to fly and in 1951, while he was operating a crop-dusting company at Mercedes, Texas, he bought a Curtiss P-40E. It cost the now ridiculous sum of $1,500 and Nolen showed a proper sense of priorities by investing in the Warhawk before buying his wife her first washing machine!

The P-40E was sold to provide funds for the purchase of a P-51 Mustang, but the Korean War resulted in all airworthy P-51s being pressed into service with the USAF, and it was not until 1957 that Nolen managed to buy a P-51D that had been used in the film "Battle Hymn". Subsequently, he sold shares in this Mustang to several friends, and the idea of adding other World War II types to the collection slowly grew. Two Navy-surplus F8F Bearcats were bought for $805 apiece and Nolen and his confederates had the nucleus of their air force, which today totals nearly 70 aircraft.

As more and more enthusiasts — mostly pilots — joined in, the group set itself the objective of obtaining and flying one example of each of the major US fighter types of World War II. The search lasted four years and at times was heartbreaking, as the group discovered just how many famous aeroplanes had apparently been consigned to the scrap yards and disappeared forever. A very rare FG-1D Corsair was rescued from a junk dealer in Arizona just as it was about to be compacted.

Nolen traced his original P-40 and bought it back; an FM-2 Wildcat and an F6F-5 Hellcat were found, together with a P-38 Lightning with photo nose. In South America, a P-63 was retrieved from Honduras and a P-47 from Nicaragua.

By 1963, the CAF had nine fighters in its collection and had also acquired a North American T-6 and a B-25 Mitchell. A great deal of hard work went into these acquisitions and their restoration; a little light relief served as a safety valve for all concerned and the Confederate Air Force image was developed by the appointment of a mythical commander, Colonel Jethro E Culpeper, and by making all contributing members full Colonels in the organisation, with certificates of membership. The CAF was incorporated as a tax-exempt museum with membership open to all persons having an interest in preserving aircraft in flying condition, and a recruiting campaign began in earnest.

With 170 members in 1965, the CAF took the first steps in the creation of a Bomb Wing, adding an A-26, B-17 and B-24. The original location at Mercedes became too small and an invitation was accepted from Harlingen to base the Ghost Squadron, as the flying segment of the CAF became known, at that city's new International Airport. Rebel Field, as the CAF section at Harlingen has been named, now has three large hangars and a World War II vintage Army Air Corps office; one hangar is devoted to maintenance and one each to the Bomb Wing and the Fighter Wing, while the office building houses an indoor museum, offices, Officer's Club and visiting officer's quarters.

The Confederate Air Force now has more than 1,000 colonels and Nolen considers the collection to be complete. New types will be added if the opportunity arises, but the primary objective now is to "keep 'em flying". About 10 per cent of the membership is rated to fly and 50 mechanics and 100 other personnel

VETERAN & VINTAGE

(Above) One of the Confederate Air Force B-25 Mitchells and one of the A-26 Invaders in loose formation, as seen from another B-25 during one of the regular CAF presentations. (Below) Lloyd Nolen's personal P-51D, purchased in 1957, that formed the nucleus around which the Confederate Air Force grew.

Representing the whole family of Chance Vought Corsairs, the CAF example is a Goodyear-built FG-1D, used in the Ghost Squadron's recreation of the Marianas Turkey Shoot, one of many famous World War II actions that the CAF recalls with its flying demonstrations at Harlingen.

provide active support for the flying activities, all on an entirely voluntary basis.

The way in which the CAF has acquired some of its aircraft reads almost like a detective novel. The Douglas SBD Dauntless (one of only two flying in the world, the other being in the US Marine Corps Museum) was purchased from the Planes of Fame collection in California. It had originally been sold as government surplus after the end of the war and taken to Mexico where it was used extensively as a high altitude camera platform. The SB2C Helldiver was also purchased from Planes of Fame and the colours and markings on the aircraft were still original, the aircraft never having been painted since the war. The very rare P-51C in the CAF was found on static display in Billings, Montana, and its first "fighter-nosed" P-38 was found in high grass behind an old hangar outside Yukon, Oklahoma and was obtained in outright exchange for the "photo-nosed" example previously mentioned.

The CAF now has no fewer than seven P-47 Thunderbolts. Six were brought back from Peru in 1969 and they now fly together, representing every major theatre of war. The remains of a very rare P-39 were found behind a hangar at Hobbs, New Mexico and the only flyable F-82 Twin Mustang in the world now belongs to the CAF.

The B-24 in the collection was originally a British LB-30, serial AM927, being No 18 off the line in 1940. Involved in an accident on its delivery flight to Canada in 1941, it was later rebuilt as a C-87 for use as a company aircraft. After the war it was sold to the Continental Can Company and flown as an executive transport for about ten years, whereupon it was purchased by Mexico's national oil company, PEMEX, and flown in Latin America until the CAF bought it in 1967 for the price of the engines, $24,000. PEMEX was going to sell the engines and scrap the airframe, even though it was still in excellent condition.

The B-17 was a PB-1W in service with the US Navy until it was released at NAS, San Diego, California after flying with Squadron VW-1. An aerial photo company then used it in Philadelphia until the CAF bought it.

The prize exhibit of the Bomb Wing has to be the Boeing B-29 Superfortress. The search for a Superfort began in 1966, and one was located at the Naval Weapons Center, China Lake, California. This came as quite a surprise to the Air Force, since the B-29 had been considered long gone. After some negotiation, the USAF (which still owned the example in question) turned over B-29 serial number 44-62070 to the CAF and after a lengthy restoration job at China Lake it was flown to Harlingen in 1971 with no mechanical malfunctions and no maintenance troubles, after 17 years on the ground.

The Mosquito Mk 35 was brought to Rebel Field from England. It was ferried via Spain, the Azores, Newfoundland, Nova Scotia and across the US between 11 December 1971 and 2 January 1972. Both Spitfire IXs were acquired privately, one in 1969 and the other in 1965, the second then being leased for the filming of "Battle of Britain". The Spanish Bf 109s (actually, HA-1112-M1Ls) had been eyed hungrily in Spain since the early 'sixties and four were bought in 1967, some weeks before the search began for aircraft that could be used in filming the *Battle of Britain*. These

(Above) The B-24 — actually an original British LB-30 converted to a C-87 transport — is seen in company with "Zero-Sen" replicas based on T-6 airframes. (Below) The Curtiss P-40 Warhawk, in the colours of the American Volunteer Group, the Flying Tigers, as used in China in 1941. (Bottom left) The Curtiss SB2C and Republic P-47D in formation.

aircraft were also then leased for use in that film; four CAF pilots went along for what they still regard as some of the most memorable flying ever.

As well as the flying Ghost Squadron, the CAF now possesses a small collection of post-war aircraft in a static collection, and several World War II-type trainers. The Indoor Museum has a large display of wartime memorabilia, photos, maps, guns, flags and similar items, grouped in sections for the US Army Air Force, US Navy and Marine Corps, and Archives. The members of the CAF have shown that they are fiercely dedicated to the preservation and flying of their collection of 30-40 year old aeroplanes and that they will stop at almost nothing to obtain aircraft representing the 1939-1945 period. Founder Lloyd Nolen describes the basic purpose of the collection as being to preserve "a part of American heritage. The aircraft represent a time when the entire nation was working together — it had to for survival. Hitler and the Japanese revealed something worth fighting for and these were the tools we used". □

Flying Aircraft	
B-17 Flying Fortress (PB-1W)	Spitfire IX (two)
B-24 Liberator (LB-30 converted to C-87)	Mosquito 35
	C-45 Expediter
B-25 Mitchell (three)	C-47 Skytrain
B-26 Marauder	BT "Val" (two TORA replicas)
A-20 Havoc	T-6 "Kate" (TORA replica)
A-26 Invader (two)	T-6 "Zero" (five TORA replicas)
Lockheed Hudson (Lodestar)	PT-19 Cornell
B-29 Superfortress	PT-22 Recruit
P-38 Lightning (three)	PT-26 Cornell
P-39 Airacobra	N2S-3 Kaydet (two)
P-40 Warhawk	BT-15 Valiant
P-51C Mustang	L-5 Sentinel
P-51D Mustang (two)	T-6 Texan (three)
P-63 Kingcobra	
F-82 Twin Mustang	**Static Aircraft:**
P-47 Thunderbolt (seven)	C-124 Globemaster
F4U Corsair (FG-1D)	C-54 Skymaster
F4F Wildcat (FM-2)	C-119 Flying Boxcar
F6F Hellcat	F-89 Scorpion
F8F Bearcat	A-1E Skyraider
SB2C Helldiver	B-47 Stratojet
TBM Avenger	HU-16 Albatross
SBD Dauntless	B-57 Canberra
Messerschmitt Bf 109 (four, Spanish)	C-97 Stratocruiser
Messerschmitt Bf 108	F-84 Thunderjet
Focke-Wulf Fw 44 Stiegletz	F-102 Delta Dagger
Junkers Ju 52/3m	

Marakesh last year, followed by cold-weather testing in Norway early this year and another period of icing trials in Denmark. For the Marakesh trials, in temperatures up to 44 deg C, sand filters were fitted, causing a slight loss of performance, but there have been no handling problems or engine malfunctions in any of the environment testing to date.

The powerplant

The engine that powers the Lynx in all its versions to date, the Rolls-Royce/Turboméca Gem, originated as a design concept late in 1966 at what was then the Small Engine Division of Bristol Siddeley Engines at Leavesden, near Watford. BSE subsequently became part of Rolls-Royce (and, to complete the historical perspective, its SED was originally part of the de Havilland Engine Co, producing the Gipsy range of piston engines and the T58 turboshaft under licence as the Gnome). The SED at Leavesden has recently become Rolls-Royce's Helicopter Engine Division, and the Gem is now its most important production commitment.

Following the selection of the Westland WG 13 as the third component of the Anglo-French helicopter package, the Gem, under its original designation BS.360, was confirmed as the power plant, Turbomeca was named as partner for production (although Rolls-Royce retained complete authority for design and development), and design activity began in earnest in January 1968. The Gem, like the Lynx, has been designed from the outset for reliability and ease of maintenance, the other primary design objectives being safety and a low specific fuel consumption, with a minimum contingency rating of 900 shp to meet the initial Lynx requirements.

The Gem* has a two-spool gas generator, a four-stage LP compressor and single-stage HP compressor, both independently driven by single-stage axial flow turbines; a reverse flow combustion chamber with air atomiser fuel sprays; a two-stage free power turbine; an epicyclic reduction gearbox mounted within the annular air intake with forward drive and an accessory gearbox mounted on the compressor casing and driven from the HP spool. Construction is modular, in seven major units, to simplify maintenance and overhaul; each module is designed to be mechanically and aerodynamically interchangeable. Comprehensive provision is made for in-flight and on-ground condition monitoring.

The Gem control system is hydromechanical and comprises a gas generator fuel flow control unit and a free power turbine governor. In the event of loss of power from one engine in the Lynx installation, power is increased automatically on the other, up to the engine's limit, through a sensing unit that detects any reduction in main rotor speed. The engine has a net dry weight of 330 lb (150 kg) and an sfc of 0·52 lb (0,24 kg) per shp/hr at the 2½-min contingency rating of 900 shp. The 1-hr intermediate contingency and 5-min maximum rating is 830 shp, and the maximum continuous output is 750 shp.

The Gem first ran in September 1969 but the full specification power could not be achieved until a redesign of the HP compressor was undertaken. Subsequently, there have been considerable development problems, chiefly concerned with the oil seals and with achieving the required sfc. Basic type approval was obtained in March 1972 and the first 150-hr endurance test was completed in January 1973. For development, a batch of 50 engines was built, of which 10 were for bench testing only and the other 40 for the flight development programme; delivery of production Gems, which meet the specification requirements, began at the end of 1975.

For the RN, Army and *Aéronavale* Lynx, the 900 shp model is known as the Gem 100, its commercial and export equivalent

* The name chosen for the BS.360 breaks with the Rolls-Royce tradition of "river" names and is regarded as the first in a new family of "precious stones" to be used by the Helicopter Engine Division. It meets the requirement of being understandable both in English and French and, as it happens, continues the original DH Leavesden practice of choosing names beginning with "G" for all its engines.

Westland Lynx Development Aircraft

XW835 First prototype, basic configuration. Flown on 21 March 1971 (all yellow finish). Used for initial handling trials and vibration survey. After receiving damage in a heavy landing, was used for certain static tests.

XW836 Second prototype, basic configuration, but the fourth to fly, after completing vibration tests suspended in a hangar. First flown on 24 March 1972 (grey finish) and used as the primary vehicle for vibration testing. After completion of programme, airframe incorporated in mock-up of civil Westland 606.

XW837 Third prototype, basic configuration, flown on 28 September 1971 (red finish). Used for automatic flight control system development and for environmental testing overseas.

XW838 Fourth prototype, basic configuration, and third to fly, on 9 March 1972 (blue finish). First to have production-type monobloc rotor head. Used for performance testing, with strain gauging and air-to-ground telemetry system fitted. Reverse direction tail rotor tested. Damaged following failure of rear gearbox in flight through lack of lubrication, and not rebuilt.

XW839 Fifth and last of batch of basic development airframes, first flown on 19 June 1974 (peach finish). Used to test all new production items including revised tail pylon and tail rotor, servo controls etc. Transferred to A & AEE Boscombe Down, end-75.

XX153 First development aircraft in utility (Army) configuration and camouflage and fifth to fly, on 12 April 1972. Used by Westland and A & AEE for engineering, performance and handling trials. Established FAI Class Ele records in June 1972 for speed over a straight course, at 199·92 mph (321,74 km/h) and over a 100-km closed circuit at 197·909 mph (318,504 km/h).

XX469 First development aircraft in naval (RN) configuration and finish. Flown on 25 May 1972 and used for trials on rolling platform at RAE Bedford and initial hot-weather performance

assessment at Marignane. Preliminary trials aboard the *Tourville* in harbour, August 1972. Subsequently destroyed in a heavy landing accident.

XX510 Second naval (RN) trials aircraft, flown on 5 March 1973. Used for AFCS and general handling development. Made sea trials aboard the RFA *Engadine*, starting in June 1973, and used to make air-launches of dummy Sea Skua ASMs. Sea trials under operational conditions aboard the *Tourville*, spring 1974.

XX910 Third naval (common) development aircraft, flown 23 April 1974. Used by A & AEE, Boscombe Down, for radio, navigation, radar, TANS development and by Westland for rescue winch trials.

XZ166 Final naval (RN) trials aircraft, to replace XX496, first flown 5 March 1975. Used to demonstrate compliance with specification and destined for continued weapons trials by the manufacturer.

XX904 First development airframe in naval (*Aéronavale*) configuration, flown on 6 July 1973. Also carried French registration F-ZKCU and, later, 0503. Transferred to Aérospatiale for testing of French rôle equipment (see XX911 also).

XX911 Second development airframe in naval (*Aéronavale*) configuration, flown on 18 September 1973. French registration F-ZKCV and, later, 0504. Transferred to Aérospatiale for testing (with XX904) of automatic transition to hover, sonar, navigation system and rôle equipment.

XX907 In utility (Army) configuration and camouflage, flown 20 May 1973 and transferred to Rolls-Royce Bristol Engine Division at Patchway, Bristol, for engine development.

XZ227 First production Lynx, in naval (RN) configuration, first flown 10 February 1976. To be used for ship trials (HMS *Sheffield* and other small ships) later in 1976.

being the Gem-2. Turboméca is responsible for about 25 per cent of production (by cost), making the air intakes, accessory gear box and some other non-rotating items for all Gems, and in due course will set up a final assembly line for the engines to be used in the French aircraft, and for their subsequent overhaul.

In January 1975, Rolls-Royce announced that it was going ahead with an uprated Gem; this is being developed at present as a private venture, as the Gem-4, at a contingency rating of 1,050 shp, with an sfc of 0·50 lb (0,23 kg) per shp/hr. The increase is obtained by restaggering the LP compressor blades to obtain about 10 per cent more air mass flow, and by a small increase in TET. Running of the Gem-4 began on the test-bed towards the end of 1975, by which time total Gem running (including flight time in the Lynx) exceeded 20,000 hrs.

The future

The immediate objective, now that production Lynxes are flying, is to clear the aircraft for service use, with the Royal Navy playing a leading rôle as its aircraft are first off the line. Nominated crews for the IFTU are expected to be integrated into the production test flying schedules, in order to obtain piloting experience on the type; they will move to RNAS Yeovilton in September with the initial batch of aircraft to proceed with the work of the IFTU itself. Small-ship trials are scheduled for later in the year, on HMS *Sheffield* and other vessels and the Lynx should become fully operational with the Royal Navy in 1977, by which time Westland will have completed the outstanding weapons trials and other work.

Deliveries will this year begin also to the *Aéronavale* (whose helicopters will be flown to France with a minimum equipment fit, for completion by Aérospatiale), the British Army and the Royal Netherlands Navy, with the first aircraft for Brazil appearing early in 1977.

At an engineering level, possible future developments include the elimination of the last feathering hinge in the rotor head — perhaps by using an elastomeric joint — and of the damper; using more GRP or other composite materials to replace some titanium components and completing the design of a Pratt & Whitney PT6B engine installation. The last-mentioned possibility was first considered some years ago when the Gem development problems were at their worst, and were continued when Westland assessed the potential market for a civil Lynx project, known as the Westland 606. Offering approximately the same power as the Gem-2, the PT6B-34 is of potential interest to future Lynx customers and could well become a firm option later this year, possibly backed up by a trial installation in one of the development Lynx airframes.

The Westland 606 civil Lynx proposal, which is currently dormant, was proposed with a lengthened fuselage but the same rotor/gearbox/transmission as the military models, and choice of Gem or PT6B engines. A retractable undercarriage was considered but the tubular skid type was preferred for the Westland 606 as initially presented to potential customers during 1974, at which time the gross weight was 9,500 lb (4 309 kg).

The higher gross weight that will be cleared in due course for military Lynx variants could certainly be usefully applied to the Westland 606. It would also allow the Lynx to meet the LAMPS-III mission as originally defined by the US Navy and for which Westland, in conjunction with Sikorsky, offered the Sea Lynx. The US Navy has subsequently revised its LAMPS objective to the point where a much larger (UTTAS-type) helicopter is needed, but there are doubts about the ability of such a large machine to operate effectively from small ships and many navies — perhaps, in the end, including the US Navy itself — may opt for aircraft of Lynx size to fulfil the LAMPS rôle, which combines submarine search and strike capabilities.

Whilst such naval applications represent part of the future market for Lynx — perhaps 50 aircraft up to 1980 — it is

(Above) Accessibility of the Rolls-Royce Gem engines is clearly shown here; the engines themselves are of modular construction in seven major components. (Below) A close-up of the Ferranti Seaspray radar in the nose of a Naval Lynx.

the Army utility variant that has the greater sales potential, with up to 150 likely to be sold outside Britain and France by 1980. The Middle East represents a specially strong market for the utility Lynx and there are prospects of sales to at least two more countries in the area apart from Egypt. Negotiations with the latter nation completed a year ago provided in principle for the Lynx and the Gem to be built at new production centres near Cairo, with full British and French technical assistance, but the need to bring the Arab Organisation for Military Industries (representing Egypt, Saudi Arabia, Qatar and the United Arab Emirates) into the financial side of the negotiations has delayed completion of the contract.

At a time when several British and French production programmes seem to be nearing an end, the Lynx offers the aerospace industries of both nations an opportunity to gain useful new business for a number of years ahead. By the late summer, production should be running at 7-8 a month against the existing contracts, with an allowance for future sales to allow an 18-24 month lead-time to be offered. In Japan, 1976 is the Year of the Dragon: in Europe it could well be the Year of the Lynx! □

PLANE FACTS

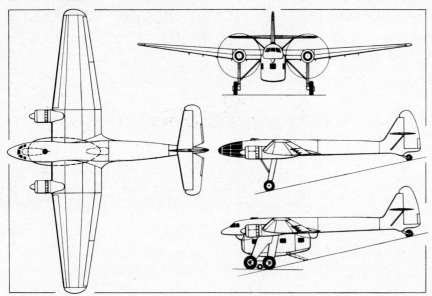

A three-view drawing of the Fieseler Fi 333 transport with extra side-view (centre right) of the projected maritime patrol version.

"Pack-Plane" Fieseler

I have recently completed reading the monumental "Warplanes of the Third Reich" in which the author, in making general remarks concerning the Gerhard Fieseler Werke, mentions the Fi 333 which, it is stated, was an aircraft of "pack-plane" concept — later adopted by Fairchild for that company's XC-120 — of which three prototypes were actually built. Can you please satisfy my curiosity by publishing further details of the Fi 333 in your "Plane Facts" column?

G H Terwiel
Zoetermeer 2280, Netherlands

The multi-purpose Fieseler Fi 333 transport project dated from 1942, and was extremely novel in concept in that it was intended to carry its entire payload in a detachable pack or pod, interchangeable packs accommodating troops, casualty stretchers, freight, a lifeboat or even a dismantled fighter being slung beneath the fuselage, the necessary ground clearance being provided by an exceptionally tall fixed undercarriage, each member of which had two independently-sprung wheels in tandem. Power was provided by two 1,000 hp BMW Bramo 323D radial engines and accommodation was provided for a crew of two in the slender fuselage, the internal dimensions of which were 6 ft 6¾ in (2,0 m) by 7 ft 0¾ in (2,15 m) by 24 ft 7¼ in (7,5 m). Overall dimensions included a span of 98 ft 5 in (30,0 m), a length of 72 ft 2⅛ in (22,00 m), a height of 19 ft 0 in (5,8 m) and a wing area of 1,088 sq ft (101,8 m²), empty weight, including a typical pod was 13,448 lb (6 100 kg), normal loaded weight was 20,172 lb (9 150 kg) and maximum take-off weight was 25,574 lb (11 600 kg).

In addition to its transportation rôle, the Fi 333 was also envisaged for maritime patrol and anti-shipping tasks, this version having an equally tall but much simplified undercarriage, an extensively-glazed nose section with the stepped windscreen eliminated and defensive armament. Both versions made extensive use of high lift devices, permitting

a minimum speed of 40 mph (65 km/h) and exceptional short-field performance. Maximum speed was 186 mph (300 km/h) at 13,125 ft (4 000 m). Three prototypes of the Fi 333 were allegedly built although no details of the test programme presumably conducted with these aircraft would seem to have survived and no photographs are known to exist. The prototypes were apparently not fitted with the special tandem-wheel undercarriage, although a scaled-down version of the undercarriage was tested on an Fi 156 Storch.

Ill-fated Viking

I have never seen a photograph of the Vickers Viking in which Ross Smith planned to fly around the world after World War I. Could you publish a history of the Viking, plus a general arrangement drawing of Smith's aircraft and a photograph if one exists?

R Warrington
New Orleans, Louisiana, USA

The volume *Vickers Aircraft Since 1908* by C F Andrews (Putnam 1969) contains a half-

tone reproduction of Sir Ross Smith's Viking IV which, the caption claims, is the "only photograph of Ross Smith's round-the-world Viking, in erecting shop at Weybridge." Notwithstanding this statement, the Smith Papers held by the State Library of South Australia contain six photographs of the Viking, two of which are reproduced herewith by kind permission of Lady Keith Smith; a third photograph from this series was published in Sir Grenfell Price's biography of Ross and Keith Smith, *The Skies Remember* (Angus and Robertson 1969).

The history of the Vickers Viking began in late 1919 when the prototype G-EAOV, designed by Rex Pierson and fitted with a 275 hp Rolls-Royce Falcon, made its first flight at Brooklands. Vickers chief test pilot Sir John Alcock was killed in this aircraft when he made a forced landing in fog near Rouen while en route to the Paris Aero Show on 18 December 1919 — eight days after Ross Smith completed the first England to Australia flight in the Vickers FB27A Vimy IV, G-EAOU, ex F8630. Two other sole versions were the Viking II, G-EASC, with a 360 hp Rolls-Royce Eagle VIII, and the Viking III, G-EAUK, with a 450 hp Napier Lion. The latter aircraft won the Air Ministry Competition for amphibians in 1920 and, the following year, it carried out deck-handling and operational trials aboard HMS *Argus* as N147.

A production line was subsequently laid down for fleet-spotter, military and commercial versions of the next model, the Viking IV. The naval variants were equipped with folding wings for storage, and the commercial Vikings usually had an enclosed pilot's cabin as against the open cockpits of the other two types. Twenty-six Viking IVs were constructed between 1921 and 1923, and these aircraft

Two rare views of the Vickers Viking IV amphibian G-EBBZ in the erecting shop at Weybridge in 1922, with Sir Ross Smith alongside the aircraft in the picture above.

were fitted with either Napier or Rolls-Royce engines. Another six Vikings were built by Canadian Vickers at Montreal between 1922 and 1924.

An optional fitting on the Viking IV was the new T64 high-lift wing section which facilitated take-off from restricted water areas, but had a vicious tip stall. This drawback, together with the adverse effect caused by the low drag component of the hull and high thrust line, made the Viking with the T64 wing section a difficult aircraft to handle. It was nose heavy with engine on, and tail heavy with engine off. Consequently the Viking IV had to be flown with caution — particularly by pilots accustomed to landplanes — to avoid flat spins inherent with aircraft of comparatively low speeds.

During 1921 Sir Ross Smith formulated plans for a flight around the world from England through Europe, Asia, India, Burma, China, Japan, Aleutian Islands, Alaska, Canada, Newfoundland, and across the North Atlantic or via the Azores to Portugal. Vickers prepared a special Type 60 Viking IV, G-EBBZ, for Sir Ross, his navigator Sir Keith Smith and engineer Lieutenant J M Bennett. Although G-EBBZ was a commercial type with non-folding wings, it was fitted with open cockpits in place of the usual pilot's cabin. Other modifications included long-distance tanks and storage compartments which occupied the normal passenger area.

On Thursday 13 April 1922 Captain S Cockerell, Vickers test pilot, flew G-EBBZ from Brooklands with Sir Ross and Bennett as passengers. After a demonstration Cockerell left the aircraft and Sir Ross and Bennett then took the Viking up on a second test flight. The amphibian climbed to an estimated height of between 1,000 and 2,000 ft (300-600 m) and, while over the south side of the motor track, Sir Ross Smith executed a sharp and almost vertically banked turn to the right through 180 degrees from which a flat spin immediately developed. The Viking appeared to lose about half its height in the spin before rotation decreased and a more spiral path was initiated. The pilot was heard to open up the engine but closed it again as a fast spinning nose dive occurred. The spin was checked again just above the ground when engine power was momentarily applied. The aircraft was too low to recover, however, and it crashed into the back of the motor track near the River Wey killing both occupants. Sir Keith had just made a belated arrival from London and witnessed his brother's death.

The cause of the accident was believed to be due to the pilot's unfamiliarity with the amphibian, particularly in regard to engine on-off conditions and the tendency of the T64-section wing to tip stall. Ironically, the two pilots who gained fame and knighthoods for their pioneering Vimy flights — Sir John Alcock and Sir Ross Smith — both lost their lives in a Viking.

The Vickers Type 60 Viking Mk IV, G-EBBZ, was powered by a 450 hp Napier Lion engine. Dimensions included a span of 50 ft (15,25 m), a length of 34 ft 2 in (10,41 m), a height of 14 ft (4,27 m), and a wing area of 635 sq ft (58,99 m²). The empty weight was 4,040 lb (1 834 kg), and the loaded weight was 5,790 lb (2 630 kg). Maximum speed at sea level was 113 mph (182 km/h), and the aircraft could climb to

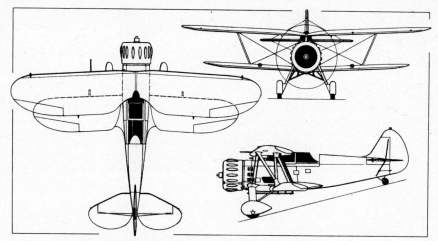

(Above) A three-view of the Waco S2HD and (below) photograph of the sixth of 10 Waco JHDs supplied to the Uruguayan Aeronautica Militar, shown in July 1938.

3,000 ft (915 m) in 3·2 min. Range, with long-range tanks, was 925 ml (1 487 km).

The D-type Waco

I shall be grateful if you will publish details, including a three-view drawing, of the Waco fighter-bomber biplane that was used pre-WW II by the Cuban Air Force. Did this aircraft type see service in the USAAF or any other air force?

Peter J Garland
Epsom, Surrey KT19 8RE

The only Waco-manufactured biplane supplied to Cuba's *Aviación de Ejercito*, or Military Aviation, prior to WW II which could remotely be described as a "fighter-bomber" was the Model D which was delivered as a general-purpose military aircraft and was also supplied to several Latin American air arms but was *not* utilised by the USAAF. Introduced in 1936, and manufactured in small numbers during 1937-38, the Model D was offered to a variety of equipment standards and with various engines in the 350-450 hp range, the equipment standard and power plant being signified by the letter or letter-and-number prefix to the model designation. At least one example (and possibly three) of the Model D was exported to Cuba, this being the S2HD version with a nine-cylinder Pratt & Whitney Wasp Junior SB rated at 450 hp for take-off. It was fitted with two USAAC A3 type bomb racks mounted in tandem beneath the fuselage and carrying a total of 10 25-lb (11,34-kg) bombs or two 125-lb (56,7-kg) bombs on the front rack only, and gun armament comprised one 0·30-in (7,62-mm) machine gun with 1,000 rounds in each lower wing and a similar Browning on a flexible mounting in the rear cockpit with 500 rounds. The tandem cockpits were provided with complete dual controls and instru-

ments, empty and loaded weights were 2,585 lb (1 173 kg) and 3,800 lb (1 724 kg) respectively, and overall dimensions were: span, 32 ft 9 in (9,98 m); length, 25 ft 6 in (7,77 m); height, 8 ft 11 in (2,74 m); wing area, 256 sq ft (23,78 m²). Performance included a max speed of 175 mph (281 km/h) at sea level and 188 mph (303 km/h) at 9,000 ft (2 743 m), cruising speeds of 150 mph (241 km/h) at sea level and 158 mph (254 km/h) at optimum altitude, an initial climb rate of 1,300 ft/min (6,6 m/sec) and a service ceiling of 18,000 ft (5 486 m).

The JHD version of the Model D differed from the S2HD supplied to Cuba in having a nine-cylinder Wright R-975-E-1 Whirlwind rated at 365 hp at sea level enclosed by a smooth NACA-type cowling (whereas the cowling of the Wasp Junior of the S2HD was fluted) and in having only one (starboard wing) fixed forward-firing 0·30-in (7,62-mm) machine gun. A similar flexibly-mounted Browning was mounted in the rear cockpit. A3 type bomb racks were provided and fuel capacity was similar (74 Imp gal/336,5 l distributed between two underfloor tanks and one aft of the engine firewall). Ten examples of the JHD version were supplied in 1937 to the Uruguayan *Aéronautica Militar*. Another military customer for the Model D was the Nicaraguan *Fuerza Aérea de la Guardia Nacional* which received at least three examples of the WHD version, this being similar to the JHD apart from having the R-975-E-3 version of the Whirlwind rated at 450 hp for take-off.

Apart from the Waco Model Ds supplied to the *Aviación de Ejercito*, Cuba acquired three Waco UMF-3 tandem two-seat trainers in late 1937 for use by the *Marina de Guerra*.

IN PRINT

"The Unknown Mustangs"
by John R Beaman, Jr
28 pp, 8½ in by 11 in, illustrated
INTENDED primarily as an aid for model-makers, this booklet can also be recommended to enthusiasts with a special interest in the P-51 Mustang. Specifically, it deals with the early Allison-engined versions, the P-51, P-51A and A-36, and Mr Beaman has produced a series of finely-detailed drawings to depict these variants (with notes to show where various P-51 kits are wrong and how they can be corrected).

There are also side-view drawings showing the markings of seven different A-36s and four P-51As. Copies can be ordered from the author at 2512 Overbrook Drive, Greensboro, NC 27408, USA, price $2·25 for the USA or Canada, or $2·75 for all other countries, both prices inclusive of postage.

"Fight for the Sky"
by Douglas Bader
Fontana, London, £1·95
168 pp, 7¼ in by 9½ in
PAPERBACK edition of Bader's story of the Spitfire and Hurricane. It was first published in 1973, casebound (see *In Print*/March 1974) and offers an interesting account of the development and wartime careers of two great aircraft — with extra contributions from eight of Bader's compatriots, all of whom were in the thick of the fighting. The eight pages of colour photographs are noteworthy, although less so than the 32-pp colour section in the original edition.

"Pioneer Bush Pilot"
by Ira Harkey
University of Washington Press, Seattle, $12·95
308 pp, 6 in by 9 in, illustrated
THIS is the story of Noel Wien, founder of Wien Alaska Airways and a pioneer of flying in Alaska. He arrived there in 1924, with a background of stunt-flying and barnstorming, and as one of the first aviators in the territory, he soon found plenty of opportunity both to demonstrate his flying skills for the benefits of the local populace, and to undertake typical "bush" flying activities carrying supplies and passengers between communities.

As Alaska developed, the opportunities for aviation to serve the growing communities expanded also, and Wien — later joined by his brothers Ralph and Sigurd — took full advantage of the opportunities that offered. Wien Alaska Airways — the first of two companies to bear the name — was formed in 1927, followed by Wien Airways of Alaska in 1932 and the second Wien Alaska Airways in 1935. As Wien Air Alaska, the company continues today.

This account of Noel Wien's flying life is well told, with Wien's full co-operation, and makes interesting reading.

"Pilot's Flight Operating Instructions"
No 1, Stearman N2S-3
No 2, D.H. Mosquito 41
AeroGraphics, Tucson, Arizona, USA
8½ in by 11 in
THESE are the first two in a new series of facsimile reprints of the Flight Handbooks for various aircraft of the 1930-1960 period. Each is an exact copy, including the cover, of the original, with no editing or additional material.

A considerable amount of data, plus cockpit and system diagrams, are included in Flight Handbooks of this type, and the success of similar reprints of WW II Pilot's Notes already published in the UK shows their popularity with enthusiasts. AeroGraphics indicates that the series will continue with handbooks on the P-59A Airacomet and the A-20 Havoc.

The N2S-3 Handbook costs $1·95 and the Mosquito (the Mk 41 was an Australian-built PR variant), $2·95, plus 30 cents postage in each case for UK and European orders. The publisher's address is P.O. Box 4656, Tucson, Arizona 85717, USA.

"Civil Marine Aircraft"
by John Stroud, £2·50
"Great Pioneer Flights"
by Oliver Tapper, £2·95
Bodley Head, London
128 pp each, 9½ in by 7¼ in, illustrated
ADDITIONS to the Putnam World Aeronautical Library, these volumes in landscape format combine a good collection of photographs with readable text, pleasantly laid out and printed on good quality paper. Not quite in the category of reference volumes for the enthusiast, these books can be recommended to the general reader with an interest in aviation, and for the younger enthusiast. The reputations of the two authors ensure the accuracy of the text.

"Civil Aircraft Registers of Africa, 1975"
by Ian P Burnett, David Partington and Ken Smy
Air-Britain, £2·10
140 pp, 7 in by 9¼ in, illustrated
NO FEWER than 57 territories in the African continent are represented in this latest addition to the series of civil aircraft registers compiled and published by Air-Britain. The information is up to date to the end of October 1975 and includes details, for each registered aircraft, of the type, c/n, previous identity, date of registration, owner and probable base.

Copies can be ordered, post free, from Air-Britain Sales Department at Stone Cottage, Great Sampford, Saffron Walden, Essex. For air mail delivery outside Europe, add £1·50.

"World War II Fighter Conflict"
by Alfred Price
Macdonald and Jane's, London, £3·25
160 pp, 6 in by 8¾ in, illustrated
ANOTHER title in the Macdonald War Illustrated Studies that amply maintains the authority of this recently-launched series of relatively slender hard-backs and confirms the importance of the series as a whole, which already contains other excellent titles. *Fighter Conflict* is described as a "comparative study on the evolution of aircraft and tactics", covering the major fighters of the UK, USA, USSR, Germany, Japan, France and Italy.

The book has three main parts. First there is a discussion of overall fighter evolution between 1939 and 1945, covering such aspects as aerodynamics, power plant, structure, armament and performance. Secondly, and perhaps the most interesting section, there are detailed direct comparisons of the performance of four famous types of fighter — the Fw 190A-3, P-51B Mustang, Tempest V and Mitsubishi A6M5 Zero-Sen — when matched against their principal adversaries. The third part of the book is devoted to the tactics employed by the various fighter forces.

In addition to many photographs, the book contains a number of diagrams showing the arrangement of armour and armament in the principal fighters of the period.

A cannon-armed North American P-51 bearing the "Snoopers" emblem of the 111th Tactical Reconnaissance Squadron serving in Italy in 1943 — one of the units illustrated in "The Unknown Mustangs" noted above.

INDIA

HINDUSTAN AERONAUTICS HPT-32

THE HPT-32 is a piston-engined primary trainer, the design of which has been completed by Hindustan Aeronautics at Bangalore in accordance with the projected requirements of the Indian Air Force. A mock-up was built during 1975, but no go-ahead has yet been given for construction of a prototype, since the Civil Aviation Department is pressing for adoption of the Revathi II in the same rôle. The latter is a two/three-seat lightplane, flown in prototype form in 1967 but not, apparently, favoured by the Indian Air Force, which is eager for development of the HPT-32 to proceed.

Fully-aerobatic, the HPT-32 is stressed for +6g and −3g at its normal take-off weight of 2,645 lb (1 200 kg) and is of all-metal construction. It has side-by-side seating with full dual controls, and a third seat in the rear of the cockpit, good all-round visibility being obtained from beneath the aft-sliding bubble canopy. With an endurance of 4½ hrs on its standard fuel capacity, the HPT-32 can carry an additional tank in the rear of the cockpit in place of the third seat, increasing endurance to 7 hrs. The airframe is designed for a fatigue life of 6,500 hrs and conforms to the requirements of FAR-23. The undercarriage is designed to absorb a rate of descent of 9 ft/min (2,75 m/sec). Four wing hardpoints will be provided, to carry assorted ordnance or supply packs.

Prototypes and early production models of the HPT-32 will have a Lycoming engine, but it is intended that a 260 hp, six-cylinder engine should be developed in India for the principal production version, this engine being related in design to the 400 hp HPE-4 that is under development for use in the HA-31 Basant agricultural aircraft.

Power Plant: One Lycoming AEIO-540-D4B5 flat-six direct fuel-injection engine rated at 260 hp for take-off, driving a Hartzell two-bladed constant speed propeller. Fuel in two integral wing tanks, capacity 25 Imp gal (114 l) each, plus provision for one 30-Imp gal (136 l) tank in rear cockpit.

Performance (at normal all-up weight): Max speed, 191 mph (307 km/h) EAS at sea level; initial rate of climb, 1,570 ft/min (7,9 m/sec); service ceiling, 21,300 ft (6 500 m); take-off to 50 ft (15,2 m), 920 ft (280 m); landing from 50 ft (15,2 m), 1,280 ft (390 m); range, 620 mls (1 000 km) at 6,560 ft (2 000 m); endurance (standard tankage), 4½ hrs, (max fuel), 7 hrs.

Weights: Empty (no avionics), 1,870 lb (850 kg); normal take-off and landing, 2,645 lb (1 200 kg); max external load on four wing pylons, 660 lb (300 kg).

Dimensions: Span, 31 ft 2 in (9,5 m); length 25 ft 4 in (7,72 m); height, 9 ft 7½ in (2,93 m); wing area, 161 sq ft (15,0 m²); aspect ratio, 6.0:1; dihedral, 5 deg constant; incidence, 2.5 deg at front spar; undercarriage track, 10 ft 10 in (3,3 m); wheelbase, 5 ft 7½ in (1,71 m).

Accommodation: Instructor and student side-by-side in adjustable seats and full dual control. Optional third seat in rear of cabin. Luggage compartment alongside rear seat.

Armament: Four wing pylons to carry up to 560 lb (225 kg) of ordnance or 660 lb (300 kg) of airdrop supplies.

USA

BEECHCRAFT KING AIR B100

AN all-round improvement in performance is offered by this newest addition to the King Air range of business twins, the King Air B100. This differs from all previous King Airs, four other versions of which are included in the range of Beechcrafts offered for sale in 1976, in having Garrett AiResearch engines in place of Pratt & Whitney PT6As.

Certified by the FAA in November, the King Air B100 was to be available for de-

The Beech King Air B100 which differs from earlier King Airs in having Garrett AiResearch engines in place of PT6As.

liveries starting this month (January). Apart from the engines, the aircraft is similar to the King Air A100, offering up to 15 seats in a pressurized fuselage. The engines are derated from a maximum of 840 shp to obtain a good TBO, starting at 3,100 hr for the entry-into-service standard.

Power Plant: Two Garrett AiResearch TPE 331-6-252B axial flow turboprops, flat rated at 715 shp each. Hartzell four-bladed constant speed fully feathering propellers, diameter 7 ft 6 in (2,29 m). Total fuel capacity, 470 US gal (1 779 l).

Performance: Cruising speeds (max cruise power at 10,500 lb/4 762 kg), 306 mph (493 km/h) at 10,000 ft (3 050 m) and 297 mph (478 km/h) at 21,000 ft (6 400 m); initial rate of climb, 1,985 ft/min (10,1 m/sec); single-engined climb, 425 ft/min (2,1 m/sec) at max weight at sea level; service ceiling, 25,200 ft (7 681 m); single-engined ceiling, 11,000 ft (3 353 m); take-off distance to 50 ft (15,2 m), 2,800 ft (853 m); landing distance from 50 ft (15,2 m), 2,400 ft (731 m); cruising range (with reserves) 1,515 mls (2 438 km).

Weights: Empty, 7,127 lb (3 233 kg); useful load, 4,747 lb (2 153 kg); max take-off, 11,800 lb (5 352 kg); max landing, 11,210 lb (5 085 kg).

Dimensions: Span, 45 ft 10¼ in (13,99 m); length, 39 ft 11¼ in (12,18 m); height, 15 ft 4¼ in (4,68 m); wheelbase, 14 ft 11 in (4,55 m); undercarriage track, 13 ft (3,97 m); dihedral, 7 deg constant; incidence, 4·85 deg at root to nil at tip.

Accommodation: Pilot and six to 13 passengers according to cabin arrangement. Cabin pressurization, 4·6 psi (0,324 kg/cm²).

GATES LEARJET CENTURY III SERIES

ALL six models of the Learjet offered in the 1976 range by Gates Learjet benefit from a series of wing improvements introduced under the series name of "Century III". Details of the new series, named to mark their introduction in the US Bicentennial year (1976), were announced last October, and deliveries will begin in July.

The new wing features a recambered leading edge as far back as the second of the eight spars in the Learjet wing, which, basically, deepens the nose section of the profile on its underside. Coupled with other innovations that include an improved stall warning/prevention system, the new profile increases the aircraft's lateral stability and handling qualities at the lower end of the speed range, this in turn permitting substantial reductions in take-off and landing weights.

The six-model range comprises the Model 24E and 24F, respectively equivalent to the Model 24D/A and 24D; the Model 25D and 25F, equivalent to the Model 25B and 25C; and the Model 35A and 36A, replacing the

A three-view drawing of the projected Hindustan Aeronautics HPT-32 primary/basic trainer.

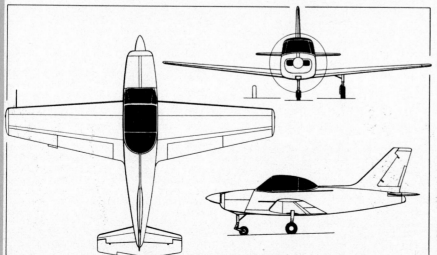

Model 35 and 36. The first four mentioned models have General Electric CJ610 engines and all will comply with FAR 36 noise standards, without using sound suppressors. Thrust reversers will be available as options on all Century III series Learjets.

Other new features include a high energy brake system, new cockpit seats and lighting and engine synchronizers for Models 35A and 36A, with the last-mentioned optional on the other four models; increased VMO (max operating speed) for the Model 25D and 25F; a new partial flap setting for the Model 25D and 25F to give an increase of more than 2,000 lb (908 kg) in take-off weight in hot and high conditions, and an increase of 1,000 lb (454 kg) in max take-off weight of the 36A. The Model 24E is heralded as an addition to the Learjet range, being essentially a low-cost variant of the Model 24 family with restricted gross weight and is offered at $897,500 (about £433,500) fully equipped for all-weather IFR operation in accordance with FAR 135. Brief details of the "Century III" models follow:

LEARJET 24E and 24F
Power Plant: Two General Electric CJ610-6 turbojets each rated at 2,950 lb st (1 340 kgp). Optional thrust reversers. Fuel capacity 840 US gal (3 180 l) in integral wing and wing-tip tanks.
Performance: Max speed, 548 mph (882 km/h); high speed cruise, Mach = 0·82, 534 mph (859 km/h); balanced field length, max weight (24E), 2,590 ft (790 m), (24F), 3,200 ft (976 m); balanced field length (four passengers for 690 mls/1 110 km), 2,550 ft (778 m); initial rate of climb (24E), 7,500 ft/min (38,12 m/sec), (24F), 6,800 ft/min (34,57 m/sec); single-engined climb rate (24E), 2,350 ft/min (11,95 m/sec), (24F), 2,100 ft/min (10,67 m/sec); operational ceiling, 45,000 ft (13 725 m); single-engined ceiling, 29,000 ft (8 845 m), time to 45,000 ft (13 725 m) (24E), 18 min, (24F), 21 min; approach speed, 96 kt (178 km/h); landing distance at typical weight, 2,450 ft (747 m); range with four passengers and 45-min reserve (24E), 1,525 mls (2 454 km), (24F), 1,865 mls (3 000 km).
Weights: Max take-off (24E), 12,499 lb (5 670 kg), (24F), 13,500 lb (6 124 kg); typical landing, 8,600 lb (3 900 kg).
Dimensions: Span, 35 ft 7 in (10,84 m); length, 43 ft 3 in (13,18 m); height, 12 ft 3 in (3,73 m); wing area, 231·77 sq ft (21,53 m²); wheelbase, 16 ft 2 in (4,93 m); undercarriage track, 8 ft 3 in (2,51 m).
Accommodation: Two seats side-by-side on flight deck and up to six passengers in cabin.

LEARJET 25D and 25F
Power Plant: As Models 24E and 24F. Fuel capacity (25D) as Models 24E and 24F. Fuel capacity (25F), 1,044 US gal (3 952 l) in integral wing, wing-tip and fuselage tanks.
Performance: Max speed, 565 mph (909 km/h); high speed cruise, Mach = 0·82, 534 mph (859 km/h); balanced field length, max weight, 3,950 ft (1 205 m); balanced field length (four passengers for 690 mls/1 110 km), 2,700 ft (824 m); initial rate of climb, 6,050 ft/min (30,75 m/sec); single-engined climb rate, 1,750 ft/min (8,89 m/sec); operational ceiling, 45,000 ft (13 725 m); single-engined ceiling, 23,500 ft (7 168 m); time to 41,000 ft (12 505 m), 19 min; approach speed, 99 kt (183 km/h); landing distance at typical weight, 2,500 ft (763 m); range with four passengers and 45-min reserve (25D), 1,905 mls (3 065 km), (25F), 2,233 mls (3 593 km).
Dimensions: As for Model 24E and 24F except length, 47 ft 7 in (14,50 m) and wheelbase 19 ft 2 in (5,84 m).

Accommodation: Two seats side-by-side on flight deck and up to eight passengers in cabin.

LEARJET 35A and 36A
Power Plant: Two Garrett AiResearch TFE 731-2 turbofans rated at 3,500 lb st (1 587 kgp) each. Thrust reversers optional. Fuel capacity (35A), 921 US gal (3 486 l), (36A), 1,109 US gal (4 198 l).
Performance: Max speed, 565 mph (909 km/h); high speed cruise, Mach = 0·83, 534 mph (859 km/h); balanced field length max weight (35A), 4,300 ft (1 312 m), (36A), 4,950 ft (1 510 m); balanced field length (four passengers for 690 mls/1 110 km), 2,820 ft (860 m); initial rate of climb (35A), 5,100 ft/min (25,92 m/sec), (36A), 4,800 ft/min (24,40 m/sec); single-engined climb (35A), 1,475 ft/min (7,50 m/sec), (36A), 1,300 ft/min (6,61 m/sec); operational ceiling, 45,000 ft (13 725 m); single-engined ceiling, 23,500 ft (7 168 m); time to 41,000 ft (12 505 m) (35A), 18 min, (36A), 21 min; approach speed, 101 kt (187 km/h); landing distance at typical weight, 2,650 ft (808 m); range with four passengers and 45-min reserve (35A), 2,858 mls (4 600 km), (36A), 3,410 mls (5 487 km).
Weights: Max take-off (35A), 17,000 lb (7 711 kg), (36A), 18,000 lb (8 165 kg); typical landing, 10,000 lb (4 536 kg).
Dimensions: Span, 39 ft 6 in (12,04 m); length, 48 ft 8 in (14,83 m); height, 12 ft 3 in (3,73 m); undercarriage track, 8 ft 3 in (2,51 m); wing area, 253·3 sq ft (23,53 m²).
Accommodation: Two seats side-by-side on flight deck and up to eight passengers in cabin.

PIPER PA-23-250 AZTEC F
A SERIES of improvements has been made by Piper to the classic Aztec to introduce the new Aztec F in the 1976 range. The important new features include optional tanks in the wing tips to increase the range by about 350 mls (563 km); a new flap-to-stabilator trim interconnect and an all-new brake assembly. The whole fuel system has been redesigned, and now includes external fuel gauges that measure the combined fuel content of the outboard and tip tanks; Navajo-type flush filler openings and caps and one-way flow baffles in each tank to help stabilize fuel flow.

The Aztec F is available in both normally-aspirated and turbocharged versions. Both benefit from a number of improvements to the cabin, including a redesigned panel arrangement and a one-piece glareshield to eliminate light reflections onto the windshield. Re-designed seats give the occupants greater leg room.

Aztec F
Power Plant: Two 250 hp Lycoming TO-540-C4B5 flat-six air-cooled engines driving Hartzell constant-speed two-blade propellers, diameter 6 ft 5 in (1,96 m). Fuel capacity,

A Piper Aztec F, 1976 model of the long-established Piper twin.

144 US gal (544 l) standard plus 40 US gal (152 l) in optional outer wing tanks.
Performance: Average cruising speed, best power at 3,850 ft (1 170 m), 206 mph (331 km/h); average cruising speed, best economy at 7,000 ft (2 150 m), 173 mph (278 km/h); take-off run (max effort), 945 ft (288 m); take-off distance to 50 ft (15,2 m) (normal effort), 1,980 ft (604 m); landing distance from 50 ft (15,2 m) (normal effort), 1,585 ft (483 m); initial rate of climb, 1,400 ft/min (7,1 m/sec); single-engine climb rate, 235 ft/min (1,2 m/sec); service ceiling, 17,600 ft (5 368 m); single-engine absolute ceiling, 6,250 ft (1 906 m); range (best economy at 7,000 ft/2 150 m), 985 mls (1 824 km) with standard fuel, 1,320 mls (2 444 km) with max fuel.
Weights: Standard empty, 3,049 lb (1 383 kg); max take-off, 5,200 lb (2 360 kg); max zero fuel, 4,400 lb (1 198 kg).
Dimensions: Span, 37 ft 4 in (11,4 m); length, 31 ft 2¾ in (9,52 m); height, 10 ft 4 in (3,15 m); wing area, 207·5 sq ft (19,28 m²); undercarriage track, 11 ft 4 in (3,45 m); wheelbase, 7 ft 6 in (2,29 m).
Accommodation: Pilot and five passengers in two pairs of individual seats and rear bench seat. Dual controls. Rear luggage compartment capacity 25·4 cu ft (0,71 m³); forward luggage compartment capacity 21·3 cu ft (0,60 m³).

Turbo Aztec F
Power Plant: Two 250 hp Lycoming TIO-540-C1A flat-six air-cooled engines with AiResearch turbochargers, providing constant manifold pressure up to 22,000 ft (6 700 m). Propellers and fuel as Aztec F.
Performance: Average cruising speed, best power at 3,850 ft (1 170 m), 247 mph (398 km/h); average cruising speed, best economy at 20,000 ft (6 100 m), 190 mph (272 km/h); take-off run (max effort), 945 ft (288 m); take-off distance to 50 ft (15,2 m) (normal effort), 1,980 ft (604 m); landing distance from 50 ft (15,2 m) (normal effort), 1,585 ft (483 m); initial rate of climb, 1,470 ft/min (7,5 m/sec); single-engine climb rate, 225 ft/min (1,5 m/sec); service ceiling, over 24,000 ft (7 320 m) single-engine absolute ceiling, 17,000 ft (5 185 m); range (best economy at 20,000 ft/6 100 m), 835 mls (1 546 km) with standard fuel, 1,145 mls (2 120 km) with max fuel.
Weights: Standard empty, 3,188 lb (1 447 kg); max take-off, 5,200 lb (3 260 kg); max zero fuel, 4,500 lb (2 043 kg).
Dimensions: Span, 37 ft 4 in (11,4 m); length, 31 ft 2¾ in (9,52 m); height, 10 ft 4 in (3,15 m); wing area, 207·5 sq ft (19,28 m²); undercarriage track, 11 ft 4 in (3,45 m); wheelbase, 7 ft 6 in (2,29 m).
Accommodation: Pilot and five passengers in two pairs of individual seats and rear bench seat. Dual controls. Rear luggage compartment capacity 25.4 cu ft (0,71 m³); forward luggage compartment capacity 21.3 cu ft (0,60 m³).

AIR
International

Volume 10   Number 5   May 1976

Managing Editor	William Green
Editor	Gordon Swanborough
Modelling Editor	Fred J Henderson
Contributing Artists	Dennis Punnett
	John Weal
Cover Art	W R Hardy
Contributing Photographer	
	Stephen Peltz
Editorial Representative, Washington	
	Norman Polmar
Publisher	Donald Hannah
Circulation Director	Donald Syner
Subscription Manager	Claire Sillette
Advertising/Public Relations	
	Elizabeth Baker
Advertising Manager	Jim Boyd

Editorial Offices:
The AIR INTERNATIONAL, PO Box 16, Bromley, BR2 7RB Kent.

Subscription, Advertising and Circulation Offices:
The AIR INTERNATIONAL, De Worde House, 283 Lonsdale Road, London SW13 9QW. Telephone 01-878 2454. US and Canadian readers may address subscriptions and general enquiries to AIR INTERNATIONAL PO Box 353, Whitestone, NY 11357 for onward transmission to the UK, from where all correspondence is answered and orders despatched.

MEMBER OF THE AUDIT BUREAU OF CIRCULATIONS   ABC

Subscription rates, inclusive of postage, direct from the publishers, per year:

United Kingdom	£5·50
USA	$17·50
Canada	$17·50

Rates for other countries and for air mail subscriptions available on request from the Subscription Department at the above address.

The AIR INTERNATIONAL is published monthly by Fine Scroll Limited, distributed by Ducimus Books Ltd and printed by William Caple & Co Ltd, Chevron Press, Leicester, England. Editorial contents © 1976 by Pilot Press Limited. The views expressed by named contributors and correspondents are their own and do not necessarily reflect the views of the editors. Neither the editors nor the publishers accept responsibility for any loss or damage, however caused, to manuscripts or illustrations submitted to the AIR INTERNATIONAL.

Second Class postage pending at New York, NY. USA Mailing Agents: Air-Sea Freight Inc, 527 Madison Avenue, New York, NY 10022.

CONTENTS

WRENDEZVOUS WITH WREN

"I said, that's their new Quiet V/STOL."

AIRSCENE

MILITARY AFFAIRS

BELGIUM

After protracted delay resulting from budgeting problems between the Ministries of Communications and Defence, the 15ème Wing de Transport et Communications of the Force Aérienne Belge (FAéB) at Melsbroek, Brussels, has finally accepted delivery of two ex-SABENA Boeing 727-29QCs as replacements for the unit's two DC-6As and two DC-6Cs. Two of the aged Douglas transports have already been withdrawn and the remaining two will be phased out within the next few months.

BRAZIL

The final 20 of the 80 EMBRAER EMB-110 (C-95) Bandeirante general-purpose light transports currently on order for the Fôrça Aérea Brasileira (FAB) are now to be of the new EMB-110K version, a freighter with a 31·5-in (80-cm) fuselage stretch, a strengthened freight floor, an enlarged cargo door and revised avionics. The EMB-110K will be capable of accommodating up to 20 troops. The FAB is also to receive four examples of the EMB-110B (RC-95) photographic version of the Bandeirante which will have cabin floor apertures for various aerial cameras, Doppler and inertial navigation equipment and a crew including three camera operators, and an order on behalf of the FAB for 16 examples of the EMB-111 maritime patrol derivative of the Bandeirante has now been confirmed. The EMB-111, which will commence its flight test programme at the end of this year, with production following on completion of current FAB orders for the EMB-110, will have 750 shp Pratt & Whitney (Canada) PT6A-34 turboprops, AN/APS-503(C) search radar, a ventrally-mounted searchlight and provision for eight air-to-surface rockets. The EMB-111 will begin to replace the FAB's remaining aged SP-2E Neptunes from 1978.

CHILE

Among new contracts recently received by Northrop from the USAF for single-seat F-5E Tiger IIs and two-seat F-5Fs totalling $85·8m (£45·1m) was an allocation for Chile. Deliveries are scheduled to commence this month (May) against a contract placed mid-1974 for 15 F-5Es and three F-5Fs for the Fuerza Aérea de Chile (FAC), this being valued at $60m (£31·5m), including spares, support equipment and training, but it is not clear at the time of closing for press if the recent allocation covers these or additional aircraft. Official sources in Santiago were referring, last year, to the FAC's intention of forming a second F-5E Grupo in view of the continuing build-up of the armed forces of neighbouring Peru.

Six Garrett TSE331 turboshaft-powered Sikorsky S-55T helicopters (remanufactured S-55s) have recently been delivered from the USA by the Helitec company to the FAC at a unit cost of $175,000 (£92,100). The Chilean government is reportedly negotiating the purchase of three EMBRAER EMB-110 Bandeirante utility transports to replace Beech 18s operated by the small air component of the Chilean Navy.

DUBAI

Continuing its policy of confining procurement for its Air Wing to Italian sources, the Persian Gulf Sheikdom of Dubai has recently placed an order with Aeritalia for one G 222 general-purpose transport and has taken an option on a second. Dubai placed a repeat order with Aermacchi late last year for a batch of four MB 326s, the delivery of which later this year will bring to eight the number of aircraft of this type in the inventory of the Sheikdom's fledgeling air arm.

EGYPT

The bulk of the equipment of the Egyptian armed forces would, said President Anwar Sadat on 14 March, be "nothing but scrap" owing to lack of spares. If something of an exaggeration, this statement nevertheless reflected the growing problem confronting the country's armed forces in general and the Egyptian Air Force in particular owing to the Soviet Union's refusal to continue to supply spares, support equipment and replacements for the Soviet-equipped services in view of Egypt's inability to settle debts reportedly totalling £3,700m on which a moratorium was requested and refused. While there is some evidence that President Sadat is overstating the difficulty that Egypt is facing in keeping the bulk of the Soviet equipment operable over the next two years or so, the problems are undoubtedly genuine and particularly pressing in so far as the Egyptian Air Force is concerned. It is known that the Soviet Union halted the supply of spare Tumansky R-13 turbojets for the EAF's MiG-21s some 20 months ago, extending the embargo to virtually all aircraft spares shortly afterwards, and the progressive deterioration of relations between Egypt and the Soviet Union — which culminated on 15 March in the abrogation by the former of the 15-year treaty of "friendship and co-operation" between the two countries originally signed in May 1971 — has resulted in Egyptian attempts to procure spares from other sources. Five months ago, the Egyptian government requested assistance with MiG-21 spares from India where the aircraft is manufactured under licence, but an Indian request to the Soviet Union for permission to export spares to Egypt was rejected by the Soviet government which informed India that any supply of MiG-21 parts to Egypt, overtly or covertly, would result in cancellation of the Indian MiG-21 manufacturing licence and would seriously disrupt diplomatic relations between the two countries. President Sadat was expected to request the aid of President Tito in obtaining MiG spares during his visit to Yugoslavia in April — the Yugoslav Air Force has upwards of 100 MiG-21s in its inventory and the Yugoslav industry reportedly undertakes limited spares manufacture — presumably on the assumption that Yugoslavia was likely to operate more independently of Moscow than India, and the Sino-Communist government has agreed to furnish Egypt with 30 "Chinese copies" of the Tumansky engine and a substantial quantity of Chinese-manufactured MiG-21 spares as a "gift". However, while existing stocks, the Sino-Communist aid and possible assistance from Yugoslavia may enable the EAF to maintain the day-to-day servicing of its Soviet equipment, major overhauls and repairs are another matter. The possibility of re-engining the MiG-21 with the Rolls-Royce Spey Mk 202 has apparently now been discarded as a result of a Rolls-Royce study which indicated that such would be both time-consuming and cost-ineffective. Meanwhile, EAF MiG-21 and Su-7 flying time has been drastically curtailed — Egyptian pilots are now getting fewer than 10 hours per month flying time in order to conserve their aircraft — and the one EAF squadron of MiG-23s is understood to have been grounded following the withdrawal of Soviet technicians who were still attached to the unit.

As a result of the unfavourable cost and time factors associated with the re-engining of MiG-21s with the Rolls-Royce Spey, some high-ranking factions in the EAF have been pressing President Sadat to authorise the initiation of the design of an indigenous Egyptian fighter that could use the Spey and, later, the RB.199 engine when this becomes available. While it is admitted that such a project would entail the recruitment of a foreign design team and possibly the manufacture of the component parts for the prototypes abroad, it is suggested that this would enable a warplane tailored to EAF requirements to be ready for production by the time the proposed Arab aircraft manufacturing industry centred on Egypt is finally established.

French press reports following the visit to France of the Egyptian Defence Minister, Gen Abdel Ghani Gamassi, and the C-in-C of the EAF, Maj Gen Mahmoud Shakir Abdel Moneim, that the Egyptian government has signed a purchase order for the Alpha Jet trainer are understood to have been premature, although the possible purchase of French fighters, trainers, helicopters and missiles is known to have been discussed by Gen Gamassi and Jean Laurens Delpech, the French Deputy Minister of Defence for Armaments. French press reports have also referred to the creation of a consortium of Dassault-Breguet, SNECMA and Thomson-CSF to assist Egypt in building up the Arab aircraft manufacturing industry, which, to be based initially on existing Egyptian production facilities, has made little progress over the past two years owing primarily to difficulties in defining the administrative and decision-making rôles of each of the several participating Arab countries. It will be recalled that the French press gave considerable publicity more than a year ago to an EAF "order" for 42 Mirage F1s, a firm contract for which has still to be signed. In so far as the EAF requirement for a new trainer is concerned, this apparently possessing highest priority on the Egyptian shopping list, it would seem that the contest between the Alpha Jet and the Hawk remains wide open.

There are signs in the USA that opposition to the sale of military aircraft for use by the EAF is receding and that discussions concerning the sale of the six Lockheed C-130 Hercules transports requested by the Egyptian government (see Airscene/April) will terminate in approval being given to their supply — possibly in the form of grant aid rather than as a straight commercial transaction owing to the limited funds currently available to the Egyptian government for equipment procurement. The contract is likely to be worth between $35m (£18·3m) and $40m (£21·1m), and this could open the door to the supply of other military aircraft, the first of which could be 20-40 Northrop F-5E Tiger IIs on a government-to-government basis, the F-5E having been requested by President Sadat and being considered by the US government to be purely defensive in rôle.

FEDERAL GERMANY

During the autumn, the Luftwaffe is scheduled to take delivery of the last four of 46 MBB Hansajet 320s built since the first production model flew 10 years ago, on 2 February 1966. The Luftwaffe currently operates eight Hansajets, six with the Flugbereitschaftstaffel at Wahn and two with the Erprobungsstelle 61 at Manching, but the four additional aircraft currently on the final assembly line are being specially equipped for electronic counter-measures tasks. With their delivery, the Hansajet production line is to close down.

The *Luftwaffe* is reportedly **considering** increasing its **procurement of** the Dassault-Breguet/Dornier **Alpha Jet** by ordering a quantity of the **training version.** Previously, the *Luftwaffe* has only evinced interest in the close air support version. The *Armée de l'Air*, hitherto committed only to the trainer model is studying the possibility of procuring a quantity of close support Alpha Jets equivalent to the quantity of trainers ordered for the *Luftwaffe*.

FRANCE
In the final report on the third five-year programme (3ᵉ PLT), which terminated on 31 December, was included a precise **equipment inventory** of the *Armée de l'Air* covering, apart from the more minor support types, all aircraft, their average age and their estimated remaining service life. According to this inventory, the *Armée de l'Air* has a current principal establishment of some 1,637 aircraft. On 1 January, the *Armée de l'Air* had a total of 345 Mirage IIIs and 5s in service, these comprising 44 Mirage IIIB trainers (10 years old), 55 Mirage IIIC interceptors (now 14 years old), 139 Mirage IIIE strike fighters (now nine years old), 41 Mirage IIIR tactical reconnaissance aircraft (now 14 years old), 18 Mirage IIIRD tactical reconnaissance aircraft (now eight years old) and 48 Mirage 5F ground attack fighters (three years old). The report considered that the Mirage IIICs possessed only four years further useful life and the Mirage IIIRs a further six years with the IIIRDs remaining in service until at least 1986. Replacement of the Mirage IIIE is scheduled to commence in 1978, although the last aircraft of this type are unlikely to be phased out until 1985. The relatively new Mirage 5Fs had an estimated 15 years service life from the beginning of the current year. The potential remaining service life of the Mirage IIIBs is calculated at nine years, although their replacement is scheduled to commence in 1982. The 50 Mirage IVA strategic bombers remaining in the inventory are to continue in service until 1985 and will not be replaced, and by the beginning of the year, 52 of the 105 Mirage F1s ordered for the *Armée de l'Air* had been delivered into the inventory, their potential service life being estimated at 16 years. Of the few other combat types, the 35 remaining Vautour bombers will be retired by 1977, and the last of 52 F-100 Super Sabres will have given place to the Jaguar by 1978. The 48 Super Mystères will all have been replaced by Mirage F1s by 1977. The 105 Mystère IVA fighters currently serving in the advanced training rôle will be replaced from 1 July 1978 onwards by the first production Alpha Jets, the 200th and last of which currently scheduled for delivery to the *Armée de l'Air* is expected to enter the inventory in December 1983, by which time it will have completely replaced the 156 Lockheed- and Canadair-built T-33As, the phase-out of which will commence in 1980. Successors will be sought for the 317 Super Magister trainers currently in *Armée de l'Air* service and scheduled to remain until 1984-85, and for the 52 MD 311 and 312 Flamant light twins, which, recently refurbished and fitted with new avionics, are to remain until at least 1981. During the current year, the service will take delivery of its fourth DC-8F transport; its fleet of 48 Transall C.160s is considered good until at least 1995, and no replacement date has yet been established for 11 (10-year-old) C-135F tankers. The existing fleet of 172 Noratlas transports is currently undergoing modification and refurbishing to extend its useful life for a further nine years to 1985.

IRAN
The Iranian **government** has apparently de-cided **not to take up** its **option on** a **third batch of** 40 Grumman F-14A **Tomcat fighters** owing, according to Gen Hassan Toufanian, the Vice-Minister for War, to their extremely high unit price of approximately $22m (£11·5m), but deliveries of the 80 Tomcats currently on firm order will not be affected. These are being delivered at a rate of two per month to the Khatami AFB, Isfahan, the delivery tempo being scheduled to increase to three per month at the beginning of next year and continue at that rate until the completion of the contract mid-1978. Fifty of the Tomcats will now be based at Khatami and the remaining 30 will operate from Shiraz, plans to establish a third base for Tomcat operation having now been discarded. Despite Iranian threats to reduce arms purchases from the USA unless arms prices were cut or more oil purchased — a threat to which the US government failed to react — Gen Toufanian is understood still to favour earlier plans to purchase up to 300 General Dynamics F-16 fighters with deliveries commencing 1979-80.

ITALY
Following the recent re-equipment of the 6° *Stormo* of the *Aeronautica Militare* (AMI) with Aeritalia-built F-104S Starfighters, the **service has** now **phased out** virtually all of its original **F-104Gs,** although a few RF-104Gs are still operated by the 3ᵃ *Aerobrigata*. At least 20 of the surplus F-104Gs were transferred to Turkey in February (see *Airscene*/April) and it seems probable that additional aircraft will be disposed of in similar fashion. The AMI has received some 180 F-104S Starfighters which serve with *squadriglie* of the 4°, 5°, 6°, 9°, 36°, 51° and 53° *stormi*.

The 207° *Gruppo della Scuola* at Latina, which is responsible for the initial grading of AMI pilots, has begun **replacing** its 27 aged Piaggio **P.148** primary **trainers with** the 20 SIAI-Marchetti **SF 260s** ordered to date. About a dozen of the P.148s are expected to be retained in AMI service as towplanes for the sailplanes of the *Scuola Militare di Volo* at Vela.

JAPAN
The three Self-Defence **Forces** are currently **formulating** their proposed weapons **procurement programmes** for the 5th five-year Defence Build-up Programme (which commences in April next year) which are to be submitted to the Ministry of Finance before September. In the wake of the Lockheed bribery scandal, it is anticipated that every proposed weapon purchase from a foreign company will be subjected to particularly searching scrutiny with decision delays resulting from the ensuing contention. The major items of aircraft procurement envisaged during the 5th DBP are as follows: (P-XL) A replacement for the P-2J maritime patrol aircraft for which it was originally planned to purchase some 70 P-3C Orions of which 50 would have been procured during the period of the new DBP (see subsequent news item); (F-X) A successor to the F-104J Starfighter with the McDonnell Douglas F-15 Eagle currently seen as frontrunner in the 100-aircraft programme but with the General Dynamics F-16 becoming a steadily stronger contender in view of the £1,050m-£1,300m anticipated cost in the event of selection of the F-15; (AEW-X) An airborne early warning aircraft for which the Grumman E-2C Hawkeye has been selected by the ASDF with 10-15 planned for procurement during the DBP for deployment at five air bases; (HH-X/CH-X) As successors to the Kawasaki-built V-107-II helicopter, the ASFD and GSDF have respectively selected the Sikorsky S-65A (CH-53) and Boeing Vertol 234 (CH-47C), the ASDF hoping to procure some 30 S-65As during the latter years of the DBP for the air-sea rescue rôle and the GSDF anticipating the acquisition of only two Boeing Vertol 234s for the medium transport rôle during the final year of the DBP with principal procurement in the following DBP; (RH-X) As a replacement for the V-107-II mine-sweeping helicopters of the MSDF the Sikorsky RH-53D has been selected and it is planned to procure 12-14 to equip two squadrons during the DBP; (AH-X) As an attack helicopter the GSDF has selected the Bell AH-1G and is proposing purchase of 50-60 of which 20-25 will be procured during the new DBP to equip two squadrons; (MASH-X) To replace the MSDF's Gyrodyne DASH drone helicopters, the service has selected the Kaman SH-2F and is proposing the procurement of 15 to equip seven frigates. Apart from the previously listed new types, the ASDF hopes to acquire 15 Kawasaki C-1 transports in the 5th DBP to supplement the 28 funded in the previous DBP with five more special versions for flight check and electronic countermeasures training rôles. The MSDF, in addition to four-five Kawasaki C-1s modified for the mine-laying rôle, hopes to procure nine more Shinmeiwa PS-1 maritime patrol flying boats and six more US-1 rescue amphibians during the 5th DBP (22 PS-1s and three US-1s have so far been funded) to enable three 12-aircraft (nine PS-1s and three US-1s) units to be formed.

Although the general consensus of informed opinion in Japan is that **procurement of** the Lockheed **P-3C Orion** maritime patrol aircraft for the MSDF is **no longer possible**, Mr Michita Sakata, the Defence Minister, told parliament on 5 March that he was still appreciative of the outstanding capabilities of the Lockheed aircraft and that the feasibility of continuing with the planned procurement of the Orion should be given further consideration. Mr Yoshio Kohmoto, Minister of International Trade and Industry, disagreed, advocating the acceleration of development of Kawasaki's projected turbofan-powered PX-L rather than any further consideration be given to the Orion. However, it has been pointed out that even if Kawasaki is given a "go ahead" immediately, it will be 1982 before the first two prototypes can be completed and at least 1984 before the first production deliveries of an indigenous maritime patrol aircraft can commence. One faction in the MSDF is proposing continuation of the P-2J production line at Kawasaki's Gifu plant, possibly with more advanced ASW equipment, in order to fill the gap. The final six of the 83 P-2Js currently scheduled to be delivered to the MSDF are now on the line with the last to be completed before March next year. Gen Yoshiharu Shirakawa, Chief of Joint Staffs, has proposed a marriage of the projected Kawasaki PX-L airframe with US-developed ASW equipment in order to reduce the timescale before an indigenous maritime patrol aircraft could be phased in. Only one aspect of the P-XL programme would seem certain and that is that no definitive decision will be taken in time to meet the budget deadline.

On 21 March, the MSDF retired the **last** of the six Grumman **Albatross** amphibians that it has operated in the ASR rôle. The six amphibians were supplied to the MSDF by the US Navy in 1961, and have now been replaced by SH-3 helicopters, but the unit will begin to phase in the Shinmeiwa US-1 amphibian in 1978.

JORDAN
During March-April, a Royal Jordanian Air Force procurement **mission** led by the C-in-C, Brig Aboud Salim Hassan, and the C-in-C of the Jordanian defence forces, Gen Zein Abu Shaker, made a three-week visit **to the US aerospace industry** with a shopping list of items considered necessary to complete Jordan's air defence system, following on approval last year of 14 Hawk missile batteries worth $260m

(£135m) and Vulcan anti-aircraft gun systems worth $87m (£45·5m). Both Litton Industries and Hughes have reportedly submitted proposals for the integration of the RJAF's F-5E Tiger II interceptors, Improved Hawk and Redeye SAMs and Vulcan gun systems into a complete air defence network, but Jordan still requires additional equipment to carry through such a programme, including radars, communications equipment, electronics and additional Northrop F-5E Tiger II fighters. The RJAF took delivery of 22 F-5Es last year but is understood to require at least a similar quantity (possibly including several two-seat F-5Fs) for delivery during the course of the next 18-24 months, with a third batch following over the course of 1979-80. The RJAF is currently operating a total of 36 Northrop F-5As and F-5Bs on indefinite loan from the Iranian government in the close-support rôle. Other equipment sought by the procurement mission is reported to include two Lockheed C-130H Hercules transports to supplement the two C-130Bs currently included in the transport inventory and Hughes TOW wire-guided anti-tank missiles. The RJAF has now taken delivery of the first two of its recently-ordered four CASA 212A Aviocar STOL transports and will be one of the first military customers for the Sikorsky S-76 helicopter, four having been ordered for late 1978 delivery. Jordanian arms purchases are being underwritten by Saudi Arabia.

NEW ZEALAND
Despite proposed defence expenditure cuts, it now seems probable that New Zealand's National Party Government will proceed with the **procurement** proposed by the last Labour Government **of** 10 **ex-RAF** Hawker Siddeley **Andover** tactical **transports** for the RNZAF at what are referred to as "bargain rates" (see *Airscene*/November).

PAKISTAN
A Pakistan Air Force evaluation team recently visited the USA to evaluate several types of combat aircraft prior to the **possible purchase of one or more** of the **types** examined. The purchase may cover as many as 100 aircraft and is being funded by the Iranian government. Types evaluated by the team during March and April comprised the F-5E Tiger II, the Vought A-7 Corsair II, the McDonnell Douglas A-4 Skyhawk II and the Fairchild A-10. Restrictions on the sale of military hardware to Pakistan were removed in February last year, but any sale will still require congressional approval.

SOVIET UNION
The Soviet Navy's **first** aircraft **carrier,** the 45,000-ton *Kiev,* has reportedly completed her **final** Black Sea **trials** and is expected to appear in the Mediterranean shortly. A third *Kiev*-class carrier is now under construction in the Nikolayev (South) yard, near Sevastopol, alongside the second carrier, the *Minsk,* tending to confirm the belief that up to six carriers of this type may eventually be built for the Soviet Navy.

The V-VS is arming its latest fighters with a **new family of** long-range air-to-air **missiles.** The MiG-25 *(Foxbat)* in its interceptor version carries four so-called AA-6 *Acrid* missiles, these being solid-fuelled, having an approximate overall length of 19 ft (5,80 m), a diameter of 1 ft (30,50 cm) and a range of some 23 miles (37 km). The MiG-23 *(Flogger)* carries both the AA-7 *Apex* and the AA-8 *Aphid,* both being solid-fuelled and having approximate ranges of 17 miles (27 km) and 5 miles (8 km) respectively. No details of the guidance systems are available.

SWITZERLAND
On 16 March, the Swiss National Council,

Lower House of Parliament, **approved** a credit of £234m for the **purchase of** 66 Northrop F-5E **Tiger IIs** and six two-seat F-5Fs after receiving assurances that there was no indication of bribery on the part of the Northrop Corporation. This was the final hurdle in the procurement of the aircraft for the *Flugwaffe* and formal signing of the purchase contract followed in Berne on 30 March. Deliveries will be made over the period 1978-81, with the first 19 aircraft being delivered by the parent company and the remaining 53 being assembled at Emmen.

AIRCRAFT AND INDUSTRY

BRAZIL
EMBRAER has **postponed** the first flight of the pressurized Bandeirante derivative, the **EMB-121 Xingu** (*AirData File*/March 1976) to June, but static and fatigue test specimens are being completed almost simultaneously and it is still hoped to have a pre-production Xingu in the air by the end of the year. Development of the supercritical wing for the EMB-120 and EMB-123 versions is expected to take another full year at least and these two pressurized versions may be subject to a greater delay. Preliminary design work is also being undertaken by EMBRAER on a jet executive type under the designation **EMB-13X**. The Piper Cherokee Lance has been added to the EMBRAER licence-built range as the **EMB-721 Sertanejo.**

CANADA
Less than a year after first flight, the **de Havilland DASH 7** quiet STOL airliner prototypes completed 500 hrs of **testing** on 7 February. The total continues to grow rapidly, with 48½ hrs achieved in 15 flights in one week late in February. The No 1 DASH 7 is devoted to stability and control testing while the No 2 aircraft is testing performance and systems, having recently had a water-methanol injection system fitted.

A de Havilland Canada DHC-5D **Buffalo** has broken **time-to-height records** for Group 2 Turboprop aircraft in the unlimited weight class C1 (previously held by a Lockheed P-3 Orion) and in a new 12 000-16 000-kg (26,430-35,240-lb) class C1H. Flying from Downsview on 16 February, the Buffalo — one of the new production batch with General Electric CT64-820-4 engines — reached 3 000 m (9,836 ft) in 2 min 12·75 sec, 6 000 m (19,672 ft) in 4 min 27·5 sec and 9 000 m (29,508 ft) in 8 min 3½ sec.

FRANCE
Aérospatiale has adopted the name **Ecureuil** (Squirrel) for its new **AS 350** five-seat helicopter (see *AirData File*/page 259). Two prototypes of the AS 350 are currently in flight test at Marignane, one with Turboméca Arriel and the other with Lycoming LTS-101 turboshaft engine; the latter is a rebuild, with modifications intended to be introduced in the production model, of the original prototype flown in June 1974 and illustrated in *Airscene*/November 1975.

Turboméca is launching **production of the Arriel** turboshaft to meet the planned requirements of Aérospatiale's Helicopter Division. It is used in the twin-engined SA 365 Dauphin and one version of the newly-announced AS 350 Ecureuil (see *AirData*/page 259). Pre-production engines will be delivered between November 1976 and June 1977 and production engines will be available in July 1977. By 1 March, Turboméca had built 17 Arriels and these had completed 3,108 test hours, including 524 airborne, the first flight in a test-bed having been made on 25 January 1975. The name **Makila** has been given to Turboméca's new 1,800 shp turboshaft destined for use in the SA 331 Super Puma.

The first **production** model Avions Fournier **RF-6B** (*Airscene*/June 1975) made its **first flight** on 4 March at Athée-Nitray. Compared with the prototype, which was powered by a 90 hp RR-Continental C-90 engine, the production RF-6B has a 100 hp O-200A, resulting in a number of small changes to the appearance of the aircraft. The first RF-6B is scheduled to be delivered to the Aeroclub de Saint-Galmier at Auvergne following a short period of testing by the CEV.

Testing of the **Astafan IV-F.6** turbofan **in** the Rockwell **Commander 690** has been under way since 24 January, following conversion of the airframe (the second Astafan-Commander) by the CGTM, a Turboméca subsidiary at Pau. The Astafan IV-F.6 has a take-off thrust of 2,356 lb st (1 070 kgp) and a max continuous rating of 2,200 lb st (1 000 kgp), and the Commander 690 test-bed has a maximum cruising speed of 345 mph (555 km/h) at 20,000 ft (6 100 m).

INTERNATIONAL
The Chiefs of Air Staffs of the three countries participating in the Panavia **MRCA** meeting in Munich on 10 March agreed that development flying to date justified their recommending a **"go-ahead" for full production** to their respective governments. At the meeting it was also agreed that the **name "Tornado"** be officially **adopted.** It will be recalled that during an address at Manching on 21 September 1974, Mr Brynmor John, Under-secretary of State for the RAF, first referred to the MRCA as the Tornado (see *Airscene*/November 1974).

On 5 March, Mr Roy Mason, Secretary for Defence, announced that full-scale **development of** the **Air-Defence Variant (ADV) of** the Panavia **Tornado** (MRCA) for the RAF had been **authorised** after the evaluation of project definition studies and a stringent review of UK air defence requirements. No estimate of the Tornado ADV development costs has been published — although it is understood to be slightly in excess of £100m at current prices — but giving evidence to the parliamentary Expenditure Committee in November, the Minister of State for Defence, Mr William Rodgers, said that the unit production cost (excluding R & D) was put at £6·5m in terms of 1976-77 prices compared with £5·29m for the standard interdictor-strike aircraft. Current planning calls for the RAF to receive 155 Tornado ADVs which will begin to enter service in 1983-84. The new intercept radar for the Tornado ADV, for which Marconi-Elliott Avionic Systems and Ferranti are prime contractors, has been undergoing trials in prototype form in a Canberra since last autumn. Externally, the Tornado ADV is expected to differ from the interdictor-strike version in having a 4-ft (1,22-m) stretch for additional internal fuel and AAM fit requirements.

MEXICO
The **Mexican** government is in the final stages of negotiation with Israel Aircraft Industries for the establishment of a jointly-owned **factory for** the assembly of the **IAI 201 Arava** light STOL transport. The factory, which is to be established at the invitation of the Mexican government, will assemble and provide after-sales support for Aravas sold to Latin-American countries where this Israeli multi-rôle aircraft is enjoying some success, customers including Guatemala, Honduras, Bolivia, Ecuador, Nicaragua and Salvador, as well as Mexico, and it has been unofficially reported that Peru is among other countries currently negotiating Arava purchases.

SOVIET UNION
The Mil bureau is reported to have flown a **new "gunship" helicopter** with tandem gunner/pilot

seating and a radar-directed 23-mm gun in a chin-mounted turret. The helicopter apparently employs a different rotor system to that of the Mi-24 *(Hind)* and will mount a new missile, which, currently under development, is believed to possess a maximum range of about six miles (10 km).

UNITED KINGDOM

Flight trials have begun at Bembridge of a **water-bomber** version of the Britten-Norman **Islander.** A tank of 176 Imp gal (800 l) capacity is installed in the fuselage with four quick-release doors in the floor, the whole installation being quickly removable.

A **Hughes FLIR** (forward-looking infra-red) sensor, as developed for the USAF's fleet of B-52s, is **under test** and evaluation in a Canberra **at the RAE** Farnborough. RAF is interested in the FLIR for possible application to the Jaguar and/or Tornado.

Marconi-Elliott Avionic Systems Ltd has introduced a **digital navigation system of** particular value to helicopters, jet strike/trainers and executive transports. The AD620 system makes use of widely-used radio aids on the ground, such as VOR/DME and TACAN — normally providing only range and bearing information from a ground beacon — to provide, through its miniature computer, all the information a pilot needs to fly along any course without manual calculations or reference to maps. Existing cockpit instruments are used to display all the information the pilot needs to steer towards any designated target or turning point. The system comprises a small digital computer to standard ARINC dimensions and a miniature cockpit-mounted control unit. The AD620 system is already used by the *Luftwaffe* in the MBB Hansajet 320 and is believed to have considerable potential, especially for the new generation of strike/trainers.

USA

The Rockwell **XFV-12A** thrust-augmented wing V/STOL research aircraft has suffered further delays and the first of two prototypes is not now to commence its **flight test programme** (in the conventional mode) until September, two years later than originally projected (see *A New Vertical Approach/ February 1974*). The US Navy has provided $12m (£6·315m) in Fiscal 1976 funding and another increment of funding is expected from reprogramming action. Last year, $1·6m (£842,000) was pared from the programme and if that amount is restored as a result of reprogramming, a further increment of $2·7m (£1·42m) will still be required to get the two prototypes to flight test status. The first XFV-12A now in final assembly in the Columbus facility is scheduled to be rolled out in July and to commence its flight test programme in September, in which month the second XFV-12A is expected to be rolled out. The initial conventional mode test phase is aimed at clearing the low-speed conventional envelope and prior to embarking upon this, the first XFV-12A will have been tested on a hover rig to trim the nozzles for initial flight and to check vertical lift. The second XFV-12A will be tested on a railway flatcar to run the aircraft up to speeds of about 50 knots (93 km/h), the purpose being to operate the aircraft in a tethered mode through the low-speed conversion envelope and transition from vertical to forward flight. For the high-speed conversion envelope, the XFV-12A will be flown at altitudes above 10,000 ft (3 050 m) to transition from conventional to vertical flight. Rockwell International anticipates completing the conversion test programme by the end of the year.

Contract discussions preceding a development

go-ahead for the McDonnell Douglas **AV-8B** improved Harrier have resulted in the **first contract** being awarded, McDonnell Douglas receiving $3·15m (£1·657m) for the full-scale wind tunnel investigation of AV-8B performance. The work is scheduled to commence during the course of this summer and will be followed by the aerodynamic modification of two AV-8As to represent the AV-8B, this entailing the addition of strakes and fences beneath the fuselage to enhance lift, the addition of an all-composite supercritical wing and redesigned air intakes for the F402-RR-401 (Pegasus 11) engine. The AV-8B is expected to offer double the range and payload of the AV-8A and is expected to operate with 7,500 lb (3 402 kg) of internal fuel, seven weapons stations and two gun pods. The flight demonstration aircraft will have an operating weight of 12,400 lb (5 624 kg). The supercritical wing will have an area of 230 sq ft (21,37 m²), or 14 per cent greater than that of the AV-8A. Flight testing of the modified AV-8As is scheduled for late 1978.

British Ministry of Defence representatives have recently been briefed in the USA on the **F-18L Cobra II**, a land-based version of the future McDonnell Douglas/Northrop F-18 shipboard fighter. The F-18L, which is being evolved in parallel with the US Navy's F-18, employs the same wing with folding mechanism deleted, and commonality between the two models is 90 per cent. Several governments have expressed interest in the F-18L in which Northrop will be prime contractor if development proceeds.

The first **Boeing 747SP** was **delivered** to Pan American on 5 March and entered service immediately, flying a load of cargo from Seattle-Tacoma to New York. The 2,800th commercial jetliner delivered by Boeing since Pam Am accepted its first 707-120 on 15 August 1958, the 747SP was to go into service between Los Angeles and Tokyo on 25 April and New York and Tokyo on 26 April. Further deliveries of 747SPs were made on 12 March, when the first for Iran Air was handed over in Seattle, and on 23 March when the first for South African Airways was flown non-stop from Seattle to Cape Town. The last-mentioned flight represented a world record distance for commercial aircraft at 10,290 mls (16 546 km), the 747SP taking off at a gross weight of 713,000 lb (323 533 kg), some 50,300 lb (22 836 kg) above the normal operating weight.

The US Army took **delivery** of the three prototypes of each of the **UTTAS helicopters,** the Sikorsky YUH-60A and the Boeing Vertol YUH-61A, on 20 March. Brief acceptance ceremonies took place at Fort Benning, Georgia, after which two helicopters of each type were transferred to Fort Rucker, Alabama, for testing under tactical conditions, the others going to Edwards AFB, Calif, for testing by the Army's Aviation Engineering Flight Activity. The first YUH-61A had resumed flight testing on 19 February, after repair (see *Airscene/April*). Minor changes have been made to the YUH-60As since first flight, including the addition of small sponsons on the front fuselage ahead of the under-carriage attachments.

Fairchild Aircraft Service Division has received a $2·5m (£1·3m) **contract to convert** another 29 Convair F-102As to **PQM-102A target drones.** The company has previously received contracts for 38 similar conversions, including four manned QF-102As. After a six-month period on the ground for overhaul and modification, the PQM-102As are flown to Tyndall Air Force Base, Florida, where Sperry Flight Systems, the programme manager, installs auto-pilots, flight controls and low

altitude radar. The work done by Fairchild, at Crestview, includes installation of a smoke system to allow ground observers to track the drones visually at high altitude, and a remotely-controlled destruct system.

The US **Forestry Service** is currently **evaluating** a Rockwell **OV-10A** Bronco, on loan from the US Marine Corps, as a command and control aircraft for use during forest fire-fighting operations. Meanwhile, the Columbus Aircraft Division is continuing to develop the YOV-10D prototypes in the NOS (night observation surveillance) configuration. These two aircraft were originally OV-10As modified as NOGS (night observation gun-ships) for the Marine Corps with a 20-mm turret under the fuselage, and they are now back at Columbus for installation of Texas Instruments FLIR in the nose and 1,040 shp Garrett AiResearch T76-G-420/421 turboprops. First flight with the new engines is expected in October.

McDonnell Douglas Corp has won a contract from Rockwell International to supply advanced concept **ejection-seats** (ACES) **for the B-1.** Features of the seat include an automatic sequencing system to deploy the recovery parachute at correct speed and altitude, a stabilization system and a divergence system to deploy the seats away from each other during simultaneous ejection so that parachutes cannot become fouled. The ACES are required initially for the fourth prototype of the B-1, due to fly early in 1979, and eventually for production aircraft, in place of the escape module used in the first three aircraft.

By 3 March, the **Rockwell B-1** had made 26 flights totalling 126 hrs 26 min of which 4 hr 38 min was supersonic. Highest speed attained remains Mach 1·6 at 34,000 ft (10 370 m), maximum altitude 50,000 ft (15 250 m) and longest single flight 8 hr 19 min. The **26th flight** was the first after a planned lay-up period during which installation was completed of an air induction control system (AICS) and automatic flight control system (AFCS) to permit the flight envelope to be extended to Mach 2+.

First flight of the **second** prototype Rockwell **Commander 700** was made at Wiley Post Airport, Bethany, on 25 February. This was also the first flight of the type in the USA, the first prototype having flown, as the Fuji FA-300, in Japan. Preliminary data and a three-view drawing for the Commander 700 are included in *AirData File* on page 260.

A plan to convert Scottish Aviation **Jetstreams** in the USA **to have** Garrett AiResearch **TPE331-3U-303 engines** in place of their present Turboméca Astazou XVIs is being supported by Apollo Airways of Santa Barbara, which has ordered 30 of the TPE331s for this programme. Apollo itself owns seven Jetstreams, which are used on scheduled services between Santa Barbara and San Jose, and one of these is now undergoing conversion at Van Nuys by the Volpar company, with first flight scheduled for 21 June. The TPE331 installation is based on Volpar experience in fitting such engines in its own Turboliner conversion of the Beech 18, although the original Handley Page drawings for the similarly-engined C-10A version of the Jetstream are also available. Two Jetstreams have been converted to have flat-rated Astazou XVIF engines by the Riley company and a third such is being converted for Sierra Pacific Airlines, operating scheduled services in the Burbank area. One earlier conversion by Riley features Pratt & Whitney PT6A-34 engines and this is now in process of certification.

Flight Systems, Inc. of Newport Beach, Calif, has developed a **drone conversion of the F-86E**

Sabre and has demonstrated the first two QF-86E target drones under US Army contract. The Army plans to use the QF-86Es as targets for the Stinger shoulder-fired SAM and is expected to order a further quantity. Basic aircraft used for conversions are 55 ex-RCAF F-86Es purchased in Canada two years ago by Flight Systems, Inc. When converted, the QF-86Es remain man-rated — ie, they can be flown by a pilot, either with or without provision for control, a remote operator, or they can be flown Nolo (no live operator) under command from a ground station.

CIVIL AFFAIRS

GHANA
Hughes Airwest has concluded a **technical assistance contract** with Ghana Airways, to help improve its scheduled service between nine points in West Africa. The airline is the seventh to sign such an agreement with Hughes in the past six years, four of these having current assistance contracts.

INTERNATIONAL
British Airways and Air France have announced their intention of inaugurating commercial **flights by Concorde** across the North Atlantic **to Dulles Airport, Washington,** on 24 May, with the first return flights operating the following day. Air France will provide a frequency of three flights a week immediately and British Airways will start with one flight a week, building up to two in mid-June and three in mid-September. Flight times on the London-Washington route will be 3 hr 55 min westbound and 3 hr 50 min eastbound, and the single fare will be £352, £61 more than the first-class subsonic fare. The two airlines have also announced that they are seeking a declaratory judgement in the US Federal Courts on their legal right to operate into New York, which has not been accepted by the Port Authority of New York and New Jersey. Late in March, an attempt in the US Senate to pass a resolution completely banning Concorde at US airports was easily defeated. British Airways took delivery of its second Concorde, G-BOAC, on 13 February and this aircraft operated its first services to and from Bahrain on the 16th. Production aircraft No 7, F-BVFB, made its first flight at Toulouse on 6 March and the prototype 002, G-BSST, made its 439th and last flight on 2 March when it was delivered from Fairford to RNAS Yeovilton for permanent exhibition there.

UNITED ARAB EMIRATES
Gulf Air inaugurated **service with** its first two Lockheed L-1011 **TriStars** on 1 April on routes between the Arabian Gulf and Europe. Arranged to carry only 211 passengers — 40 six-abreast first class and 171 eight-abreast economy class — the TriStars have a separate first-class dining saloon, swivel chairs to form conference areas during flight and an air-to-ground telephone for first-class passengers and other special features. Tri-Stars are operating five non-stop services a week between the Gulf and London, and Gulf Air has also now introduced four non-stop services a week with its VC10s to serve Amsterdam and Paris.

UNITED KINGDOM
British Airways has assigned its two most recently-delivered L-1011 **TriStars** (Alpha Juliet and Alpha Kilo) to the Overseas Division for operation on routes **to the Middle East and India** starting in early April. A number of changes have been made for OD use, including installation of Litton LTN-5P inertial sensor systems and a new interior configuration.

London-Edinburgh is the route chosen by British Airways for its second **Shuttle service.**

Starting on 1 April, regular no-booking guaranteed-seat services have been operating at two-hourly intervals in each direction. The Shuttle is operated by 146-seat Trident Threes with 100-seat Trident Ones as back-up aircraft. Trident Ones that are surplus to British Airways' requirements for the Shuttle operation are now in process of being scrapped, no purchasers having been found for these aircraft withdrawn from service over a year ago.

British Airways and Air France are combining to offer an **"Air Bridge" on** the **London-Paris** route, the objective of which is to provide a streamlined high-frequency service, with simplified check-in and boarding facilities always using the same gates at London Heathrow and Paris Charles de Gaulle. British Airways' services to Orly have been transferred to the latter airport and at peak periods during the summer flights will be operated (mostly by TriStar and A300) at 30-min intervals. A total of 1·6m passengers is expected to use the "Air Bridge" during the first year.

CIVIL CONTRACTS AND SALES

Airbus A300: Lufthansa has taken up one of its nine options to make four on firm order.

Beech Super King Air: Indonesia Air Transport has acquired two, for use on charter work and general purpose missions. with 12 passenger seats and two pilots.

Boeing 707: Pacific Western has acquired another convertible 707 and will place it in service for regular passenger charters when a new interior has been installed. □ Alia has acquired one 320C from World Airways.

Boeing 727: Trans Australia has ordered its seventh 727-200, for delivery in November 1976; six 727-100s are also in service. □ Royal Air Maroc ordered three Advanced 200s for delivery from December 1976; four other 727s are already in service. □ Air Algerie ordered a sixth Advanced 727 for November delivery. □ Western Airlines has ordered five more -200s for March-May 1977 delivery.

Boeing 737: Olympic Airways ordered four Advanced 737s for delivery in June (2), October and November. The order is Olympic's first for the 737. □ Air Algerie has ordered three more Advanced 737s for delivery in December, January and April; 10 had been ordered previously.

Bristol Britannia: Young Cargo of Charleroi-Gosselies is buying three more ex-RAF Britannias to make a total fleet of six. □ City Airways of Coventry bought two.

Dornier Skyservant: The German aerospace research and experimental establishment, the DFVLR, has taken delivery of a Skyservant specially modified for remote sensing of earth resources.

EMBRAER EMB-110 Bandeirante: Recent customers include the Banco de Noroeste, a Brazilian private bank, which bought one EMB-110E executive model and the Road Construction Department of the Amazonas State, which bought one EMB-110P. Another EMB-110E was ordered by the J P Mattins company of Rio de Janeiro. □ A third-level operator in Colombia is negotiating to buy two, and Federal Express in the USA, which recently failed to obtain CAB approval to operate DC-9s, is reported to be investigating the purchase of a fleet of 35 Bandeirantes, including 18 of the EMB-110K freighter version with longer fuselage.

Fokker F27: Aramco has ordered another Mk 500 CRF (Cargo Rough Field) version, for delivery next February. The first of the type was recently delivered to Aramco in Saudi Arabia and two others were to follow in May and June.

Hawker Siddeley Argosy: Management Jets International has purchased one ex-RAF Argosy for conversion to a water bomber at Lincoln, Nebraska. The aircraft concerned had been converted to the prototype Argosy T Mk 2 navigation trainer by Hawker Siddeley at Bitteswell before the RAF requirement for this variant was cancelled.

Lockheed L-1011 TriStar:, Cathay Pacific Airways is leasing one from Eastern, pending delivery of another that it is buying from the same company. The latter will be converted to L-1011-100 version with extra tankage by Lockheed, and delivered to CPA next year. Purchase of a second L-1011 from Eastern is on option. □ The two L-1011s purchased by Saudia from TWA (this column, last month) are now known to be additional to the four the Saudi Arabian airline had on order already.

McDonnell Douglas DC-8: Cyprus Airways has leased one Srs 52 from the manufacturers, ex-Iberia, to operate non-stop services to European destinations. □ Aero America has acquired one DC-8 in cargo configuration, to be based in the Middle East.

McDonnell Douglas DC-10: Swissair ordered one more Srs 30 to make nine in all. Delivery will be in the last quarter of 1977.

Swearingen Metro II: European Air Transport of Brussels has taken delivery of a Metro II, to operate in Sabena colours on services linking Brussels with Eindhoven and Cologne at a frequency of three times a day from 1 April.

Vickers Viscount: Intra Airways of Jersey has leased one Srs 708 from Alidair for one year. □ Cyprus Airways has leased one Srs 812 from Field Aviation.

MILITARY CONTRACTS

Boeing 737-200S: The *Fuerzas Aéreas Venezolanas* has procured one Boeing 737 for use as a VIP transport at a reported cost of £6·3m including spares, ground support equipment and crew training.

EMBRAER EMB-111: An order has been placed on behalf of the *Fôrça Aérea Brasileira* for 16 EMB-111 maritime patrol aircraft for delivery from 1978.

EMBRAER EMB-110: The *Fôrça Aérea Brasileira* has converted the final 20 of its order for 80 EMB-110 (C-95) Bandeirante general-purpose light transports to the stretched EMB-110K freighter version (see *Military Affairs* news item) and has placed an order for four EMB-110B (RC-95) photographic models.

Lockheed L-100-20 Hercules: The *Fuerza Aérea del Peru* has placed an order with the Lockheed Aircraft Corporation worth in excess of £10m for three L-100-20 Hercules for delivery between this November and January 1977. The aircraft will be employed on para-military operations and will supplement the existing FAP Hercules fleet (two L-100-20s acquired in 1970 and four C-130Es in 1971-72).

McDonnell Douglas DC-9CF: The Kuwait government has ordered two convertible passenger/cargo DC-9s for operation by the Kuwait Air Force with delivery at the end of this year.

WINGED SPRINGBOK

TAKES ON MUSCLE

W ITH THE VICTORY in Angola of the Soviet-sponsored Cuban forces and the likelihood of eventual confrontation along the border between Angola and South West Africa (Namibia) between these same forces and those of South Africa — the latter possibly confronted simultaneously by Soviet-supported and Cuban-stiffened forces of the fiery Marxist President Machel of Moçambique with which the South African Republic shares a common border — the military threat to South Africa would seem to have escalated dramatically in recent months. Strategists for the most part agree, however, that, short of full-scale Soviet-backed invasion, South Africa is hardly likely to be reduced by force of arms, and certainly the Republic's armed forces do not seem unduly perturbed, despite the traumatic shock induced by the débâcle of the South African-supported UNITA faction in Angola, evincing no less confidence in their ability to contain the menace from the north, greater or no.

It is perhaps the longer-term economic threat posed by protracted military confrontation that has given rise to most

South African anxiety following events in the former Portuguese territories. South African defence spending is, understandably, rising rapidly, both as a result of inflation, which is currently running at 15 per cent, and of increased procurement and operating costs — approximately £813m for the 1976-77 Fiscal Year it has virtually trebled in three years and its proportion of total government spending, more than one-sixth, bids fair to increase substantially in FY 1977-78 — but it is the possible strangulation of the flow of much-needed foreign capital into the Republic that might result from any major escalation of militancy on South Africa's northern borders and the economic stagnation that could follow in its wake rather than militancy itself that is causing the greatest concern.

Compounding the problem in so far as the South African government is concerned is, of course, the fact that virtually no country in the world will overtly afford support — though many covertly sympathise — and this has, and is continuing to, complicate procurement of some of the equipment vitally

The Dassault-Breguet Mirage F1CZ (head of page) is the latest addition to the operational inventory of the SAAF and now equips No 3 Squadron at Waterkloof Air Station, and the single-seat MB 326K Impala Mk 2 (below) is now being phased in and, together with the two-seat Impala Mk 1, will eventually equip the majority of the Active Citizen Force squadrons.

necessary to maintain and, indeed, accelerate the modernisation and expansion of the South African armed forces. Nevertheless, despite the procurement strictures resulting from the United Nations' embargo, South Africa's defences have taken on considerable muscle in recent years, for France and Italy, the Republic's principal source of military supplies, have paid no more than lip service to the embargo and French President Valery Giscard d'Estaing appears to have been merely juggling with semantics last year when he announced during a visit to Zaïre that the sale of French military equipment to South Africa was to be halted.

Most important, South Africa has steadily moved towards increasing self-sufficiency in a wide range of weaponry during the 'seventies under the Armaments Development and Production Corporation (Armscor), and is now manufacturing AMX tanks, Panhard AML60 and 90 armoured cars, Matra-Thomson Crotale surface-to-air missile systems, SS-11 anti-armour missiles, 90-mm field guns, a range of bored and rifled cannon, 1,000-lb (453,5-kg) general-purpose bombs, napalm bombs and air-to-surface rockets. But it is on the South African Air Force (SAAF), or *Suid-Afrikaanse Lugmag,* that indigenous hardware production is having the most far-reaching effect, despite the greater sophistication of its equipment than that of its fellow armed services, and by the

end of the decade, the vast bulk of its aircraft inventory will have been part- or wholly-manufactured by one of the Armscor subsidiaries, the Atlas Aircraft Corporation.

Stage set for expansion

The SAAF, commanded by 54-year-old Lt Gen R H D Rogers, has seen little growth in the numerical sense during the first half of the present decade, but it has witnessed a dramatic increase in potency in the rôles to which it now assigns primary importance, namely ground attack, close support, counter-insurgency and air mobility. If the programme of modernisation has perforce been progressing in relatively low key, it has now attained a stage at which, with the bulk of the service's obsolescent equipment phased out, a sound basis has been established for the steady expansion that is anticipated throughout the remainder of the 'seventies and into the 'eighties. This expansion will naturally include progressive increase of personnel strength, currently totalling some 5,500 regulars, referred to as the Permanent Force, backed by conscripts and Active Citizen Force trained reservists, and for the first time efforts are being made to recruit to the service Indians and Black Africans.

Defence Headquarters on Potgeiter Street in Pretoria — from where are administered the four operational commands: Strike, Maritime, Light Aircraft and Transport — would seem little perturbed by rumours that multi-rôle MiG-21 fighters similar to those seen in Angola and presumably similarly flown and maintained by Cuban personnel have appeared in Moçambique, within easy flying time of Pretoria and Johannesburg. The larger part of the SAAF's Strike Command is deployed in the Transvaal; the newly-acquired Mirage F1CZ interceptors of No 3 Squadron, with their Cyrano IV radar fire control and Matra 550 Magic AAMs, are now based at Waterkloof Air Station, adjacent to Pretoria, sharing this base with No 2 Squadron whose Mirages have both intercept and fighter-bomber capability, while further north, at the Pietersburg Air Station, are now the surviving Sabre Mk 6s interceptors, which, taken into the inventory of No 85 Advanced Flying School and primarily utilised for operational training, possess a secondary intercept rôle.

It is the consensus of service opinion that this force is more than capable of coping with anything that is likely to intrude into Transvaal skies from Moçambique or elsewhere in the foreseeable future. It is capability against guerilla infiltration

The Shackleton MR Mk 3 maritime patrol aircraft of No 35 Squadron (above) are now being progressively resparred. (Below) One of No 12 Squadron's Canberra B(I) Mk 12s which now sport a new overall PRU-Blue finish.

The Buccaneer S Mk 50 (below) has now seen more than a decade of service with No 24 Squadron at Waterkloof and only about half of those originally delivered now remain on strength, the UK government having consistently refused the supply of additional aircraft.

The tandem two-seat Mirage IIIBZ conversion trainer (seen above in the insignia of No 2 Squadron) has recently been supplemented in the SAAF inventory by the Atar 9K-50-powered Mirage IIID2Z which serves with No 85 Advanced Flying School, the service also having several two-seat Mirage IIIDZs.

(Above) One of the Mirage IIIRZs of No 2 Squadron still sporting the NATO style camouflage in which it was originally delivered. This may be expected to give way to the standard SAAF tactical camouflage seen on a Mirage IIIR2Z of the same unit (below).

Bearing much of the logistic support commitment of the SAAF, the Transall C.160 (above) serves alongside the C-130B Hercules in the inventory of No 28 Squadron at Waterkloof, Pretoria. (Below, left) An SA 330 Puma of No 19 Squadron's "A" Flight which is permanently assigned to Swartkop Air Station.

across the Angolan and Moçambique borders that is of more immediate concern to the SAAF; greater importance is attached to strengthening air-to-ground capability to face the anticipated threat of the years immediately ahead than to expanding air defence capability to meet a danger that is assessed as being unlikely to take on really serious proportions much before the end of the present decade. Thus, the principal current production programme engaging the Atlas Aircraft Corporation and its numerous sub-contractors is the licence manufacture of the Aermacchi MB 326K Impala Mk 2 single-seat ground attack aircraft; a relatively unsophisticated, thoroughly reliable little warplane, which, not overly demanding on maintenance time in the field nor exorbitantly expensive to operate, can tote a formidable load of ordnance.

Impalas and Mirages

Production of the Impala Mk 2 followed on the phase-out last year of production of the lower-powered tandem-seat MB 326M Impala Mk 1 basic trainer and this type is envisaged as the SAAF's primary counter-insurgency aircraft for the next decade. The first seven MB 326K single-seaters were delivered to the SAAF by the Italian parent company from late 1974, these being followed by 15 in knocked-down parts for Atlas assembly, and the South African factory is now well into an initial batch of 50 aircraft of this type, which, scheduled for completion during the course of this year, will be followed by a second batch of at least a further 50 aircraft with deliveries continuing into 1978 and possibly longer. The cannon-armed MB 326K Impala Mk 2 has the Viper Mk 632-43 turbojet of 4,000 lb (1 814 kg) thrust, self-sealing fuel tanks, pilot armour and a zero-zero rocket ejection seat, and it can lift a wide variety of external ordnance — up to 4,000 lb (1 814 kg) with reduced fuel — on six underwing pylons.

The first Impala Mk 2s were assigned to the Flying Training School at Langebaanweg Air Station, north of Cape Town, and during the course of last year this type was also allocated to the former Sabre Mk 6-equipped No 1 Squadron at Pietersburg Air Station, although only as interim equipment as this is the first squadron to work up on the Mirage F1AZ ground attack fighter and has already passed its Impala Mk 2s to the Active Citizen Force squadrons. No 1 Squadron flew the Canadair Sabre Mk 6 for some 19 years, 34 fighters of this type having been originally acquired in 1956, and a dozen or so of these are still flying, although no longer possessing an operational rôle. The surviving Sabres were supplemented in No 1's inventory by Impala Mk 1s which have since been passed on to No 6 Squadron, the Sabres going to No 85 AFS. The majority of the Impala Mk 2s will be assigned to the six Active Citizen Force squadrons possessing a dual counter-insurgency/refresher training rôle and manned by both permanent and reserve personnel, and these are all expected to be operating a mix of two-seat Impala Mk 1s and single-seat Impala Mk 2s by the late 'seventies.

Apart from its Impala Mk 2 programme and production of 40 C4M Kudu STOL light utility transports for the SAAF's Light Aircraft Command, Atlas is gearing up for the assembly and progressive manufacture of the Mirage F1AZ ground attack fighter with the EMD Aida II fire control system and laser range-finder. The Dassault-Breguet company is delivering several complete aircraft against the initial SAAF order for 32 Mirage F1AZs, the remainder following in knocked-down form and incorporating an increasing proportion of Atlas-manufactured components, production of which has already been initiated. The knocked-down sets will begin arriving at the Atlas factory for assembly from late this year and the first Atlas-assembled Mirage F1AZ (expected to be given a South African appellation) is scheduled to be handed over to the SAAF next year.

These will serve as pattern aircraft and the indigenous content will be progressively increased until only the most sophisticated components have to be imported from France, and the SAAF has been unofficially reported as having a requirement for about 100 fighters of this type, but the only official comment has been made by the president of the South African Armaments Board who said that production would be continued by Atlas for as long as the Mirage F1 "remains one of the best fighters in the world". Although the disposition of the substantial quantity of Mirage F1AZs that the SAAF anticipates taking into its inventory during the 1977-80 period must, at this point in time, remain a matter for pure supposition, it is generally assumed that at least two and possibly three new fighter squadrons will be formed on these aircraft within Strike Command by the end of the decade.

The SAAF has, of course, received a substantial number of earlier delta-winged Mirage IIIs over the last 13 or so years, commencing in 1963 with 16 Mirage IIICZ interceptors which remained in the inventory of No 2 Squadron until recent reassignment of the survivors for the advanced training task. To these were added three two-seat Mirage IIIBZ trainers, and No 2 was later to take on strength four Mirage IIIRZ tactical reconnaissance aircraft. During 1965-66, 18 Mirage IIIEZ fighter-bombers and three two-seat Mirage IIIDZs were acquired for No 3 Squadron, and in 1972, 13 Atar 9K-50-powered Mirage IIID2Z aircraft were ordered for No 85 Advanced Flying School, the substantial increase in thrust of the -50 engine affording marked improvements in take-off, climb, acceleration and manoeuvrability, and runway arrester hooks being fitted to both these and the four Mirage IIIR2Zs for No 2 Squadron.

Since the re-equipment of No 3 Squadron with the Mirage F1CZ interceptor, No 2 is now the primary operational delta-winged Mirage unit, fulfilling both fighter-bomber and reconnaissance rôles, but various types of Mirage are included in the inventory of No 85 Advanced Flying School (IIIDZ, IIIEZ, IIID2Z, etc). Having now seen some 10 years of SAAF service, it can be assumed that the Mirage IIIEZ will be relegated to the training rôle with the advent of the Mirage F1AZ within the next two years or so, but the relatively new Atar 9K-50-powered aircraft may be expected to remain in the first-line inventory well into the next decade.

Soldiering on

The remaining first-line combat squadrons of the SAAF are unfortunately not so well placed in so far as existing equipment or chances of re-equipment are concerned as they operate aged British equipment for which the most suitable replacements are only available from the UK or USA, both of which firmly adhere to the UN embargo. Within Strike Command are the two strike-reconnaissance squadrons, Nos 12 and 24, which

The Wasp of No 22 Flight (above) was recently rebuilt after crashing in Table Bay and spending a night underwater. (Immediately below) The AM-3C Bosbok now equips two units of the Light Aircraft Command, this example belonging to No 42 Squadron at Potschefstroom.

(Above right, centre) An MB 326M Impala Mk 1 of No 8 Squadron at Bloemspruit, Bloemfontein, with (immediately above, right) a colourfully-marked C-47 employed by No 25 Squadron at Ysterplaat for target-towing duties. (Below) No 1 Squadron at Pietersburg until recently included a number of Canadair Sabre Mk 6s on strength, these having now been refurbished and transferred to No 85 Advanced Flying School.

are both Waterkloof-based. The former operates the aged Canberra B(I) Mk 12, six of which were ordered in 1962, together with three refurbished ex-RAF Canberra T Mk 4s, but which have still some way to go before reaching the end of their fatigue lives, and the latter operates the survivors of the almost equally-aged Buccaneer S Mk 50 maritime strike aircraft of which 16 were delivered from late 1965 onwards and about half remain on strength. The most suitable successor to the Canberra would appear to be the SEPECAT Jaguar and in so far as the Buccaneer is concerned . . . newer Buccaneers! However, the chances of the SAAF acquiring the Jaguar would seem remote at this point in time and successive British governments have consistently refused to supply additional quantities of Buccaneers.

More ancient than either Canberra or Buccaneer is Maritime Command's Shackleton MR Mk 3 purchased mid-1957. Operated by No 35 Squadron primarily from D F Malan Air Station, Cape Town, the Shackletons will soon have fulfilled the maritime patrol rôle in SAAF service for a score of years and in view of the vital importance attached by the SAAF to the maritime rôle their replacement has for long given cause for considerable concern. The seven Shackletons have had their radar and ECM equipment updated from time to time, but without a successor in prospect, the SAAF has had no recourse but to initiate its own re-sparring programme. This is being undertaken by service technicians at Ysterplaat as each individual aircraft comes up against the end of its fatigue life and involves the virtual disassembly of the Shackleton and its reconstruction from scratch. The first two re-sparred aircraft have now been returned to service with the probability that they will soldier on through the end of the decade.

Undertaking coastal patrol and fishery surveillance duties in addition to light transport and liaison tasks, No 27 Squadron at Ysterplaat Air Station is equipped with a dual-rôle version of the Italian P.166 light twin developed specifically to SAAF requirements by Piaggio and known as the P.166S Albatross. Equipped with search radar and other items for the over-water rôle, the Albatross was purchased in two batches of nine.

Much of the equipment of the SAAF's Transport Command is as elderly as that employed for strike-reconnaissance and maritime patrol, a fact which, too, gives rise for some concern in view of the increasingly heavy commitment to the support of the ground forces in operations against infiltrators and the importance attached to air mobility. Long-range heavy logistic support is provided by No 28 Squadron based at Waterkloof and operating a mix of Lockheed C-130B Hercules, seven examples of which were delivered to the SAAF in 1963, and Transall C.160Zs, seven of which followed from mid-1969. Governmental transportation tasks are performed by No 21 Squadron at Swartkops with four Hawker Siddeley HS.125s, known to the SAAF as the Mercurius, a single Vickers Viscount 781 and six Merlin IVAs. The bulk of the 30 or so examples of the venerable Douglas C-47 Dakota transport remaining in the SAAF inventory are operated by Nos 25 and 44 squadrons, the former serving as a Fleet Requirements Unit from Ysterplaat and the latter, which has a dual Permanent and Citizen Force function, operating this type from Swartkop alongside five ex-South African Airways DC-4s, and with No 86 Advanced Flying School (formerly the Multi-engine Conversion Unit) at Bloemspruit.

Transport Command would certainly like some new Hercules transports and has reportedly evinced some interest in the potential of the Aeritalia G.222, but a successor to the ubiquitous C-47 still appears to be well over the horizon. The latest addition to the transport inventory has been the small number of Fairchild Swearingen Merlins but there have been rumours of an intended purchase of Britten-Norman Islanders, presumably in Defender configuration.

Counter-insurgency capability

An increasingly heavy workload has been imposed on the helicopter component of the SAAF, some Alouettes and Pumas having been deployed to Rhodesia over the past couple of years to support Rhodesian ground forces in operations against infiltrating Black guerrillas along the border with Moçambique, but more recently major effort has been called for in support of the South African defence zone on both sides

continued on page 248

Dark green and dark earth camouflage is now being applied to most SAAF helicopters and an Alouette III of No 16 Squadron at Port Elizabeth (above left) and an SA 321L Super Frelon 'casevac' helicopter of No 15 Squadron's "A" Flight at Swartkop are seen here in this new finish.

T-34 CHARLIE : A BETTER MENTOR

THERE is nothing derogatory in calling the newest Beechcraft trainer a Charlie — it just happens to be the phonetic description for the "C" model of the T-34 Mentor, soon to enter service at the US Navy's primary training units at NAS Pensacola. In fact, the T-34 "Charlie", with a turboprop power plant married to a modernised version of a 28-year-old airframe design, has been received enthusiastically by the Navy personnel responsible for its evaluation and there are signs that the joint Navy/Beech programme to develop the T-34C has produced a primary trainer of particular merit and excellent sales prospects. The Navy's own requirement is for some 400 aircraft, of which 149 have been funded in defence budgets up to and including FY77; in addition, one export order, from Morocco, has already been concluded by Beech and others are under negotiation.

The production of military training aircraft, whether for primary, basic or advanced rôles, is good "bread-and-butter" business for any company and this market therefore tends to be hotly contested. Beech Aircraft Corporation experienced this situation to the full when it embarked on the marketing of the original Model 45 Mentor — the basis of the T-34 — during 1948, suffering not only the competition of other manufacturers but considerable indecisiveness on the part of the USAF, which was using, at that time, the well-proven and greatly admired North American T-6 Texan as its primary trainer; thousands had been built during World War II and at least 2,000 were still in the USAF inventory, to be operated at low cost and backed by massive stocks of spares. Prospects for selling a low-powered T-6 replacement depended, at least in part, on a change in USAF training philosophy in favour of using a light primary trainer for the first 30 hours or so of the flight training syllabus. The alternative — certainly practicable but possibly more costly — was to use a heavier, more powerful type for both *ab initio* and intermediate stages of the syllabus, and in conformity with this system the USAF had

already, in 1948, ordered prototypes of the 800 hp North American T-28 to replace the 600 hp T-6.

The Beech entry in this competitive and apparently ill-defined market was a variant of its Model 35 Bonanza, a four-seat lightplane with a novel and distinctive V-tail arrangement that appeared in 1946 and was to become as synonymous with the name Beechcraft in the post-war years as the Model 17 Staggerwing had been before the war. Although the V-tail had several claimed advantages and imposed no unusual control characteristics, Beech designers concluded that it would be unacceptable to military users and conventional vertical and horizontal surfaces were adopted for the Model 45; the other major change concerned the crew accommodation, with two seats being provided in tandem under a long "glasshouse" enclosure. Most of the wing structure and many fuselage components were identical with those of the Bonanza and could be produced on the same tooling.

The design philosophy behind the Model 45, according to a Beech statement made at the end of 1948, was to "offer the

(Below) The original Beechcraft Model 45 Mentor N8591A, first of three civil prototypes that preceded the military production models and (above) one of the two YT-34C prototypes in inverted flight.

(Above) The three YT-34 Mentors used by the USAF in 1950 to evaluate the Beech basic trainer, resulting eventually in production of 450 T-34As. (Below) A production model T-34A in a vertical climb.

military services a high performance trainer that would incorporate all the controls and characteristics of heavier, more advanced combat craft, yet could be operated and maintained at a minimum cost". Among its special features were an ultimate manoeuvring load factor of 10 g (and 6·67 g for landing); a high level of performance including a top speed of 176 mph (283 km/h) on 205 hp; immediate availability because of its commonality with the Bonanza and a unit cost of below $20,000 assuming quantity production was launched and economy of operation. The gross weight, at this stage, was 2,650 lb (1 200 kg).

By the time it made these claims public, Beech had already "put its money where its mouth was" by building a prototype Mentor*, in which company chief test pilot Vern Carstens made the first flight on 2 December 1948 at Wichita. Civil-registered (as N8591A), it was powered by a 205 hp Continental E-185-8 engine and was followed during 1949 by two more demonstrator/prototypes, the last of which had a 225 hp Continental E-225-8 engine that boosted the top speed

*The name came from Greek mythology: Mentor was the "trusted servant" in whose care Odysseus left his son Telemachus during his 20 years absence at the Trojan War. Under Mentor's instruction, Telemachus grew to be equally outstanding in character, in scholastic accomplishment and in the art of war.

to 189 mph (304 km/h). In addition to being used to obtain civil certification (confirmed by the CAA on 17 July 1950) these original three Mentors were used extensively for demonstrations across the USA, particularly for the benefit of USAF and USN representatives but also at civil air displays and for potential overseas buyers.

These demonstrations — which included a particularly memorable aerobatic display at Chicago's National Air Fair in 1949 by 22-year-old international aerobatic champion Betty Skelton — were made against a background of continuing uncertainty as to USAF requirements. At one point in 1949, for example, the Air Force had ordered 100 of the 280-hp Fairchild T-31 primary trainers (a version of the XNQ-1 design originally built on US Navy contract), but this order was then cancelled and acquisition of a jet-powered primary was favoured for a time. Early in 1950, these plans also were dropped and a new evaluation of light-piston-engined primaries was initiated, although procurement of the T-28 was going ahead and there was still no certainty that a lower-powered type would be required in addition.

The 1950 evaluation was to include the Fairchild XT-31 and, for the first time, the Beech Mentor and a Temco design. Three examples each of the Beech and Temco trainers were ordered, respectively with the designations YT-34 and YT-35, and these were to be used, together with the XT-31, at Randolph Field, Texas, where Air Force cadets would follow a standard basic training curriculum on each type and the results achieved would be compared with those on the T-6. Following this evaluation, a similar programme was to be followed at NAS Pensacola, in the hope that a single type could be adopted by both the USAF and USN.

Beech flew its first YT-34 in May 1950, followed by the second and third in June and July, and pilots of the 3512th Basic Pilot Training Squadron ferried two of this trio to Randolph Field at the beginning of August. Lingering uncertainty within the USAF over the rôle of a light primary trainer combined with the exigencies of the Korean war resulted in the Randolph evaluation being abandoned before any conclusions had been reached, however, and the modernization of several hundred Texans to T-6G standard was pressed ahead as a stop-gap measure.

A year later, in August 1951, USAF began yet another evaluation of the YT-34 and YT-35, the XT-31 having meanwhile been abandoned by Fairchild, which was busy with other programmes. The evaluation was won by Beech, but more than a year was to elapse before the USAF finally announced, on 4 March 1953, that production was to be allowed to proceed. The YT-34s differed in detail from the prototype Model 45 Mentors, being powered by the 225 hp Continental E-225-8 engine like the third prototype but having a gross weight of 2,750 lb (1 250 kg) as a result of equipment changes. At a gross weight of 2,600 lb (1 180 kg), with fuel tanks half empty, the max speed at sea level was 188 mph (302 km/h) and the cruising speed at 10,000 ft (3 050 m) on 60 per cent power was 167 mph (269 km/h); initial rate of climb was 1,210 ft/min (6,2 m/sec), service ceiling was 21,200 ft (6 466 m) and the cruising range on 50 US gal (189 l) was 770 mls (1 238 km).

Beech engineering pilots reported that the YT-34 had a rapid rate of roll and required little correction for yaw. A single snap roll could be executed at 120 mph (193 km/h) with less control force than needed by most other aircraft and the slow, or aileron, roll could be accomplished at very low airspeeds as well as with usual entry at near-cruising speed. The Beechcraft trainer could actually be rolled inverted at 100 mph (161 km/h) IAS and then climb 300 ft (92 m) before stall occurred. Normal slow rolls were "easy on the arm" and required a minimum of correction for directional control. Stall and spin performance was positive; power-on stalls with gear and flaps extended came at 50 mph (80 km/h) IAS, with a noticeable tail buffeting effect, and spin recovery, using standard techniques, required less than one turn.

Production models

The USAF planned total procurement of 450 T-34A Mentors and, once the decision to use the type had been taken, wanted them quickly. Consequently, contracts were placed simultaneously both with Beech at Wichita and with the Canadian Car and Foundry Co at Fort William, Ontario. Making good its claim that production aircraft could be made quickly available through use of Bonanza tooling, Beech rolled out its first T-34A in the last week of September 1953 and deliveries to the USAF began early the following year; the company eventually built 350, with another 100 entering USAF service from the CCF production line.

The T-34A, powered by a 225 hp O-470-13 engine (military designation of the E-225), was an all-metal monoplane of conventional construction. The wing was a two-spar structure with built-up ribs, the leading edge being attached to the front spar by piano hinges to provide ease of access for service and repair. Magnesium alloys were used for the ailerons and NACA slotted flaps, these and the wing trailing edge having corrugated skins. Similar skins were used for all tail surfaces, both fixed and movable, these also being of magnesium construction. Adjustable trim tabs were incorporated in all control surfaces.

The retractable tricycle undercarriage was similar to that of the Bonanza, using Beech air-oil shock struts with Goodyear wheels and single disc hydraulic brakes. When retracted, each main wheel was enclosed by two doors, the inner portions closing also when the gear was down to prevent dirt ingestion into the well. Undercarriage and flap operation was electrical, using a 28-volt DC system powered by an engine-driven generator with a stand-by battery.

Fuel was contained in two tanks, each with a capacity of 25 US gal (94,6 l), located in the wing leading edges close to the fuselage. The cockpit, with full dual controls and individually adjustable seats, was heated and ventilated. The USAF avionics fit included ARC-12 VHF transmitter/receiver equipment.

In USAF service, the T-34As equipped a number of primary training schools and were used to give 30 hours of *ab initio* training before student pilots went on to the T-28A. They became redundant in 1960/61 when the USAF introduced all-through jet training (on the Cessna T-37) and a number were then assigned to other nations through Mutual Aid Programs while others went into store. In fact, the long-debated all-through training scheme proved, in USAF experience, more expensive and in 1965 the syllabus was again changed to introduce a light piston-engined primary, the Cessna 172 being chosen and entering USAF service as the T-41A. By the time

the T-34A was phased out of the USAF, however, it had become firmly established in service with the US Navy and with a number of overseas air forces.

Navy interest in the Mentor dated back to 1950 when, as already mentioned, plans were first made for standardization of training between the USAF and USN. This plan began to be implemented in 1952 when the Navy ordered T-28B versions of the North American basic trainer, and about a year later the Navy began a new evaluation of a light primary. The Beech and Temco designs were once again in competition as the performance of Navy student pilots was assessed on each type at NAS Pensacola; also in the running was a Ryan trainer, but this was soon eliminated as it had side-by-side seating which the Navy found unacceptable. Repeating its success with the USAF, the Beech Mentor was named winner of the Navy competition on 17 June 1954 and the first of an eventual total of 423 T-34Bs was delivered exactly six months later, on 17 December the same year.

Originally delivered in an overall yellow finish and later repainted in the Navy's current white-and-red training colours, the T-34Bs were virtually identical with the USAF's T-34As, although the engine designations changed to O-470-4. The T-34Bs have now been in use for over 20 years as the type on which all Navy, Marine Corps and Coast Guard pilots have learned to fly. For this task, they were assigned initially to

(Above) A few examples of the Beech Mentor have served with civil agencies in the USA. The aircraft shown here is a T-34B used by the US Forest Service.

Production T-34Bs for the US Navy were delivered with an overall yellow finish (below) but were later repainted in the white and red colours carried on the YT-34Cs. The T-34B above used as a station "hack" carried a special blue-and-white finish in 1966.

The two YT-34Cs — converted T-34B airframes — have been subjected to an extensive flight test programme, as described in this article, to establish satisfactory spinning characteristics. Up to two minutes of inverted flight is possible.

Training Squadron One (VT-1) at NAS Saufley Field — a satellite of NAS Pensacola which is the home of Naval Training Air Wing Six (TraWing 6). By the end of the 'fifties, VT-1 had the T-34B firmly established in its syllabus; with an establishment of 135 aircraft, the squadron expected to have 127 T-34Bs either in the air or on standby at all times and by 1969 available statistics indicated that the squadron was completing over 100,000 hrs a year on its Mentors. Indicating the kind of flying to which the typical primary trainer is subjected, one T-34B with 5,115 hours on its airframe had made 16,459 landings, had been stalled 17,904 times and had made 3,401 spins and 4,604 loops.

More recently, a second squadron, VT-5, has joined VT-1 at Saufley Field, to share the *ab initio* training task. Typical students receive 11 weeks of Aviation Officer Candidate training at Pensacola before reaching VT-1 or VT-5, where a course of ground instruction precedes the first flight. The flying syllabus, for which the ratio of students to instructors is four to one, normally comprises 19-20 flights, the first 12 being pre-solo. After going solo on the 13th flight, the student usually makes six more flights in the T-34B to practice precision aerobatics, half of these being solo, and covering wingovers, loops, rolls and spins. At nearby Pensacola, Naval Flight Officers (NFOs — crewmen for two-seat aircraft) receive four flights in T-34Bs of VT-10 for familiarisation purposes.

Exports and other developments

Whilst the USAF and Navy have been the best customers for the Mentor — without including the new Navy buy of T-34Cs — Beech found a useful addition to its market in overseas sales, which included three licence production arrangements. The first export order came only three months after the T-34A had been selected by the USAF and was for 36 similar Model B45s for the Chilean Air Force, subsequent orders bringing the total for Chile to 66. Columbia soon followed Chile, purchasing 32 for use at the *Escuela de Aviacion* at Cali, and other Central and South American nations to acquire the type were El Salvador, which bought three, Mexico, buying four, Venezuela, which acquired 34 for its air force and seven for the government-operated civil flying school in 1958/59, and Argentina, which received 90, all but the first 15 of these being assembled from kits and components supplied by Beech at the *Fabrica Militar de Aviones* at Cordoba. Beech also supplied 20 T-34s to Indonesia and 20 to the Philippines.

As already noted, when the USAF first selected the T-34A, arrangements were made for production of the type in Canada. This was a direct deal undertaken by the US government, which had the rights to assign production as it wished. In April 1954, however, Beech concluded an agreement with the Canadian government permitting the latter to assign production of the T-34 to Canadian Car & Foundry Co to meet a contract for 25 for service with the RCAF. These aircraft were delivered in 1955 and were used in place of North American T-6s for *ab initio* training but the results, assessed on the first two courses completed on the type, were considered not to show sufficient improvement to justify a permanent change being made. Under the terms of MDAP, 24 of the RCAF T-34As were then transferred to Turkey (the 25th having been written off in Canadian service) where they replaced ancient Miles Magisters in air force service.

Several other nations have received T-34s through US government aid programmes, these including Ecuador, Peru (with about six used to train non-jet pilots), Uruguay (one T-34B in use at *Escuela de Especializacion Aeronaval*), and Spain (using 25, with the local designation E-17, at the *Academia General del Aire* at San Javier).

The biggest overseas user of the Beech trainer, however, has been Japan, which was also the first nation to negotiate a licence for production of the type directly with Beech, this event occurring in November 1953. The B45 was chosen by Japan as the first air equipment for the National Security Force *(Hoantai)* that preceded the formation in 1954 of the three Self-Defence Forces (Ground, Maritime and Air). The company chosen to handle B45 Mentor assembly and, eventually, production in Japan was Fuji Heavy Industries Ltd, successor to the pre-war Nakajima company, and an initial contract was placed for 60 aircraft. Deliveries began in August 1954, 11 being in service for a short time before being passed to the JASDF and the remaining 49 being delivered direct to the latter service; they were followed by another 64 T-34As for the JASDF, of which 40 incorporated Beech components, and Fuji also supplied 36 to the Philippine Air Force and one to the Indonesian Air Force, supplementing those supplied to the latter two countries by Beech.

Taking advantage of the terms of its licence, Fuji set about development of the B45, initially to meet the requirements of the JGSDF for a four-seat liaison aircraft. This emerged for a first flight on 6 June 1955 as the LM-1 Nikko, using the same wings, landing gear and tail unit as the Mentor with a new centre fuselage including a cabin with four seats in side-by-side pairs. Twenty-seven LM-1s were built for the JGSDF, plus two civil prototypes; some of these were later converted to LM-2 standard with 340 hp Lycoming engine. A similar engine installation had initially been made in the single KM

prototype, converted from a civil LM-1 and flown on 1 December 1958.

For the JMSDF, Fuji developed the KM-2, also with the 340 hp Lycoming but with a cabin seating only two, side-by-side. With deliveries starting in July 1962, the KM-2 retained the same structural provisions as the KM, and had wing strong points to permit its use in local ground support operations; 30 were in service with the JMSDF in 1975, together with a dozen T-34As transferred from the JASDF, and small scale production of the KM-2 is continuing, eight having been ordered in the 1976 Fiscal Year budget. Fuji's development of the Beech trainer came full circle in 1974 when it flew the prototype (on 26 September) KM-2B, which is essentially the KM-2 with wide fuselage but the original tandem seating. Powered by the 340 hp Lycoming IGSO-480-A1A6 and with increased fuel capacity in the wings, the KM-2B was selected in August 1975 as the JASDF's new primary trainer, an initial order for 12 being placed and ultimate production of 60 projected.

Compared with Fuji's efforts to develop the T-34, the parent

(Above) One of the Canadair-built, ex-RCAF, Mentors in service with the Turkish Air Force. (Below) The first of 15 Mentors supplied to Argentina prior to production of the type being initiated at the Fabrica Militar de Aviones at Cordoba.

(Above) The first foreign air force to select the Mentor was the Fuerza Aérea de Chile, a line-up of the initial batch of aircraft being seen prior to delivery in 1959. (Below) The Fuerza Aéreas Venezolanas eventually purchased 34 Mentors, starting in 1966, when this line-up was photographed at Wichita awaiting delivery.

company did little to the basic design until evolution of the T-34C itself began in 1973. One relatively minor step, taken in 1951, was the addition of armament to one of the YT-34As for demonstrations to the US Army and USAF. A 0·30-in (7,7-mm) gun was fitted on each wing, and hard points were fitted to allow either six rocket projectiles or two 150-lb (68-kg) bombs to be carried under the wings. None of the T-34s produced by Beech made use of this feature, but the design details were made available to Fuji for incorporation of hard points in the KM-2s.

The only other Beech development of the Model 45 airframe was much more radical, and was undertaken during 1955 when the USAF showed that it was again interested in introducing a jet primary trainer for "all-through" jet training. As a private venture to known USAF requirements Beech produced a

Beechcraft T-34C Specification

Power Plant: One Pratt & Whitney (Canada) PT6A-25 turbo-prop derated from 715 shp to 400 shp up to 18,000 ft (5,490 m). Hartzell three-blade reversing and feathering propeller, diameter 7 ft 6 in (2,29 m).

Performance*: Max speed, 350 kts (648 km/h) at sea level, 280 kts (518 km/h) at 20,000 ft (6 100 m); max cruising speed, 185 kts (342 km/h) at sea level, 208 kts (385 km/h) at 10,000 ft (3 050 m) and 226 kts (418 km/h) at 17,500 ft (5 338 m); initial rate of climb, 1,430 ft/min (7,27 m/sec); rate of climb at 17,500 ft (5 338 m), 1,260 ft/min (6,4 m/sec); service ceiling, over 30,000 ft (9 150 m); take-off distance to 50 ft (15,2 m) using short field technique, 40 per cent flap, 1,270 ft (387 m); landing distance from 50 ft (15,2 m), full flaps, no reverse pitch, 1,800 ft (550 m); range (5 per cent and 20 min reserve), 787 mls (1 265 km) at 220 mph (354 km/h) at 17,500 ft (5 338 m), 915 mls (1 470 km) at 222 mph (357 km/h) at 25,000 ft (7 625 m).

Weights: Approx empty, 2,940 lb (1 335 kg); max fuel, 840 lb (381 kg); useful load, 1,360 lb (617 kg); max take-off and landing, 4,300 lb (1 952 kg).

Dimensions: Span, 33 ft 4 in (10,15 m); length, 28 ft 8½ in (8,74 m); height, 9 ft 11 in (3,02 m); wing area, 179·9 sq ft (16,71 m²); wheelbase, 7 ft 11 in (2,41 m); undercarriage track, 9 ft 6½ in (2,91 m).

Accommodation: Pupil and instructor in tandem.

*Based on prototype flight trials.

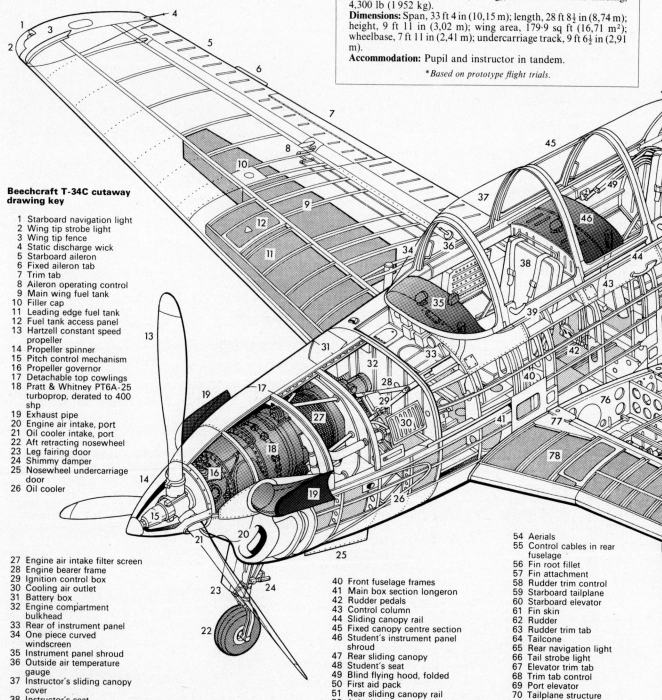

Beechcraft T-34C cutaway drawing key

1 Starboard navigation light
2 Wing tip strobe light
3 Wing tip fence
4 Static discharge wick
5 Starboard aileron
6 Fixed aileron tab
7 Trim tab
8 Aileron operating control
9 Main wing fuel tank
10 Filler cap
11 Leading edge fuel tank
12 Fuel tank access panel
13 Hartzell constant speed propeller
14 Propeller spinner
15 Pitch control mechanism
16 Propeller governor
17 Detachable top cowlings
18 Pratt & Whitney PT6A-25 turboprop, derated to 400 shp
19 Exhaust pipe
20 Engine air intake, port
21 Oil cooler intake, port
22 Aft retracting nosewheel
23 Leg fairing door
24 Shimmy damper
25 Nosewheel undercarriage door
26 Oil cooler

27 Engine air intake filter screen
28 Engine bearer frame
29 Ignition control box
30 Cooling air outlet
31 Battery box
32 Engine compartment bulkhead
33 Rear of instrument panel
34 One piece curved windscreen
35 Instrument panel shroud
36 Outside air temperature gauge
37 Instructor's sliding canopy cover
38 Instructor's seat
39 Canopy handle

40 Front fuselage frames
41 Main box section longeron
42 Rudder pedals
43 Control column
44 Sliding canopy rail
45 Fixed canopy centre section
46 Student's instrument panel shroud
47 Rear sliding canopy
48 Student's seat
49 Blind flying hood, folded
50 First aid pack
51 Rear sliding canopy rail
52 Avionics compartment
53 Rear fuselage structure

54 Aerials
55 Control cables in rear fuselage
56 Fin root fillet
57 Fin attachment
58 Rudder trim control
59 Starboard tailplane
60 Starboard elevator
61 Fin skin
62 Rudder
63 Rudder trim tab
64 Tailcone
65 Rear navigation light
66 Tail strobe light
67 Elevator trim tab
68 Trim tab control
69 Port elevator
70 Tailplane structure
71 Ventral fin
72 Tailplane root fillet

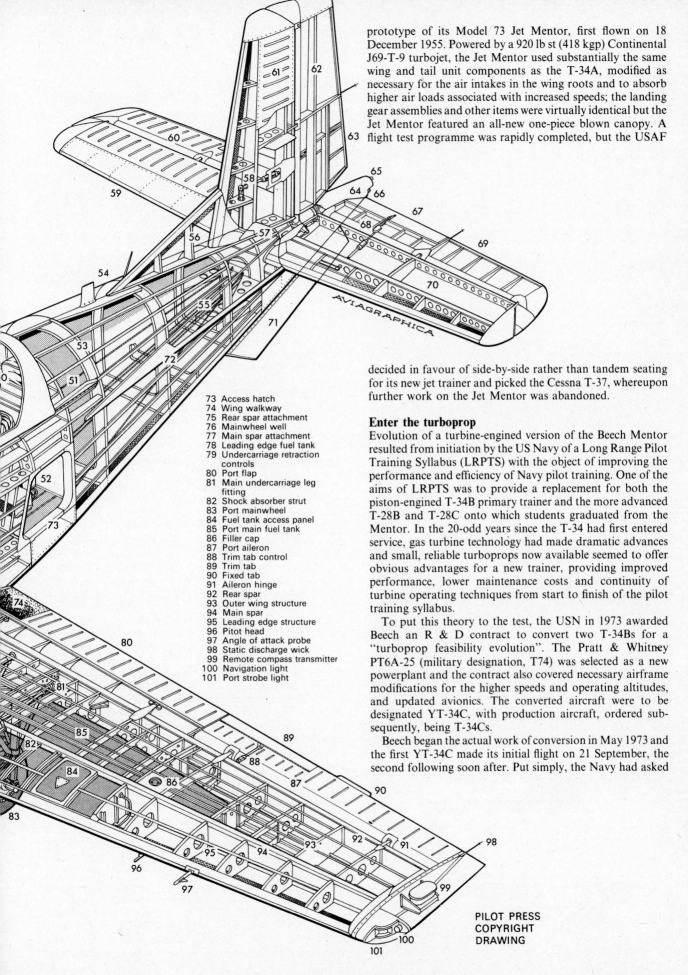

prototype of its Model 73 Jet Mentor, first flown on 18 December 1955. Powered by a 920 lb st (418 kgp) Continental J69-T-9 turbojet, the Jet Mentor used substantially the same wing and tail unit components as the T-34A, modified as necessary for the air intakes in the wing roots and to absorb higher air loads associated with increased speeds; the landing gear assemblies and other items were virtually identical but the Jet Mentor featured an all-new one-piece blown canopy. A flight test programme was rapidly completed, but the USAF

decided in favour of side-by-side rather than tandem seating for its new jet trainer and picked the Cessna T-37, whereupon further work on the Jet Mentor was abandoned.

Enter the turboprop

Evolution of a turbine-engined version of the Beech Mentor resulted from initiation by the US Navy of a Long Range Pilot Training Syllabus (LRPTS) with the object of improving the performance and efficiency of Navy pilot training. One of the aims of LRPTS was to provide a replacement for both the piston-engined T-34B primary trainer and the more advanced T-28B and T-28C onto which students graduated from the Mentor. In the 20-odd years since the T-34 had first entered service, gas turbine technology had made dramatic advances and small, reliable turboprops now available seemed to offer obvious advantages for a new trainer, providing improved performance, lower maintenance costs and continuity of turbine operating techniques from start to finish of the pilot training syllabus.

To put this theory to the test, the USN in 1973 awarded Beech an R & D contract to convert two T-34Bs for a "turboprop feasibility evolution". The Pratt & Whitney PT6A-25 (military designation, T74) was selected as a new powerplant and the contract also covered necessary airframe modifications for the higher speeds and operating altitudes, and updated avionics. The converted aircraft were to be designated YT-34C, with production aircraft, ordered subsequently, being T-34Cs.

Beech began the actual work of conversion in May 1973 and the first YT-34C made its initial flight on 21 September, the second following soon after. Put simply, the Navy had asked

73 Access hatch
74 Wing walkway
75 Rear spar attachment
76 Mainwheel well
77 Main spar attachment
78 Leading edge fuel tank
79 Undercarriage retraction controls
80 Port flap
81 Main undercarriage leg fitting
82 Shock absorber strut
83 Port mainwheel
84 Fuel tank access panel
85 Port main fuel tank
86 Filler cap
87 Port aileron
88 Trim tab control
89 Trim tab
90 Fixed tab
91 Aileron hinge
92 Rear spar
93 Outer wing structure
94 Main spar
95 Leading edge structure
96 Pitot head
97 Angle of attack probe
98 Static discharge wick
99 Remote compass transmitter
100 Navigation light
101 Port strobe light

AVIAGRAPHICA

PILOT PRESS
COPYRIGHT
DRAWING

(Above) The Fuji KM-2 was one of several Japanese developments of the Beech Mentor, having a 340 hp Lycoming engine and being operated as a two-seater although retaining the basic four-seat cabin designed for the LM-1. (Below) The LM-2, used by the JGSDF, also had the uprated engine and four-seat cabin.

(Below) The Fuji LM-1 Nikko, flown in June 1955, was the first Japanese derivative of the Mentor, having the same engine but a new centre fuselage seating four in two pairs of side-by-side seats.

(Above) From the LM-1, Fuji developed the KM-1, the first variant to have the uprated Lycoming engine. A few examples were built for civil use, leading to adoption of the similar KM-2 by the JASDF. (Below) As its new primary trainer, the JASDF has recently adopted the KM-2B, final Fuji derivative of the original Beech design.

for an aeroplane they could "fly a lot and not have to fix very much"; in other words, high reliability and ease of maintenance were of primary importance. One way of achieving this was to derate the engine, which has a basic output of 715 shp at sea level, to 400 shp by means of a mechanical torque limiter; this power is available at altitudes up to 18,000 ft (5 490 m) or so in standard day temperatures, so the student pilot does not have to worry about over/under boost, overtorque or overtemperature, even with a failed torque limiter, and extra power will be available, if required by future weight growth, for example, by resetting the torque limiter.

The engine is installed in the T-34C offset slightly to starboard and down from the aircraft centreline, cancelling out much of the torque effect of the airscrew and thereby enhancing the jet-like feel of the aircraft. The propeller is auto-feathering, the blades being spring-loaded in the feathered position with engine oil pressure overcoming the spring force; if engine oil pressure is lost, the propeller therefore feathers automatically. An inverted oil system is fitted, permitting more than two minutes of inverted flight. Fuel capacity, in bladder tanks in the wing torsion box, has been increased from the T-34A's 50 US gal (189 l) to a total of 125 US gal (473 l).

Externally, the T-34C differs from its predecessor in the power plant installation, the addition of about 6 in (15 cm) to the overall wing span, and enlarged dorsal fin and — as eventually adopted for production — two ventral fins angled out from the undersides of the lower fuselage and long fairing strakes extending forwards from the tailplane leading edge roots. These last-mentioned modifications were associated with the spinning characteristics of the YT-34C, the exploration of which occupied a major part of the 700-hr test programme preceding the taking of a production decision.

Like the earlier Mentor, the T-34C has mechanically-actuated flight controls and trim tabs, by cables and push rods, and the landing gear and flaps are electronically actuated, with manual back-up for the former only. A 28-volt DC electrical system is provided with a 250-amp starter-generator on the engine and two 250 VA solid-state inverters are fitted, only one being in use at any given time. A high pressure oxygen system is provided, sufficient for 3·5 hrs use by two pilots.

An important new feature of the T-34C is the addition of a Freon-type air conditioner for cockpit cooling. This provides 100 per cent ground cool-down, even at engine idling speeds, and makes it unnecessary for the cockpit canopy to be open at any time from brakes off to brakes on. Other detail improvements include the addition of high intensity strobe flasher lights on the wing-tips and tail, a stall-warning rudder shaker, cockpit annunciator warning system, fire detection system, angle-of-attack indicators and indexer in each cockpit and an advanced, solid state avionics package. The last-named includes UHF communications, Collins TCN-40 TACAN with RMI and bearing selector with provision for area navigation equipment addition, omni receiver for nav/com back-up, code transponders with altitude reporting in each cockpit and an emergency locator transmitter. The T-34C has been designed to have a 16,000-hr fatigue life, sufficient for 20 years' service at the anticipated utilisation of 800 hrs/yr.

Spinning trials

Before flight testing of the two YT-34Cs began, models were subjected to tests in the NASA spin tunnel at Langley. These tests showed that the aircraft had a neutral (near-zero) inertia yawing movement parameter (IYMP), for which the optimum spin control for recovery could not be predicted analytically. The NASA report on the model tests said, in part: "The spinning motion is very complicated and involves simultaneous rolling, yawing and pitching while the airplane is at high angles of attack and sideslip. Since it involves separated flows in the region beyond the stall, the aerodynamic characteristics of the airplane are very non-linear and time-dependent: and hence, at the present time, the spin is not very amenable to theoretical analyses".

It was clear from this report that considerable attention would require to be paid to spinning during flight testing. To provide a measure of security, NASA developed two devices, either of which promoted a stable, recoverable, moderate spin mode, and both were fitted in the prototype used for the spin trials, the second YT-34C being used as chase aircraft because of its compatible performance and common UHF communication. The spinning trials were conducted by Beech engineering test pilot Robert R (Bob) Stone, and the details that follow are based on his own account published in *Approach,* the US Naval Aviation Safety Review.

The first intensive two-month period of flight testing included 175 spins, and defined the safe flight envelope for the subsequent evaluation by USN pilots. It was soon discovered that the YT-34C, in common with other IYMP straight-winged aircraft, had an "aggravated spin mode" from which

recovery was impaired because of pilot disorientation in the high spin rate and by difficulty of control action. This "aggravated mode" was produced by holding the rudder pro-spin, and pushing the stick full forward from a stable spin. The aircraft then transitioned from a 160 deg/sec spin rate in a 45-deg nose-down spin attitude to a 70-deg plus nose-down attitude with a spin rate in excess of 300 deg/sec. Furthermore, this new spin mode was very stable and reversing the rudder (which completed the stick forward, rudder anti-common spin recovery control position) did *not* bring about recovery. The only way to recover was to go back: pro-spin rudder, stick aft for one turn and *then* apply a normal recovery.

At the end of this initial phase of flight testing, the YT-34C was submitted for its first NPE (Navy Preliminary Evaluation), which consisted of 55 flights but included only one spin flight, comprising six spins, one of which was "aggravated". Results of the NPE showed that "The YT-34C exhibited excellent potential to perform the primary training mission" and "Installation of a turboprop engine, angle-of-attack indicator and upgraded avionics package makes the YT-34C a superior trainer to the present trainer airplanes" which it would replace. However, the Navy declined to enter a production contract because of the "spin and spin recovery characteristics" and certain other NPE deficiencies.

Beech then embarked on a seven-month development programme, supported by testing in the NASA Langley spin tunnel, which consisted primarily of spin development and included 1,200 spins (one of which required deployment of the anti-spin parachute for recovery). Some 15 aerodynamic configurations were tried, and several difficult dynamically oscillated spin recoveries were made.

After achieving reliable, consistent rudder primary recoveries in all conditions, the final YT-34C spin characteristics were compared with those of the T-34B, T-28, and T-37 by in-flight evaluation and were found to be superior to all. The new model would still "aggravate", but from a stable rate of only 100-120 deg/sec. The "aggravation" brought the rate up to less than 180 deg/sec and recovery was effected in less than two turns with rudder only. The T-28 rudder-only recovery from its "aggravation" took 3·5 to 4 turns to recover, and the T-37

Three-view drawing of the Beechcraft T-34C.

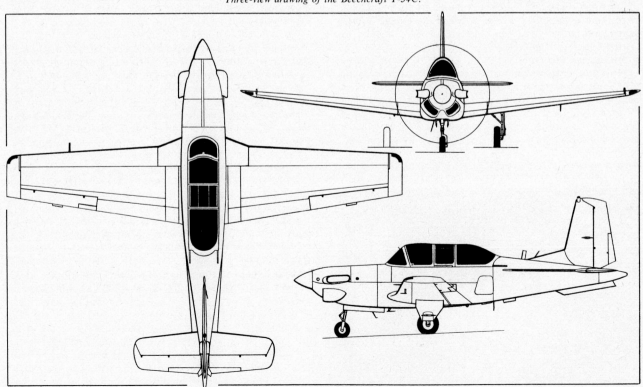

required the complicated "back pro-spin" recovery technique from much higher "aggravated" spin rates.

With this refinement of the YT-34Cs spinning characteristics completed, the Navy was ready to undertake a second NPE, which consisted of 48 flights, over half of which included spins. The report on this NPE showed that all earlier deficiencies had been corrected, and that the YT-34C "continued to exhibit excellent potential to perform the primary training mission and should prove to be a vast improvement over present trainer airplanes".

Both YT-34Cs were then submitted to NAS Pensacola for an OPEVAL (Operational Evaluation) that was planned to comprise 120 flight hours in six weeks. Thanks to 100 per cent aircraft availability, excellent training time efficiency and the enthusiasm of participating instructor pilots, the whole OPEVAL schedule was concluded in 97·4 hrs and three weeks. Favourable analysis of the data cleared the way for the Navy to begin procurement of the T-34C, and although some consideration had earlier been given to converting existing T-34B airframes, this proved not to be cost effective and plans have been made instead to replace the Navy's training fleet of T-34Bs and T-28s with a force of about 400 new-build T-34Cs over a five-year period.

To get production under way, an initial order was placed for 18 T-34Cs in April 1975 on a fixed-price contract worth about $7·1m (£3·5m), with deliveries to begin in March 1976. Subsequently, a second batch of 75 was ordered with FY76 funds; further quantities of 23 and 33 are included in the Transition and FY77 Defence Budgets, and 103 will be requested in FY78. Final production batches to meet USN requirements are expected to be ordered in FY79 and FY80, but export orders could well keep the newest Beech trainer in production into the 'eighties. An early indication of overseas interest in the type has been given by the order placed, towards the end of 1975, by the Royal Maroc Air Force, for 12 examples. Other deals are under negotiation and the Beech T-34C, with its unique blend of a 'fifties-era airframe with mid-'seventies engine and avionics technology, is already a worthwhile addition to the current spectrum of training aircraft. □

Viewed from the Cockpit

by John Fricker

GENERATIONS of US Navy pilots have received their introduction to flying via the sturdy wings of the Beech T-34, which, having been in service since 1954, has already surpassed the longevity of such classic trainers as, for example, the Avro 504 in the RAF. Just as the rotary engine in the 504K was replaced with the passage of time by the Lynx radial of the 504N, however, the USN is now turning from the air-cooled piston engine to the turbine with its new T-34C, while retaining with little other change the thoroughly-proven airframe of the T-34B.

In place of the original 225 hp Continental flat-six engine, the T-34C has a Pratt & Whitney PT6A-25 turboprop of a very closely similar weight, but with almost twice the available power. In fact, with its PT6A-27 gas-generator normally developing 715 shp, the PT6A-25 is flat-rated to maintain 550 shp (580 ehp) up to ambient temperatures of 33°C (91·4°F), or about 22,000 ft (6 705 m). This represents the design limit of the PT6A-20 gearbox used by the hybrid -25 engine, but as the USN requires only 400 shp for the T-34C, production aircraft will incorporate a torque controller to restrict power to this level.

Introducing the writer to the YT-34C 0861, the second of the two prototypes which had been converted from standard T-34B airframes, Beech project pilot Bob Stone pointed out the engine controls for the PT6 in a quadrant on the port side of the big tandem cockpits. Engine handling is through conventional throttle and pitch levers, although primary power indication is through a torque meter, in conjunction with a propeller rpm gauge. The PT6A-25 develops its 400 shp in the T-34C at 950 ft/lb torque and 2,200 rpm, but with no automatic limitation in the prototypes, power regulation had to be monitored with some care. The prototypes can, in fact, use up to 550 shp at a maximum 1,320 ft/lb torque, which Bob Stone utilized with much élan during his spectacular aerobatic displays at last year's Paris air show where the T-34C made its international début.

Power margins are, therefore, unlikely to prove a problem, despite the increase in gross weight from the 2,975 lb (1 349 kg) of the original Navy Mentor to around 4,300 lb (1 950 kg) for the T-34C. Much of this extra weight results from the thirst of the PT6A compared with the piston engine that it supplants, this having necessitated more than doubling the original fuel capacity. The airframe is also beefed-up to maintain the normal load factor limits of +6 g and −3 g at the higher weight, and achieve a minimum fatigue life of 16,000 flying hours and 30,000 landings at descent rates of up to 17 ft/sec (5,1 m/sec).

Since the prototypes are simply converted T-34Bs with 21 in (53,3 cm) extended forward fuselages primarily to accommodate the longer engine, they are not entirely structurally representative of the definitive T-34Cs, which are being built from new production tooling. To strengthen them to T-34C standard, the prototypes use several off-the-shelf items, such as the ailerons and main undercarriage units of the Beech Duke light twin, and have Baron 58 wings with 123 Imp gal (559 l) fuel capacity. As a matter of interest, Beech is using the same test airframe for both fatigue testing and undercarriage drop trials — a particularly severe combination.

In view of the fact that the Mentor was derived directly from the four-seat Bonanza, its twin cockpits are unusually spacious, and yet all controls come conveniently to hand. Not unexpectedly, prototype instrumentation is largely 1950-ish, with the addition of such new engine references as N_1 gas generator percentage rpm, turbine temperature gauge and fuel flowmeter. As a modern USN trainer, 0861 also has the standard angle of attack indicator, graduated from 0 to 30 degrees, on the port coaming, together with a comprehensive avionics fit, including UHF. Production aircraft will also have TACAN, plus wiring for R-nav.

From the front cockpit, just behind the wing leading-edge, all-round visibility is exceptionally good and I found that the normal seating position was high enough above the long nose for the latter not to be too obtrusive. Rear cockpit visibility is obviously acceptable, although not conforming to current

The first prototype YT-34C after modifications to the tail unit that had to be made to provide acceptable spin characteristics.

The airline that taught the world about "altiports"
reports on the Twin Otter:

"Great STOL performance... high-altitude performance... and short-haul economy."

"That's what we looked for when we bought our first Twin Otter," says Michel Ziegler, President of Air Alpes, "and that's what we got. So now our fleet includes seven Twin Otters."

Air Alpes began operating in 1962, with a single plane flying skiers into the Alps. Now it is one of Europe's leading regional carriers with passenger traffic of 202,000 in 1974. And along the way the Air Alpes people have been consulted by countries from Nepal to Peru because of their expertise in the development and use of small, high-altitude fields or "altiports."

One of the most spectacular of these is 2,000 m. up in the Alps at Courchevel, shown above, where Twin Otters fly scheduled service into a 340 m. strip

with unusually steep gradients. The Twin Otters, with their exceptional STOL performance and control, are able to take advantage of the terrain by making all landings uphill and takeoffs downhill.

As Ziegler says, "There aren't many planes that can operate there to begin with. And none that can touch the Twin Otter's economics on the shorter runs."

The de Havilland Twin Otter. Making money ... and aviation history ... from Courchevel to Los Angeles to Indonesia. That's why sales have already reached the 500 mark.

The de Havilland Aircraft of Canada Limited, Downsview, Ontario M3K 1Y5. Telex: 0622128 Cable: Moth, Toronto.

Twin Otter: the standard of dependability and profitability in 50 countries.

de Havilland

The right concept for today and tomorrow!

The Viggen attack version was first introduced in the Swedish Air Force in 1971. This multi-role Viggen is now also in production in reconnaissance and fighter versions. The latter will enter into service in 1978 and continue in production at least until 1985. Today, yet another Viggen version is proposed by Sweden's defence planners for service starting in the mid-eighties. Tentatively designated the "A 20" it is a multi-role development of the new advanced technology JA37 fighter now in initial production.

SAAB
A product from Saab-Scania, Sweden

Scania medium-heavy and heavy diesel trucks, buses and diesel engines.

Saab-Scania AB, Scania Division, S-151 87 Södertälje, Sweden. Tel +46 0755-341 40.

Saab passenger cars in several models. The Saab 99 series, the Saab 95L and the Saab 96L.

Saab-Scania AB, Saab Car Division, S-611 01 Nyköping, Sweden. Tel +46 0155-807 00.

Saab aircraft, guided missiles, avionics and space equipment.

Saab-Scania AB, Aerospace Division, S-581 88 Linköping, Sweden. Tel +46 013-12 90 20.

Datasaab computers, terminal systems and other advanced electronics.

Saab-Scania AB, Datasaab Division, S-581 01 Linköping, Sweden. Tel +46 013-11 15 00.

Nordarmatur valves and instruments for the process industry, steam- and nuclear power plants and ships.

Saab-Scania AB, Nordarmatur Division, S-581 87 Linköping, Sweden. Tel +46 013-12 90 60.

Financial summary 1975
Consolidated sales
total   Skr 7,900 millions
Sales to markets
outside Sweden   42 %
Number of employees   37,500

Saab-Scania AB, Head Office, S-581 88 Linköping, Sweden. Tel +46 013-11 54 00.

standards achieved with stepped-up tandem seating. Rudder pedals can be cranked back and forth to allow for varying leg lengths, so that cockpit comfort is outstanding. In anticipation of the hot and humid conditions in Florida, where the USN's primary training schools are located, production aircraft will be further improved by the installation of Freon air conditioning.

Unusually in a single-engined aircraft, the PT6 in the T-34C retains its feathering facility, and starting is from the feathered blade position. The start sequence is automatic after holding in the button until N_1 speed reaches 12 per cent, and then about 110 ft/lb of torque gets the aircraft rolling on its long-stroke oleos. Unlike the USAF T-34As, the Navy versions do not have nosewheel steering, but taxying is simple enough with the effective toe brakes. Reverse pitch from beta blade angles is also available to check rolling speeds and provide additional ground control. The beta release switch on the engine control quadrant is to be modified in production aircraft to obviate its inadvertent selection in the air, although this would in any case be possible only at the moment immediately before the stall.

On opening up to the required torque limit, the T-34C fairly leaps off the ground, after the shortest of ground runs, in a great surge of thrust. It has little apparent tendency to swing, despite its power; the rudder becomes effective almost immediately from the slipstream, and a gentle rotation results in a positive unstick at about 80 knots (148 km/h) IAS. Trim changes with gear retraction are small and in fact remain so throughout the flight envelope. The doll's eye indicators for each undercarriage leg brought back to this writer fond memories of RAF aircraft of the 1950s. At anything between 120 and 150 knots (222-278 km/h), a comfortable cruise climb of around 2,000 ft/min (10,16 m/sec) can be maintained all the way up to 22,000 ft (6 705 m) if required. An economical cruise speed of 240 knots (444 km/h) could be achieved at that height, although for its more normal lower-level operations, the T-34C hums along effortlessly at around 200 knots (370 km/h) at a typical power setting of around 1,000 ft/lb and 1,800 rpm.

Cruising in the YT-34C at about 2,500 ft (762 m) above the peaceful French countryside, the fuel flow at this setting was about 260 lb/h (118 kg/h), although it can average as little as 25 Imp gal (113,61) per hour. In the air, the T-34C is extremely pleasant to fly, with light, responsive and well-harmonised controls which retain their effectiveness throughout the remarkably wide speed range. This was demonstrated with considerable verve from the rear seat by Bob Stone, who treated the occupants of a remote French village, as well as myself as a somewhat closer observer, to his full five-minute Paris air show aerobatic routine — a smooth and precise combination of loops, rolls, hesitation rolls, flick rolls, spins and inverted flying in bewildering succession.

As I then discovered for myself, the T-34C performs most aerobatic manoeuvres from a constant power setting of around 1,000 ft/lb torque and the resulting level speed of around 190 knots (352 km/h). No power changes or other engine handling are necessary, and negative g fuel supply is available for a long, long two minutes, so that the T-34C goes, and with some zest, virtually anywhere you point it. After two minutes of inversion, the PT6 will flame-out from fuel exhaustion, but will auto-relight, regardless of throttle position, within 10 seconds of the aircraft rolling level. If you were persistent enough to hold the T-34C inverted for $3\frac{1}{2}$ minutes, the oil pressure would drop and the PT6 would auto-feather itself before roll-out. Since the PT6 will also be automatically protected, in the production T-34C, from over-torqueing, engine handling, even by sprog naval pilots, would seem to be virtually idiot-proof.

Exploration of the T-34C's low-speed handling was approached with some interest in view of the spin problems encountered during the initial $400,000 (£200,000), six-month, prototype development phase. With its new nose and slab-

Production models of the T-34C are expected to reach US Navy units in the near future with the first training courses on the new type starting later this year. A prototype YT-34C is illustrated.

sided fuselage with rounded corners, the T-34C exhibited very interesting characteristics at the start of its spin trials, with a tendency to enter a stable and almost flat autoration at the alarming rate of around 320 degrees per second. In the aggravated spin mode, with the stick moved forward for the start of recovery, rotation rates were so high that fuel in the tanks distended the wing skins through centrifugal force.

Beech subsequently spent some seven months and $2m (£1m) of its own money in taming the T-34C's suddenly savage spin. After more than 1,200 test spins, during which it was necessary to deploy the tail-recovery parachute on only one occasion, the present combination of tailplane/fuselage leading-edge strakes and twin ventral fins was evolved, following 14 less successful fixes. The present configuration was further tested by Bob Stone in another 300 or so spins, resulting in the achieving of unlimited spin clearance. If my experience in 0861 is any indication, the T-34C now has completely classic spin entry and recovery characteristics. Clean and power off, it stalled with very little aerodynamic buffet, although artificial warning is provided by a rudder pedal shaker. After making uneventful spin checks in both directions, in which the airspeed stabilised at about 70 knots (130 km/h) IAS, I lowered undercarriage and flaps below their respective limits of 152 knots (282 km/h) and 122 knots (225 km/h), with virtually no change of trim, and found that some lateral control remained right down to the mild stall breakaway, which occurred at only 50 knots (92 km/h) IAS.

At the other end of the speed range, a brief dive to the V_{NE} of 250 knots (463 km/h) IAS showed no untoward heavying-up of control or aeroelastic effects. The altitude performance of the T-34C is such that this never-exceed speed will translate, in production aircraft, to about Mach = 0·64 above about 10,000 ft (6 100 m) — a stimulating limit for a primary trainer.

In the circuit, however, the T-34C reverts to typical lightplane handling and performance, motoring sedately around at about 85 knots (157 km/h) and approaching at 80 knots (148 km/h). In the course of half-a-dozen circuits and bumps on both runway and grass at the small French airfield of Persan-Beaumont, the T-34C proved no more demanding than the average flying-club trainer, and the combination of a responsive elevator and squashy oleos made for flattering landings. The already minimal ground run could be further reduced, if required, by the judicious use of beta propeller braking.

In its simplicity and docility of handling, the T-34C is thoroughly representative of the current generation of primary trainers, although it is unique at the moment as a production item in pioneering the concept with turboprop power. Future USN — and many foreign — students will thus derive the dual benefits of turbine handling and classic flying characteristics, backed by the experience of untold thousands of hours in the air of the original piston-engined airframes. □

TOOTH-CUTTER FOR THE JAGDFLIEGER
...the Heinkel He-51

Viewed from the Cockpit

To the group of relative novices at the stick and rudder bar in which the writer was included on that cold winter morning early in 1943, the rakish biplane on the hard standing was little short of awe inspiring. Its close-cowled twelve-cylinder vee engine and fixed-pitch two-bladed propeller seemed immense to those of us whose experience was limited to such low-powered, lightly-loaded and readily forgiving types as the Bücker Bü 131 Jungmann or the Focke-Wulf Fw 44 Stieglitz. If no longer in the first flush of youth — indeed, long since overtaken by technological development and by now something of an anachronism — this elegant aircraft to which we were being somewhat nonchalantly introduced by our instructors was, nevertheless, a very different bird from those to which we were still barely accustomed. It was this self-same aircraft, the Heinkel He 51, that had entered service as the first genuine fighter of our then still-clandestine *Luftwaffe* some eight years earlier and, soon afterwards, had been flown in combat over Spain to provide the platform from which most of our leading 'aces' had gained their first 'kills' — small wonder

Physically, the Heinkel He 51 was merely a sturdy, thoroughly orthodox fighter biplane possessing a performance capability undistinguished from those of its more run-of-the-mill contemporaries; spiritually, it symbolized both nationally and internationally the renaissance of German military aviation. Forty years ago, in August 1936, it appeared in Spanish skies to become the first German combat aircraft to fire its guns in anger for 18 years; it was the warplane on which the fighter component of the Luftwaffe metaphorically cut its teeth. Its first-line career was destined to be relatively short, but as a fighter-trainer the He 51 was to soldier on well into WW II, providing many of Germany's fighter pilots with their first experience of flying relatively high-powered single-seat aircraft. On these pages, a former Luftwaffe pilot, Harro Kortbein, records at AIR INTERNATIONAL'S invitation his recollections of the He 51 gained during flying training early in 1943.

that our awe was tinged with something akin to reverence.

The He 51 was not a large aircraft by the standards of the day, but with its steep ground angle resulting from what seemed an inordinately tall undercarriage — every inch of which was, in fact, needed to provide adequate clearance for the massive wooden propeller — it towered above us, the leading-edge of the lower mainplane reaching almost to shoulder height. It was allegedly mettlesome; it was said to be unforgiving and none suggested that it suffered tyros gladly. Small wonder if we tyros experienced some trepidation at the thought that we would soon be clambering into this monster.

Powered by a glycol-cooled BMW VI 7,3Z twelve-cylinder vee engine which was coaxed into giving a shattering 750 hp for one minute at 1,700 revs but possessed a normal rating of 550 hp at 1,530 revs, the He 51 had a rectangular welded steel-tube fuselage structure which was faired to an oval at top and bottom, and covered forward by detachable light metal panels and aft by fabric. The metal two-spar wings were fabric covered, the upper planes carrying the ailerons and the lower planes carrying the plain trailing-edge flaps. A pair of synchronised 7,9-mm MG 17 machine guns were installed in the upper decking of the forward fuselage, ammunition tanks containing 500 rpg being attached to the rear face of the firewall, and a 46 Imp gal (210 l) fuel tank was mounted beneath the pilot's feet, provision being made to supplement this with a 37·4 Imp gal (170 l) drop tank on the fuselage centreline.

My turn finally came to hoist myself into the cockpit of an He 51, comforted somewhat by the obvious age of this fearsome beast, or, rather, by the thought of the number of ham-fisted pupils that must have flown it and survived the experience over the four or five years that had elapsed since it had been pulled out of first-line service and relegated to the training rôle. The open cockpit proved surprisingly commodious, the T-shaped instrument panel seemed hardly more complex than those of the very much lower-powered trainers that I had been flying and the cockpit drill was — as I was to appreciate in later years — extremely simple. After a somewhat erratic start, the big BMW engine settled down to a comforting deep-throated growl, the propeller flailing apparently slowly around and the aircraft rocking gently against the chocks. Forward visibility in the three-point attitude was totally obscured by the broad engine cowling and any attempt to peer around the tiny excuse for a windscreen set one's cheeks literally flapping in the slipstream. The chocks were signalled away, a quick precautionary check of the control surfaces, a shouted Hals-und-Beinbruch from the instructor, and I was gathering speed in this totally strange, powerful and still seemingly enormous aircraft.

My take-off was not too untidy as I experienced little difficulty in keeping the He 51 straight and once the tail came up forward visibility between the centre-section struts and bracing wires was not too bad. Acceleration was greater than I had anticipated and I was quickly airborne and making a tightish climbing turn. While it would be untrue to say that I immediately felt at home in the cockpit and thereupon initiated a series of aerobatics with gay abandon, the first few airborne minutes were by no means as traumatic as I had anticipated. The controls were light and very responsive and for a beginner such as myself the maximum attainable speeds in excess of 200 mph (320 km/h) were breathtaking, being twice as high as anything that I had flown to that time. The circuit of the field — which was the ordered extent of my initiation — seemed to take no time at all and I was making my approach before I had even mentally adjusted to having successfully taken-off.

At this stage in my training I could risk nothing more than a conservative straight-in approach and attempt a three-pointer. The He 51 was prone to bouncing severely on touch-down and a ground loop was a serious hazard. It was by no means

The Heinkel He 51 in its heyday (at head of opposite page) in service with I Gruppe of Jagdgeschwader 132 "Richthofen" based at Döberitz in 1935 and (below) with I Gruppe of Jagdgeschwader 134 "Horst Wessel" at Werl in the following year. The twin-wire undercarriage bracing and drop tank identify the aircraft below as He 51B-1s whereas that illustrated opposite is an He 51A-1 with single mainleg bracing wires and no drop tank provision.

Heinkel He 51B-1 cutaway drawing key

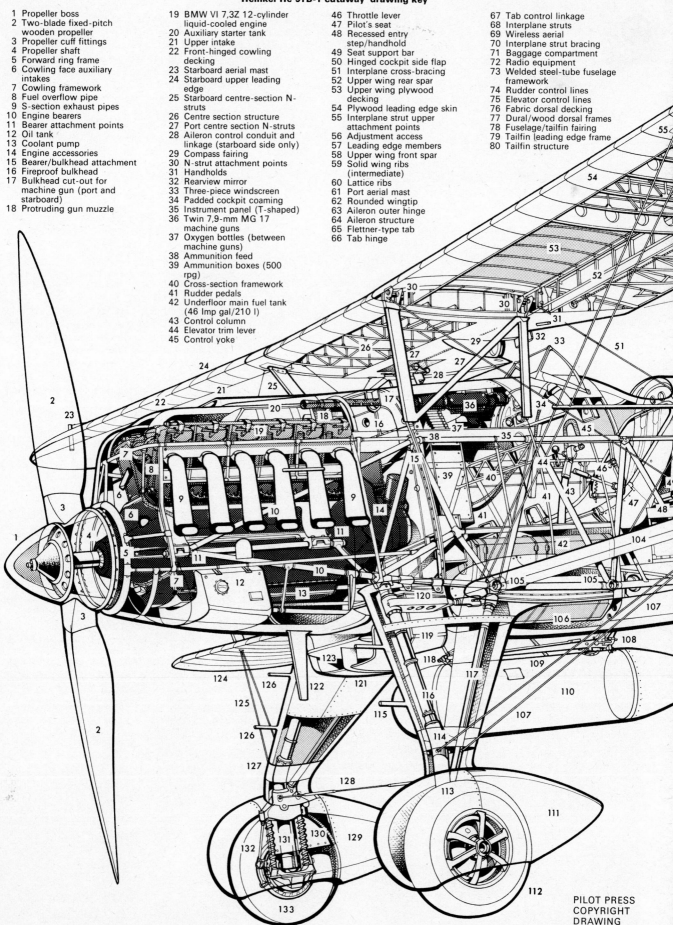

1 Propeller boss
2 Two-blade fixed-pitch wooden propeller
3 Propeller cuff fittings
4 Propeller shaft
5 Forward ring frame
6 Cowling face auxiliary intakes
7 Cowling framework
8 Fuel overflow pipe
9 S-section exhaust pipes
10 Engine bearers
11 Bearer attachment points
12 Oil tank
13 Coolant pump
14 Engine accessories
15 Bearer/bulkhead attachment
16 Fireproof bulkhead
17 Bulkhead cut-out for machine gun (port and starboard)
18 Protruding gun muzzle

19 BMW VI 7,3Z 12-cylinder liquid-cooled engine
20 Auxiliary starter tank
21 Upper intake
22 Front-hinged cowling decking
23 Starboard aerial mast
24 Starboard upper leading edge
25 Starboard centre-section N-struts
26 Centre section structure
27 Port centre section N-struts
28 Aileron control conduit and linkage (starboard side only)
29 Compass fairing
30 N-strut attachment points
31 Handholds
32 Rearview mirror
33 Three-piece windscreen
34 Padded cockpit coaming
35 Instrument panel (T-shaped)
36 Twin 7,9-mm MG 17 machine guns
37 Oxygen bottles (between machine guns)
38 Ammunition feed
39 Ammunition boxes (500 rpg)
40 Cross-section framework
41 Rudder pedals
42 Underfloor main fuel tank (46 Imp gal/210 l)
43 Control column
44 Elevator trim lever
45 Control yoke

46 Throttle lever
47 Pilot's seat
48 Recessed entry step/handhold
49 Seat support bar
50 Hinged cockpit side flap
51 Interplane cross-bracing
52 Upper wing rear spar
53 Upper wing plywood decking
54 Plywood leading edge skin
55 Interplane strut upper attachment points
56 Adjustment access
57 Leading edge members
58 Upper wing front spar
59 Solid wing ribs (intermediate)
60 Lattice ribs
61 Port aerial mast
62 Rounded wingtip
63 Aileron outer hinge
64 Aileron structure
65 Flettner-type tab
66 Tab hinge

67 Tab control linkage
68 Interplane struts
69 Wireless aerial
70 Interplane strut bracing
71 Baggage compartment
72 Radio equipment
73 Welded steel-tube fuselage framework
74 Rudder control lines
75 Elevator control lines
76 Fabric dorsal decking
77 Dural/wood dorsal frames
78 Fuselage/tailfin fairing
79 Tailfin leading edge frame
80 Tailfin structure

PILOT PRESS
COPYRIGHT
DRAWING

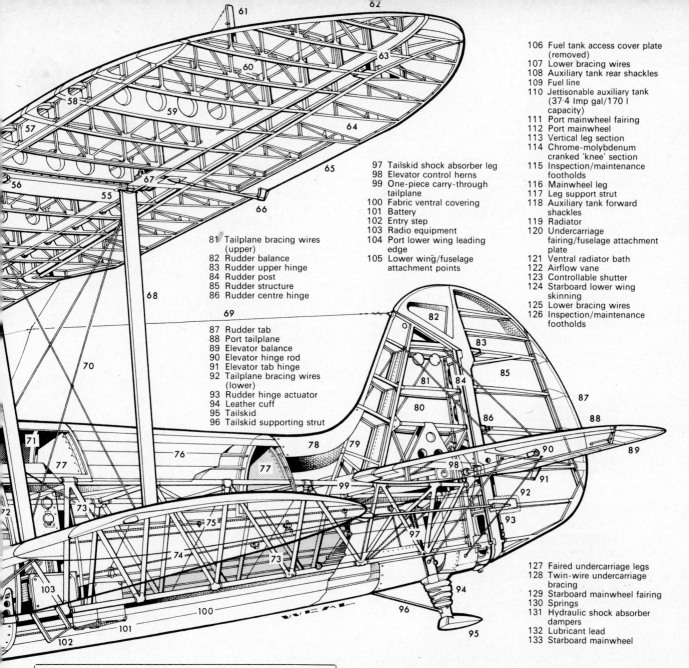

61
62
63
60
58
59
57
56
64
55
65
67
66
68
69
70
71
77
76
78
79
72
73
75
74
103
100
101
102

106 Fuel tank access cover plate (removed)
107 Lower bracing wires
108 Auxiliary tank rear shackles
109 Fuel line
110 Jettisonable auxiliary tank (37·4 Imp gal/170 l capacity)
111 Port mainwheel fairing
112 Port mainwheel
113 Vertical leg section
114 Chrome-molybdenum cranked 'knee' section
115 Inspection/maintenance footholds
116 Mainwheel leg
117 Leg support strut
118 Auxiliary tank forward shackles
119 Radiator
120 Undercarriage fairing/fuselage attachment plate
121 Ventral radiator bath
122 Airflow vane
123 Controllable shutter
124 Starboard lower wing skinning
125 Lower bracing wires
126 Inspection/maintenance footholds

97 Tailskid shock absorber leg
98 Elevator control horns
99 One-piece carry-through tailplane
100 Fabric ventral covering
101 Battery
102 Entry step
103 Radio equipment
104 Port lower wing leading edge
105 Lower wing/fuselage attachment points

81 Tailplane bracing wires (upper)
82 Rudder balance
83 Rudder upper hinge
84 Rudder post
85 Rudder structure
86 Rudder centre hinge

87 Rudder tab
88 Port tailplane
89 Elevator balance
90 Elevator hinge rod
91 Elevator tab hinge
92 Tailplane bracing wires (lower)
93 Rudder hinge actuator
94 Leather cuff
95 Tailskid
96 Tailskid supporting strut

82
83
85
81 84
80
87
88
86
89
90
98
91
92
93
94
96
95

127 Faired undercarriage legs
128 Twin-wire undercarriage bracing
129 Starboard mainwheel fairing
130 Springs
131 Hydraulic shock absorber dampers
132 Lubricant lead
133 Starboard mainwheel

WEAL

Heinkel He 51B-1 Specification

Power Plant: One BMW VI 7,3Z 12-cylinder vee liquid-cooled engine rated at 750 hp at 1,700 rpm for take-off and possessing a normal max rating of 550 hp at 1,530 rpm. Fixed-pitch two-bladed wooden propeller of 10·17 ft (3,10 m) diameter. Internal fuel capacity of 46 Imp gal (210 l) and provision for one 37·4 Imp gal (170 l) drop tank.

Performance: Max speed, 205 mph (330 km/h) at sea level, 193 mph at 13,125 ft (4 000 m), 177 mph (285 km/h) at 19,685 ft (6 000 m); speed at 85% max continuous power, 174 mph (280 km/h) at sea level, 162 mph (260 km/h) at 13,125 ft (4 000 m), 137 mph (220 km/h) at 19,685 ft (6 000 m); range (at full throttle), 174 mls (280 km) at sea level, 267 mls (430 km) at 13,125 ft (4 000 m), 342 mls (550 km) at 19,685 ft (6 000 m), (at 85% max continuous power), 242 mls (390 km) at sea level, 354 mls (570 km) at 13,125 ft (4 000 m), 435 mls (700 km) at 19,685 ft (6 000 m); optimum range, 460 mls (740 km); time to 3,280 ft (1 000 m), 1·4 min to 6,560 ft (2 000 m), 3·1 min, to 13,125 ft (4 000 m), 7·8 min, to 19,685 ft (6 000 m), 16·5 min; ceiling, 25,260 ft (7 770 m); take-off distance, 110 yds (100 m); landing distance, 165 yards (150 m); landing speed, 59 mph (95 km/h).

Weights: Empty, 3,247 lb (1 473 kg); normal loaded, 4,189 lb (1 900 kg); wing loading, 14·34 lb/sq ft (70 kg/m²).

Dimensions: Span, 36 ft 1 in (11,00 m); length, 27 ft 6¾ in (8,40 m); height, 10 ft 6 in (3,20 m); wing area, 292·78 sq ft (27,20m²).

Armament: Two synchronised 7,9-mm MG 17 machine guns with 500 rpg.

uncommon to see one of the Heinkel biplanes traversing the field in spine-jarring leaps as a result of a poorly judged approach and touch-down. However, with stick held firmly back into the pit of the stomach I succeeded in restricting the incipient bounce and keeping the grass more or less firmly under my wheels while I mentally recovered from my first experience of a 93 mph (150 km/h) approach speed.

That the Heinkel had its eccentricities I knew, but at least it had been ladylike enough not to reveal these during our first acquaintance and having successfully accompanied this bird into the air and regained *terra firma* intact, my earlier trepidation was forgotten and I looked forward to further experience with the He 51 with pleasurable anticipation. We were now required to carry out a dozen so-called aimed landings each from an altitude of 2,300 ft (700 m) and each occupying no more than three-four minutes, and then two *Spitzenflüge,* or "ceiling flights", with a barograph, climbing to an altitude of 9,840 ft (3 000 m) and then gliding down in a total elapsed time of no more than 15 minutes.

By this time, I had established considerable rapport with the elderly Heinkel fighter and savoured every flight. It undoubtedly possessed its faults but, having had no opportunity

The He 51B-1 saw only brief first-line service with the Luftwaffe as a fighter, some being utilised as interim equipment for Stukagruppen before relegation to the Jagdfliegerschulen.

to fly other aeroplanes of comparable vintage, power and intended rôle, I was unable to assess its merits as compared with its contemporaries. One thing that I am sure was common to virtually all aircraft of similar configuration was the poor forward and downward visibility offered from its cockpit. This restriction in view was dramatically demonstrated in tragic fashion at an early stage in our training course. One of our group of trainees was far too high during a landing approach, two red flares being fired as a signal for him to go around again. He attempted to comply but because of the poor view forward and downward he failed to see a slower trainer that was still climbing just after taking off, and his propeller chewed through the cockpit of the other aircraft, killing its pilot.

The climax of our training programme with the He 51 was reached with two so-called high-altitude flights of 45 and 55 minutes duration respectively at an altitude of 11,800 ft (3 600 m), and it was customary to complete the second of these flights with a near-vertical dive to circuit flight altitude — a sort of *adieu* to the Heinkel biplane. This practice was officially frowned upon but *unofficially* permitted. At 1630 hours on 21 February 1943, I took-off for my final flight in the He 51 and, of course, my diving finale. Conditions were absolutely ideal with a perfectly cloudless sky — essential prerequisites for these graduation flights which had to be observed continuously from the ground — but after 30 minutes a bank of cloud moved in from the south-west and rapidly obscured the field.

The cloud was unbroken but for a funnel which, though it seemed to fluctuate in diameter, remained almost stationary over a nearly-circular lake some six miles (10 km) south of the airfield at Königsberg. By this time, I had completed the specified endurance flight and so I put down the nose of the He 51, aiming at the small blue-black lake framed by the cloud. Plummeting down that funnel in the cloud was an eerie and unforgettable experience; the surrounding vapour rendered everything unreal and distances deceptive, and although I believed the aircraft to be standing on its nose, I suddenly began to wonder if I might not have actually passed the vertical — I was told afterwards that the most difficult thing in diving is to avoid overestimating the dive angle which invariably feels much steeper than it actually is. What really got the adrenalin flowing, however, was the realisation that my altimeter was not unwinding as rapidly as it should have been and thus I would not know if I still had sufficient altitude to recover from the dive until I broke through the cloud level!

Less than half-a-minute elapsed between putting down the nose of my aircraft and screaming out of that cloud funnel, with, happily, sufficient altitude for a safe recovery. My only problem was a splitting headache as, in my excitement, I had forgotten to swallow to compensate for the change in pressure on my eardrums, and the dressing down that I received from my instructors on landing hardly served to alleviate the condition. From their angle on the ground they could not see the cloud funnel that had afforded me a reasonable safe descent and had been under the impression that I had committed the cardinal folly of putting my aircraft into a screamer through solid cloud.

Altogether, I had flown the He 51 a total of 26 times and although I was subsequently to fly a variety of aircraft types, ranging from maritime reconnaissance flying boats to Me 262 jet fighters on which I was being schooled at the war's end, few flights were more exciting or more memorable. I still have a self-portrait that I made with a camera that I secretly took along with me on one occasion when I was flying the Heinkel biplane. I held the camera at arm's length above that tiny windscreen and in the full force of the slipstream which very nearly whipped it from my grasp. Unfortunately, I had forgotten to wind on and my helmeted head is superimposed on an aerial view of the sun-shimmering River Oder that I had taken a moment or two before. That now-faded double-exposure brings back vividly my attempt to hold the camera steady against the slipstream while gripping the control column with my knees so that the barograph would reveal no sudden change of altitude; it also recalls the affection that I felt for that ageing Heinkel fighter which, by rights, should have long been consigned to some technological scrapheap. □

The He 51Bs that served with the Jagdfliegerschulen during the war years had, like that illustrated below, the tailskid replaced by a tailwheel. This aged fighter served throughout WW II in the training-rôle.

SPAD STORY

A comprehensive account, by J M Bruce, of the Spad 13 and its relatives

ONE OF THE earliest scandals to rock the aviation world centred upon the French industrialist Armand Deperdussin, a silk importer and boat manufacturer whose personal interests lay in aviation. In the years preceding the war of 1914-18, the Deperdussin was one of the great *marques,* a line of many sturdy monoplanes culminating in the magnificent racing monoplanes of 1913. These were distinguished by exceptionally clean lines: each had a superb monocoque fuselage designed by Louis Béchereau, with a large spinner of excellent form and a well cambered engine cowling that, together, made the installation of the 160 hp Gnome rotary engine remarkably clean. Speeds were phenomenal: in the 1913 Gordon Bennett trophy the Deperdussin flown by Maurice Prévost attained a speed of 200,5 km/h (125·3 mph).

But in 1913, when the monoplanes built by his *Société provisoire des Aéroplanes Deperdussin** were at the acme of their fame and success, Armand Deperdussin was accused of embezzling 28 million francs and arrested; he was imprisoned on 5 August 1913. Judgement on Deperdussin was not given until 30 March 1917, when he was found guilty and sentenced to five years penal servitude. Given the benefit of France's First Offenders Act, he was immediately released, but he did not re-enter aviation. His company, however, did not collapse completely with his arrest; a brave display of three handsome monoplanes formed a striking part of the Paris Aero Salon that opened on 5 December 1913. One of these aircraft had been flown by Prévost to win the Gordon Bennett race on 29 September 1913.

According to one contemporary report, it was thought that the Deperdussin business would be kept going by the engineering firm of Delaunay-Belleville, but an official receiver (M Raynaud) was appointed and he subsequently acted for Armand Deperdussin in applying for patents on armament installations in tractor aircraft. These included the notable *Brevet* No. 475.151, applied for on 22 January 1914, in which Deperdussin sought to patent the idea of installing a machine gun to fire forward through the airscrew disc of a tractor

aeroplane. He did not detail the mechanism that was to accomplish this, but in any case he was not the first to conceive this idea and his patent, although frequently cited as an example of advanced thinking, has little historical significance.

In August 1914 a group of industrialists headed by Louis Blériot set up a new company that acquired the assets of the former Deperdussin concern. According to legend its title, *La Société anonyme pour l'Aviation et ses Dérivés,* was designed to retain the initials S.P.A.D., though why this should have been regarded as of such apparent importance has never been made clear. Perhaps the most important asset acquired by the new S.P.A.D. concern was the design talent of Louis Béchereau. By then, of course, France was at war, and Béchereau was obliged to design military aircraft, a task for which his long experience of high-performance aircraft made him remarkably well equipped.

News of the company's change of name seems not to have penetrated immediately to England. At that period, the English weekly aeronautical journal *Flight* incorporated an entertaining (and often remarkably informative) gossip column entitled "Eddies", presided over by *Aeolus,* and in the issue dated 7 May 1915 the following cryptic note appeared: ' . . . and the Deperdussin *(sic)* works are hard at it with a highly original biplane, details of which, however, for the moment must be veiled'.

Anyone who could have had privileged access to the confidential files of the *Office national de la Propriété industrielle* might have been able to forecast the appearance of the new Spad* aeroplane from the specification of Patent No. 498.338, applied for on 27 February 1915. As Béchereau's erstwhile master had not actually invented the means of firing a machine gun through a rotating airscrew, the designer was obliged to find other means of providing armament on a tractor aircraft, and the patent drawings depict a tractor biplane on which the airscrew rotated in line with the leading edges of the wings to permit the attachment, ahead of the airscrew, of a frontal nacelle housing an observer. The original

---

**According to French convention this title could be abbreviated as S.P.A.D., but if this was done at that time the abbreviation found no general use; the monoplanes were universally known as Deperdussins.*

**Although the name of the company was usually rendered as S.P.A.D. its aircraft were, in French and other contemporary documents, sensibly named Spad. To present an aircraft designation as, eg, S.P.A.D. (or SPAD) 7.C 1 is a needless latter-day affectation.*

patent showed the nacelle as being stayed to the leading edges of upper and lower wings, but it was soon realised that this would make access to the engine and airscrew difficult. The installation was therefore redesigned, and *Addition* No. 22.088 to Patent No. 498.338 was applied for on 7 June 1915. This provided for the frontal nacelle to be hinged to the forward undercarriage legs and attached to the forward end of the airscrew shaft by a special fitting incorporating double ball bearings.

Another S.P.A.D. patent of greater significance was applied for on 4 June 1915. This was No. 488.191, which described a system of interplane bracing for biplanes. The essence of the invention was the provision of two-part articulated auxiliary struts at the intersection points of the landing and flying wires in a bracing bay. It was claimed that this could reduce the number of true interplane struts required, allowed greater ease of adjusting the bracing wires and reduced the vibration (and therefore the drag) of the wires. In effect, it allowed a biplane of relatively long span to be braced as a single-bay structure.

The first Spad biplane appeared in May 1915 and embodied both patents. It was a compact little single-bay biplane with intermediate auxiliary struts; its power unit was an 80 hp Le Rhône rotary engine installed in line with the front spars of the mainplanes, and a small nacelle for the observer was mounted in front of the airscrew. A characteristic method of actuating the ailerons was employed. Rods were used throughout; spanwise elements linked to the pilot's control column ran along behind the rear spars of the lower wings and were pivoted to one arm of an externally mounted bell crank. To the horizontal arm of the bell crank was attached a vertical rod that linked with the actuating levers mounted on the upper and lower ailerons. The tail surfaces were of distinctive shape and set a pattern for subsequent Spad designs.

This biplane was designated Spad A-1 and apparently made its first successful flight on 21 May 1915. The type was put into production and several variants were built. Surviving records are sketchy and contradictory, but it seems that the most numerous sub-type was the Spad A-2, of which 42 were supplied to the French *Aviation militaire* and 57 to the Imperial Russian Air Service. The Spad A-3 was reported to have dual control and machine-guns fore and aft, but remains cloaked in obscurity. Of the Spad A-4, which had the 110 hp Le Rhône engine, eleven were built; one was delivered to the French *Aviation militaire* and ten to the Imperial Russian Air Service.

Some details of the Spad design were communicated to RFC Headquarters in a report dated 2 August 1915, written by an anonymous officer who had seen a dismantled example. This contained the significant observation "It would be expensive in observers if piloted by indifferent pilots"; yet went on to suggest that the aircraft should be tested when re-assembled. There is no record that the RFC ever tested any Spad A sub-type, however.

In the spring of 1916 a Royal Flying Corps general report on current French aircraft described a single-seat development of the Spad in which the frontal nacelle was used as a housing for a heavy Hotchkiss *mitrailleuse d'infanterie* with a belt of 1,000 rounds. A speed of 100 mph (160 km/h) at 6,600 ft (2 000 m) was quoted, that altitude being attained in 7 minutes 15 seconds. This must have been the Spad Type G, Béchereau's first attempt at a single-seat fighter. Not surprisingly, it seems to have failed to find favour. Indeed, the front-nacelle Spads saw very limited service with French units and on 1 February 1916 there were only four at the front plus a further five with (presumably) training units.

(Above) The Spad A-1 prototype, displaying characteristic profiles of fuselage and tail unit, distinctive interplane bracing and rod-and-crank aileron controls.

(Above right) Production Spad A-2, S.19, in operational use. The engine installation has been improved and the design of tailplane and elevators revised. (Below and heading picture p 237) Spad 12 S.459 with the final form of mainplanes, having blunt tips. The slight stagger that distinguished the Spad 12 is clearly shown.

our trail in the sky

The G222 is today the
only medium range military transport
aircraft available on the market today.
Wide operational capabilities
and high reliability even in critical
flight conditions are guaranteed by the
advanced G.E. T64 P4D turbo-engines.
The most sophisticated avionics systems
and airborne instrumentation enable the aircraft
to operate in all weather conditions independently
of ground assistance. The G222 is certified
for operation with a crew of two and
can take-off and land on grass strips.
Its large volumetric capacity allows it to carry a wide range
of loads (up to 20,000 lbs.) or 44 fully equipped soldiers
and to parachute 32 paratroopers or to
air drop heavy loads up to 11,000 lbs.
The G222 can be rapidly converted to fulfil
rescue missions, aeromedical transport,
aerophotogrammetry, fire fighting and radio calibration.
And all the above at a very low operational cost.

AERITALIA

DIREZIONE GENERALE
80125 NAPOLI
PIAZZALE V. TECCHIO 51
TEL. 619.522 TELEX 71370

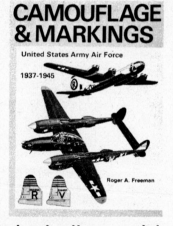

(Above) A typical Spad 7 C 1, S.3281, in the markings of Escadrille *Spa.99. (Below left) A close look at the engine installation and the observer's perilous perch on a Spad A-2.*

The early Béchereau Spad designs were given letter-form designations in alphabetical order. Two, the Types I and J, were to have been single-seat tractor fighters, respectively a biplane and monoplane, armed with a fixed, synchronized, forward-firing gun. Neither was completed, however, because the rotary engine for which they were designed, unnamed but of high performance, was never delivered. A truly great aero-engine was by then in existence, however, and its availability was to enable Béchereau to design his masterpiece. The historic power unit in question was an eight-cylinder water-cooled V-8 designed by Marc Birkigt, a Swiss engineer who, in 1904, had opened a factory in Barcelona to manufacture motor-cars, the bi-national nature of the company being directly reflected in its title, the *Sociedad Hispano-Suiza.*

Birkigt started work on the design of the new aero-engine in November 1914, and test running of the prototype began at the Barcelona works in February 1915. The new Hispano-Suiza was innovatory in several ways and marked a great step forward in aero-engine design. It pioneered monobloc cylinder construction, its two blocks each of four cylinders being cast in aluminium alloy; into these blocks were screwed steel cylinder liners that were threaded over their entire length, thus providing full-length contact between liner and block and improving cooling. All gas and water passages were formed as integral parts of the monobloc castings; this eliminated external water pipes, made the engine lighter and permitted the use of a lighter crankcase. Overhead camshafts were employed; their housings were a distinctive external feature of the engine and their design was that evolved by Birkigt in 1914.

Performance of the engine was highly promising, for it delivered 140 hp at 1,400 rpm for a weight of only 330 lb (150 kg). Birkigt had set up a French subsidiary company, the *Société Hispano-Suiza,* in April 1911; the French factory began life with a brief occupancy of a disused tramway depot at Levallois-Perret, but soon moved to Bois-Colombes. News of the new Hispano-Suiza aero-engine soon reached the French authorities, and a two-man mission, in the persons of *Commandant* Grard and *Capitaine* Martinot-Lagarde, was sent to Barcelona in May 1915 to examine and report on the engine. As a result the French government ordered two examples which were thoroughly tested at Chalais-Meudon. Testing began on 21 July 1915 and proved completely satisfactory; 50 engines were then ordered from the parent company, and later 1,600 were ordered from other French engineering companies.

In August 1915 a British order for 50 Hispano-Suizas was placed and by early November 1915 the employment proposed for these superb engines was to install them in B.E.2c's. In fact, the first British installation of a Hispano-Suiza was made in a B.E.2c at St Omer early in March 1916.

The French authorities had more practical ideas on the use to which this light, compact and powerful engine could be put, as indicated in this passage from *La Victoire des Cocardes* by Albert Étévé:

"The Swiss engineer Birkigt had established a factory at

Courbevoie, where he was producing the light aero-engine that had become known as the Hispano-Suiza. General Headquarters requested that this 150 hp engine should be used to power fighter aircraft. Louis Béchereau undertook the design of such an aircraft. In 1915 there could be seen in the S.P.A.D. works a fuselage in which a mock-up of a Hispano engine had been mounted, and all the aces came to see it."

The new Hispano-powered Spad was given the designation, still in the company's alphabetical series, of Type V. The prototype appeared in April 1916, in appearance being clean, compact and purposeful; structurally it was one of the strongest aircraft in the Allied armoury. In its airframe the new Spad incorporated many physical and detail resemblances to the A-2 and A-4, but was a wholly conventional tractor biplane. As on the earlier nacelle biplanes, the mainplanes were braced as a single-bay structure but had the articulated intermediate struts that gave the bracing a two-bay appearance. The rod-and-crank method of actuating the ailerons was employed and the tail surfaces resembled those of the Spad A-1 prototype.

In the mainplanes the main spars were set close together, their proximity virtually dictated by the unusually thin aerofoil section that was used. They were carefully designed to provide maximum strength: at the attachment points of the interplane and intermediate struts the spars were of appreciably thicker cross section than over the remainder of their length. In the upper wing a third spar was provided to carry the ailerons, which were fitted to that wing only; the upper wing was mounted close to the fuselage. The fuselage structure was conventional and much of its strength lay in the sturdy channel member of fretted plywood that served as the engine bearers at its forward end. The Hispano-Suiza engine was encased in metal cowlings and when the prototype first appeared its airscrew had a large spinner with frontal opening to admit cooling air. To ensure clean blending of the spinner with the lines of the fuselage, a circular radiator installation embodying an octagonal radiator in an annular cowling was fitted. Although the Spad quickly discarded its spinner, it retained its characteristic circular radiator cowling and this remained a distinctive feature of production aircraft and subsequent developments. Indeed, in all essential geometry, structure and proportions the first Spad wrote the signature of a whole series of great fighting aircraft.

The new Spad prototype was flying in April 1916, and in the course of one flight during its maker's trials it was timed at a speed reported as 213 km/h (133 mph) over a measured distance of 1 km. Wind speed and direction were not quoted, however, and a note in an RFC file dated 19 April 1916 said of the Spad, more realistically,* that: "It is stated to climb 3 000 m (9,840 ft) in 9 minutes and to go a speed of 170 km/h (105·4 mph)".

Britain's Royal Flying Corps knew about the Spad before it underwent its official trials and was acutely interested in it. The officers of the British Aeronautical Supply Depot (BASD) in Paris and at RFC Headquarters maintained an interest in aviation developments that was far more lively, intelligent and resourceful than certain self-appointed, clamorous but chairborne critics in England would ever have acknowledged. Thanks to their persistence and persuasiveness the RFC received its first Spad within days of the delivery of the first production aircraft to the French *Escadrille* N.3, a remarkable achievement when viewed against the circumstances of the time. An RFC report dated 29 April 1916 stated that the prototype was then doing its official trials. These were conducted at Villacoublay and apparently continued into May. The results recorded were so impressive that the French authorities placed an immediate order for 268 aircraft with the S.P.A.D.

*Test results that subsequently became available gave a speed of 178 km/h (111 mph) at 10,000 ft (presumably derived from 3 000 m).

The production aircraft were designated Spa.7.C 1* officially, the suffix 'C 1' indicating that the aircraft was a single-seat fighter *(monoplace de chasse)*. It is not known whether this designation came wholly from the *Service des Fabrications de l'Aviation* (SFA) and its derivation is obscure. These aircraft were armed with a single Vickers gun synchronized by a simple but effective mechanism designed by Marc Birkigt; this was driven from the starboard camshaft of the Hispano-Suiza engine. Structurally the production Spad 7 resembled the prototype, but may have had the number of ribs in the mainplanes greatly increased. The type became widely subcontracted and came to be used by the RFC and by the Belgian, Italian, Russian and American flying services. It was also built in Britain and Russia and saw extensive service on several fronts. Its history is a major component of the full history of the aerial warfare of 1914-18 and deserves full treatment by itself. This narrative, however, is primarily concerned with the Spad 13.C 1, and it is to the history of that type that this story must now move forward.

It did not take very long for the Spad 7 to be overtaken by the opposition. The Spads in general had undistinguished climbing performance, especially the Spad 7 in its original form with the basic 150 hp Hispano-Suiza 8Aa. By December 1916 Georges Guynemer, France's immortal leading ace, told Louis Béchereau: "The 150 hp Spad is not a match for the Halberstadt. Although the Halberstadt is probably no faster it climbs better, consequently it has the overall advantage. More speed is needed: possibly the airscrew might be improved."

A worthwhile improvement was effected by replacing the 150 hp engine with the 180 hp Hispano-Suiza 8Ab. This was substantially the basic direct-drive engine with the compression ratio increased from 4·7 to 5·3 and different carburettors. Clearly, however, Béchereau could not rely on this modest increase in power to keep the Spad 7 ahead of its German counterparts; moreover, its single gun was inadequate against the twin-gun German fighters that had entered service almost contemporaneously with the Spad itself. Fortunately, Marc Birkigt was developing the Hispano-Suiza engine. The existence of a geared engine rated at 200 hp was known at RFC Headquarters as early as 7 May 1916. On 17 May a British official document recorded that the 200 hp engine had not yet undergone official (French) trials at that time but was expected to do so at the end of that week. However, a subsequent report noted that these trials were expected to start on 3 June or

---

This is the precise rendering of the designation as it appears in the official French Liste d'Appellations des Avions, *prepared by the* Section Technique de l'Aéronautique militaire, Ministère de la Guerre, *and dated 15 October 1917. The use of Roman numerals in the designations of many French aircraft types became quite common, even in French publications, but it seems that this undesirable practice lacked official acceptance. It will therefore be avoided in this article, and clarity will be better served thereby.*

Georges Guynemer's Spad 12 Ca 1 at St Pol, summer 1917. This aircraft had the original form of wings with well rounded tips.

In this photograph of the Spad 12 S.440 the plywood 'pocket' extensions on the wing tips can be seen clearly. As noted in the text, these primitive modifications were made to both Spads 12 and 13.

shortly thereafter. By 11 June the engine had just completed its official 50-hour run, and the Hispano-Suiza company had made three of the new geared engines by 30 June 1916. Even at that early date the BASD in Paris was making strenuous efforts to secure an example for the RFC: at home in England the Bailhache enquiry into the administration and command of the RFC had just had some four days of its deliberations monopolized by the egregious Noel Pemberton Billing, whose preposterous charges in the House of Commons had led to the setting up of that major enquiry almost on the eve of the Battle of the Somme.

The new Hispano-Suiza engine had the same bore and stroke (120 × 130 mm) as the original 150 hp 8Aa; it also had the same compression ratio of 4·7. The major difference lay in the spur reduction gear and the higher normal rpm (2,000) at which the engine ran; as time went on various gear ratios were employed, but it seems that the original ratio was 24:41, with the airscrew shaft normally running at 1,170 rpm. Later French-made engines had gear ratios of 21:28 and 26:39; the Wolseley-made engines (named Wolseley Adder) mostly had ratios of 35:59 but a few had 28:37. The basic designation of the new engine was Hispano-Suiza 8B; subsequent detail refinements and modifications were reflected in differing sub-type designations.

By dint of much persuasive perseverance the British Aeronautical Supply Depot, largely in the person of Captain Lord Robert Innes-Ker, managed to secure a number of Spad 7s for the RFC. Initial deliveries were from the parent company, but French demands for the aircraft were so substantial and of such priority that the French authorities advised the BASD to place its orders for Spads with a sub-contractor. For this purpose the RFC was recommended in September 1916 to try the *Ateliers d'Aviation L Janoir* of Saint-Ouen. Apparently nothing came of this, but an RFC contract for 60* Spads was eventually given to the *Avionnerie Kellner et ses Fils,* 185 route de Versailles, Billancourt, a firm that had not previously built aircraft.

Late in March 1917, before Kellners had delivered their first Spad to the RFC, Brigadier General Brooke-Popham had asked the officers of the BASD to investigate the possibility of having the firm substitute the 200 hp Hispano-Suiza from the 26th production aircraft onwards. Not surprisingly, Kellners demurred, for they had already made major components for most of the Spads and the 200 hp engine required different fittings.

Brigadier General Brooke-Popham's request may have been inspired by the report forwarded to RFC Headquarters on 20 February 1917 by Major F N Scholte of the British Aviation Commission: "For your information, it is notified that Messrs Spad have now on order for the French Government twenty 200 hp (with geared-down propeller) Hispano-Suiza single-seater Spads which are to be fitted with two Vickers guns, mounted upon the cowling and firing through the propeller to the right and left, respectively, of its axis. The interrupter mechanism is the same as on the single-gun Spad, the right-hand gun being served by the camshaft of the right-hand block of cylinders and vice-versa. Separate disintegrating belts are fed to the breech of each gun from a common box. Two Bowden operated triggers upon the "cloche" permit firing of either or both guns at will." In a subsequent follow-up report dated 13 March 1917, Major Scholte gave a brief description of the fuselage and armament of the 200 hp twin-gun Spad, and concluded: "The first machine is now ready and awaiting favourable weather for trials. A considerable further number are almost completed at the works." But this is to anticipate our history somewhat. The aircraft to which Major Scholte referred was the new Spad 13.C 1, but it was not the first new 200 hp Spad to have been designed by Béchereau.

A cannon-armed Spad

Guynemer's concern over the mediocre performance of the original 150 hp Spad 7.C 1 has already been mentioned above. Late in 1916 he asked Béchereau to build him a fighter capable of carrying a 37-mm Hotchkiss shell-firing gun; presumably he also specified a performance better than that of the Spad 7. In doing this Guynemer was following the same line of thought that had inspired Charles Nungesser to ask Armand Dufaux, a Swiss aviation pioneer then working in France, to build him a fighter with a 37-mm gun. For Nungesser, Dufaux designed the ingenious aircraft with transversely mounted twin 110 hp Le Rhône engines that was the subject of his French patent No. 503.114, for which he applied on 27 November 1916*. It is not known whether Guynemer was merely following Nungesser's example or had hit on the same idea independently. What is certain is that the combined talents of Birkigt and Béchereau led to the creation of a new single-seater of enormous potential. There was nothing new in the idea of installing a gun to fire through a suitably disposed hollow airscrew shaft: the earliest known proposal was that of Dufaux's compatriot Franz Schneider, put forward in August 1911 and developed into a practical arrangement by January 1912. A later French patent covering the concept of mounting a gun to fire through a hollow crankshaft and airscrew shaft was applied for by Marcel Echard on 10 January 1916 (Patent No. 502.830).

The configuration of the 200 hp Hispano-Suiza engine, with its spur reduction gear, lent itself well to the fitting of a gun between the cylinder blocks with its muzzle in line with the elevated airscrew shaft. This is precisely what Birkigt did, and the engine designated Hispano-Suiza 8C had a 37-mm Hotchkiss gun fitted in this way. The gun barrel had to be shortened to produce an installation of acceptable length. For this engine Béchereau designed a new single-seat biplane that was very similar in appearance to the Spad 7, and the existence of the cannon-armed fighter design was recorded in an official document dated 10 December 1916. The document concerned made no mention of any other 200 hp Spad single-seater at that date. The overall dimensions of the new type were slightly larger than those of the earlier single-seater, its wing area was proportionately greater and it was significantly heavier. The engine cowling was so shaped that it enclosed the engine without recourse to the characteristic fairings over the camshaft housings that had appeared on the Spad 7; and the high thrust line of the geared engine made the exhaust

---

*The RFC's total order on the Kellner company as at 1 August 1917 was for 150 Spads, of which 30 were to be taken as spare parts, 60 were to be Spad 7s and 60 Spad 13s.

*See the author's book, Warplanes of the First World War, *Vol IV, pp.98-100, (Macdonald, 1972), for a description of the Dufaux* avion-canon.

manifolds emerge relatively low down on the flanks. A single Vickers gun was mounted in a trough on top of the fuselage, offset to starboard. The mainplanes had slight stagger and originally had well rounded tips. In the tail unit the shapes of all surfaces resembled those of their counterparts on the Spad 7, but the rudder had a slightly curved trailing edge. The complete aircraft had a kind of elegance not quite attained by any other Spad.

The new cannon-armed fighter was officially designated Spa.12.Ca 1 and was ordered in quantity for the *Aviation militaire*. It seems that 300 were ordered but it is doubtful whether all were completed; certainly only a handful saw operational use and the type never formed the equipment of any operational unit. Guynemer had his Spad 12 by July 1917 and soon named it his *avion magique*; with it he is reported to have won his 49th, 50th, 51st and 52nd victories. René Fonck (75 victories) flew the Spad 12 *S.445* during his operational career and won eleven of his combat victories on it. Another leading French fighting pilot who flew the Spad 12 was Albert Deullin (20 victories) and the type was also flown by *Sergents* Fernand Chavannes and Lionel de Marmier of *Escadrille Spa.112*.

Despite the alleged total order of 300 Spad 12s the type was never numerous. On 1 August 1917 only one was on the strength of the *Aviation militaire,* apparently with an operational *escadrille*. This must almost certainly have been Guynemer's aircraft. The total of operational Spad 12s on 1 April 1918 was only five, and on 1 October it had risen to eight; but to the end it was regarded as a standard type of fighter and it underwent progressive modifications, presumably in step with the contemporary Spad 13. When the high-compression version of the geared engine, the 220 hp Hispano-Suiza 8Bc, was developed, the *moteur-canon* version was similarly modified to deliver the same power. As will be related in the history of the Spad 13, an extraordinarily makeshift addition to the wing tips was at one time introduced; this was also

applied to some of the Spad 12s and even when a new design of upper wing with blunt tips was introduced the wing-tip 'pocket' additions were still used on the lower wings. Finally, new lower wings with blunt tips similar to those of the upper wings were fitted.

Like the Spad 13, S.E.5a and Sopwith Dolphin, the Spad 12 suffered from the assorted malaises that plagued the geared Hispano-Suiza. These ailments will be discussed in the history of the Spad 13, but a particularly serious drawback on the Spad 12 was the engine's vibration, which inevitably affected the accuracy of the shell-gun. Apart from this, however, pilots found the single-shot gun a considerable handful in combat; the technique of using the Vickers as a sighting device and firing the *canon* at precisely the critical instant called for superhuman piloting skill and marksmanship, and reloading demanded equal coolness and dexterity while engaged in combat. In addition to all this the gun had a heavy recoil; its shortened barrel reduced muzzle velocity and impaired accuracy and its fumes discharged into the cockpit. Small wonder that most pilots preferred the twin Vickers guns of the Spad 13.

It is a little-known fact that a Spad 12 was delivered to the RFC. This was *S.449* (engine No 9523) which had been allocated for the RFC early in January 1918 and was reported to be at Buc being tested and tuned up on 5 January. Carburettor troubles delayed delivery until 9 March, when it was flown from Buc to No 2 Aircraft Depot at Candas by *Adjudant* de Courcelles. It was allotted the British serial number B6877. Its presence at No 2 AD caused some local mystification, but it was apparently seen by Major-General Trenchard on 12 March and on the following day a telegram from the Air Ministry commanded that the Spad 12 should be flown to Martlesham Heath as soon as possible. On 18 March it was flown to England by Flight Sergeant Piercey and apparently went to Martlesham Heath, where it was not highly thought of. Thence it was sent to the Isle of Grain, presumably for practical testing of the 37-mm gun; but it crashed on 4 April while on its way there. Thereafter the record is mute, and it seems that the RAF made no subsequent attempt to repair or replace B6877.

In view of the US Air Service's heavy commitment to the Spad 13 it is not surprising that that service was also interested in the Spad 12. One example was acquired by the USAS in July 1918 and was issued to the 13th Aero Squadron, commanded by Major C J Biddle. According to Biddle the aircraft was originally intended to go to the 139th Aero Squadron to be flown by Lieutenant D E Putnam but was re-allocated after Putnam's death on 14 September 1918. In the 13th Aero Squadron, Biddle himself flew the Spad, which was marked as the Commanding Officer's aircraft.

(To be concluded next month)

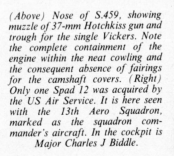

(Above) Nose of S.459, showing muzzle of 37-mm Hotchkiss gun and trough for the single Vickers. Note the complete containment of the engine within the neat cowling and the consequent absence of fairings for the camshaft covers. (Right) Only one Spad 12 was acquired by the US Air Service. It is here seen with the 13th Aero Squadron, marked as the squadron commander's aircraft. In the cockpit is Major Charles J Biddle.

Is it goodbye to Ground Attack?

PERSONAL VIEW

ROY M BRAYBROOK

HEADING north out of Beirut, the road takes you along the Lebanon's beautiful coastline to the ancient town of Byblos, where the ruins date back far beyond biblical times. One day in 1973, Israeli F-4s came in low off the sea, flying eastwards. As they swept over this oldest port in the world they made a truly impressive spectacle. Bombs on the racks. Gas levers into the firewall. Trails of black smoke. Noise like the end of the world. Almost as impressive as the SAMs which destroyed one F-4 after the other, as they reached the Syrian border a few moments later, pulling up to search for targets.

In the first three days of the Yom Kippur War, very heavy losses were undoubtedly sustained by the Israeli air arm (*Heyl Ha'Avir*), which, in 1967, had been a leading exponent of ground attack, immobilising Arab air forces on their airfields and knocking out countless Egyptian tanks in the Sinai desert. Despite Israeli claims to have destroyed the SAM belts by the end of the 1973 hostilities, and recent assertions that they will soon have a weapon giving a high kill probability against SAM sites, the credibility of all ground attack aircraft was seriously damaged in that war and is still being questioned today.

Accepting that the full details of the 18-day conflict have never been made public and that in some respects (eg, weather and terrain) the action was not representative of other important scenarios, further analysis of the ground attack lessons of 1973 may still prove instructive. In particular, there are good reasons to discuss in the light of that war how viable ground attack is today and whether there is any point in designing a specialist ground attack aircraft for the future.

Numbers game

Before going into the qualitative lessons, one must first ask what loss rate the Israelis actually suffered in ground attack aircraft. The total number of aircraft lost was reportedly 103, but this included all types and all causes. It was said initially that approximately 80 per cent were lost to SAMs and flak, 10 per cent in accidents and the remainder in air combat. The Israeli's CAS (General Peled) has since stated that the average loss rate was 1·1 per cent (ie, just over one aircraft destroyed per hundred sorties) which, he pointed out, compared

favourably with the 1·4 per cent attrition of 1967, when his service achieved its most spectacular successes.

These overall statistics are interesting, but hardly illuminating. What is slightly more helpful is the CAS's statement that, in October 1973, only five aircraft were lost in 4,000 air superiority sorties, compared with 10 aircraft lost in 637 such sorties in the previous war. By inference, in 1973 some 98 aircraft were lost in rather more than 5,000 other sorties (mainly ground attack), giving an average attrition rate of 1·8 per cent. Comparing this to the 1967 loss rate of 4·0 per cent in the pre-emptive strike, it seems to be in the right ballpark: nasty, but not suicidal.

Overall loss rate in ground attack missions was therefore probably quite acceptable. However, eyewitness accounts of the first weekend's action suggest that attrition due to SAMs and flak at that stage bore no resemblance to the 18-day average. The Israelis had issued mobilisation orders only four hours before hostilities began. In the north, 150 Israeli tanks faced an attack by 2,100 Syrian tanks, while in the south the Egyptians were putting nine divisions across the Suez Canal, with a total of 2,640 tanks. The Israeli Air Force's priority task was to stop the Syrian tanks, and their aircraft had to go in without SAM/flak suppression.

Some indication of the initial ground attack attrition may be gained if Israeli losses are broken down into aircraft types. When the balloon went up on Saturday, 6 October, the service had a total strength in the region of 500 aircraft (accounts range from 488 to 550). Of these, the modern ground attack component took the form of approximately 300 McDonnell Douglas A-4s and F-4s. By Israeli admission, 33 F-4s and 53 A-4s were lost overall, and Moshe Dayan (then Defence Minister) has stated that 50 aircraft were lost in the first three days, presumably in ground attack missions. What emerges from these clues is a picture of an air force losing almost 20 per cent of its attack strength right at the outset of a war of indefinite length. Moreover, if allowance is made for aircraft damaged too badly to return to action for several days (and it was a characteristic of the SA-7 *Grail's* 3·9-lb (1,8-kg) warhead, that it damaged many more aircraft than it

destroyed), then the Israelis may well have lost the use of *30 or even 40 per cent* of their ground attack aircraft by the end of the third day!

Heavy initial losses were thus quite consistent with official statements from the Israelis. In the circumstances it is hardly surprising that they hit the panic button and screamed for help from Washington. However, before anyone reads too much into these figures, it must be emphasised that in the early missions the Israeli air arm got everything wrong. It went into action against a modern defensive system that it had completely underestimated, without first knocking out its surveillance radars or suppressing the defences, then attempted to make dive bomb attacks! However, the other side was far from perfect. Syrian SAMs are reported to have shot down 20 "friendly" aircraft in a single day, including several Jordanian Hunters relying on British IFF!

In trying to read across from the last Middle East War to a European war, it may be more meaningful to estimate that the overall (18-day) Israeli ground attack attrition of about two per cent should only have been doubled in the early missions, when Arab defences were still in good shape. The question is then whether a loss rate of around four per cent is acceptable, and whether this order of attrition is likely to increase or decrease in the future.

What loss rate is "acceptable" clearly depends on many factors. An attrition rate used in long-term planning bears no relation to what might be endured in a real war situation. In the last eight months of the war in Europe, all German fighters except the Me 262 are reckoned to have had the astronomical loss rate of over 30 per cent, whereas in planning a new fighter generation one tenth of that figure would be regarded as quite serious.

Looking for some sort of historical guidelines, RAF

(Above) The Fairchild A-10A, newest ground attack aircraft in the USAF armoury, carries a 30-mm GAU-8 rotary-barrel cannon designed specifically for the close air support rôle and to ensure a high probability of tank kill on a single strafing pass. (Below) The Hunting BL755 cluster-bomb, adopted by six NATO countries, provides "shot-gun" coverage of ground targets, each 600-lb (272-kg) bomb ejecting over 100 "bomblets". This McDonnell Douglas Phantom FGR Mk 2 of No 41 Squadron, RAF, is carrying seven BL755s in addition to four Sparrows and four Sidewinders.

A Fairchild A-10 demonstrates the lethality of its GAU-8 cannon in a practice attack on a captured Soviet T-62 battle tank. Using a mix of armour-piercing and high-explosive incendiary ammunition, the A-10 hits the T-62 and sets fire to its internal ammunition store.

Bomber Command appears to have aimed for an attrition of no more than three per cent in night raids over Germany, which would have given crews a better-than-40 per cent chance of completing a tour of 30 missions. Although individual missions suffered far higher losses, the general conduct of the bombing campaign suggests that when monthly attrition approached 10 per cent, a change of tactics or equipment was regarded as essential. Taking an example from the USAAF side, toward the end of 1943 attrition of the B-17 Fortress had reached 9·1 per cent, but the introduction of the P-51 Mustang long range escort quickly brought this down to 3·5 per cent.

Historical guidelines

Looking at the effect of attrition on aircrew morale, it seems logical to argue that, since the sortie rate for fighters is much higher than for long-range bombers (perhaps by a factor of three), the critical loss rate for the fighter should be correspondingly lower. In the bitterly fought Battle of Britain, loss rates were 2·6 per cent for the Bf 109, 3·3 for the Bf 110, 4·4 for the Spitfire, and 5·7 for the Hurricane. Digressing slightly, the loss rate for German bombers was 8·6 per cent, which was unacceptably high, so they were switched to night attacks. The fighter data might be taken to suggest that as a general planning figure for a long term conflict the aim should be to keep attrition below one per cent, and that a rise to three per cent should trigger a change in tactics if not equipment. In short, the attrition criteria for a tactical fighter should possibly be only one-third as high as those for deep penetration aircraft, since the fighter pilot will be flying at three times (or more) the latter's sortie rate.

These suggested figures for a generally "acceptable" attrition are, of course, only a subjective interpretation of historical data. In reality there are many factors that influence an air force's assessment of what losses can be accepted: eg, how long the conflict is expected to proceed, at what rate aircraft and crews can be replaced and (above all) how "worthwhile" are the positive results obtained by continuing the missions.

Bearing such reservations in mind, the discussion so far might be summarised as follows:

(a) The Israelis should have suffered a loss rate of about four per cent in the initial ground attack sorties, but in reality

probably did worse. It should be remembered that for deep penetration the Israelis could fly around the border SAM belt and thus only met defences in the target area.

(b) For the one-sortie-per-day deep interdictor, a loss rate of three per cent is acceptable and nine per cent is about the limit.

(c) For the three-sorties-per-day close support aircraft, the generally acceptable loss rate may be only one per cent and the upper limit about three per cent.

So what? Well, the numbers support the assertion that if the Israelis had not changed their tactics, *Heyl Ha'Avir* might have been wiped out as a ground attack force before new equipment

One example of the growing use of electronic countermeasures equipment in Europe is provided by the fitting of Westinghouse ALQ-101 jamming pods to RAF Buccaneers.

and replacement aircraft arrived from the US. More importantly, the numbers imply that if a major war should break out in Europe today, then ground attack might be a very marginal exercise. Before discussing what can be done to achieve an acceptable loss rate tomorrow, it may be worthwhile to summarise the new technical considerations that are currently working against ground attack.

To say that the advent of SAMs has produced an unacceptable attrition rate in ground attack aircraft would be an oversimplification. In reality, various new means of active and passive defence have combined to increase the aircraft's loss rate, and simultaneously degrade its effectiveness. In the 1973 war the SA-2 *Guideline* and SA-3 *Goa,* which had appeared in Vietnam eight years earlier (destroying the first aircraft, an F-4, in July 1965), were complemented by the highly mobile SA-6 *Gainful* and the man-portable SA-7 *Grail,* plus radar-directed ZSU-23-4 quadruple 23-mm flak. Earlier defences were only designed for medium and high altitudes, giving the attacker a reasonable chance of intruding successfully at low level, or of staying high and jamming and manoeuvring. However, the new Soviet defence system covered the entire altitude spectrum. In addition, the later missile radars proved difficult to jam, while the weapons themselves probably had a much faster reaction time. Considering equivalent Western systems, the French Crotale has a reaction time of only six seconds, which clearly places minimal demands on radar detection range. In the less open terrain of Europe, conventional radar warning would be very short, but could be boosted by airborne early warning: ie, the Tu-126 *Moss* which was allegedly used as far back as the Indo-Pakistan conflict of 1971.

A good modern defence system leaves no loophole for the attacker, who must carefully weigh attrition against effectiveness. At present the tendency is for Americans to go all out for effectiveness and for Europeans to emphasise survivability. There is an analogy here to armed helicopter design philosophy: the Americans put the sighting system low, because it enables them to use heavy multiple sensors, but Europeans put the sight on the cabin roof, so they can fire missiles while hull-down.

As discussed in December's AIR INTERNATIONAL, the USAF attitude is that it is impossible to live with flak at low level (unless you stay so low that the target is invisible), hence the only viable approach is to go high and jam the enemy's radars. The European philosophy is that the effectiveness of ECM is unreliable and that some SAMs have reasonably good optical stand-by guidance systems. The only viable solution is, therefore, to deliver weapons from such a low level that warning time is marginal. One fundamental difference

between the systems is that, *if* the American concept works, the USAF can attack virtually any target (and conceivably even loiter to find one), whereas the European system is only viable against pre-planned targets, which require a minimal pop-up time. American sources claim that these low-level attacks with CBU will average only 0·3 per cent tank kills per sortie, against three for their own high attacks with Maverick or PGM (precision-guided munitions).

So much for the effect on attack tactics of modern active defences. Turning to passive defences, in 1973 the Arab air forces made widespread use of concrete shelters and aircraft dispersal, which (together with flak positioned to stop bombing runs along the runways) made Israeli attacks on their airfields a losing game. There have also been many reports of quick runway repair techniques, although the writer has yet to be convinced of their effectiveness or even the need for such repairs: it takes heavy and sustained bombing to prevent a modern fighter taking off from a standard NATO base. Runway bombing is more of a threat where the runways are short and narrow, and secondary runways even worse (eg, Switzerland).

While trends in active and passive defences are combining against ground attack aircraft, the leading armies are reducing their dependence on air forces for close support. Aside from the armed helicopter, which appears set for large-scale procurement (rightly or wrongly), various services are developing rockets for area bombardment and investigating the potential of the RPV in reconnaissance, target marking and weapon delivery (including laser-guided bombs). The US Army is meanwhile seeking to improve its supporting fire capability with long-range rocket-boosted shells, the Martin Marietta 155-mm CLGP (cannon-launched guided projectile), and LTV's TGSM (terminally-guided sub-missile), which homes on to tanks after release from the Lance battlefield support missile. The overall aim is not to replace the fixed-wing aircraft completely in the close support rôle, but rather to limit its application to situations in which there is no cheaper means of providing quick support in a critical area and to the delivery of special types of weapons.

Future developments

All the signs indicate that, provided the ground attack aircraft can survive the defences and deliver armament effectively, there will be a continuing demand for its services. However, it appears that this demand will be significantly reduced in regard to close support, and airfields may well be scrubbed from the list of interdiction targets.

For USAF aircraft to continue with their form of ground attack, it requires only improved radar sensing (ESM), eg, ALR-46 and -62, and ECM, such as the Northrop ALQ-135 internal countermeasures set, providing automatic jamming for the F-15. On the European side, ESM equipment is already in evidence on many RAF tactical fighters, while ECM equipment is instanced by the Westinghouse ALQ-101 jamming pod being fitted to Buccaneers. There is also a great deal of European development on flare and chaff dispensing.

However, the low level tactic really demands improved means to find the target and destroy it. Even with a modern weapon, such as the Hunting BL755 cluster bomb which can be released in a low level pass, the pilot still has to pull up from tree-top height, sight the target, turn his aircraft to overfly it and give his weapon aiming system a few seconds to compute the release point.

Aircraft weapon system development may be categorised as: (a) armament giving enhanced damage effect, (b) better accuracy of weapon delivery and (c) means to reduce the risk to the parent aircraft. In the first category come the later series of retarded bombs and cluster weapons, minelet dispensers and FAE (fuel air explosives). For scenarios with smaller airfields one promising development is the Matra Durandal runway-piercing bomb. There is an urgent need for a defence-suppression weapon and a dual-sensor anti-radar missile. Delivery accuracy is being enhanced by improved weapon release point computation, better display of aiming information and the use of guided weapons (including laser-homing bombs). It is vitally important to have a delivery accuracy that is not degraded in wartime: the F-105 Thunderchief was reported to have a bombing accuracy of 125 ft (38 m) in practice, but this changed to 575 ft (175 m) against heavily-defended targets in North Vietnam!

Ideally, the pilot should be able to sight an objective (such as a group of tanks) without pulling up and attack without overflying the target. In the limit, this would not only make the aircraft impossible to detect, but it would also take it outside the range of point defences. As a first step to improved target acquisition, RAF Harriers and Jaguars are now receiving the Ferranti LRMTS (Laser Ranger and Marked Target Seeker). It is conceivable that some day a pilot will be able to glimpse a target off to one side and track it with his helmet sight for a second, enabling a computer to establish the target's position, then (without climbing or turning) fire an inertially-guided missile at it. As a stepping-stone in that direction, a helmet sight may be used to direct a laser-designator pod with a TV lock-on facility, keeping the target illuminated as a weapon homes on it. This is essentially what is under development by Northrop as the LATAR (Laser Augmented Target Acquisition Recognition) system, which is currently flying in pod form on an F-5E Tiger II and will be tested on an F-4 Phantom in October. A night attack version is in prospect.

For certain targets, aircraft vulnerability may be reduced by the use of long-range stand-off missiles, just as the Egyptian Air Force used *Kelt* in anti-radar strikes. The turbojet-powered Harpoon already provides for long range attacks on ships and the projected SOM (Stand-Off Missile) with two J402 engines will presumably further extend range and provide for other targets. Also some way in the future, SIM (SAM Intercept Missile) will be used to protect tactical fighters, up to 16 being carried by the F-15 Eagle and 14 by the F-4 Phantom. Thought is also being given (especially in the US) to supersonic penetration and bomb delivery, which involves either internal weapons (F-111) or conformal carriage (F-4, F-15).

Summary
Before attempting to reach any conclusions from this hot-war discussion, it must be emphasised that in most regions of the world the defences are still limited to manually-directed automatic weapons. Ground attacks can generally be carried out by (say) time-expired MiG-17s, with negligible losses. The reason to use more modern aircraft is that they carry much bigger warloads over longer radii, from shorter fields.

Within the next few years, radar-directed light flak and SA-7 missiles may see much wider service, but the only impact of this will be to emphasise the need to stay low and keep the speed up. The Israelis found that the older models of A-4 Skyhawk could not be used against heavily defended targets, but that the better-powered versions had an acceptable loss rate when used correctly. If guided weapons such as Rapier, Crotale and Roland ever come into really general use, the ground attack aircraft will remain a viable proposition in most regions (especially in less open areas), although it will then need ESM, ECM, chaff, flares, etc.

Turning to the Central European scenario with WarPac forces on constant alert with the whole range of SAMs and flak, plus AEW, then the viability of ground attack aircraft is more in doubt. The USAF contribution seems likely to remain impossible to assess (unless war breaks out), since it depends very largely on the effectiveness of ECM. The European ground attack effort appears to avoid the chance of total disaster, but not all such aircraft currently have ESM and ECM equipment and it is debatable whether exposure time in the pop-up manoeuvre favours the aircraft or the ground defences. In the longer term the low level concept will only be viable if much more advanced air-surface weapons are developed to permit the aircraft to remain at tree-top height.

However, finding a means by which the ground attack aircraft may continue to function effectively (and with a low attrition) is a far cry from proving that the manned aircraft is more cost-effective than the RPV in attack and reconnaissance rôles. The writer's own feeling is that the RPV has received disproportionate attention due to the PoW problem in the Vietnam War. It may be significant that even now the USAF only has one RPV squadron, the 11th Tactical Drone Sqdn at Davis-Monthan AFB.

In the long term the use of manned aircraft in ground attack will doubtless continue (alongside the RPV) by virtue of the flexibility of rôle and other special capabilities that derive from having a Grade-A human being right where the action is. Reverting to intuition, it is conceivable that the manned aircraft will prove more attractive in night operations, when the SAM's fall-back guidance mode will hopefully be ineffective, and a two-man ship (possibly even a Hawk or Alpha Jet) can cruise around at rather more than tree-top height, jamming all the radars and zapping everything that moves. What else? I can't be sure, but my tailbone says to go back to designing real fighters and leave ground attack for the secondary rôle. □

The USAF expects to achieve a major increase in the effectiveness of its ECM force with the introduction of the EF-111A, subject to satisfactory completion of tests. An aerodynamic prototype of the EF-111A, without the fin-tip radome to be fitted eventually, recently entered flight test after conversion by Grumman Aerospace.

The close family relationship between the Italian-manufactured and South African-assembled AM-3C Bosbok (above) and the Atlas-built C4M Kudu (below) is apparent in these photographs. Both types are now serving with the SAAF's Light Aircraft Command.

SPRINGBOK———————————*from page 220*

of the border between Angola and South West Africa, and it is becoming increasingly obvious that substantial expansion of the SAAF's helicopter force is not only desirable but vitally necessary.

Apart from the handful of Westland Wasps operated by the South African Navy's No 22 Flight*, all the helicopters currently in the inventories of the South African armed forces are of French origin. In so far as the SAAF is concerned, about half of the 100 or so Alouette IIIs supplied to South Africa are on the strength of Nos 16 and 17 squadrons home-based at Bloemspruit Air Station with flights deployed as necessary, the latter squadron having a detached flight permanently assigned to Swartkop where 'A' Flight of No 19 Squadron is also based, this unit, which received 20 SA 330 Pumas, having its 'B' Flight based at Durban. Alouette IIIs are also operated by No 87 Advanced Flying School (formerly the Helicopter Conversion Unit) at Ysterplaat. The remaining SAAF helicopter unit is No 15 Squadron which has 15 SA 321L Super Frelon medium transport helicopters at Swartkop. In view of its escalating counter-insurgency commitment, the SAAF would like to have a modern LOH available in some numbers plus

The Wasps of No 22 (Naval) Flight operate from South African Navy frigates. Having lost half of its original complement of 10 Wasps, the South African Navy succeeded in placing a follow-up contract in the UK for seven more of which six had been delivered before the British Labour Government vetoed the order, the seventh Wasp remaining in storage in the UK.

armed helicopters, although it sees no immediate requirement for a helicopter possessing anti-armour capability. Interest has been displayed in the SA 341 Gazelle and the SA 360 Dauphin and there is a likelihood that helicopter procurement will be extended to Agusta in Italy shortly, although Atlas has long-term plans for initiating licence manufacture of helicopters and at one time it was anticipated that a manufacturing licence would be acquired for the SA 319 Alouette III.

The backbone of the SAAF's counter-insurgency force remains, of course, the Active Citizen Force squadrons which have now largely replaced their Harvard IIAs, IIIs and T-6G Texans with the Atlas-built MB 326M Impala Mk 1. It may be said that Atlas cut its teeth on this extremely successful Aermacchi trainer of which upwards of 150 left the Atlas assembly line, up to 80 per cent of the content of later batches of aircraft being of South African origin. Apart from the Flying Training School at Langebaanweg and the Flying Training School at Dunottar (formerly the Central Flying School), the Impala Mk 1s have, for the most part, been assigned to the ACF squadrons, No 4 Squadron at Water-kloof being the first to convert from the Harvard, Nos 5 (Durban), 8 (Bloemspruit) and 6 (Port Elizabeth) following suit in that order, and No 7 at Ysterplaat likely to convert in the near future. Another ACF unit to undergo re-equipment recently was No 41 Squadron at Grand Central, Johannesburg, which, performing forward air control, tactical reconnaissance, light transport and casualty evacuation tasks, converted to the Aermacchi AM-3C Bosbok (Bushbuck), as did also No 42 Squadron of the Permanent Force at Potschefstroom, these units passing their Cessna 185s to two newly-established squadrons, No 11 at Potchefstroom and No 43 at Durban, all components of the Light Aircraft Command.

Forty Bosboks were acquired, and after delivery of the first few as complete aircraft by the parent company, the remainder were assembled from component sets by Atlas, this programme being completed last year when the Bosbok was succeeded on the Witwatersrand assembly line by the Kudu which is now being delivered to the Light Aircraft Command. The Kudu possesses considerable commonality with the Bosbok, mating the wings, tail assembly, undercarriage and power plant to a boxlike fuselage essentially similar to that of the Aermacchi-Lockheed AL.60 utility aircraft. The Kudu, which is virtually entirely built by Atlas, will be seen in increasing numbers in SAAF markings in the years ahead, its excellent STOL performance, ability to use semi-prepared strips and very useful payload rendering it an ideal vehicle for the type of anti-infiltration operation with which the SAAF appears likely to be increasingly concerned in the years ahead. The Kudu, which is eventually to re-equip No 43 Squadron, will probably see some service with the Air Commando squadrons; auxiliary units operating under SAAF control and comprising civil light aircraft. There are currently 12 Air Commando squadrons (Nos 101-112) performing liaison, communications and support duties in times of emergency with a wide variety of light aircraft types, but as a proportion of current Kudu production is for commercial sale, its eventual appearance with the Air Commandos would seem assured.

Airfield protection has been greatly improved as a result of the purchase from Jordan mid-1974 of more than 500 Short Tigercat surface-to-air missiles which now supplement the longer-range Cactus (alias Crotale) all-weather missile system which is intended to intercept aircraft flying at speeds of up to Mach 1·2 at low altitudes. However, the likelihood of the SAAF being engaged in full-scale all-out aerial warfare in which its bases will be under attack would seem remote, at least, for the remainder of the present decade, and the Mirage-Impala mix on which the service will largely rely in the years immediately ahead should be capable of coping with any threat currently envisaged. In so far as the strike-reconnaissance and maritime patrol rôles are concerned, much will depend on the continuance of the United Nations' embargo. One thing is certain and that is that the SAAF will assume steadily increasing importance in ensuring the continued survival of the South African Republic. □

(Above) MB 326M Impala Mk 1s of No 6 Squadron, one of the most recent Active Citizen Force units to have converted from T-6s, these particular Impalas having previous supplemented the Sabre Mk 6s of No 1 Squadron until replacement by the Impala Mk 2. (Below) The C-130B Hercules transports of No 28 Squadron now sport dark green and dark earth camouflage.

TALKBACK

Viastra fiasco

IN SEEKING information on the Vickers Viastra (*Plane Facts* Vol 9 No 9, September 1975) Mr G Hoole added that he believed the type "was supplied to Australia." Although the *Viastras various* reply presented a concise history of the entire five Viastra aircraft, it featured photographs only of the three British registered versions. Assuming that Mr Hoole — and, perhaps, other interested readers — may wish to see the Viastra in Australian markings, I am forwarding the accompanying photographs and the following notes to correct one or two errors that have appeared in print about these aircraft.

Western — subsequently changed to West in the late 1920s — Australian Airways Ltd was founded by Major N Brearley in August 1921. During the next eight years WAA used a variety of G-AU registered aircraft — an Avro 504J in 1921, eight Bristol Tourers between 1921-24, six D.H.50/D.H.50As (three of the latter being built by WAA) between 1924-27, a Curtiss JN-4D Jenny in 1926, two D.H.60s and one D.H.60X in 1927, and four D.H.66s in 1929. In addition, Sir Alan Cobham's ex-Jaguar engined D.H.50J, G-EBFO, which had made the first England-Australia-England flight in 1926, was acquired in September 1929 as the Nimbus engined D.H.50, G-AUMC. When VH superseded G-AU as Australia's international identification letters, the WAA aircraft still in service were automatically re-registered in late 1929; G-AUMC, for example, became VH-UMC. The first *new* aircraft of WAA to carry a VH registration, however, was the Vickers Viastra VH-UOO.

On 31 July 1930, Major Brearley wrote to the Controller of Civil Aviation requesting that registrations be allotted to "the two twin-engined monoplanes which are being constructed by Messrs Vickers Ltd", so that the Australian identification letters could be painted on the machines before they left the English workshops. On 6 August the Controller, Lieut-Col H C Brinsmead, advised that "the registration markings VH-UOM and VH-UOO have been reserved for the two twin-engined monoplanes at present under construction in England . . ."

In the event, when the first Vickers Viastra II, Type 198 (c/n 1), was wheeled out it appeared with the second registration VH-UOO. This aircraft completed its tests at Brooklands in late 1930, but did not appear on the Australian Register of Civil Aircraft until 18 February 1931, two days after it arrived by ship at Fremantle, Western Australia. It was assembled in the WAA hangar at Maylands Aerodrome on the Swan River about two miles from Perth. VH-UOO went into service as a replacement airliner for the slower D.H.66 Hercules three-engined biplane, and made its first flight between Perth and Adelaide, South Australia, on 2-4 March (although Sir Norman Brearley's autobiography *Australian Aviator* inexplicably states that the flight commenced on 22 February). This inaugural flight was completed in about 11 flying hours at an average speed of 125 mph (201 km/h), as against the Hercules speed of 100 mph (161 km/h) and an average time of 14-15 hours. Although

(Above) Viastra II, VH-UOO, on trials in the UK before being shipped to Australia in 1931. To improve performance, the Townend rings were removed in October 1932 and the slots in March 1934. (Below) A rare photograph of Viastra II, VH-UOM, at Parafield, South Australia, in 1933. Note the nose landing-light and the unringed engines. Apparently this second WAA Viastra was delivered without wing slots.

plagued by recurring failures of the geared Bristol Jupiter XIF engines, VH-UOO remained in service for five years until its certificate of airworthiness was allowed to expire on 17 February 1936. On 1 July 1936 WAA was taken over by Australian National Airways, and VH-UOO was subsequently sold as a redundant aircraft.

The second Vickers Viastra II, Type 198 (c/n 2), arrived in Australia during September 1931 and was entered on the register as VH-UOM on 8 October. It operated, literally speaking, for the next two years and two days with VH-UOO on the Perth-Adelaide run. Then, on Wednesday 11 October 1933 (Sir Norman inadvertently states the 10th in his book), while the Viastra was climbing out of Maylands for the east, the port engine seized and shattered the wooden propeller, which sliced through the fuselage. The pilot, H Baker, put the Viastra down in a market garden in the suburb of Redcliffe, damaging the undercarriage and part of the fuselage. The aircraft was taken by road back to Maylands where it languished in a hangar and was removed from the register on 31 October 1934. The damaged Viastra was used for spare parts to keep VH-UOO serviceable and, as from 1936, it lay abandoned at Maylands until June 1939 when it was sold for scrap.

In regard to Vickers Viastra VI, Type 203 (c/n 1), the single-engined Jupiter XIF freighter that was ordered, but not accepted, by WAA, an error has been perpetuated over the years by an assumption made by historians that it was "registered VH-UON"; that is, between VH-UOM and VH-UOO. In fact the registration VH-UON was not, even tentatively, reserved for WAA but was allotted to a de Havilland aircraft in August 1930 — the

same month that the registrations VH-UOM and VH-UOO were allocated in advance to the Viastra IIs, and *eight* months before the Viastra VI first flew on 22 April 1931 with the Supermarine Class B registration N-1. The freighter subsequently completed its tests with the Vickers Class B marking O-6, as pictured in "Plane Facts", and was eventually allotted the British registration G-ABVM. This latter identification was not used, however, and the Viastra VI was scrapped in 1932 still marked as O-6.

For information, the aircraft that became VH-UON was the first production D.H.80A Puss Moth (c/n 2001), ex G-AATC, and the first of its type in the Antipodes. It was shipped to Australia and was assembled at the de Havilland workshops, Mascot Aerodrome, Sydney, early in August 1930 — and not December as recorded in some histories. An application for registration was submitted on 7 August, and the certificate for VH-UON was forwarded to de Havilland Pty Ltd on the 16th. Meanwhile, on 13 August, Major Hereward de Havilland flew the three-seat, high wing monoplane from Sydney to Melbourne with the registration letters applied to the fuselage. The following morning he demonstrated the aircraft at Essendon Aerodrome and, before the day was over, orders were received for four Puss Moths. VH-UON had three other Sydney owners — H R Clarke as from 26 October 1930, J J Leahy as from 2 April 1933, and R G Whitehead as from 23 March 1934 — before it was transferred on 16 January 1935 to the New Zealand register as ZK-ADU.

Gp Capt Keith Isaacs AFC, RAAF (Retd)
Lyneham, ACT,
Australia

A case of force majeure

IT IS A FACT OF LIFE that few readers of magazines, be they esoteric or exoteric in subject matter, take pen to paper and write to the editor unless they are particularly incensed by something that *has* appeared or they believe *should* appear in the pages of the publication whose editor finds himself in their firing line. Thus, editors become more accustomed to brickbats than to plaudits and usually console themselves — not with a bottle of the hard stuff as popular fiction would have us believe — by misquoting an old adage: "You can *please* some of the *readers* all of the time and all of the *readers* some of the time, but . . . !"

This reflection was prompted by a letter from reader Chris Guscott of Liss, Hampshire, who has concluded that your columnist is heavily biased in favour of a certain period of aviation history, namely, World War II — Oh, how wrong can you be, Mr Guscott — and has a strong predilection for aeroplanes with fans; that the *Model Enthusiast* column is obsessed with WW II aircraft and that either this 'obsession' should be exorcized or the act of exorcization should be performed on the modelling editor! Our correspondent supports his contention with statistics concerning the subjects of the colour profiles that accompany this column, pointing out that, over the past five years, no fewer than 41 — whoops, 42 if we count this issue — have been WW II aircraft, whereas only 14 have been postwar types, a mere four have been 'tween wars subjects and but one has been an aircraft of WW I vintage.

Mr Guscott points out justifiably that the amount of information available on aircraft finishes of the WW II period is enormous, whereas far less published material relates to the 'tween wars period, or, indeed, the 'fifties and 'sixties. Ergo, the colour content of *Model Enthusiast* should be slanted towards the periods in aviation history that are less adequately catered for. Our correspondent ends his letter " . . . perhaps a wider view would be beneficial, not least to the modelling editor."

The sincerity of Mr Guscott is not doubted but we would venture to suggest that it is the *wider* view that *he* lacks. Firstly, let it be said that your columnist is *not* responsible for the final selection of the subject chosen for colour representation in each issue, this being a collective decision on the part of the editorial team. Secondly, we would stress that our personal penchant in modelling is for the more esoteric aircraft types of the 'twenties and 'thirties, but the aircraft of WW II . . . *niemals* . . . *jamais* . . . never! Thirdly, we would express our sympathy for the viewpoint expressed by Mr Guscott as an *individual* modeller — one that we have no doubt is shared by a number of readers of this column. However, having said all this, we return to the question of the width of our correspondent's view.

Upwards of 100,000 people all over the world read AIR INTERNATIONAL and although not a *modelling* magazine, we like to think that a substantial proportion of these readers peruse this column each month. Assuming this to be so and coupling this assumption with the results of readership analyses and the correspondence that we receive, we have long since concluded that such readership as this column is proud to possess represents a broad cross-section of modelling; in other words, modellers with tastes ranging across the complete spectrum from the pedestrian to the ultra exotic. It is an editor's task to cater for as many of his readers as possible, however much the interests of the minority may coincide with his own — a sound reason for the modelling editor not having the entire responsibility for selecting the subject matter of the colour content of *Model Enthusiast*. Thus, over the months and years, the balance of the colour subjects offered to readers must perforce reflect a cross-section of subject interest proportionate to kit *popularity*. Mr Guscott takes pains to point out that over the last half-decade we have offered colour profiles of three times as many WW II aircraft types as postwar aircraft types, and kit releases over this same period of time have favoured the former category of aircraft over those of the latter by — surprise, surprise — three to one, or thereabouts!

Whether we or Mr Guscott like it, the fact remains that by far the most popular subjects for modelling remain the aircraft of WW II, a point that we have made in this column on numerous occasions — see, for example, the August 1975 issue — and for every one query we receive concerning an aircraft of another period, we receive a dozen relating to the aircraft of 1939-45. In October, we devoted our colour pages to an aircraft of World War I for the first time, simultaneously stating our reasons for not having done so before. These pages generated more correspondence than any before or since and the preponderance was *unfavourable*. Ask yourself, Mr Guscott, why it is that kits of WW II aircraft outsell all others many times over. If *you* take the "wider view", you will perhaps admit that while it is a simple matter for an individual to express his tastes by writing to the editor, they are his *personal* tastes and by no means necessarily those of the vast majority. It is the editor's function to ascertain to the best of his ability the tastes of the *majority* and in trying to cater for these he must fall foul of the minority. Indeed, an editor's job is not (necessarily) a happy one!

An 'Ilyusha' from Russia

The small number and generally poor quality of plastic aircraft kits produced in the Soviet Union has always presented something of a mystery as we know that there is very considerable interest in modelling in that vast country and that those few kits that do appear are eagerly snapped up irrespective of quality. It *may* be due to Soviet difficulties in producing dies of adequate quality — the dies for the kit of the battleship *Potemkin* marketed in the Soviet Union were produced in France — but what few kits of Soviet origin *have* come our way have featured odd scales, indifferent accuracy, a lack of detail and low grade plastic. We were particularly pleased, therefore, to receive recently through the kindness of one of our Czechoslovak readers, Mr J Hornát of Prague, a sample of a Soviet kit of the Ilyushin Il-2 *shturmovik* which certainly displays a higher standard than previous efforts and is worthy of serious consideration.

The Czechoslovak Kovozavody Prostejov has produced a very nice 1/72nd scale kit of the later Il-10, but hitherto the Il-2 had been modelled only by Airfix, and very inaccurately at that. The packaging and presentation of the Soviet kit is quite deplorable and the instruction sheet was missing when it reached us, although the component parts were complete. The scale adopted is decidedly odd at 1/57th, and it would not, therefore, fit into any standardised collection, but it is reasonably accurate, consists of 32 parts which have been reasonably well moulded, primarily in off-white plastic of good quality with some of the smaller component parts moulded in light blue.

The surface detailing is really quite fine, and includes outlines of the star insignia on each side of the fin and below each wingtip. The most noticeable outline error is a curved rudder trailing edge resulting from an overly narrow tip, and the cockpit interior is a complete void. This model represents the two-seat version and the canopy is acceptably clear. There is a rudimentary machine gun for the rear cockpit. The undercarriage is rather disappointing as it consists only of the wheels which are intended to be cemented into slots in the housings to represent the retracted position. The fuselage aft of the cockpits is a little on the shallow side, but the overall appearance of the finished model is quite reasonable.

We received no decals with our kit, but if previous experience is any guide, the omission of such was no great loss and, in any case, the markings are simple. Until some enterprising manufacturer in Europe or the USA comes up with a better kit, this, despite its odd scale, is the only reasonably accurate kit of the Il-2 available, but modellers wishing to acquire an example will have to do so through East European pen-friends as this kit is unlikely to become available elsewhere.

This month's colour subject

The availability of powerful German liquid-cooled engines revolutionised the Italian fighter scene during WW II. As airframe designers, the Italians were second to none and the opportunity to mate their airframes with really first-class and powerful engines produced several outstanding warplanes which, unfortunately for the *Regia Aeronautica,* did not for the most part become available in quantity prior to the Armistice of 1943. One such was the Macchi C.205 Veltro (Greyhound), a progressive development of

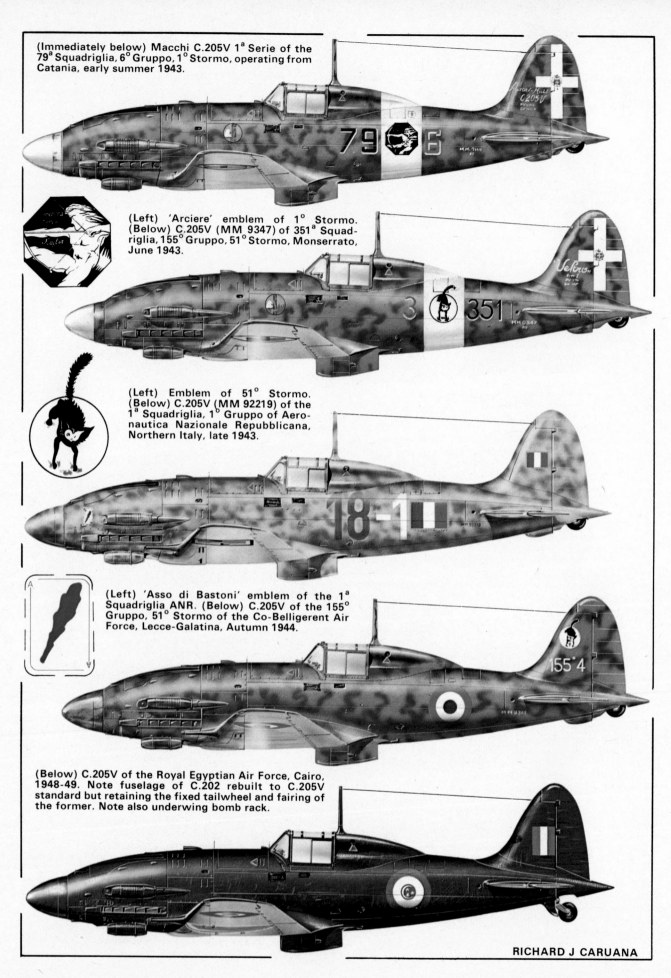

(Immediately below) Macchi C.205V 1ª Serie of the 79ª Squadriglia, 6° Gruppo, 1° Stormo, operating from Catania, early summer 1943.

(Left) 'Arciere' emblem of 1° Stormo.
(Below) C.205V (MM 9347) of 351ª Squadriglia, 155° Gruppo, 51° Stormo, Monserrato, June 1943.

(Left) Emblem of 51° Stormo.
(Below) C.205V (MM 92219) of the 1ª Squadriglia, 1° Gruppo of Aeronautica Nazionale Repubblicana, Northern Italy, late 1943.

(Left) 'Asso di Bastoni' emblem of the 1ª Squadriglia ANR. (Below) C.205V of the 155° Gruppo, 51° Stormo of the Co-Belligerent Air Force, Lecce-Galatina, Autumn 1944.

(Below) C.205V of the Royal Egyptian Air Force, Cairo, 1948-49. Note fuselage of C.202 rebuilt to C.205V standard but retaining the fixed tailwheel and fairing of the former. Note also underwing bomb rack.

RICHARD J CARUANA

the C.202 Folgore from which it differed primarily in having the Daimler-Benz DB 605A alias Fiat RA 1050 RC 58 Tifone engine. First flown on 19 April 1942 at Lonate Pozzolo (Varese), the Veltro was a superbly agile, fast and sturdy fighter, and first achieved service a year later, in April 1943, with the 1° *Stormo* based on Pantelleria, production deliveries having begun during the previous October and 99 having been completed by 8 September 1943, when Italy capitulated, 66 being on *Regia Aeronautica* strength of which 35 were serviceable. Approximately two-thirds of a further batch of 150 Veltros were completed after the Armistice for the air arm of the Repubblica Sociale Italiana, subsequently seeing extensive operational usage and gaining the reputation of being among the few Axis fighters capable of matching the redoubtable P-51D Mustang. As late as 1949, the Royal Egyptian Air Force acquired a mixed bag of 48 C.202 Folgore and C.205V Veltro fighters, some of the latter actually utilising rebuilt Folgore airframes.

A model of the C.205V Veltro makes an interesting, marginally off-beat addition to any collection of WW II fighters and the most readily available kit of this type is a product of the Italian Supermodel concern and is to 1/72nd scale. This is a fairly recent product and is to a very high standard in every respect. The moulding and detailing are very good, such refinements as separate black vinyl tyres are included in the kit and the decals are of rub-on type and of fine quality. Attention to detail goes as far as including separate transparencies for the wingtip navigation lights, and we particularly commend the provision of actuating struts for both the main under-carriage members and their fairing doors.

There are a few very minor inaccuracies deserving of comment. The canopy is about $\frac{1}{32}$ in (0·80 mm) too deep, an error which can be corrected by fairing the canopy smoothly into the fuselage and then taking the paint line above the frame; the spinner should be slightly lengthened behind the propeller and the starboard wingtip needs slight trimming — the span of each half-wing was unequal to counteract torque. This kit should certainly be obtainable in the UK from the larger model shops, priced at around 65p. One other kit of the C.205V Veltro to 1/72nd scale has been marketed to our knowledge, this being a product of the Italian Delta concern, but we have not seen an example.

The off-beat from Airmodel . . .
There is now no more prolific a manufacturer of vacuum-formed kits than the Federal German Airmodel concern, and the latest consignment of releases received from this company includes two fascinating German WW II experimentals, the Blohm und Voss BV 238 V1 flying boat and the Messerschmitt Me 209 V5 (A-1) fighter, their esoteric nature suggesting that, at this rate, it will soon be possible to build to 1/72nd scale a collection embracing not only WW II *Luftwaffe* service aircraft but the numerous experimental types that never reached production status.

The BV 238 V1 six-engined boat was indeed a whopper and with a span of almost 2 ft 9 in (83 cm) this must surely be just about the largest 1/72nd scale aircraft kit yet produced. The hull, almost 2 ft (61 cm) long, comes in four sections and must be well reinforced and very carefully lined up before assembly. The

wing consists of eight sections and calls for insertion of a substantial spar to ensure rigidity. Large apertures must be cut in the lower surfaces of the outer panels to form the wells for the retractable stabilising floats and some careful internal structural details must be introduced in these wells if one does not wish to be left simply with gaping holes. The kit includes the six Daimler-Benz DB 603 engines, the stabilising floats, tailplane, vertical surfaces and a clear canopy for the flight deck, and the accompanying instruction sheet is very good, including a full-size 1/72nd scale general arrangement drawing printed in four sections, detailed assembly information and notes on finish and markings. The sheer size of this model provides a good case for detachable wings — without such the storage problem could be acute.

Truly impudence to the dignity of the previously-reviewed BV 238 on the score of size, the Me 209 V5 — which, in fact, had no relationship to early Me 209 prototypes other than a common design origin — was basically a Bf 109 derivative and, initially at least, had approximately 65 per cent airframe com-monality with the earlier fighter. Bearing some resemblance to the Focke-Wulf Fw 190D owing to its combination of anular engine cowling and wide-track undercarriage, the Me 209 V5 enjoyed a relatively brief test career and is perhaps an odd choice for a kit. All the major airframe parts are provided, including a clear canopy, and again ample drawings and information accompany the kit, full details being provided of the parts that must be made by the modeller.

. . . and the more orthodox
Making up an oddly assorted quartet of kits in this batch of offerings from Airmodel are the Bristol Brigand and the Sikorsky CH-37A Mojave, but variety is the spice of life and certainly a kit of the Brigand from one or other of the major manufacturers has been long overdue. Although too late to see service in WW II, the Brigand served for a number of postwar years with the RAF and saw some action in Malaya during the early 'fifties. The Airmodel kit provides all the major parts, with the exceptions of wheels, engines and propellers, and it is suggested that Airfix's Bristol Freighter kit will provide a suitable source for both the four-bladed propellers and the cooling fans which, largely hiding the engines, render detailing of the Centauruses unnecessary. This one really does call for a lot of work, but all the necessary information is provided and if Federal Germany is an unlikely source from which to acquire a kit of an important RAF aircraft that has never found favour with British kit manufacturers, this Airmodel product is still welcome.

The CH-37A Mojave must surely have been one of the ugliest helicopters ever to attain quantity service, with its outrigged engine pods and bulbous fuselage nose, and what with twin-wheeled retractable main undercarriage units and a five-bladed rotor assembly, it

presents quite a complex modelling subject and a challenge that no chopper model buff will be able to resist. Airmodel provides the fuselage, engine pods, stub wings, stabiliser and transparencies, leaving plenty to be added by those aspiring to include this one in their collections. The general standard of the mouldings of the four Airmodel kits reviewed here is good, and the amount and quality of the surface detailing variable, but we have nothing but praise for the presentation and for the drawings and information accompanying each kit. Airmodel kits are stocked by most major model shops but prices of those previously listed were unavailable at press-time.

A couple of nice 'uns from Modeldecal
The latest pair of decal sheets to reach us from Modeldecal are, if such was possible, even better than this concern's previous issues and these were superlative. Packed in a clear plastic bag and with very clear and comprehensive drawings of each type of aircraft represented, together with fully comprehensive painting information and affixing details for even the tiniest of the decal subjects, these are a boon to any modeller yearning for authenticity in his models. Suitable kits are suggested and conversion details provided where appropriate, so Modeldecal offers a very comprehensive service.

The biggest problem is, perhaps, that of separating the hundreds of small items from the sheet and we would recommend that not so much as a chocolate liqueur be permitted to pass one's lips on the night before tackling this task for a steady hand with the scissors is vital! The decals are not difficult to affix but demand careful handling for they are quite thin and adhere like a coat of paint, following the shape of the model to which they are attached remarkably well. Location is greatly assisted by the dozen photographs that accompany each kit and these are also extremely useful in providing modelling detail. The size of each sheet is $7\frac{3}{8}$ in by $5\frac{5}{8}$ in (18,73 mm by 14,28 mm) and each is simply a mass of useful markings, including instrument panel decals. Where kit decals are to be used in conjunction with those from Modeldecal this fact is duly noted.

Sheet No 29's subject matter is the RAF and NATO, covering a Danish C-130H Hercules, a Dutch Republic F-84F Thunderstreak, a Norwegian RF-84F Thunderflash and two RAF Jaguars, a GR Mk 1 and a T Mk 2, both of No 14 Squadron based at Brüggen. Sheet No 30 provides markings for Javelin FAW Mk 8s of No 41 and No 85 Squadrons, a Jaguar GR Mk 1 and a T Mk 2 of No 17 Squadron and Phantom FGR Mk 2s of Nos 29 and 54 Squadrons. In addition, there are markings for a Dutch Navy US-2N Tracker and an SP-2H Neptune, both of No 320 Squadron. The price of each sheet is 60p plus 15p postage on up to two sheets and 18p for three or more. These are obtainable from Modeltoys of 246 Kingston Road, Portsmouth, Hants. □

F J HENDERSON

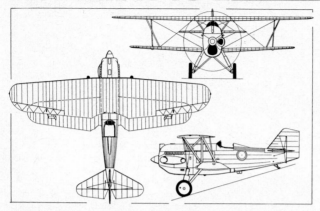

(Above and below) The P-6A which differed from the original P-6 in having ethylene glycol rather than water cooling. Eight P-6s were brought up to P-6A standards.

CURTISS P-6 TO P-6D USA

Installation of the new 600 hp Curtiss V-1570-1 Conqueror engine in a P-2 airframe for participation in the September 1927 air races at Spokane led to the application of the designation XP-6, a similarly-powered aircraft utilising a P-1A fuselage, XPW-8A wings and surface radiators becoming the XP-6A. A third Conqueror-powered conversion with a P-1C airframe for a New York-Alaska flight in July 1929 was assigned the designated XP-6B. Although these aircraft were intended purely to prove the Conqueror engine, the success of this power plant prompted a USAAC order for 18 P-6s on 3 October 1928, these being powered by the 600 hp water-cooled V-1570-17 and, although generally similar to the P-1 in construction, embodied extensively revised fuselage contours. Deliveries commenced in October 1929, but with the 11th aircraft Prestone (ethylene glycol) cooling was introduced, the designation changing to P-6A and the V-1570-23 engine having a similar rating to the -17 that it supplanted; armament remained unchanged at two 0·3-in (7,62-mm) guns. In service, eight of the Army Air Corps P-6s were brought up to P-6A standards, and eight additional P-6s were delivered to the Netherlands East Indies and one to Japan under the export designation Hawk I. Subsequent to being converted as a P-6A, the first production P-6 was fitted with a side-mounted turbo-supercharger on its V-1570-23 engine as the XP-6D, and in 1932, 10 P-6As were fitted with the F-2F supercharger as P-6Ds. In addition, two aircraft originally ordered as P-11s (P-6 airframes with the unsatisfactory 600 hp Curtiss H-1640 Chieftain engine) were completed as P-6Ds. The P-6D was 269 lb (122 kg) heavier than the P-6A and featured a three-blade propeller, and performance included max speeds of 190 mph (306 km/h) at 10,000 ft (3 050 m) and 197 mph (317 km/h) at 13,000 ft (3 960 m), service ceiling being 32,000 ft (9 755 m). The following data relate to the P-6A.

Max speed, 178 mph (286 km/h) at sea level, 173 mph (278 km/h) at 10,000 ft (3 050 m). Time to 10,000 ft (3 050 m), 5·8 min. Empty weight, 2,389 lb (1 083 kg). Loaded weight, 3,172 lb (1 439 kg). Span, 31 ft 6 in (9,60 m). Length, 23 ft 7 in (7,19 m). Height, 8 ft 7 in (2,62 m). Wing area, 252 sq ft (23,41 m²).

CURTISS P-6S (CUBAN HAWK) USA

During 1930, Curtiss offered for export a version of the basic P-6 fighter powered by a 450 hp Pratt & Whitney Wasp nine-cylinder radial air-cooled engine. The Cuban government placed a contract for three fighters of this type, which was referred to both as the P-6S and as the Cuban Hawk and should not be confused with the more powerful Hawk II (which see), four examples of which were to be delivered to Cuba some three years later. Max speed, 157 mph (253 km/h) at sea level. Initial climb, 1,820 ft/min (9,24 m/sec). Loaded weight, 2,910 lb (1 320 kg). Span, 31 ft 6 in (9,60 m). Length, 22 ft 10 in (6,96 m). Height, 8 ft 6 in (2,59 m). Wing area, 252 sq ft (23,41 m²).

(Above) One of the 10 P-6s completed and (below) the turbo-supercharged P-6D (a converted P-6A).

(Below) The P-6S, also known as the Cuban Hawk, was an export derivative of the Conqueror-powered P-6, three being built.

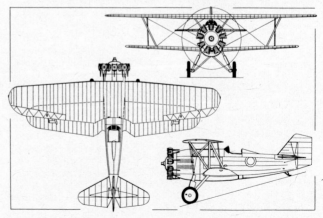

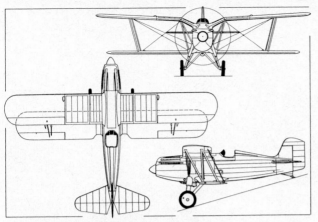

(Above and below) The XP-10 bore no relationship to members of the Hawk family, other than a common design origin, and placed emphasis on aerodynamic cleanliness.

CURTISS XP-10   USA

On 18 June 1928, the USAAC placed a contract with Curtiss for one prototype of the XP-10 single-seat fighter powered by a 600 hp V-1570-17 Conqueror engine. Of mixed construction with fabric-covered steel-tube fuselage and plywood-covered wooden wings, the XP-10 placed emphasis on aerodynamic cleanliness and utilised surface evaporation wing radiators and a gulled upper wing. Delivered in August 1928, the XP-10 was tested until October 1930, but continuous problems with the cooling system prevented further development. Max speed, 173 mph (278 km/h). Loaded weight, 3,700 lb (1 678 kg). Span, 33 ft 0 in (10,06 m). Length, 24 ft 6 in (7,47 m).

CURTISS XP-17   USA

The XP-17 comprised the airframe of the first P-1 mated to the new 480 hp Wright V-1460-3 Tornado inverted inline air-cooled engine and was intended primarily to test the power plant rather than extend the service life of the P-1 design. The conversion of the airframe was undertaken by the US Army and flight

The XP-17 (below) was a P-1 Hawk airframe mated to a Wright Tornado air-cooled in-line engine and was intended primarily as a power plant test bed.

testing was initiated in June 1930. Max speed, 165 mph (265 km/h) at sea level, 161 mph (259 km/h) at 5,000 ft (1 525 m). Time to 10,000 ft (3 050 m), 8·0 min. Empty weight, 2,204 lb (1 000 kg). Loaded weight, 2,994 lb (1 358 kg). Span, 31 ft 7 in (9,63 m). Length, 22 ft 10 in (6,96 m). Height, 8 ft 7 in (2,61 m). Wing area, 252 sq ft (23,41 m²).

CURTISS YP-20   USA

During the course of 1928, the 600 hp Curtiss H-1640 Chieftain 12-cylinder air-cooled radial appeared to show promise as a fighter power plant and Curtiss was assigned the task of mating this engine to the P-6 airframe, being allocated a USAAC contract for three aircraft which were designated P-11s. In the event, the Chieftain proved unsatisfactory, and the P-11 was abandoned (together with the projected Curtiss XP-14 that had been designed around this engine), two of the airframes that had been ordered in January 1929 being completed as P-6Ds and the third, which was fitted with a 575 hp Wright R-1820-9 Cyclone, being assigned the designation YP-20 on delivery in October 1930. It was later to be fitted with the V-1570 engine of the XP-22 (which see), complete with cowling, and the cantilever main undercarriage members and three-blade propeller of this aircraft to become the XP-6E. Max speed, 187 mph (301 km/h) at sea level, 184 mph (296 km/h) at 5,000 ft (1 525 m). Initial climb, 2,400 ft/min (12,19 m/sec). Empty weight, 2,477 lb (1 124 kg). Loaded weight, 3,233 lb (1 466 kg). Span, 31 ft 6 in (9,60 m). Length, 23 ft 9 in (7,24 m). Height, 9 ft 2 in (2,79 m). Wing area, 252 sq ft (23,41 m²).

The YP-20 (above and below) was originally built as a P-11 and, after reconstruction, was eventually to become the XP-6E.

CURTISS XP-21   USA

After being flown in the National Air Races of 1929, the XP-3A was re-engined with a Pratt & Whitney R-985-1 Wasp Junior with which it was somewhat misleadingly redesignated XP-21. It later underwent further conversion to P-1F standards. The original XP-3A (converted from a P-1A airframe) was similarly re-engined as XP-21A in December 1930, but trials with these aircraft were not associated with the further development of the basic fighter design, despite the allocation of an "Experimental Pursuit" designation.

PLANE FACTS

The mysterious Pirate

Is it possible to publish a three-view drawing and details of the Vought F6U-1 Pirate which I believe to have been developed at the same time as the North American FJ-1 Fury. T Hadden
Clevedon, Avon, BS21 6BU

Can you please publish whatever details are available concerning the Chance Vought Pirate, together with a three-view drawing and photograph. Robert Briggs
Hinckley, Leics, LE10 0DP

The Vought XF6U-1 was designed as a general-purpose single-seat fighter for use in escort, combat air patrol and ground support missions, and despite the fact that it achieved production status, mystery has surrounded its test programme and the ultimate fate of the production examples. The designation XF6U-1 was initially assigned to a proposed long-range shore-based or shipboard fighter powered by two Pratt & Whitney R-2800-E two-stage air-cooled radial engines on which the Chance Vought design team was engaged early in 1944. However, the US Navy Bureau of Aeronautics lost interest in fighters of this category and at a conference held by the Bureau in September 1944 indicated interest in a single-seat fighter powered by a single Westinghouse 24C axial-flow turbojet and making extensive use of Metalite skinning — a material developed by the Chance Vought company and comprising two sheets of high-strength aluminium alloy bonded to a balsa wood core — which promised to eliminate skin wrinkling and make possible a saving in structural weight as its use appeared to call for fewer ribs and stiffeners. The design proposal submitted by Chance Vought was accepted and on 29 December 1944 a letter of intent was received by the company for three prototypes to which the designation XF6U-1 was now assigned.

(Above and left) The first XF6U-1 (BuNo 33532) as originally flown in February 1946 from Muroc Dry Lake, and (below) the second XF6U-1 (BuNo 33533) flying with wingtip tanks.

The head-on, plan and lower centre side profile drawings illustrate the production F6U-1 Pirate in its definitive form. The side profile drawings to the left illustrate (top to bottom) the first XF6U-1 in its initial form, the second XF6U-1, the third XF6U-1 and the first XF6U-1 after modification to test the Solar afterburner. The side profile top centre depicts the production F6U-1 Pirate in its initial form.

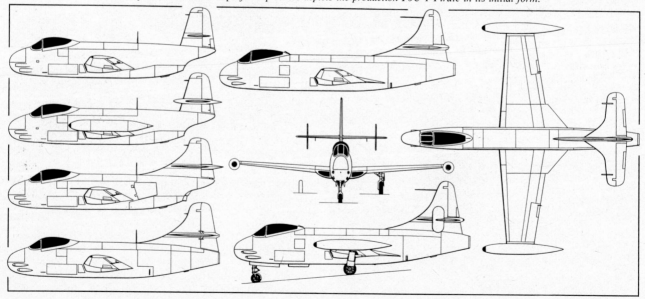

(Above) The third XF6U-1 (BuNo 33534) which featured an extended jetpipe, fuselage-mounted air brakes, redesigned vertical tail surfaces and extended horizontal tail surfaces. The first XF6U-1 is illustrated (below left) after application of similar but taller vertical tail surfaces to those tested by the third aircraft and the Solar afterburner extension.

The XF6U-1 was of conventional construction, apart from the ¼-in (6,35-mm) Metalite skinning of the fuselage, wing and vertical fin surfaces, and was powered by a Westinghouse 24C-4B (J34-WE-22) turbojet rated at 3,000 lb (1 360 kg) thrust. Provision was made for 308 Imp gal (1 400 l) in two fuselage tanks plus two 116·6 Imp gal (530 l) jettisonable wingtip tanks, and normal combat and take-off gross weights were estimated at 9,026 lb (4 094 kg) and 10,940 lb (4 962 kg) respectively, calculated maximum speeds being 541 mph (871 km/h) at sea level, 542 (872 km/h) at 2,000 ft (610 m) and 523 mph (840 km/h) at 20,000 ft (6 095 m). The first XF6U-1 (BuNo 33532) was flown on 10 February 1946 from Muroc Dry Lake (Edwards AFB) by Edward Owens. Although no details of the flight test programme have ever been revealed, aerodynamic and stability problems were apparently encountered from an early stage and performance was reportedly seriously down on original estimates, partly as a result of greater duct losses than had been calculated and partly owing to some weight growth, normal combat and take-off gross weights being 9,306 lb (4 221 kg) and 11,125 lb (5 047 kg). A substantial acorn fairing appeared at the fin/tailplane junction of the second XF6U-1 (BuNo 33533), which was the first prototype to be flown with tip tanks, while continuing stability problems resulted in major redesign of both vertical and horizontal tail surfaces of the third XF6U-1 (BuNo 33534) which also featured fuselage-mounted air brakes and a projecting jet tailpipe.

Meanwhile, Chance Vought had received a production contract for 30 F6U-1s (BuNos 122478-507), the first of which was flown by Robert Baker on 3 May 1948. Apart from featuring some further redesign of the tail surfaces, an extended forward fuselage, a revised canopy and wing root trailing edge extension, the F6U-1 had the Westinghouse J34-WE-30A (24C-4C) rated at 3,150 lb (1 420 kg) thrust boosted to 4,100 lb (1 860 kg) by a

Solar A-103B afterburner extension which had been first tested by the first XF6U-1 during the previous month, this prototype having been fitted with a new aft fuselage of stainless steel construction, taller fin and broader rudder surfaces, and additional elevator mass balances. The Chance Vought company had meanwhile moved from Stratford to Dallas where the runways were too short for use by the F6U-1. Therefore, production aircraft were disassembled and trucked a couple of hundred miles to a former USAF training field at Ardmore, Oklahoma, where they were reassembled and, after acceptance testing,

flown to Quonset Point NAS where some testing was conducted. Several were apparently assigned briefly to VX-3 at Atlantic City for armament testing, but none was issued to a fleet squadron and most appear to have been transferred to technical training schools for use as ground instructional airframes, the last F6U-1 delivery being made in February 1950.

The F6U-1s were to receive a further modification at an early stage in the production run, persistent stability problems dictating the addition of auxiliary vertical surfaces to the tailplane. The F6U-1 had an empty weight of 7,320 lb (3 320 kg), a normal combat weight of 11,060 lb (5 017 kg) and a max take-off weight of 12,900 lb (5 851 kg). Internal fuel capacity totalled 350 Imp gal (1 590 l) and armament comprised four nose-mounted 20-mm cannon with a total of 600 rounds. Overall dimensions included a span of 32 ft 10 in (10,01 m), or 36 ft 8 in (11,18 m) over tip tanks, a length of 37 ft 8 in (11,48 m), a height of 12 ft 11 in (3,94 m) and a wing area of 203 sq ft (18,95 m²).

While no details of actual performance attained by the F6U-1 under test are available, Bureau of Aeronautics calculated performance as at 1 May 1949 was as follows: (at a gross weight of 11,060 lb/5 017 kg and at combat power) max speed, 596 mph (959 km/h) at sea level, 550 mph (885 km/h) at 31,000 ft (9 450 m); initial climb rate, 8,060 ft/min (40,94 m/sec); time to 30,000 ft (9 145 m), 5·4 min; service ceiling, 46,300 ft (14 110 m).

(Above) The first production F6U-1 Pirate (BuNo 122478) as originally flown — note angled trailing-edge wing root extensions — and (below) the thirteenth production F6U-1 (BuNo 122490) with definitive wingtip tanks and auxiliary fins on the tailplane.

IN PRINT

"The Speed Seekers"
by Thomas G Foxworth
Macdonald and Jane's, London, £12
560 pp, 11 in by 9½ in, illustrated

AT FIRST GLANCE, this weighty volume, of somewhat unusual format, might be assumed to fall into the "coffee-table book" category. It is lavishly illustrated, well laid out and printed on good quality paper — the kind of book that is a pleasure to handle and a delight to browse through.

However, the book deserves to be considered as a much more significant addition to aviation literature than this first impression might suggest. Tom Foxworth has set out to present a slice of aviation history in a novel way, by describing the quest for speed in the air from 1919 to 1926. In so doing, he not only describes the great aerial events of the period, in which flamboyant fliers of many nations vied for laurels, but also traces in satisfying detail the technical effort of designers and engineers to provide high-speed aircraft and the engines that powered them.

The book falls into several distinct but interconnected parts — first, an account of the great races, then a discourse on the technical problems of developing engines and airframes, followed by a country-by-country and type-by-type description of racing aeroplanes, and a series of appendices listing the results of all major races and aircraft and aero-engine specifications. There are three-view line drawings of all the aircraft, and a quite remarkable collection of photographs. Anyone with a feel for these early formative years of flight, when opportunities for individualism still abound, will love this book. If you can't afford to buy one — and despite the apparently high price this volume offers excellent value for money — then insist that your local library obtains a copy!

"Early Supersonic Fighters of the West"
by Bill Gunston
Ian Allan Ltd, Shepperton, £4·95
256 pp, 5¾ in by 9 in

THIS is the third volume in which Bill Gunston tells the stories of a group of aircraft of the 'fifties and 'sixties. The 10 aircraft which he covers in this book are those with which he was professionally concerned as technical editor of "Flight International" at the time of their early development and entry into service. Because of security restrictions, much of the story could not be told at the time, but the author obviously feels under no such restraints now, and he writes freely of the technical problems and the political and economic influences on these aircraft, comprising the Lightning, Saro SR.53 and SR.177, Mirage III and 5, Draken, CF-105 Arrow, F-100 Super Sabre, F-102 Delta Dagger, F-104 Starfighter, F4D Skyray and F-8 Crusader.

There is much good material here, and Gunston presents his story in a readable way, although this reviewer finds his constant use of the personal pronoun irritating in what is presumably intended to be a factual account rather than a personal view of events. The biggest criticism must concern the lack of illustrations. In a volume as expensive as this, even allowing for current inflation, the reader

is entitled to expect more than a 12-pp insert with one illustration of each type described.

"Concorde"
by John Costello & Terry Hughes
Angus & Robertson, Lewes, Sussex, £3·80
302 pp, 5¾ in by 9 in, illustrated

ANOTHER book about Concorde — but certainly one of the more useful to appear so far. Neither a paean of praise for a technological marvel nor a bitterly-biased criticism of the project (examples of both having already been published) this is an attempt to trace the whole story of the effort to develop Concorde in the face of difficulties and set-backs both from within and without. The attempt is successful.

The authors — who are not aviation professionals but who previously collaborated to write the best-selling "D-Day", record with reasonable objectivity and eminent readability the many stages through which the Anglo-French SST has progressed. The rôles of many personalities — technical, industrial and political — are related and the several efforts to "kill the Concorde" in the UK, France and, more recently, the USA, are described. The book draws no conclusions, but cannot fail to help its readers reach their own; it is also valuable as a historical record of aspects of the Concorde story that have been very fully reported in the daily press but have not previously been brought together and analysed.

"Aichi M6A1 Seiran"
by Robert C Mikesh
Monogram Aviation Publications, Massachusetts, $3·95
32 pp, 8¼ in by 10¼ in, illustrated

TO PROVIDE No 13 in the Monogram Close-up series, Bob Mikesh, Assistant Curator of Aircraft at the National Air and Space Museum, Washington, has assembled a detailed account of one of the most fascinating Japanese wartime projects. The Seiran was a two-seat single-engined floatplane designed exclusively to be launched from specially-developed submarines in a one-time attack on the strategically important Panama Canal. Had the war lasted a few more weeks, the attack might well have been made.

Seiran was the only attack aircraft ever developed to be launched from submarines. Its development was initiated in May 1942 and was brought to the point of operational deployment by August 1945. When Japan surrendered, two submarines carrying three Seirans each were at sea in preparation for an attack on the US fleet, hope of the assault on the Panama Canal having been abandoned. The story is a fascinating one, well and fully told here, with many exclusive illustrations.

"Jane's Weapon Systems 1976"
Edited by Ronald T Pretty
Macdonald and Jane's, London, £19·50
872 pp, 8½ in by 12½ in, illustrated

AS ONE OF the Jane's Yearbooks of principal interest in aviation circles — second only, perhaps, to All the World's Aircraft —

Weapons Systems appears to grow in stature year by year. It provides extensive and authoritative details of the whole range of weaponry, both "basic" and highly sophisticated, now available to the world's defence forces. Much of this, obviously, is related to aircraft, being intended either to be air-launched or used in defence against air attack.

Additional sections deal with radar equipment — ground, naval and airborne — electronic warfare equipment, sonar and other items. Much useful data is condensed in analytical tables at the back of the volume, which has grown by 20 pp since last year.

In his introduction, Editor Ron Pretty makes a veiled reference to the probable development, in both the USA and the Soviet Union, of a "death ray" in the shape of high energy lasers. This led to the appearance of the volume receiving considerable publicity of a somewhat sensational kind; but its value for reference will remain long after such transient stories are forgotten.

"Strategic Air Command"
by David A Anderton
Ian Allan Ltd, Shepperton, £4·95
316 pp, 5½ in by 8½ in, illustrated

USAF's Strategic Air Command occupies a unique position within the US defence structure and makes up two-thirds of the Triad forces, providing the bomber aircraft and the underground ballistic missiles that, together with the US Navy's fleet ballistic missile submarines, control strategic weapons with nuclear warheads. Its history dates back to 1946 as a discrete Command, born of experience gained in World War II, and in the 30 years of its existence it has passed through several phases to reach its present status.

David Anderton's account provides both an historical survey of SAC and a detailed description of its present organisation and equipment. His writing style, using very short paragraphs that are often only a single sentence long, may prove a slight distraction to British readers, but the story he tells is always interesting, and the book is heavily illustrated throughout. Production of the volume unfortunately appears to have taken a very long time, however, and the only reference to the B-1 — SAC's all-important new swing-wing supersonic bomber — is that the first flight "was to take place in mid-summer 1974". The book was published in December 1975.

"Ju 188E-1 Flugzeug Handbook"
Richard P Lutz Jr, California, USA
5½ in by 8½ in, illustrated

ANYONE with a special interest in the aircraft of the Luftwaffe will welcome the appearance of this facsimile reprint of the Ju 188 handbook. In German throughout, it provides a detailed description of the airframe and equipment, with many line illustrations. Aircraft specifications are, however, not included.

Copies can be ordered direct from Mr Lutz at 3950 W 226th Street, No 110, Torrance, California 90505, USA, price $6·60 including surface postage; add $3·25 for airmail delivery. Mr Lutz also has copies of many other German World War II handbooks available for reprinting if there is sufficient demand.

FRANCE

AEROSPATIALE AS 350 ECUREUIL

PRELIMINARY data have now been released by Aérospatiale's Helicopter Division in respect of the AS 350 light helicopter (see *Airscene*/November 1975), two prototypes of which are now in flight test. The AS 350 is a five/six-seat helicopter designed to sell at less than one million francs (£110,000) when deliveries begin early in 1978. It is regarded by Aérospatiale as the first in a family of new light helicopter designs, and is aimed primarily at the market in which the Alouette II/III series have achieved considerable success. Emphasis has been placed upon commercial rather than military prospects, and an Aérospatiale survey indicates a possible market, over the next 10 years, for some 6,000 five-seat helicopters with a single turboshaft engine for civil use.

The AS 350 features the new Aérospatiale Starflex rotor, which has only 62 pieces including nine rotating joints and three laminated rotor blades; by comparison, the Gazelle's simplified NAT (semi-rigid) rotor has 202 parts and that of the Alouette, 377. Much use is made of plastics construction throughout.

The first prototype of the new helicopter made its initial flight on 27 June 1974, and was powered by a 600 shp Lycoming LTS-101 turboshaft. This engine will be used in production models destined for the North American market, and it is intended that these helicopters will be assembled and equipped in the USA by Aérospatiale Helicopter Corporation, a subsidiary of the French manufacturer. Another prototype of the AS 350, flown on 14 February 1975, is powered by a 650 shp Turboméca Arriel, this being the engine intended for the helicopter assembled in France by Aérospatiale for sale throughout the world. The original AS 350 with LTS-101 engine is now flying with some detail refinements intended to be introduced in the production version, including additional windows in a longer cabin with an increase of 6 in (16 cm) in fuselage length. The name Ecureuil (Squirrel) has been adopted.

Power Plant: One Turboméca Arriel turboshaft rated at 650 shp for take-off and with a max continuous rating of 600 shp, or one Avco-Lycoming LTS-101 turboshaft rated at 600 shp for take-off and with a max continuous rating of 510 shp. Fuel capacity, 117 Imp gal (530 l).

Performance (LTS-101 engine): Max speed (V$_{NE}$), 159 mph (256 km/h) at sea level, 143 mph (230 km/h) at 4,920 ft (1 500 m); cruising speed, 143 mph (230 km/h) at sea level, 136 mph (219 km/h) at 4,920 ft (1 500 m); vertical rate of climb, 1,593 ft/min (8 m/sec) at sea level, 944 ft/min (4,8 m/sec) at 4,920 ft (1 500 m); inclined climb rate, 1,770 ft/min (9 m/sec) at sea level, 1,338 ft/min (6,8 m/sec) at 4,920 ft (1 500 m); hovering ceiling IGE, 9,015 ft (2 750 m); hovering ceiling OGE, 6,560 ft (2 000 m); service ceiling, 19,015 ft (5 800 m); range, 460 mls (740 km) at sea level, 510 mls (820 km) at 4,920 ft (1 500 m).

Weights: Empty, 2,090 lb (950 kg); useful load, 1,900 lb (880 kg); max slung load, 1,980 lb (900 kg); max take-off weight, 4,185 lb (1 900 kg).

Dimensions: Rotor diameter, 35 ft 0½ in (10,69 m); tail rotor diameter, 6 ft 0 in (1,83 m); overall length, 42 ft 8 in (13 m); fuselage length, 35 ft 9 in (10,91 m); overall height, 9 ft 8 in (2,94 m); undercarriage track, 6 ft 10 in (2,10 m).

Accommodation: Pilot and co-pilot or passenger side-by-side (with dual controls) and three-four passengers in rear of cabin.

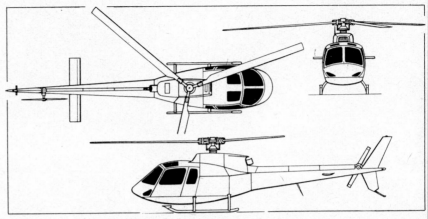

A three-view drawing of the Aérospatiale AS 350 Ecureuil (Squirrel) in its proposed production version.

USA

CESSNA 421C GOLDEN EAGLE

CESSNA has introduced a new "wet wing" and several other new design features on its 1976 model Golden Eagle, the 421C. Whereas the previous Golden Eagle featured wing tip tanks, the Model 421C provides greater fuel capacity in integral wing tanks without using tip tanks, and also has optional provision for "locker" tanks in one or both of the wing baggage bays. The wing is totally new from the nacelles outboard, and uses metal-to-metal bonding to achieve a smooth finish as well as the necessary security for integral fuel stowage.

With the same basic engines as before, the Model 421C has modified turbochargers that increase the critical altitude from 18,000 ft (5 490 m) to 20,000 ft (6 100 m). Undercarriage retraction is now hydraulic instead of electric, using a 1,500 psi (105,5 kg/cm²) system, and the wheels are now located on the outside of the leg, increasing the track and helping to prevent foreign objects being thrown into the wheelwell. To improve directional control and reduce rudder pedal forces, the height of the fin and rudder has been increased by 10 in (25,4 cm).

A number of other detailed improvements has been introduced, several of these being common throughout the Cessna twin-engined range, and the Golden Eagle is available in a basic model, in Golden Eagle II form with a package of 11 optional items of equipment plus IFR avionics factory-installed, or as the Model 421 Executive Commuter with special interior.

Power Plant: Two 375 hp Continental GTSIO-520-H flat-six geared, fuel injection engines with turbochargers, driving Cessna constant speed three-blade fully-feathering propellers of 7 ft 6 in (2,29-m) diameter. Standard fuel capacity, 213·4 US gal (808 l) plus one or two optional "locker" tanks in wings with capacity of 28·4 US gal (108,5 l) each.

Performance: Max speed, 295 mph (474 km/h) at 20,000 ft (6 096 m); max cruising speed at 75 per cent power, 239 mph (385 km/h) at 10,000 ft (3 050 m) and 276 mph (445 km/h) at 25,000 ft (7 620 m); initial rate of climb, 1,940 ft/min (9,8 m/sec); single-engine climb, 350 ft/min (1,8 m/sec); service ceiling, 30,200 ft (9 205 m); single-engine ceiling, 14,900 ft (4 542 m); take-off distance to 50 ft (15,2 m), 2,323 ft (708 m); landing distance from 50 ft (15,2 m), 2,293 ft (699 m); range (with standard fuel), 1,080 mls (1 740 km) at 25,000 ft (7 620 m) at 75 per cent power and 1,252 mls (2 017 km) at 10,000 (3 050 m) at recommended lean mixture; range (with max fuel), 1,440 mls (2 319 km) at 25,000 ft (7 620 m) at 75 per cent power and 1,712 mls (2 756 km) at 25,000 ft (7 620 m) at recommended lean mixture.

Weights: Standard empty, 4,501 lb (2 042 kg); empty (with II package options), 4,729 lb

A three-view drawing of the Cessna 421C Golden Eagle. A photograph appears on the next page.

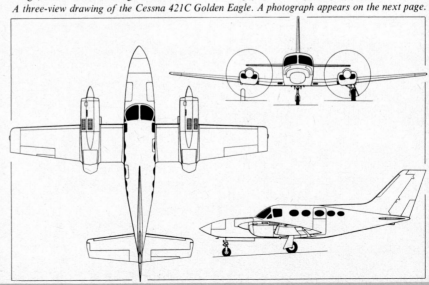

The Cessna 421C Golden Eagle II has new integral wing tanks, making unnecessary the tip tanks used by previous Golden Eagle models.

to begin next February.

Power Plant: Two Lycoming TIO-540-R2AD flat-six air-cooled engines rated at 340 hp each. Hartzell fully-feathering constant-speed propellers, diameter 6 ft 9 in (2,06 m).

Performance: Estimated high speed, 268 mph (430 km/h) at 20,000 ft (6 100 m). No other performance data revealed.

Weights: Empty, 4,500 lb (2 040 kg); max take-off and landing, 6,600 lb (2 990 kg); max taxi weight, 6,640 lb (3 010 kg).

Dimensions: Span, 42 ft 5½ in (12,92 m); length, 39 ft 4 in (12 m); height, 12 ft 9 in (3,98 m); wing area, 200 sq ft (18,6 m²); undercarriage track, 16 ft 6½ in (5,03 m); wheelbase, 10 ft 4 in (3,15 m); cabin length, 16 ft 5 in (5 m); cabin width, 4 ft 9 in (1,44 m); cabin height, 4 ft 9 in (1,44 m).

Accommodation: Pilot and five to seven passengers in cabin pressurized to 5·5 psi (0,39 kg/cm²) differential. Baggage compartments in nose and at rear of cabin, both pressurized, with capacity of 53 cu ft (1,50 m³).

(2 145 kg); max take-off, 7,450 lb (3 379 kg); max landing, 7,200 lb (3 266 kg).

Dimensions: Span, 41 ft 1½ in (12,53 m); length, 36 ft 4½ in (11,09 m); height, 11 ft 5½ in (3,49 m); wing area, 215·0 sq ft (19,97 m²); dihedral, 5 deg constant; undercarriage track, 17 ft 11½ in (5,47 m); wheelbase, 10 ft 5¼ in (3,19 m).

Accommodation: Two seats side-by-side for pilots or pilot and passenger, plus provision for up to six passengers in individual seats in the cabin. Total baggage capacity, 1,500 lb (680 kg) in nose compartment, rear cabin and wing lockers; if fuel tanks are fitted in the lockers, the baggage capacity is reduced by 400 lb (182 kg).

ROCKWELL COMMANDER 700

A FIRST FLIGHT was recorded by the second Rockwell Commander 700 at Oklahoma on 25 February, following which some initial data for the type have been made available. The first prototype had flown in Japan, as the Fuji FA-300, last December. Product of a joint design effort by Fuji and Rockwell, the Commander 700 is intended to be produced primarily in Japan, with final assembly lines being set up in both Japan and the USA and Rockwell marketing the type in almost all areas outside of Japan.

The Commander 700 is a pressurized twin of conventional layout, designed to seat six including the pilot. It is to be certificated to FAR 23 Amendment 14 standards, which specify stringent conditions for production of various components and equipment, as well as requiring more comprehensive handling demonstrations than previously. Rockwell and Fuji plan to complete certification by October, using six aircraft, three each in Japan and the USA. Customer deliveries are expected

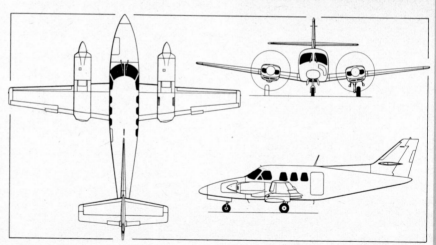

The second prototype of the Rockwell Commander 700 is shown in the photographs below and top right, and is depicted also in the three-view drawing above.

AIR International

Volume 10   Number 6   June 1976

Managing Editor   William Green
Editor   Gordon Swanborough
Modelling Editor   Fred J Henderson
Contributing Artists   Dennis Punnett
                       John Weal
Cover Art   W R Hardy
Contributing Photographer
                       Stephen Peltz
Editorial Representative, Washington
                       Norman Polmar
Publisher   Donald Hannah
Circulation Director   Donald Syner
Subscription Manager   Claire Sillette
Advertising/Public Relations
                       Elizabeth Baker
Advertising Manager   Jim Boyd

Editorial Offices:
The AIR INTERNATIONAL, PO Box 16,
Bromley, BR2 7RB Kent.

**Subscription, Advertising and
Circulation Offices:**
The AIR INTERNATIONAL, De Worde
House, 283 Lonsdale Road, London
SW13 9QW. Telephone 01-878 2454.
US and Canadian readers may address
subscriptions and general enquiries to
AIR INTERNATIONAL PO Box 353, White-
stone, NY 11357 for onward transmis-
sion to the UK, from where all corres-
pondence is answered and orders
despatched.

MEMBER OF THE AUDIT
BUREAU OF CIRCULATIONS   ABC

Subscription rates, inclusive of postage,
direct from the publishers, per year:
United Kingdom   £5·50
USA $17·50
Canada $17·50

Rates for other countries and for air mail
subscriptions available on request from
the Subscription Department at the
above address.

The AIR INTERNATIONAL is published
monthly by Fine Scroll Limited, distributed by Ducimus Books Ltd and
printed by William Caple & Co Ltd,
Chevron Press, Leicester, England.
Editorial contents © 1976 by Pilot Press
Limited. The views expressed by named
contributors and correspondents are their
own and do not necessarily reflect the
views of the editors. Neither the editors
nor the publishers accept responsibility
for any loss or damage, however caused,
to manuscripts or illustrations submitted
to the AIR INTERNATIONAL.

Second Class postage approved at New
York, NY. USA Mailing Agents: Air-Sea
Freight Inc, 527 Madison Avenue, New
York, NY 10022.

CONTENTS

WRENDEZVOUS
WITH WREN

AIRSCENE

MILITARY AFFAIRS

AUSTRALIA

Reports from Canberra suggest that the likelihood of the purchase of two **different aircraft** types **to meet** the RAAF's ground **attack and air superiority missions** has markedly increased as a result of reappraisal of future requirements and current thinking that the advantages of commonality offered by a single type are outweighed by the enhanced operational capability gained by the acquisition of two distinct types each optimised for one specific rôle. The RAAF is known to favour the SEPECAT Jaguar International for the ground attack mission and the McDonnell Douglas F-15 Eagle is frontrunner in meeting the service's air superiority requirement. It is currently planned that an Australian evaluation team will visit prospective suppliers during the course of this year with a definitive choice being scheduled for the first half of 1977, deliveries commencing towards the end of the decade.

The Royal Australian Navy's **carrier** HMAS *Melbourne*, which has recently undergone an $A6m refit to extend its operational life until at least 1985, is expected **to be returned to service** shortly, re-commissioning having been delayed by a strike at the Sydney naval dockyard. The recently-delivered Wessex AS Mk 31s of No 817 Squadron — officially commissioned with seven helicopters on 2 February — will be included in the complement of the *Melbourne* when the vessel commences working-up trials.

The Pilatus **Turbo-Porters** and Bell **Sioux helicopters** of the Army Aviation Corps' 183rd Reconnaissance Squadron and the three RAAF DHC-4 Caribou transports that have been deployed to Papua New Guinea have now **returned to** their **home bases** (see page 297).

AUSTRIA

The *Luftstreitkräfte* is to receive 12 Bell Model 206B **JetRanger** light observation helicopters under a $2·8m contract to supplement a similar quantity of Bell and Agusta-Bell Model 206A JetRangers currently included in the inventory of *III Geschwader*. This element of *Fliegerregiment* 1 is also receiving a second batch of a dozen Pilatus **Turbo-Porter** light STOL transports ordered last year (see *Airscene*/June 1975) at a cost of Sch 7m, six having recently been delivered into the *Luftstreitkräfte* inventory with the remaining six scheduled to follow next year. Although Dassault-Breguet has recently demonstrated the Mirage F1 to the *Luftstreitkräfte* at Langenlebarn air base, the service is understood to still favour the Northrop F-5E Tiger II to fulfil its long-standing interceptor requirement.

BELGIUM

The *Force Aérienne Belge* (FAéB) officially took **delivery of** its first Swearingen **Merlin IIIA** at San Antonio, Texas, on 2 April. Four FAéB pilots are currently undergoing ground school and flight training on the Merlin IIIA with the Swearingen Aviation Corporation and 18 ground personnel are receiving airframe, avionics and power plant training with Swearingen and AiResearch. The remaining five Merlin IIIAs are now scheduled to be delivered to the FAéB by August.

EGYPT

As earlier forecast (see *Airscene*/May), the US Congress refused to block the sale of six **Lockheed C-130 Hercules** transports to Egypt,

the total cost of which (including spares, ground support equipment and the training of Egyptian Air Force personnel in the USA) is now put at $65m (£35·6m). Although Dr Kissinger has stated that the supply of C-130s to the EAF does not commit the US to a long-term arms supply programme for Egypt, the US administration has refused to assure Congress that these transports will be the only military equipment supplied to Egypt. No indication has yet been given as to when C-130 deliveries to the EAF will begin, but current planning calls for the training of EAF personnel in the USA to commence this summer.

At the time of closing for press, initial **deliveries** of the Aérospatiale SA 342 **Gazelle** helicopter to the Egyptian armed forces was reported to be imminent. Forty-two Gazelles have been ordered by Egypt and these are to be equipped to launch Aérospatiale/MBB HOT wire-guided anti-tank missiles.

The **Egyptian** government is currently considering the **purchase of** up to 20 **Hawker Siddeley 748** Series 2A transports with the wide freight door for operation by the EAF in the trooping and cargo transportation rôles and is also showing interest in the HS 748 Coastguarder (see page 267 *et seq*), reportedly having a requirement for at least two squadrons of aircraft in this category.

FEDERAL GERMANY

The three VFW-Fokker **VFW 614** transports on order for the *Flugbereitschaftstaffel* of the *Luftwaffe* as replacements for the Convair CV-440s already withdrawn from service (see *Airscene*/March) are scheduled **to be delivered** in February, July and August of **next year.** The aircraft to be supplied to the *Luftwaffe* are to be equipped with additional navigational equipment which will include inertial navigation and a ground proximity warning system. Programme cost of the VFW 614 procurement will be DM78·6m.

The *Luftwaffe* now anticipates taking **delivery of** the first of its 200 Dassault-Breguet/Dornier **Alpha Jet** light strike aircraft in October 1978 when a training unit will be formed at Fürstenfeldbrück.

Twenty-two **shipboard** ASW **helicopters** are expected **to be ordered** shortly for the *Marineflieger*, the choice resting between the Agusta-Bell AB 212AS and the Westland Lynx. The helicopters will be used to equip six new frigates.

GREECE

On 1 April, the Hellenic Air Force took **delivery of** three additional Canadair **CL-215** multi-purpose amphibians at Montreal, these joining two CL-215s supplied earlier against a contract placed in 1973 (see *Airscene*/December 1973). While the HAF CL-215s fulfil a forest protection rôle they also possess a secondary logistic support and troop transportation rôle.

The Hellenic **Air Force** is reportedly **negotiating** with the Israeli *Heyl Ha'Avir* the **purchase of** the latter's remaining score or so of Nord 2501 **Noratlas** transports now surplus to requirements. The HAF currently operates 30 plus Nord 2501D in its 355 and 356 *Mire* at Eleusis, these having been transferred to the HAF by the *Luftwaffe* under the 1967 NATO military air agreement.

IRAN

The Iranian Imperial Air Force is scheduled to

start taking **delivery of** its two-seat Northrop **F-5Fs** this month (June). The first production F-5F effected its maiden flight at Palmdale, California, in April. The quantity of F-5Fs on order for the IIAF has not been announced.

JAPAN

The **Kawasaki-designed P-XL** maritime patrol aircraft project is now considered to have a greatly **enhanced chance** of receiving a prototype contract in the near future as a result of the virtual abandoning of plans to procure the P-3C Orion as an *interim* P-XL. Consideration is currently being given to the retention of the P-2J production line and the dispensing with the earlier scheme for the licence manufacture of an interim type. It is now calculated that the development cost of the Kawasaki P-XL will be of the order of £110m and the unit price (excluding ASW systems) will be about £7·6m, the fully-equipped unit price being between £15·5m and £18m, these unit costs allegedly comparing favourably with those anticipated for the licence-built P-3C Orion.

The Air Self-Defence Force had completed the Mitsubishi **FS-T2kai** close-support fighter flight **test programme** by the end of March and the designation 'F-1' is now to be assigned to this type in October. The first F-1 squadron is expected to be formed within the 3rd Air Wing at Misawa AB early in the 1977 Fiscal Year, and the type will progressively replace the F-86F Sabres of the 3rd and 8th squadrons.

NEW ZEALAND

Following the completion of deliveries against the RNZAF's repeat order for six BAC Strikemaster Mk 88s, the single McDonnell Douglas A-4K and three TA-4K **Skyhawks** that have been operated by No 14 Squadron have now been **transferred to No 75 Squadron** which will, in future, carry out the strike conversion rôle. No 14 Squadron's 16 Strikemasters will continue to be used for the advanced flying training stage in the newly-introduced advanced flying training programme from which the advanced flying stage on the Devon has now been eliminated. RNZAF student pilots now complete basic training on the CT-4 Airtrainer before converting to the Strikemaster for the advanced stage of 103 hours over a period of five-six months.

The RNZAF's two forward air control **Harvards** which are included in the inventory of No 14 Squadron are **to be phased out** during the course of this year, together with all other Harvards remaining in RNZAF service. An RNZAF spokesman has said that it is unlikely that any of the service's 13 CT-4s will be used in the FAC rôle.

NIGERIA

The Nigerian government has entered into preliminary **negotiations** with the Brazilian Aerotec concern **for** the supply of approximately 40 **Uirapuru** primary **trainers** for the Federal Nigerian Air Force. The production rate of the Uirapuru is being increased to three-four per month as from this month (June) to meet home demand and prospective export orders.

PERU

A top-level evaluation team of the *Fuerza Aérea del Peru* (FAP) visited the Soviet Union in April to discuss terms and conditions of a Soviet **offer to provide** MiG-21 fighters financed by a long-term, low-interest loan. The FAP visit reflects the frustration felt over financing arrangements and delivery times quoted by the US in a letter of offer covering the purchase of 24 Northrop F-5E Tiger IIs which was subsequently allowed to lapse (see *Airscene*/February 1975). The Soviet Union has been offering the FAP MiG-21s since 1974, but the service has consistently expressed a preference for the Tiger II.

The 100th Fokker F.28 **Fellowship** which was **delivered** on 30 March was the first of four examples ordered by the *Fuerza Aérea del Peru* for passenger and cargo transportation tasks. Arranged to accommodate up to 48 passengers, these F.28s are equipped specifically for operations under Peruvian conditions and feature additional fuel tankage and ground proximity warning systems — the first F.28s so fitted.

SAUDI ARABIA
According to the US Assistant Secretary of State, Saudi arms purchases have included an hitherto unannounced **order for** 400 Bell **HueyCobra** gunship helicopters of which more than 200 have already been delivered. Deliveries of 70 Northrop F-5E Tiger IIs to the Royal Saudi Air Force are continuing and deliveries of 20 two-seat F-5Fs (to supplement 20 two-seat F-5Bs supplied earlier) will commence later this year. The RSAF is showing a renewed interest in the McDonnell Douglas F-15 Eagle and the Grumman E-2C Hawkeye, and on 10 March awarded Northrop a massive $1,464m (£800m) fixed-price contract for modernising the entire infrastructure and support organisation.

SINGAPORE
The Republic of Singapore Air Force (formerly Singapore Air Defence Command) is the most recent target in an endeavour to export Israel Aircraft Industries' Kfir fighter. The **Kfir** is being **offered as a successor to the Hunters** currently operated by Nos 140 and 141 Squadrons and is in competition with the F-4 Phantom and the F-5F Tiger II for SAF orders. The first SAF Skyhawk unit, No 142 Squadron which is operating both the A-4S and TA-4S versions, is now at an advanced stage of working up and a second Skyhawk squadron will be formed later this year or early next year. The other current SAF squadrons are No 120 (Alouette IIIs), No 121 (Skyvan 3Ms), No 130 (Strikemasters) and No 150 (SF-260MS).

TURKEY
At the time of closing for press, the approval of the US Congress was awaited concerning the proposed **US-Turkish agreement** under which US bases in Turkey would be reopened in exchange for $250m (£137·3m) per year in military aid over the next four years. Clauses in the proposed agreement include Turkish retention of control of the bases, an additional $70m (£38·4m) a year in Export-Import Bank loans for the purchase of US products and the loan of 14 F-4 Phantoms for use by the Turkish Air Force until 14 new-production aircraft can be delivered. If the agreement receives Congressional approval, the Turkish government is to request (in addition to the previously-mentioned 14 F-4E Phantoms which are extra to the 40 aircraft of this type being purchased from Fiscal 1976 defence budget funds — see *Airscene*/March) 36 air defence fighters of either F-15 or F-16 type, 20 advanced trainers of unspecified type and 72 helicopters of unspecified type. The Turkish Foreign Minister, Mr Caglayangil, has stressed that these aircraft will supplement those included in the 1976 defence budget and that if congressional approval of the agreement is not forthcoming, the US bases in Turkey will be closed permanently.

It is now known that the **quantity of** Dassault-Breguet/Dornier **Alpha Jet trainers** under negotiation between the Turkish and Federal German governments is 40 aircraft and not 60-65 as was earlier reported by Turkish sources. The agreement had not been finalised at the time of closing for press and, in view of the comparatively small quantity of aircraft involved, there is now little likelihood of Turkish industrial participation in their manufacture.

There is apparently some **confusion regarding** the type of light **utility transport** that is to be adopted by the Turkish Air Force (see *Airscene*/April) following the sudden retirement of the C-in-C, Gen Emin Alpkaya. Gen Alpkaya — who retired after allegations of irregularities concerning his handling of sums of money ostensibly paid to him by Aeritalia for Turkish earthquake victims — had reportedly confirmed that an agreement had been reached for the licence manufacture in Turkey of the Air Metal AM-C111 (as the TC-111) at a factory at Kayseri, but the Federal German government's refusal of a guarantee covering Air Metal requested by the Turkish government has since apparently halted the procurement process. Fresh tenders have been sought and submitted but no definitive choice of aircraft had been announced at the time of closing for press. The specification calls for a 20-seat pressurized aircraft with STOL capability and some form of co-production.

UNITED KINGDOM
Near East Air Force (NEAF) was **disbanded** by the RAF on 31 March in a brief ceremony at Akrotiri, Cyprus, and the Command's Queen's Colour is to be laid up in St Clements Dane Church, London. The disbandment is part of the general contraction of British commitments overseas, and RAF units continuing to operate in the Eastern Mediterranean are now controlled by a new Air HQ, Cyprus, which has the status of a Group within Strike Command.

As additional Wessex helicopters are introduced by the RAF in the search-and-rescue rôle, some **changes** are being made **in** the designations of the Whirlwind and Wessex **SAR flights.** Thus, the Whirlwind unit at RAF Leuchars, previously C Flight of No 202 Squadron, has recently become B Flight of No 22 Squadron, and will shortly re-equip with the Wessex. This, in effect, was an exchange of plates with the SAR Flight at Coltishall, which has now become C Flight of No 202 Squadron. Other Wessex units will also be in No 22 Squadron — that already flying the type at Manston will become E Flight in June, and the SAR Flight at Valley, Anglesey, to receive Wessex in October, is already in No 22 Squadron.

After serving in home-based RAF fighter squadrons for 16 years in a natural metal finish, **BAC Lightnings** are now being painted **in** a green and grey **camouflage scheme.** Lightning F.2As based in RAF Germany have had a dark green finish on upper and side surfaces since 1972, but the predominantly high-altitude role of the UK-based Lightning squadrons made such a finish unnecessary. More recently, however, the Lightnings of No 5 and 11 Squadrons at RAF Binbrook have increasingly operated in a low level air defence rôle, often in association with AEW Shackletons of No 8 Squadron, over the North Sea. Four different schemes have been evaluated at Binbrook since last August, including overall dark sea grey, overall dark green and overall greyish pale blue, as well as that now adopted, comprising dark sea grey with the addition of a dark green camouflage pattern. Red and blue roundels are used in conjunction with the new finish. A similar green and grey finish is also in process of being applied to the RAF's fleet of Hercules transports, which are now almost totally committed to operating in the European theatre, this scheme replacing the earlier two-tone brown finish.

The Vickers **Varsity ended** 25 years of **service** with the RAF on 2 April, when an aircraft of No 6 FTS at RAF Finningley, Yorks, landed after a routine training flight. The training task previously fulfilled by the Varsity has now been taken over by the HS.125 Dominie T Mk I navigation trainer.

AIRCRAFT AND INDUSTRY

CANADA
Canadair has negotiated with William P Lear to buy exclusive design, production and marketing **rights in the LearStar 600** twin-jet transport that Lear has been developing privately for the last few years. The deal requires approval of the Canadian government, which at present temporarily owns Canadair and its implementation depends upon the results of a major feasibility and marketing study, to be directed for Canadair by James B Taylor, who was until recently responsible for marketing the Cessna Citation and, before that, the Dassault Falcon in North America. The LearStar 600 has a supercritical wing and two rear-fuselage-mounted Avco Lycoming ALF-502 turbofans; it will seat 14 passengers in an executive interior, with a range of up to 4,000 mls (6 436 km) cruising at Mach = 0·85 at 45,000 ft (13 725 m), or up to 30 passengers as a commuter when it can make five 100-ml (161-km) sector flights without refuelling, cruising at 20,000 ft (6 100 m) at Mach = 0·80. More details will appear in *AirData File* next month.

Trident Aircraft Co of Vancouver now appears to have sufficient funds in hand to complete **certification of the TriGull** six-seat amphibian with a 285 hp Tiara engine (*AirScene*/September 1975). Certification of the prototype before the end of this year will allow production to start, against orders (backed by deposits) for 32 and the promise of an order for 100 from a single source when production begins.

Pratt & Whitney Aircraft of Canada has delivered its **9000th** example of the **PT6A turboprop.** A PT6A-27, it is destined to be used in an EMBRAER EMB-110 Bandierante for the Brazilian Air Force.

FEDERAL GERMANY
Modifications proposed by VFW-Fokker to adapt the **VFW 614** to the medium-range **sea surveillance rôle** — including the specific requirements of the US Coast Guard — include the provision of an air-openable hatch in the rear cabin floor for dropping of supplies, dinghy packs, markers, etc, in flight and the addition of a ventral radome to house the search radar aerial. Cabin layout provides seats for two observers with blister windows at the forward end and a surveillance system console with operator's seat on the port side farther aft. Passenger seats would be fitted to starboard, there being ample room in the VFW 614 for all required equipment plus passengers. Growth items for possible later application include forward-looking infra-red, microwave radiometry (useful for detecting oil spills), laser sensors (housed in an underwing pod, also useful for oil slick detection), cameras, visual displays and computers,

FRANCE
Suffering a serious shortage of work, **Aérospatiale** is reported to have concluded a **"letter of intent" with Boeing** covering the joint development of new versions of the Boeing 737 and the Airbus A300. The former, referred to as the 7N7-100 (see news item under "USA" heading) would have a lengthened fuselage, CFM-56 engines and a new wing developed by Aérospatiale. The Airbus in question is the A300BB10 (see under "International" head-

ing) with some Boeing input and possibly RB.211 engines. Consummation of the deal appears to depend upon decisions taken by the governments of France, Germany and the UK in respect of development of new civil aircraft in Europe, based on the recommendation of the "Group of Seven". Other possible new work for Aérospatiale includes the relaunching of production of the Transall to meet an *Armée de l'Air* requirement for 25-30 aircraft, continuing production of the Nord 262 and launching the Fouga 90, this being the new designation of the modernised Magister with Turboméca DF600 turbofans (see *AirData File*/September 1975).

The Aérospatiale **SA 360C** Dauphin single-engined helicopter received its French **certificate of airworthiness** on 18 December, for day and night VFR flight. Similar certification has subsequently been granted by the FAA. With a 1,050 shp Turboméca Astazou XVIIA turboshaft, the SA 360C is cleared initially for operations at a weight of 6,400 lb (2 900 kg), to be increased to 6,615 lb (3 000 kg) in the near future. Two prototypes and the first production Dauphin have totalled more than 1,350 hrs to date.

Production of the Aérospatiale **Corvette is to end,** at least temporarily, with completion of 40 aircraft. Work will be resumed at some future date if market demand justifies such a step being taken. One recent Corvette delivery was to Air Intergulf, which now has two.

Among the new projects currently under consideration in France and offered as the basis for collaborative development is a military **STOL transport by Dassault-Breguet.** Based in part on experience gained with the Breguet Br 941 prototypes, the new project has a high wing with an advanced system of leading and trailing-edge high-lift devices and is powered by two SNECMA/GE CFM-56 turbofans. With a span of 99 ft 4 in (30,3 m), the gross weight of the project is expected to be 110,000-132,000 lb (50-60 tonnes) and it would be designed to operate from the same field lengths as the Transall, but having much improved overall performance characteristics.

INDIA

Two flying **prototypes** and a static test model **of** the tandem two-seat **Ajeet trainer** derivative of the Gnat are now to be built and the first prototype is scheduled to commence its test programme early in 1979.

The Indian Air Force has finally emerged victor in its battle to have the HAL HPT-32 trainer (*AirData File*/April 1976) developed rather than the DGCA's Revathi, and two **prototypes of** the HPT-32 have now been put **in hand** with the first scheduled to fly early next year.

The prototype of the HAL **Kiran Mk II** with de-rated Orpheus 701 turbojet, built-in gun armament, updated avionics and four wing hardpoints is now expected **to fly in October. A** second prototype will follow within six months.

The extraordinary tenacity of the HAL design team in persisting with the **development of** the basic **HF-24** to meet the IAF's deep penetration strike requirement is illustrated by the fact that, having now virtually abandoned proposals to use the SNECMA M53 owing to several factors including cost, preliminary studies are once again being conducted **for** the use of a **Soviet engine.** The actual type of engine has not been specified but is understood to be of some 15,430 lb (7 000 kg) thrust.

INTERNATIONAL

No further **production of Concordes,** beyond the 16 already authorised, was sanctioned at the 29 March meeting between Marcel Cavaille. French secretary of state for transport, and Gerald Kaufmann, British minister of state for transportation. Production tooling is to be maintained in good condition, however, and work on a spares backlog has been approved, to help keep the work forces together in both Toulouse and Filton. Air France took delivery of its third Concorde (No 207) on 8 April at Charles de Gaulle airport, Paris, this being the aircraft in which, on 31 March, André Turcat had made his final Concorde test flight before retiring as head of Aérospatiale's Flight Test Division. On 9 April, Air France opened its second Concorde route, with a once-a-week service between Paris and Caracas, Venezuela, with a refuelling stop in the Azores. Concorde 201 was used from 6 to 13 April for a final series of flights from Kuala Lumpur to confirm the autopilot modification that had been required for British certification.

A version of the **Airbus A300 with** Rolls-Royce **RB.211-524 engines,** the A300B10, has emerged as favourite in the studies conducted by the "Group of Seven" European airliner manufacturers (BAC, HSA, Aérospatiale, VFW-Fokker, MBB, Dornier and — a late-comer to the group — Dassault-Breguet) for the Type A requirement of European airlines, represented in particular by British Airways, Air France and Lufthansa. For the smaller Type B the Group proposes a version of the Mercure 200 or One-Eleven 800 with two ten-tonne engines. As an alternative to joint European development of the A300B10, however, France is closely considering a joint Aérospatiale/Boeing development known as the A300BB10, using a Boeing-designed supercritical wing, and to be undertaken as part of a package deal in which Aérospatiale would also participate in development of the Boeing 7N7-100, a Boeing 737 derivative with up to 170 seats and CFM56 engines. The B10 and BB10 Airbus variants have a shorter fuselage than the current B2 and B4, with about 210 seats, and a similar fuselage is proposed for the Airbus A300B11, a long-range variant which is now planned with a totally new wing using an advanced aerofoil, 4 deg more sweepback (32 deg) and a span of 172 ft 5 in (52,59 m), 25 ft (7,63 m) more than the present wing. Four ten-tonne engines would be used in underwing pods.

First flights of the 23rd and 24th examples of the **Airbus A300** took place respectively on 12 February and 3 March. The aircraft are both B4 versions, being the eighth for Air France and the third for Korean Airlines respectively and were delivered on 14 April and at the end of the month respectively. No 25 flew on 23 March and is being used to complete certification of the B4 at its new gross weight of 346,916 lb (157 500 kg). No 26, the third B2 for Lufthansa, was delivered at the beginning of May and No 28 flew (out of sequence) on 16 April, being the fifth B4 for Korean Airlines.

ISRAEL

Israel Aircraft Industries has projected a **maritime reconnaissance** version of the Eleven-24 **Westwind,** known as the Model 1124N and powered, like its civil counterpart, by Garrett-AiResearch TFE731-3 turbofans. Unlike the various turboprop aircraft now offered in the MR rôle, such as the HS.748 Coastguarder and the Fokker F27 Maritime, the 1124N offers an attack capability as well as surveillance and search-and-rescue. The 1124N would carry Litton AN/APS-503 high-power search radar in a ventral randome offset to port; a retractable MAD boom in the rear fuselage, retractable forward-looking infra-red (FLIR), low light level TV (LLLTV), a searchlight at one wing-tip and other sensors and special avionics. Ordnance would be carried in pods on underwing pylons. With crew of two pilots and four sensor operators/observers and 2,190-lb (994-kg) of mission equipment in the fuselage, the 1124N would operate within the Westwind's normal gross weight of 22,850 lb (10 374 kg).

NETHERLANDS

First **flight of** the **Fokker F27MPA Maritime** test bed and demonstrator was made at Schiphol on 25 March. This aircraft is Mk 100 No 68, originally delivered to THY, and will be used to prove the new features of the maritime patrol version prior to delivery of the first production model in the summer of 1977. The F27MPA carries Litton AN/APS-503F search radar, with a small radome under the forward fuselage; Litton LTN-72 long-range INS, a Smiths SEP-2E autopilot, a radar altimeter and other new avionics equipment. Observation stations with blister windows are located at the rear of the cabin, each side, adjacent to a marine marker launcher, and the cabin also contains the main display consoles for the radar operator and navigator. A crew of six is normally carried and the F27MPA, with 2,250 shp Dart 536-7R engines, carries centre section and underwing fuel tanks to bring the total capacity to 2,460 US gal (9 310 l) and the endurance to 11 hrs, equivalent to a range of up to 2,300 naut mls (4 262 km). One F27 Maritime has been ordered by the Icelandic Coast Guard and two by an unidentified South American operator.

SOVIET UNION

Construction of the **prototype Ilyushin Il-86** large-capacity widebody airliner is now nearing completion and first flight is expected before the end of the year (a little earlier than previously indicated), while assembly of a second prototype has now begun.

SWEDEN

A full-scale **mock-up** of the Saab-Scania **light transport** project (*AirScene*/December 1975) is to be constructed and it has been confirmed that the power plant will comprise four 320 hp Continental Tiaras. At one time referred to as the Mulas, the design is now known as the Transporter.

SWITZERLAND

Pilatus Aircraft Ltd has announced the sale of five PC-6 Turbo-Porters to the Thai Ministry of Agriculture, primarily for artificial rain-making, these being among **10 Turbo-Porters sold** in the first quarter of this year. Other recent customers are in Africa and South America, and production is now running at 2-3 a month.

UNITED KINGDOM

Scottish Aviation has recently received a **contract for** nine **Bulldogs** for delivery to the Kenya Air Force. The new aircraft are identified as Model 127s, a previously unused type number. Kenya ordered five Bulldog 103s in October 1969, the change in the model number indicating a new equipment standard. Bulldog sales now total 290 to customers in Sweden, Kenya, Malaysia, Ghana, Nigeria, Lebanon and Jordan as well as the RAF.

The MEL Equipment Company has confirmed the selection by Hawker Siddeley Manchester of its **MAREC II** airborne radar system as standard equipment **for the HS.748 Coastguarder.** A prototype of the Coastguarder, intended for maritime rôles such as reconnaissance, search and rescue, fishery and off-shore rig protection and tactical ASV and ASW rôles — is to be produced by converting an HS.748 airframe and will be available for demonstration next year (see pp 267 et seq). MAREC II is a high-powered dual-pulse-width system with a 36-in (92-cm) high gain antenna installed in a radome beneath the forward fuselage, which provides a full 360-deg azimuth scan together with a sector scan facility. Maximum range is 200 naut miles (370 km).

Ten years after joining with Rolls-Royce to develop and produce the **M45H turbofan** for the VFW614, SNECMA is reported to have negotiated a **revised agreement** under which it becomes a sub-contractor instead of a partner. One consequence of the change is that Rolls-Royce becomes responsible for any further development costs, which because of the limited sales of the M45H have been considerably above estimate.

US certification of the Rolls-Royce **RB.211-524** was obtained late in March, at an initial rating of 50,000 lb st (22 700 kgp), and this milestone was followed by the first flight of a -524 in a TriStar prototype for a five-hr flight on 10 April that covered speeds up to Mach = 0·90 and altitudes to 35,000 ft (10 675 m); it will also be tested in the tail installation. First production -524 was to be delivered in May for installation in a Saudia L-1011-200, and initial services will be flown in 1977, at a rating of 48,000 lb st (21 792 kgp). The first RB.211-524 for use in a Boeing 747 reached Seattle on 13 April and first flight of the Rolls-Royce engined version of the 747-200 for British Airways is scheduled for August, with deliveries of four on order to start early in 1977. Meanwhile, Boeing and Rolls-Royce have announced their agreement to offer versions of both the Boeing 747SP and the 747SR with RB.211-524 engines. All variants of the 747 are therefore now available with a choice of three engines — JT9D, CF6-50 or RB.211.

A second Tiger Moth floatplane has recently been completed, to join the collection of Leisure Sport Ltd at Thorpe Water Park (see S-5 replica story, November 1975). Purchased from the Tiger Club, this Tiger Moth has been painted to represent a Royal Navy aircraft and fitted with a pair of Short-built floats from a Fox Moth — slightly oversize for a Tiger Moth. The original Sea Tiger, operated by the Tiger Club, has meanwhile been almost totally rebuilt in the past two years and was relaunched on a lake close to Lydd Airport during the autumn.

USA
The first prototype of the **General Dynamics YF-16** has been flying since 16 March after modification **for** a series of **CCV** (control configured vehicle) **trials** to be conducted by USAF's Flight Dynamics Laboratory at Edwards AFB. For these trials, two triangular fins have been added under the fuselage, close to the dorsal air intake lip and each at an angle of about 45 deg to the vertical; these surfaces were not fitted, however, for the first post-modification flight made on 16 March at Fort Worth by Neil R Anderson.

Boeing is using the designation **7N7** to cover a series of **design studies** for new versions of the Boeing 707, 727 and 737. Among the possibilities are the use of the SNECMA/GE CFM56 turbofan on any of these models, with or without other refinements that might include supercritical wing sections. The 7N7 effort has taken the place of the 727-300 project, now in abeyance, and Boeing is seeking partners from outside the USA. Particular interest centres upon a 737 derivative with new engines and wing to meet Japan's requirements for a YS-11 replacement (see *Airscene*/March 1976). Included in the range of studies is the 7N7-100, which is a stretched 737 to carry 155 passengers over range of up to 2,300 mls (3 700 km), powered by CFM-56 or JT10D-2 "ten-tonne"

engines and making use of a new wing that would be designed by Aérospatiale if the proposed collaboration between the two companies on the 7N7 and the Airbus A300BB10 (see news item under "International") comes to fruition. The 7N7-200 project is a 707 lengthened by about 10 ft (3 m) with four CFM-56 engines and the 7N7-500 is a 707 lengthened by more than 23 ft (7 m) and using uprated CFM-56 or JT10D engines.

McDonnell Douglas is building an **enlarged wing** to test **on** one of its **YC-15** AMST prototypes, to assess the aircraft's potential as a strategic transport. The new wing, with the same supercritical airfoil, has a span of 110 ft 4 in (33,64 m), 22 ft (6,71 m) more than the present prototype. In six months since first AMST prototype (on 26 August 1975) the two prototypes have totalled more than 200 hrs on 93 flights (the second flew on 5 December). Key points already demonstrated include a landing speed of 75 knots (139 km/h), stop distance of 700 ft (213 m) and a non-stop flight of 2,246 mls (3 613 km) in 4 hr 35 min, reaching an altitude of 33,000 ft (10 058 m).

The Hughes **YAH-64** AAH completed, in a four-day period late in March, its first series of **weapon firing tests,** both in the hover and in forward flight. In 16 test flights, a total of 1,040 rounds was fired from the Hughes-developed 30-mm XM230 Chain Gun — an external-powered single-barrel weapon — and 84 2·75-in rockets were launched from four wing-mounted pods, at forward speeds of up to 100 knots.

Eight **proposals** have been made by six companies competing **for** the US **Coast Guard MRSA** (medium-range surveillance aircraft) requirement. Needing 41 aircraft to replace Grumman HU-16 Albatross amphibians in the SAR rôle, the USCG originally proposed to buy Sabreliners but Congress blocked funds for the deal because the order had not been put out to competitive bidding. When it was, only Rockwell and VFW-Fokker responded, but contractual negotiations with Rockwell broke down late in 1975 and further submissions were invited for a 19 March deadline, with selection of the winning design expected by July. Rockwell and VFW-Fokker have again proposed versions of the Sabreliner and VFW 614, the former in a considerably-modified ternational Computer Exchange) proposes a and more internal fuel. Lockheed has proposed two versions of the JetStar II, with four TFE731-3 engines (as in the forthcoming commercial version) or two General Electric TF34s. Grumman proposed Gulfstream IIs with the standard Speys or TF34 turbofans. Dassault-Breguet, through the Falcon Jet Corporation, its US marketing organisation, proposes a version of the Falcon 20 with ATF3-6 engines and — the most novel entry — ICX Aviation (a subsidiary of ICX International with Avco-Lycoming ALF-502 turbofans modified Yak-40 called the X-Avia with three TFE731-2 turbofans, Collins autopilot and US interior wiring.

First flight of the **second Rockwell B-1** was made on 2 April at Palmdale. The flight lasted 4 hr 54 min and reached a speed of Mach = 0·85.

Garrett Corporation's AiResearch Aviation Company announced the **first flight of** a "production" **731 JetStar** on 18 March, at Los Angeles International Airport. The 731 JetStar is a re-engined Lockheed JetStar I with four TFE731-3 turbofans and the first aircraft was to be delivered to a customer in May; the company has a firm backlog of 34 JetStars to be modified — all but one for customers in the USA. Meanwhile, Lockheed is nearing completion of the first production JetStar II, which

has similar features to the 731 conversion and is scheduled for roll-out in June and first delivery in September.

Rockwell International's Columbus Aircraft Division has completed the mock-up of a **four-seat version of** the **T-2 Buckeye.** Designed to meet the requirements of the US Navy for a trainer for NFOs (Naval Flight Officers), the modified T-2 has a new widened fuselage housing two pairs of side-by-side seats, but is otherwise similar to the T-2C now in Naval service.

General Electric's Aircraft Equipment Division has developed a new radar system, **AN/APS-125,** to replace the AN/APS-120 early warning radar **in the** Grumman E-2C Hawkeye. Currently in the production design phase, the AN/APS-125 has increased sensitivity in noise and clutter environments, allowing it to operate as effectively over land as over water, and also has better long-range capability to detect small targets. The new radar will be fitted in new production E-2Cs and will also be retrofitted in earlier aircraft.

At year-end, McDonnell Douglas had 850 firm **orders for the DC-9,** including 40 military C-9 versions, and another 18 were on conditional order or option. The 800th DC-9 was delivered during January, this being the first of Finnair's DC-9 Srs 50s. The **DC-10 sales total** is now 230, plus 34 on conditional sale or option, with 212 delivered by January. McDonnell Douglas needs to sell another 170 DC-10s to "complete the 400-unit DC-10 accounting pool" (ie, to break-even).

Name of the Aérospatiale subsidiary that markets its range of helicopters in the USA has been changed to **Aérospatiale Helicopter Corp.** It was previously Vought Helicopter Corp, and originally an LTV subsidiary before being acquired by Aérospatiale.

Boeing is studying a number of possible **"stretches" of the Model 747,** for possible long-term development. Assuming the availability of engines with a thrust of 60,000 lb (27 240 kg), these could have fuselages 50 ft (15,2 m) longer than the present model, to seat 526-704 passengers compared with 385-500, and/or a supercritical wing. Gross weights of up to 1,000,000 lb (454 000 kg) are thought to be feasible for these developed 747s.

Rockwell **Sabreliners** have received FAA approval for operation **from gravel runways,** subject to installation of a modification kit and additions to the flight manual. The kit comprises a shield attached to the nose landing gear to deflect gravel away from the fuselage, and is applicable to Sabreliner Models 75A, 60 and 40.

Rockwell International's General Aviation Services division has developed long-range "slipper" tanks to give the **Turbo Commander 690A** an **extended range.** Flush-fitting under the wings of the Commander just outboard of the engine nacelles, the tanks have a capacity of 50·3-US gal (190 l) each and give the aircraft an increased range of about 350 naut mls (648 km) to nearly 2,000 naut mls (3 700 km) with reserves. Modification of the aircraft's fuel system takes about five days and costs $25,000 (£13,000); the tanks can be removed when not required. First delivery of an extended-range Turbo Commander 690A was made recently to ETS Air Transport in Switzerland and the same modification can be made on the Commander models 680V, 680W, 681 and 690.

FAA certification of the Cessna **Citation** at its **new gross weight** of 11,850 lb (5 380 kg) was confirmed at the beginning of February, and availability of a Rohr thrust reversers was announced at the same time. The weight increase, combined with a 54-lb (24,5-kg) saving on a new Sperry/Collins avionics package) allows the Citation to carry six passengers and full fuel, sufficient for a range of 1,400 mls (2250 km) with VFR reserves. Aircraft from No 276 onwards can be operated at the new gross weight; the 300th Citation was delivered in January, to the Mercedes Benz distributor in Austria. The thrust reversers have an estimated installed weight of 125 lb (57 kg) and are of the target type, hydraulically operated. They give improvements of 13 per cent on a wet runway and 43 per cent on an icy runway.

USAF is investigating the development and production of a **long life cycle cost avionics** (LLCCA) system to be **applied to** SAC's fleet of 271 B-52G/H Stratofortress bombers. It is claimed that the LLCCA, currently the subject of a design definition contract by Boeing, would extend the service life of the B-52s by 15 years. The programme, if financed, would provide a first flight of an LLCCA installation on 1 July 1979 and initial operational capability in the B-52 fleet by 1 June 1983. Although the major objective of the LLCCA effort is to reduce the operating and maintenance costs of the B-52s, important improvements in capability are also expected. Features of the LLCCA are expected to include the use of FLIR (forward-looking infra-red) a laser range-finder (in one of the two chin turrets of the newly-installed electro-optical viewing system), an inertial navigator, doppler and radar altimeter, terrain following/avoidance radar and an improved automatic flight control system.

Soloy Conversions Ltd, having previously engineered **turboshaft versions of the Hiller UH-12** helicopter, has now made a similar installation of the Allison 250-C20 in a **Bell 47 G-3B1.** First flight was made in January, the engine being derated from its basic 400 shp to 280 shp at sea level; at a gross weight of 2,950 lb (1 340 kg) the helicopter has improved performance in all respects compared with the original piston-engined version. Subject to FAA certification, Soloy expects to offer turboshaft conversion kits applicable to the Bell Models 47G-3, 47G-3B, 47G-3B1, 47G-3 B2 and 47G-4A. The UH-12 conversion, using the Allison 250-C20 derated to 350 shp, are known as the UH-12J3 and UH-12J5, the former being a four-seat model based on the UH-12D or UH-12E, and the latter a five-seater based on the UH-12E4. Both these models have been certificated and 17 UH-12Js have been sold to date.

An experimental **supersonic rocket launcher** has been developed at the Air Force Armament Laboratory and built by Hughes Aircraft Co. Designed for use on aircraft at supersonic speeds, the pod carries 18 folding-fin (2·75-in (700-mm) rockets and has many novel design features, including extensive use of aluminium, urethane foam and epoxy glass fibre composites to provide the required strength at low weight. It is built in three modules to facilitate maintenance and repair, comprising a front section incorporating the aerodynamic nose and main structural support; a middle portion housing electrical firing contacts and other mechanisms, and a hollow aerodynamic rear fairing.

CIVIL AFFAIRS

BELGIUM
Belgian tour operator Sunair has helped to found a new charter airline, **Sun Airways,** based at Brussels National Airport with an initial fleet of two Boeing 737-200s. Sunair

holds 75 per cent of the shares. Abelag Aviation the other 25 per cent and Britannia Airways is providing technical assistance. Another new Belgian operator is reported to be in process of formation at Liege with the name **Transactions Air Service International** (TASI). The company plans to order two Yak-40s and to concentrate on charter and third-level operations.

BRAZIL
With increasing overseas sales for its aircraft in prospect, **EMBRAER** is setting up a small repair and maintenance **facility** plus a spares stock **in Mali** to support any aircraft sold in Africa. An EMB-110P Bandeirante is to be demonstrated in Africa in June and the area also appears to be one in which the EMB-201 Ipanema could find acceptance. The company is also planning to demonstrate the Bandeirante and possibly the Ipanema at Farnborough in September.

NEW ZEALAND
Mount Cook Airlines has announced the **termination of** its **amphibian services** from Auckland to Hauraki Gulf and the Bay Islands, and from Invercargill to Stewart Island. Grumman Goose and Widgeon amphibians have been operating on these routes at a loss for some years and will be withdrawn before the end of the year.

UNITED KINGDOM
The appointment of **members of** the Organising Committee for **British Aerospace** — which will be responsible for managing the nationalised portion of the industry, expected to be effective later this year — has been announced by the Secretary of State for Industry. They include Alan H C Greenwood, present chairman of BAC and to be appointed deputy chairman of British Aerospace; G R Jefferson, chairman and managing director of BAC Guided Weapons Division; E G Rubython, general manager of HSA; John T Stamper, technical director, HSA; L W Buck, president of the Confederation of Shipbuilding & Engineering Unions; Bernard Friend, formerly chairman and managing director of Esso Chemicals (to be full-time Finance Member) and Dr A W Pearce (who will be a part-time member). Chairman of Esso Petroleum.

USA
A **merger between Trans International and Saturn Airways** has been approved by the CAB and President Ford, creating the largest US supplemental with rather more than 40 per cent of the total market shared by five such airlines. Combined fleet of TIA and Saturn will be 35 aircraft, including three DC-10s, 11 DC-8s, 12 Hercules L-100-30s and nine Electras. The merger is not expected to take effect for a few months, while necessary legal and other provisions are fulfilled, and Trans International will emerge as the surviving name.

Pan American was to make an unusual record-breaking **round-the-world flight** as this issue closed for press, **with** its first **Boeing 737SP,** named *Clipper 200 — Liberty Bell Express.* The flight was to operate from New York, with stops only at Delhi and Tokyo before returning to New York, and was expected to take 40 hrs for the 22,864-ml (36 788-km) distance. Revenue passengers were to be carried, the round-the-world service departing the US daily but this takes 70 hr 51 min for the journey, with nine stops (including an overnight transit in Hong Kong). Competing with Pan Am's 747SP service between New York and Tokyo, which was inaugurated on 26 April and has a flight time of 13 hr 40 min for

the 6,754-ml (10 867-km) journey, Japan Air Lines at the end of March flew a standard 747 with 18 tons of freight (but no passengers) from Tokyo to New York, the first commercial non-stop flight on this route.

CIVIL CONTRACTS AND SALES

Airbus A300: Transavia of Holland has decided to acquire one A300B4.

BAC One-Eleven: Olympic Airways has two on lease from British Caledonian, under terms negotiated with Boeing when the Greek carrier ordered 737s recently.

Boeing 720B: Five 720Bs sold by Continental to AAR of Illinois are reported to be intended only for use as a source of spares.

Boeing 737: Piedmont has purchased a second-hand Srs 200 from Interlease Finance Corp, previously used by United Airlines. □ Frontier Airlines bought two from United, for delivery in July and September.

Boeing 747: National Airlines sold its two 747s plus spares to Northwest, for immediate delivery.

EMBRAER EMB-110 Bandeirante: Two EMB-110E executive models were sold to the *Departamento Nacional de Estradas de Rodagem* (National Department of Road Building, Ministry of Transport) for delivery before October.

Fairchild FH-227: Interlease Finance Corp has acquired one FH-227B from Piedmont.

Fokker F27: Air Anglia added two more to its fleet, ex-Bangladesh-Biman, to make six in all.

McDonnell Douglas DC-10: Overseas National Airways has ordered two Srs 300 for delivery next spring, with a third under negotiation. They will replace two ONA DC-10s that were destroyed in separate accidents last year. The new aircraft will be powered by 52,000 lb (23 835 kgp) CF6-50E engines with provision for later uprating to 54,000 lb (24 516 kgp) and will have a gross weight of 572.000 lb (259688kg).

Vickers Viscount: British Airways is leasing two Srs 814s from British Midland Airways for use on local routes in Scotland, replacing two Srs 700s recently withdrawn from service.

MILITARY CONTRACTS

Bell Model 206B JetRanger: A contract for 12 Model 206B JetRanger II helicopters valued at $2·8m (£1·53m) has been placed on behalf of the Austrian *Lüftstreitkräfte.*

Bell UH-1N: Bell Helicopter Textron has been awarded a contract valued at $16·3m (£8·95m) for a further 24 UH-1N (Twin Two-Twelve) helicopters for the US Navy and USMC with deliveries commencing in January 1977 and continuing throughout the year.

De Havilland Canada DHC-6 Twin Otter: Two DHC-6 Twin Otters have been purchased by the US Army under the designation UV-18A for use in western and northern Alaska.

Lockheed C-130H Hercules: The Royal Maroc Air Force *(Al Quwwat Aljawwiya Almalakiya Marakishiya)* ordered six C-130Hs, adding to three purchased previously.

Northrop F-5E Tiger II: An order has been placed on behalf of the Royal Thai Air Force for 16 F-5E Tiger II fighters at a contractual cost of approximately $50m (£27·4m).

The Versatile HS.748...

FEEDERLINER WITH A FUTURE

THE BENEFITS bestowed upon society as a whole by air transportation are widely appreciated and the design and manufacture of commercial aeroplanes needs no other justification. Nevertheless, at a time when there is growing awareness that the earth's resources are not limitless, it is relevant to question the demands made upon those resources by any aspect of contemporary technology, and to relate such demands to the contribution made to the community at large. So far as aviation is concerned, three significant resources are time, land and fuel.

The Hawker Siddeley 748 twin-turboprop feeder-liner is environmentally acceptable on all three counts. Its simple construction and ease of maintenance ensure that the manhours spent in constructing and operating the 748 are low. Good airfield performance means that the 748 makes only modest demands on the areas of land that need to be allocated to airfields and their access systems. And over the short stage lengths for which the 748 was designed to operate, it is particularly fuel efficient, consuming little more per passenger per mile than a large car.

These are, of course, somewhat unusual criteria on which to judge the merits of an aircraft, and it is not suggested that the 748 is unique in the low demands it makes on these resources, although it is certainly a great deal better than some. They are pointers, however, to at least some of the reasons for the 748's success, which in more conventional commercial terms can be expressed as the sale of over 300 examples in the 15 years since the first order was placed, with production continuing and prospects of continued sales good. The HS.748 is, in fact, one of a small number of transport aircraft designed in Britain post-war that can be counted an unequivocal commercial success, the others being the Vickers Viscount and BAC One-Eleven and further down the scale, the HS.125 and Britten-Norman Islander.

Today, production of the HS.748 is one of the principal activities of the Manchester works of Hawker Siddeley Aviation Ltd, and the aircraft is in service in some 40 different countries with over 60 operators, both military and civil. It has been produced in several different versions, to meet specific market needs and to take advantage of power plant improvements, and it is assembled under licence in India. Work is continuing actively on the development of the airframe for new rôles, and a jet-powered derivative is currently one of the most interesting prospects for future production within the nationalized British aircraft industry. If some other, more specific, claim to historic significance for the type is sought, then it can be recorded that it was the last completely new design to emerge bearing the famous Avro name, for it was as the Avro 748 that the type was designed, first flew and entered service. Avro was already then a part of the Hawker Siddeley

(Top of page) A standard production HS.748 Srs 2A of Royal Nepal Airlines and (below) the original Avro 748 prototype demonstrating at an SBAC Display at Farnborough.

Jet derivatives of the basic 748 design have been studied since 1962; the current proposal, known as the Series 5, is depicted here and some details are given at the end of the article.

Group and although types up to the 784 were projected under the Avro name before it disappeared in favour of Hawker Siddeley in 1963, none of these later types was built.

The ultimate Avro

The history of this last Avro aircraft goes back almost two full decades to 1957, when the appearance of the infamous Sandys White Paper of Defence, with its forecast of no more manned military aircraft, marked a watershed in the affairs of many companies in the industry. The A V Roe company, with its extensive works in the Manchester area and final assembly and flight test facilities at nearby Woodford, had concentrated upon military aircraft since shortly after the end of World War II, when production of the York, Lancastrian and Tudor had met with only limited success in the commercial field. Seeing

the writing on the wall, the company set about the task of re-entering the civil market and chose to do this with the development of a short-haul twin-turboprop transport in the category of a replacement for the ubiquitous DC-3 as well as the newer Viking and Heron.

Some early attention was given to the possibility of an aircraft operating from city centres — a 40-seater capable of taking-off and landing at 3,000 ft (915 m) strips that might be established on the roofs of railway stations or in other clear spaces. This concept was soon realised as being over optimistic, but a study of DC-3 operations at that time showed the need for an aircraft that would operate from semi-prepared airfields of not more than 4,000 ft (1 220 m) in length in hot conditions. The principal design objectives therefore evolved as follows:

1. Full payload to be carried over 400 naut mls (740 km), with provision for longer stages to be flown.

2. Ability to operate from any airfield used by the DC-3, allowing for inherent deficiencies in facilities for servicing, refuelling, navigational aids and communications.

3. Flying characteristics to be very good for operation in uncertain terrain and difficult airfields.

4. Cabin to be pressurized.

5. Structure to have good fatigue life, with complete failsafe characteristics and ease of repair in the field.

6. Reliable civil engine to be selected, easy to maintain.

7. Aircraft systems to be simple and based on existing well-proven components, with low maintenance costs and easy accessibility.

8. Flexible internal cabin layout for high density load factors with mixed freight capacity.

9. Highest standards of British and US airworthiness requirements to be met.

10. Low noise levels inside the cabin and in the far field.

This set of design objectives could be met, of course, by any one of several possible aircraft configurations, and the first thoughts of the Manchester design team favoured a high-wing layout with two small turboprop engines. Such a layout offered good propeller/ground clearance, ease of freight loading and, of less importance, good downward view from all passenger windows; these factors were thought to outweigh the disadvantages of a main spar passing through the cabin and a weight penalty in the fuselage to support the wing, and also to be of greater benefit than the advantages that came from a low wing arrangement, such as ease of control, stability at low airspeeds, ease of maintenance, short and sturdy undercarriage, passenger protection in the event of a belly landing and increased ground clearance resulting in less likelihood of damage to the pressure shell when operating from rough fields. In favouring the high wing layout, as represented by the first project to bear the Avro 748 type number, in mid-1958, the team was in good company, for both Handley Page and Fokker had adopted similar layouts for, respectively, the Herald and the F.27, two aircraft in a similar

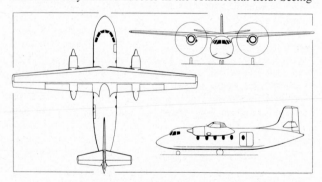

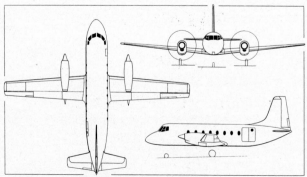

(Above left) The original high-wing Avro 748 project compared with (below left) the original low-wing 748 proposal in 1958. (Below right) The second prototype 748, G-ARAY, after conversion to Srs 2 with uprated engines.

Development of the wide rear door and freight handling equipment in the cabin has enhanced the value of the HS.748 to military operators, such as the Fuerza Aérea Ecuatoriana (above). An air drop from an HS.748 with wide door is seen from the inside of the cabin (below).

category to the 748 which had already been launched. At about this time, too, the de Havilland company at Hatfield began to study an aircraft of similar layout and comparable characteristics, the D.H.123*.

The high-wing 748 proposal was an aeroplane of only 20 seats, having a gross weight of 18,000 lb (8 172 kg) and a span of 71 ft (21,66 m). Powered by turboprop versions of either the de Havilland Gnome or Armstrong Siddeley P.182 engines of about 1,000 shp — derived from then-current helicopter engines — this project was used as the basis for a preliminary approach to prospective airline customers. It soon became apparent that a low-wing configuration would be more acceptable to airlines in general, the great majority of civil airliners since the DC-3 having been of this type, and a re-examination of the claimed advantages for the high-wing layout began to show that these did not, in fact, outweigh the disadvantages. By the autumn of 1958, the Type 748 was a low-wing monoplane of 18,500 lb (8 400 kg) gross weight, carrying a 4,500 lb (2 043 kg) payload a distance of 410 naut mls (760 km) on two 1,100 shp P.182 turboprops.

Further airline inputs led to the conclusion that this project with a cabin only 7 ft 6 in (2,29 m) wide and a headroom of 5 ft 10 in (1,8 m), was too small, and by the end of 1958 the project had been revised upwards to have two 1,600 shp Rolls-Royce Dart engines — already established in airline use throughout

* Eventually, de Havilland, like Avro, abandoned the high wing in favour of a low wing layout; after the former company became part of the Hawker Siddeley Group, by which time the 748 had already been launched, the Hatfield project for a feederliner underwent a lengthy period of design refinement that finally produced the HS.146 with, once again, a high wing in favour. Details of the evolution of the HS.146, which also involved the Manchester design team with jet versions of the 748, will be found in the January 1974 issue, Vol Six No 1.

Hawker Siddeley HS.748 Series 2C Cutaway Drawing Key

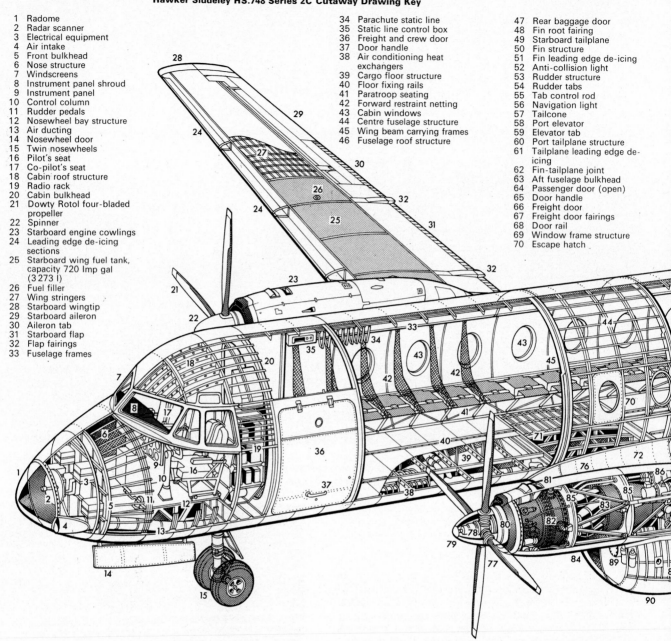

1 Radome
2 Radar scanner
3 Electrical equipment
4 Air intake
5 Front bulkhead
6 Nose structure
7 Windscreens
8 Instrument panel shroud
9 Instrument panel
10 Control column
11 Rudder pedals
12 Nosewheel bay structure
13 Air ducting
14 Nosewheel door
15 Twin nosewheels
16 Pilot's seat
17 Co-pilot's seat
18 Cabin roof structure
19 Radio rack
20 Cabin bulkhead
21 Dowty Rotol four-bladed propeller
22 Spinner
23 Starboard engine cowlings
24 Leading edge de-icing sections
25 Starboard wing fuel tank, capacity 720 Imp gal (3 273 l)
26 Fuel filler
27 Wing stringers
28 Starboard wingtip
29 Starboard aileron
30 Aileron tab
31 Starboard flap
32 Flap fairings
33 Fuselage frames

34 Parachute static line
35 Static line control box
36 Freight and crew door
37 Door handle
38 Air conditioning heat exchangers
39 Cargo floor structure
40 Floor fixing rails
41 Paratroop seating
42 Forward restraint netting
43 Cabin windows
44 Centre fuselage structure
45 Wing beam carrying frames
46 Fuselage roof structure

47 Rear baggage door
48 Fin root fairing
49 Starboard tailplane
50 Fin structure
51 Fin leading edge de-icing
52 Anti-collision light
53 Rudder structure
54 Rudder tabs
55 Tab control rod
56 Navigation light
57 Tailcone
58 Port elevator
59 Elevator tab
60 Port tailplane structure
61 Tailplane leading edge de-icing
62 Fin-tailplane joint
63 Aft fuselage bulkhead
64 Passenger door (open)
65 Door handle
66 Freight door
67 Freight door fairings
68 Door rail
69 Window frame structure
70 Escape hatch

A close-up of the wide freight door of an Ecuadorian HS.748, showing the passenger loading section of the door open and the folding air-stair extended.

the world and therefore more immediately acceptable than the "unknown" Armstrong Siddeley unit — and a gross weight of 29,000 lb (13 166 km) at first, soon growing to 33,000 lb (14 980 kg). The cabin width and height increased to 8 ft 1 in (2,46 m) and 6 ft 5 in (1,97 m) respectively allowing four-abreast seating for 36 passengers and the max payload of 9,650 lb (4 380 kg) could be carried a distance of 580 naut mls (1 075 km). The wing span increased from 71 ft (21,66 m) to 95 ft (28,98 m) and the aspect ratio from 10 to 11·35. To obtain the required ground clearance for the four-bladed propellers whilst retaining a short undercarriage, the designers adopted an overwing location for the engines, the nacelles being extended beneath the wings only to provide housings for the main undercarriage when retracted.

In this form, the Avro 748 received the backing of the Hawker Siddeley Group Board, which in January 1959 authorized the construction of two flying prototypes and static and fatigue test specimen airframes — the latter to be subjected to testing in a water tank while the cabin was pressurized and flight loads were applied to the wings and other parts of the structure in a regular cycle to simulate

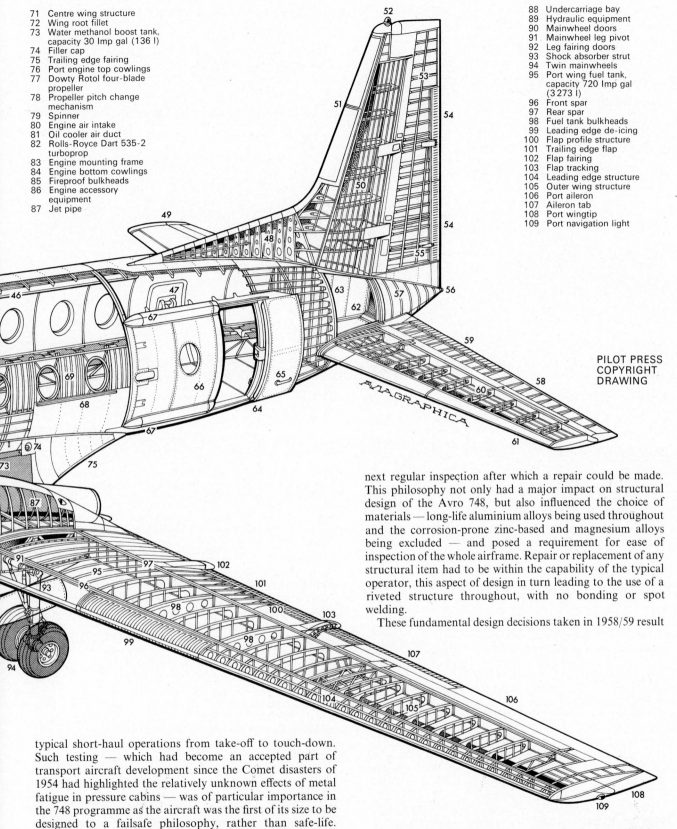

71 Centre wing structure
72 Wing root fillet
73 Water methanol boost tank, capacity 30 Imp gal (136 l)
74 Filler cap
75 Trailing edge fairing
76 Port engine top cowlings
77 Dowty Rotol four-blade propeller
78 Propeller pitch change mechanism
79 Spinner
80 Engine air intake
81 Oil cooler air duct
82 Rolls-Royce Dart 535-2 turboprop
83 Engine mounting frame
84 Engine bottom cowlings
85 Fireproof bulkheads
86 Engine accessory equipment
87 Jet pipe

88 Undercarriage bay
89 Hydraulic equipment
90 Mainwheel doors
91 Mainwheel leg pivot
92 Leg fairing doors
93 Shock absorber strut
94 Twin mainwheels
95 Port wing fuel tank, capacity 720 Imp gal (3 273 l)
96 Front spar
97 Rear spar
98 Fuel tank bulkheads
99 Leading edge de-icing
100 Flap profile structure
101 Trailing edge flap
102 Flap fairing
103 Flap tracking
104 Leading edge structure
105 Outer wing structure
106 Port aileron
107 Aileron tab
108 Port wingtip
109 Port navigation light

PILOT PRESS
COPYRIGHT
DRAWING

next regular inspection after which a repair could be made. This philosophy not only had a major impact on structural design of the Avro 748, but also influenced the choice of materials — long-life aluminium alloys being used throughout and the corrosion-prone zinc-based and magnesium alloys being excluded — and posed a requirement for ease of inspection of the whole airframe. Repair or replacement of any structural item had to be within the capability of the typical operator, this aspect of design in turn leading to the use of a riveted structure throughout, with no bonding or spot welding.

These fundamental design decisions taken in 1958/59 result

typical short-haul operations from take-off to touch-down. Such testing — which had become an accepted part of transport aircraft development since the Comet disasters of 1954 had highlighted the relatively unknown effects of metal fatigue in pressure cabins — was of particular importance in the 748 programme as the aircraft was the first of its size to be designed to a failsafe philosophy, rather than safe-life. Whereas the latter, then widely-accepted, technique involved establishing the maximum number of flight hours that could be expected of any structural component or piece of equipment before replacement or, at least, inspection, was necessary, fail-safe implied that if a crack or other failure occurred in the structure during the aircraft's normal working life, then the loads would be carried by other parts of the structure, allowing the aircraft to remain in service until the

today in the 748 making only modest demands on the time resource, as already noted. The emphasis placed upon airfield performance as one of the other basic design features, with consequent low demand on the land resource, has been no less relevant in the sales success of the 748, the take-off and landing field lengths of which today, in current production versions with higher payloads than in the 1959 specification, are significantly lower than those claimed in the original brochure.

British Airways has so far purchased two HS.748 Srs 2As, for use primarily on routes in the north of Scotland. They are the most fully equipped 748s to date and have allowed the airline to achieve a new standard of punctuality and reliability on such difficult routes as the Aberdeen-Sumburgh service, where poor weather, short daylight hours and short runways combine to impede operations.

So far as the third resource, fuel, is concerned, the aircraft has been fortunate to benefit from the continued development of the Rolls-Royce Dart, one of the most efficient and successful turboprops so far produced, but additional benefit derives from the effort made to minimize drag at the initial design stage.

In line with consistent Hawker Siddeley policy, the 748 was launched as a private venture and although some obvious benefits have subsequently been derived from the sale of versions of the design to the British government, no government aid has been provided of the kind that helped launch most of the other British post-war civil transports. In line with the philosophy of achieving low first cost, low operating and maintenance costs and high utilization rates, the 748 was designed to use proven components wherever possible, with the majority of system components grouped for ease of access below the cabin floor. Forward of the engine fireproof bulkhead, the complete nacelle and sub-frame of the Viscount 800 was adopted — the design being purchased from BAC — and the Dowty Rotol accessory gearbox was also a Viscount standard unit. The Dowty Rotol propellers used hubs similar in design to those of the AW Argosy.

An intensive period of detail design began in January 1959, with first metal cut in February, at which time the first flight target date was just a year later. First flight was in fact achieved a little later than this target, on 24 June 1960, but this was still a creditable performance, more especially for a design and production unit that, despite its long experience with large military aeroplanes, was breaking new ground in a number of respects. The first prototype (G-APZV) was assigned the primary certification tasks while the second (G-ARAY) was intended as the back-up and company demonstrator; airframe

No 2 was the static test specimen and No 4 the fatigue specimen. Completion of the second flying prototype (airframe No 3) was delayed when it suffered serious damage in a factory fire at Avro's Chadderton works in 1960, and first flight did not take place until 10 April 1961, by which time 'PZV had completed about 360 hrs of the planned total of 1,000 for certification. The static tests began in April 1961 and the water tank test in August the same year; in the latter, the loads of a typical 1¾-hr flight were simulated in each cycle, and 57,500 such cycles were applied to demonstrate a crack-free life of at least 30,000 hrs, with a safety factor of three. Additional static and fatigue testing has been undertaken in respect of subsequent design development and other special cases.

The overall configuration of the Avro 748 as it was first built has already been described. Key design features included a relatively high aspect ratio, dictated primarily by the "engine cut at take-off" case; use of well proven NACA aerofoil sections to achieve a docile stall — these being 23018 at the root and 4412 at the tip — and very large high-performance flaps to achieve the required field performance. The flaps were basically of Fowler type, having a single slot and moving aft as well as down when selected out; however, the Fowler concept was modified by the addition of a hinge that allowed a tab comprising the rear 35 per cent of the flap chord to rotate down a further 27·5 deg relative to the main flap angle, primarily to increase drag in the landing run although this hinged section also gives a small increment of lift. The flaps occupied 30 per cent of wing chord over 58 per cent of the semi span and when selected down at 27·5 deg for landing they gave the wing a C_L max of 3·1 — an excellent figure for a late 'fifties design although bettered by newer, more complicated STOL designs.

(Above) The original Avro 748 prototype converted to HS.748MF configuration as an aerodynamic prototype for the Andover C Mk 1 which (below) had a redesigned rear fuselage with air-openable loading ramp and doors.

(Below) The HS.748 demonstrator G-AZJH was the first to fly with the air-openable wide freight door and was sometimes referred to as the Srs 2C.

The wing had 2 deg 55 min of sweepback at the quarter-chord line and a relatively high angle of dihedral — 7 deg — which helped to achieve the required propeller clearance. The size of the fin and rudder derived from the "engine failure at take-off" case, propeller diameter of 12 ft (3,7 m) was also influenced by the engine-out take-off performance, while the landing field length called for the use of anti-skid units (Dunlop Maxarets) on the main wheels, plus ground fine pitch on the propellers.

All flying controls were manually operated, with electric operation of the flaps and a 2,500 psi (176 kg/cm²) hydraulic system operating the undercarriage, wheel brakes, nose-wheel steering, propeller brake and (optional) airstairs. All three undercarriage legs were designed to free-fall after emergency mechanical release of the uplocks in the event of hydraulic failure, with the doors mechanically linked to the legs to achieve reliable and trouble-free operation. The cabin was pressurized to a differential of 4·2 psi (0,30 kg/cm²) to allow a normal operating ceiling of 20,000 ft (6 100 m) and airframe de-icing was by inflatable rubber boots on the wing, tailplane and fin leading edges, using engine compressor bleed air, with electric de-icing for the engine air intake, propeller and spinner de-icing mats and windscreen.

Fuel was located in integral wing tanks occupying the entire torsion box from outboard of the engine nacelles to the tips. Water methanol was used to restore engine power at high temperatures and altitudes, and an optional APU installation was provided in the starboard nacelle aft of the engine and driving into the normal accessory gearbox (through a Spragg clutch) so that all the main aircraft accessories could be run off the APU. The fuselage emerged with a circular cross section and no taper over the length of the cabin, which could therefore offer maximum flexibility through the use of moveable bulkheads positioned at any point. Basic accommodation was for 40 passengers at a seat pitch of 36 in (92 cm) or 48 at 30 in (76 cm), four-abreast with a central aisle, and a freight loading door was incorporated in the forward port side ahead of the propeller, this being large enough to allow loading of a spare Dart engine.

Certification and service

By November 1961, all flying trials required for certification of the Avro 748 had been completed, the two prototypes having accumulated 683 and 367 flying hours respectively. A Transport Category certificate of airworthiness was awarded on 9 January 1962, and production deliveries began in the same month. As certificated, the aircraft had a gross weight of 36,200 lb (16 435 kg) compared with the 34,500 lb (15 663 kg) at which the first prototype had started its flight trials, and was powered by 1,600 shp Dart 514s — variants of the R Da 6 model. Production models were delivered to this initial specification, but had an increased wing span, compared with the prototypes, of 98 ft 6 in (30,04 m) and the power available from the Dart 514s was increased slightly.

Production of the Avro 748 had been put in hand towards the end of 1959 when the Hawker Siddeley Board approved the construction of jigs and tooling and an initial batch of 10 aircraft, plus long lead time items for another 10; since that time, the production commitment has been constantly "topped up" in the light of the back-log of firm orders plus projected future sales, and production continues in 1976 on the same basis of laying down small batches — usually 20 — of aircraft "on spec" to preserve competitive delivery dates. Hawker Siddeley was encouraged to make its initial production commitment by the level of interest shown in the 748 well before first flight. The first order actually came from the Indian government, and involved the purchase of a licence agreement permitting the assembly and eventual local manufacture of the Avro transport in a factory to be set up for the purpose at Kanpur (and subsequently taken over by Hindustan Aeronautics Ltd). This Indian production line, intended to satisfy the requirements of, primarily, the Indian Air Force and, to a lesser extent, Indian Airlines Corporation, was brought into use with the help of Avro personnel almost at the same time as the parent company began production and the first aircraft assembled at Kanpur (wholly from imported components) was flown on 1 November 1961.

The first British production aircraft had flown, meanwhile, on 30 August 1961 and was in the colours of Skyways Coach Air — the first airline to announce its intention to buy the type, although the contract, for three aircraft, was not formalised until 31 May 1961. By then, a more important order had been received from Aerolineas Argentinas, which contracted for nine 748s on 25 January 1961 and was the first customer to take delivery and to inaugurate service with the type, these milestones being achieved on 18 January and in April 1962 respectively. Skyways eventually took delivery in April 1962 and began operating its 748s on the Coach-Air service between London and Paris, the air segment of the journey being between Ashford (Lympne) Airport, Kent — a grass field — and Beauvais to the north of Paris. Although Skyways eventually foundered, this operation was continued by Dan Air with virtually no interruption and 748s continue in service on the route to this day — an unusually long period, in airline terms, for one type to operate a given route.

While production was being launched and the type was being established in service, design development was under way and new versions of the 748 began to receive public mention, although not all were to come to fruition. The most important development, so far as future sales were to be concerned, proved to be the decision to adopt the uprated Dart R Da 7 in what became known as the Series II, the initial production configuration then becoming the Series I. With an initial rating of 1,910 shp (since increased), the Dart R Da 7 allowed the 748 to operate at significantly higher weights, which translated as greater payloads over a given range or more range with a given payload; equally significant, there was a major improvement in the take-off performance at high altitude airfields and in elevated temperatures. With an initial take-off weight of 43,500 lb (19 750 kg),* the Series II required some structural strengthening of the wing and undercarriage; in addition, the cabin pressurization was increased to a differential of 5·5 psi (0,39 kg/cm²) to permit operations up to 25,000 ft (7 625 m) and this called for some strengthening of the fuselage structure.

Soon after completion of the initial certification trials, the second prototype was converted to Srs 2 standard and resumed flying in this guise on 6 November 1961, the engines taking the designation Dart 531 in this application. It was used to obtain certification of the Srs 2 (in October 1962) and then became a company demonstrator, being leased in succession to LAV (Venezuela), LIAT (Leeward Islands), Varig (Brazil) and PAC (Philippines), all of which companies subsequently ordered 748s. The Srs 2 rapidly became the most important production version, only 23 Srs 1s being completed including the first five aircraft from the Kanpur assembly line; the first Srs 2 assembled in India flew on 28 January 1964.

Before the Srs 2 had flown, Avro had announced details of a proposed stretched fuselage version as the 748E, this being basically a Srs 2 with a 6 ft (1,83 m) fuselage stretch to allow up to 60 passengers to be carried over short ranges. A 748 Super E was also proposed using 2,400 shp Dart R Da 10s with the long fuselage, but neither of these projects saw the light of day. Other early designations which fell into disuse included 748X, an executive model of the Srs 2 proposed in 1962 with extra fuel for a range of 2,250 mls (3 618 km) and 748M for the military freighting version exemplified by the aircraft for the Indian Air Force which had a reinforced cabin floor. This model was more accurately the Avro Type 757, and the company also proposed for IAF use the Type 758 which was a

high wing freighter using the wing of the 748 Srs 2 with Dart R Da 7 engines in underslung nacelles and a fuselage of 10 ft 9 in (3,28 m) diameter having a rear loading ramp and the undercarriage on the fuselage sides.

Military models

A simpler and cheaper modification of the basic 748 to suit it to the military freighting rôle was offered, however, in the 748MF or, more properly, the Type 780, designed specifically to meet an RAF requirement for a medium tactical freighter. This retained the low wing configuration and the same fuselage cross section but had a new rear fuselage incorporating loading doors and ramps for vehicles to drive in and drive out; a kneeling undercarriage was fitted to bring the rear opening closer to the ground and 2,970 shp Dart R Da 12s (Mk 301) were required to match the take-off weight of 50,000 lb (22 680 kg). The well-used prototype G-ARAY played a part in winning the RAF order for this variant — which was in competition, during 1962, with the Handley Page Herald — by demonstrating the ability to operate in deep mud at Martlesham Heath.

Definitive design work on the Type 780 began in October

---

* Subsequent structural and fatigue testing, plus routine development, has allowed the max take-off weight of the Series 2 to increase to 46,500 lb (21 110 kg) while that of the Series 1 grew eventually to 39,500 lb (17 933 kg). Max landing weights have always been relatively high in ratio to take-off weight for the 748, permitting the operation of several short flight sectors without intermediate refuelling, and are currently 39,500 lb (17 933 kg) for the Srs 1 and 43,000 lb (19 522 kg) for the Srs 2.

Hawker Siddeley HS.748 Series 2A Specification

Power Plant: Two Rolls-Royce Dart 535-2 (R Da 7) turboprops rated at 2,080 shp each at 15,000 rpm for take-off, driving Dowty Rotol four-blade constant speed feathering propellers of 12-ft (3,66-m) diameter. Fuel capacity 1,440 Imp gal (6 546 l) in two integral wing tanks; water methanol capacity 60 Imp gal (272 l) in two tanks in wing root fillets.

Performance: Max cruise (at 40,000 lb/18 145 kg), 278 mph (448 km/h); initial rate of climb (at 40,000 lb/18 145 kg), 1,320 ft/min (6,7 m/sec); service ceiling, 25,000 ft (7 620 m); take-off balanced field length, 5,380 ft (1 640 m); landing field length, 3,390 ft (1 033 m); range with max payload, (230-ml/370-km diversion plus 45-min hold), 845 mls (1 360 km); ferry range with max fuel (reserves as before) 1,978 mls (3 182 km).

Weights: Empty equipped, passenger aircraft, 26,920 lb (12 211 kg); empty equipped, freight aircraft, 25,418 lb (11 529 kg); max passenger payload, 11,580 lb (5 253 kg); max freight payload, 13,082 lb (5 934 kg); max take-off, 46,500 lb (21 092 kg); max landing, 43,000 lb (19 504 kg); max zero fuel, 38,500 lb (17 463 kg).

Dimensions: Span 98 ft 6 in (30,02 m); length, 67 ft 0 in (20,42 m); height, 24 ft 10 in (7,58 m); wing area, 810·75 sq ft (75,35 m²); undercarriage track, 24 ft 9 in (7,54 m); wheelbase, 20 ft 8 in (6,30 m); usable freight space, 1,725 cu ft (48,8 m³).

Accommodation: Typical layouts, all with four-abreast seating and centre aisle, for 44 passengers at 33-in (84-m) pitch or 52 passengers at 28-in (71-m) pitch with 264 cu ft (7,47 m³) freight space or 60 passengers at 28-in (71-cm) pitch with 165 cu ft (4,67 m³) freight space.

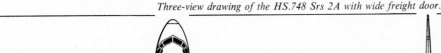

Three-view drawing of the HS.748 Srs 2A with wide freight door.

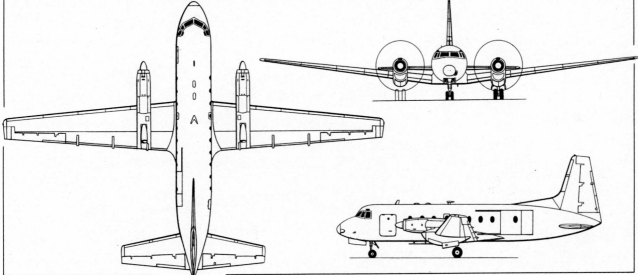

1962, and a production contract was awarded for 31 aircraft in April 1963, the RAF giving this type the name Andover C Mk 1. To test the new aerodynamic configuration, which included a dihedral tailplane to clear the propeller slipstream and a wider centre section to accommodate the larger-diameter propellers — the wing tips being cropped by 18 in (46 cm) each side to retain the same overall span — the original 748 prototype G-APZV was converted and flew in its new guise on 21 December 1963, followed by the first production Andover C Mk 1 on 9 July 1965. CA Release was obtained in May 1966, whereupon the type entered service, primarily with No 46 Squadron; its operational record proved highly satisfactory but the type was withdrawn from RAF service in 1975 to implement the defence expenditure cuts ordered earlier that year, and the entire fleet is, at the time of going to press, available for sale, some interest in the purchase of 10 of these aircraft having been expressed by the Royal New Zealand Air Force.

Many examples of the basic HS.748 have been sold for military or para-military use around the world, including six to the RAF as Andover CC Mk 2s for general communications duties, two of these being assigned to Queen's Flight and having special interiors. Ten purchased by the RAAF and two by the Royal Australian Navy as navigation trainers were non-standard in that they had 2,250 shp Dart R Da 8 (Mk 550-2) engines, but most of the military 748s have been standard Srs 2s in structural and power plant details, with special interiors according to rôle. The Indian Air Force is the largest military customer, having ordered 55 (all from the Kanpur assembly line); the *Força Aérea Brasileira* has purchased 12, the Belgian Air Force purchased three, the *Fuerza Aérea Ecuatoriana* bought five, some of these being used by the air force-operated airline TAME, and the *Fuerza Aérea Colombiana* similarly bought four for use by Satena. For VIP or Royal Flight use, the Royal Thai Air Force has two, the Venezuelan government, one, the Argentine government, one, the Zambian Air Force, one, the Sultan of Brunei, one, the Korean government, two and the Nepal Royal Flight, one.

The military attractiveness of the HS.748 was enhanced in 1972 when a large freight door was introduced as an option. Combined with the passenger entrance door, which forms the rear part of the freight door and is altered to open rearwards along the side of the fuselage, the new door provides an opening of 5·64 ft by 8·75 ft (1,72 m by 2,67 m), allowing large items of freight to be carried. A suitable freight-carrying floor, with roller equipment, can be provided. The door can be opened in the air, for dropping of paratroops and/or supplies, and several of the air forces listed have bought the "large door" 748, for use in the paradrop rôle. The prototype, a company demonstrator (G-AZJH), first flew on 31 December 1971 and the designation Srs 2C was used temporarily for civil cargo versions with the large door. Hindustan Aeronautics also developed a military freighter version with the large freight door, referred to as the HS.748M and flown on 16 February 1972; this became the subject of a provisional IAF order for 48 in 1973 but the requirement for a tactical transport was subsequently reconsidered and the order was in abeyance at the time of writing, 10 Srs 2 having been ordered in the interim.

Of the 310 HS.748s sold to date, in fact, 138 are for military operators in 14 countries. The balance of 172 have been sold to 49 customers in 36 countries, including 15 for use in an executive or non-airline rôle. Since mid-1967, the basic aircraft has been the Srs 2A, this designation indicating the introduction of further engine improvements. Two slightly different versions of the Dart R Da 7 are applicable to the Srs 2A, the mark numbers being 534-2 and 535-2 (at first known as the 532-2L and 532-2S respectively) with a rating of 2,080 shp.

Special rôles

While the rôle of the HS.748 Srs 2A as a well-proven low-cost short-haul civil transport remains unchallenged, the market for the type is capable of extension by the introduction of new versions adapted for special rôles. Reference has already been made to military potentiality and this may be extended to provide a genuine multi-rôle aircraft. The basic HS.748 military transport on offer today is equipped with the fixed rôle fittings required to undertake troop transport (up to 58 troops in forward-facing four-abreast seats) or cargo carrying duties, with an on-board freight handling system including a roller table at the rear freight door and roller conveyor tracks along the cabin floor, plus an optional air transportable hoist with a lifting capacity of 5,600 lb (2 540 kg). Rapid conversion for

continued on page 308

Transgabon is typical of the smaller airlines throughout the world that have found the HS.748 ideally suited to their needs for a reliable, low-cost feederliner.

THE SOVIET AIR FORCES

An Offensive Posture and Expanding Capability

INTELLIGENCE PROGNOSES of Soviet air capability in the years immediately ahead have of late made increasingly gruelling reading for western eyes. The steadily rising perturbation of NATO military leaders faced with major upgrading of the Air Forces of the USSR and allied Warsaw Treaty Organisation air arms in qualitative if not quantitative terms, compounded by a transformation of posture from basically defensive to highly mobile offensive, is being reflected by their ever more numerous public expressions of concern, echoed by the recently-published British Defence White Paper which stressed the growing imbalance between NATO and Warsaw Pact forces.

The gradual erosion of NATO air capability as a result of swingeing budgetary restrictions on defence expenditure is overtly acknowledged; the concomitant growth in capability of the opposing Warsaw Pact forces accelerating the adverse trend in military balance is tacitly admitted. This heightened threat is greatest in Central Europe, where, for example, every tactical combat aircraft fielded by NATO is faced by 2·3 aircraft of the potential opponents. But quantitatively, the Warsaw Pact air forces have for long possessed a very considerable edge; it is the rapidity with which the qualitative supremacy, for long considered a traditional advantage in the West, is eroding away that proffers NATO leaders the most unpalatable aspect of the currently-evolving situation. Frightening implications are inherent in the recent comments of the RAF Chief of Air Staff, Air Chief Marshal Sir Andrew Humphrey, to the effect that Soviet industry is now manufacturing 1,800 advanced combat aircraft annually — a rate that could re-equip the entire RAF with warplanes approximating in calibre to the *future* Panavia Tornado within *five months* — and that production is concentrating on *offensive* tactical aircraft to the virtual exclusion of defensive interceptors.

In view of the measure of *détente* achieved in recent years, Soviet sustainment of a substantial real growth rate in military aviation capability provides something of an enigma. If Soviet air power was markedly inferior to that of the West or if a serious external threat to the Soviet Union existed, the momentum of capability enhancement could perhaps be accepted with some equanimity; the apparently irrational and disproportionate emphasis that is being placed on air power growth can only be viewed with alarm. Conclusions concerning Soviet intentions do not come within the scope of this survey and it suffices to say that the Air Forces of the USSR protect the world's largest state, which stretches some 7,000 miles (11 265 km) east-to-west and 3,000 miles (4 830 km) north-to-south, NATO's forward defence forces abutting the Warsaw Pact buffer zone — the loyalty of which is dependent

Now being deployed in increasing numbers in Eastern Europe, the reconnaissance version of the high-altitude, deep-ranging MiG-25, the Foxbat-B (head of page and immediately below), can overfly West European NATO countries with impunity, no currently deployed NATO SAM system or interceptor being capable of challenging it at its operational ceiling. Ports and dielectric panels for optical and other sensing devices may be clearly seen in the forward fuselage (Photos courtesy Flug Revue).

The MiG-23S (Flogger-B) interceptor (illustrated above) has now been in service with the V-VS for five years and normally carries a mix of AA-7 Apex and AA-8 Aphid AAMs plus a twin-barrel GSh-23 cannon. With a 90-cm AI radar, the MiG-23S reportedly has a combat thrust/weight ratio of the order of 0·8 : 1·0 and is rapidly replacing the late-model MiG-21s deployed by the FA in Eastern Europe.

The MiG-23B (Flogger-D), seen immediately above, has been optimised for low-level strike and differs in a number of respects from the MiG-23S, having fixed engine air inlets, a sturdier undercarriage with low-pressure tyres, a Gatling-type gun, repositioned stores pylons and a nose-mounted laser designator. (Below) The two-seat MiG-23U (Flogger-C) is included in the inventory of all V-VS MiG-23 squadrons, operating in the combat proficiency training and, allegedly, ECM rôles (Photos courtesy Flug Revue).

to some extent on the maintenance of a strong Soviet presence — and a hostile China sharing Siberia's long southern frontier. Huge tactical air establishments are thus, perhaps, understandable, although many western strategists contend that Soviet air power now far exceeds what is required for deterrence and defence — of course, Soviet ideas on "how much is enough" may differ significantly from those held in the West.

The organizational structure of the Soviet forces is unlike anything to be found in the West and the Soviet equivalent of the USAF — the only other of the world's air arms comparable in size — comprises the Air Forces of the USSR, or *Voenno-vozdushniye Sily* (V-VS), with one of its components, the Naval Air Force*, or *Aviatsiya Voenno-morskovo Flota* (AV-MF), excluded; the manned interceptor element of the Anti-aircraft Defence of the Homeland, or *Protivo-vozdushnaya Oborona (Strany)*, which is a separate command of the Armed Forces of the USSR, and the Strategic Rocket Forces, or *Raketny Voiska Strategicheskovo Naznacheniya*, which, too, is a separate command. Collectively, these comprise what is, in terms of personnel strength and

* This aspect of Soviet air power was dealt with in detail two years ago, in June 1974 — see "Stronger Sealegs for Soviet Air Power" by Norman Polmar.

equipment inventory, the largest of the world's air arms. For obvious reasons, detailed numerical precision is not possible, but the consensus of western intelligence agencies suggests that the personnel strength of the aerospace forces (ie, V-VS, P-VO and RVSN) is currently 1·3m-1·4m and that the firstline combat aircraft strength of the V-VS (excluding the AV-MF) and the P-VO *Strany* is approximately 11,000 warplanes. The principal components of the V-VS are the Frontal Aviation (*Frontovaya Aviatsiya*), the Long-range Aviation (*Aviatsiya Dal'nevo Deistviya*) and the Transport Aviation (*Voenno-transportnaya Aviatsiya*), plus, of course, the previously mentioned naval air element, the AV-MF, overall command of the V-VS being invested in Chief Marshal of Aviation Pavel Kutakhov, responsible to the Minister of Defence, Marshal of the Soviet Union A A Grechko, the V-VS Chief-of-Staff being Marshal of Aviation A P Silantiev.

Emphasis on TacAir upgrading

Since the early 'seventies, the highest priority has been assigned to the enhancement of the capabilities of the tactical component of the V-VS, the *Frontovaya Aviatsiya* (FA), which is immersed in a thoroughgoing re-equipment programme. The traditional Soviet emphasis on air defence in its tactical air elements has, in recent years, given place to concentration on aircraft optimised for the interdiction and counterair rôles with a dramatic improvement in capability. The FA is currently fielding roughly 25 per cent more tactical strike fighters than the USAF and US Marine Corps combined, and according to US intelligence assessments, more than half of the counterair and some 80 per cent of close air support aircraft now in the inventory have been phased in over the past five years.

The FA currently possesses marginally more than 5,000 first-line combat aircraft, plus about 3,000 obsolescing tactical-type aircraft that are utilised primarily in training rôles, and these are deployed within the various military and frontier districts according to their importance and with the Forces Groups based in other Warsaw Pact countries, strong elements being deployed in Czechoslovakia, Poland, Hungary and East Germany — upwards of 800 FA aircraft are based on East German airfields alone. The FA has undergone a certain amount of reorganisation in recent years and the Frontal Aviation Army (*Frontovaya Aviatsionnaya Armiya*) now possesses a purely organisational significance — there are currently 16 assigned to 12 Military Districts and the four Forces Groups deployed outside the Soviet Union proper —

as do also its component Aviation Corps (*aviatsionny korpus*), the largest operational formation being effectively the Division (*divisiya*) comprising three and sometimes more regiments (*polki*), each of which possesses three squadrons (*eskadrilii*) of 12-16 aircraft.

All squadrons in each Regiment operate the same aircraft type and the inventory of each squadron usually includes two or three dual-rôle aircraft (ie, equipped to fulfil both combat proficiency training and operational tasks). The regiments of each Division all usually perform one primary rôle (eg, counterair, tactical reconnaissance, air superiority, close support, etc) but not necessarily with only one aircraft type. Transport and support components are assigned at divisional level, and communications and liaison elements at regimental level.

FA elements attached to a specific Military District or Forces Group are referred to by the designation of the District or Group (eg, Aviation of the Northern Group of Forces, or *Aviatsiya Severnoi Gruppi Voisk*). The principal Military Districts are Moscow, Leningrad, Baltic, Kiev, Volga, Trans-Caucasion, North Caucasian, Carpathian, Ural, Odessa, Byelo-Russia, Central Asia, Turkistan, Trans-Baikal, Siberian and Far East. The Forces Groups comprise the Northern Group of Forces with Headquarters at Legnica, Poland; the Southern Group of Forces with Headquarters at Tokol, Hungary; the Central Group of Forces with Headquarters at Milovice, Czechoslovakia, and the Group of Soviet Forces in Germany with Headquarters at Wünsdorf. In addition, there are a number of Frontier Troop Districts (eg, Eastern Frontier District) to which FA elements are assigned.

Over the past three years, the infusion of more effective combat aircraft into the ranks of the FA — and particularly the elements facing NATO in Central Europe — has accelerated rapidly, and the capabilities of these new tactical aircraft have necessitated major re-evaluation of western projections of V-VS tactical capability over the remaining years of the present decade, and it is primarily these re-evaluated projections that have resulted in NATO's current concern.

Rapidly becoming numerically the most important combat aircraft in FA elements deployed with the Forces Groups in the buffer zone of satellite countries along the Soviet western periphery and in the three westernmost Military Districts of European Russia is the very effective variable-geometry MiG-23 fighter of which some 1,200 have now reportedly been delivered into the V-VS inventory. Two basic versions of this aircraft are widely used, the MiG-23S (*Flogger-B*) which is optimised for the air superiority and intercept rôles and the MiG-23B (*Flogger-D*) which is intended primarily for battlefield interdiction. The former totes a 23-mm twin-barrel GSh-23 cannon and a quartet of infrared- and radar-homing AA-7 *Apex* and AA-8 *Aphid* AAMs, and features a 90-cm AI radar, and the latter replaces the twin-barrel weapon with a six-barrel rotary cannon of similar calibre and has terrain avoidance radar and a laser designator.

Even more significant among new generation FA tactical aircraft is the Sukhoi Su-19 (*Fencer-A*), which, perhaps best described as a slightly scaled-down F-111, is the first Soviet fighter optimised for the long-range interdiction rôle and the first to be capable of lifting an offensive load comparable to those carried by current generation western aircraft. Capable of attacking any NATO airfield, including those in the UK, from East German bases with a 6,000-lb (2 720-kg) warload, the Su-19 began to enter FA service during the course of 1974, and several hundred are now thought to have been delivered. This,

The Tupolev Tu-22 (Blinder), which has now seen 10 years of service with the ADD and almost as long with the AV-MF, still forms an important item in the V-VS inventory, the example illustrated below revealing a number of modifications recently introduced. The remotely-directed tail gun turret has apparently been deleted, this and its attendant radome having been replaced by a tail cone incorporating electronic "bulges" presumably associated with passive jamming or decoy equipment, and aft-looking bomb-damage-assessment camera ports now appear aft of the main undercarriage wells. The outline of the AS-4 Kitchen ASM may just be seen, this being the normal armament associated with the bulged radome (peculiar to the Blinder-B). The operational training version, the Tu-22U (Blinder-D) is illustrated above right.

together with the previously-mentioned MiG-23, is likely to form the backbone of the FA over the next decade, although yet a third new tactical fighter has been absorbed by the FA inventory in recent years, this being the Sukhoi Su-17 (*Fitter-C*), a variable-geometry derivative of the obsolescent Sukhoi Su-7 (*Fitter-A*) which is in process of being phased out. Although retaining much of the structure of the earlier fighter and enjoying only marginal increases in fuel capacity and power, the Su-17 represents a marked improvement, possessing greater versatility than its predecessor and offering better shortfield performance.

For reconnaissance at extreme altitudes, the FA is deploying with its Northern Forces Group Aviation and with the Aviation of the Group of Soviet Forces in Germany the spectacular MiG-25 (*Foxbat-B*), which is used in its interceptor version by the IAP-VO *Strany*. Possessing short-endurance $M = 3.0$ capability and capable of overflying any portion of Western Europe with — as yet — relative immunity, NATO possessing no air defence weapon capable of reliably intercepting it, the reconnaissance MiG-25 features a battery of cameras in the nose and dielectric panels are much in evidence. The air superiority and intercept rôles are being steadily taken over by the MiG-23S, but a substantial number of late-production third-generation MiG-21s (eg, the MiG-21SMT) with upgraded avionics and augmented internal

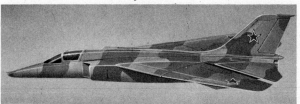

Two of the latest additions to the V-VS inventory are the medium-to-long-range Backfire-B and the variable-geometry two-seat Sukhoi Su-19 Fencer-A illustrated above and below respectively by provisional artist's impressions.

fuel capacity are likely to remain in service with frontline FA squadrons for a further two or three years. The phase-out of obsolescent aircraft types is proceeding at a pace commensurate with the introduction of the previously-mentioned types. The Yak-27R (*Mangrove*) has been retired and the Yak-28 (*Brewer*) is being progressively withdrawn, although the electronic countermeasures escort version (*Brewer-E*) is expected to remain in the inventory for some time to come. The Su-7BMK and aircraft of similar vintage are gradually being relegated to Military or Frontier Districts of minor importance.

There is a continuing and significant build-up of FA helicopter forces which now total some 2,500 rotorcraft, mostly of the Mil Mi-8 (*Hip*) type which, while primarily intended for the transport rôle, is extensively employed as a gunship with strut-rigged UV-32-57 rocket pods and a 23-mm cannon on a flexible mounting, but there are now several hundred of the formidable Mi-24 (*Hind*) attack and assault transport helicopter, and a new two-seat anti-armour helicopter with a radar-directed 23-mm chin turret gun and advanced anti-tank missiles is expected to be introduced by the FA by 1978.

FA deployments between Groups of Forces or Military Districts vary to some extent with changes in world tension. For example, there are 18 to 20 FA divisions with between 2,000 and 2,200 aircraft permanently assigned to the Military Districts bordering on Chinese territory, between Tadzhikistan (Central Asian MD) and the Pacific, but any increase in tension can, it is alleged, produce reinforcement of at least 50 per cent within five-seven days.

Strategic bombing and airlift capabilities

While the strategic bombing capability of the V-VS as represented by the *Aviatsiya Dal'nevo Deistviya* (ADD) was progressively declining in importance with growing equipment obsolescence and the transfer of emphasis to the Strategic Rocket Forces, it began to take on renewed significance last year with the introduction of the potentially intercontinental-capable *Backfire-B* variable-geometry bomber which has provided one of the primary bones of contention during the Strategic Arms Limitation Talks. Reported to have attained a delivery tempo of five-six monthly earlier this year, the 286,600-lb (130 000-kg) *Backfire-B* is, by virtue of its size and configuration alone, a strategic weapon and one which US military observers view as an unacceptable threat to the USA; it is the subject of deliberate obscurantism on the part of the Soviet Union which insists that the *Backfire* is a *tactical* weapons system, yet its capability compares closely with and in some aspects exceeds that of the Rockwell B-1, an aircraft

Although now being progressively phased out in favour of more advanced all-weather interceptors, the Yak-28P (Firebar), illustrated below, still possesses an important place in the inventory of the IAP-VO Strany and is unlikely to disappear from the manned interceptor force until late in the present decade.

The Mil Mi-24 (Hind) anti-armour and assault transport helicopter is now serving in substantial numbers with the FA. Possessing a generally similar power plant arrangement to that of the Mi-8, the Mi-24 is, in fact, a somewhat smaller and lighter helicopter and is seen here with four UV-32-57 rocket pods on the underwing pylons. The twin rails on each wing-tip hardpoint each carry an AT-2 Swatter anti-tank missile but may presumably also carry the wire-guided Sagger missile.

that the Soviet Union accepts as being a *strategic* bomber.

Only some 45-50 *Backfires* were expected to have attained operational status with the ADD by mid-1976 — approximately half of production deliveries are currently being diverted to the AV-MF — and these join a force of upwards of 300 Tupolev Tu-22s (*Blinder*), which, with a tactical radius of 1,370 miles (2 200 km) in a hi-lo-hi mission profile, is only a medium-range bomber. Intelligence of the expansion of production facilities for the *Backfire* gained from reconnaissance satellites indicates that the ADD inventory of this advanced bomber will, by the mid 'eighties, substantially exceed the 250-300 aircraft that has hitherto been projected by western intelligence agencies. The Tu-22s are augmented by a declining force of fewer than 150 obsolescent Tu-16 (*Badger*) medium bombers and a similar quantity of aged Myasishchev M-4 and Tupolev Tu-20 heavy bombers which, with the latter preponderant, have for long been little more than symbolic.

The ADD, which is commanded by General Colonel of Aviation Vasily V Reshetnikov, a Deputy Commander-in-Chief of the V-VS, still possesses a strategic reconnaissance commitment, emphasis during the early 'seventies being placed on the surveillance of those areas of China bordering on the USSR, such types as the An-12 (*Cub-C*) being employed for ELINT missions. The largest component of the ADD is the Division which normally consists of three regiments each with three 10-aircraft squadrons with attached flight refuelling tanker elements.

While the V-VS continues to place less emphasis than the USAF on strategic military transports, the primary logistic support component of the V-VS, the *Voenno-transportnaya Aviatsiya* (V-TA), has progressively increased its airlift capability in recent years commensurate with the increase in emphasis on vertical envelopment tactics and possesses some 800 Antonov An-12 (*Cub*) tactical transports. There are currently approximately 60 strategic transports in two V-TA divisions, two-thirds of which are Antonov An-22s (*Cock*), production of which terminated in 1974, the remainder being Ilyushin Il-76s (*Candid*) which entered the operational inventory last year and a flight refuelling tanker variant of which is now in production. There is some evidence indicating that more effort is now being exerted to afford the V-TA a more sophisticated airlift capability for the support of operations in Africa and elsewhere, and western analysts are of the

opinion that the Il-76 is providing the cornerstone of this development.

Commanded by General Lieutenant of Aviation G N Pakilev, the V-TA has a primary commitment to the airborne forces which include seven 7,000-man airborne divisions of which more than half, together with their support elements, can be lifted simultaneously over short-to-medium ranges.

Strategic air defence

By far the most massive and expensive air defence system in the world, with 9,500 surface-to-air missile launchers, 2,700 interceptor fighters and in excess of 5,000 radars, the Anti-Aircraft Defence of the Homeland is an independent service commanded by Marshal of the Soviet Union P F Batitskiy. Responsible for the air defence of the main centres of industry, its very substantial manned interceptor force, the *Istrebitel'naya Aviatsilya P-VO Strany*, or IAP-VO *Strany*, commanded by General Colonel of Aviation A Ye Borovykh, has traditionally enjoyed priority in equipment with new combat types, a priority which, over the past two years, has apparently been transferred to the FA.

While the numerical strength of the IAP-VO *Strany* has been declining at an average annual rate of 100 aircraft over the past decade, the overall capability of the force has grown steadily during this period with the phasing in of progressively more sophisticated interceptor fighters. The P-VO *Strany* Headquarters in Moscow exercises overall control of the Warsaw Treaty Organisation air defence and warning system and deploys its forces in two P-VO Districts, the *Moskovsky Okrug P-VO* (Moscow) and the *Bakinsky Okrug P-VO* (Baku). Elsewhere in the USSR, IAP-VO formations are assigned for the defence of specific centres of industry and population, and for peripheral defence, mounting standing patrols over areas not screened by surface-to-air missiles.

Older interceptors, such as the Sukhoi Su-11 (*Fishpot-C*) and Yak-28P (*Firebar*), are believed to equip about 40 per cent of the strategic defence fighter component, the most important interceptor being the Su-15 (*Flagon*), a markedly improved version of which (*Flagon-E*) having been phased in two years ago and making up, in part, a low-altitude intercept deficiency which has been the major weakness of the P-VO *Strany*. Generally acknowledged to possess good intercept capabilities at high, medium *and* low altitudes, the *Flagon-E* is substantially more powerful than earlier versions of the Su-15; embodies a number of aerodynamic improvements, including a revised wing; standardises on the GSh-23 twin-barrel cannon which it uses in concert with a mix of both infrared- and radar-homing late-generation AAMs, and has upgraded avionics. Phased into IAP-VO *Strany* service simultaneously with the growth version of the Su-15 was the interceptor version of the MiG-25 (*Foxbat-A*), which has a dash speed in excess of $M = 3.0$ and mounts a quartet of massive AA-6 *Acrid* 23-mile (37-km) range AAMs, two being semi-active radar homers and two being infrared homers. The *Fox Fire* radar system of the MiG-25 interceptor is being developed to incorporate an extensive look-down capability but it is uncertain as to what stage this programme has reached.

Considerable effort is being expended in developing defences against the USAF's short-range attack missile (SRAM), these calling for the SRAM carriers to be attacked and destroyed at the earliest possible penetration stage and a prerequisite thus being early detection. A small number — possibly as few as a dozen — of Tu-126 (*Moss*) AWACS (Airborne Warning and Control System) aircraft have been utilised for several years but provide only limited airborne controlled intercept capability. The Tu-126 is believed to be reasonably effective in overwater operations but to have strict limitations in the more challenging overland task. It may be assumed that effort is being directed towards the development of a more effective AWACS capable of tracking intruding aircraft at low altitudes over land but such is thought unlikely to achieve operational status much before the end of the decade. The Il-86 (*Candid*) presents itself as a possible carrier for such a system. Peripheral standing patrols are apparently still mounted by the ageing Tupolev Tu-28P (alias Tu-128), but reports persist that this type is being progressively replaced by a long-range intercept derivative of the Tu-22.

The training organisation

The V-VS training organisation embraces a very large number of technical and specialist schools under the command of General Colonel of Aviation Ye M Gorbatyuk, combat training being provided by a separate organisation under General Colonel of Aviation P S Kirsanov. The P-VO *Strany* has its own training organisation under General Colonel of Aviation V N Abramov, with combat training being the responsibility of General Colonel of Aviation N D Gulayev. Pupil pilots for both the V-VS and the IAP-VO *Strany* normally receive both primary and basic instruction (on the Yak-18 and Yak-11) with the schools of the para-military DOSAAF (Volunteer Society for Co-operation with the Army, Aviation and the Fleet) organisation prior to induction

by one or other of the services. DOSAAF is headed by Marshal of Aviation Aleksandr Pokryshkin, a leading Soviet WW II "ace".

The DOSAAF training permits specialization at a relatively early stage in the service programme. An all-through jet training syllabus has been employed by the V-VS since 1965, basic instruction being provided on the Czechoslovak L 29 Delfin (*Maya*) and, more recently, the L 39 Albatross. From this point, V-VS and IAP-VO *Strany* pupil pilots are assigned to the advanced flying schools operated by the individual services, future fighter pilots having already completed advanced conversion on the MiG-15UTI (*Midget*). Type conversion is conducted on two-seat versions of the various operational aircraft, such as the MiG-21U (*Mongol*), the MiG-23U (*Flogger-C*), the Su-7U (*Moujik*), the Su-11U (*Maiden*), or the Yak-28U (*Maestro*). Combat training is undertaken on type at specialist flying combat training schools.

Flying and technical training schools are distributed throughout the USSR, and the training organisation includes three academies, the *Voenno-vozdushnaya Inzhenernaya Akademiya im Prof N Ye Zhukovsky*, which has components in both Moscow and Shchelkovo, north-west of Moscow; the *Voenno-vozdushnaya Akademiya im Yu A Gagarin* at Monino, near Shchelkovo, which is a command staff and tactical academy, and the VIRTA (*Voennaya Inzhenivnaya Radiotekhnicheokaya Akademiya*), the radio and electronic engineering academy at Kharkov named after Marshal of the Soviet Union L A Govorov. One of the most important flying schools is the *Kachinskoya Vyshee Voennoye Aviatsionnoye Uchilishshce im A F Myasnikov* near Volgograd, believed to be the largest military flying school in the world, and there are Pilots' Higher Schools at Borisoglebsk and Barnaul, and a combined Pilots' and Navigators' Higher School at Stavropol. Other V-VS advanced flying training schools include those at Tambov, Orenburg, Balashov (near Saratov), Syzran, Chernigov, Kharkov and Yeisk (near the Sea of Azov). There are advanced navigational schools at Chelyabinsk and Voroshilovograd, and there are aeronautical technical schools at Tambov, Riga, Vasilkov (near Kiev), Archinsk, Irkutsk and two at Kharkov.

Students pass out from these schools with the rank of lieutenant. From the higher schools the qualification is Pilot (Navigator), Engineer (Diploma), etc. The P-VO *Strany* organisation includes an advanced flying training school at Armavir, a technical aviation school at Daugavpils, radio-technical schools at Vilnyus and Krasnoyarsk, a command-electronics school at Pushkin, near Leningrad, and anti-aircraft rocket schools at Engels, Opochka (near Pskov), Gorky, Yaroslavl, Ordzhonikidze and Zhitomir.

According to leading US strategists, if the present tempo of V-VS modernisation is maintained, the Soviet Air Forces will have established decisive superiority in both tactical and strategic power by the early 'eighties when the Soviet Union could well have gained all the preconditions that would enable it to opt for global conflict should diplomatic pressures exerted from strength fail to attain its goals. The development of a highly capable offensive tactical air force that can strike deep into western Europe and takes the place of the predominantly defensive force deployed in the past has already reached an advanced stage; there are indications that a sophisticated airlift capability is being created that will be able to support effectively direct or indirect military action in Africa and elsewhere, and the manned strategic bombing force is being resuscitated and bids fair to pose, by the end of the decade, a formidable threat. In view of the dramatic advances to be seen in V-VS equipment in recent years, which have been paralleled by the Soviet Union's land and sea forces, and the emphasis on kill hardware coupled with a change in posture from defensive to offensive, it is small wonder that NATO military leaders are becoming increasingly perturbed. □

The Tu-126 (Moss) AWACS aircraft (below) serves in the V-VS in small numbers but provides only limited airborne controlled intercept capability and development of an appreciably more advanced system may be assumed to be in progress.

JAPAN'S FINAL SWORD STROKE...

THE STORY OF SHUSUI

BY YOSHIO IMAGAWA*

IT IS SAID of the Japanese national character that fanaticism and fatalism are innate ingredients. Assuming this allegation to contain at least an element of truth, no excessive stretch is imposed on the imagination to conceive the impact that the exotic Messerschmitt Me 163B undoubtedly had on the Japanese military and naval attachés in the autumn of 1943, when they witnessed a demonstration of this extraordinary warplane at an airfield near Bad Zwischenahn in Oldenburg. To these representatives of the Japanese services, with such inborn predilections, the attraction of so audacious a concept, spiced with the element of risk imposed by the unstable nature of the rocket fuels and unpredictable behaviour of the rocket motor, must surely have been irresistible. Certainly the hazards that it imposed on pilots and ground staff alike — and concerning which their German hosts had expounded at length — found little prominence in the highly enthusiastic reports that they subsequently transmitted to their respective headquarters; was not this beyond any doubt the weapon with which to counter the bombing offensive against the Japanese home islands that was being increasingly overtly predicted?

These reports and the associated proposals for licence manufacture of the Me 163B in Japan were not to receive universal approbation, however, for serious misgivings were expressed concerning Japanese industry's ability to produce the vast quantities of hydrogen peroxide, the principal ingredient of the primary rocket motor fuel, and the hydrazine hydrate employed by the catalyst, the manufacture of which demanded the expenditure of inordinate quantities of electrical power. There was, too, much criticism of the strictly limited endurance of the rocket-powered fighter, necessitating its production in vast numbers if it was to provide an effective antidote to the threat posed by the B-29 Superfortress, and it was argued that Japanese industry could ill afford to devote the proportion of its capacity that such production would demand to so radical and as yet still operationally unproven a weapon.

While the arguments concerning the pros and cons of adopting the Me 163B continued among Army and Navy aviation engineers and air tacticians, negotiations for the

acquisition of manufacturing licences for both the Me 163B airframe and its Walter HWK 509A bi-fuel rocket motor, *Reichsmark* 20m being demanded for the latter alone. Nevertheless, agreement was finally reached under which Germany was committed to supplying Japan with complete blueprints and manufacturing data for the Me 163B and its power plant, one complete airframe, two sets of sub-assemblies and components, and three complete HWK 509A rocket motors by 1 March 1944. The Japanese were to be permitted to study German manufacturing processes for both airframe and power plant, and facilities were to be afforded the Japanese joint-service mission to permit the study of *Luftwaffe* operating techniques for the rocket-propelled interceptor as these evolved.

Events conspired to prevent Germany from fulfilling many of the terms of the agreement, but in each of March and April 1944, an allegedly complete set of technical data on the Me 163B airframe, its engine and the manufacturing processes of the fuels for the latter was passed to the Japanese joint-service mission, the first set being consigned to the care of Cdr Kikkawa for transfer to Japan aboard the submarine *Satsuki* and the second set being passed to Cdr Iwaya aboard the submarine *Matsu*. Both submarines set sail for Japan, but the *Satsuki* was sunk en route by the Allies and, after an extremely hazardous voyage, the *Matsu* reached Singapore on 14 July 1944. Immediately the submarine docked, Cdr Eiichi Iwaya and his precious blueprints were transferred to an aircraft and flown to Tokyo.

Following Cdr Iwaya's arrival, staff officers of the 1st Naval

(Head of page) The two prototypes of the Akikusa glider after completion by the Navy Air Technical Arsenal, and (below) Lt Cdr Inuzuka after completing the initial test flight of the first Akikusa glider.

---

* "Yoshio Imagawa" is the nom-de-plume of a well-known Japanese aircraft engineer, who, while with the Mitsubishi Jukogyo KK, was closely associated with the Shusui programme.

Air Technical Arsenal, the *Dai-Ichi Kaigun Gijitsusho*, in Yokosuka met on a daily basis to discuss the practicalities of adapting the German aircraft and its engine for Japanese manufacturing techniques and mass production, but whether or not the Me 163B *would* be built in Japan had still to be finally resolved. Although Vice Admiral Jisaburo Ozawa's crushing defeat in the Battle of the Philippine Sea and the obvious imminence of Allied capture of the Marianas — which would place the Japanese home islands in easy striking range of B-29 Superfortresses — had engendered a psychological state of receptiveness to any weapon, however revolutionary, that offered some chance of success, strong doubts were still being expressed as to the wisdom of committing so much effort to so radical a warplane. Finally, the balance was tipped by the personal efforts of the CO of the Arsenal, Vice Admiral Misao Wada, who, pleading that a desperate affliction called for a desperate remedy, reminded the committee of the Japanese Navy's traditional adventuresomeness in engineering, suggesting that the rocket-powered point defence interceptor was no more innovatory a concept than others that the service had pioneered.

Mitsubishi had meanwhile been assigned the task of developing a Japanese version of the Me 163B but had been reluctant to initiate a full-scale effort while some element of doubt that the project would be pursued remained. However, the Navy now issued a 19-*Shi* (19th year of the Showa regime, or 1944) specification for a rocket-propelled point defence interceptor fighter based on the Me 163B, assigning it the

Mitsubishi J8M1 Shusui Cutaway drawing key
1 Wingtip bumper
2 Elevon outer hinge
3 Starboard elevon
4 Trim tab
5 Wooden wing construction
6 Fixed leading edge wing slot
7 Elevon mounting
8 Rocker bar
9 Elevon actuation push rod
10 Control bell crank
11 Wing rear spar
12 Starboard inboard trim flap
13 Trim flap hinge control
14 Flap control rod
15 Starboard underwing landing flap
16 Main Otsu (C-Stoff) wing tank
17 Wooden box-type mainspar
18 Otsu leading edge tank
19 Wing tank connecting pipe
20 Connecting pipe fairing
21 Otsu feed pipe
22 Toko Ro.2 (KR 20) motor turbine
23 Engine bearer frame
24 Trailing edge fillet
25 Combustion chamber support brace
26 Tailwheel steering control
27 Axle pivot mounting
28 Steering fork
29 Tailwheel oleo
30 Tailwheel fairing
31 Rocket thrust orifice
32 Tailpipe fairing
33 Cooling slots
34 Rudder trim tab
35 Rudder construction
36 Horn balance

AVIAGRAPHICA

designation J8M1, and the project, having been a joint Navy-Army venture from the outset, was also allocated the *Kitai* or Experimental Airframe designation Ki.200 by the Army, the somewhat emotive appellation of Shusui (Sword Stroke) being given to the warplane in keeping with its exotic nature.

On 27 July, a full-scale meeting was held of all the service, industry and ministerial factions involved in the Shusui programme, and it was decided that the German data for both airframe and power plant would be adhered to closely. The Me 163B airframe had proven aerodynamic qualities and, in so far as the rocket motor was concerned, Japan had no alternative but to adhere religiously to the German specifications, having little experience with bi-fuel rocket motors. It had meanwhile been ascertained that the German data were very far from complete in respect of the airframe, detailed information on major structural areas and certain component parts being lacking and material specifications inadequate. This fact led to some dissension between Navy and Army representatives, the latter suggesting that, in view of the inadequacy of the data supplied and the amount of experimental work that would be thus entailed, little time would be lost in completely redesigning the airframe in order to achieve a desired improvement in powered endurance. The Navy representatives demurred and the Army was overruled, although, in the event, while ostensibly accepting the directive that the Shusui should adhere closely to the Me 163B in every respect, the service clandestinely ignored it.

Overall supervision of the Shusui airframe was assigned to

Mitsubishi's Nagoya plant and a team was assembled under the leadership of Mijiro Takahashi, comprising Tetsuo Hikita, Shunichi Sadamori, Isao Imai, Makoto Kuroiwa, Sadao Dori and Toshihiko Narahara. Naval Air Technical Arsenal engineers involved included Cdr Iwaya, who had brought the technical data from Germany and had spent some time at Messerschmitt's Regensburg factory, Cdr Koshino (from the Science Division) and Lt Kumamoto (from the Test Division). Lt Cdr One was assigned to the project as test pilot from the Yokosuka Naval Air Group.

The final full-scale meeting concerning airframe planning was held on 7 August and from this point on, in sharp contrast to the half-hearted approach to the project that had been displayed in the preceding months, the Shusui development tempo accelerated at a tremendous pace. Inspection of a full-scale cockpit mock-up took place on 8 September and of a mock-up of the entire aircraft 18 days later on 26 September, and during the previous month, the Navy and the Army had finalised a production schedule which called for the completion of 155 aircraft by March 1945, 1,300 by the following September and no fewer than 3,600 by March 1946.

Meanwhile, Mijiro Takahashi and his team, eating and sleeping by their drawing boards, were endeavouring to compensate for the lack of detailed information relating to

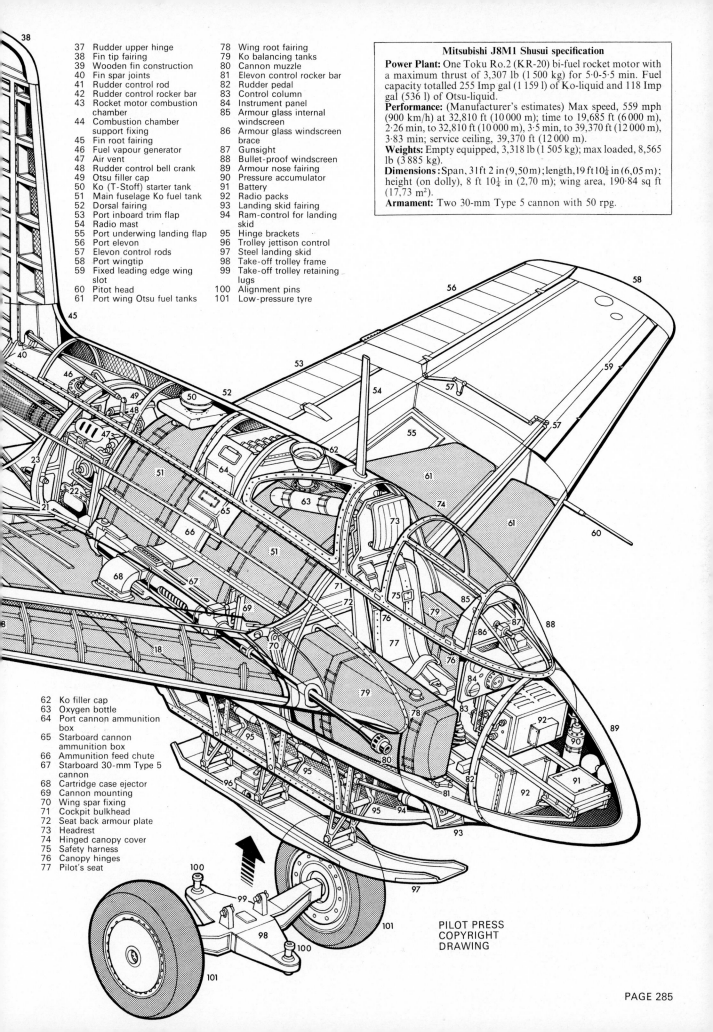

37 Rudder upper hinge
38 Fin tip fairing
39 Wooden fin construction
40 Fin spar joints
41 Rudder control rod
42 Rudder control rocker bar
43 Rocket motor combustion chamber
44 Combustion chamber support fixing
45 Fin root fairing
46 Fuel vapour generator
47 Air vent
48 Rudder control bell crank
49 Otsu filler cap
50 Ko (T-Stoff) starter tank
51 Main fuselage Ko fuel tank
52 Dorsal fairing
53 Port inboard trim flap
54 Radio mast
55 Port underwing landing flap
56 Port elevon
57 Elevon control rods
58 Port wingtip
59 Fixed leading edge wing slot
60 Pitot head
61 Port wing Otsu fuel tanks

78 Wing root fairing
79 Ko balancing tanks
80 Cannon muzzle
81 Elevon control rocker bar
82 Rudder pedal
83 Control column
84 Instrument panel
85 Armour glass internal windscreen
86 Armour glass windscreen brace
87 Gunsight
88 Bullet-proof windscreen
89 Armour nose fairing
90 Pressure accumulator
91 Battery
92 Radio packs
93 Landing skid fairing
94 Ram-control for landing skid
95 Hinge brackets
96 Trolley jettison control
97 Steel landing skid
98 Take-off trolley frame
99 Take-off trolley retaining lugs
100 Alignment pins
101 Low-pressure tyre

Mitsubishi J8M1 Shusui specification

Power Plant: One Toku Ro.2 (KR-20) bi-fuel rocket motor with a maximum thrust of 3,307 lb (1 500 kg) for 5·0-5·5 min. Fuel capacity totalled 255 Imp gal (1 159 l) of Ko-liquid and 118 Imp gal (536 l) of Otsu-liquid.
Performance: (Manufacturer's estimates) Max speed, 559 mph (900 km/h) at 32,810 ft (10 000 m); time to 19,685 ft (6 000 m), 2·26 min, to 32,810 ft (10 000 m), 3·5 min, to 39,370 ft (12 000 m), 3·83 min; service ceiling, 39,370 ft (12 000 m).
Weights: Empty equipped, 3,318 lb (1 505 kg); max loaded, 8,565 lb (3 885 kg).
Dimensions: Span, 31 ft 2 in (9,50 m); length, 19 ft 10¼ in (6,05 m); height (on dolly), 8 ft 10¼ in (2,70 m); wing area, 190·84 sq ft (17,73 m²).
Armament: Two 30-mm Type 5 cannon with 50 rpg.

62 Ko filler cap
63 Oxygen bottle
64 Port cannon ammunition box
65 Starboard cannon ammunition box
66 Ammunition feed chute
67 Starboard 30-mm Type 5 cannon
68 Cartridge case ejector
69 Cannon mounting
70 Wing spar fixing
71 Cockpit bulkhead
72 Seat back armour plate
73 Headrest
74 Hinged canopy cover
75 Safety harness
76 Canopy hinges
77 Pilot's seat

PILOT PRESS
COPYRIGHT
DRAWING

The MXY8 Akikusa (above and below) was a faithful full-scale wooden replica of the Shusui rocket-propelled interceptor and it will be noted that even the rocket exhaust pipe was simulated.

certain aspects of the airframe with educated guesses — no time was available for full-scale testing of each item — and as the drawings were completed they were passed to the workshops where parallel construction was proceeding on three airframes, one being a structural test specimen and the other two being intended as so-called "heavy gliders", their purpose being to evaluate the flying characteristics of the Shusui with ballast replacing rocket motor and fuel. Takahashi's team followed the structural design of the German original faithfully, the only changes of any consequence being those dictated by Japanese equipment. For example, the 17-*Shi* 30-mm Type 5 cannon were both larger and heavier than the similar calibre Rheinmetall Borsig "pneumatic hammers" that they replaced, necessitating the extension of each wing root by 3·94 inches (100 mm) and increasing overall span by 7·88 inches (200 mm). The nose cone, too, had to be lengthened by a similar amount in order to accommodate the more space-consuming Japanese radio pack and battery.

The Japanese were, of course, unfamiliar with the handling characteristics of aircraft lacking a conventional horizontal tail and to provide a means of expediting the training of pilots eventually to be assigned to the rocket-driven fighter, the Scientific Division of the Navy Air Technical Arsenal at Yokosuka had been assigned the task of creating a full-scale wooden glider version of the Shusui. While definitive design work and prototype construction proceeded at Nagoya, Hidemasa Kimura — who had been responsible for the Tachikawa-built A-2600 that had created a new international closed-circuit distance record — developed the glider which was known as the MXY8 Akikusa (Autumn Grass). This was flown for the first time at the Hyakurigahara airfield, the base of the 312th Naval Air Group which, it had been decided, would be the first recipient of the Shusui. This event took place on 8 December, its pilot being Lt Cdr Toyohiko Inuzuka who had taken the place of Lt Cdr One as the project test pilot after the latter had been taken ill. The Akikusa glider was towed into the air by a Kyushu K10W1 and its handling characteristics received a highly favourable report from Inuzuka. The second Akikusa was sent to the Army Aerotechnical Research Institute, the *Rikugun Kokugijutsu Kenkyujo*, at Tachikawa

where it was tested by Col Aramaki with similarly successful results.

On 1 December, the completed structural test specimen was inspected and approved by both services, but a week later, on 7 December, the Tokai district, in which Nagoya was situated, was wracked by strong earth tremors and the airframe, which was undergoing loading tests, was overstressed and suffered distortion, On 18 December, the Ohe plant in which the "heavy gliders" were being built suffered a heavy attack from B-29 Superfortresses* and it was decided to transfer the salvaged airframes, together with the structural test specimen, to a plant that had been created in a mountain cave at Taura, Yokosuka, although the Ohe plant continued, together with the Nanko plant, to build a number of pre-series Shusui interceptors. Despite these setbacks, the first "heavy glider" Shusui was test flown by Lt Cdr Inuzuka at Hyakurigahara airfield on 8 January 1945, after being towed into the air by a Nakajima B6N1 Tenzan attack bomber.

For the initial flight, the engineless Shusui weighed 2,286 lb (1 037 kg) and the CG was situated at 16·8 per cent of the aerodynamic mean chord, Inuzuka confirming that there was no difference between the handling characteristics of this "heavy glider" and the Akikusa apart from a minor change of trim at take-off. During subsequent flights, some elevon vibration was experienced at gliding speeds in excess of 184 mph (296 km/h) but this was eradicated when the gap between the wing and elevon was reduced and the Frise balance near the elevon tip shortened. Various problems were encountered in the oil pressure system, but these were quickly resolved and in March all Navy flight testing of the "heavy glider" was to be pronounced satisfactorily completed. The second "heavy glider" was tested by the Navy at the Kashiwa airfield, Chiba, and this was eventually to be tested also by the Army. However, this service was apparently of the opinion that no useful purpose would be served in hurrying these tests which, in the event, were not to commence until August, and at an early stage in the trials, the Shusui parted company with its towplane prematurely and crashed in a pine forest, its pilot suffering injuries.

The first pre-series Shusui was completed by the Ohe plant in late December 1944, and, fitted with a dummy rocket motor, was sent to the Naval Air Technical Arsenal at Yokosuka. However, while progress with airframe design and manufacture had been quite startlingly rapid, work on the rocket motor was proving less easily accomplished.

Power plant development

Development and manufacture of the copy of the Walter HWK 509A bi-fuel rocket motor was assigned to Mitsubishi's aero engine division under the supervision of the Army and with the close co-operation of the Engine Division of the Naval Air Technical Arsenal and Mitsubishi Juko's Nagasaki Arms Manufacturing Company, the designation Toku Ro.2 being allocated to the power plant, although it was also to be known as the KR-20. Production of the *Ko*-liquid (as the *T-Stoff* was known) — 80 per cent hydrogen peroxide (H_2O_2) plus oxyquinoline and pyrophosphate as a stabilizer — and *Otsu*-liquid (*C-Stoff*) — 30 per cent hydrazine hydrate (N_2H_4) in methanol (CH_3HO) and water with a little copper potassium cyanide — was assigned to the Navy's 1st Fuel Arsenal and the Mitsubishi Kasei and Edogawa Kagaku industrial chemical companies. Subsequent to the first B-29 attack on Mitsubishi's Nagoya complex, the development of the turbine and pump-related systems of the Toku Ro.2 was taken over by the 11th Naval Air Arsenal, the *Dai-Juichi Kaigun Kokusho,* at Hiro under the guidance of Prof Kasai of the Kyushu University, with the component parts being

---

* *Sixty-three B-29s were involved in this operation, bombing mostly by radar as thick cloud obscured the target. More than 17 per cent of the roofed area was destroyed.*

Outstanding books on every aspect of warfare

Perhaps because no other field of human activity has played such a major part as war in man's development, there is today an enormous demand for books covering every aspect of warfare. If man's military history – or any facet of it – is your particular interest, then THE MILITARY BOOK SOCIETY is designed specially for you. Membership brings you the choice of a wide range of titles dealing with war on land, sea and in the air. Famous books, as well as new releases, carefully selected from the lists of leading publishers. Biographies of military personalities; important works on notable campaigns and special operations as well as on the tools and dress of war. Superbly produced books, often lavishly illustrated . . . exactly the same as publishers' editions except in one respect – the price is much less! Members of THE MILITARY BOOK SOCIETY enjoy a substantial saving on every book – never less than 20%, usually more.

You decide which books to have.

As a member of the Society you need take only the books you want. Every month you receive a free copy of the Society's *Bulletin* telling you all about the forthcoming Main Choice and a selection of other books too. It is you who decide whether or not to accept the Main Choice, take an alternative or have no book at all in any one month. All that is asked of you is that you accept a minimum of four books from dozens offered during the course of a year. Here is a wonderful opportunity to build a specialised home library to be proud of – or to add to your existing collection at low cost.

Take any 2 of these fine books for just 39p each plus postage and packing

as your introduction to
The Military Book Society

MARINE

The Chiefs of the Air Staffs of Britain, Germany and Italy have named their new Multi-Role Combat Aircraft

Tornado

The Chiefs of the Air Staffs of the United Kingdom, Air Chief Marshal Sir Andrew Humphrey; of the Federal Republic of Germany, Generalleutnant Gerhard Limberg; and of Italy, Generale S. A. Dino Ciarlo; and the representative of the Chief of Staff of the German Navy, Konter Admiral von Schröter, met in Munich today for one of the regular reviews of the MRCA project.

The Chiefs of the Air Staffs reached agreement that the encouraging evidence provided so far from the Development Test Flying Programme justifies recommendation to their respective Governments to authorise full production go-ahead.

During the meeting, it was also agreed that the aircraft will be named TORNADO.

March 10th, 1976.

MESSERSCHMITT-BÖLKOW-BLOHM

Those that made the grade...

and some that didn't.

Can you identify them all? The aircraft currently used by the RAF and those which have been rejected for service.

They're all in the Royal Air Force Yearbook 1976. Plus many more fascinating features. Altogether, there are 72 pages packed with information, diagrams and full colour illustrations covering all aspects of the RAF and aviation, as it was, and today.

At only 50p you can't afford to miss the Royal Air Force Yearbook for 1976. So order your copy now from your newsagent or bookseller, or direct from RAF Yearbook, 283 Lonsdale Road, SW13 9QW, price 65p post paid.

Published by the RAF Benevolent Fund. Proceeds to the RAF Benevolent Fund and the Royal Air Forces Association.

manufactured by the Washino, Hitachi, Ishikawajima and Mitsubishi Kyoto concerns. The first-mentioned company, which was a precision machine manufacturer, was responsible for the fuel-adjustment equipment and the *Ko*-liquid relief valve.

The basic planning for the major part of the rocket motor had been completed by early October 1944, and late in the month Mitsubishi-Nagasaki began combustion trials, achieving success during November. Simultaneous trials by Mitsubishi-Nagoya with the turbine and pump were somewhat less successful, however, owing to cavitation phenomena and it was at this point that Prof Taijiro Kasai was called in, satisfactory results finally being achieved just as Mitsubishi-Nagoya received its first visit from B-29 Superfortresses, a force of 71 aircraft attacking the facility on 13 December. This resulted in the transfer of the engine development programme to the former Navy underground laboratory at Natsushima, Yokosuka, where it came under the supervision of the 11th Naval Air Arsenal.

Numerous problems were encountered, some of these being the result of Japanese industry's inability to meet some of the German material specifications. For example, an attempt was made to use 13-chrome steel in place of the specified 18-8 stainless steel for the injection nozzle, the fuel adjustment valve and the rod of the *Ko*-liquid relief valve, but as soon as running began the motor seized and exploded. The *Ko*-liquid pump shaft fulcrums of the KR-20 version of the engine were arranged in a similar fashion to those of the HWK 509A, but development was undertaken in parallel of a pump in which the distance between the shaft fulcrums was increased, intermediate bearings being added, and the version of the motor with this pump was referred to as the KR-22. The development of two different types of pump simultaneously complicated the programme, but after an explosion occurred during the running of the KR-22 version, apparently as a result of *Ko*-liquid leaking into the intermediate bearings and reacting with the bearing grease, all further effort was devoted to the KR-20.

On 11 April 1945, development of the Toku Ro.2 motor now being some three months behind schedule, the CO of the 312th Naval Air Group which was to fly the Shusui, Capt Shibata, convened a conference with the aim of finding ways and means of expediting development of the rocket-propelled fighter. At this conference it was decided that, if the Ro.2 motor could be run efficiently for two minutes, an initial flight test with a powered Shusui would be attempted on 22 April. Every effort was made to meet this schedule, but during the two-minute engine run the Ro.2 exploded. As there was some fear that Natsushima would be attacked, the Navy power plant development group transferred to Yamakita, Hakone, late in May, while the Mitsubishi-Nagoya group moved to Matsumoto where the Army had completed a test centre in collaboration with Mitsubishi, the intention being that the two groups would undertake parallel development work with a cross-feeding of test results. In mid-June, the Yamakita group succeeded in running the Ro.2 for four consecutive minutes while the Matsumoto group completed a three-minute run.

As a result of these successes, it was decided that it would be possible to use these bench-run motors for actual flight testing, and that the Yamakita Ro.2 should be installed in the first Shusui airframe and the Matsumoto Ro.2 in the second airframe. Both rocket motors were accordingly transported to Natsushima late in June and installed in the airframes. Thus, at the beginning of July, the first Shusui, complete with Ro.2 power plant, was taken to the nearby Yokoku airfield. This was a relatively small coastal field and was selected partly for its proximity to the Natsushima facility, partly because of the risk of air attack involved in transporting the aircraft a greater distance, but primarily because it was believed that if the rocket motor failed immediately after take-off, the pilot would

have a chance of alighting in the sea and surviving whereas a crash landing anywhere else would almost certainly result in the explosion of the highly volatile fuels.

Poor results were obtained from initial ground runs, uneven combustion being achieved as was indicated by the colour of the hot gases emitted from the tailpipe — the gases were faintly red when combustion was incomplete but were slightly yellow-green when combustion was complete — but after adjustments satisfactory results were achieved on 5 July and it was decided that a test flight would be attempted two days later. The Shusui was tanked up with 127·5 Imp gal (580 l) of *Ko*-liquid and 35 Imp gal (160 l) of *Otsu*-liquid, loaded weight being 5,401 lb (2 450 kg), and at 1655 hours on 7 July, Toyohiko Inuzuka started the rocket motor. After an 11-second 350-yard (320-m) run the Shusui left the ground quite smoothly, the jettisonable take-off dolly being dropped from an altitude of about 33 feet (10 m). The aircraft continued to climb smoothly and the assembled spectators were elated. All seemed to be going well. On reaching about 1,150 ft (350 m), the engine emitted puffs of dark smoke, faltered and stopped. The Shusui continued climbing to approximately 1,640 ft (500 m) and then Inuzuka levelled off, made a starboard turn and began gliding back towards the field.

The *Ko*-liquid streamed from the emergency release valve as the aircraft began its approach after a series of turns to port

(*Above*) *The first J8M1 Shusui airframe to be fitted with an Ro.2 rocket motor at Natsushima prior to delivery to the Yokoku airfield.*

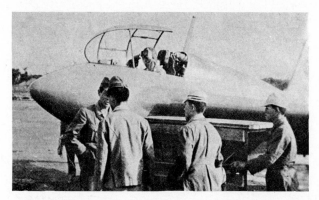

(*Above*) *Lt Cdr Inuzuka in the cockpit of the Shusui at the Yokoku airfield immediately prior to his sole and, in the event, fatal rocket-powered flight, and (below) the Shusui about to commence its take-off run at the Yokoku airfield.*

(Above) A Shusui fuselage found by the Allies in a rather crude structural test rig at Mitsubishi's Ohe factory, and (below) a completed Shusui that had been used at Ohe for structural testing.

and starboard, but Inuzuka had lost too much speed and realising that the Shusui would hit a house near the perimeter of the field, he pulled up the nose and deliberately stalled the aircraft. The starboard wing dropped, just touched the roof of a building and the Shusui cartwheeled, both wings being torn off and the remainder of the aircraft finally coming to rest in an open space to the south-west of the airfield. The forward portion of the fuselage, including the fuselage, was heavily damaged and Inuzuka suffered injuries from which he died.

It was concluded that the rocket motor had stopped as a result of fuel starvation. The *Ko*-liquid feed outlet was at the base of the tank which had been less than half full for the initial flight test and it appeared that the steep climb angle and strong acceleration had combined to tip the fuel so that it did not reach the feed outlet. A few days later, an Ro.2 exploded at the Yamakita test centre, one of the test personnel, Lt Shoda, losing his life. A similar explosion took place shortly afterwards at the Matsumoto centre, leaving only one complete rocket motor. This was to be installed in the second Shusui which had been allocated to the Army and was at the Kashiwa airfield, Chiba, awaiting completion of the installation when hostilities ended and with them the Shusui programme.

At this time, four Shusui airframes had been completed by the Ohe and Nanko factories and six more were virtually complete on the assembly line. Four production Ro.2 rocket motors had been completed, another two were virtually complete and major components had been manufactured for a further 20. Production of the MXY8 Akikusa had meanwhile been assigned to the Maeda Aircraft Institute (*Maeda Koku Kenkyujo*) and it had been proposed that some of these training gliders should be fitted with water ballast tanks so that they would more closely approximate to the handling characteristics of the fully-loaded Shusui. The Navy was also investigating the possibilities of a powered version of the Akikusa which had been dubbed Shuka (Autumn Fire) and which it was proposed should be powered by a Tsu.11 ducted fan of 441 lb (200 kg) thrust, but the prototype of this model had still to be completed when the Pacific War came to an end on 15 August 1945.

On that morning design work had been completed at the Naval Air Technical Arsenal for a modified version of the interceptor, the J8M2 Shusui-Kai, which had one of the wing-mounted cannon deleted and a revised fuel tank system which offered a marginal increase in powered endurance, and design was also virtually complete at the Army Aerotechnical Research Institute for that service's own Shusui-Kai. The Army had never been convinced of the wisdom of endeavouring to produce a facsimile of the Messerschmitt fighter, believing that substantial performance gains, particularly in respect of powered endurance, could result from major redesign. It had acceded to the prime directive of absolute commonality between the versions of the rocket-propelled interceptor for the two services with some reluctance — the Army's Ki.200 differed from the Navy's J8M1 almost solely in the type of cannon installed, the former having the 30-mm Ho-105 — and on 1 March, the Army finally decided to ignore the directive, and launched a major redesign to which was given the designation Ki.202 Shusui-Kai, this being considered as the Army's priority interceptor for service from 1946 onwards. The intention was to establish operational procedures and tactics with the Ki.200 Shusui and, at the earliest possible stage, phase in the Ki.202 Shusui-Kai. However, as previously related, on 15 August 1945, hostilities terminated — one year, one month and one day after the submarine *Matsu* had docked at Singapore with its cargo of blueprints and manufacturing data for the radical German warplane. □

(The editors wish to acknowledge their gratitude to Koku Fan, with whose permission this feature is reproduced.)

(Below) One completed Shusui airframe (apparently without the Ro.2 rocket motor) was transported to the USA after the end of hostilities but was not subjected to any tests.

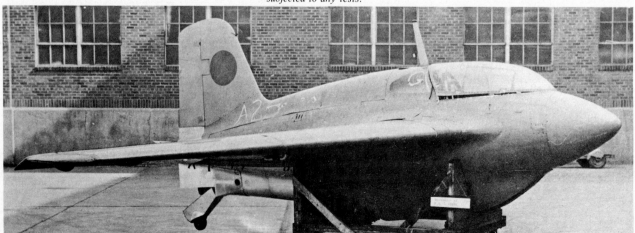

SPAD STORY

Part Two of the account, by J M Bruce, of the Spad 13 and its relatives

As noted already, the initial batch of Spads 13 were nearing completion in mid-March 1917. What has been reported as the first aircraft of this type, *S.392,* was flown at Buc on 4 April, piloted by *Sous-Lieutenant* René Dorme, and an early demonstration to French fighter *escadrilles* was given by Maurice Prévost. The Spa.13.C1 was a completely separate and structurally different aeroplant from the Spa.12.Ca 1, yet it bore a strong family resemblance to the cannon-armed fighter and to the earlier Spa.7.C 1. All major dimensions were somewhat larger than those of the Spad 7: the span was 27 ft 1 in (8,250 m) as compared with the 25 ft 8 in (7,822 m) of the Spad 7; length was 20 ft 4 in (6,20 m) compared with 19 ft 11 in (6,08 m); heights were 7 ft 6 in (2,30 m) and 7 ft 2½ in (2,20 m) respectively; chord of upper wing 4 ft 11 in (1,50 m) and 4 ft 7 in (1,40 m) respectively and of lower wing, 4 ft 7 in (1,40 m) and 4 ft 2 in (1,275 m) and the wing area was 227·2 sq ft (21,11 m²) compared with 192 sq ft (17,85 m²). Weights had gone up, too: a typical Spad 13 *(S.512)* tested in September 1917 weighed 1,888·5 lb (856,5 kg); the standard corresponding figure for the Spad 7 was 1,554·5 lb (705 kg).

In its structural characteristics the Spad 13 embodied many features employed on the Spad 7, notably the single-bay bracing with intermediate struts, the rod-and-crank actuation of the ailerons, the circular cowling round the radiator, the triangular fin of low aspect ratio and the dorsal and belly deckings on the fuselage, with the fuel tank shaped to form part of the belly fairing. The Spad 13 differed from its single-gun predecessor in being armed with twin Vickers guns with 400 rpg; it was widely referred to in contemporary official documents as the Spad *bi-mitrailleuse.* Apart from its larger dimensions, the Spad 13 as first built was distinguished by its markedly rounded wing tips and inversely tapered ailerons, while the rudder and elevators had rounded trailing edges. The centre-section struts had forward stagger and were supplemented by a drag-wire running from the top of the forward strut to the upper longeron on each side. Fuel capacity was 24 Imp gal (110 l) of petrol and 4-4·4 Imp gal (18-20 l) of oil.

The power unit was the 200 hp Hispano-Suiza 8Ba, and the earliest known performance figures for the early Spad 13 exist in a note, apparently made in April 1917, in a RFC file. This quoted a speed of 124 mph (200 km/h) at 13,000 ft (approximately 4 000 m), to which altitude the time of climb

was 11 minutes. Tests of *S.512* made in September 1917 produced a maximum speed of 135·5 mph (218 km/h) at 6,560 ft (2 000 m) and 130 mph (209 km/h) at 13,120 ft (4 000 m), the climbing times to these heights being 4 min 40 sec and 12 min 10 sec respectively. The appraisement of the aircraft was good without being enthusiastic; significantly, the report commented that the view from the cockpit left something to be desired.

A fact that seems to have escaped the attention of historians is that, by the standards of the 1914-18 war, the introduction of the Spad 13 into full operational use was a remarkably slow

(Top of page) Ten aircraft of Spa.151, of which two are Spad 7s and the remainder Spad 13s. The nearest Spad 13, No 13, has the plywood 'pocket' extensions on the wing tips. (Above) A typical early production Spad 13, S.497 of Escadrille Spa.159, with rounded wing tips and initial form of radiator cowling. The aircraft is here seen in German hands. (Below) The first few hundred Spad 13s were built with fully rounded wing tips, as seen on this aircraft.

(Above) An early production Spad 13 of Escadrille Spa.65. (Below left) This late-production Spad 13 of Escadrille Spa.3 was photographed at Germersheim on 22 October 1919. The detachable side panel marked "Photo" proclaimed that the aircraft could, when required, carry a camera installation for photographic reconnaissance.

(Below) Cockpit and armament of an early Spad 13 of Escadrille Spa.65. A rear-view mirror is mounted in the upper-wing trailing edge above the windscreen.

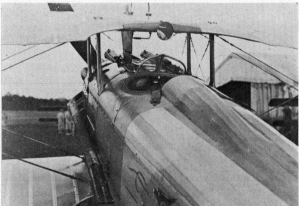

and protracted business. This is the more remarkable when viewed against Major Scholte's reports of 20 February and 13 March 1917, quoted above, which suggested that, presumably to speed up the operational introduction of the Spad 13, the French authorities had ordered a batch of 20 aircraft rather than expend valuable time on developing a small number of prototypes. At least one Spad 13 was operational by 27 April 1917, at which date it was at La Bonne Maison aerodrome near Fismes. On that date Brooke-Popham instructed Captain C K C Patrick to visit La Bonne Maison on 29 April for the purpose of inspecting the new aircraft and reporting back to RFC Headquarters. Patrick was told he was not to fly the Spad

or even ask to fly it, but was to report on the pilot's view, amount of ammunition carried, ease of access to the guns, and the aircraft's performance. His report, dated 1 May 1917, was as follows:

"The machine is larger at all points than the standard 150 hp Spad. The span is greater, the tail plane is larger, the wing tips are rounded, and the fuselage, though much the same breadth, is considerably deeper, the radiator being an oval rather than a circle.

"Owing to the greater depth of fuselage the two guns are set deeper in the cowling.

"The wing section is different to the 150 hp Spad, being flatter beneath and more cambered above.

"*Visibility*. Practically identical with 150 hp Spad.

"*Ammunition*. 800 rounds carried (400 rounds per gun).

"*Jams*. The right hand gun is in much the same position for getting at as the gun on the 150 hp Spad. Without moving the windscreen and sights, it would be impossible to remedy any but the simplest jams on the left hand gun.

"*Fittings*. The guns are fired by two separate triggers. The old type of ejector tubes are being used.

"*Climb*. The service climb is:

4 000 m	11 minutes
5 000 m	16 minutes
6 000 m	21$\frac{1}{2}$ minutes
7 000 m	28 minutes

The pilot had not had the machine above 7 000 m, but there was no noticeable loss in the climb at that height.

"*Speed*. At 4 000 m the speed is 120 mph.

"The machine is said to be less handy near the ground, but considerably handier at a height than the 150 hp Spad."

A related official note, dated 30 April 1917 and recording the visit of inspection, noted that "The French pilots were very enthusiastic over the 200 hp geared Hispano-Suiza Spad". So, it seems, were the French authorities, who promptly ordered 250 Spad 13s and proposed to build the aircraft on such a scale that the forecast deliveries to 31 March 1918 were expected to total 2,230. It was fortunate that production of the Spad 7 was not abandoned in this enthusiasm for the Spad 13, for grave troubles lay ahead and the production forecasts were not realised.

One reason why the Spad 13 was so slow to come into operational use in numbers was that production took some time to get under way. By 1 August 1917, only 17 Spad 13s were with French *escadrilles* and acceptance parks, and six more were with the *Réserve générale aéronautique* (RGA); at least one more had been delivered and had been allocated to the RFC, but of that aircraft, more presently. At that same date, 445 Spad 7s were with French *escadrilles* and acceptance parks. A Royal Flying Corps report dated 10 September 1917 records that, in the case of the Blériot works, only Spad 13s were being built at that date, a fact that was contributing to a shortage of spares for Spad 7s.

Added emphasis on the need to produce large numbers of Spads was provided by the decision of French General Headquarters dated 22 October 1917 that the obsolete Nieuport scouts must be withdrawn and replaced by Spads or the then-untested Nieuport 28s. This followed a blunt letter from *Général* Pétain in which he stated unequivocally that the Nieuports then in operational use were inferior to all opposing enemy types. When the Nieuport 28 was abandoned by the *Aviation militaire* everything depended on the Spad designs.

The whole history of French aviation at that time seemed to consist of unattained production targets and downward revisions of planned output. The Spad 13 was no exception to this: the estimated output of Spad single-seaters for December 1917 was 250, but only 131 were delivered; the figure for January 1918 was to be 300, but up to 20 January only 79 had been received. Whereas a total of 2,230 Spad 13s by 31 March had been optimistically estimated in 1917 the deliveries actually made by that date amounted to no more than 764. By contrast, the forecast output of Spad 7s was almost completely realised: of the estimated total of 1,276 all but 56 were delivered by 31 March 1918. On 1 April 1918, almost a full year after the type's operational début, the *Aviation militaire* had on its strength a total of only 372 Spad 13s; of these, 290 were with *escadrilles,* 64 were in reserve and 18 were at aircraft parks.

Like its British contemporary the S.E.5a, the Spad 13 suffered from the defects of the geared Hispano-Suiza engine, and did not enjoy the full exploitation of its excellent performance at the time when it would have been most telling in the skies of France. In a substantial report dated 20 November 1917 Colonel Duval, *Chef du Service aéronautique au Grand Quartier Général,* informed the Commander in Chief of the Northern and North-Eastern Armies that among the aircraft then in service were "Other types which, like the Spad two-seater (ie, the Spa.11.A 2), are condemned to unserviceability two days out of every three, because the 200 hp Hispano with which they are equipped is not satisfactory and is not running." Looking ahead to the spring of 1918, Colonel Duval predicted of the *Aviation de Chasse:* "This will probably consist wholly of Spad single-seaters. No two-seat fighters. And the Spad single-seater, fitted with the 200 hp Hispano

motor, is at present incapable of giving dependable service."

This was confirmed in the penetrating and merciless survey of French aviation contained in the report submitted to the Army Commission on behalf of the Sub-Commission on Aeronautics by the Sub-Commission's president, M d'Aubigny, on 3 May 1918. Analysing with cold realism the numbers of truly up-to-date and serviceable aircraft in operational use at 1 April 1918, the d'Aubigny report stated: "This figure of 1,237 is a maximum, for it takes no account of the unserviceability caused by the shortcomings of the Hispano engine which, by virtue of the repairs thus necessitated in the *escadrilles,* immobilize two-thirds of 200 hp Spad aircraft."

The geared Hispano-Suiza suffered from more than one ailment. Trouble was experienced with the reduction gearing, especially in those engines made by Automobiles Brasier of Ivry-Port. Vibration proved to be especially troublesome in the Spad 13 and lubrication was unsatisfactory and erratic. The vibration was reduced somewhat by the primitive expedient of staying the ends of the camshaft covers, by means of clip-anchored wires, to the lower longerons. To improve the engine's lubrication, a larger-diameter feed pipe was fitted between the oil tank and the oil pump and the vent holes in the partitions of the crankcase were enlarged to permit freer movement of oil.

A piquant aspect of the troubles experienced with the Hispano-Suiza is that the Spad company had built examples of the Spad 11 and Spad 13 fitted with the 190 hp Renault 8Gd, obviously as an insurance against the possible failure of the geared Hispano-Suiza. This is recorded in a memorandum dated 10 May 1917 from the British Aviation Commission in France to the Controller of the Technical Department. The memorandum stated that "Messrs Spad have turned out two machines similar aerodynamically to the two-seater 200 hp

(Above right) S.706, the Spad 13 that had the Rateau turbo-supercharger installation. This aircraft had the plywood 'pocket' additions to the wing tips. (Below) a Spad 13 of the final production form in service with an unidentified escadrille. *This photograph shows clearly the lower end of the chute for empty cartridge cases. On late-production aircraft its outlet was in the fuselage flank, below the mid-point of the exhaust pipe. A similar chute served the starboard gun.*

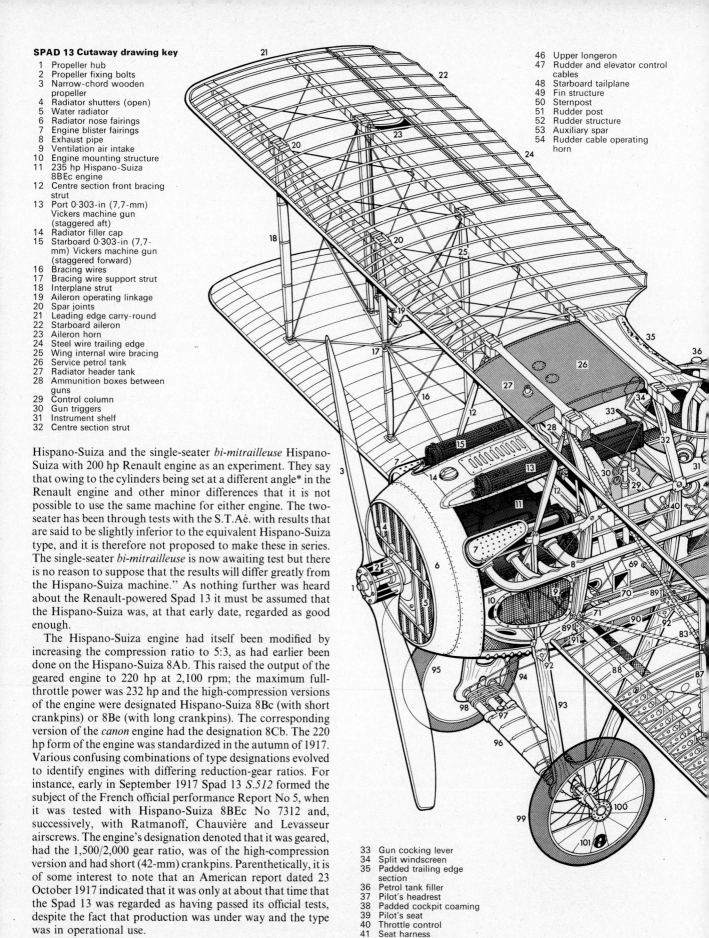

SPAD 13 Cutaway drawing key

1 Propeller hub
2 Propeller fixing bolts
3 Narrow-chord wooden propeller
4 Radiator shutters (open)
5 Water radiator
6 Radiator nose fairings
7 Engine blister fairings
8 Exhaust pipe
9 Ventilation air intake
10 Engine mounting structure
11 235 hp Hispano-Suiza 8BEc engine
12 Centre section front bracing strut
13 Port 0·303-in (7,7-mm) Vickers machine gun (staggered aft)
14 Radiator filler cap
15 Starboard 0·303-in (7,7-mm) Vickers machine gun (staggered forward)
16 Bracing wires
17 Bracing wire support strut
18 Interplane strut
19 Aileron operating linkage
20 Spar joints
21 Leading edge carry-round
22 Starboard aileron
23 Aileron horn
24 Steel wire trailing edge
25 Wing internal wire bracing
26 Service petrol tank
27 Radiator header tank
28 Ammunition boxes between guns
29 Control column
30 Gun triggers
31 Instrument shelf
32 Centre section strut

46 Upper longeron
47 Rudder and elevator control cables
48 Starboard tailplane
49 Fin structure
50 Sternpost
51 Rudder post
52 Rudder structure
53 Auxiliary spar
54 Rudder cable operating horn

Hispano-Suiza and the single-seater *bi-mitrailleuse* Hispano-Suiza with 200 hp Renault engine as an experiment. They say that owing to the cylinders being set at a different angle* in the Renault engine and other minor differences that it is not possible to use the same machine for either engine. The two-seater has been through tests with the S.T.Aé. with results that are said to be slightly inferior to the equivalent Hispano-Suiza type, and it is therefore not proposed to make these in series. The single-seater *bi-mitrailleuse* is now awaiting test but there is no reason to suppose that the results will differ greatly from the Hispano-Suiza machine." As nothing further was heard about the Renault-powered Spad 13 it must be assumed that the Hispano-Suiza was, at that early date, regarded as good enough.

The Hispano-Suiza engine had itself been modified by increasing the compression ratio to 5:3, as had earlier been done on the Hispano-Suiza 8Ab. This raised the output of the geared engine to 220 hp at 2,100 rpm; the maximum full-throttle power was 232 hp and the high-compression versions of the engine were designated Hispano-Suiza 8Bc (with short crankpins) or 8Be (with long crankpins). The corresponding version of the *canon* engine had the designation 8Cb. The 220 hp form of the engine was standardized in the autumn of 1917. Various confusing combinations of type designations evolved to identify engines with differing reduction-gear ratios. For instance, early in September 1917 Spad 13 *S.512* formed the subject of the French official performance Report No 5, when it was tested with Hispano-Suiza 8BEc No 7312 and, successively, with Ratmanoff, Chauvière and Levasseur airscrews. The engine's designation denoted that it was geared, had the 1,500/2,000 gear ratio, was of the high-compression version and had short (42-mm) crankpins. Parenthetically, it is of some interest to note that an American report dated 23 October 1917 indicated that it was only at about that time that the Spad 13 was regarded as having passed its official tests, despite the fact that production was under way and the type was in operational use.

*The Renault was a 60-deg V-8, whereas the Hispano-Suiza was a 90-deg V-8 engine.

33 Gun cocking lever
34 Split windscreen
35 Padded trailing edge section
36 Petrol tank filler
37 Pilot's headrest
38 Padded cockpit coaming
39 Pilot's seat
40 Throttle control
41 Seat harness
42 Plywood decking
43 Headrest fairing
44 Dorsal structure
45 Dorsal stringers

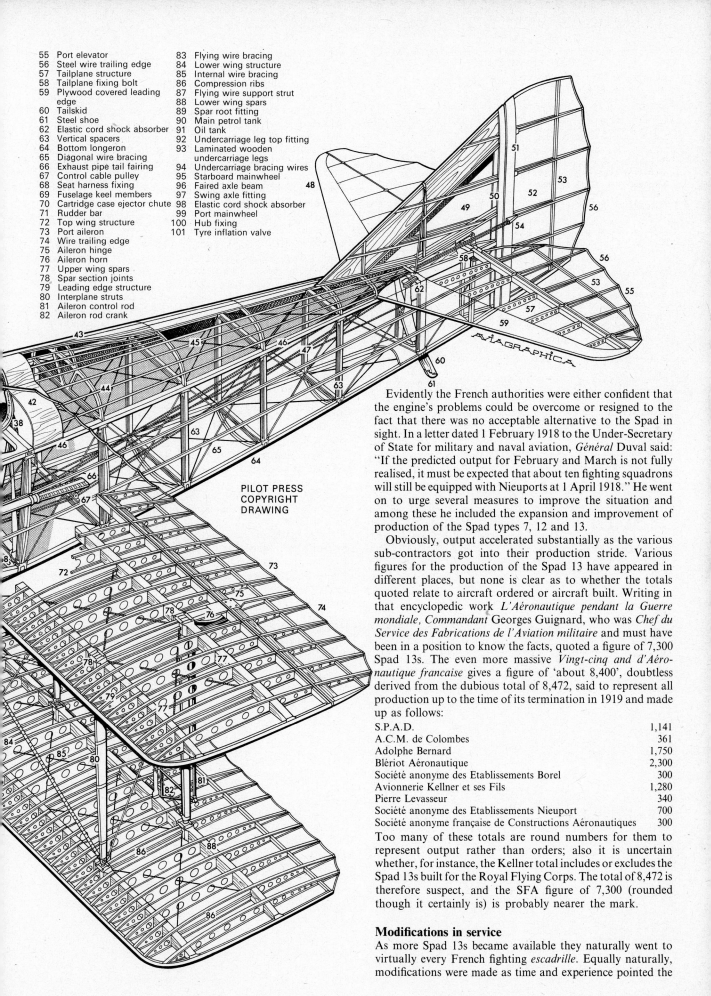

55 Port elevator
56 Steel wire trailing edge
57 Tailplane structure
58 Tailplane fixing bolt
59 Plywood covered leading edge
60 Tailskid
61 Steel shoe
62 Elastic cord shock absorber
63 Vertical spacers
64 Bottom longeron
65 Diagonal wire bracing
66 Exhaust pipe tail fairing
67 Control cable pulley
68 Seat harness fixing
69 Fuselage keel members
70 Cartridge case ejector chute
71 Rudder bar
72 Top wing structure
73 Port aileron
74 Wire trailing edge
75 Aileron hinge
76 Aileron horn
77 Upper wing spars
78 Spar section joints
79 Leading edge structure
80 Interplane struts
81 Aileron control rod
82 Aileron rod crank
83 Flying wire bracing
84 Lower wing structure
85 Internal wire bracing
86 Compression ribs
87 Flying wire support strut
88 Lower wing spars
89 Spar root fitting
90 Main petrol tank
91 Oil tank
92 Undercarriage leg top fitting
93 Laminated wooden undercarriage legs
94 Undercarriage bracing wires
95 Starboard mainwheel
96 Faired axle beam
97 Swing axle fitting
98 Elastic cord shock absorber
99 Port mainwheel
100 Hub fixing
101 Tyre inflation valve

PILOT PRESS
COPYRIGHT
DRAWING

Evidently the French authorities were either confident that the engine's problems could be overcome or resigned to the fact that there was no acceptable alternative to the Spad in sight. In a letter dated 1 February 1918 to the Under-Secretary of State for military and naval aviation, *Général* Duval said: "If the predicted output for February and March is not fully realised, it must be expected that about ten fighting squadrons will still be equipped with Nieuports at 1 April 1918." He went on to urge several measures to improve the situation and among these he included the expansion and improvement of production of the Spad types 7, 12 and 13.

Obviously, output accelerated substantially as the various sub-contractors got into their production stride. Various figures for the production of the Spad 13 have appeared in different places, but none is clear as to whether the totals quoted relate to aircraft ordered or aircraft built. Writing in that encyclopedic work *L'Aéronautique pendant la Guerre mondiale, Commandant* Georges Guignard, who was *Chef du Service des Fabrications de l'Aviation militaire* and must have been in a position to know the facts, quoted a figure of 7,300 Spad 13s. The even more massive *Vingt-cinq and d'Aéronautique francaise* gives a figure of 'about 8,400', doubtless derived from the dubious total of 8,472, said to represent all production up to the time of its termination in 1919 and made up as follows:

S.P.A.D.	1,141
A.C.M. de Colombes	361
Adolphe Bernard	1,750
Blériot Aéronautique	2,300
Société anonyme des Etablissements Borel	300
Avionnerie Kellner et ses Fils	1,280
Pierre Levasseur	340
Société anonyme des Etablissements Nieuport	700
Société anonyme française de Constructions Aéronautiques	300

Too many of these totals are round numbers for them to represent output rather than orders; also it is uncertain whether, for instance, the Kellner total includes or excludes the Spad 13s built for the Royal Flying Corps. The total of 8,472 is therefore suspect, and the SFA figure of 7,300 (rounded though it certainly is) is probably nearer the mark.

Modifications in service

As more Spad 13s became available they naturally went to virtually every French fighting *escadrille*. Equally naturally, modifications were made as time and experience pointed the

Spad Specifications

Power Plant (Spad 12.Ca 1, 14.Ca 1 and 24.Ca 1): 200 hp Hispano-Suiza 8Ca or 220 hp Hispano-Suiza 8Cb.
Power Plant (Spad 13.C 1): 200 hp Hispano-Suiza 8Ba, 8Bb or 8Bd (8BCa, 8BDa, 8BEa, 8BCb, 8BDb, 8BEb, 8BCd, 8BDd or 8BEd according to ratio of reduction gear); or 220 hp Hispano-Suiza 8Bc or 8Bc (8BCe, 8BDc, 8BEc, 8BCe, 8EDe or 8BEe according to ratio of reduction gear); or 190 hp Renault 8Gd (experimental) or 300 hp Hispano-Suiza 8Fb (experimental).
Power Plant (Spad 17.C 1, 21.C 1 and 22.C 1): 300 hp Hispano-Suiza 8Fb.
Dimensions (Spad 12): Span, 8,00 m (26 ft 3 in); length, 6,40 m (21 ft 0 in); height, 2,55 m (8 ft 4½ in); wing area, 20,2 m² (217·43 sq ft).
Dimensions (Spad 13): Span, originally 8,25 m (27 ft 1 in), later 8,08 m (26 ft 6 in); length, 6,25 m (20 ft 6 in); height, 2,60 m (8 ft 6½ in); wing area, originally 21,11 m² (227·23 sq ft, later 20,2 m² (217·43 sq ft).
Dimensions (Spad 14): Span, 9,80 m (32 ft 1⅓ in); length, 7,40 m (24 ft 3⅓ in); height, 4,00 m (13 ft 1½ in); wing area, 26,2 m² (282 sq ft).
Dimensions (Spad 17): Span, 8,08 m (26 ft 6 in); length, 6,25 m (20 ft 6 in); height, 2,60 m (8 ft 6½ in); wing area, 20 m² (215·28 sq ft).
Dimensions (Spad 21*): Span, 8,435 m (27 ft 7¼ in); length, 6,40 m (21 ft); height, 2,415 m (7 ft 11 in); wing area, 23,5 m² (253 sq ft).
Armament (Spad 13, 17, 21 and 22): Two 7,65-mm Vickers machine guns with (on Spad 13) 400 rounds per gun, or 320 rpg with disintegrating-link Mk II belt.
Armament (Spad 12, 14 and 24): One 7,65-mm Vickers machine-gun and one 37-mm Hotchkiss shell-firing gun.

* These dimensions converted back to metric from a British official document of October 1918. Their accuracy is therefore suspect.

need for them. Until early 1918 all Spad 13s were delivered with the amply rounded wing tips, but it seems that lateral control was considered to be inadequate, for steps were taken to increase the area of existing wings and ailerons. The method of doing this was of hair-raising crudity and was quite lucidly described in a report sent by the British Air Force Representative in the Ministry of Munitions Paris office to RFC Headquarters on 6 February 1918, which read as follows:

"Attached herewith blue print, showing modifications which Messrs Spad have instructed their sub-contractors to carry out to the type 13 machine.

"The addition of three-ply corners to the tips of the trailing edge of each wing and aileron is stated to be for the purpose of increasing wing and aileron surface.

"Messrs Kellner have been instructed to carry out these modifications on our Spads from No 3251 *(sic)* onwards, but they will not modify these machines if this should be contrary to your wishes, and unless you are of opinion that the aileron control of the present machines is not satisfactory. I consider that the modifications should not be embodied since, although approved by the French Section Technique, they appear to be carried out in an unsatisfactory manner.

"The corners consist of two pieces of three-ply in the shape of a triangle, the edges of two sides of which are joined, thus forming a pocket which slips over the wing and is laced thereto along the third side by means of twine passing through eyelet holes in the wood.

"The execution of the work is badly carried out and should the twine rot or fray, the three-ply corner would become detached, probably jamming or damaging the aileron."

Two days later the AQMG at RFC Headquarters sensibly replied: "We agree with you that the design of this is very poor indeed and we shall not wish to make use of this modification." The RFC were therefore spared the dangers implicit in this fearsome modification, but numbers of Spad 12s and 13s were built with it.

It may have been short-lived, however, for on 7 March 1918 the Air Force Representative reported to RFC Headquarters that ". . . machine No 4563 (that is, *S.4563*) is fitted with square tipped planes — latest type *not* with three-ply additions — but it would not appear that these planes are ready for fitting to all machines yet as No 4564 has the ordinary type."

WEIGHTS AND PERFORMANCE

	Spad 12	Spad 13	Spad 13, *S.512*			Spad 13, B3479 *(S.498)*		Spad 17	Spad 21
Power plant	220 hp H-S 8Cb	200 hp H-S 8BEa	220 hp H-S 8BEc	220 hp H-S 8BEc	220 hp H-S 8BEc	200 hp H-S	200 hp H-S	300 hp H-S 8Fb	300 hp H-S 8Fb
Propeller	—	Chauvière 222H	Ratmanoff 6727	Chauvière 2223	Levasseur 586	—	—	—	—
Date of trial	—	24 March 1917	12 September 1917	6 September 1917	—	7 June 1917	8 June 1917	—	—
Weight empty, kg (lb)	587 (1,295)	—	601·5 (1,326)	601·5 (1,326)	601·5 (1,326)	—	—	687 (1,515)	750·5 (1,670)
Weight loaded, kg (lb)	883 (1,947)	—	856·5 (1,888)	856·5 (1,888)	856·5 (1,888)	—	—	942 (2,077)	1,047·5 (2,309)
Max speed, km/h (mph) at									
1 000 m (3,280 ft)	—	211 (131)	—	—	—	—	—	—	—
2 000 m (6,560 ft)	203 (126)	208·5 (129·5)	218 (135·5)	213 (132·5)	217 (135)	—	—	217 (135)	221 (137)
3 000 m (9,840 ft)	198 (123)	205·5 (128)	214 (133)	211 (131)	215 (133·5)	—	—	214 (133)	217 (135)
3 050 m (10,000 ft)	—	—	—	—	—	221 (137)	222 (138)	—	—
4 000 m (13,120 ft)	190 (118)	201 (125)	209 (130)	205 (127)	210 (130·5)	—	—	211 (131)	214 (133)
4 575 m (15,000 ft)	—	—	—	—	—	225 (140)	216 (134)	—	—
5 000 m (16,400 ft)	177 (110)	190 (118)	203 (126)	194 (120·5)	198 (123)	—	—	201 (125)	205 (127)
5 500 m (18,000 ft)	—	—	—	—	—	216 (134)	186 (115·5)	—	—
6 100 m (20,000 ft)	—	—	—	—	—	206 (128)	184 (114·5)	—	—
Climb to									
1 000 m (3,280 ft)	—	2 m 20 s	1 m 55 s	2 m 30 s	2 m 00 s	—	—	—	—
2 000 m (6,560 ft)	6 m 03 s	5 m 17 s	4 m 40 s	5 m 10 s	4 m 40 s	—	—	5 m 24 s	5 m 40 s
3 000 m (9,840 ft)	10 m 02 s	8 m 45 s	7 m 50 s	8 m 20 s	8 m 00 s	—	—	8 m 20 s	8 m 51 s
3 050 m (10,000 ft)	—	—	—	—	—	9 m 12 s	9 m 06 s	—	—
4 000 m (13,120 ft)	15 m 42 s	13 m 05 s	12 m 10 s	12 m 45 s	12 m 20 s	—	—	12 m 32 s	13 m 03 s
4 575 m (15,000 ft)	—	—	—	—	—	16 m 18 s	16 m 15 s	—	—
5 000 m (16,400 ft)	23 m 13 s	20 m 10 s	18 m 30 s	19 m 15 s	18 m 35 s	—	—	17 m 21 s	18 m 18 s
5 500 m (18,000 ft)	—	—	—	—	—	—	23 m 50 s	—	—
6 100 m (20,000 ft)	—	—	—	—	—	—	34 m 00 s	—	—
Ceiling, m (ft)	6 850 (22,500)	6 800 (22,300)	—	—	6 850 (22,500)	—	—	7 175 (23,500)	7 000 (23,000)
Endurance (hours)	1·75	2	—	—	1·66	—	—	1·25	1·66

Doubtless Béchereau had recognised the dangers in the plywood 'pocket' extensions, especially on the upper wing, for which it had to be made in two articulated parts to fit both wing and aileron. Completely new wings with blunt, near-square tips were therefore designed and were fitted to later production aircraft. Nevertheless, as noted above, some Spads were given new upper wings only and retained the old lower wings with the absurd plywood additions. One such survives to the present day; it is *S.7689, Smith IV* of the American 22nd Aero Squadron, preserved in the Smithsonian Institution, Washington. The fact that the revised wings with blunt tips were not introduced until early 1918 means that several hundred Spad 13s, not merely an initial production batch, were built with the original rounded tips.

Another external modification was the fitting of a wooden fairing to the drag wire that ran from the top of the forward centre-section strut to the upper longeron on each side; the drag wire itself may have been of increased thickness. This gave the appearance of an additional strut. Many production Spad 13s had modified fuselages to permit the installation of a camera for photographic-reconnaissance duties. This followed the similar provision made in earlier Nieuport 17s and Spad 7s, and the modified aircraft had the word 'Photo' painted on the fuselage as a distinguishing mark.

By 1 October 1918 French *escadrilles de chasse* had a total of 764 Spad 13s on their strength, but significantly they still had a total of 324 Spad 7s. The total of Spad single-seaters of all three types then in service was 1,096; by 11 November it had risen to 1,152.

One of the most important contributions to aero-engine development was made in France by Professor Auguste Rateau who, in 1916, first applied a turbosupercharger* to an aero-engine. The advantages of supercharging the engines of military aircraft were obvious, and Rateau's work was developed throughout 1917. In that year, details of his work were sent to the US Army, which proceeded to persuade the General Electric Company to develop a turbosupercharger under the direction of Sanford Moss. In Britain, much original work on supercharging had been done at the Royal Aircraft Factory by J E Ellor, who promptly sent for a Rateau installation as soon as he learned of the French professor's promising work and tested it in a modified RE8.

In France, one of the aircraft in which a Rateau supercharger installation was made was the Spad 13 *S.706*. The arrangement must have been rather peculiar, for it appears that the turbosupercharger was located immediately behind the pilot's seat, some considerable distance from the engine; liberal louvres were provided in the side panels of the fuselage, fifteen holes were made in the sides of the rear fuselage under the tailplane to help in heat dissipation and the supercharger's exhaust protruded below the fuselage in line with the rear edge of the cockpit. The Rateau Spad 13 weighed 220 lb (100 kg) more than the standard aircraft. It was subjected to trials on 3 September 1918, but was apparently not taken to a greater altitude than 9,840 ft (3 000 m). Its performance was inferior to that of the standard Spad 13, but it was understood that these tests were wholly unrepresentative and inconclusive. After these trials, *S.706* was reported to be in the hands of the STAe for engine repairs, and its subsequent activities are not known. Other known Rateau installations were made in Breguet 14s and in a Nieuport 29 and Spad 11.

A more powerful engine

Marc Birkigt was meanwhile continuing work on the development of the Hispano-Suiza engine. In the summer of 1917 he proposed a 16-cylinder engine that was virtually a

---

The concept of the turbosupercharger for internal combustion engines was first put forward in 1906 by the Swiss engineer Alfred Buechi of the Brown-Boveri company. Initial tests of a device of this kind were made in 1911.

One of the small number of Spad 17s that were built was S.733.

double-size 200 hp Hispano-Suiza; its output was expected to be 400 hp and one had been made by 1 July 1917 but had not run at that date. This engine was reported to be under test by mid-October 1917 but was not developed, doubtless because of its size. Birkigt had, at about the same time, completed the design of a further development of the eight-cylinder engine that would develop 300 hp. The initial design had bore and stroke of 140 × 140 mm and was designated Hispano-Suiza 8Fa; this was known by early November 1917, by which time it had already been superseded by the 8Fb, in which the stroke was increased to 150 mm.

In his *Review of French Airplanes as of October 23, 1917* Lieutenant Colonel T H Bane of the US Signal Corps reported: "A very interesting design is now being studied by Béchereau, wherein he is hard at work with M Birkigt, the

Flying characteristics of Spad 13	
Extract from French official Report No 5 on Spad 13 S.512 with Ratmanoff airscrew, Series 6727	
Report on handling trials	
Effect of controls	
1 Longitudinal	Good.
2 Lateral	Good.
3 Directional	The aircraft does not naturally assume the angle of bank. On the contrary it tends to
4 Turning	hunt.
Control response	
1 Longitudinal	The aircraft is tail heavy.
2 Lateral	Fairly stiff at low altitudes, improves as height is gained; nevertheless the response is good.
3 Directional	.. .. ..
4 Overall	.. .. ..
Stability	
1 Longitudinal	Near the ground the aircraft is markedly tail heavy.
2 Lateral	Good.
3 Directional	.. ..
Take-off	
Ground handling	The aircraft has no ground looping tendencies.
Ease of take-off	Gathers speed quickly and takes off well.
Landing	
Ease of touchdown	Easy. The aircraft settles well on the tailskid and wheel simultaneously.
Braking on landing run	Good.
Risk of overturning	Tail heavy.
Other remarks	
Visibility	The view from the cockpit leaves something to be desired; it could be improved to the sides.
Observations	It would be advantageous to increase the area of the fin.

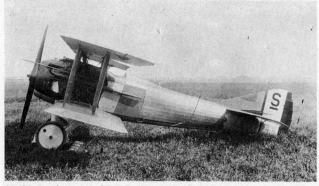

(Left) Another view of S.733, illustrating the heavier appearance of the Spad 17 and showing the fully faired fuselage. (Right) The remarkable wing planforms of the Spad 22 can be seen here; note also the horn-balanced elevators.

Hispano-Suiza engine designer, attempting to fit the new 300 hp Hispano-Suiza to an existing *bi-mitrailleuse* Spad, and to also place this Hispano-Suiza 300 in a new airplane which he is designing especially for it. This gives considerable promise, and also embodies the feature that the cannon can be used in this engine." This is confirmed by the British monthly report of French experimental aeroplanes dated 1 November 1917, in which two new Spad designs were reported to be under study. The first was to have "Similar fuselage to Type 13 with two guns"; the second was to be "As above but with a 37-mm *canon* in addition." Both were to have the 300 hp Hispano-Suiza.

Evidently a 300 hp engine was installed in a Spad 13, for the report dated 1 December 1917 records that such an aircraft had crashed. This must have been an early prototype engine, for it is recorded that the 300 hp Hispano-Suiza had only just finished its bench tests by 24 February 1918. It seems that the second 300 hp Spad design never materialized. The *canon* version of the 300 hp engine, designated Hispano-Suiza 8G, was reported to be still under test in September 1918, and Herbemont abandoned his Spad 18 *canon*-armed design, intended for the Hispano-Suiza 8G, in favour of the Spad 20, which had the Hispano-Suiza 8Fb. This, the standard 300 hp engine, was in fact a direct-drive power unit in which a *canon* installation was impossible. It seems that vibration was still a problem on the 300 hp Hispano-Suiza 8G and prevented its successful development before the war ended.

The resourceful Béchereau was not defeated, however, for he proceeded to revise the basic Spad design formula yet again to produce a new design with the 300 hp Hispano-Suiza 8Fb as its power unit. This new type was designated Spa.17.C 1 and

(Above) The Spad 21 had wings of equal span and chord, and there were ailerons on both upper and lower wings. (Below) Another view of the Spad 21 S.777, showing that the ailerons had compound taper.

was undergoing tests in April 1918 (at which time only ten 300 hp Hispano-Suizas had been completed). Recorded results suggest that its performance was little better than that of the Spad 13; nevertheless, limited production was ordered and it appears that twenty were built before the Armistice. Perhaps this was a further case of a development batch of twenty, as had apparently been built in the case of the Spad 13. The Spad 17's operational trials were flown by *Capitaine* de Slade in June 1918, and the few known serial numbers for the type suggest that the production aircraft were built by the parent Spad company. It appears that the Spad 17s were allocated only to *Les Cigognes*; and it is known that René Fonck (75 victories) flew one late in the war.

In general appearance, the Spad 17 closely resembled its immediate predecessor; indeed, its overall dimensions were identical with those of the Spad 13. However, its structure incorporated a strengthened wing cellule with a proven factor of safety of 9 (that of the Spad 13 was only 7); the fuselage was bulkier than that of the earlier type; the larger diameter of the radiator was slightly emphasized by the camber of its cowling and the fuselage sides behind the cockpit were faired with numerous stringers. So full was the fairing of the fuselage sides that it did not converge to form a vertical knife-edge at the stern-post. Instead, the lower part of the rudder incorporated a bulbous fairing that continued the contours of the fuselage smoothly back to the trailing edge of the rudder. In the tail unit, enlarged horizontal surfaces, strut-braced from below, were fitted and auxiliary flying wires connected the under-surface of the lower wings to special attachment points on rearward extensions of the apices of the undercarriage V-struts.

Almost contemporary, indeed almost identical, with the Spad 17 was the Spad 21. This was virtually a Spad 17 on which the upper and lower wings were of equal span and chord and both were fitted with ailerons. As on the Spad 17, there were auxiliary flying wires running from rearward extensions of the apices of the undercarriage V-struts to the main spars of the lower wing directly under the intermediate struts. A connecting link between upper and lower ailerons was housed in a fairing behind the rear interplane strut on each side. Surviving records suggest that the Spad 21 may have been slightly larger in its major dimensions than the Spad 17, but this seems unlikely. Possibly it was hoped to improve both manoeuvrability and climbing performance, but in the latter respect at least the Spad 21 was inferior to the Spad 17. Performance generally was disappointing; although slightly faster than the Spad 17, the Spad 21 was slower on the climb despite its greater wing area. Test results for the type were known in October, but it was abandoned in November. Two were reportedly retained for experiments with Tempier (*sic*: possibly Tampier misspelt) fuel equipment in the immediately post-war period. One of the Spad 21s bore the serial number *S.777.*

continued on page 310

THE "BIRD-OF-PARADISE" AIR ARM

A MONG THE MOST YOUTHFUL of the world's air arms, the air component of the Papua New Guinea Defence Force, whose aircraft sport this newly independent nation's flamboyant yellow bird of paradise emblem on concentric rings of black, red and green, has now assumed responsibility for the tasks hitherto performed by a contingent of the Royal Australian Air Force. With an initial strength of four ex-RAAF Douglas C-47s, delivered last year as part of a $A 16·4m Australian defence aid programme, the PNGDF air component is seen as the nucleus of an air force, the anticipated expansion of which during the remainder of the present decade will involve the procurement of STOL transports and support aircraft, such as the GAF Nomad 'Mission Master', and helicopters.

The Papua New Guinea Department of Defence began operating on 1 October 1974, in preparation for the transfer of responsibility in defence matters from Australian to its own armed forces, and 10 years of Australian military aviation in Papua New Guinea came to an end recently with the withdrawal of two flying units of the RAAF and the Australian Army Aviation Corps. The detachment of three DHC Caribous based at Port Moresby in support of the PNGDF has now been withdrawn, having flown a total of 26,500 hours during its stay in the country, and the Army Aviation Corps' Pilatus Turbo-Porters and Bell 47G Sioux helicopters contributed 10,000 and 16,000 flying hours respectively up to the time of their withdrawal.

The proposed PNGDF defence organisation is based on a personnel force of some 3,500 officers and men, this comprising two infantry battalions of Pacific Islands Regi-

ment, plus seagoing and air elements. Initial training and formation costs have been financed by the Australian government, and New Zealand has also provided military aid, including the secondment of Army and RNZAF instructors to the PNG Joint Services College at Lae. The PNGDF air component has bases available at Port Moresby, Lae,

Madang, Rabaul and Wewak, plus numerous strips. All training of air component personnel has so far been conducted by the RAAF, which may be expected to continue to furnish advanced instruction in the foreseeable future, but it is anticipated that *ab initio* and basic instruction will eventually be provided by a flying school to be established in Papua New Guinea. □

FIGHTER A TO Z

The XP-22 (above) was the true forerunner of the production P-6E but was eventually returned to P-6A standard.

CURTISS XP-22   USA

In 1931, the third production P-6 (which had been converted to P-6A standard) was withdrawn from service and returned to Curtiss for extensive modification as the XP-22. Retaining the V-1570-23 engine, the XP-22 was cleaned up aerodynamically and featured cantilever main undercarriage legs and wheel spats, plus a redesigned engine cowling with, initially, an annular radiator. The radiator was subsequently returned to a position beneath the rear of the engine. On 30 June 1931, the XP-22 demonstrated a level speed of 202·4 mph (326 km/h) and on 10 July a USAAC contract was placed for 45 Y1P-22s. These were subsequently redesignated as P-6Cs, but prior to the start of production deliveries the designation was to be changed once more to P-6E, by which time the engine of the XP-22, complete with cowling and three-blade propeller, plus the main undercarriage members, had been grafted on to the YP-20 which had thus become the XP-6E while the XP-22 was returned to P-6A configuration. Max speed, 202 mph (325 km/h) at sea level, 195 mph (314 km/h) at 10,000 ft (3 050 m). Initial climb, 2,400 ft/min (12,19 m/sec). Empty weight, 2,597 lb (1 178 kg). Loaded weight, 3,354 lb (1 521 kg). Span, 31 ft 6 in (9,60 m). Length, 23 ft 7 in (7,19 m). Height, 8 ft 10 in (2,69 m). Wing area, 252 sq ft (23,41 m²).

CURTISS F9C (SPARROWHAWK)   USA

Designed to meet a lightweight shipboard fighter requirement, other contenders being the Berliner Joyce XFJ-1 (see *Fighter A to Z*/May 1973) and General Aviation XFA-1, the XF9C-1, flown on 12 February 1931, failed to gain acceptance as a carrier-based aircraft, but its small dimensions commended it for use from the dirigibles *Akron* and *Macon* which had been designed with internal hangar bays. The XF9C-1 was subsequently fitted with the so-called "skyhook" which engaged the retractable trapeze featured by the dirigibles, some directional instability resulting from the hook dictating the enlarging of the vertical tail surfaces. A second prototype,

The XF9C-1 (below) was designed as a lightweight shipboard fighter but was rejected for carrier operation.

the XF9C-2 with single-strut main undercarriage members, was built at Curtiss expense prior to the placing of a US Navy contract for six F9C-2s which featured a similar tripod undercarriage strut arrangement to the XF9C-1, the XF9C-2 later being purchased by the US Navy and modified to F9C-2 standard. The F9C-2 was powered by a 438 hp Wright R-975-E3 radial engine and carried an armament of two 0·3-in (7,62-mm) Browning machine guns. Originally intended to provide fighter protection for the dirigibles, the F9C-2s were used primarily to extend the reconnaissance capabilities of the parent craft. The *Macon* was lost on 12 February 1935, together with four of the F9C-2s. Max speed, 176 mph (284 km/h) at 4,000 ft (1 220 m). Initial climb, 1,700 ft/min (8,63 m/sec). Range, 350 mls (563 km). Empty weight, 2,089 lb (947 kg). Loaded weight, 2,770 lb (1 256 kg). Span, 25 ft 5 in (7,75 m). Length, (6,27 m). Height, 10 ft 11½ in (3,34 m). Wing area, 173 sq ft (16,07 m²).

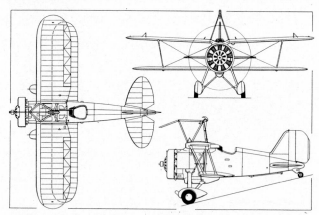

The F9C-2 (above and below) was an air-launched fighter operated from the dirigibles Akron *and* Macon.

CURTISS P-6E   USA

When the V-1570-23 engine of the XP-22, complete with three-blade propeller and the cowling, plus the cantilever main undercarriage members of the XP-22 were grafted on the YP-20 airframe in the autumn of 1931, the result of this marriage being assigned the designation XP-6E, and the 45 Y1P-22s ordered during the previous July and which were briefly to be referred to as P-6Cs, being designated as P-6Es by the time deliveries began on 2 December 1931. Powered by the same 600 hp Curtiss V-1570-23 Conqueror engine, the P-6E carried an armament of two 0·3-in (7,62-mm) Browning machine guns and 17 surviving examples were eventually assigned to ground schools during the summer of 1939. In the spring of 1932, the XP-6E was returned to Curtiss for a turbo-supercharged V-1570-55 engine of 675 hp, a fully-enclosed cockpit with aft-sliding canopy being fitted at the same time and the designation being changed to XP-6F. This attained 225 mph

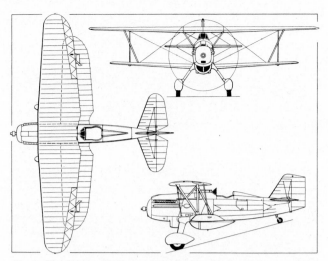

The P-6E (above and below) was the final production derivative of the basic P-6 design.

The XP-6F (below) had previously served as the XP-6E, the designation being changed after the application of a turbo-supercharger and a fully-enclosed cockpit.

planform mated to an all-metal monocoque fuselage of very clean aerodynamic form and a turbo-supercharged, geared GIV-1570C Conqueror engine. Delivered to the USAAC in February 1932, the XP-23 offered too insignificant advance in performance over the P-6E to warrant further development, and the troublesome turbo-supercharger was removed, the three-bladed propeller was replaced by a two-blader and the aircraft was returned to the USAAC in April 1932 as the YP-23. It was then returned to Curtiss and its wings used for the XF11C-1. The following data relate to the XP-23. Max speed, 223 mph (359 km/h) at 15,000 ft (4 570 m). Initial climb, 1,370 ft/min (6,96 m/sec). Range, 435 mls (700 km/h). Empty weight, 3,274 lb (1 485 kg). Loaded weight, 4,124 lb (1 870 kg). Span, 31 ft 6 in (9,60 m). Length, 23 ft 10 in (7,26 m). Height, 9 ft 6 in (2,89 m). Wing area, 252 sq ft (23,41 m²).

The XP-6H (above) was an adaptation of the first production P-6E with four wing-mounted guns.

(362 km/h) at 18,000 ft (5 485 m) during tests. One P-6E was temporarily assigned the designation XP-6G while being used as a test-bed for the V-1570-51 (F-series) engine, while the first production P-6E was also fitted with this engine and experimental wing armament as the XP-6H. The wing armament comprised two 0·3-in (7,62-mm) guns in both the upper and lower wings, these firing outside the propeller disc and augmenting the twin synchronised fuselage guns. The following data relate to the P-6E. Max speed, 193 mph (311 km/h) at sea level, 180 mph (290 km/h) at 15,000 ft (4 570 m). Initial climb, 2,460 ft/min (12,49 m/sec). Normal range, 285 mls (458 km). Empty weight, 2,699 lb (1 224 kg). Loaded weight, 3,436 lb (1 558 kg). Span, 31 ft 6 in (9,60 m). Length, 23 ft 2 in (7,06 m). Height, 8 ft 10 in (2,69 m). Wing area, 252 sq ft (23,41 m²).

CURTISS XP-23   USA

The last fighter biplane to be developed by Curtiss for the USAAC, the XP-23 was considered to be the ultimate refinement in this category. Ordered in July 1931, the XP-23 introduced fabric-covered metal wings of standard P-6

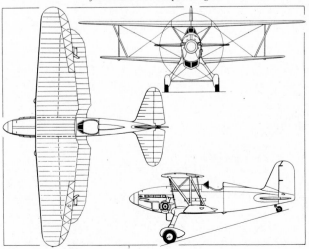

The XP-23 (above and below) was the final fighter biplane to be developed by Curtiss for the USAAC, was of all-metal construction and featured a turbo-supercharger.

BRAZIL'S "LITTLE BUG"

T HE BRAZILIAN aircraft industry is generally regarded as being one of the world's youngest, albeit fast-growing to meet the expanding demands of both military and civil users in Brazil and neighbouring countries. It is certainly true that the industry as constituted today is relatively new and that for many years both before and after World War II attempts to mass-produce aircraft met with little success. Nevertheless, Brazilian pioneers — among whom the name of Albert Santos Dumont is the best known — have been actively designing, building and flying prototypes since 1910. In the 66 years since then, it is estimated that as many as 1,000 different aircraft have been projected in Brazil and between a quarter and a third of these reached at least the prototype stage.

Of all those prototypes, one of the most intriguing — and certainly the smallest — was the Bichino (Little Bug). Designed as a private venture in the late 'thirties, the Bichino subsequently served as a test-bed for the IPT (*Instituto de Pesquisas Tecnológicas* or Technological Research Institute) of the São Paulo State University. Four examples were built and, remarkably, one of these not only still survives but is still airworthy, being flown (on special occasions and with loving care) by instructors at the Rio Claro aeroclub.

In 1938, the IPT's Aviation Research Department was, by a fair margin, the most important aviation research centre working in Brazil and had completed a long series of studies of the use of native Brazilian woods in aircraft. A special technique had been developed for producing in industrial quantities a new kind of plywood for aircraft using Brazilian pine, and studies had been made of freijo, a Brazilian hardwood 20 per cent stronger and heavier than spruce.

One of the principal researchers at the IPT was Frederico Abranches Brotero, who was also a gifted designer. In company with Orthon Hoover, an American who had come to Brazil as a demonstration pilot for Curtiss in 1911 and had decided to stay, Brotero set about putting freijo and the new plywood to the test in a light aircraft. Hoover had previously participated, with Santos Dumont's nephew and another pilot, Fritz Roesler, in development of a light aircraft in São Paulo; this, the Ypiranga, became the prototype of the highly successful Paulistinha,

more than 1,000 examples of which were eventually to be built.

Work on Brotero's tiny wooden aeroplane, designed around a 60 hp Walter Mikron engine, began late in 1939 in a workshop of the São Paulo Polytechnic School under IPT supervision and it was transferred to Rio Claro city aero club for completion and first flight. The latter was effected in 1940 and is recalled by one of the mechanics who worked on the project, Balbino Romero, now 71 years of age and still living in Rio Claro. Both Hoover and Brotero were "laughing like children", he says, "when the ex-Curtiss demonstration pilot started the engine and after a very short run took off without problem".

A three-view drawing of the Bichino in its original form and extra side view showing version with enclosed cockpit.

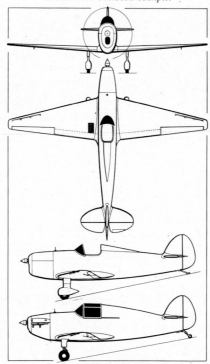

The flight lasted 27 minutes. On the second flight, Hoover took the Bichino to 3,200 ft (1 000 m) and began a series of aerobatics ending with a high speed dive "that made us nervous", Balbino Romero recalls. "We were afraid that the wooden structure would break under the strain, but the Bichino buzzed safely over our heads with a smiling Hoover at the controls".

Technical novelty

The Little Bug was of all wood construction, the cantilever low-wing being a two-spar structure with a Clark Y aerofoil; the spars were of paumarfim*, ribs of freijo and covering of Brazilian pine plywood. Ailerons were fabric covered; fixed letter-box slots were incorporated ahead of the ailerons and split flaps extended along each trailing edge from aileron to fuselage. The wooden monocoque fuselage structure had guapuruvu longerons and freijo reinforcements with plywood construction. Tail unit construction was of freijo with fabric covering for the elevators and rudder; there was a controllable trim-tab in the starboard elevator.

The fixed landing gear had rubber-in-compression shock absorbers and a steel tail skid. Phenolic resin was used to bond the wooden components. The open cockpit was just wide enough for a pilot of average build, but was comfortable and afforded good visibility.

In 1943, the Bichino prototype (PP-THH) was purchased by the IPT to be used as a flying test bed and three more examples were put in hand, with some structural redesign to reduce weight and improve performance. The three new Bichinos had 65 hp, 75 hp and 85 hp Continental engines respectively. By this time, IPT had completed other prototypes designated the IPT-1, IPT-2 and IPT-3, and the Bichino was consequently given the designation IPT-0, the three new examples becoming the IPT-0-A, -B and -C respectively. The fourth and last was completed in 1947 and proved to be the best performer and most pleasant to fly. In the same year, the Bichino

* *Botanical names for the woods used in the Bichino are as follow: paumarfim, balfourodendrun riedelanum; Brazilian pine, araucaria brasiliensis; freijo, cordia goeldiana and guapuruvu, squisoloblum excelsum.*

VETERAN & VINTAGE

was given official Type Approval and plans were made for its production, but these came to nought.

The first Bichino had already been retired in 1945 and the third was later destroyed in an accident while the fourth (PP-ZPA, later PP-AOA) was eventually scrapped. The surviving example (PP-ECM) is the second, still in its original green and yellow colours. It has been refurbished and modified three times and differs from the original in having an enclosed cockpit. As already noted, all four aircraft had different engines, with Brazilian wooden propellers although the fourth flew for a time with a manually controlled variable pitch Beech Aircraft propeller.

The Bichino has a span of 22 ft 4 in (6,80 m), length of 19 ft 4 in (5,90 m), height of 5 ft 3 in (1,60 m) and wing area of 66·74 sq ft (6,20 m²). Empty weight is 616 lb (280 kg) and take-off weight, 970 lb (440 kg). Max speed with the 65 hp engine is 150 mph (240 km/h) and cruising speed 130·5 mph (210 km/h). An endurance of 3 hrs is achieved on the fuel capacity of 20 Imp gal (90 l) and take-off and landing runs are 755 ft (230 m) and 1,050 ft (320 m) respectively on unpaved surfaces. □   ROBERTO PEREIRA

The three colour illustrations show the surviving IPT-0 Bichino at the Rio Claro city aero club, where it is kept in flying condition. Above, the original Bichino flying over São Paulo in 1940.

IN PRINT

"To Fly Like a Bird"
by Keith Sherwin
Bailey Bros & Swinfen Ltd, Folkestone, £3·95
182 pp, 8¾ in by 5 in, illustrated

ALREADY the author of a definitive manual on the practical aspects of man-powered flight, Keith Sherwin now provides a more general treatise on the same subject. Largely, this is a history of all the efforts that have been made to achieve flight using the energy of the pilot to propel the aircraft. Such efforts began as early as 1913, when the Peugeot company in France offered prizes for successful flights in a man-powered aircraft; they were never won, as the required minimum distance and height were never achieved. Similarly, a prize offered by the Polytechnische Gesellschaft of Frankfurt in the mid-thirties set minimum standards that proved unattainable.

Interest in man-powered flight revived in the UK in 1956 and was further stimulated in 1959 when the Kremer prize was offered. With £50,000 still waiting to be won, the Kremer prize is today the principal stimulus for man-powered flight activities throughout the world, and these are all clearly described in Mr Sherwin's book. There are also chapters on man-powered flight as a sport, and on the construction of such aircraft as student projects at high schools, colleges and universities.

"Man Powered Flight"
by Keith Sherwin
MAP/Argus Books Ltd, Herts, £2·95
192 pp, 5¾ in by 8¼ in, illustrated

A SECOND edition, this time in paperback, of a volume that was considered to be one of the best in its field when first published in 1971. All aspects of man-powered flight are dealt with, special attention being given to practical aspects, and the most successful projects to date are described. Recommended reading for anyone with an interest in this branch of aviation.

"RAF Fighters 1918-1937"
by G R Duval
D Bradford Barton Ltd, Truro, £3·50
96 pp, 8 in by 8½ in, illustrated

UNIFORM with nine previous volumes by this publisher, this is essentially a collection of well-captioned photographs, nicely printed on good quality paper. As such, it appears a little expensive, even by today's inflated standards, but usefully supplements other publications that deal at greater length with the various aircrafts' histories.

"Regia Aeronautica: Balcani e Fronte Orientale"
"Regia Aeronautica: Colori e Insegne"
by Angelo Emiliani, Giuseppe F Ghergo and Achille Vigna
Intergest, Milan, L3000 and L3800 respectively
230 pp each, 9½ in by 6¾ in, illustrated

ITALIAN-language volumes devoted, respectively, to the operations of the Italian Air Force on the Balkan and Eastern Front, and the colours and markings used by its aircraft between 1935 and 1943, these soft-cover books are in a series entitled *Immagini e Storia dell'Aeronautica Italiana 1935-1945* (Italian Aviation in Words and Pictures, 1935-1945).

The emphasis is upon illustrations, including some colour photographs and drawings, and many of the details given in the text can be deduced by the average enthusiast even with no knowledge of Italian. Sole UK distributor for the series is Bivouac Books Ltd, from whom copies are available at 104 Kilburn Square, London NW6 6PS, the post-inclusive price being £2·25 and £2·75 respectively.

"Spagna 1936-39: l'Aviazione Legionaria
by Angelo Emiliani, Giuseppe F Ghergo and Achille Vigna
Intergest, Milan. L2,200
210 pp, 9¼ by 6¾ in, illustrated

ANOTHER title in the series referred to in the previous note, this volume describes operations of the Italian units in the Spanish Civil War. The post-inclusive price from Bivouac Books is £1·65.

"Fiat CR.42 Falco"
by Italo de Marchi
Stem Mucchi, Modena, Lire 500
24 pp, 9¼ in by 8¾ in

LATEST of the profiles in *Le Macchine e la Storia* series, provides a selection of photographs, a three-view in colour, and Italian text describing the construction, production and operational use of the Fiat CR.42, the last of Italy's fighting biplanes.

"Heathrow Airport, London"
by Bernard Henry
J M Dent & Sons, London, £2·95
120 pp, 5¼ in by 8½ in, illustrated

FOR most passengers using them, modern airports are large, noisy, impersonal, sometimes dirty places to be endured as a necessary part of the process of getting from A to B. This volume presents London's Heathrow in a somewhat different light, as an almost self-contained city where thousands work to provide the many different services associated with more than a quarter million aircraft movements each year.

"Annalar Islenskva Flugmala 1931-1936"
by Arngrimur Sigurdsson
Bokautgafa Aeskunnar, Iceland
200 pp, 8½ in by 11 in illustrated

SECOND volume in a history of aviation in Iceland, covering the years from 1931 to 1936. In Icelandic throughout, the history is of limited value outside that country, but it does include a good collection of photographs of value to anyone with a specialist interest in the subject.

"Scale Model Aircraft in Plastic Card"
by Harry Woodman
Argus Books Ltd, Kings Langley, Herts, £2·95
148 pp, 5½ in by 8¼ in, illustrated

IN THIS very detailed dissertation, Mr Woodman explains a method for modelling aircraft that allows the modeller greater opportunity to display his personal skill than is necessarily required in the construction of a typical plastic kit. He goes so far as to suggest that modelling in plastic card is a natural successor to the "real modelling" of pre-war days, when balsa or other wood, razor blades, sandpaper, wood glue and wire were the materials and the achievement of accuracy in a finished model often depended upon the modeller's ability to scale up or scale down a three-view drawing reproduced in the aviation press.

Whether the claim is a fair one or not, this book certainly indicates that modelling in plastic card offers plenty of scope for deployment of old skills (or the learning of new ones) to produce the correct overall shapes and manufacture all the many items of equipment for a well-finished model. The illustrations show what can be achieved by the patient modeller.

"The Achievement of the Airship"
by Guy Hartcup
David & Charles, Newton Abbot, Devon, £6·50
296 pp, 5¼ in by 8½ in, illustrated

THIS is another history of the airship, a theme that has attracted the attention of several authors in recent years, and one that can be recommended to general reader and specialist alike. As the 12-page list of references at the back of the volume attests, the author has researched his subject with particular care and thoroughness, digging deep into unpublished material in the Public Records Office as well as the published records in the UK, USA and Germany.

A short closing chapter describes possible future opportunities for the airship, but the author indicates his detachment from the subject by adding a question mark to the chapter title "A Rôle for the Future". This detachment allows him to record the history of the airship fairly without losing sight of the disadvantages that were apparent quite early on and are still more obvious today.

"Civil Aircraft Registers of France, 1975"
"The Benelux, Swiss and Australian Civil Registers, 1975"
"United Kingdom & Eire Civil Registers, 1975"
Air-Britain Publications
7 in by 9¼ in, illustrated

THREE 1975 editions of civil aircraft registers, prepared by enthusiasts for enthusiasts. Each contains information updated to early 1975, including details of aircraft ownership, c/n, previous identities and probable bases. There is also a guide to civil airfield location in each volume. Copies can be ordered from the Air-Britain Sales Department, at Stone Cottage, Great Sampford, Saffron Walden, Essex CB10 2RS: prices (post free) are £1·50 for the French register, £1·35 for the Benelux volume and £1·45 for the UK edition.

"Bombers and Transports in Service since 1960"
by Kenneth Munson
Blandford Press, Poole, Dorset, £2·10
160 pp, 4½ in by 7 in, illustrated

ANOTHER revised edition of one of the titles in Blandford's "Pocket Encyclopaedia of World Aircraft in Colour". The "bombers" title embraces attack aircraft (such as the A-4 and A-7), and patrol and reconnaissance types are also included, while "transports" extend down the scale to such aircraft as the Beagle Basset (now discarded by the RAF) and the Neiva Regente. Colour profiles depict side and plan views of each type described.

The (h)itch in scratch-building

LONG, LONG AGO, during our salad days which happened to coincide with the infancy of the plastic model aircraft construction kit, the manufacturer chancing his arm in this youthful and still undeveloped modelling market invariably offered a kit for a specific aeroplane of a specific type and that was precisely what we built — a miniature replica of that one individual machine and no other. Sets of decals offering a variety of alternative markings were far in the future and most of us cutting our teeth in this still novel pastime were content enough. But as we modellers began to proliferate and the kit manufacturers steadily increased their output (ie, the *quantity* of individual kits rather than their *variety*) the cult of personalising models began to grow; the modification by modellers of the component parts of standard kits to create different variants at one extreme to the mere marking change at the other. The individuality that is an innate part of the make-up of every true modeller was beginning to reveal itself.

The kit manufacturers were not slow to appreciate the possibilities that this trend presented from the viewpoint of sales and were soon offering two, three and even more sets of alternative decals with their kits. Sophistication accompanied maturity and soon kit producers were beginning to include extra parts so that the modeller was no longer restricted to one sub-type of a particular aircraft if he did not resort to introducing his own modifications. All well and good, but it did render the task of truly personalising a model that much more difficult. The *aficionados* now took the process a stage further, producing models of aircraft not available in kit form by making some component parts from scratch and marrying these with suitably adapted components from several kits, a process which soon evolved into pure scratch-building.

Today, the ranks of the scratch-builders are swelling at a rate of knots, but there is one major hitch; an impediment that looms larger as the retail prices of kits rise. The vast majority of scratch-builders still utilise *some* component parts from commercially-produced kits; parts that are time-consuming and difficult to produce from scratch, such as engines, cowlings, propellers, wheels, seats, etc. Therein lies the rub, or, perhaps more appositely, the irritation, for to obtain the desired components it is necessary to purchase the complete kit, the unused portions of which are of little or no value in the spares box.

There are now a goodly number of specialist decal producers providing an invaluable service to the modelling fraternity. Is it beyond the realms of possibility that some enterprising company will endeavour to cater for the ever-growing ranks of the scratch-builders by offering kits of standard components (engines, cowlings, etc)? A market for such certainly exists and the availability of kits of this nature could do much to eliminate the *financial* hitch that is currently inhibiting the scratch-building movement. Quite obviously, the major kit manufacturers are unlikely to consider potential sales sufficient to justify such a venture, and yet Faller, the substantial German concern specialising in kits for HO and N gauge model railway buildings, has for many years enjoyed a brisk trade in packs of scale doors, windows, walls, etc, for the use of the railway scratch-builder. If it is not economical to produce such model aircraft components in plastic, then why not use white metal castings? With the range of adhesives now available, the old problem of mating dissimilar materials no longer exists.

Building from scratch

Two months ago, we presented a case for scratch-building and promised that, from time to time, we would be offering a few tips that we believe to be helpful in putting theory into practice. Commencing with first principles, it is obviously necessary to decide what aircraft is to be modelled and, as an initial scratch-building venture, it is wise to select a relatively simple subject possessing a preponderance of straight lines in its plan and elevations. Not that one is restricted to modelling straight lines, but the more curvaceous the subject the more complex the construction of the model.

Having chosen the subject, it is then necessary to obtain an adequate selection of reference material in the form of general arrangement drawings and photographs — as detailed as possible — in order to ascertain the precise shapes of the original. Assuming that you have the good fortune to unearth a set of drawings to the required scale, you are in business, but the chances are that the drawings will have to be enlarged or reduced photographically in order to obtain the scale in which you wish to work. The next stage is to consider the method of construction and the materials to be used. Basically, the material will be sheet polystyrene plastic which is readily obtainable in a good range of thicknesses from ·005-in up to ·125-in, and it would be wise to lay in a stock of several different thicknesses, the most useful being ·010-in, ·020-in and ·030-in. This sheet is available in black, white and various colours, but we would recommend that only the white be used as this not only provides a good base for painting but is the most easily marked with pencil when setting out the parts.

The most useful adhesive is methylethylketone, available in model shops under various brand names as liquid cement — tube plastic cement will be needed for some of the heavier joints, such as at wing roots, but the liquid will be neater and cleaner for most purposes. Clear polystyrene and acetate sheet will also be needed, and a small stock of strip and block balsa, obechi or other easily-carved wood will serve a number of purposes. Finally, you will need a selection of fine gauge nickel silver wires.

The tools required for scratch-building are much the same as for kit building — craft knives with a selection of blades, small files, a pin-vice with some small drills, "wet n'dry" emery paper, etc — but there are some important additions, such as a good steel straight-edge and a small steel square, plus a firm, smooth board upon which to cut.

From this point, the decision must be taken as to the best method of construction to be used to achieve the correct shape of the aircraft. There are two main methods: vacuum forming as used for the commercially-available vacuformed kits, but best kept for smaller components unless special equipment is available, and building up in sheet from a basic framework. The former corresponds roughly to monocoque construction in a full-scale aircraft while the latter more closely approximates to the method of construction with formers and stringers widely used prior to WW II. We propose to go into the subject of vacuum-forming at a later date and for the moment will confine ourselves to the built-up method.

A start is made by constructing a box upon which to build up the eventual shape of the fuselage, and this will comprise the top, with suitable openings left for cockpit, cabin, etc; the bottom, the sides and such bulkheads as are required to provide stiffness. All these parts may be drawn in pencil straight on to plastic sheet of suitable thickness, reducing the width of top and bottom to compensate for the thickness of the sides. The accuracy of this basic structure is vital to the successful outcome of the operation and it must be precisely squared. This box core should be assembled with liquid cement and allowed to dry overnight, and upon this may be built up such formers, bulkheads and longerons as are necessary to support the outer covering in the correct shape and with adequate strength.

The external covering, usually made from the thinner sheet, such as ·010-in, can now be cut out in suitable sections or panels, corresponding, as far as is practicable, with those of the original. The plastic sheet can be ruled from the inside with the point of an empty ballpoint pen to represent the rib and stringer effect under the fabric-covered areas and scribed with a steel scriber to represent panel lines on metal-skinned areas. A fair degree of single and even double curvature may be achieved by moulding the plastic between the fingers and thumbs, provided that the sections of panelling are kept reasonably small.

Interior details must, of course, be added during the fuselage construction and can, for the most part, be made from the sheet material — seats may require from two to as many as six parts each in order to achieve the correct shape, but most other parts are easier, being pieces of sheet or rod, either commercially prepared and obtainable in packets or heat-stretched sprue to which we will be referring later.

We have not as yet mentioned scale and it is

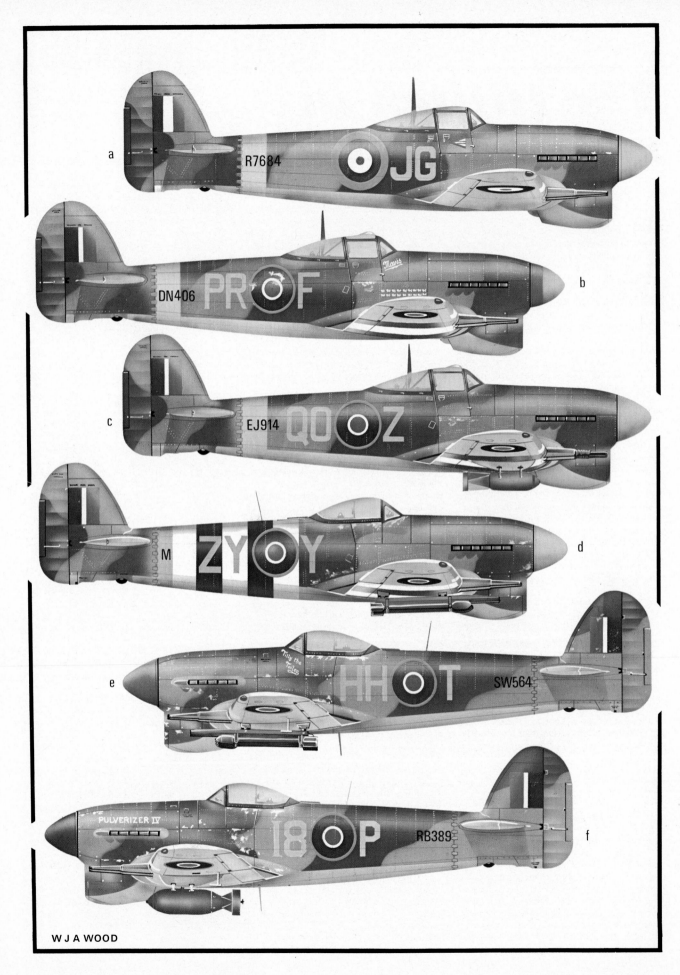

a R7684 ◉ JG

b DN406 PR ◉ F

c EJ914 QO ◉ Z

d M ZY ◉ Y

e HH ◉ T SW564

f 18 ◉ P RB389 PULVERIZER IV

intended that these notes on scratch-building shall be applicable over a wide range, for we have seen very successful scratch-built models in scales from 1/72nd up to 1/24th, the main consideration not being so much the method of construction but the thicknesses of the materials used, these having to be commensurate with the size of the model. Scales from 1/48th upwards are eminently suitable for scratch-building, but, using the thinner gauge sheets, it is possible to obtain very fine results, even with the smaller 1/72nd scale subjects.

Returning to the fuselage construction, it is advisable to reinforce the structure at all points where attachments have to be made, such as wing roots and undercarriage members. Furthermore, a laminated nose block will provide a secure anchorage for the engine, or, in the case of an inline profile, the propeller. If scoring of panel lines is necessary at this stage, it will be found useful to have a flexible metal typewriter eraser shield as a guide for the scriber, as this will be adaptable to the curvature of the surface in most places. In a future column we propose to consider the construction of the wings and tail surfaces.

This month's colour subject

Although acquiring a reputation as a fighter of dubious reliability during the early stages of its career, the Hawker Typhoon overcame an inauspicious service début with maturity to enjoy widespread acclaim as one of the Allies' most potent weapons — a close-support fighter destined to turn the tide in many a land battle and overturn many land warfare concepts. The heaviest and most powerful single-seat, single-engine warplane envisaged at the time of its design, the massive, rather bulbous Typhoon makes an excellent modelling subject and has received more than adequate coverage in so far as model kits are concerned, maintaining a presence in the catalogues these many years past.

The earliest of the Typhoon kits were products of Frog and Airfix, both to 1/72nd scale and the latter being still available, Frog having recently replaced its offering with a completely new kit for the Mk IB, this being easily the best available in this scale and recommended with confidence. Some years ago, Monogram produced a very fine 1/48th scale Typhoon Mk IB and this, again, is still available. It is a kit that belies its age and is unlikely to be bettered in the foreseeable future.

Continuing up the scales, we have a 1/32nd kit from Revell which is one of the best in this company's large scale series. The Airfix and earlier Frog kits represented, as also does the Monogram kit, the "bubble" canopy version of the Mk IB, whereas the Revell and later Frog kits depict the version with the earlier framed canopy and car-type entrance door.

Depending entirely upon your scale preference, you can safely buy the Revell, Monogram and current Frog kits, all three being included in the respective current catalogues, and these should be readily obtainable wherever their manufacturers' products are distributed.

Nichimo's "Dragon Slayer"

The distribution of Nichimo aircraft kits in the UK would seem to be somewhat erratic which is unfortunate in view of the high standards attained by this Japanese company's products. Occasionally a sample new release reaches us and the latest to do so is a truly beautiful kit to 1/48th scale of the Kawasaki Ki.45-KAI-Hei Toryu (Dragon Slayer) twin-engined fighter. This is the first kit of Toryu in this scale, and for all practical purposes, may be considered definitive. There are no fewer than 100 component parts, all extremely cleanly moulded in light grey plastic and embellished with the finest of surface detailing. Just about everything that could reasonably be included, both exterior and interior, is here, and the result is the sort of kit that could tempt even the most diehard of 1/72nd scale addicts to venture into quarter-inch scale.

Toryu was a handsome aircraft and Nichimo has captured its lines to perfection. The cockpit interiors account for 17 of the component parts and it is impossible to find anything of importance that can be added. The very clear five-piece canopy enables the interior to be seen to advantage. The undercarriage is built up from many very finely moulded components, each unit being mounted on a floor section to be built into the nacelles, while the two-row radial engines have separate cylinder blocks fitting over the crankcase, each having an individual exhaust collector assembly. The obliquely-mounted cannon are faithfully modelled and are visible through the canopy transparencies. Despite detailed completeness, this is not a difficult kit to build, everything fitting together with satisfying precision. The decal sheet is matt finished and offers markings for two different aircraft of the 53rd *Sentai*, one being from the 3rd *Chutai* and the other from the *Shinten* attack component of the *Sentai*. Unfortunately, at the time of closing for press we have received no information regarding availability and retail price.

Ferocious feline. . .

The latest in Grumman's long line of fighting 'cats', the F-14A Tomcat, is a massively impressive piece of aeronautical hardware from any angle and a natural for the plastic kit manufacturer. About four years ago, Monogram made a somewhat abortive take-off with a 1/72nd scale kit, obviously hurriedly and unquestionably poorly conceived, which added little lustre to a distinguished name, and thus the market has been wide open for a really good kit of this supremely expensive but fantastic felid. Two British kit manufacturers, Airfix and Lesney (Matchbox), have been busily preparing their submissions for filling

this void and the former company's 'cat' has streaked past the metaphorical post by a whisker and fang. To 1/72nd scale, this Airfix kit will surely be hard to better, doing full justice to the full-scale original.

The kit, nicely moulded in clean white plastic, comprises no fewer than 110 component parts. The standard of the surface detailing, although mostly of the raised-line variety, is very high, the intricate shape of the fuselage is effectively captured and the variable-geometry wings are an ingenious operating feature, the sections interlocking firmly and leaving no ugly gaps around the slots — the triangular vanes in the leading edges extend as the wings are swept and the all-moving tailplane operates smoothly, the two halves being linked through the rear fuselage. The cockpit interiors are very good, with realistic ejection seats and two well-sculptured crew figures. The undercarriage may be assembled either extended or retracted and is delicately modelled to scale.

External stores are, of course, an important feature and Airfix offers four AIM-7E and six AIM-54A AAMs. The flight-refuelling probe can be fixed in deployed or retracted positions, as may also be the rear-fuselage air brakes, and the very clear cockpit canopy can be fixed open or closed. The decal sheet is a fine one, offering the colourful markings for the first two US Navy units to get with this 'cat', VF-1 and VF-2. In Series 5, this highly attractive and thoroughly recommended kit retails in the UK at £1.05.

. . . and its prop-driven predecessor

Predating the Tomcat by more than two-and-a-half decades, the Bearcat did, in some respects, provide as noteworthy an advance in shipboard fighter equipment in its day as does its current descendant. Of course, the Bearcat arrived on the scene at a time when the fan-up-front was already being considered as *passé* for the fighter. Nevertheless, from the commencement of its service phase-in in May 1945, it served with first-line US Navy units for more than four years, its withdrawal commencing mid-1949; it saw its share of action with the *Armée de l'Air* and it did stints with both the Thai and Vietnamese air forces.

The Grumman F8F Bearcat, which now appears in a new 1/72nd scale kit from Frog, has been modelled, and very successfully, by Monogram, and anyone having the earlier kit may be happy enough with it, although, on balance, we feel that this new effort is preferable. Comprising 39 component parts moulded suitably enough — always assuming that you do not have a penchant for the natural metal-finished examples flown by the Thais and Vietnamese — in the usual Frog dark blue-grey plastic with fine raised panel lines, the result is effective. We have a personal preference for engraved detail as the raised type tends to get obliterated when joints are smoothed down. There is a modicum of flash on the mouldings, but they are generally clean and the trailing edges of the flying surfaces are acceptably fine.

The cockpit interior could make good use of a lot more detail and we must admit to some misgivings over the massive locating lugs inside the wheel wells for the main undercarriage members — perhaps a little judicious trimming would not be entirely out of place. The undercarriage itself is a little on the *continued on page 307*

PLANE FACTS

The recce Romeos

After reading "Air War over Spain" and volume three of "Mediterranean Air War", I would like to obtain some details or the Meridionali Ro 37 and Ro 37bis reconnaissance and army co-operation aircraft referred to in these books. Details of their float-equipped derivatives, the Ro 43 and Ro 44, seem readily available but facts related to the earlier aircraft would seem singularly obscure. Can you publish a general arrangement drawing, photos and information?

Richard Fowkes
Perry Barr, Birmingham, B42 1QF

The IMAM Ro 37 two-seat reconnaissance biplane was the first aircraft of original design produced by the SA Industrie Meccaniche e Aeronautiche Meridionali (IMAM) in large numbers, this company having become, in 1936, the successor to the SA Industrie Aeronautische Romeo (all IMAM designs subsequently retaining the "Ro" prefix). Designed by Giovanni Gelasso, the first of two prototypes (MM 220 and 221) was flown on 6 November 1933 with a 600 hp Fiat A 30 RA 12-cylinder water-cooled inline engine. An unequal-span staggered single-bay biplane, the Ro 37 had a welded steel-tube fuselage with duralumin and fabric skinning, and fabric-covered wings of mixed construction (dur-alumin spars and wooden ribs). Pilot and observer were seated in tandem cockpits, fuel tanks in the fuselage and upper wing centre section contained a total of 159 Imp gal (742 l) and armament comprised either one or two synchronised forward-firing 7,7-mm Breda-SAFAT machine guns with 500 rpg, a similar weapon on a flexible mounting with 500 rounds in the rear cockpit and provision for two 79·4-lb (36-kg) bombs or 72 4·4-lb (2,0-kg) anti-personnel bombs.

From the outset, the Ro 37 was designed to take a 560 hp Piaggio P IX RC 40 nine-cylinder air-cooled radial engine as an alternative to the inline water-cooled Fiat A 30, the radial-engined model being designated Ro 37bis, and both versions were ordered into production for the *Regia Aeronautica,* some production being subcontracted to Caproni-Taliedo and Avio Industrie Stabiensi (AVIS). A pre-production batch of 12 (MM 10566-77) A 30-powered Ro 37s was delivered by IMAM during July-September 1935, after which IMAM con-centrated on the Ro 37bis until February 1937, producing 152 aircraft of this type (MM 10698-749, 10753-802 and 10805-854) before reverting to the Ro 37 and building a batch of 130 aircraft (MM 10855-984). Subsequently, IMAM was to build 86 more Ro 37bis aircraft (MM 11234-63, 11319-24, 11328-69 and 11426-33), production being completed in March 1939. Caproni-Taliedo built 150 Ro 37s (MM 10985-11134) and 19 examples of the Ro 37bis (MM 11162-77 and 11325-7), while AVIS built solely the Ro 37bis, delivering 118 (MM 10805-854, 11178-83, 11289-318, 11401-424 and 11434-41), total production (including prototypes) thus amounting to 669 aircraft (ie, two prototypes, 292 production Ro 37s and 375 production Ro 37bis's), and of these a number were exported to Afghanistan, Ecuador, Hungary and Uruguay.

The Ro 37 and Ro 37bis were adopted as standard equipment by the *Gruppi Osser-*

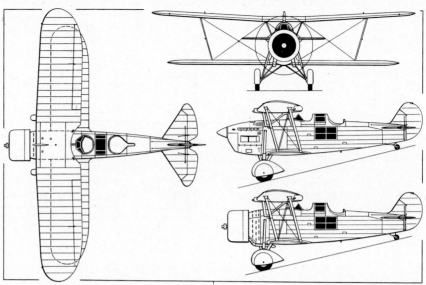

The front, plan and lower side elevations above illustrate the Ro 37bis and upper sideview depicts the Ro 37. (Immediately below) Ro 37bis of the XXII Gruppo OA (120ª Squadriglia) of the Aviazione Legionaria, and (bottom left) an A 30-powered Ro 37.

vazione Aerea of the *Regia Aeronautica,* and equipped the *XXII Gruppo Autonomo OA "Linci"* of the Italian *Aviazione Legionaria* sent to the assistance of the Spanish Nationalists, this *Gruppo,* which operated the Ro 37bis, comprising two *squadriglie,* the first of these (the 120ª) joining combat in October 1936 and the second (the 128ª) following in February 1937. The first *squadriglie* to re-equip with the Ro 37 and Ro 37bis were the 103ª and 108ª respectively, the latter participating in operations against Ethiopia from October 1935, being joined by the similarly-equipped 109ª and 110ª *squadriglie,* and subsequently by the Ro 37-equipped 103ª and 105ª *squadriglie.* By 10 August 1940, a total of 296 Ro 37s and Ro 37bis's remained in the first-line inventory of the *Regia Aeronautica,* these subsequently serving on virtually every front on which the service operated. In North Africa, the

principal *Gruppi* operating these types were the 64º (122ª and 136ª *squadriglie),* the 67º (73ª and 115ª *squadriglie),* and the 73º (127ª and 137ª *squadriglie),* while in the Balkans were the 5º (31ª and 39ª *squadriglie),* the 63º (41ª and 113ª *squadriglie),* the 70º (25ª and 114ª *squadriglie),* and the 72º (42ª and 120ª *squadriglie).* Attrition was high and by March 1942, only 146 Ro 37s and Ro 37bis's remained, 61 having been lost on operations and 85 in accidents.

The Ro 37 and Ro 37bis were employed as much in the close-support and assault rôles as for reconnaissance and observation tasks, proving extremely sturdy, although the Piaggio engine of the latter proved trouble-some under desert conditions. Consideration was given to adapting the Ro 37 as a single-seat assault aircraft and one example (MM 10868) was converted and tested at the Centro di Furbara in 1941.

The Ro 37bis (Piaggio P XI RC 40 engine) attained a maximum speed of 205 mph (330 km/h) at 14,765 ft (4 500 m) and possessed a range of 932 miles (1 500 km). An altitude of 13,125 ft (4 000 m) was attained in 11 min and service ceiling was 24,605 ft (7 500 m). Empty equipped and maximum loaded weights were 3,230 lb (1 465 kg) and 5,071 lb (2 300 kg) respectively, and overall dimensions were: span, 33 ft 4¼ in (11,08 m); length, 28 ft 1⅔ in (8,57 m); height, 10 ft 2⅔ in (3,11 m); wing area, 344·44 sq ft (32,00 m²).

Natacha or Rasante

I shall be grateful if you will publish details of the S-Z Rasante aircraft used by the Republican side during the Spanish Civil War. I have long been puzzled as to the positive identification of this particular aircraft and will be pleased if you can supply a three-view drawing, a specification and a photograph.

M C Richards
Woodbridge, Suffolk, IP12 4LZ

There has been some confusion regarding the appellation bestowed upon the S-Z (more usually referred to as the R-Z or R-Zet) light reconnaissance-bomber employed in some numbers during the Spanish Civil War, this perhaps being due to its external similarity to its progenitor, the R-5, which was also utilised in quantity during that conflict. The R-Z (alias S-Z) was in fact known as the *Natacha* whereas the earlier R-5 was known as the *Rasante*. The R-Z was a modernized and more powerful derivative of the basic Polikarpov R-5 light reconnaissance-bomber of 1928, which, during the early 'thirties, had become one of the most widely used of all Soviet combat aircraft. Evolved by D S Markov and A A Skarbov in 1935, the R-Z differed from the R-5 primarily in having an M-34RN liquid-cooled engine of 820 hp in place of the M-17F of 730 hp of later production R-5s (eg, R-5Sh and R-5SSS), redesigned tail surfaces and semi-enclosed cockpits.

The R-Z began to reach Spain during the late autumn of 1936, being joined early in 1937 by the R-5, and both types were to see considerable service throughout the conflict. The R-Z normally carried an armament of one 7,62-mm PV-1 machine gun on the portside of the upper fuselage decking and a ShKAS machine gun of similar calibre on a flexible mount in the observer's cockpit, and provision was made for two 275·5-lb (125-kg) and four 110-lb (50-kg) bombs on underwing racks. Empty and normal loaded weights were 4,425 lb (2 007 kg) and 6,944 lb (3 150 kg)

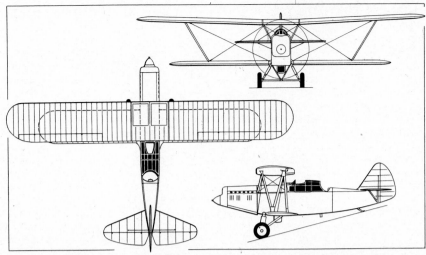

(Above and below) The R-Z (or R-Zet) light reconnaissance-bomber known in Spain as the 'Natacha' was a derivative of the Polikarpov R-5 which was known in Spain as the Rasante.

respectively, and performance included a max speed of 196 mph (316 km/h) at 9,840 ft (3 000 m) and 171 mph (276 km/h) at sea level, a range of 620 mls (1 000 km) and a ceiling of 28,545 ft (8 700 m), an altitude of 9,840 ft (3 000 m) being attained in 6·6 min and 16,405 ft (5 000 m) in 11·8 min. Overall dimensions were: span, 49 ft 10¼ in (15,20 m); length, 31 ft 10¾ in (9,72 m); height, 11 ft 3⅜ in (3,45 m); wing area, 457·68 sq ft (42,52 m²). A total of 1,031 R-Z aircraft was produced as compared with a total of 4,995 R-5s.

MODEL ENTHUSIAST — from page 305
chunky side but not excessively so, and the wheels are nicely formed. External stores comprise a centreline drop tank, two bombs and four rockets. The engine is a one-piece moulding but looks well enough, being set well back inside the cowling, while the two-piece canopy is extremely clear and sits well on the fuselage.

The variant depicted is the F8F-1B and the excellent decal sheet offers markings for an aircraft of the US Navy's VF-72 in 1950, based at NAS Quonset Point, and for a Bearcat of GC 1/21 *Artois* of the *Armée de l'Air* in Indo-China in 1952. Our sample kit was provided, incidentally, by G W Jones Bros & Company of 62 Turnham Green Terrace, London W4, who are retailing it in the UK at 55p (plus 20p postage).

Teutonic lightning

One of the most dramatic developments in the annals of WW II aviation was the début of the first operational turbojet-powered bomber in the form of Arado's Ar 234B Blitz (Lightning), which, fortunately for the Allies, achieved

service in insufficient quantities to offer more than an annoying toothache. A kit of the Ar 234B to 1/72nd scale was produced many years ago by Lindberg and, for its time, assembled as quite an acceptable model. Now Frog has come up with a new Blitz to the same scale and which we anticipate will find widespread acceptance.

Adaptability would seem to be the keynote of this kit which has 90 component parts moulded in Frog's now apparently standard dark blue-grey plastic. A full complement of alternative parts is provided so that any one of three versions may be modelled — the twin-jet Ar 234B-2, the four-jet Ar 234C-2 and the essentially similar multi-purpose Ar 234C-3, the kit including alternative single- and twin-turbojet engine nacelles and alternative nose sections. A good selection of external stores is provided, comprising one SC 1000 and two AB 500 bombs, two drop tanks, two podded *Rauchgeräte* and, oddly enough, a complete Fieseler Fi 103 flying bomb. We say oddly enough advisedly, for the idea of launching the Fi 103, alias V-1, from a dorsal cradle (raised for the actual launching by a series of

hydraulically-actuated arms) was no more than a paper study and would seem somewhat out of place in a kit representing hardware that actually existed. Another odd item among the 'extras' in this kit is the presentation of the Walter HWK 500A-1 assisted-take-off rocket packs which bear little resemblance to the units that they are intended to portray, lacking the wing attachments and being moulded as solid sections!

The trailing edges of the wings call for thinning down as do also those of the rudder which are exceptionally thick, but assembly is simple enough, with well-fitting parts and an adequate instruction sheet with an elaborate — perhaps *too* elaborate — system of symbols. The choice of markings must perforce be strictly limited as only the Ar 234B-2 achieved service status, but the decal sheet covers an aircraft of this sub-type operated by III/KG 76 from Achmer and offers merely national markings for the C-series aircraft. All in all, a praiseworthy effort, which, with a little more care on the part of its manufacturer, could have been rated as outstanding. □

F J HENDERSON

HAWKER SIDDELEY HS.748 —— *from page 276*

paratrooping (48 troops and dispatcher with seats along both sides, dropped through the rear freight door) or supply dropping (using the roller conveyors and rear door) is possible, and 24 stretchers plus nine seats can be accommodated. All necessary fittings for these varied rôles can be carried in the aircraft for rapid conversions in the field.

Another specialised rôle already fulfilled by the HS.748 is that of radio and navigation calibration and flight inspection. With the technical ability to make Cat 2 ILS approaches (decision height 100 ft/30,5 m and RVR 1,200 ft/366 m, with coupled descent in visual conditions to 50 ft/15 m), the flight inspection 748 is capable of checking and calibrating these radio and radar aids: ILS, VASI, PAR, VOR, TACAN, Marker Beacon, surveillance radar, NDB, DME, and UHF and VHF communications and DF. Two examples of the HS 748 are used in this rôle by the Civil Aviation Flying Unit in the

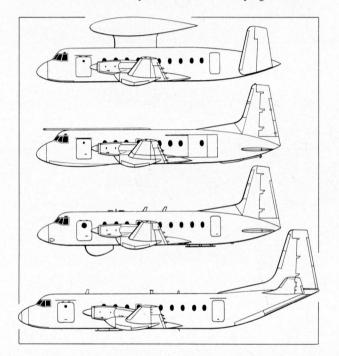

UK and after initial satisfactory experience with two examples by the West German *Bundesanstalt für Flugsicherung*, five more were ordered and delivery of these was completed early in 1976.

Several HS.748s have been purchased for use as specialised trainers, especially to train navigator/air electronics officers. Ten aircraft used in this rôle by the RAAF are equipped to train six students and carry two instructors, consoles being arranged all down one side of the cabin. Observation domes, periscopic sextants, drift-sights, vertical cameras and special avionics are all fitted for this specific training rôle. Other projected military variants have included one for carrier on-board delivery and one for airborne early warning. The COD project had a new undercarriage for deck landing, catapult and arrester hook fittings, a flight refuelling probe and folding wings, with a single upward hinge outboard of each nacelle to reduce the span to 48 ft 6 in (14,8 m). Such a variant was of only limited application but was an interesting example of the 748's adaptability. Rather more attention was given, some years ago, to the AEW version, with a rotodome above the fuselage and twin fins and rudders, but current RAF interest centres on an AEW Nimrod variant as the only viable European alternative to the Boeing E-3A AWACS.

Of all the special rôle HS.748s, the most promising at the time of writing appeared to be the Coastguarder, a variant intended for maritime reconnaissance not so much in the conventional military sense but rather to cover the whole gamut of surveillance and coastal patrol duties to detect smuggling, invasion of fishing rights, illegal entry, search and rescue, shipping surveillance and pollution detection. Based on a standard Srs 2A airframe, the Coastguarder has been defined in basic form and with a number of options; it is now on firm offer to potential customers and one of the 748 demonstrators is to be converted to this configuration, with first flight early in 1977.

The basic Coastguarder has a crew of five comprising two pilots, a navigator/radar operator and two observers/stores despatchers. MEL Marec search radar is fitted, with a 36-in (91,5-cm) scanner located in a radome beneath the forward fuselage, where it enjoys an uninterrupted 360-deg scan. It can also be used for weather radar display with pilot repeater presentation. The radar display is presented on a flat desk top with 17-in (43-cm) square plotting surface, located in

(Above left) The side view drawings show, top to bottom, the projected AEW version of the HS.748; the COD proposal; the Coastguarder variant currently under development and the HS.780 Andover C Mk 1. (Below) Three of the jet-powered derivatives of the HS.748 are (left to right) the three-engined HS.778, the twin-Trent HS.806 and the currently proposed HS.748 Series 5 with M45 engines.

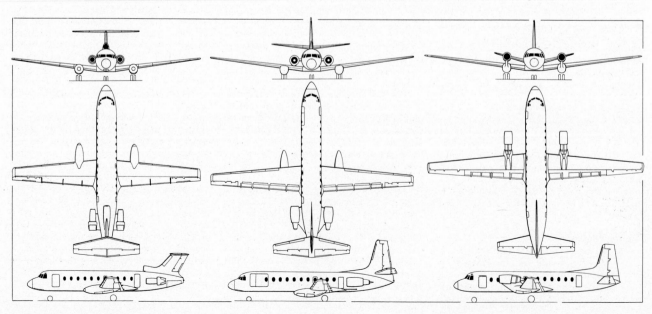

the rear half of the cabin, leaving space forward for various of the options. A Decca TANS 9447 navigation computer is fitted, plus a Decca 72 Doppler and radio altimeter. Nimrod-type bubble windows are fitted each side at the front of the cabin for beam observers, and one window on each side at the rear can be opened in flight for photographic purposes. The Marec radar is a variant for fixed-wing use of a helicopter radar already in service worldwide, and in the Coastguarder it has the capability of spotting in a sea state of 3-4 (a moderate sea), a ship of cruiser size at a distance of 125 naut mls (232 km) from 10,000 ft (3 050 m), a frigate at 70 naut mls (130 km) from 3,000 ft (915 m) or a patrol boat at 40 naut mls (74 km) from 1,000 ft (305 m).

A stores launch area is located at the rear of the cabin, stowage being provided for flares and sea markers which can be launched through a chute. One of the options, for search and rescue duties, is the carriage of four-man dinghies which can also be dropped through this chute; larger dinghies would be dropped through the large rear freight door, which is another option. Other possibilities are the fitting of four underwing strongpoints for the carriage of external stores, rescue equipment or air-to-surface weapons, or a searchlight pod mounted on a pylon on the inner strongpoint of the starboard wing; a passive ECM system could be installed, and extra fuel could be carried in tanks in the inner wing to give an endurance of 13½ hrs and range of 2,000 naut mls (3 700 km). Apart from the increased fuel option, the Coastguarder has the same overall parameters as the HS.748 Srs 2A.

Jets and STOL

The HS.748 has excellent field performance, as already described, but it is not in what is now generally considered to be the STOL category. Consequently, over the years since the aircraft was launched, a number of proposals has been studied for improving the take-off and landing performance, including the provision of full VTOL. The latter projects are now largely of academic interest, since the applications for a VTOL transport, either civil or military, have declined, but the introduction of versions with better STOL performance is still a possibility for the future. One way of achieving this would be to fit the more powerful R Da 10 Dart engines driving reversing propellers of 13 ft 6 in (4,1 m) diameter. Aerodynamic changes would comprise the use of lift dumpers, a long travel undercarriage, new wheels and brakes with touchdown protection, a revised flap/tab arrangement and larger fin and rudder. This would allow a take-off field length of 2,350 ft (717 m) to be achieved and the landing distance from 50 ft (15,2 m) would be less than 1,200 ft (366 m). As a first step towards such STOL performance, lift dumpers could be fitted to the standard Srs 2A airframe without these other modifications.

One VTOL variant studied was an Andover C Mk 1 airframe with the addition of 10 Rolls-Royce RB.162-31 lift jets of 5,600 lb st (2 542 kgp) each, mounted transversely in two underwing pods; roll and pitch control nozzles would have been required at the wing tips, nose and tail, and a total hovering time of 15 min would have been possible. A later VTOL study, conducted in 1969, was based on one of the HS.748 jet variants, with NGTE circulation control rotors fitted at each wing tip where they were powered by lightweight turboshaft engines, while forward propulsion came from high by-pass ratio turbofans on the rear fuselage. In this project, little of the HS.748 remained save some of the wing structure, but a number of simpler jet-powered derivatives of the basic transport have been studied and one of these is again, at the time of writing, under active consideration.

The first "jet 748" appeared as early as 1962 in the shape of the Avro 778, which had three 4,000-lb st (1 815-kgp) General Electric CF700 engines grouped at the rear, Trident-style. The fuselage to the rear of the cabin was basically unchanged and the wing structure was the same although the span was reduced

An impression of the HS.748 Coastguarder, a variant now under development that promises to extend the market for the 748 by a substantial number of aircraft.

to allow a cruising speed of 374 kt (693 km/h) with a payload of 9,200 lb (4 177 kg) for 500 naut mls (927 km). Pods were retained on the wings, at the original nacelle locations, to house the undercarriage.

Engine availability and market requirement were the two critical factors in evolving a jet feederliner during the 'sixties and the Manchester design team, working both independently of and in association with their colleagues at Hatfield, studied the application of several possible powerplants in rear-engine arrangements, at first as the HS.806 and then as the HS.860, on which considerable effort was expended. The HS.806 had two Rolls-Royce RB.203 Trent engines and a lengthened 748 fuselage, whereas the HS.860 — also with Trents — had a new fuselage with increased diameter of 9 ft 5 in (2,87 m) and could seat up to 72 passengers. The HS.860 was submitted to the HSA Board for comparative evaluation with the Hatfield-designed HS.136, and subsequent development (after the Trent had been dropped) led eventually to the Hatfield-designed HS.146.

The demise of the latter left the way open for Manchester to refocus its attention on a jet development of the 748, seen as a means of staying in the civil market without the need for massive launching expenditure. The right aircraft, with 50-60 seats, could be a potential replacement for the 1,700 piston-engined twins still in service and, in the longer term, for a thousand or so turboprop twins of the HS.748 and Fokker F27 type. Thus, there is considerable incentive to get this aeroplane right and to get it under way. Although all the earlier jet versions had rear mounted engines, the current Series 5 proposal* has the much simpler arrangement of two turbofan engines mounted overwing on the same structure that carries the Dart nacelles. The first such project envisaged using Avco Lycoming ALF 502 turbofans — the same engine that had been selected for the HS.146 — but more recent studies have favoured the Rolls-Royce M45.

Eventual production of a jet version of the HS.748 could well serve to prolong the longevity of the basic type well towards the end of the century; even without such a development, however, there is confidence at Manchester that the HS.748 itself, with the help of the special-purpose variants described in the foregoing account, will find a useful market continuing into the 'eighties. The production rate is currently being increased from one to two a month to meet actual and expected orders and, if sales figures for the HS.748 do not quite match those of the DC-3, this low cost/low fuel demand feederliner must certainly be rated as one of the most successful of the many attempts made to produce a replacement for the ubiquitous Douglas twin. □

* *The original project designation was HS.748/502 to indicate ALF 502 engines. When the latter were dropped, the "502" was changed to just '5'; hence, Series 5 does not imply the existence of a Series 3 or 4 version.*

(Above) A typical Spad 14, photographed at St-Raphael. (Below) The Spad 24, a landplane conversion of the Spad 14.

SPAD STORY ———————————— *from page 296*

As the Spad 21 was being declared to be abandoned, the Spad 22 was being assembled at Buc. This was an extraordinary development of the Spad geometry, designed to improve the pilot's field of view and possibly inspired, in part at least, by the Descamps C 1 that had appeared in September 1918. In the Spad 22 the fuselage was apparently that of the Spad 17 but the design of the mainplanes was drastically revised: the upper wing had pronounced sweepback and the lower had equally pronounced sweep-forward. This produced very marked stagger at the fuselage and brought the leading edge of the lower wing well aft so that the pilot's downward view was improved; stagger at the tips was almost nil. The interplane bracing had to be extensively redesigned to cope with this arrangement and the upper wing evidently had three main spars; the lower wing, as on the Spads 17 and 21, was braced from the undercarriage V-struts. In the tail unit, the fin and rudder appeared to be identical with those of the Spads 17 and 21, but new horizontal surfaces were designed. These incorporated horn-balanced elevators and the tailplane was strut-braced by inverted V-struts. Ailerons were fitted to the upper mainplanes only; they had marked inverse taper.

Last in the line of wartime Spad single-seaters of Béchereau origin was the Spad 24. This was a landplane conversion of the Spad 14, which in its turn had been a seaplane development of the Spad 12 and was similarly armed with a 37-mm *canon* firing through the hollow airscrew shaft, together with a Vickers machine-gun. The Spads 14 and 24 had long-span wings with true two-bay bracing, and the area of the vertical tail was appreciably increased to compensate for the side area of the floats of the Spad 14.

The Spad 14 had first flown on 15 November 1917, the prototype having been built by Pierre Levasseur. Forty production aircraft were built for fighter units of the *Aviation maritime* and the type saw limited service. A speed of 128 mph (205 km/h) was recorded by the prototype and this was claimed as a speed record for seaplanes at that time. The Spad 24 did not fly until 5 November 1918, too late to be developed into the shipboard fighter that it was apparently intended to be.

What the Spad 17 might have done in 1919 had the war continued remains conjectural, but the war's end was timely as far as the Spad 13 was concerned. Writing on 3 October 1918, Major J P C Sewell, a British liaison officer, said: "The 200 hp Hispano-Suiza Spads are becoming more outclassed every day. Their visibility is bad and their climbing powers insufficient. No new single-seaters seem likely to be turned out in numbers until (at the earliest) the summer of 1919 when Spads, Nieuports and Dolphins with 300 hp Hispano-Suiza engines will probably be in use." These three types were, respectively, the Herbemont-designed Spad 20, the Nieuport 29.C 1 and the French-built Sopwith Dolphin II.

One of the Spad 13 *escadrilles* continued on a war footing after the Armistice. This was Spa.162, which went to Poland with Haller's army in May 1919. Together with six other French units, Spa.162 was fully absorbed into the Polish forces in September 1919 and became the Polish 19th Squadron. It had fifteen Spad 13s and was based at Warsaw-Mokotów. In August 1920 it was briefly re-equipped with Sopwith Dolphins but reverted to Spad 13s in the following month.

Operations with the RFC

The Spad 13 was introduced to the RFC at a remarkably early date. As noted already, arrangements were made for Captain C K Cochran-Patrick, RFC, to inspect a Spad 13 at La Bonne Maison at the end of April 1917. Little more than four weeks later, an example of the new type, *S.498,* was handed over to the BASD by the French government. This Spad 13 was promptly sent by road to No 2 Aircraft Depot at Candas where it arrived on 1 June 1917; it was soon allotted the British serial number B3479. At Candas the new Spad was subjected to performance trials, and on 7 June returned a true air speed of 140 mph (225 km/h) at 15,000 ft (4 575 m), to which height it had climbed in 16 min 18 sec. Subsequent tests provided less spectacular results, but the performance was by any standards outstanding for mid-1917.

B3479 was sent to No 19 Squadron, then equipped with Spad 7s, for operational evaluation; it reached the squadron on 9 June, and was subjected to more tests on 13 June. For this purpose it returned to No 1 AD at St Omer, but was flown by Lieutenant G S Buck of No 19 Squadron. Buck was again flying the Spad 13 on 15 June, when he accompanied a patrol of the squadron and shot down an enemy aircraft despite several gun stoppages. On 13th July, Captain F Sowrey took B3479 into combat and drove an enemy aircraft down out of control. He had three No 3 stoppages on his guns and, in a common fault inherited from the Spad 7, his aircraft's radiator leaked, leading to overheating at lower altitudes. On 22 July, Sowrey forced a German two-seater to land and 'drove one EA scout down obviously out of control'. Six days later, Sowrey, again on B3479, forced another enemy aircraft to land.

No 19 Squadron's solitary Spad 13 apparently left the unit shortly after the trouble experienced by Captain Sowrey on 10 August, when serious knocking in the engine compelled him to return from patrol. It was found that the reduction gearing was loose. The aircraft was by no means discarded, however, for it subsequently went to No 23 Squadron and survived until 23 March 1918, when it was destroyed after flying for a total of 85 hours 19 minutes; it was formally struck off RFC strength on 30 March.

The test results obtained from B3479 obviously inspired RFC Headquarters to want Spad 13s rather than Spad 7s. Inevitably, the Service had to look to the Kellner company for its aircraft. As noted previously, the position at 1 August 1917 was that Kellner had RFC contracts for 60 Spad 7s, 60 Spad 13s and the equivalent of 30 further aircraft in spares. It seems, however, that the 60 Spad 13s were in fact a change in a contract that had originally called for that number of Spad 7s as a follow-on to the first 60 of that earlier type. To the contract for 60 Spad 13s was added a written undertaking to order a further 100 for the RFC.

Although deliveries of the RFC's Spad 13s were first (and

very optimistically) hoped for by August 1917, Major General Trenchard had resigned himself to deliveries not starting until November and had recognised that this might make it impossible to maintain the RFC's two Spad squadrons. A further complication that was to retard deliveries to the RFC was the fact that, after the British contract had been placed, the Kellner firm accepted large orders from the French government for Spads 7 and 11. This led to the situation, in December 1917, where the French authorities instructed the Kellner firm that for every Spad 13 delivered to the RFC one must be delivered to them. An understandably aggrieved note in the BASD's weekly report on supplies from Paris for the week ending 5 January 1918 observed: "Therefore of the 40 machines now going through the works which, according to Messrs Kellner's contract were laid down for the RFC, twenty will be delivered to the French. Complaints have been made to the French government upon this subject but the matter has been passed from Department to Department evidently with a view to procrastination until a large number of machines have actually been delivered to the French."

Deliveries of the Kellner-built Spad 13s for the RFC began in November 1917. The first, *S.4311*, was reported on 10 November to have been at Villacoublay for several days " . . . but cannot be started, it being practically impossible to start a high-compression 200 hp Hispano-Suiza when cold by means of the low-tension Bristowe exciter and Dixie magneto as fitted to the engines supplied to Messrs Kellner. A number of French magnetos, however, are being forwarded by RFC HQ in the Field, and some standard French high-tension exciters are being obtained from the French government. This will alleviate the difficulties as regards the November deliveries of machines. The second machine has gone to the aerodrome today where it is being assembled, and should be ready for reception as soon as the new magnetos can be fitted."

It was expected that the 60 Spad 13s would be delivered by the end of 1917, but there were production delays. After initial shortages of aluminium sheet, aluminium tubing and fabric had been overcome, deliveries of the RFC's Kellner-built Spad 13s continued until late March 1918. During the week ending 23 March, *S.4570* was officially accepted and was apparently regarded as the last delivery under the first contract. Strangely,

however, the BASD seemed to have got their sums wrong, for that was in fact the 61st Spad to be delivered.

In the first week of April 1918, *S.4571* and *S.4575*, described as "the two first machines off the second contract for 70, reduced to 25", were at Villacoublay awaiting reception action, but they, together with *S.4336* and *S.4570*, were not in fact taken on by the RAF, owing to official instructions that no more Spads were wanted. Instead, they were diverted to the US Air Service and never acquired British identities.* The decision to reduce the second contract to 25 aircraft had been conveyed to the President of the British Aviation Commission on 7 March 1918, but it seems that all the Spads not wanted by the RAF were delivered without engines to the United States Air Service.

With very few exceptions, the Spad 13s delivered to the RFC had the original rounded wing tips. Although Headquarters had rejected the primitive 'pocket'-form extensions to the wing tips on 8 February 1918, word of this had evidently not reached the Fifth Brigade or No 23 Squadron, for on 28 February, Brigade HQ wrote to RFC HQ: "I understand that all 200 Spads in the French 6th Army and, I believe, in all the French armies, have square wing and aileron tips fitted. The fitting of these tips is very simple and all French pilots appear to agree that the manoeuvring powers of machines are very much improved by them. I should be glad if permission could be given for one machine in No 23 Squadron to be fitted in this manner for trial. Arrangements can be made with the French for the provision, unofficially, of all necessary material, and for obtaining instruction about fitting."

Following this request RFC Headquarters asked the British mission in Paris to obtain two sets of detachable wing tips for test. It is not known whether these were ever supplied, but it seems unlikely that they were tested, for on 22 March 1918, RFC Headquarters wrote to the Fifth Brigade: "Reference Spad wing tip extensions. I believe wings are now made with increased area at the wing tips and ailerons, and we are trying to obtain some for your squadron." The belief in the existence of the revised form of mainplanes was probably based on the delivery of *S.4563*, fitted with the new wings. This is recorded in the note dated 7 March 1918, of which the text is reproduced above, concluding that not all Spad 13s were then being supplied with the modified wings, because *S.4564* had been delivered with the original form. *S.4563* went from Buc to No 2 Aircraft Depot on 17 March 1918, and acquired the British identity of B6882; it was probably the only Spad 13 of its kind

*The 63 Kellner-built Spad 13s delivered for the RFC had the French identities S.4311-S.4350, S.4451-S.4453, S.4551-S.4552, S.4554-S.4561, S.4563-S.4571 and S.4575. Known British serial numbers for RFC Spad 13s are B3479, B6731-B6739, B6835, B6838-B6862, B6864-B6867, B6872-B6875, B6878-B6886 and B9445. There is good reason to believe that, in fact, B6838-B6887 were all Spad 13s with the possible exception of B6871 and the known exception of B6877, the RFC's only Spad 12.

(Above left) A late production Spad 13 of the 22nd Aero Squadron, American Expeditionary Force. (Below) The Spad 13s of No 23 Squadron, RFC. Aircraft N is B3479, the first Spad 13 to be delivered to the RFC. It appears to be the only aircraft to have been finished in P.C.10; all the others retain their French camouflage.

to go to No 23 Squadron, in which it was apparently known as the 'clipped wing experimental' Spad. It was allocated to the squadron on 27 March 1918. Had production for the RFC and RAF continued, however, more aircraft with the revised wings would have been delivered, for it was intended that all the Spad 13s of the second Kellner contract would have had the improved mainplanes.

In the RFC, only No 23 Squadron was equipped throughout with the Spad 13, replacing the Spad 7s that had formed the unit's equipment, and all but a few of the known aircraft passed through the squadron's hands at some time from December 1917 onwards. There were undercarriage troubles: tailskids broke frequently during frosty weather and landing wheels buckled on landing. The latter fault was remedied by replacing the original French wheels with SE5 wheels. Panels of aluminium and asbestos had to be fitted to the fuselage sides behind the exhaust pipes to eliminate the danger of charring.

It seems that the only Spad 13 to go to No 19 Squadron, RFC, was the early B3479, and the unit flew Spads 7 until it was re-equipped with Sopwith Dolphins. Re-equipment began in December 1917 and was completed in January 1918. It was intended that No 23 Squadron would be similarly re-equipped by the end of March 1918, and plans were proposed for sending to England those Spads that were not required in France. But by 2 March 1918 it had been decided that No 23's re-equipment would be postponed until June in order to avoid delaying the arrival of No 85 Squadron (SE5a's) and other Dolphin squadrons. In the event, No 23 Squadron was completely re-equipped with the Sopwith type by 4 May 1918, and the RAF in France ceased to have operational Spads on its strength.*

It has been reported that the British Blériot and Spad Company of Addlestone, Surrey, was building a 200 hp twin-gun Spad in 1917, but it is not clear whether this was a much-modified Spad 7 or a true Spad 13. The possibility that the company were merely modifying a Spad 13 (apparently Constantinesco synchronizing gear was being installed, an unusual departure on a Spad) cannot be excluded, for one

---

The Spad 13s returned to the depot by No 23 Squadron were as follows: on 29 April, B6739, B6847, B6851, B6853, B6855, B6882, B6883 (wrecked) and B6885; on 30 April, B6736, B6884 and B6886; and on 1 May, B6838 and B6865.

(Above) A Spad 13 in Czechoslovakian service in the post-war period. (Below) A Spad 13, or Hei 1, in Japanese service.

other Spad 13 had been delivered to the RFC in 1917. This was *S.505*, which received the British serial number B9445 and is known to have been at Brooklands by 8 September 1917. At that date the aircraft was expected to go to the Aeroplane Experimental Station at Martlesham Heath, but apparently it spent September undergoing or awaiting AID inspection. It was last mentioned in Martlesham's weekly report of 6 October 1917, still to be collected when finally inspected by the AID, but it seems that it never reached Martlesham. Perhaps this aircraft had been sent to England to serve as a model for production of the Spad 13 by the Blériot and Spad Company. English-built Spad 7s were considered by the RFC to be inferior to French-built aircraft, however, and any idea of English production of the Spad 13 may have foundered for that reason.

Other combatant nations using the Spad 13 operationally were Italy, Belgium and the USA. Relatively few went to Italy and Belgium, however; it appears that only two Italian *squadriglie* (the 77ᵃ and 91ᵃ) were equipped with the type, and only the 10ᵉ *Escadrille* of the *Aviation militaire belge* was equipped with Spad 13s. Of the great Italian aces, Francesco Baracca flew both the Spad 7 and the Spad 13 and scored many of his combat victories on the latter. When the Battle of Vittorio Veneto began on 27 October 1918, the Italian *squadriglie* had an operational total of 48 Spads, presumably of both types. Much larger numbers of Spad 13s were used by the US Air Service than by any other of France's allies. At the time of the Armistice, no fewer than sixteen Aero Squadrons were equipped with the type, and there were 328 Spad 13s with American units. Altogether, 893 were delivered to the American flying service and most of the famous American fighter pilots flew the type with considerable success. A few USAS Spads were armed with Marlin guns in place of the Vickers and this weapon would probably have been standardized on Spads in US service if hostilities had continued into 1919.

Had the war lasted longer, there might also have been American-built Spad 13s in service. Reference sources are not in complete agreement over the proposed extent of American production: one states that 6,000 Spads (possibly of more than one type) ordered from American contractors were cancelled at the Armistice; another avers that 3,000 were cancelled in mid-1918 because it was found that the Spad was unsuitable for the Liberty engine. Whatever the truth of the matter, no Spad of any kind was built in the USA; and in fact no Spad 13 was built outside France.

After the war the Spad 13 remained one of France's standard single-seat fighters until 1923, and numbers continued to serve in the USA. Italy and Belgium also retained their Spad 13s as first-line types in the post-war years: about 100 served with the newly formed *Regia Aeronautica* and in Belgian service the type survived until 1922, when it was replaced by the Nieuport 29.

A Spad 13 was exhibited on the Pierre Levasseur stand in the 1919 Aero Salon in Paris. Whether this inspired other countries to acquire the type is not known, but Spad 13s helped to equip the air forces of Czechoslovakia, Poland, Spain and Japan, where it was designated Type *Hei* 1 after its official adoption by the Japanese army in December 1920.

At the time of writing, very few known specimens survive. Three are in the USA, one in Italy, one in the *Musée de l'Air* in Paris and another in the *Musée royal de l'Armée et d'Histoire militaire* in Brussels. Perhaps the Spad 13 has been somewhat over-glamorized by the pulp magazines and by the historical fact that there was a time when French fighter pilots could choose only between the outclassed Spad 7 and the Spad 13 with its refractory engine, limited outlook from the cockpit, poor climbing performance and somewhat deficient manoeuvrability. But great things were done by Spad 13s and their gallant pilots, and the type remains one of the immortals. □